JESUS

By
CHARLES GUIGNEBERT
**Professor of the History of Christianity
in the Sorbonne**

Translated from the French by
S. H. HOOKE
**Samuel Davidson Professor of Old Testament Studies
in the University of London**

UNIVERSITY BOOKS *New Hyde Park, New York*

Printed in the United States of America

Library of Congress Catalog Card Number: 56-7837

CONTENTS

PART I

THE LIFE OF JESUS

IV CONTENTS

CONTENTS

FOREWORD

IT WAS NOT UNTIL THE FIRST third of the last century, as an historical attitude became commonplace in all fields of study, that a systematic effort was made to amplify on a purely historical plane what was considered to be known about the founder of the most successful religion in history; it was Protestant thought, especially in Germany, that took up the figure of Jesus as a subject of study and went on from there to an examination of the general problem of the origins of Christianity itself.

Since everything we know about Jesus Christ comes to us through the pages of the New Testament — pagan and Jewish sources tell us practically nothing — this so-called Critical movement eventually concentrated on the material contained in this slim volume, in which the only substantial information is further reduced to the Four Gospels. On this narrow foundation a truly monumental work of analysis, exposition and speculation was erected by the scholars of many countries, spreading rapidly from Germany to Great Britain and the United States, and consummated, perhaps, by the last generation of French scholars.

This exhaustive investigation of the historical Jesus was embarked on in simple-minded faith. It seemed to the trail-blazing generation of scholars that no religious problem was being raised by this probing into Jesus' life on earth: they thought it could do no more than deepen our understanding of the real nature of his message, clarify the circumstances of his career, and elucidate the obscurer passages concerning him.

As Albert Schweitzer put it, in his own massive *Quest of the Historic Jesus,* "startling revelations were in store for them." The Gospels, whose simplicity had been taken for granted for so long, proved to be a labyrinth of complexities, and the movement of Criticism brought about the utter disintegration of their apparent smoothness and matter-of-factness. It became increasingly obvious that the Gospels were not written from any historical point of view at all, but were rather a catechesis for the instruction of the first Christian generations. The Evangelists were not in the least concerned with the *biography* of Jesus but were composing a manual of ritualistic indoctrination.

As a result the credible facts about the life of Jesus were reduced to a bewilderingly small number. It became increasingly evident that scholarly zeal had got a tiger by the tail. Even in those scholars who were most diligent in their pursuit of objectivity there was often a strong emotional bias from which, indeed, they derived the energy

VII

to carry on their work. It was rare to find a scholar whose interest was purely historical: most investigators were in the grip of some religious predisposition, avowed or not.

Charles Guignebert, the author of this book, is one of the few exceptions. As he says himself: "The historian must permit himself to be swayed by no other presupposition save that he may believe nothing and that he knows nothing, he is nothing more than a seeker." (p. 411) He is in search only of "historical truth," and he "relies upon nothing save textual sources." (p. 315)

This splendid statement of principles — which many, to be sure, might express, though few live up to — is a precise description of Guignebert's scholarly criteria: the reader of this book will be persuaded that it is not possible to have a more magisterial, all-embracing control of a mass of material which is, after all, studendous. Guignebert must be considered one of the finest examples of European scholarship and a model for scholars in all fields.

Guignebert spent a lifetime of research into the genesis of all forms of religious belief; toward the end of his life he held the chair of the History of Christianity at the Sorbonne. His present work is a masterpiece of historical erudition whose distinction is made all the more evident by an unusual readability.

All Guignebert's qualities — the urbane limpidity of his prose, his painstaking yet elegantly borne erudition, his utter detachment — combine to present us with an insight that is arresting in its simplicity:

We know nothing at all of the personality of Jesus, scarcely anything of the facts of his life, little as to his teaching, and can only speculate as to his career.

This is indeed a reversal of tradition, which is so pervasive that even nowadays many people who consider themselves quite free of traditional piety will speak of the Gospels as documents which depict a personality of utter charm and compelling goodness. The Gospels are generally spoken of as though it were somehow possible to regard Jesus as of universal significance quite independently of the Christian tradition; that despite the admitted "gaps" or disagreements of "detail" in the Gospel account there is something "basic" which emerges.

Guignebert, impartially summing up the results of a century and a half of intensive scholarship, demolishes this notion. He will convince any unbiased reader that we can recover nothing from our source-books which will give us a glimpse, however slight, into the character of a flesh-and-blood human being.

Some shreds of Jesus' message, to be sure, survive a rigorous study of the texts; some probabilities emerge about his career; some speculations about the circumstances of his life, and even the general cast of his thought, may seem more or less persuasive.

But the man himself, Jesus the historical personage, has vanished beyond restoration. There is simply not enough to build on: Guignebert, in laying the evidence of the record before us as simply and modestly as possible, establishes this conclusively.

For the main point about the evidence is its scantiness. It is impossible to ignore the extreme poverty and confusion of the Gospel contents, especially if taken as the pious account of a man considered to be a vessel of divinity: a few comings and goings, some miracles, and a number of sayings that appear to bear mostly on a cataclysm of the imminent future. Moreover, the space of time actually covered is so short; a few weeks would be more than enough for all of Jesus' actions to have been performed.

It is possible that Jesus' brief public career was just this and nothing more, but it is far more likely, after all, that this scantiness represents the indifference of the Evangelists to history as we understand it. The Evangelists did not bother to conserve anything that did not directly serve their own ends, that is to say, anything that did not bear directly on doctrine, ritual, or apologetics.

It is this striking absence of evidence, complicated still further by the discrepancies woven into the very fabric of the earliest tradition, that obliged Guignebert to entitle his book simply *Jesus,* rather than the *Life of Jesus.* After reading Guignebert we can only raise our eyebrows at the latter title as an example of presumptuous question-begging.

To select only one example: after laying before us all the data concerning Jesus' birth and family, in 132 pages of lucid exposition, Guignebert shows us that all the evidence boils down to one engagingly simple statement: "Jesus was born somewhere in Galilee in the time of the Emperor Augustus, of a humble family, which included half a dozen or more children besides himself." (p. 132)

The force of this simple sentence arises organically out of Guignebert's clearing away the dense undergrowth in which the entire Gospel tradition is entangled: our eyes, made indifferent by the repetition and pseudo-familiarity due to our upbringing, thanks to Guignebert perceive the value of brief statements in the Gospels which otherwise they would skip over uncomprehendingly. It is just because the evidence is so skimpy that the few statements in the Gospels with an authentic ring about them finally ₃tand out so convincingly. The proper weight is then given, for instance, to the astonishment of Jesus' immediate family and neighbors at the beginning of his mission: "When his friends heard it, they went out to seize him, for they said, 'He is beside himself.'" (Mk 3:21) "Many who heard him were astonished, saying, 'Where did this man get all this? What is the wisdom given to him?'" (Mk 6:2)

Guignebert's magisterial tranquility, in short, has the effect of a blockbuster. He takes up one theme after another — the Virgin Birth, Jesus' family and education, his career as Messiah, his message for Israel and the world, his view of himself and of his mission, whether he thought he was the Messiah or the Son of God, his betrayal by

Judas, his trial, his crucifixion by the Romans — and we are led enthralled into the thick of the baffling labyrinth.

The whole of Guignebert's *Jesus* leads up to its last sentence: "The Christian religion is not the religion which filled the whole being of Jesus; he neither foresaw nor desired it . . . Enthusiasm engendered Christianity, but it was the enthusiasm of the disciples, not that of Jesus." (p. 538)

This statement rolls open a vast gate and reveals a totally strange country. Sentences like this, so simple yet so explosive, are characteristic of Guignebert's writing. Here is another shattering summing up: *"The genuine teaching of Jesus did not survive him* . . . Although Christianity may be said to have its origin in him, since the new religion grew out of speculations concerning his person and his mission, he was not its founder. It had never even entered his mind." (p. 407: Guignebert's italics)

This conclusion is, in fact, the end-result of the investigation launched during the last century — the definitive scission between Jesus and Christianity.

The early scholars — and most of their successors — held Christianity to be essentially a Jewish phenomenon, and the figure of its founder, however original, was to be explained in one way or another by his reaction to the Jewish milieu into which he was born. The Jewish world at the time of Jesus' birth was considered to be a universe secluded from its Hellenistic and Asiatic surroundings by the impenetrable hedge of Judaism. Jesus, accordingly, was taken to be a startling and quite original genius, who was rejected by his own people because of his intensely original *reformistic* innovations, even though he was actually carrying on an authentic Jewish tradition. Because of this rejection — which in essence, perhaps, remained rather mysterious after all — the seed of his inspiration was thought to have been capable of blossoming fully only after transplantation to Hellenistic terrain. In short, Christianity was considered a Jewish movement subsequently extended to the Greco-Roman world.

The figure of St. Paul and the uniqueness of his contribution was considered to parallel in the Greek Diaspora of the Jews the role ascribed to Jesus on the soil of Palestine as the initiator of Christianity.

A further parallel assumption, constituting the apex of this symmetrical and ultra-personal view of Christian origins, was that the elaboration of Christian doctrine was in its turn the result of the influence of Greek thinkers on the exotic Jewish import. It was assumed that since the new faith arrived unencumbered by any complex body of doctrine it was natural for the lush atmosphere of Greek speculation to serve as matrix for a completely new and original world religion.

The realization that the historicity of the Gospels is nil led responsible scholars to discard such a view of Christian origins. This resulted not only in the perception that no *Life of Jesus* was possible; Jesus

FOREWORD XI
vanished not only as a man but, consequently, as the architect of
Christianity.

Guignebert's book is the antithesis of a negation; it is poles removed from that species of debunking shallow minds find entertain-
ing. His *Jesus* is fascinating precisely because it unfolds the actual
process of the formation of the Christian mythology; he lays bare the
active principle of the myth. He causes to emerge with striking clarity
the following complex tradition embodied in the New Testament:

Jesus regarded himself as having a message (whatever it may
have been in detail) for no one but the Jews. On this point the texts
are unequivocal.

> "... 'Go nowhere among the Gentiles, and enter no town of
> the Samaritans, but go rather to the lost sheep of the house
> of Israel.' " (Mt 10:5,6)
>
> "... One of the scribes ... asked him: 'Which commandment
> is the first of all?' Jesus answered: 'The first is, "Hear, O
> Israel; the Lord our God, the Lord is one: And you shall love
> the Lord your God with all your heart, and with all your soul,
> and with all your mind, and with all your strength." ' " (Mk
> 12:28-30)
>
> "(A Gentile woman) came and knelt before him, saying,
> 'Lord, help me.' And he answered, 'It is not fair to take the
> children's bread and throw it to the dogs.' " (Mt 15:25,26)
>
> " 'Think not that I have come to abolish the Law and the
> Prophets; I have come not to abolish them but to fulfil them.' "
> (Mt 5:17)
>
> "(Jesus) answered: 'I was sent only to the lost sheep of the
> house of Israel.' " (Mt 15:24)

The reason these texts have an overwhelming authenticity is
precisely because they *fail* to fit in with the generally anti-Jewish pro-
pagan tendency of the Evangelists, who were writing and editing the
early documents at a time when the Jews had been abandoned as
prospects for conversion and the only hope of the early Christian
community lay in proselytization among the pagans. Accordingly, for
these texts to have survived the doubtless rigorous process of selection
and editing implies that they were very early elements too solidly
embedded in the tradition as handed down to be tampered with. They
plainly contradict those portions of the New Testament which express
a message of universal salvation, and so must be taken as anterior and
consequently genuine.

Jesus regarded himself essentially as a Herald of the Kingdom of
God, which was *at hand* (Mt 10:7). In fact this may well have been
his primordial message: it is, at any rate, the only aspect of his basic
attitude which is incontrovertible. By "at hand," also, he meant something to be taken quite literally: though its duration varies somewhat
in the Gospels its utmost limit cannot be more than a generation
(Mk 9:1, 13:30), to say nothing of still another passage in which

Jesus predicts the advent of the Kingdom of God before the Apostles shall have passed through the cities of Israel (Mt 10:23).

Jesus came to Jerusalem, in the final act of the tragedy, not to die, but to act.

His action in Jerusalem (whatever doubts may envelop its aim) ended in a fiasco.

All these elements taken together — once again, we repeat, they are unmistakable in intent precisely because they are at variance with the prevailing tendency of the New Testament as a whole — clearly boil down to this:

Jesus was a prophet in the Jewish tradition, who prophesied the imminent advent of a celestial transformation of significance only to the Jewish people, who came to Jerusalem to help bring it about, and who was there destroyed by the secular authorities — the Romans.

But it is the Resurrection that is the primordial factor in the formation of Christianity: as St. Paul says: "If we preach not Christ Resurrected our preaching is in vain." St. Paul also referred to the Crucifixion itself as "a stumbling-block for the Jews and a folly to the Gentiles."

For Jews, that is, the notion of a Messiah "hung on wood" was a grotesque and monstrous absurdity (Deuteronomy 21:23: "He that is hanged is cursed of God"). In any case a Messiah should be victorious by definition.

For Gentiles, on the other hand, the idea of a Jewish Messiah as such was meaningless: it was a specifically Jewish national conception, and when this exotically parochial notion was associated with an earthly fiasco its irrelevance to the Greco-Roman world was simply heightened *ad absurdum*.

Accordingly, Jesus was sacrificed to Christ. The Church was quite right to adopt as its *de facto* motto the words of St. Paul: "If we have known Christ after the flesh yet henceforth we know him no more."

It is this dynamic change of perspective that clarifies a great deal of the haziness in the present structure of the Gospels. Their treatment of Jesus remains enigmatic only as long as we take their historical character at face-value and becomes clear when we see them in the perspective of a transcendental event — Christ Crucified and Glorified.

Perhaps the best way of summing up is to say that it was the failure of the Kingdom of God to appear that produced the Church. In Guignebert's words, "the Church was brought into being by the persistence of the temporal order, which compelled it to ask and to answer questions which Jesus had never foreseen." (p. 246). The failure of the Kingdom of God is, in fact, the inner history of Christianity to this day.

Christianity thus represents an explosive resolution in the Greco-Roman world of a phenomenon that among the Jews could only remain an incomprehensible contradiction — a failed Messiah. It is true that it launched the new religion on a fabulously triumphant career, but it was not Jesus the man who was being borne aloft on the standards of the spreading religion, but Christ the Savior — unforeseen by and incomprehensible to the humble Galilean.

One can, perhaps, appreciate the sardonic pithiness of St. Augustine's remark: "I should not believe in the Gospels if I had not the authority of the Church for so doing."

Because of this inherent contradiction the split with Judaism was unavoidable. For if there was still salvational value in the Jewish Law — as Jesus believed! — what was the point of his death to begin with? And if his death was pointless, how could there be a new religion?

But a new religion was already, a generation after his death, functioning in fact, it encompassed the minds of the Evangelists and the editors of those texts which have come down to us in the New Testament. Even the very first texts that concern Jesus were not written down until a generation after his death, when the perspective of the Crucifixion and Resurrection was already established in the actual cult of the new religion, and when its principal opponents were to be found among the Jews for whom Jesus himself thought he had a unique message.

As Schweitzer points out, "we must be prepared to find that the historical knowledge of the personality of Jesus will not be a help, but perhaps even an offense to religion." When Schweitzer then goes on to speak of the grotesque, repellent and startling figure that might very well confront us if an attempt at historical reconstruction were conceivably to be successful, we are bound to sympathize with the despair that must arise in the heart of any fairminded theologian who penetrates into the sources of his faith. Schweitzer's *The Quest of the Historic Jesus,* which is a monumental investigation of the *"Lives of Jesus"* that had been written up to his time — some 30,000! — ends up on the note of hopelessness suggested above, at the irreconcilability of Jesus' outlook with that of the whole of organized Christianity since. This is a contradiction which no apologetics can palliate or bypass.

The very fullness of Guignebert's exposition makes unmistakable the gap in our knowledge of Jesus' career which the development of Christianity as a cult has plastered over. Absorbing as material for the analysis of the primitive Christian Church, the Gospels are manifestly inadequate as a portrait of real events.

The discovery more than ten years ago of the so-called Dead Sea Scrolls has thrown this inadequacy into still bolder relief. The furore aroused by the Scrolls has been due primarily to a widespread feeling that at last some light might be cast on Jesus' environment. These documents, which arose during the first century before Jesus in a secluded Jewish sect near the Dead Sea now called the Qumran community, are generally agreed to be the earliest actual documents of the period.

Many pious Christians were alarmed at what was widely interpreted as a possible threat to the "uniqueness of Christ" arising out of the various historical parallels rightly or wrongly adduced from evidence of the Scrolls. But pious apprehensions were swiftly allayed. Most religious-minded scholars, after seeing that the historical parallels were of necessity eked out by inferences, deductions, questionable interpretations, etcetera, felt justified in maintaining that the uniqueness of Christ did not depend on any such historical data, but was in fact guaranteed by passages in the New Testament that are outside the sphere of the information contained in the Scrolls. Historically minded scholars, on the other hand, quickly found themselves debating specialists' points in which the larger issues that had alarmed lay opinion were lost to sight.

All this misses the point.

It is quite irrelevant to say, as Millar Burrows does in his *More Light on the Dead Sea Scrolls,* that "what for the community of Qumran was at most a hope was for the Christians an accomplished fact, the guarantee of all their hopes . . . The resurrection experience . . . confirmed the disciples' faith in Jesus as the Messiah."

To make this conventional claim that the Resurrection and all its implications constitute the primordial uniqueness of Christianity is simply to continue the Christology that has stood between ourselves and history for so long. As Guignebert points out so convincingly, it has plainly nothing to do with the history of Jesus the man.

The interest of the wealth of historical suggestions in the Scrolls does not lie in their providing us — at least as yet — with any precise historical data concerning Jesus personally, but in illuminating the obscurity of the generations before and after Jesus.

The vacuum in our knowledge makes speculation irresistible. Guignebert heroically resists it and his book is all the better for this. But we may be forgiven if we close this foreword with a suggestion for a reinterpretation of Jesus' life. Let us, accordingly, turn back to the New Testament, with the help provided by the Dead Sea Scrolls in acquainting us with other Messiahs, "Teachers of Righteousness," fanatical sectarians, etc., who thus reaffim the turbulence of the times.

Now, if we simply begin, as the Evangelists began, with the fact of the Crucifixion (abandoning the Resurrection to theology) we collide with an insoluble mystery, which may be outlined as follows:

The Gospels (despite their obvious anti-Jewish and pro-Roman bias) leave no doubt in the reader's mind that it was the Roman authorities who actually carried out the sentence of crucifixion, which was a characteristically Roman (and non-Jewish) form of punishment, originally reserved for slaves and later extended to thieves, criminals in the provinces, etc.

In the case of Jesus, furthermore, the charge was quintessentially political: he was crucified by the Romans as "King of the Jews," i.e., a rival sovereign. The Romans were in any case notoriously indifferent to the purely religious squabbles of the peoples they ruled.

Certainly Jesus did nothing, according to the Gospels, that would have warranted his *execution* by the Jewish authorities. He was not, *in fact,* executed by them but by the Romans, and on a politically formulated charge.

Force was involved — there are scattered indications that Jesus' followers were armed (Mt 26:51 is typical — "One of those who were with Jesus . . . drew his sword, and struck the slave of the High Priest and cut off his ear"). Further, the Temple itself was actually held for three days, and one recalls that it was guarded by a Roman legion, and was the second seat of authority in the country. It is clear that a mere harangue on the part of Jesus would have been futile as a means of clearing it.

Accordingly, the following speculation would seem justified:

If Jesus' followers were armed, and held the Temple against a Roman legion, and Jesus was crucified by the Romans on a purely secular, political charge, it becomes at least likely that there was an element in Jesus' activity which the Romans interpreted politically and responded to by bloody reprisals. In all this, to be sure, they may well have had the collaboration of the Jewish aristocracy, especially the Temple priesthood, for whom Jesus would also have been a troublemaker.

Nor does this in any way preclude other aspects of Jesus' activity: he might himself have been *primarily* interested in proclaiming the imminence of the celestial cataclysm, and then gone to Jerusalem to help bring it about.

What seems certain is that it was just the political motif in Jesus' career that the Gospels have omitted or suppressed. Writing when they did, the Evangelists would have found embarrassing or incomprehensible any indication that the object of their veneration had been put to death by the Romans on a charge of insurrection, especially an insurrection that failed. It is perhaps most likely, indeed, that it was this political fiasco that caused Jesus' first followers to erase the secular elements of Jesus' activity from their memories and retain only the transcendental ones. Quickly transplanted in any case to Greco-Roman soil, the doctrine of Jesus' paradoxical glorification struck root at once and left his earthly career behind. So completely behind, indeed, as Guignebert's great book shows, that it remains beyond our ken.

Joel Carmichael, M.A. (OXON.)
New York City, 1958

JESUS

INTRODUCTION

A

THE PROBLEM OF THE ORIGINS OF CHRISTIANITY: THE PAST AND THE PRESENT

THE historical problem to the study of which the present work is a contribution is that of the birth of the Christian religion and its establishment in the ancient world.

The triumph of Christianity, its persistence, and even its power of propagating itself, are largely the result of causes which do not depend upon its origins; like every other human institution, it has maintained itself through the course of the ages by means of transformation and adaptation.[1] Nevertheless, it is to its origins that we must go in order to determine its fundamental characteristics, and consequently to understand the spirit and direction of its development.

The belief that Christianity came into being and has survived in a different manner from the various other religions which have, before and after it, shared the allegiance of the hearts of men; that it has been exempt from the laws that regulate them all, and the chances that sway them; that its nature is unique and exclusive—is a religious belief, worthy of respect for the feeling that inspires it, still possessing a certain practical (or pragmatic) interest, but nevertheless historically erroneous. Ever since investigators, unbiased by religious motives, first applied themselves to the study of the problem of Christianity, not one has failed to reach the fundamental conclusion that the traditional explanation, the orthodox account of Christian origins, will not bear critical examination. As opposed to this negative conclusion, many different and even contradictory theories have been offered in place of the one

[1] The author has developed this statement in three essays entitled: *L'évolution des dogmes*, Paris, 1910; *Le christianisme antique*, 1921; *Le christianisme médiéval et moderne*, 1922.

1

discredited, but when put to the test none has yet finally proved itself acceptable in its entirety.

There is no reason for astonishment in this, and still less hope of turning it to the advantage of the traditional view.[1] Since science is, in essence, the process of approximation towards perfection, it is therefore always changing, and the more it learns and understands, the more it is compelled to alter its standpoints, to regroup the constituent elements which its analysis has isolated, and to modify the patterns which had seemed to emerge from the development of the facts, and which served as the basis of their organization. In other words, it is continually forced to destroy and rebuild its explanatory scheme, which is thus never anything but provisional. It does not follow that nothing remains of each of its successive attempts at synthesis, still less that the facts it has established, the empirical conclusions it has laid down, lose any of their certainty. Because, for instance, the exegetes have, as the result of their researches, put forward conflicting explanations of the growth of the " Easter faith," the contradictions and impossibilities which they have found in the gospel accounts of the resurrection of Christ do not thereby become any more consistent or probable. Again, from the fact that one scholar has proposed a theory which more complete information causes another to reject, and has risked a hypothesis which is afterwards seen to be too ambitious or too frail, it would be wrong to conclude that these gropings, these unsatisfactory experiments, these unsuccessful attempts, prove that the history of ancient Christianity is doomed to irremediable uncertainty. No doubt the study of the subject will never discover all that could be wished, but its patient endeavours, even those that seem only futile and disappointing, are slowly but surely bringing into relief and order the solid grounds of a completely satisfying explanation.

Such an explanation, indeed, is not entirely in the making. A considerable part of it is already achieved and may be said to be substantially unassailable. The number of important points and general principles on which independent scholars seem to have reached a definite agreement, already deserves respect and inspires confidence. The facts to be studied are complicated and confused ; our means of approaching and unravelling them are treacherous and difficult to handle. This

[1] The Catholic apologists have not, however, given up this hope, witness the book of Father Lagrange, *Le sens du christianisme d'après l'exégèse allemande*, Paris, 1918. The method followed in this work seems hardly admissible.

is being increasingly recognized, and its realization constitutes an important guarantee of progress.

We need not refer to the orthodox outline of Christian origins ; it is a matter of common knowledge. Nor would an enumeration of all the successive opinions with regard to the whole problem of Christianity that have been held by modern historians for more or less brief periods yield a gain commensurate with the expenditure of time involved.[1] We shall only indicate here in broad outline the differences between the historical account that prevailed towards the end of the nineteenth century and that which tends to be accepted today.

It was natural that, as soon as their science attained self-consciousness, towards the end of the eighteenth century, the critics should have first set themselves to the examination of the Gospels and the study of the figure of Jesus. They were still too much dominated by the traditional views not to believe that to understand Christianity was, essentially, to understand Christ, and on the other hand, they were too uncertain of their method, too ignorant of the religious life of the Orient to put the fact of Christianity in its true perspective ; hence they confined their study of it to that which it appeared to be, that is to say, a Jewish movement subsequently extended to the Greco-Roman world. This point of view prevailed in general throughout the nineteenth century. Scholars worked desperately to " restore the historical Christ." They sought in the most praiseworthy way to discover in Israel the whole secret of the Christian movement, to trace in the evolution of Greco-Roman thought the ideas and tendencies which prepared the way for it in the midst of paganism, and to understand the nature and origin of the resistance which the new faith nevertheless encountered.[2] At the period above mentioned, round about 1900, people continued, in general, to attribute to the initiative of Jesus, to his genius, which was regarded as unique

[1] A full and intelligent statement of the traditional account of the origins will be found in Bibl. **V.** For the various schools, more or less liberal, see Bibl. **CLXXVI** and **CLXXVII** ; **CCCXI** ; Jordan, *Jesus und die modernen Jesusbilder,*[2] in *Biblische Zeit- und Streitfragen,* 1909, no. 36 ; Holtzmann, **L,** 2nd ed., i. 5 ; *Entwickelungsgeschichte* ; Bibl. **DCG,** appendix to vol. ii ; and **LIII.** It will also be helpful to read the Introduction to **LXVII,** 1–13, together with the bibliography, which, though almost exclusively German, is exceedingly well chosen and suggestive, and M. Goguel's essay, *Critique et histoire à propos de la vie de Jésus.*

[2] Renan's *Vie de Jésus* (1863), and in a general way his *Histoire des origines du christianisme* (1863–83) together with Ernest Havet's *Le christianisme et ses origines* (1871–84), will suffice to illustrate these statements.

and original, a primary and essential importance, not only in the actual evangelical work of the very beginning—which, of course, was, and still is, taken for granted—but in the formation, if not of the doctrine at least of the spirit of Christianity, and of its initial impulse. It was commonly agreed that Jesus was a Jew, and that if he had extended the horizon of his people he had probably not gone beyond it. Moulded in the environment of Palestine, his thinking, by whatever personal boldness it was characterized, could only have followed the forms of Jewish life. Hence his teaching, as we find it in the Synoptic Gospels, is clearly Jewish in aspect. The vesture of parables in which it is for the most part clothed was woven in Palestine, and the characteristic expressions of the Aramaic language spoken by the Galileans and Judæans at the beginning of our era, are plainly perceptible beneath the laborious Greek of the first two Gospels. Convinced that Christianity was sprung from Jewish seed and rooted in Jewish soil, scholars devoted themselves to an exhaustive investigation of that soil, to the analysis of its elements, and to the discovery of a formula that would reveal their true relations.

Such a preoccupation was natural and logical. It inspired works which are still of fundamental importance [1] and its fruitfulness therefore cannot be disputed. Nevertheless, it had not yet succeeded in freeing itself from certain traditional opinions not far removed from prejudices. Its point of departure was always the idea of Israel that seemed to be dictated and justified by the Bible : a closed world, narrowly hemmed in by the impassable hedge of its legalism, a unique exception in the Semitic Orient, in total contrast to the Hellenized part of Asia. Of course it was recognized that the life, even the religious life, of Palestine was no longer, in the first century B.C., a mere reflection of the Pentateuch. In order to find out what it really was, recourse was had to Josephus and Philo, to the books last admitted to the Scriptural canon, known to us as the Deutero-Canonical, or to those left on its outskirts, the Apocrypha of the Old Testament. Above all, special attention was given to the ideas of the Jewish milieu apparently derivable from the New Testament, without observing that to regard these as typical, to rely upon them as sources of historical information concerning Palestinian Judaism, was almost equivalent to begging the question, since it was these very ideas that were in need of comprehension and elucidation. In fact, the Talmudic literature was utilized as a source of illumination, and

[1] All these may be said to be summed up in the great work of E. Schürer, Bibl. **XXIX**, of which the first edition appeared in 1886.

especially of confirmation, without sufficient allowance for the dangerous uncertainties of its chronology.

Further, it was taken for granted that Christianity, intended by Jesus as a Jewish religious reformation, and presented by him as the traditional doctrine, purified and adapted to the imminent Messianic Age, had preserved this same character in the propaganda of his Apostles. Preached by them in their native country, it had merely vegetated there, between the hostility and the indifference of the Jews, until the day when chance carried it into the synagogues long established on Greek soil, which were much more disposed than those of Judæa to consider it seriously. Almost at the same time it fell in with Saint Paul, another original and powerful genius, a Jewish genius likewise, but imbued with Hellenism, with a mind broadened by a profound practical experience of life, and fully conversant with the Judaizing communities of Greek Asia. By the combined effect of his thought and his activities, St. Paul succeeded in transforming the primitive faith and adapting it to the needs of the Greco-Romans. Thus its career began, and hence scholars paid almost as much attention to the figure of the apostle of the Gentiles as to that of Christ himself,[1] an emphasis which was to lead, in the opening years of the twentieth century, to a controversy so clamorous that the echoes of it reached even the general public, usually quite indifferent to the quarrels of the learned.[2] It became a violently disputed question whether the true founder of Christianity was not Paul rather than Jesus. While that conclusion did not meet with general acceptance, Paulinism was regarded as the second stage in the progress of the new faith—a stage of the greatest importance since it was during that pause in its advance that it began to formulate its dogmatic system, and, setting itself up in opposition to the Judaism which repudiated it, began to take shape as an independent religion. On the other hand, on the strength of the evidence of the Acts of the Apostles and of some vigorous assertions in the Pauline Epistles,[3] Paul of Tarsus was regarded as a pure Jew, a Pharisee, a rabbi brought up " at the feet of Gamaliel," that is to say, educated in one of the great religious schools of Jerusalem under a famous master,

[1] This explains how Schweitzer could write a *Geschichte der paulinischen Forschung*, which, although it begins, naturally, with the Reformation, is more than half of it devoted to the exegetes of the period with which we are concerned.

[2] We shall have occasion to refer again to this controversy, which reached its height about 1907. *Cf.* **CLXXVI**, 543 *ff.*

[3] In particular Acts vii. 58 ; xxii. 3 ; Phil. iii. 5 ; 2 Cor. xi. 22.

and belatedly transformed, by means of a sudden illumination, into a herald of the universalistic Gospel. It was not, indeed, very easy to understand by what road a man so imbued with the narrow legalism of Palestine, a " schoolman," and proud, no doubt, of his learning, had come to share the convictions of ignorant Galileans, and what is more, to crystallize in some fashion around the name, the cult, and the myth of Jesus, hopes that were prevalent among the Jews of the Dispersion, but the difficulty was evaded by appealing to the peculiar and mysterious tendencies of an exceptional religious temperament.

The third stage, and the one which determined the future of Christianity, was to be seen developing after the pattern of Hellenic thought. It was the result of the intercourse, obscure to us but evidently active from the first half of the second century, between Christian catechists and Greek thinkers. The new religion, still elementary and indefinite as regards doctrine, gave a ready reception to philosophic speculation, which, without abandoning its own principles, *dogmatized*, deepened, and enriched with its commentaries the affirmations of the faith, making them capable of indefinite development. The frail little Jewish plant, transplanted into this fruitful Hellenistic soil, quickly became a luxuriant tree. The period that saw the beginning of the first theological disputes could be regarded as closing the period of origins.

Starting from the main outline just sketched, numerous students with praiseworthy industry exhaustively explored the domain of early Christian history within the limits thus fixed. It would be unjust, and even absurd, to deny that their efforts yielded important and permanent results. But there is no doubt that the most valuable of these results for the progress of knowledge was the increasingly convincing, though almost involuntary, proof of the fact that the basis laid down was too narrow for so vast a problem. Moreover, rightly or wrongly [1] more than one scholar came to think that the known texts had been drained of their content, the problems exhausted, and that it was necessary to begin to look for something new, to set on foot and systematize the quest for fresh documents, to broaden the inquiry, and to look outside the old controversies. Now as soon as study was seriously undertaken in this spirit, conclusions became evident which have determined, in essentials, the positions on which the pioneers of today take their stand.

[1] Wrongly, of course, for it may be said that the study of the New Testament texts was begun over again twenty-five years ago, both from the point of view of philology and of exegesis.

Of these conclusions the following may be regarded as the chief :

1. In proportion as they became more completely emancipated from the subtle and tenacious bonds of tradition, exegetes began to read the Gospel texts with different eyes. They lost confidence, to a large extent, in their historicity ; they seized with growing precision upon their inaccuracies and omissions with regard to the life and teaching of Jesus ; finally they came to recognize that both had reached us in such a distorted state that all hope of recovering them as a whole would have to be given up. As a natural and inevitable consequence, they found themselves led to believe that the personal importance of Christ in the formation of Christianity, though indisputable, was unascertainable in any absolute sense, that at any rate this original impetus was accompanied by many others, and that it had not been so abnormal, so exceptional, so unique, as had so long been believed. The extreme limit of this new idea of Christ was attained in the negation of his existence—an opinion, indeed, more than a hundred years old, but which it was now sought to revive by setting it forth as the inevitable result of scholarship. The sensible critics refused to go so far, and it will be shown later why they were wise to do so. But they did, at least, become more and more firmly convinced that Jesus had conformed to his environment rather than distinguished himself from it.

On the other hand, this background itself on closer examination appeared to be, both in range and in depth, much less homogeneous than had been supposed, and than Paul, Acts, and the gospel tradition seemed to indicate. At the same time the oldest portions of the New Testament, corresponding to the first period of Christian history, seemed to be losing a good deal of their fundamental Judaism, inasmuch as a better knowledge of Hellenistic speech, due to a thorough study of Asiatic inscriptions and Egyptian papyri, revealed the fact that a large proportion of their supposed *Aramaisms* were, in fact, simply *Hellenisticisms*. This meant, since words are only the vehicles of ideas, that currents of thought wholly foreign to the Judaism of the Bible and of Jesus became evident in the very fabric of the tradition embodied in these ancient writings, thus showing its complexity to be infinitely greater than had previously been·suspected.

2. A corresponding alteration took place in the picture of Judaism itself. The beautiful unity which had been attributed to Israel crumbled away, the famous enclosing hedge began to reveal gaps, with the result that it became possible to describe

as *syncretistic* [1] this Palestinian world in which Jesus had been born and lived, and his Apostles likewise, and in which the first Christian community had taken shape. Not only did the whole system of religious ideas which the canonical texts present as orthodox Judaism reveal itself as much more complex, and above all much more permeated by foreign elements, than had been supposed, but other manifestations of Judaism were discovered on its outskirts. Sects came to light that were always Jewish in intention, and probably also in spirit, but that were full of ideas arising from speculations far removed, both in origin and essential nature, from the true Mosaic law. It even came to be seriously considered whether it were not from one of these sects that Jesus himself had sprung.

Outside the field of Palestine itself, this valuable idea of syncretism was turned to the illumination of the Jewish colonies scattered about the Greco-Roman world, the communities of the *Diaspora*.[2] It revealed in full progress an interesting effort of the two contiguous worlds, the Jewish and the Greek, at mutual adaptation. And it revealed also the preparation, unconscious but none the less active, for the Christian preaching of salvation. The Greco-Romans, while continuing to observe the old cults of the City, were little by little losing their interest and their faith in them. They found them too barren, too exclusively ritualistic, too narrow ; they turned towards religious practices and beliefs that were more sympathetic and emotional, cults in which the individual counted for more than in the ancient civic religions, and which also offered, *whatever a man's birth and social status*, an easier access than the exclusive *Sacra*, bound up as these were with the cult of ancestors of the City. Their religious aspirations crystallized round an old metaphysical conception, the Orphic idea of the *salvation* of the human soul, that is to say, of its eternal survival in a blessed future. But as they despaired, in their feeble humanity, of attaining this immortality by their own efforts, they clung more and more

---

[1] The word *syncretism* designates a *mixture*, a combination, of religious beliefs, tendencies, and practices of diverse origin. It seems improbable, however, that it comes from the root κεϱάννυμι—I mingle, which would have given the form *syncratism*. It is more plausibly referred to Crete, the island of a hundred cities perpetually eager for a unity which their constant rivalries perpetually prevented. People said συγκϱητίζειν as they said ἑλληνίζειν and λακωνίζειν, and συγκϱητισμός as one would say ἑλληνισμός and λακωνισμός. *Cf.* J. Wackernagel, *Vorlesungen über Syntax*, Basle, 1920, 301.

[2] A Greek work meaning *dispersion*. The Epistle attributed to James (i. 1) is addressed ταῖς δώδεκα φυλαῖς ταῖς ἐν τῇ διασποϱᾷ—*to the Twelve Tribes of the Dispersion*. *Cf.* also 1 Peter i. 1.

to the hope of a divine intercession, a merciful act of succour, by means of which a Saviour (*Soter*) would aid their weakness. They believed in the sovereign efficacy of the initiations into the various Mysteries which contained the revelation of the true means of salvation.

3. It came to be supposed that Christianity, transported in an embryonic state to this quickening and fruitful soil, and taking root there, had proceeded to develop in ways that were much less simple than had previously appeared. The forces that favoured its growth and moulded its future are seen today to have been more numerous, more complicated, and more widespread than was once believed. The influence of particular and exceptional factors is now obliterated, or at any rate considerably overshadowed, by that of collective ideas. Saint Paul, for instance, has ceased to be regarded as an independent and original agent, and has given place to *Paulinism*, which is something that goes beyond his mere personality. Paulinism is a combination of widely differing elements, a *syncretistic* product, in which genuinely Jewish ideas mingle with metaphysical syntheses grown in the soil of the *Diaspora* and beliefs taken over from the immortality Mysteries.

4. It has been established that it was not primarily by means of reflective and speculative thought, as much philosophical as actually theological, the influence of Hellenism made itself felt upon the Christian faith. It was rather through its religious feelings, its rites and hopes of salvation, the spirit of its Mystery cults.

5. The result of this depreciation—which is generally accepted by independent historians—of the determining influence of *individuals* in the founding of Christianity, and of the corresponding enhancement of that of *communities* and *environments*, is that we are coming more and more to regard Christianity as a *socialized phenomenon*. That is to say, it now appears to be the creation, as well as the expression, of the needs of a civilization, or at any rate of a social environment.[1] But when it is a matter of analysing a social environment, or rather, as is the case here, various social environments, we are faced with a complicated problem whose solution calls for delicate shading and careful reservations ; the beautiful simplicity of the traditional explanations has gone for ever. The

[1] Some very sound ideas, unfortunately combined with others of a fanciful type to form extravagant conclusions, have been developed, on the subject of the social genesis of Christianity, by Kalthoff. *Cf.* especially his three studies : *Das Christus-Problem, Grundlinien zu einer Sozialtheologie,* and *Die Entstehung des Christentums,* Leipzig, 1904.

fundamental basis of our study has become immeasurably more extended, since now, instead of Judaism alone, it covers the whole of the Hellenistic Orient.

To sum up, the change of perspective whose definition is here attempted has been brought about by a threefold advance of scholarship in relation to the ancient world. First, a philological advance, which by giving us a better understanding of Hellenistic language has clarified for us the thought of those who spoke it, and at the same time has established with greater precision the relation of the New Testament to the secular environment in which it was cradled. Next, an advance in the strictly historical sense, which has penetrated further into the obscure and fertile field in which, by the workings of syncretism, the emotions and hopes of the Mystery cults became associated with the transcendental systems of Gnostic cosmology. We have thus acquired terms of comparison which have enabled us to discover hitherto unsuspected aspects of the Christian story. Finally, an advance in comparative method, or the method of inferring, from the comparison of the similar beliefs, opinions and practices that are found in various settings, useful information with regard to their origin and the direction and manner of their evolution. This method is as dangerous as it is tempting. But the serious errors to which it has sometimes given rise must not cause us to underestimate the services which it is capable of rendering when it is handled with proper caution and controlled by the true historical spirit.

Viewed thus, in its actual life and setting, Christianity by no means appears to be, as was so long believed, *a break in the ancient religious pattern*. On the contrary, it quite naturally assumes its place in that pattern. It is a logical step in the religious development of the Greek Orient. Far from emerging as an unexpected phenomenon, unique, exceptional, and miraculous, which was to revolutionize the spiritual progress of humanity, it has every appearance of an expression, a positive realization, of historical antecedents and forces, which can be defined and analysed and shown to contain the explanation of its origin.

That does not mean, of course, that the analysis is always easy and the explanation simple. Both will perhaps seem so some day, but many patient efforts by many investigators will be necessary before that happy consummation. Meantime, awaiting the completion of the inquiries that will give us a proper knowledge of all the aspects of the problem—or destroy all hope of it—we must be content to leave gaps in our interpretation of the birth and establishment of Christianity.

As our *knowledge* advances we are better able to realize the conditions which the desired explanation will have to fulfil. It cannot, obviously, be too rigid and absolute ; it will have to admit both uncertainties and doubts. It will avoid schemes that are too complete, and perhaps even general ideas that are too clear-cut, the more we recognize how numerous, complicated, subtle, and difficult to apprehend and to gauge, are the influences, and, so to speak, the constituent elements, of which the religion of Jesus Christ is composed.

This book does not claim to be a *Life of Jesus*. It aims only at presenting to the reader a critical study of the problems which historical research concerning the existence, the activity, and the teaching of the Nazarene, offers for our study. It would be a mistake to suppose that points of importance have been treated in excessive detail. Only close observation will yield a comprehensive grasp of the character of the subject as a whole. A middle course has been steered between a so-called popular scientific treatment and pedantry. Numerous references have been given in footnotes to enable anyone who is interested in the subject to go more deeply into it than has been possible within the limits imposed.

THE SOURCES FOR THE LIFE OF JESUS [1]

I

THE PAGAN TESTIMONY

THE lack of pagan and Jewish testimony concerning the person and life of Jesus seems incredible to many of our contemporaries. How could a person who played so large a part in history, at least through his spiritual descendants, have been so completely unnoticed during his lifetime ? It is, they say, wholly improbable, utterly inconceivable. Some solve the difficulty by maintaining that the silence of the texts is only apparent, others by concluding that Jesus never really existed, that he is nothing more than the personification of a myth.

Only a firm resolve and an intense desire to extract information at any cost from a witness who has nothing to tell, could discover in a few meagre phrases of Tacitus, Suetonius, Pliny the Younger, Celsus, and a false Pilate thrown in, an assurance

[1] For a general bibliography and survey, the former not quite up to date, and the latter a little old-fashioned on some points, but still valuable, see **HRE,** ix, §§ 6 and 7, and **EB,** art. " Gospels." All the important works relating to Jesus contain a bibliographical index and a more or less detailed critical study of the documents. Note should be made of the numerous *Introductions* to the New Testament, especially those of Goguel (**XLV**) and Jülicher-Fascher (**LIV**), the two most recent, and of the great *Commentaries* of Meyer, Holtzmann, Loisy, Bousset-Heitmüller, Lietzmann, Lagrange, and Montefiore. It must not be forgotten that each book of the New Testament has been the subject of special studies and commentaries, the most important of which will be found mentioned in our notes. The following are a few of the standard books on the subject : **CLXXVI, LIII, CLXXII, LXXXIII,** all conservative works ; **LXXIII,** which is reactionary in comparison with the above-mentioned article, " Gospels," in which the author collaborated ; **CLXXXV, LXXVI, LXXV, LXXIX, CLVI** and **CLVI**–*a,* and, by the same author, *Critique et histoire à propos de la vie de Jésus, Cahiers de la* **RHPR,** no. 16, 1928 ; **CLVII,** i, book i, which is written from the Catholic point of view ; and finally, two books which represent, as it were, the culmination of two methods : **LXXXIV,** in which internal criticism is made to yield its utmost ; and **LXXXVI,** a forcible application of the *Formgeschichtliche Methode,* of which we shall have something to say later.

of the historical existence of Christ and a few fragments of information about his life.[1]

Tacitus (*Annals*, 15, 45) relates that Nero, disturbed by the derogatory rumours which charged him with the burning of Rome (July, A.D. 64), tried to throw the responsibility for the catastrophe upon those whom *the common people called Christians*. " *Their name*," he adds, " *comes from Christ, who in the reign of Tiberius was condemned to death by Pontius Pilate*." Various critics, including Drews, have endeavoured to prove that the passage in question was only an interpolation by a Christian hand. They have not succeeded ; on the face of it a Christian would have spoken of his co-religionists in a different tone. But the authenticity of the passage is not, of itself, proof of its reliability. It remains to be asked where Tacitus got the information that Christ was executed under Pontius Pilate. It has been suggested that his source was a report by the Procurator himself in the State Archives. But it is hardly probable that he could have had a direct knowledge of this, for the Archives, as he himself tells us,[2] were not available to private individuals. An indirect knowledge, by hearsay, is of course possible, but there is nothing to prove it. It has been further suggested that he might have taken it from some pagan narrative like the lost *Histories* of Pliny the Elder. But this also is unfortunately only a hypothesis ; we do not even know whether Pliny ever mentioned the death of Jesus. On the other hand, if we date the *Annals* about A.D. 115, it is abundantly clear that the elements of the Christian tradition concerning the life of Christ must by that time have been sufficiently well known for the statement of Tacitus to be no more than an echo of popular opinion. And so long as there is that possibility, the passage remains quite worthless.

[1] Aufhauser, *Antike Jesus Zeugnisse*, Bonn, 1913 (Kleine Texte) ; Kurt Link, *De antiquissimis veterum quae ad Jesum spectant testimoniis*, Giessen, 1913 (*Religionsgeschichtliche Versuche und Vorarbeiten*, ed. Wunsch and Deubner, XIV, i) ; Seitz, *Christuszeugnisse aus dem klassichen Altertum und unglaubigen Sekten*, Cologne, 1906. The alleged evidence of a certain Thallus the Samaritan, whose *History* was written somewhere between A.D. 29 and 221, is, in the opinion of the writer, completely valueless. According to Julius Africanus (in a fragment preserved by the Byzantine chronicler, George Syncellus, which may be found in **XXIX**, iii, 369) Thallus is supposed to have explained as an eclipse the darkness which, according to Mark xv. 33, and the Synoptics, covered the earth from the sixth to the ninth hour. This proves merely that he was acquainted with the account of the Crucifixion given by the Christians of his time. (*Cf.* **CLIV**, ii. 138 *ff.*, and **CLVI**–*a*, 70 *ff.*, whose conclusions appear to go further than the text justifies.)

[2] Fabia, *Les Sources de Tacite*, Paris, 1893, 324 *ff.*

The authority of Suetonius is of even less value. In his *Life of Claudius* (ch. 25) he writes : " *He drove out of Rome the Jews, who were perpetually stirring up trouble at the instigation of Chrestus.*" Nowadays it seems to be generally agreed that this Chrestus was Christ himself, of whom believers were wont to insist that he lived and worked *in their midst.* It is easy to see how a man who did not know very much about them might have taken literally what for them had a spiritual meaning. But if the book of Suetonius may go to prove that there were Christians at Rome about the year A.D. 50, or some twenty years after the traditional date of the death of Jesus, and that they were spreading propaganda amongst the Jews, it hardly offers any warrant for the death of Christ, or even for his historical existence.

The letter (*Ep.* x, 96) written in A.D. 112 to the Emperor Trajan by Pliny the Younger, then governor of Bithynia, on the subject of the Christians whom he had discovered in his province, is well known. It informs us that he had had a certain number of people arrested, and that they had confessed that they held meetings before daybreak to sing to Christ, as god, a hymn in alternating strophes. Only the most robust credulity could reckon this assertion as admissible evidence for the historicity of Jesus.

Celsus, who wrote, about A.D. 180, a book against the Christians, of which the essentials seem to have been preserved to us in Origen's refutation, written in the middle of the following century, knew, at least superficially, the traditional history of Christ, and makes very clear allusions to it. But as he was obviously not unacquainted with the evangelical literature, and nothing gives us any reason to believe that he had any other source of information about Jesus, what he says of him is worth no more than the evangelical tradition itself, and proves nothing.

There remains Pilate, whose testimony on the subject of the Passion was invoked by the Christians themselves, who referred their adversaries to a report which the Procurator is supposed to have addressed to Tiberius. Justin is the first to put forward this belief in an official document, and Tertullian follows him consistently.[1] The problem is not to determine whether such a report by Pilate ever existed—it may be granted, if one will, that it probably did [2]—it is to prove that one, at

---

[1] Justin, 1 *Apol.*, 35, 9 ; 48, 3 ; etc. ; Tertullian, *Apolog.*, 21.

[2] S. Reinach, *A propos de la curiosité de Tibère*, **CCXCII**, iii. 16 *ff.*, believes, on the contrary, that in that case " it would have been known," and the Christians would not have found it necessary to forge the

least, of the Christians who affirmed its existence actually saw
it, really had first-hand acquaintance with it. But everything
tends to show that Justin—probably the first to do so—merely
assumed that there was such a report, that Tertullian took it
on trust from Justin, without verification, and that then, someone much later, in the fourth or fifth century, on the authority
of Tertullian, forged the document that has come down to us,
and in which, incidentally, the name of Claudius replaces the
expected one of Tiberius. (Πόντιος Πιλάτος Κλανδίῳ χαίρειν
is what we actually read at the head of the letter.)[1] We cannot, at all events, place any reliance upon an obvious forgery.
The same may be said of the notorious *letter of Lentulus*, so-
called *Governor of Jerusalem*, addressed *to the Senate and People
of Rome*, concerning the personal appearance and teaching of
Jesus. It is a preposterous forgery of mediæval origin, though
even today some are still deceived by it.[2]

It may be repeated that there is no occasion for surprise
at the wretched scantiness of this secular evidence. The pagans
of the first century and the first half of the second had not
our reasons for being interested in Jesus. No doubt from the
time of the first Antonines they had, for the most part, heard
his name, associated with various malicious charges and wild
rumours. But after all, his birth in a remote little Galilean
town, in poor circumstances and amongst those despised and
downtrodden Jews, his short and insignificant career, terminated by a commonplace act of authority, his teaching, which
neither in matter nor in form appealed to the Greeks and
Romans—there was nothing in all this to hold the attention
of a historian of that century, even if by chance it had been

document if it had been in the archives. But in the second century
they may well have had no means of consulting these.

[1] The Greek text of the letter, accompanied by a Latin translation
and an interesting extract from Tertullian, may be found in **XII²**,
605 *ff.*, and a German translation of it in **CXXXIV**, 76. The substitution of the name of one emperor for that of another is probably to be
explained by the fact that in early Christian times there was some
uncertainty regarding the date of the death of Jesus. It was associated,
of course, with the name of Pilate, but the exact period of Pilate's
governorship of Judæa was not too well known. Moreover, some,
under the influence of John viii. 37, as we shall see, believed that Christ
was fifty years old at the time of his death, and accordingly assigned
a later date to that event. This error is to be found in Irenæus, *Demonstratio*, 74.

[2] For the text, history, and examination of the document, see **CC**,
319 *ff.* In the opinion of Eisler, the portrait contained in the letter
is a reflection of the *description* appended to the *warrant of arrest* issued
by Pilate against Jesus. This requires a powerful effort of imagination.
We are not even aware that any such " warrant " ever existed.

momentarily aroused. To be convinced of this one need only note the brief mention with which Tacitus contents himself. It can hardly have been until the latter half of the second century that the growth of the Church aroused the curiosity of men of letters ; and by that time their interest would be much more concerned with the doctrine and life of the Christians than with the historical figure of their Lord.

II
THE JEWISH TESTIMONY [1]

The silence of Jewish writers regarding Jesus is still more striking. There is, to begin with, Philo of Alexandria, undoubtedly a man of wide outlook and learning, who interested himself in the welfare of Israel. He was born about thirty years before the beginning of the Christian era, and did not die until fifty-four years after it. Yet in the more than fifty works by him that have come down to us, it is impossible to find even a single allusion to Jesus or his followers. It may be urged that Alexandria, where he lived, probably had little intercourse with Galilee, and that a philosopher would hardly think it worth while to devote attention to outbreaks of local fanaticism, such as he doubtless considered the movement of Jesus to have been ; hence he may either have heard nothing about it, or have held it beneath his notice. We may admit the probability of such a conclusion. But we are then faced with the problem of Justus of Tiberias, who was himself born in Galilee about the supposed date of the Crucifixion, and who lived in that country, amongst men who, it is natural to suppose, were still powerfully stirred by the gospel preaching, and whom he encouraged and commanded in their revolt against Rome. Yet in his two great works, a history of the war of independence and a chronicle of events from Moses to Agrippa II (d. A.D. 100), he has not made the smallest reference to Christ. Photius, who knew both books, gives positive evidence on the point. It is sometimes asserted that we are in better case with regard to Josephus, the great Jewish historian, who was born in A.D. 37 or 38, and died towards the end of the century, and who knew the history of Galilee thoroughly. We read in his *Jewish Antiquities* (18, 3, 3) the following remarkable passage : " At that time lived Jesus, a holy man, *if man he may be called,* for he performed wonderful works, and taught men, and they

[1] On the Jewish literature concerning Jesus, *cf.* J. Klausner, *Jesus of Nazareth*, London, 1925, 18–54. The author is a rabbi.

joyfully received the truth. And he was followed by many Jews and many Greeks. *He was the Messiah* (ὁ Χριστὸς οὗτος ἦν). And our leaders denounced him. But when Pilate had caused him to be crucified, those who had loved him before did not deny him. *For he appeared to them after having risen from death on the third day. The holy prophets had, moreover, predicted of him these and many other wonders.* The race of Christians takes its name from him, and still exists at the present time." [1] We have italicized the phrases that no Jew could ever have written, save one, indeed, who was on the verge of conversion to Christianity. Their glaring improbability was attacked as early as the beginning of the eighteenth century by a Swiss philologist called Otto, and nowadays all the critics take them for what they are worth. [2] The question, however, is still open whether we have here an authentic rhetorical outburst of Josephus, amended by a Christian, [3] or, as the writer inclines to believe, a pure Christian forgery.

It may be admitted that the style of Josephus has been cleverly imitated, a not very difficult matter, but the short digression, even with the proposed corrections, interrupts the thread of the discourse into which it is introduced. And if the forgery is early, since Eusebius, at the beginning of the fourth century, knew our text and accepted it without suspicion, [4] yet the earliest of the Church Fathers were unacquainted with it. Origen, for example, tells us that Josephus did not believe that Jesus was the Messiah. [5] He could not, therefore, have read in his copy of the *Antiquities* the ὁ Χριστὸς οὗτος ἦν italicized above. Hence it may perhaps be inferred that the interpolation was inserted in the second half of the third century.

In another place in the *Antiquities* (20, 9, 1) we find a further short sentence containing the name of Jesus. It is in connexion with James, who is stated to have been " *the brother of Jesus, called Christ* " (τὸν ἀδελφὸν Ἰησοῦ τοῦ λεγομένου Χριστοῦ). It is maintained that for Josephus to have thus referred to Jesus in passing, without any explanation, he must already

[1] **XXIX**, i, 544 *ff.*, gives a full bibliography of the discussion to which this passage has given rise. See also **CLIV**, i, 3 *ff.*

[2] The reader is referred to **XXIV**, i, 206, which mentions a number of recent studies on the subject.

[3] This theory is strongly upheld by Th. Reinach in **REJ**, xxxv, 1897, 1 *ff.*, and somewhat more cautiously, by **CLVI**, 38, and, above all, by **CLIV**, i, 84–8.

[4] Eusebius, *H.E.*, i, 11, 7 ; *Demonstratio evangelica*, iii, 3, 105 *ff.*

[5] *Contra Celsum*, i, 47. There are in existence three Greek manuscripts of the *Antiquities*, but as the oldest dates only from the ninth century, their evidence on the subject is of no value ; they naturally give the later text.

have spoken of him before, and in detail.   The argument would
be valid only if the authenticity of the allusion were beyond
doubt.¹ An attempt has been made to support it by the
authority of Origen, who is supposed to have known it, and
to refer to it three times.   But the event to which Origen refers
three times, quoting Josephus, is the death of James, *brother
of Jesus called Christ,* and since, on each of these occasions, he
accompanies this reference, still, as he says, quoting Josephus,
with a mention of the divine punishments which the death of
" James the Just " brought down upon the Jews, concerning
which our text of the *Antiquities,* 20, 9, 1, is silent, there is
reason to believe that he was using an edition quite different
from our own and very much Christianized.   It is objected
that he might have quoted from memory and confused his
recollections of Josephus with a memory of Hegesippus, who
does actually connect the death of James with the fall of the
Holy City.   Such a statement is easily made ; but it is hard
to believe that Origen would have been guilty of the same
confusion three times.²

The passage of Hegesippus of which Origen is supposed to
have been thinking, is known to us through Eusebius (*H.E.,*
2, 23, 4 *ff.*).   Now Eusebius quotes (*H.E.,* 2, 23, 20) as from
Josephus, a passage quite analogous to that which Origen may
have known, and which is no longer in our manuscripts.   It
has been suggested that he must simply have borrowed it from
Origen, but this is decidedly improbable, for he plainly says
that it is a direct quotation, and some slight differences from
the *Contra Celsum* prove that he is speaking the truth.   By
comparison with the aforesaid three passages it becomes perfectly apparent that Origen neither mixed up his recollections
nor confused his sources, but that he was, on each of the three
occasions, referring directly to *his* Josephus, which was not
identical with ours.

It seems probable that Josephus did not name Jesus anywhere ; that the Christians—and perhaps the Jews also, for a
different reason—were very early surprised and pained by this
silence, and did their best to rectify it by various glosses, at
various times and in various places, of the different manuscripts
of the Jewish chronicler.   This would explain why Origen did
not find in his copy of the *Antiquities* the text of 18, 3, 3, trans-

¹ The view that it is, is held by, amongst others : Goguel, **CLVI,** 40 ;
Norden, *Neue Jahrbücher f.d. Klass. Altertum,* **XXXI,** 1913, 649, 1 ;
and contested by Schürer, **XXIX,** i, 548 and 581.
² The three passages from Origen are to be found in *Comment. in
Matth.,* **17** (on Matt. xiii. 55), and in the *Contra Celsum,* 1, 47, and 2, 13.

lated above, while Eusebius did find it in his ; why Origen,
and Eusebius after him, read in a context different from ours
the mention of Christ which our manuscript gives in *Antiquities*,
20, 9, 1 ; and also why other supposed fragments of Josephus
relating to Christianity have been discovered elsewhere.

Such an explanation would apply, for instance, to the fragment which runs as follows : " *Josephus, your historian, who
has spoken of Christ as a just and good man, full of divine grace,
who by his miracles and wonders did good to many.*" [1] Similarly
also, to the fragments translated into German and published
by Berendts in 1906 from an old Slavonic text. [2]

The spuriousness of the latter seemed to have been agreed
upon at the time of their appearance on the strength of a study
by Schürer which was regarded as decisive by practically all
the critics. [3] Recently, however, Robert Eisler has appealed
against this judgment, and has brought to the reinstatement
of the *Slavonic Josephus* a laudable tenacity, supported by a
vast erudition and an inexhaustible ingenuity. [4] He has made
some converts, amongst them Salomon Reinach. But up
to now he has not, as far as we know, convinced any of the
New Testament scholars, whom he ought to have converted
first of all. The conclusions of Eisler seem, to put it flatly,
quite unacceptable, and the method by which he has arrived
at them is, in the judgment of the writer, the antithesis of
both criticism and history. We shall have, however, an opportunity later to discuss some of the assertions here rejected
in toto.

Without going off into paradox and maintaining, as some
have done, [5] that the silence of Josephus is perhaps our best
guarantee of the existence of Jesus, it is possible to discover
sufficiently good reasons for it.

It may be remarked at once that Josephus is very far from
being a scrupulous writer. He had, it appears, written his
Jewish War in the first place for the use of his compatriots,

[1] **XXIX**, i, 549.

[2] Berendts, *Die Zeugnisse vom Christentum in Slavischen de Bello
judaïco des Josephus*, in *Texte und Untersuchungen*, N.F., xiv, 4.

[3] **TL**, 1906, col. 262.

[4] After a number of articles and communications to learned societies,
he published, in support of this object, an immense work entitled
ΙΗΣΟΥΣ ΒΑΣΙΛΕΥΣ ΟΥ ΒΑΣΙΛΕΥΣΑΣ (Jesus, the king who never
reigned). For favourable and unfavourable discussion of this book, see
respectively, S. Reinach, in **REJ** (1929), and M. Goguel, **RH** (1929).
The writer is decidedly of the opinion of M. Goguel.

[5] Pascal (*Pensées*, 604, ed. Brunschvig) was the first to put forward
this idea, and Bousset followed him (**CXLIII**, 16).

and in their language.[1] But it is not this version that has
come down to us (for we are not convinced by Eisler that
the so-called Slavonic Josephus gives us the most important
parts of it). What we possess is a work which was intended
for the Greco-Romans, and which, being especially concerned
to win them to a more favourable attitude towards Israel and
its religion, would naturally avoid calling their attention to
anything that might be offensive or uncongenial to them.
Accordingly we see our apologist disguising as philosophical
opinions the various religious conceptions of his compatriots
which might seem strange to the *goyim*, or again, completely
obliterating the hope of the resurrection, so vital in the
Palestine of his day, but which he knew to be distasteful
to the West. Both in the *Antiquities* and the *Jewish War*, it
is only possible to discover here and there a few brief references
to things connected with the great expectation of the Jewish
people. John the Baptist, for example, is introduced in a fairly
circumstantial manner, but no allusion is made to his Messianic
preaching, without which he is unintelligible. In fact, there
is no mention of him except in connexion with the difficulties
which the death of the prophet created for the Tetrarch Herod
Antipas (*Ant.*, 18, 5, 2). Nevertheless, Josephus is convinced
that a day will come when all men will accept the *Torah*, and
that belief is too directly connected with the Messianic hope
not to imply it.[2] Hence it required no little audacity for this
brazen renegade to hail in the career of Vespasian the realization of the Messianic illusions which had incited and sustained
the great rebellion.[3] Obviously, then, it was not to be expected
that he should make any reference to the movement of one of
those dangerous visionaries who had followed a will-o'-the-wisp,
and of whom the Roman authorities had rid themselves by
execution.[4] It has been pointed out [5] that Josephus no doubt
knew of the Christian sect at Rome, and if he said nothing
about it, it was probably because he thought it reflected discredit on his people. The same fear may have kept him from
speaking of Jesus.

A simpler and preferable solution is that Josephus, like
Justus of Tiberias, did not think the movement initiated by
Jesus worthy of attention, since it had, in fact, occupied only
an insignificant place in the Jewish history of his day. Moreover, Josephus does not name other individuals whom we now
consider of importance, such as Gamaliel, Hillel, Jochanan ben

[1] *B.J.*, Preamble, i. [2] **CCLXX**, 69.
[3] *B.J.*, 6, 5, 1. [4] **XXIX**, i, 548; **CCXVII**, 2 *ff.*
[5] **CLX**, 4.

Zakkaï, all of whom are quite likely to have been of more consequence in his eyes than Jesus ever was. Hence the silence
of the Jewish chroniclers regarding Jesus cannot be used as
an argument against his existence.

Scholars have sought information in the Rabbinical literature, where Jesus is sometimes mentioned. But the oldest
portions of the *Talmud*, which are composed of ethical maxims
supposedly drawn from the teachings of the old masters,[1]
though they may help us to understand the religious and intellectual character of the Nazarene, tell us nothing of his life.
They are as little help as an anthology of the aphorisms of
Goethe would be if it were a question of proving the existence
of Frederick the Great and constructing his biography. Probably about the year A.D. 80, at the instigation, it is said, of
Rabbi Gamaliel II, there was introduced into the *Eighteen
Benedictions* (*Shemoneh Esreh*), a prayer which the pious Jew is
supposed to repeat three times a day, a malediction against
the apostates and the *minim*.[2] The definition of the word
minim has been, and still is, much debated. There is reason
for maintaining that it signified heretics in general, because
the *Jerusalem Talmud* speaks of twenty-four sects of *minim*.[3]
But it is difficult to dispute that from a very early period the
heretics *par excellence* were, in the judgment of the Jewish
divines, the Christians. The Church Fathers, at any rate, were
perfectly clear that it was against Christ and his followers that
the malediction of the Synagogue [4] was launched. In any case,
it tells us nothing about Jesus himself. As for the Jewish
legend of the adultery of Mary with the soldier Panthera, or
Pandera, which was in circulation as early as the second century
(Celsus knew it [5]), it is obviously explained by the polemical
necessity of giving a derogatory interpretation to the story of
the virgin birth, and certainly does not represent any independent tradition. The same is true of the malicious defama-
tions of Mary which have been found in the Talmud.[6] As a
matter of fact, the Talmudic legend of Jesus, which was still
growing up to the fifth century, only began to take shape after

[1] They are collected in the *Pirke Aboth*, the *Sayings of the Fathers*.
[2] It is *Benediction* xii. *Cf.* **XXIX**, ii, 463 and notes. **CCXVII**, 294,
quotes the Palestinian text which specifically names the *Nazarenes*
between the *apostates* and the *minim*. *Cf.* **XXII**, 467.
[3] *Sanhedrin*, 29, c ; **CCXI**, no. 24.
[4] Justin, *Dial.*, 16 and 17 ; Epiphanius, *Hær.*, 29, 9 ; Jerome,
Ad Is., 5, 18–19 ; 49, 7 ; 52, 4 ; etc. *Cf.* **XXIX**, ii, 463, n. 139.
[5] Origin, *Contra Celsum*, 1, 32 ; 33, 69. *Cf. Bab. Talmud*, *Shabbat*,
104, b ; *Sanhedrin*, 67, a.
[6] **CCXVIII**, 17–19 ; **CCXI**, 40–43.

the separation of Christianity and Judaism, that is to say, after the formation of the Christian tradition.   It is simply a defamatory distortion from which the historian of Jesus has nothing to gain.[1]

III

The Christian Testimony

Admitting, then, that all the pagan and Jewish testimonies, so-called, afford us no information of any value about the life of Jesus, nor even any assurance that he ever lived, let us turn to the Christian documents.   It will be convenient to divide them into three parts.   The first which we shall consider will comprise the New Testament writings not especially relating to Jesus ;   the second will be restricted to the four canonical Gospels ;   the third will consist of the extra-canonical and apocryphal Gospels, Epistles, and Acts, the earliest Christian documents.

Tradition, which has lately found an unexpected champion in Adolf Harnack,[2] attributes the book of the Acts of the Apostles to the physician Luke, the companion of Saint Paul, and dates its composition about A.D. 61 or 62.   A decision of the *Papal Biblical Commission* of June the 12th, 1913, states that the author of Acts is definitely Saint Luke the Evangelist, that the work cannot be attributed to more than one author, the contrary supposition having been found to be *wholly baseless*, and that its agreement with the Epistles of Paul is remarkable. It is less remarkable, however, than the audacity of such assertions, since it has been established that the author of Acts was ignorant of the Epistles of Paul, and even formally contradicts them ;[3] that he does not understand certain ancient traditions to which he refers (confusing, for instance, *glossolalia*, or *speaking with tongues*, a form of *charisma* common in the primitive communities, with the miraculous knowledge of all foreign languages) ; and, above all, that his narrative of the first years of the history of the Christian Church, whose founders he is

---

[1] Several notable works have been devoted to the study of this Jewish legend, namely, **CCXVIII, CLXI, CCXI, CCCVII.**   See also **LXX,** 6 (1900), 266 *ff.* ;   **CCXVII,** 288 *ff.* ;   **CXLII,** 452 *ff.* ;   Herford, *Christ in Jewish Literature*, **DCG,** ii, 876 *ff.*

[2] **XCIII** ;   **XCII** ;   **XCIV.**   For the contrary view, **XXXVI,** 248 *ff.* All the information relating to the study of Acts will be found in **XLV,** iii.   See also **XIII,** ii and iii, and **LXXXVIII.**

[3] *Cf.*, for instance, Acts ii. 4, with 1 Cor. xii. 10 and 30 ;   xiii. 1 ; xiv. 2 *ff.*

supposed to have known intimately, is pitifully inadequate.
If we consider that his first twelve chapters cover at least
twelve years—assuming that the death of Jesus occurred
approximately in the year 30, and the imprisonment of Peter
by Herod Agrippa in 42 or 43—and that they are mainly taken
up with apocryphal speeches, we are forced to conclude either
that the author was strangely uninterested, or that he was very
ill-informed.   He hardly mentions Jesus, an omission for which
he excuses himself at the outset (i. 1–2) by referring his reader
to another book of his dealing with the life and teaching of
the Lord.   That work is no doubt our third Gospel.

Nevertheless, the few allusions to the gospel history which
he makes in the course of his narrative, are not without significance.   They inform us (ii. 22 *ff.*; x. 38 *ff.*) that Jesus the
Nazarene, held by the Jews to be *a man chosen of God,* and
moreover, of Davidic descent (xiii. 23), revealed himself by
miracles, and went about doing good.   Then, according to the
will of God, he was delivered into the hands of his enemies,
taken by the Jews, and crucified by wicked men.   But God
raised him again from the dead, as all his followers attest, and
set him at his right hand.   He received the Holy Spirit according to the promise, that is to say, he became the Messiah.   The
main emphasis falls on the Resurrection (ii. 24 ; ii. 32 ; iii. 13 ;
v. 30 ; x. 40 ; xiii. 30) to which Peter (x. 41) adds the final
confirmation by asserting that Jesus showed himself *to witnesses
who had been chosen beforehand by God, and that he ate and drank
with them.*   It is evident that the tradition on which this passage
is based goes back to the very early period when it was believed
that the Messianic elevation of Jesus had been made manifest
by the Resurrection.   Later, the divine choice was taken back
to the Baptism (Luke iii. 22), and later still was placed before
the birth of Jesus, in the accounts of the Annunciation and
the Virgin Birth.   According to Acts, the career of Jesus begins
in Galilee, John's baptism forming its starting point (x. 37 ;
xiii. 24).   There is not the slightest allusion in it to the childhood of Christ, of which the third Gospel makes so much.

The truth is, we have no certainty who wrote our Acts,
nor when they were written.   The majority of the critics agree
in thinking that we do not possess them in their original form.
The first edition probably was the authentic work of Luke,
the companion of Paul, but the various mutilations, interpolations, and dislocations which it subsequently suffered at the
hands of some tendentious and unscrupulous adapter, have
altered it to such an extent that it seems today a very hazardous
undertaking to pick out and reassemble the pieces, as Loisy,

amongst others, has endeavoured to do. The date at which
this second version was made can only be fixed within very
wide limits.[1] When Harnack, in his *Chronology*, assigned it to
a date between 78 and 93, he was probably nearer the truth
than in his later works, and Loisy is probably right in assigning it to the first years of the second century.[2] Whatever its
date may be, it is certain that what Acts tells us about Jesus,
though testifying to a firm belief in his human existence, reveals
rather the beginning of his legend than the historical actuality
of his life. It affords more grounds for the criticism of the
former than facts for the illumination of the latter.

A similar impression is given by the Epistles of Saint Paul.
We shall for the present pass over the Epistle to the Hebrews,
whose Pauline authenticity is no longer maintained, and the
three Pastoral Letters (1 and 2 Tim. and Titus) which are
excluded from the Pauline canon by the majority of independent critics, although the Papal Commission in its communication of the 12th of June, 1913, affirms the Pauline authorship
of them to be definitely established.[3] Similarly the necessary
sifting of the evidence must be deferred for the present, and
we shall here content ourselves with Wernle's summing up : [4]
" Had all these letters been lost, we should still know hardly
less than we do about Jesus."

Paul was, apparently, the exact contemporary of Christ.
He seems neither to have known, nor even to have seen him,[5]
but he had associated with the disciples from the beginning,
and it would be difficult to conceive his not having taken pains
to obtain full information from them concerning the person,
the life, and the teaching of the Master. We do not know
whether he subsequently made use of the details of the tradition to direct and enrich his own preaching, but his letters
contain only slight traces of this tradition.[6] We learn from
them that Jesus was a Jew (Gal. iii. 16), that he was descended
from David (Rom. i. 3), that he was born of a woman (Gal.
iv. 4), and that he had brothers (1 Cor. ix. 5), one of whom,
James, was especially prominent in the community at Jerusalem. Further, that he lived *under the Law*, in other words,
as an orthodox Jew (Gal. iv. 4), that he preached only to Israel,

---

[1] **LXXXVIII**, 360.   [2] **CCLXXXII**, 108.

[3] For the history of Pauline criticism, see **CLXXVII** and **XLV**, iv.

[4] **CLXXXV**, 4.

[5] The contrary has been maintained on the strength of 2 Cor. v. 16.
We shall revert to this problem.

[6] All the Pauline allusions to Jesus are cited and commented upon
by **CIII**, i, 6 *ff*. *Cf.* also Drescher, *Das Leben Jesu bei Paulus*, Giessen,
1900.

according to the promises (Rom. xv. 8), that he was without
sin (Rom. viii. 3), and showed himself an obedient servant of
God to the point of accepting death on the cross (Phil. ii. 8);
that he chose twelve Apostles (Gal. i. 17, 19), that he instituted
the Eucharist on the night of his betrayal (1 Cor. xi. 23–6),
that he was reviled (Rom. xv. 3) and crucified (1 Cor. xv. 3;
Gal. ii. 20, iii. 13, etc.) because of the malice of the Jews (1
Thess. ii, 15), but rose again on the third day (1 Cor. xv. 4)
and showed himself to Peter, to the Apostles and others, and
to Paul himself (1 Cor. xv. 5–8), and that he now sits on the
right hand of God (Rom. viii. 34) awaiting the great day when
he shall come again.

It is not our purpose to examine the truth of these assertions, but only to give an idea of the positive picture of Jesus
that is to be obtained from the Pauline Epistles by bringing
together all the allusions and scattered references that they
contain.

This reconstruction is necessarily very incomplete, and in
strong contrast to the full Christology contained in the same
Epistles. That is to say, *Paul has deliberately sacrificed Jesus
to Christ.* Converted by a special revelation, the chosen re-
cipient of a gospel communicated to him from above, by visions
and various revelations, he stoutly maintains his apostolic
independence of those who plume themselves on the friendship
of Jesus. He holds aloof from their teaching and even, for
several years, from personal intercourse with them. He has
seen the glorified Christ, far other than the Galilean whom the
disciples knew " in the flesh " (Gal. i. 11–18). Under the
influence, unconscious but none the less active, of doctrines
derived from the syncretistic Mysteries of Asiatic paganism,
which had taken deep root in his mind, he conceives of Christ
as the Saviour God, who died and rose again for the salvation
of his worshippers and with whom they have been united by
means of a powerful rite, at once a memorial and a renewal of
his redeeming sacrifice.[1] For this reason he has really no
interest in anything but the divine status of Christ, his glorification, the interpretation of his death and resurrection as a
saving Mystery. What Jesus may have said and done on earth
became almost a matter of indifference to one who saw in him
" *the Lord* " and ruler of the world. If Paul had paid attention to the recollections of the Twelve, he would have found
them completely contradictory of his own revelation. He
implicitly admits it in 1 Corinthians xii. 3, where he says:
" *And no one can say that Jesus is the Lord save in the Holy*

[1] **CCXLII**, 91 *ff.*; **VIII**, under the word " immortality " in the index.

Spirit," that is to say, *under the inspiration of the Holy Spirit.*
It is, accordingly, only incidentally that he touches on the facts
of the life of Jesus. In general " he is absorbed in his own
hallucinations and transcendental ideas, imposing indeed, but
historically unsatisfying." [1]

As the Epistle to the Hebrews and the Pastoral Epistles are
equally dominated by the Pauline conception of Christ, they
are as disappointing as the Pauline Epistles. Careful search
may discover in them a few allusions to a real person,[2] but
they are much more serviceable to the adherents of the mythical
view, since they present us with a theological doctrine derived
from Paul, and not with an historical tradition.

The other Epistles of the New Testament, which most critics
no longer attribute to the Apostles—the two assigned to Peter,
the three Johannine, the Epistle of James, and that of Jude
—tell us nothing, and can tell us nothing. Unauthentic and
relatively late in date,[3] they seem to depend upon the traditions which we shall find in the Synoptics, but they can hardly
be said to reflect them. They too, with the exception of James,
have clearly been more or less influenced by Paul, and have
no relation to the history of Jesus. There is not much to be
gained from the fact that, besides several allusions, in the
Pauline manner, to the death and resurrection of Christ (i. 21 ;
iii. 18) 1 Peter mentions the descent of the Lord into hell to
preach to the dead (iii. 19), and 2 Peter (i. 16 *ff.*) recalls the
Transfiguration. The most that may be inferred from the
statement in 1 John v. 6, that Jesus came " by water and
blood," is that for its author the career of the Master lay within
the limits of the Baptism and the Crucifixion, and even that
is a hazardous interpretation.

Neither can we gain anything from the symbolism of the
Apocalypse and its glorification of the slain Lamb, which are
only of Christological significance.

From our rapid survey of the indirect Christian sources of
the life of Jesus, we may draw at least the valuable conclusion
that the details of that life do not seem to have held the interest
of Christians for very long. The first Christological speculations, which appeared immediately after the Master's death,
triumphed over the authentic memories he had left in the minds
and hearts of his disciples, and soon relegated them to an
insignificant place in the Christian teaching.

[1] CCL, 9.
[2] Heb. i. 2 *ff.* ; ii. 10–18 ; iv. 15 ; v. 7 and 10 ; vii. 14 and 26 ;
xiii. 12 ; 1 Tim. iii. 16 ; vi. 13 ; 2 Tim. ii. 8.
[3] They probably range between A.D. 75 and 125.

IV

THE DIRECT EVIDENCE OF THE NEW TESTAMENT : THE GOSPELS

Hence our sole remaining source of information is the Gospels, which claim to relate the salient facts in the life of Jesus and the essential features of his teaching. First of all a distinction must be made between the four Canonical Gospels.[1] The first three (Matt., Mark and Luke) have been called " Synoptic," since they are sufficiently alike for it to be possible to arrange their contents in parallel columns giving a sort of synopsis of the facts which they have in common. The fourth Gospel (John) [2] appears at first sight to be of a different type. Not only does it recount episodes that do not appear in the other three, and for which the utmost ingenuity has succeeded in finding no satisfactory place in the synoptic framework, but still more inexplicable is the divergence of its chronological scheme. While the Synoptics limit the duration of the public career of Jesus to one year at most, the Fourth Gospel extends it to two, or even three years, and locates it principally in Jerusalem instead of in Galilee. According to John, Jesus went up to the Holy City five times,[3] while the Synoptics take him there only once ; he celebrated three Easter festivals with his disciples [4] instead of only the one that preceded his arrest ; and he died on the 14th and not the 15th day of the month *Nisan*. To crown all, the Jesus of John seems quite a distinct person from the one implied by the Synoptic tradition. He is in every way different—his character, his behaviour, his consistently harsh attitude towards the Jews, and the tone of his discourses, which are solemn and lofty exhortations never understood by their hearers, and full of profound meditations on the eternal Christ instead of the familiar teachings about the *coming Kingdom* and the conditions of entrance to it.

[1] The canon is the collection of sacred books, numbering twenty-seven, accepted by the Church. The list was formed during the first four centuries, and its final establishment was the occasion of long disputes between the churches. The gospel group (*Corpus evangelicum*) was organized somewhat later than the Pauline group (*Corpus apostolicum*). From the end of the second century it appears to have been generally held that there was only *one gospel* in *four different forms*. On the history of the canon *cf.* **LX**, 301 *ff.* A full summary is to be found in **LXXII**, and shorter ones in **XLIX, XLVII,** and **LXV**.

[2] For a résumé of the history of the criticism of the Gospel of John, see **XLV**, ii, ch. 1.

[3] John ii. 13 ; v. 1 ; vii. 10 ; x. 22 ; xii. 1.

[4] John ii. 13 ; vi. 4 ; xi. 55.

It may be granted that the claims to historicity of the Fourth Gospel have no less weight than those of the three Synoptics, and seem, on the whole, quite as valid, which, of course, may be taken to mean that they are equally worthless. But the choice must be made between them, and all attempts at artificial harmonization abandoned. It is possible that the author or one of the redactors [1] of the Johannine account has here and there brought in some historical fact that is worth keeping,[2] a point which only a careful examination of each particular case can decide. But it is certain that on the whole the Gospel of John seems further removed from historical probability than the other three. The plan of it is entirely dictated by dialectical considerations. Its interest is wholly mystical and theological, and its arrangement is based on the current rules for this species of rhetoric. The Synoptic material and the Pauline teaching seem to have furnished the main substance of the book, but the special purposes and peculiar ideas of the author—or authors—have conditioned their use, and take us far from the earthly plane of human life and history.

Let us turn then to the Synoptics.[3] Originally the word " gospel " meant " good news," the Good News of which Jesus was the bearer and the embodiment,[4] namely, that of the imminence of the expected Kingdom, or of the *salvation* which later took the place of the Kingdom. The sense we give to it of *a book that expounds the Good News* is, however, very early, for we read in Mark xiv. 9 : " Wheresoever this gospel shall be preached . . . this also that she hath done shall be spoken of." It was the Jewish custom to designate a book by its first word. The first word of Mark was εὐαγγέλιον which may have been used to designate Mark and then come to be extended to other books of the same kind and having the same purpose.[5]

---

[1] A number of critics today believe that the first redaction underwent one or more subsequent recastings. *Cf.* H. Wendt, *Die Schichten im vierten Evangelium*, Tübingen, 1911 ; **CXXVII**⁹, 46 *ff.* ; **XLV**, ii, Ch. x.

[2] See, on this point, **XLV**, ii, 553 *ff.*, and, to the same effect, **CXXIV**, 142–57, and 235. The latter author, however, admits (p. 26) that the gospel narrative is an inextricably interwoven tissue of the historical and the symbolical.

[3] To the bibliography appended on this subject may be added the article by Klostermann, *Evangelien, Synoptische*, in **RGG** and **LIV**⁷, 321.

[4] **XXXVI**, 192 : " *Evangelium ist die Heilsbotschaft dass Jesus der Christus ist. Er ist der Inhalt, nicht der Träger dieser Botschaft.*" The word " gospel " already had a religious colouring in the Hellenistic language. *Cf.* **CCLII**, 276 *ff.*, and **CCLXXXVII**, *ad verbum*. A detailed study of the term is to be found in **LI**, ii, 1 *ff.* See also **CIII**, i, 3 *ff.*, 175 ; **CCLXIII**, i, 65 ; **CCLXXXVI**, note E, 141 *ff.* ; **LXXXIV**, 498.

[5] **LXXXIV**, 498.

Our Gospels are entitled "*according to Matthew*," "*according to Mark*," "*according to Luke*." From the time of Saint Augustine (*Contra Faustum*, xvii. 4) some people have interpreted this "according to" (κατὰ—*secundum*) as if the three books were the work of unknown authors merely utilizing information furnished by Matthew, Mark or Luke, but that is a misconception. Undoubtedly the expression in question goes a long way back, since it is already found, about A.D. 180, in Irenæus (1, 26, 2 and 1, 27, 2), but it does not go back to any of the three authors; it comes from some copyist or other. The clue to its true sense is given by the second line of the *Canon of Muratori*, which runs as follows : "*The third book of the Gospel according to Luke*." There is, according to this, *only one Gospel*, of which Matthew, Mark and Luke give three different versions, and "according to" simply means "by." The copyist who wrote the title of each book certainly believed himself to be giving the name of the real author, and it is, as a matter of fact, by virtue of this name that our three Synoptics found a place in the canon in preference to other evangelical writings which also were in circulation.[1] They triumphed over their rivals about A.D. 150 to 170, but that does not mean that henceforth they, including the Fourth Gospel, were the only ones used. The writings of Justin alone would suffice to prove the contrary.[2] When our apologist speaks of the *Recollections of the Apostles* (*Dial.*, 103, 22) we do not know what texts he is using, but on more than one point they obviously differ, either by excess or defect, from our Synoptics. When in the last third of the second century the Church, endorsing the choice of the majority of its communities, gave to the Synoptics the sanction of her bishops, it was certainly not because she had preserved authentic information as to their authorship—her tradition on the subject is wholly theological and legendary. She approved them because they were congenial to her, and she accepted what was said of their origin because, at a time when the apostolic tradition, real or supposed, was the supreme arbiter in matters of doctrinal doubt or disciplinary difficulty, their authenticity seemed the best guarantee of their authority. For this reason *we can hope for light on our Gospels only from their own text*.

Their date is a matter of extreme uncertainty, which is not relieved by the clues that may be discovered here and there

[1] **LII** gives a very thorough discussion of the question, together with all the necessary references.

[2] A detailed study of the gospel of Justin will be found in **CIII**, i, 34 *ff*.

between their lines because their earliest form has apparently been more or less recast several times. Here is an example of the difficulties with which we are confronted. Mark xiii. 1–2 contains the prediction of the fall of Jerusalem and the destruction of the Temple, which might naturally be regarded as a *post factum* prophecy, and therefore as subsequent to A.D. 70. But, in the first place, it may be that the little Apocalypse contained in this thirteenth chapter was interpolated at a more or less late date in a text already completed prior to the Great Revolt. In the second place, it may plausibly be maintained [1] that the pseudo-Marcan prophecy is of a very general character, and does not necessarily imply a recollection of the sack of the city by Titus, but is merely the threat of a calamity that was above all feared by the Jews. The first interpretation is preferable, but not certain, and it is perfectly true that Luke, who repeats the same prophecy, makes it much more specific.[2] Our texts afford us almost nothing on which to base even a satisfactory approximation. The earliest Christian documents have, of course, been thoroughly searched for traces of acquaintance with our Gospels, and some passages have been found which look very much like quotations, while others contain fairly specific allusions. But unfortunately the only certain instances go back no further than the end of the second century. The other references, for example those found in Justin, may easily have been derived from one of the short collections that appear to have been in independent circulation before being united into a Gospel. It is for this reason that critical opinion on the problem of chronology remains strikingly divided,[3] especially when it is a question of attempting to distinguish between the earliest form of each Gospel and the more or less revised form that has come down to us.

It seems certain that our Mark was not edited before A.D. 70. The parable of the wicked husbandmen (xii. 1–12) alone suffices to prove it. It follows that the same is true to an even greater degree of Matthew and Luke, since they are both later than Mark. A considerable interval of time must be allowed in dating Luke, whose author already had at his disposal a fairly abundant Christian literature (*cf.* the Prologue) ; its conception of Christ, of Christianity, of the Law, of the *parousia*, affiliate it rather with the writings of the second century than

---

[1] **CXLIII**, 33 ; **XCIV**, 88. The latter is very positive on the point.
[2] Luke xxi. 6, 20 and 21.
[3] **XLV**, i, 370 *ff.* (Mark), 441 (Matt.), 527 (Luke) ; **LXXXIV**, 485 *ff.* ; **LIV**, 304 *ff.* (Mark) ; 285 *ff.* (Matt.) ; 319 *ff.* (Luke). *Cf.* **CIII**, i, 14 and 82 ; **CLXXV**, 40.

with really early documents (*cf.* xxiv. 25–7, on the scriptural proof of the Messiahship of Jesus).   We shall not be far wrong if we assign the origin of our Mark to about A.D. 57, of our Matthew to about 85 to 90, and of our Luke to between 100 and 110, nor would it be surprising if, in the future, even later dates should be assigned to them.   It is to be understood that in speaking of " our Matthew," " our Mark," " our Luke," we do not include the various minor modifications to which the original versions continued to be subject up to the time when the canonization of the three books in the majority of churches practically stabilized their texts.

Accepting these moderate and reasonable views, and putting the death of Jesus approximately in the year 30, we find that the redaction of our Synoptics took place about forty-five years in the case of Mark, fifty-five to sixty in the case of Matthew, and seventy to eighty in that of Luke, later than the events which they are supposed to relate.   That is a great deal at a time when, as we shall see, the beliefs and doctrines concerning the person of Christ suddenly underwent a profound transformation, and when the interests of religion far outweighed any care for historical accuracy.

If, moreover, we were certain that the Synoptics received their definite form in the country where the gospel tradition originated, and where perhaps it was preserved in its original form longer than elsewhere, it would be some consolation.   But unfortunately the birthplace of our books remains uncertain, and the various conjectures that have been advanced all seem very unsubstantial.   The most probable conjecture with regard to Mark is that it was composed at Rome, or at any rate outside Palestine.[1]   Matthew was perhaps written in Asia Minor or Syria, Luke in some Greek community of Europe or Asia. It is useless to endeavour, as many critics have done, to be more specific.[2]   The authority of our texts has nothing to gain from such hypotheses.

On the other hand, between the redaction, properly speaking, of our Synoptics, and the time when by their inclusion in the canon their text was practically fixed, more than a century elapsed, during which they were regarded, not as personal works which had received from their authors a definite form which might not be tampered with, but as the property of the churches that adopted them.   These made use of them in accordance

---

[1] **XLV**, i, 365 *ff.* ; B. J. Bacon, *Is Mark a Roman Gospel?*, Harvard Theological Studies, 1919 ; **CLXXXVII**, 14 *ff.*   *Cf.* **CI**, xcix ; **CLXXXV**, 58 ; **XCIV**, 92.   On the tradition, **LI**, ii, 431 *ff.*

[2] **LI**, ii, 484 ; **XLV**, 441 *ff.*, 526.

with what they believed to be their own interests and the dictates of the faith, and thought nothing of " improving " them when they judged it expedient.

The necessity of having a stable text as a foundation for doctrinal controversy and liturgical order finally put a limit to this freedom of adaptation, to which the number of variants testifies. We shall not here go into the very complicated history of the synoptic text.[1] Neither shall we discuss the reasons which have secured the predominance of one family of manuscripts over another, nor why the attention of scholars has lately been drawn to the so-called *Western text*, which was long ignored in favour of the *Textus Receptus*.[2] We need only observe that our Synoptics have been in the canon longer than their text, which has suffered such deep-seated corruptions that in many places the original meaning has been lost with scant hope of its restoration.

If, moreover, we consider that the primitive tradition was originally expressed in Aramaic, and that its translation into Greek can hardly have been effected without some detriment to it ; furthermore, that our Gospels belong to a type of litera-ture in which the purpose of moral edification is paramount, in which the most obvious plagiarism is perfectly consistent with a complete lack of respect for the work plagiarized, in which an utter disregard for order, logic, and chronology is, as it were, the fundamental law, and in which depth of feeling and sincerity of intention take the place of factual accuracy, it will easily be understood that extreme caution is incumbent upon anyone who attempts to extract from such difficult docu-ments such scraps of truth as they may still contain.

The originals of our Gospels were written in Greek ; none of them have been translated from Aramaic. The Greek used is that of common speech during the Hellenistic epoch.[3] Its quality varies greatly from one Gospel to another. For example, it is very mediocre in Mark and extremely good in Luke. But even in the latter, whose author sometimes does

[1] **LII**, ii, gives a good general survey. *Cf.* **LXII, LV, LX.**

[2] The *textus receptus* (the expression of Elzevir—1633) is the term used by the Greek Church since the fifth century.

[3] The main work is still **CCLII.** The most convenient edition of the New Testament in Greek is that of E. Nestle, *Novum Testamentum Graece*⁶, Stuttgart, 1907. For a detailed study see Von Soden, *Die Schriften des N.T.*, ii, Berlin, 1913. The most practical grammar is that of Blass-Debrunner, *Grammatik des neutestamentlichen Griechisch*⁵, Göttingen, 1921. There are some good special dictionaries (Grimm's, in Latin, Thayer's, in English, Preuschen's, in German, etc.). Special mention must be made of *The Vocabulary of the Greek Testament illus-trated from the Papyri*, by Moulton and Milligan, London, from 1914.

take pains to show that he can write, there are, properly speaking, no pretensions to a literary style.   Our Gospels are akin to that group of short occasional writings that have been preserved in the papyri, more especially to the informal letters, and do not belong to literature.   The point has, however, lately been raised whether they have not been devised in accordance with certain principles of rhythm,[1] which, if it were true, would at least deprive them of that naïve spontaneity which was formerly attributed to them.   The question is being studied, but unfortunately it has been complicated and obscured by the claim of the conservatives that the strictness of the rhythm is a guarantee of the authenticity of the content.   Such conclusions seem somewhat premature ; but we shall revert to this point.

A superficial reading of our three Synoptics at once reveals certain *resemblances*.   They all three leave a similar impression of the figure of Jesus and of his teaching ; they relate, beginning with his baptism, almost the same incidents of his life ; they employ, almost in detail, the same methods of exposition, and use forms of expression that are often analogous and sometimes even identical.   Now genuine eye-witnesses, writing independently, would never coincide in this way—picking out of a life which none of them recounts in full exactly the same facts, selecting from a teaching which is only partially given by any of them exactly the same ideas, giving *precisely parallel* quotations from the Jewish Scriptures, sometimes from the Septuagint and sometimes from another translation.   On the other hand, a more attentive examination soon brings to light significant *differences* between the three books.   In the parts that are common to them all there are found degrees of variation amounting in some cases even to contradiction.   Irreconcilable differences in detail make their appearance in the same narrative.   The same saying is found not only in a different context but utilized in a different manner.   The so-called historical framework of the teaching of Jesus changes completely from one to the other, and the order of events is sometimes different.   Each of the three has portions that are peculiar to itself, and also gaps in relation to the other two, or to one of them.   To limit ourselves to one example, Mark says nothing either of the birth or the childhood of Jesus, and the two accounts of them given by Matthew and Luke are irreconcilable.[2]

[1] For the bibliography see **XLV.** *Cf.* **CLVII,** 201 *ff.* ; Père Marcel Jousse, S.J., *Études de psychologie linguistique*, Paris, 1925.

[2] The full significance of these brief remarks can be properly appreciated only with the help of a concordance.   There is a recent one in French by Père Lagrange. *Cf.* **XLV,** i, chap. iv.

The first explanation that occurs to the mind after these somewhat disturbing discoveries is that the three evangelists, without being acquainted with each other, all borrowed from previous writings, the same ones in the case of the common element in the three books, different ones in the case of the rest. Patient and minute comparison of the three texts has discredited this hypothesis, and it is now generally accepted [1] that Mark is considerably older than Matthew and Luke and was used by both of them.

The proof of the priority of Mark is based upon the following main considerations : (1) Mark represents a more elementary stage of Christian apologetic than Matthew and Luke. The Jesus of whom he gives us a glimpse possesses a truer humanity than the figure portrayed by the other two, which already shows signs of apotheosis ; (2) the whole, or almost the whole, of Mark is to be found in Matthew and Luke, often in the same terms, so that it has been pointed out (Wernle) that if we had lost Mark entirely we should still be in possession of practically all that he tells us.[2] The first and third evangelists have made very free use of the second. They have supplemented and altered him according to the requirements of their own arguments, the tendencies of their own minds, and the resources of their own special information,[3] but there is no doubt that they have both based their narratives upon his. Since the modifications of the text of Mark which are found in both Matthew and Luke show no real influence of the two latter upon one another, it is probable that they were mutually independent. It is important to note, in this connexion, that the comparison of the manuscripts proves that later copyists sometimes corrected or completed some passage in one of the Gospels by borrowing from one of the other two, which explains resemblances of detail between Matthew and

---

[1] The Catholic exegetes, such as Father Lagrange, still reject this conclusion on principle, and because they cannot do otherwise, but their opposition is not very spirited. The attempts which are made from time to time, though very rarely, to disprove the " two document hypothesis," never originate nowadays with professional critics, and none of them has succeeded in holding their attention.

[2] CLXXXV, 35, gives the list of things in Mark omitted by Matthew and Luke. They are those which did not harmonize with their special purpose. For greater detail see CXVI, the first two parts ; LXXXIII, ii, 278 ff. ; 326 ff. ; CCL, 67. We shall, for the present, leave unexamined the theory (held by P. Schmiedel, J. Weiss, etc.) which assumes Matthew and Luke to have used an edition of Mark prior to ours.

[3] Clue, The Corrections of Mark adopted by Matthew and Luke, 1911 ; CCL, 103 ff. ; CLXXV, 36 ff.

Luke which might, at first glance, seem to argue a utilization of the one by the other.

But if Matthew and Luke contain all the essentials of Mark, they also contain *in common* considerable fresh material not found in the latter ; such, for example, as concerns the baptism of Jesus, his temptation, several minor episodes, and, in particular, the substance of his gospel teaching. It must accordingly be concluded that, if they did not copy from one another, they borrowed from a common source other than Mark.[1] This source has been designated as the *logia*, or Discourses or Sayings of Jesus, since its contents are more didactic than narrative, and is usually symbolized by the letter " Q," from the German word *Quelle*, meaning " source."[2] Quite frequently in Matthew and Luke, the joins between the two documents thus combined are still clearly visible (*cf.* Matt. vii. 28 ; xi. 1 ; xiii. 53 ; xix. 1 ; xxvi. 1 ; etc.).

It is still an open question whether Mark himself knew Q. Various critics (Wernle, J. Weiss) contend that Mark reports so little of the sayings of Jesus because he does not want to duplicate the *Logia*, which he knows his own readers already possess. It is evident that Matthew and Luke found in Q a few things that they had already got from Mark, and which they consequently made use of twice, once from their first source and again from their second. The question is whether Mark had himself already taken them from Q. Some answer in the affirmative (Barth, Loisy) ; others in the negative (Harnack) ; others content themselves with a " perhaps " (J. Weiss). In short, nobody knows,[3] because Mark might easily have picked up some *logia* that were in independent circulation without having possessed a collection similar to that employed by Matthew and Luke.

Moreover, besides Mark and Q, Matthew and Luke each had independent access to certain special sources,[4] which are more abundant in the case of Luke (source " P " according to Harnack). It is not sufficiently borne in mind that sayings, parables, and episodes could easily have passed into circulation and become stereotyped individually, or in small groups, and that any gospel writer may have known them in that form. It is difficult for us to evaluate the importance of such a source,

---

[1] **LXXXVII**, ii, 1–100, makes a detailed comparison of Matthew and Luke, with a view to discovering this *Redenquelle*.

[2] **CLXXXV**, 49 *ff.* ; **XCV** ; **XLV**, i, 212 *ff.*

[3] **CLXXXV**, 59 ; **CXLI**, 16 ; **CIII**, i, 89 ; **XCV**, 136 ; **LXXXV**, 372. *Cf.* **CI**, xlix, cvii *ff.*

[4] **XLV**, i, 170 ; **LXXXVII**, iii, 89 *ff.* (on the *Sonderüberlieferung* of Luke) ; 145 *ff.* (on that of Matthew).

but it is important not to overlook the possibility of its existence, which would explain many a literal divergence of our
texts quite as naturally as the individual fancy of the authors.
For this reason the " *two document* hypothesis " might more
accurately be called " an hypothesis of the two *principal*
documents." [1]

V

The Sources of the Synoptic Gospels

Setting aside for the moment Mark and Luke, which have
at most only as much validity as their sources, let us consider
the sources themselves. The point to be decided is whether
they go back to the origins of the Christian movement or already
reflect some working over of the original tradition. Moreover,
since we are specially concerned with Mark, the question arises
whether Mark is a primary source or the work of an editor,
since it presents a consecutive narrative, while *Q* can only
have been a collection, either of sayings with a slight narrative
framework, or of entirely independent sayings. [2]

Until about the beginning of the twentieth century it was
generally held that a large, if not easily definable, part of our
Mark was directly founded upon the recollections of Peter,
and that it was, therefore, essentially primitive. But the result
of Wrede's attack on these conclusions in 1901, [3] showed them
to be unsound, and today all liberal critics admit that our Mark
is a composite work. In the words of J. Weiss, " It is not a
source, but a basin into which several sources flow," and Conybeare aptly compares it to those stars which seem to the naked
eye to be one, but which the telescope separates into two or
three. Subjected to the same critical tests as Matthew and
Luke, it reveals similar traits. It has its doublets, inexplicable
save on the theory of the utilization of two sources giving the
substance of the same account in two different forms ; [4] it has
its interpolations and dislocations which exhibit the unskilful

---

[1] **LXXXIV**, 227 *f.*, dwells at length on the reservations here briefly
indicated, and suggests four documents, representing four local traditions
(Jerusalem, Antioch, Rome, and Cæsarea) as the sources of our Synoptics. Mark would be assigned to Rome and *Q* to Antioch.

[2] **CXVII.**

[3] **CCXLI**, and the reply of J. Weiss, **LXXXV** (1903), which, on
the point with which we are concerned, reaches practically the same
conclusions.

[4] **CCL**, 51. *Cf.* Mark vi. 30–45 ; viii. 1–13 ; and viii. 17–20 ; which
Conybeare regards as four different stages of the same tradition.

combination of different elements [1]; it has its editorial additions which reveal obvious modifications of the main tradition. Thus the explanation of the Parable of the Sower (iv. 11–20) is later than the parable itself (iv. 3–10) ; and the great eschatological discourse (xiii. 3–37) appears to be only the expansion of xiii. 1–2 : " And as he went out of the temple, one of his disciples said unto him : Master, see what manner of stones and what buildings are here ! And Jesus answering said unto him : Seest thou these great buildings ? there shall not be left one stone upon another that shall not be thrown down." The parabolic discourse (iv. 1–34) has all the charac-teristics of an artificial composition derived from an earlier version. The disputes with the Pharisees (ii. 1–12, 13–37, 18–22, 23–28, and iii. 1–6) also form an artificial group, in which, moreover, occurs three times (ii. 10, 19–20, 28) the proof of the Messiahship of Jesus, and twice the expression " Son of Man " in an unmistakably Messianic sense, incon-sistent with viii. 29–30 : " And he saith unto them, But whom say ye that I am ? And Peter answereth and saith unto him, Thou art the Christ. And he charged them that they should say this to no man of him."

Further, when the parable of the sower above mentioned is compared with its editorial elements, we not only perceive that this is a composite work, arising out of the addition of foreign elements to the original " similitude " ; we also realize the underlying tendency which determined its gradual trans-formation. Where Jesus simply announced the imminent coming of the Kingdom, or of the Reign of God, the glosses present this as the revelation of a mystery, of a plan of salva-tion entrusted to the initiated : " *Unto you is given the mystery of the kingdom of God* " ($\dot{v}\mu\tilde{\imath}\nu$ $\tau\grave{o}$ $\mu\nu\sigma\tau\acute{\eta}\varrho\iota o\nu$ $\delta\acute{e}\delta o\tau\alpha\iota$ $\tau\tilde{\eta}\varsigma$ $\beta\alpha\sigma\iota\lambda\epsilon\acute{\iota}\alpha\varsigma$ $\tau o\tilde{v}$ $\theta\epsilon o\tilde{v}$), iv. 11. The fact that this idea, which, as we shall see, was far removed from anything Jesus could have said or thought, obviously influenced the final redaction of the Gospel, proves beyond question the composite nature of the work.[2]

That in several places Mark appears to be even less primi-tive than Matthew or Luke,[3] may be explained either by the theory that there were two editions of Mark, one prior to

[1] **CIII**, i, 85. *Cf.* Mark i. 2–3 ; iv. 11–12 ; ix. 13 ; which cannot be original (Wellhausen).

[2] **CLXII**, 411.—**LXXXVI** brings out strongly the influence of the communal faith on the arrangement and elaboration of Mark.

[3] **CIII**, i, 86 ; **CLXXXV**, 47 ; **CLXXV**, 27. *Cf.* Mark i. 8, and Matt. iii. 11, or Luke iii. 22 (in the Western text) ; Mark vi. 7–13, and Luke x. 1–16, or Matt. x ; Mark xiii. 18, and Matt. xxiv. 20, which restores the mention of the Sabbath.

Matthew and Luke and one subsequent to them, or on the grounds that Matthew and Luke were acquainted with the sources of Mark, and occasionally made direct use of them in preference to Mark itself. It has even been claimed that we can distinguish a first version of Mark, which was the source of Matthew and Luke, a second, which was the source of our Mark, and our Mark itself.[1] These hypotheses are attempts to explain the agreement of Matthew and Luke against Mark [2] in several instances, while maintaining, on the whole, its priority to them.

The presence of editorial corruptions in Mark is admitted. Harnack himself, for fifteen years the great champion of the conservative cause, has acknowledged that Mark has taken pains to adapt the reminiscences of Jesus at his disposal to the demands of the belief of his time, and that several stages of the tradition already lie behind him.[3] Certain scholars have attempted to ascertain and define these stages by endeavouring to distribute the material of our Mark amongst the various redactional strata which they believe to have been discovered in its text. They have not, of course, been able to do more than suggest probabilities, but their work has not been without value in that it has at least emphasized the facts at issue.[4]

If Mark is a composite work we can rely upon it only so far as we can rely upon its sources, and these, unfortunately, are unknown to us. J. Weiss, however, thinks that he can distinguish two : first, and most important, a group of narratives in which Peter figures, and which possibly are derived from him ; second, a collection of sayings, discussions, and discourses, taken in all probability from the *Logia*. The critics are not agreed as to the chronological relation between Mark and Q,[5] but for the present this may be neglected since our immediate concern is with the group of narratives. To

---

[1] A. Hoffmann, *Das Marcus-Evangelium und seine Quellen. Ein Beitrag zur Lösung der Urmarcusfrage*, Königsberg, 1904.

[2] On these agreements between Matthew and Luke, which are few in number and relatively unimportant, see the sensible remarks of **LXXXIV**, chap. xi.

[3] **XCIII**, 87.

[4] There are two especially interesting attempts : **CCXXXIV**, which aims at isolating the original basis of Mark, and that of Wendling (*Urmarcus*, Tübingen, 1905, and *Die Entstehung des Marcus Evangeliums*, 1908), which arrives at the theory of three redactional stages, the first to be assigned to an historian, the second to a poet, and the third to a theologian.

[5] The most notable adherent of the view that Mark is older than the *Logia*, is Wellhausen. Most of the critics maintain the contrary. *Cf.* **XLV**, i, 250 *ff.*

determine its value we must know its source. To avoid the possible ambiguity of the expression " *Proto-Mark* " [1] let us call this source by its German name " *Urmarcus,*" with the understanding that it refers only to a group of narratives incorporated in Mark, and not to an original edition of that Gospel.

The whole church tradition concerning the origin of our Gospels may be said to have arisen from the testimony of Papias, Archbishop of Hierapolis in Phrygia about the middle of the second century. These are his words, as preserved to us by Eusebius : [2] " And the Presbyter said this : Mark, the interpreter of Peter, wrote down exactly, but not in order, what he remembered of the acts and sayings of the Lord, for he neither heard the Lord himself nor accompanied him, but, as I have said, Peter, later on." It was, accordingly, on the basis of the recollections with which Peter enriched his teaching that Mark himself wrote, " without any other care than to omit nothing of what he had heard and to bring in nothing false." Papias continues : " As for Matthew, he made a collection in Hebrew of the sayings (τὰ λόγια) and each translated them as best he could." Ignoring the flood of literature which these few lines have evoked, let us see what can be made of the text itself. It is apparently agreed that John the Presbyter, whom Papias is quoting, was acquainted with two gospel treatises, one containing a narrative attributed to Mark and supposed to be founded on Peter, the other a collection of sayings attributed to Matthew and written in Aramaic. Unfortunately, since we do not know who the Presbyter was, we cannot determine whether he was in a position to guarantee the authenticity of the two books or not. Clearly in what Papias says there is no indication of either extreme reverence or unlimited confidence. It has even been suggested recently [3] that the object of the old Asiatic bishop was to depreciate two intruders, two new gospels, which were beginning, in his day, to rival the Ephesian gospel, that of John, which must have been accepted in Hierapolis. This, however, is nothing more than an ingenious hypothesis, but it is at least evident that

---

[1] A term which is greatly disliked by the conservatives, because it implies the secondary character of our canonical Mark, and hardly less so by those liberal critics who believe in the identity of the Mark of Papias with that used by Matthew and Luke, and with our own. **LXXXIV** has recently launched an attack upon what it calls the " phantom Urmarcus " (*passim,* and especially p. 331) which seems somewhat exaggerated.

[2] Eusebius, *H.E.*, 3, 39, 15–16.

[3] **LXXXIV**, 19 *ff.*

Papias knows nothing about the Mark and Matthew [1] referred to, and that accordingly we are in no better case.

Be that as it may, the Christians who read Papias after Mark and Matthew had become current in the Churches, did not hesitate to identify them with the two writings in question, and some critics of importance still agree with them, though admitting that neither Mark nor Matthew corresponds exactly with what Papias says of them. Loisy's opinion, that "the reference is a forgery," [2] is possible, but by no means certain. At the time when our Phrygian wrote, the Synoptics were certainly in existence, and he probably was acquainted with them. But it is not upon his own authority that he makes the statement; it is upon that of the Presbyter (καὶ ταῦθ' ὁ πρεσβύτερος ἔλεγεν) which at once takes us considerably farther back. It is true, as Loisy says, that "it may be held that the evidence put into the mouth of John the Elder is intended to justify an existing situation, to preserve the acquired prestige of a book concerning whose origin not enough was known," although the reference of Papias to the two books is a somewhat strange way of enhancing their prestige. But if it be noted : (1) that our Matthew is not translated from Aramaic, and is not merely a collection of sayings, but rather, an obvious compilation into which almost the whole of Mark has been absorbed ; (2) that our Mark exhibits a more logical arrangement than the reference implies, and that it is somewhat rash to regard it merely as the catechetical instruction of Peter or any other Apostle, it is clear that there is also the alternative possibility of interpreting the statements of John the Elder as referring to *Urmarcus* and **Q**.

While this conclusion certainly seems more probable than the other, nothing much is gained thereby, since it leaves quite untouched the problem of the authority and reliability of John the Presbyter with regard to the two original books. Neither hypothesis can be said to find much favour with modern critics. [3]

Apart from the evidence of Papias, the meaning of which, as we have seen, is doubtful, and the value slight, we possess only insignificant indications regarding the origin and relia-

---

[1] **XXIV**, i, 243.

[2] **CIII**, i, 28. *Cf.* **CLXII**, 400 *ff*.

[3] Bousset, for example, has come to the conclusion that neither of them is worth anything. See *Jüdisch-christlicher Schulbetrieb in Alexandria und Rom*, Tübingen, 1905, p. 315. It is difficult to believe that in Papias' youth, about A.D. 110 or 115, any of the actual disciples of the Lord would still have been alive. Even a man who was only twenty in A.D. 30, would by that time have been a hundred.

bility of *Urmarcus*. In Mark itself there are many incidents connected with Peter which might have come from him. There are also a few Latinisms, which may be taken as support for the tradition of its redaction at Rome.[1] On the other hand, the frequent occurrence of Aramaisms led Wellhausen to conclude that *Urmarcus* was written in Aramaic. In that case it would go back to a very early period, about A.D. 60 or 65, and would possess the authority of antiquity. But unfortunately presumption, however attractive, is not proof. A number of critics (Loisy, Spitta, J. Weiss, Wernle, Ed. Meyer, etc.) favour the theory which attributes *Urmarcus* to Mark, the disciple of Peter, but obviously, even if we follow their example and accept it, though with full reservations, it gives us no security against the corruption which the tradition of Peter may have suffered between Mark and the editor of Mark in its present form.[2] Moreover, we are still uncertain as to the exact degree of authority of this *Urmarcus*. We do not know, in other words, what is the historical value of this original collection on which our Mark was based, and which, consequently, is *almost the sole source of our knowledge of the life of Jesus*.

Nor do we possess greater certainty with regard to the origin and reliability of *Q*.[3] The identification of Matthew the Apostle with Matthew referred to by John the Presbyter rests only upon a dubious probability. It may be admitted that the collection goes back almost as far as *Urmarcus*, but that, again, does not tell us very much. Its background was probably Galilean, and its content almost entirely didactic, without any apologetic or dogmatic tendency.[4] Placing no importance on the death of Jesus, it would not have mentioned the Passion or the Resurrection, and its Messianic teaching would have been confined to a prediction of the apocalyptic return of the Master. Those are undoubtedly primitive characteristics,

[1] Eusebius, *H.E.*, 2, 15, 1–2, following the sixth *Hypotyposis* of Clement of Alexandria. On this tradition see B. J. Bacon, *Is Mark a Roman Gospel?*, and **CLXXXVII**, 14 *ff*.

[2] The editorial element in our Mark is probably to be found in the impression of mystery which it seeks to convey. Everything is presented as secret, esoteric, a veiled revelation to a little group of initiates. *Cf.* on this point the penetrating observations of **LXXXVIII**, 80 *ff*.

[3] A restoration of the *Logia* that is on the whole very probable, based on a detailed comparison of the passages common to Matthew and Luke that are not to be found in Mark, is given in **XCV**. *Cf.* **CCL**, 106 *ff*.

[4] The Old Testament also has its *Logia*. It contains several types, which may profitably be compared with those of the New Testament. *Cf.* **LXXXVI**, 39 *ff*.

earlier than, and out of harmony with the spirit of, our Gospels. But unfortunately the attribution of them to *Q* is wholly inferential.[1] Several critics (Loisy, Nestle, Wellhausen, Wernle, etc.) are convinced that the language of the original was Aramaic, which would be another argument for its antiquity. But at all events it was a Greek version that was employed by Matthew and Luke, since the amount of verbal agreement displayed by them makes it impossible that they were each independently translating from a Semitic original.

Harnack maintains that *Q* was historically superior to *Urmarcus*,[2] which is equivalent to saying that our knowledge of the teaching of Jesus is perhaps not quite so inadequate as our knowledge of his life. It is possible, but the assumption is not justified by the extent of our knowledge. We do not even know what the *Logia* contained. We can see well enough what Matthew and Luke took from them, but we have no guarantee that they omitted nothing of importance. Granting, however, that this is improbable,[3] we are still in ignorance as to the arrangement of the collection and the original order of the sayings, which Matthew and Luke obviously broke up to suit themselves. Again, it may be asked what is the true meaning in those cases where Matthew and Luke give different versions. All these questions must be left unanswered. Detached and unconnected, these *Logia* have come down to us with no temporal or local setting, and even those which have preserved a slight narrative framework afford but a doubtful contribution to the story of the life of Jesus.

VI

The Apostolic Tradition concerning the Life of Jesus

In the last analysis *Urmarcus* and the *Logia* rest wholly upon the recollections of the immediate disciples of Jesus, which is perhaps the reason why tradition connected them with two of their number. On the unproved assumption that the two books were the earliest written form of these recollections, if we assign to their composition the earliest possible

---

[1] **CXLVI**, 213 *ff.*, points out that our knowledge of the *Logia* is so uncertain that they might better be designated by the algebraic symbol for the unknown, *X*, instead of by *Q*.

[2] On the relation between the *Geschichtsquelle* and the *Redenquelle*, *cf.* **LXXXVII**, ii, 157, 203.

[3] **LXXXIV**, ch. x, advances important reasons for believing that Luke contains almost the whole of *Q* in its original order.

date, which would be about the year 50,[1] the apostolic reminiscences must have been in circulation as *oral tradition* (παράδοσις)
for about twenty years. That is a long time, especially when
we consider that during this period the Christian faith came
into existence, and began the inevitable process of glorifying
the figure of Jesus. On the other hand, it is too much to
expect that the tradition itself should have accurately preserved
all the materials necessary for a true picture of Jesus, and only
those. Between the Master whom they had known in the flesh
and the Apostles' picture of him twenty years later, lay the
drama of the Passion and the mystery of the Resurrection,
which had shifted the emphasis of their original faith, and,
at the same time, altered the perspective of the actual circumstances in which it had arisen.

During these twenty years, the minds of the Apostles had
been concentrated upon a few ideas which they had gradually
systematized, and in the light of which they had unconsciously
sorted out and interpreted all that they had remembered of the
life and teaching of Jesus. Hence the treasure of the tradition
may well have been much less rich and splendid than we are
inclined, by a kind of reaction from the gospel legend, to
imagine.[2] Since the execution of the Master did not put an
end to his activity, it must necessarily represent a culmination
and a transformation. *Jesus the Nazarene disappeared and
gave place to the glorified Christ,* and the disciples, witnesses of
the resurrection, or, in other words, fully persuaded that it
had taken place, began to preach the Christ. They went
about proclaiming that the Messianic promises made to Israel
had been fulfilled in Jesus, that he would soon return, and
that his " parousia," or manifestation, would mark the dawn
of the Kingdom which he had announced. As a consequence,
it became necessary for them to prove to themselves and to
others that Jesus was the Messiah expected by the Jews, and
that he had lived, acted, and spoken as such. It is easy to
see that such a proof, such a surprising claim, demanded more
than the Galilean tradition to support it. The idea of the
Messiah was already established, and Jesus had to be adapted

[1] It has been claimed that the most striking of the sayings were
committed to writing during the actual lifetime of Jesus, and even that
Q dated from that period. *Cf.* **CLXXII,** 171 *ff.,* and **CX,** x. These are
no more than *impressions* and have no rational foundation.

[2] The writer is inclined to agree with **CLXII,** 403 *ff.,* that little by
little two sets of narratives grew up : one in the Galilean setting, which
probably remained somewhat bare and scanty ; the other in the atmosphere of Jerusalem, richer but hardly so authentic, because it based
itself upon the death of Jesus as the essential fact of his life.

to it. Messianic expectation was sufficiently indefinite regarding the type of "the one who was to come" for this not to seem completely impossible, but it was at least necessary for the person and life of the Nazarene to carry out and justify the scriptural texts which the Jews regarded as announcing and foreshadowing the Blessed of Jahweh. Accordingly the Apostles began to discover, probably not much to their surprise, that they had not correctly understood many of the *sayings* of Jesus, that they had misinterpreted certain of his *acts*. They revised and, in the exact sense of the word, reformed their idea of him by placing it in a Messianic light. Instinctively, they dropped many recollections which did not harmonize with their present belief, and "revived" others which appropriately · strengthened it. Actually it was from their imagination and not their memory that these latter were called forth, to meet the need of their apologetic and the questions raised by their controversy with the Jews. There is, of course, no question of their good faith; but an irresistible necessity gradually effaced from their minds the outlines of the disappointing truth, and engraved in its stead a picture of the life of Jesus better adapted to the requirements of his Messiahship. With an unconscious, but inevitable logic, they revised the actual order of his life, working back from the Resurrection to the Nativity.[1]

It may be assumed that the Apostles themselves did, to a certain extent, endeavour to resist the powerful forces of suggestion which impelled them to a forgetfulness of the facts, and that if their recollections became selected, transfigured, enriched, they did not, for all that, entirely lose contact with historical truth. But the faith of their disciples was not subject to the same restraints. With no means of choosing between the various influences which tended to substitute an imaginary Christ for the real Jesus, their faith was moulded by them all : the popular Messianic ideas ; the supposedly prophetic [2] texts of the Old Testament ; the mythical motifs current throughout the Semitic Orient, and ready to crystallize about any type of religious hero ; the mystery religions of

---

[1] A very good outline of this reconstruction will be found in **CIII**, i, 176 *ff*.

[2] **CIII**, i, 336. On the subject of this anxiety to find in Jesus the fulfilment of the Scriptures, which resulted in the sheer invention of incidents, see **LXIV** in general. Harnack advances as an argument for the historicity of Mark, the fact that the Old Testament has scarcely any influence upon its tradition (**XCIV**, 95). That is true in comparison with Matthew, and especially with John, but absolutely, as we shall see, it requires qualification.

Syria and Asia, in which the Saviour God, dying and rising again, was united with his followers by powerful rites, half symbolic and half realistic, which at once commemorated and in some way re-enacted, the saving drama of his life [1]; and finally the Jewish attitude, which made it necessary for Christian preaching to produce convincing miracles by Jesus, for, as Saint Paul says, " the Jews seek after signs " (1 Cor. i. 22 ff.).

There must also be added the influence of the " prophets " —of whom Paul is the most striking example—who in all good faith confused and blended the recollections which they may have owed to a genuine tradition, with the ideas derived from their own special revelations and visions. A man like Paul would attribute at least as much historical validity and a good deal more importance to what he had " learned of the Lord " by direct communication than to what he might have gathered from the lips of one or other of the Twelve.

Hence, the first Christians who judged it desirable to put it in writing found themselves in the presence of a very much depreciated tradition, a tradition diminished in one direction and enlarged in another. They were moved to the attempt, not by any consideration for our historical curiosity, but by the ethical or cultual requirements of Christian teaching, for the sake of which the first gospel compilations were made. We must imagine the two original source-books of our Synoptic Gospels as collections of sayings or incidents made for a special purpose, and it is evident that the authors of such tendentious collections cannot be taken as trustworthy judges of the intrinsic importance of what they leave out. It is reasonable to suppose that *Urmarcus* and *Q* were not the only compilations of this sort in circulation at the time. Even if we concede the authenticity of their reputed authorship, which probably determined their survival, it must be admitted that it did not procure for their texts the respect of their readers and copyists, who had few scruples about altering them and filling them with variations of a more or less serious character.

Hence, it is legitimate to question the trustworthiness of the letter of our present texts.[2] Before their canonization had more or less fixed their text, the Gospels had enjoyed a considerable circulation, possibly to their detriment. Of course we do not possess the originals, and we know them only as copies of copies. The strict accuracy of the archetypes them-

---

[1] **XLVIII,** 64 *ff.* ; **XLI,** 30 *ff.*, 208 *ff.*, 223 *ff.* ; **CCXLVII,** 34 *ff.* ; **CCXXVIII,** 174 *ff.*

[2] On the gospel text and its history *cf.* **LX** ; **LV** ; **LII,** ii ; **LXXXIV,** part i ; **LXII,** part i, 1–59 ; **XXVIII,** i, 475–86.

selves is doubtful, and since then the carelessness, the ignorance, or, worse still, the conceit of many a copyist, have worked havoc with the unfortunate text, not to mention the mischief done by the intentional "corrections" of those who have deliberately modified it, in one direction or another, to suit their religious views.[1] The patient work of exegesis can, perhaps, by a painstaking comparison of the manuscripts, correct some of these various corruptions. But it is to be feared that there are still some which we are no longer in a position to detect. Many of the innumerable variants are of no importance, but there are some, as we shall see, that are very disturbing.[2]

Since the two source-books did not include the whole of the oral tradition, the latter continued in circulation alongside them, offering a ready reception to edifying improvements, and always tending to influence the redactors of the texts. Some, such as Papias himself, still gave it preference over the writings, because they found it fuller. They failed to observe that its riches were not all genuine, as the absurdities which were current in the time of the Phrygian bishop sufficiently demonstrate. Eusebius, who had first-hand acquaintance with the works of Papias, brings the following charge against them : He (Papias) " adds some other things, as taken from the oral tradition, certain parables from the teaching of the Saviour which are surprising, and a number of stories which are wholly mythical ($\mu\nu\theta\iota\varkappa\acute{\omega}\tau\varepsilon\varrho\alpha$)." [3]

It is probable that it was from this tradition—which, whatever it had originally been, was no longer a *tradition* in the proper sense, but merely an affirmation of the *internal evidence* of the faith [4]—that the various redactors who successively worked upon *Urmarcus* and *Q* obtained the supplementary information of which they found themselves in need. Some of these additions are obvious from a cursory examination, such as the childhood narratives in Matthew and Luke, and the conclusion of Mark (xvi. 2–20). Others are less obvious or completely concealed, but their presence is unquestionable. To many modern critics [5] the presence of this oral tradition, plastic and instinctively adapting itself to the needs of the

---

[1] Concerning the old texts of our Gospels, see **LXXXIV**, 27 *ff*.

[2] *Cf.* **LV**, index ii, 380.—*Cf.*, for example, Luke xxii. 15–20, in the classic examples furnished by the *Textus Receptus*, and in *Codex Bezae*, entitled *D*, the great representative of the so-called *Western text*.

[3] *H.E.*, 3, 39, 11. A suggestive review of the influences which affected the development of the gospel tradition will be found in **CLVI**, 258 *ff*. For details see **LXXXVI**.

[4] Cadbury, XIII, ii, 263.   [5] *Cf.* Loisy, **RHLR**, 1922, 427 ; **CCV**, 30.

growing faith, appears to be the decisive factor in the shaping of our Gospels, and for that reason they no longer attach much importance to the problem of the written sources of these books. They regard them as mere incidents in the great process of constructing the legend of Jesus Christ, which came to an end only with the establishment of the canon, and it would be hard to say that they are wrong.

Our Gospels, then, were written to serve the purposes of instruction, of controversial apologetic, and of organized worship, and strictly speaking it is from these that they had their birth.   But forty or fifty years after the death of Jesus, Christian apologetic [1] was no longer merely concerned with proving that the Nazarene had been the Messiah ; it had to take into account a developed Christology, which raised problems concerning the relation of the Lord to God and to the cosmos quite incapable of solution by the Galilean *paradosis*.   It was still subject, moreover, to the influences that had so speedily made themselves felt upon the original tradition, and to them was now added that of Jewish Apocalyptic, which had undergone a vigorous revival about the time of the Great Revolt (A.D. 67–70), [2] that of the Apocryphal Gospels, in which the edifying legends of popular belief were set forth with a complete absence of restraint or good taste, [3] and finally, perhaps above all, that of the final breach between Judaism and Christianity, which inevitably tended to invest Jesus with a person and character irreconcilable with the ideas of Israel.   We may sum up this long discussion with the conclusion that the redaction of the most important episodes of the Synoptics, the Passion, for example, was especially influenced by cultual considerations. As soon as the Christian Lord (κύριος) became an object of worship, a cultual legend became a necessity, and the Gospels, from Mark to John, show a steady progress towards this end. There is no need to call them *merely* cult legends, as some have done, [4] but that is undoubtedly one of their aspects, and perhaps

---

[1] Baldensperger, *L'apologétique de la primitive Église, son influence sur la tradition des origines et du ministère galiléen de Jésus*, Rev. de théol. et de philos., Lausanne, 1920, 5–43.

[2] **CCXCV**, 69 *ff.* ; Hollmann, *Welche Religion hatten die Juden als Jesus auftrat?*, Halle, 1905, 37 *ff.*

[3] **CLXXXV**, 7.   There is no difference in kind between the stories of the childhood to be found in Matthew and Luke and those, for instance, collected by W. Bauer in **CXLII**.

[4] **LXXXVI**, 227 : " So sind die Evangelien Kultlegenden." **LXXXII**, 124 : " Die Evangelien sind kultische Volksbücher oder auch Volkstümmliche Kultbücher."   In the opinion of **CXCII**, the Passion, recast for liturgical purposes, was probably the beginning of the gospel tradition, and **CCV**, 18 *ff.*, advances a similar view.

the principal one. It is evident that the attempt to adapt the
gospel tradition to liturgical requirements must effectively have
contributed to the introduction of mythical and the suppression
of historical elements. The tradition may have been different
to begin with,[1] but we know it only in the adapted form which
organized worship imposed upon it. We shall see later, for
example, that the institution of Holy Week is not the same
in the Synoptics as in John, and that the liturgical commemoration of Easter is appointed at different times and governed by
different practices in the Asiatic churches and in the other
communities on pagan soil. It seems probable that the surprising divergence of the Fourth Gospel from the other three
is due to, and motivated by, the necessity of justifying an
established ritual custom, and that, on the other hand, the
same thing is true of the synoptic tradition itself, which was
called upon to justify a different custom. If it is true that the
gospel tradition is " in very large part a product of the Christian
faith " (Loisy), the influence upon it of the ritual in which that
faith expressed itself, is only a special case of the general
phenomenon. There is nothing surprising in the fact that it
is more striking than the rest, for the requirements of worship
are more immediate and imperious than those of reflection,
especially at the period we are dealing with.

Moreover, the first redactors of our Synoptics, who already
had little enough inducement to adhere to historical truth,
did not even succeed in giving a final form to the gospel beliefs
and conception of Jesus, since a comparison of their three
texts and of the manuscripts which remain to us reveals that
they suffered a number of subsequent alterations before becoming relatively stabilized in the canon. We say " *relatively* "
because between the end of the second century and the period
of our oldest manuscripts (such as the *Vaticanus* and *Sinaïticus*)
which date from some time in the fourth, occur all the small
corrections and rearrangements of detail made by the various
Churches in the text as they knew it, and all the work of
revision, emendation and adjustment, accomplished during the
third and fourth centuries in the great Christian schools of
Alexandria, Palestinian Cæsarea and Antioch. It is hardly a
rash assumption that the exegetes of those times were influenced
less by the strict principles of modern textual criticism than
by the demands of their reason and of their faith.

On the whole, all the work of early Christian thought on
the oral and written tradition regarding Jesus may be summed
up in one sentence : *it tends progressively to discard historical*

[1] **CLVI,** 270 *ff.* ; **XIII,** ii, 191, n. 1.

reality and to substitute for it edifying legend. What is surprising is not that our Synoptics contain so little of the actual
life and authentic teaching of Jesus, but that they appear still
to preserve some fragments of it.[1] We have reason to be
grateful to the method of symbolic interpretation, which perhaps was the means of saving several important incidents, and
to the zest of our three Evangelists for compilation, which led
them to ignore the necessity of blending the various elements
of their collection into a coherent whole. If they had been
occupied with this aim, they would have bequeathed to us
three documents of the type of the Fourth Gospel, and of as
little help in reconstructing the historical Jesus.

Nevertheless, all liberal critics, even those most concerned
to maintain the historical reality of Christ, and the possibility
of reaching it through the Synoptics, emphasize the inadequacy
of the information contained therein. They agree that it gives
us only the outline of a *secondary* representation, namely, the
conception of the Lord Jesus which was created by the generation after the Apostles, and that it is, moreover, only a one-
dimensional picture of Jesus, so to speak, on a single plane,
showing nothing of the variety, change, and development in
which life expresses itself.

Some have attempted to minimize this latter defect, repugnant to the psychologist, by maintaining that Jesus was so
essentially simple that he would not have changed greatly,
or that his career was too short to allow him time to develop.
But it remains to be disproved that the reason he seems to us
simple is because the gospel texts conceal his true life and
character. We no longer regard the Nazarene only with the
eyes of the men who, at the end of the first century, directed
their hopes towards the glorious future of his apocalyptic
return rather than towards the reality of his earthly past,
and for whom his image was fixed in the immobility of a superhuman perfection. To questions which seem to us elementary,
the testimony which these offer gives no answer, save, possibly,
a false or an erroneous one, because these witnesses were concerned only with the requirements of their faith, and not with
the problems of history. They were exclusively interested in
the myth of salvation which they had substituted for the facts
of the existence and preaching of Jesus, and, save for a few
inadvertencies, they retained of the original tradition, of the
veridical recollections of the Galilean Master, only so much as

---

[1] **LXXXVII**, 29, extends this remark and regards the existence of
the first five books of the New Testament as a greater miracle than
any contained in them.

accorded with their conception of the Lord. Even in the Gospel of Mark " we have no longer a historical biography of Jesus, but a series of anecdotes strung together " (Bousset). Strung together *arbitrarily*, we should add, sometimes with an apologetic or cultual motive, sometimes at random. A comparative study of the parallel incidents of the three Synoptics and a close analysis of the context of each leads inevitably to the conclusion that probably not a single one of them is either perfectly accurate or in its right place historically.[1] Even the little outline of the life of Jesus given by Mark, to which the Christian tradition has adhered at all costs, is possibly only the creation of a redactor. It is small consolation to reflect that, with little exception, this was the usual mode of writing history in the ancient Orient.[2] But we are denied even that, if, as everything seems to show, it was a Hellenistic community which created, on Greek soil, the literary form of the " Gospel." [3]

VII

The Apostolic Tradition concerning the Character and Teaching of Jesus

Lacking the help of the historical life of Jesus, is there at least a possibility left of arriving at some knowledge of his character and his fundamental ideas ? It is agreed that the gospel discourses attributed to him are, for the most part, including the most famous of all, the Sermon on the Mount, the work of redactors. Assuming that the teachings and sayings which compose them really emanated from Jesus, the question is how far they have preserved their original character and meaning in becoming part of an artificial discourse. Many of the sayings of the Nazarene dealt with particular situations, and claimed no wider application. They cannot be incorporated in a connected discourse directed to a much more general object, without ignoring their essential character, and investing them with a scope which possibly they did not originally possess.

For example, when Jesus says : " Think not that I am come to destroy the Law or the Prophets " (Matt. v. 17), the probability is that he is simply protesting against a tendency to regard him as a religious reformer. Luke xvi. 17 gives the saying as an independent *logion*. Matthew, on the other

---

[1] Bultmann, lxxxvi, has made the most thorough inquiry of this sort. *Cf.* **CLVI**, 230 *ff.*

[2] *Cf.* on this point, **XIII**. ii, ch. 1.   [3] **LXXXVI**, 226.

hand, by incorporating it in the Sermon on the Mount, sets it in quite a different light.[1] Further, the authenticity of all these *words* attributed to Jesus is open to question. It is hardly reassuring to remember that before being written down they had had a wide oral circulation, that they had been adapted to the purposes of apologetics, and that they had served as controversial weapons.

The truth is, *they are judged by their present appearance*, and that is a very dangerous criterion. The *logia* of Jesus, we are told,[2] are like pebbles which the waves of tradition have rolled and polished, and thrown into chance groups and patterns, but which, like real pebbles, have remained essentially unchanged, and may still be known for what they are. Such figures of speech are misleading. There are many things we do not know about the pebble which we pick up on the beach, or pluck from the chalky matrix of the cliff. Who can tell where its substance was formed; how it was torn from its original place; what were its original size and shape; when it began its journey; and by what road it travelled before coming to rest in the place where we find it? Nevertheless, we do at least know its name and age, and the nature of the rock of which it is a fragment. But where is the infallible test that will enable us with certainty to pick out from the rest a saying of Jesus, a saying that has reached us, like the pebble, worn and polished by long usage? Conybeare,[3] a scholar who is not afraid of bold negative conclusions, maintains that the majority of the gospel *logia* have a common stamp, which a little experience makes it possible to recognize with certainty. " It seems hypercritical, not to say absurd " to regard them as a collection of sayings issuing from different persons. The same claim is made about the *parables*, whose essential unity of style and spirit is undisputable. When we read the Psalms of David or the Proverbs of Solomon, the fact that they are written by various authors is quickly apparent. " In the sayings and parables of the Gospel, on the contrary, it is everywhere the same mind that speaks and expresses itself in the originality of their similes." [4] Hence it is clear that it is the appearance of the *logia* that constitutes the criterion of their genuineness.

The acceptance of this criterion still does not compel us to conclude that, if the *logia* came from a single source, that

---

[1] *Cf.* further Luke xiv. 26 and Matt. x. 37, on the subject of filial affection.

[2] **CXLIII,** 53. [3] **CCL,** 137 ; *cf.* **XXXIII,** 176.

[4] **CLXXX,** 24.

source must be identified with the teaching of Jesus. It is known, however, that both before and after the time of Christ the Jews were in the habit of making collections of the dicta of their rabbis. The authenticity of the sayings, for example, attributed by the *Mishnah* to Gamaliel, Hillel, Eliezer, and other early Jewish Fathers, has never been disputed, though they were committed to writing at a much later date after their utterance than were the *logia* of Jesus.

Hence, after making every allowance for the editorial corruptions that are always possible, there is a chance that the *logia* which our Evangelists found in *Q* were substantially authentic. We cannot, however, feel quite so confident on the point as those critics, such as Bousset and Conybeare, who find the above argument entirely conclusive, for the reason that we do not share their certainty of being able to recognize the *stamp* of Jesus upon what they offer as specimens of the gospel teaching. Without entirely endorsing the uncompromising challenge of Steudal, who holds the mythological view: " I shall be obliged to any theologian who will bring me a saying of Jesus which I cannot prove to have been already in existence in his time," we do not always see in the *logia* ascribed to Jesus the inimitable *originality* which is still sometimes attributed to them. We would even go so far as to say that many of them would attract no attention whatever, if they had been found in some dubious collection of *agrapha* instead of in a canonical book.

Moreover, it is not quite fair to compare the preservation of our *logia* with that of the rabbinical Sayings of the Fathers. Gamaliel, Hillel, Eliezer, etc., no doubt increased in stature with the passage of time, and people may have arbitrarily attributed to them here and there some striking saying to which the tradition assigned no author. But none of them became the Christ, the Son of God. Between them and the time when their sayings were fixed in writing, as far as we know, no Saint Paul intervened, and the point is undoubtedly significant. Finally they were never appealed to in support of a faith supposed to be derived from their teaching.

Pending a detailed proof, these simple considerations will perhaps suffice to show that the texts concerning the teaching of Jesus have little more chance of having remained unaltered than those which profess to deal with his life. Both have suffered addition or omission *in essential points*. The most we can hope is that we may still possess the original gist, or something like it, of a considerable number of those moral teachings of Jesus which came into no conflict with the Christological development, and of some of his precepts concerning the love of God and trust in him.

It must be admitted that many critics are more optimistic, or rather, though they are pessimistic enough when they study the gospel texts themselves, they change their attitude when they come to interpret them historically. It is only fair to give some account of their reasons, which are not entirely without weight.

Renan, who was a master of fine distinctions, sums up his impressions of the Gospels as follows : " They are neither biographies after the manner of Suetonius nor artificial legends after the manner of Philostratus ; they are romantic biographies. I should compare them with the legends of the saints, with the lives of Plotinus, Proclus, Isidore, and other writings of the same kind, in which historical truth and the desire to present models of virtue are blended in varying proportions. Inaccuracy, which is one of the characteristics of all popular writings, is especially conspicuous in this type. Let us suppose that ten or twelve years ago [1] three or four old soldiers of the Empire had independently set themselves to write the life of Napoleon on the basis of their memories. Their narratives would naturally exhibit numerous errors and striking discrepancies . . . but something would emerge from these naïve accounts which would have a high degree of truth, namely, the character of the hero, the impression that he made on those around him. From this point of view such popular narratives would be worth more than a sober official history. We may say the same of the Gospels. Solely concerned to throw into relief the greatness of the Master, his miracles and his teaching, the Evangelists are completely indifferent to everything but the very essence of Jesus. . . . The degree of inspiration that was ascribed to the sayings of Jesus was in inverse proportion to that attributed to his chroniclers. The latter regarded themselves merely as scribes, and concentrated on just one thing : omitting nothing of what they knew." [2] This view of the Gospels, however, does not correspond with the facts, and the very penetrating observations on the necessity which transformed Jesus into a figure of legend, with which Renan follows this rhetorical outburst, are not sufficient to correct the misleading character of his judgment. It was not the essence of Jesus that interested the authors of our Gospels, it was the essence of Christ, as their faith pictured him. They are exclusively interested, not in reporting what they know, but in proving what they believe.

[1] This was written in 1863.   [2] CLXVIII, xliv.

It is curious that even the men whose efforts have done most to prove that this is indubitably the evidence of our texts, are themselves betrayed, by imperceptible stages, into agreement with Renan. An atavistic instinct, more powerful than their reason, makes the negative conclusions to which their exegesis points intolerable to them, and drives them to postulate, for the benefit of the gospel narrative, a species of truth analogous to that which Renan attributed to the story of the Passion. In his words, " *they are not literally true, but they have a higher truth.* They are truer than the bare truth in the sense that they are truth rendered eloquent and significant, truth raised to the level of an idea." It seems difficult to conceive, in the field of history, of a truth superior to accuracy, which is made manifest only through errors of detail. Furthermore, the process which claims to raise a fact to the level of an idea hardly inspires confidence, for in the domain of religion, ideas have usually no relation to facts.

With less rhetoric, and, incidentally, less elegance, than Renan, but quite as confidently, a number of important modern critics champion the great historical value of our Synoptics, and thus repudiate in sum the concessions extorted by their detailed critical analysis. Some maintain [1] that the relevant recollections of the Galilean disciples were definitely fixed between A.D. 30 and 70, and that the growth of the tradition did not affect their essential content. Such was the position of Loisy in his *Évangiles Synoptiques*, when he wrote [2] : " Notwithstanding the importance that must be assigned to the influence of traditional ideas and of gospel redaction, the first three Gospels are substantially a faithful reflection of the teaching of Jesus," though he did make the following reservation : " The evaluation of the narratives is a very delicate matter." We are told of the " solid ground " beneath the accumulation of legend,[3] or the " sound historical material " which the synoptic tradition " in general " contains,[4] or the substantial identity of the accounts (*Erzählungsstoff*) given by the various narrators.[5] Other critics, more or less inclined to be suspicious of Matthew and Luke, retain their confidence in Mark, as embodying the best form of the early tradition.[6] All these " recantations " seem to indicate the dominance of a religious complex, the more fatal to clear judgment in that

---

[1] **XCIII**, iv *ff.*
[2] **CIII**, i, 82. *Cf. Autour d'un petit livre*[2], 88.   [3] **CLXVII**, 17.
[4] **XLVII**, 64. The same impression is given by **CCXVI**, 46, and **CCXVI**-*a*, 26 ; **CXLI**, 22 ; **CXLIII**, 43.
[5] **CLXXX**, 16.   [6] **CXVII**, 12 ; **CLXXXV**, 70 ; **CLXXV**, 47.

it is unconscious. Those who realize it gradually free themselves from it, as Loisy, for instance, has done, and come to
see the desert of our knowledge in its true light, undeluded
by mirages.

One important fact is certain : the synoptic tradition still
presents Jesus as a living person. It does not translate him
into the realm of divinity, as the Pauline writings go on to do.
But if it vouches for the actuality of his life, it does not reveal
the truth of it. On the contrary, it conceals it under accretions
which have no connection with the actual facts. We are confronted by the problem of distinguishing between genuine
tradition and apologetic figments. There are liberal critics
who maintain that the legendary figure of the Lord is always
animated by the vivid experience of Jesus. This optimistic
conviction is based on the belief that *Urmarcus* and *Q* were
originally trustworthy documents, which is precisely what we
have endeavoured to show they were not. Even had they
really been so, it would help us little, because they have been
so mishandled by the gospel redactors. The contradictions in
our three texts are not, as some still seek to maintain, limited
to the arrangement and style of the narrative, they penetrate
and infect the historical substratum itself—the *Erzählungsstoff*.
It is not, as a rule, so easy as it seems to certain critics, to
distinguish " the diamond from the bit of polished glass "
(Jülicher). It is only by means of the most patient and minute
critical labour over every gospel statement, that, aided by the
oversights, the blunders, the lapses of intelligence or the slips
of logic, into which our Evangelists have fallen, we can hope
at most to reach *probabilities on certain points*—apart from
the definite negative conclusions necessarily entailed by the
impossibilities of the canonical narrative.

So far we have been concerned only with the narratives.
For the " genuineness " of the *logia,* we are referred to the
inevitable parallel of the Rabbinical literature, and the argument
runs as follows. The *logia* come from a country where the
teachings of the rabbis were committed to memory by their
disciples, and preserved by this means without essential alteration for generations. The proof of the latter is that if we
collect and compare the Talmudic traditions concerning the
great " Masters " of Israel, we obtain of each of them a characteristic and lifelike picture, which has every appearance of
truth. This unerring memory, still characteristic of the
Orientals today, together with the intellectual inertia of the
Palestinians of the time of Jesus, and the clean, sharp outlines
of the sayings and parables, provide convincing evidence of

the genuineness at issue. In those days the rabbis were engaged in splitting hairs, and despised reality. Is it to be conceived that a work so vital, so closely in touch with concrete reality, could have emanated from any but a most original personality ? On close inspection our Evangelists undoubtedly reveal themselves as interpolators ; but though they have invented details, they are certainly not creators. They have no intellectual independence, and all their work is moulded by a twofold pattern, a personality (*Vorbild*) and a document (*Vorschrift*), which are quite unintelligible unless they reflect a man and a teaching. The apologetic tendency of these Evangelists is undeniable, which makes their inclusion of so many useless details, so many anecdotes irrelevant to their purpose, quite incomprehensible except on the assumption that these were part of the tradition, and that they either did not dare or did not know how to get rid of them. Why have they preserved so many instances in which Jesus appears as a mere teacher of morals (*Sittenlehrer*), and in no wise as a divine Redeemer (*Erlösergott*), when they themselves thought of him only as the latter ? The picture of the man and his teaching unfortunately remains fragmentary, but these fragments undoubtedly represent scraps of reality, so that, though the biography of Jesus is full of yawning gaps, the figure of the Nazarene and the essence of his teaching are almost completely known to us.[1]

It is not to be denied that these arguments contain some truth, but, plausible as they appear, a close examination of the texts that are supposed to justify them reveals their illusory character. It is remarkable, for instance, that men possessing such powers of memory have not even accurately retained the names of the Twelve Apostles, or the letter of the Paternoster. On the other hand, as we have tried to show, it seems evident that *Urmarcus* and *Q*, the sole bases of the gospel edifice, embody a tradition much less reliable and much more corrupt than is realized by the opponents of Drews. We may concede that the breath of life is still discernible in our Synoptics, and that the outline of a man and the traces of an individual activity are still to be distinguished, but that falls far short of what we need to see and know in order to form any clear and certain conception of the person of Jesus.

[1] These expressions are borrowed from **CLXXX**, 25 *ff.* ; **CXLIII**, 43 *ff.* ; and **CCXVI**–*a*, 26 *ff.* ; that is to say, from polemical works directed against the adherents of the mythological view ; but they are also those employed by most of the liberal critics. *Cf.* also **XXXIII**, 176 *ff.*

VIII

THE EXTRA-CANONICAL GOSPELS [1]

There are no other sources available to us besides the two to which our only means of approach is through the Synoptics. *Urmarcus* and *Q*, as we have observed, were probably not the only books inspired by the apostolic tradition, nor were these ancient documents made use of only by Mark, Matthew, and Luke. But whatever gospel writings may have been in circulation at the same time as the two mentioned by Papias, they have, unfortunately, disappeared, and of the Gospels which were authorized in various Churches, such as the " Gospel according to the Hebrews," the " Gospel according to the Nazarenes," the " Gospel according to the Ebionites," etc., we possess only small fragments. However, as far as we can judge, these different versions made use of no sources beyond those known to the Synoptics, and were no more faithful to them than they. Our impression, at least with regard to the " Gospel according to the Hebrews " and the " Gospel according to the Egyptians," is that they are dependent on our canonical Gospels, and we can expect from them no more than a basis of comparison and criticism.[2] Still less is to be derived from the imaginary, and often fantastic compositions which go by the names of the " Protevangelium of James," the " Gospel of the Childhood," the " History of Joseph the Carpenter," etc., or from the Gnostic writings known as the " Gospel of Thomas," the " Gospel of Philip," and the " Gospel of Eve," [3] of which, in any case, we have only scattered fragments.

The Egyptian Oxyrynchus Papyri have given us a dozen or so *logia*, which were discovered by Hunt and Grenfell in 1897 and 1903 respectively.[4] They appear to have been part of a collection made about the middle of the second century, and the sources and origins of this collection have been the

---

[1] For bibliography see James, *The Apocryphal New Testament*, Oxford, 1924, 29.

[2] **CIII**, i, 200 ; **CLXXXV**, 6. *Cf.* especially A. Schmidtke, *Neue Fragmente und Untersuchungen zu den judenchristlichen Evangelien*, Leipzig, 1911.

[3] *Cf.* **CXXXIII**. The texts are to be found in **CXXXVIII** and **CXXXVI**, and a German translation, together with valuable comments, in **CXXXIV**. On the use that is to be made of these legends, see **CXXXII** and **CXLII**.

[4] All these fragments are published in **XXIII** (nos. 11 and 31). The best edition is that of **CXL**. See also Ern. Buonaiuti, *Detti extracanonici di Gesu*, Rome, 1925.

subject of much discussion.[1] It was definitely not based upon our Synoptics, because several of the *logia* it contains have no parallel in our texts, and those which do resemble them differ too widely in form to have been directly derived from them. Some critics therefore conclude that the Oxyrhynchus collection represents an independent compilation based directly upon the tradition. Others explain them as derived from our canonical texts, but more or less completely distorted by the imagination of the collector. Others again prefer the idea of an anthology taken from one or more of the extra-canonical Gospels. Support may be adduced for all these views, but the essential point is that there is no reason to believe that these *logia* omitted from the Writings (which is the literal meaning of·the word *agrapha*. by which they are designated) are any older, that is, any nearer to the original form, than those contained in our Synoptics. The collection can hardly be older than A.D. 140. It is therefore improbable that it was made under any more favourable conditions than Mark, Matthew, and Luke. We shall probably not be far wrong in describing it as a little book of extracts from one or more of the non-canonical Gospels.[2] The "Gospel according to the Egyptians," which was at first suggested, must be excluded from the possible sources, because we know that it was already infected with Gnosticism, and was related to the *Pistis Sophia*, whereas the Oxyrhynchus *logia* exhibit the characteristic Synoptic colouring. Possibly the "Gospel according to the Hebrews" was the principal source.[3] A Lucan tinge appears in at least one of these *logia*, number two, which may be translated: "And the kingdom (or reign) of Heaven is within you."[4] This is the only echo to be found in any of the texts of the famous twenty-first verse of the seventeenth chapter of Luke: "for behold, the kingdom of God is within you (or among you)."

It is probable that we have here a collection of extracts made for the private use of a few believers. The state of preservation of the papyrus is poor, and the restorations that have to be made in the text are very often mere conjecture. On the whole, this interesting find is disappointing. It tells us nothing that we did not already know, and in the opinion of the writer, there is not much hope of anything better from future discoveries.

All the ancient writings that have come down to us have been carefully searched for sayings attributed to Jesus that

---

[1] *Cf.* **CXL**, xxxviii. [2] **CXL**, xl *ff.* [3] **CXL**, lxvii.
[4] The mutilated Greek text may be restored as follows: καὶ ἡ βασ [ιλεία τῶν οὐρανῶν] ἐντὸς ὑμῶν [ἐ]στι,

are not included in the canonical books, but these *Agrapha* are open to the same objections as those just dealt with.[1] The most we can hope to obtain from them is occasional light on the details of the teaching of Jesus ; they make no contribution to his biography.

There is another vast body of literature which is full of information about Jesus, namely, the Apocrypha of the New Testament. Renan's verdict on these is as follows : " Uninteresting and puerile elaborations, based on the canonical gospels and adding nothing of value." In any case, all they have to offer is the history of the development of the legend of Jesus, and the amazing inventions of a faith which, desirous of leaving no part of the human existence of the Lord unexplored, pictured it in the terms of its own imaginings, as a dazzlingly miraculous fairy tale. One of these apocryphal writings, the *Protevangelium of James*, is exceedingly interesting from the point of view of the history of Christian piety and the inspiration of Christian art, but it is quite irrelevant to the biography of Jesus.[2]

To all appearances the generation which followed that of our Evangelists knew no more than the latter about the Lord, and the writings of the Apostolic Fathers, the first Christian authors of the period between the closing years of the first century and the middle of the second, are of little assistance. They can aid us in tracing the history of the canon and of the legend of Jesus, but that is all. Their authors were no better informed than we regarding the facts of the life of the Master, and were much less competent to make the best use of the available traditions.[3]

Some scholars are of the opinion that several of the main incidents in the gospel life of Jesus, several of the essential features of his teaching, betray some influence of Indian Buddhism on the ideas current in the Christian communities at the time of the writing of the Synoptics. Apart, however, from the fact that the question of this influence is extremely obscure, Buddhistic sources could do no more than help us to understand some of the mythical elements of the gospel narrative. We need not labour the point here ; we shall have an

[1] The best collection is **CXXXVII**, or, in French, E. Besson, *Les Logia agrapha*, Bihorel-les-Rouen, 1923.

[2] All this literature is dealt with in detail by **CXXXII** and **CXLII**. *The Protevangelium of James* is published, with a good French translation, in **CXXXVI**, i.

[3] *Cf.* Bartlett, *The New Testament in the apostolic Fathers*, New York, 1905.

opportunity to revert to it in cases where a comparison may seem to be of value.[1]

CONCLUSION

To sum up, the tradition and recollections, more or less accurate, assembled in *Urmarcus* and *Q*, are all we have on which to base our knowledge of Jesus and his teaching. Further, our only means of access to them is through our Synoptics, in which it is by no means certain that they are completely included, and in which, in any case, their arrangement, setting and connexion are quite arbitrary. It is evident on first examination that the independent sources of Matthew and Luke furnish' no supplementary information of any value, apart, possibly, from a few details, inasmuch as they are almost wholly confined to the miraculous accounts of the Nativity and the Resurrection. Even, however, if we still possessed *Urmarcus* and *Q* in their original form, we should be little better off than we are now, since *Urmarcus* was already a patch-work of traditions of varying authenticity, and *Q* a mere collection of sayings and parables with no temporal or local setting. As Wernle justly observes, traditions about Jesus are not Jesus, and *logia* attributed to him, even correctly, are not his complete teaching ; and the attempt to construct a whole out of these disjointed fragments, is in great danger of following in the footsteps of the Synoptic authors themselves and achieving complete artificiality. The more we are convinced that there is no confidence to be placed in the Evangelists' arrangement of their source-material, the more we are forced to the conclusion that a reconstruction of the life of Jesus is impossible. We may still possess some stones of the edifice (*Bausteine*) but the plan of it (*Bauplan*) is unknown to us. The most we can legitimately attempt is to discover these stones in the later constructions that made use of them, to isolate them, and to study them, and even in this we must be prepared for many disappointments. Between us and the reality is always inter-

---

[1] Everything necessary for a general study of the question may be found in **CCLXXXV**. *Cf.* **XLI**, 5 *ff.* ; La Vallée-Poussin, *Le bouddhisme et les Évangiles canoniques*, **RB**, 1906, 353 *ff.* ; A. Bertholet, *Buddhismus und Christentum*, Tübingen, 1909 ; **LI**, ii[2], 350. Several important works have been devoted to a study of the question, notably those of R. Seydel, A. J. Edmunds, and A. van den Bergh van Eysinga. The most recent one known to the writer (R. Garbe, *Indien und das Christentum*) confines the Buddhistic influence to four passages of the New Testament. As a curious parallel, we may mention the book of Jeremias, *Babylonisches im N.T.*, Leipzig, 1905.

posed the faith of the generations through which the Gospels
were handed down, and on every point on which that faith
fastened, during the forty years or so between the death of
Jesus and the establishment of our Synoptic texts, we find
ourselves faced with the most disturbing complications. Concerning the person of the Master, the eschatological drama
which he is reputed to have proclaimed, the miracles he is
supposed to have performed, and his attitude to the Jews and
their Law, we know, perhaps, what his followers of the period
in question thought or believed. But what he himself thought
we can only conjecture. For those men his whole life was
seen in the perspective of his death and resurrection, and
culminated in his ascension in glory.[1] It need hardly be pointed
out that his own point of view must have been different, and
that in reality his career cannot have been such as it was represented by the Easter faith. The celebrated German scholar,
Eduard Meyer, has recently [2] made another attempt to evade
the conclusions just put forward, by endeavouring to convince
us that the *disciples*, who in the gospel account constitute the
ordinary following of Jesus, and appear as the bearers of the
tradition, left behind them a collection of authentic recollections (*die Jünger Quelle*), as did also the Twelve (*die Zwölfer-
quelle*). These two written sources would have been known
and used by the authors of the Synoptics, so that our knowledge of the life of Jesus would not rest solely upon the ideas
of the second generation, but go much further back, to the
recollections of the very generation that had seen and known
Jesus. Unfortunately, these comforting theories are the creation of a newcomer in the field of exegesis, and have convinced
none of those critics whose support might give them some
weight.

If we are unwilling to substitute invention for knowledge,
there is only one method. We must examine each individual
episode, each parable, each *logion*, and endeavour by a careful
comparison of the attendant circumstances as they are given
by the various accounts, and of the terms in which they are
expressed, to eliminate the accretions and recover the essential
nature of the source. Even when this perilous process is completed, we are obliged to be content with a critique of probabilities, based upon a study of the environment in which Jesus
lived, and constantly and vigilantly guarded against the intru-
sion of personal prejudices. A thankless task, beset with
anxiety, and whose results must always be open to question.
It is all too easy to point out its weaknesses. If, however, we

[1] CXII, 148 ; Cadbury, XIII, ii, 263.   [2] XXIV, i, 134–48.

can manage to establish a few probabilities, it is to such a method that we shall owe our success. The credit for making this possible must be given to the patience and perseverance of liberal exegesis.

A school has recently arisen in Germany, the principal representatives of which are G. Bertram, R. Bultmann, Dibelius, and K. L. Schmidt,[1] which claims to reform the methods and supplement—in some cases to alter—the conclusions of the scientific inquiry which for more than a century has been engaged upon our texts. It is called the *Formgeschichtliche Methode*, because it is characterized by a careful study of the *form* of each paragraph, with a view to discovering underneath the present version the exact nature of the tradition it is supposed to express. In other words, it endeavours, by means of the analysis of the existing text, to get back to the period prior to the setting down of the tradition, to its pre-history. Every type of writing, borrowed from Rabbinical literature, Greek history, popular legends, etc., which has been established by a comparison of the known models, is susceptible of the same critical analysis, and must be subjected to it, disclosing in the process the artificiality of its redaction, and in most cases, its utter lack of historical foundation. This proceeding is not so entirely novel as its ingenious practitioners appear to think, and the conclusions to which it leads are not all equally convincing. Nevertheless, their efforts have not been in vain, and they have rendered exegesis the great service of systematizing methods, which, although already introduced by J. Weiss and Loisy, amongst others, were worthy of a stricter and more regular application. The *Formgeschichtliche Methode* is, of course, only a special and somewhat limited application of the historical method. It has not revolutionized anything,[2] it has filled a gap, and it is the historical method itself which remains, on the whole, our sole hope, when textual and philological criticism has said its last word.

[1] The principles of the school are set forth by R. Bultmann, *Die Erforschung der synoptischen Evangelien* (*Aus der Welt der Religion*, no. 4), but the best general account of them is that of Erich Fascher, *Die Formgeschichtliche Methode ; Eine Darstellung und Kritik*, Giessen, 1924. Well worth reading are the various reports and analyses concerning works and tendencies of the school by Goguel, which have appeared of late years in the **RHPR** of Strasbourg.

[2] It is even somewhat surprising to see as radically negative a critique as that of Bultmann in **LXXXVI**, issuing, in **CXLV**, in a kind of revival of faith, well calculated to delight the conservatives.

PART I

THE LIFE OF JESUS

CHAPTER I

THE HISTORICAL EXISTENCE OF JESUS [1]

I

THE PROBLEM

THE poverty and uncertainty of our information about Jesus long ago gave rise to the question, of first importance to us here, whether this person, of whom we know practically nothing, ever really existed, or whether that which claims to be the record of his life is anything more than a tissue of myths, allegories, and symbols. The controversy was started at the end of the eighteenth century by some of the French *philosophes*, notably Dupuis and Volney, and has continued ever since, alternately raging furiously and lapsing into periods of quiescence. It is evident that if the personality and influence of Jesus disappear from history, the birth of Christianity has still to be explained, and it is to this task that those who deny his historicity have applied themselves, with a confidence only equalled by the variety of their theories and the flimsiness of their arguments. Popular opinion, always susceptible to novelty, and entirely indifferent to the cautious reservations of scientific exegesis, impressed by their air of conclusiveness

[1] For the bibliography of the subject prior to 1914, see the small book by the present author, **CLVIII**. The following additions should be made : for the mythological case : A. Drews, *Das Markus-Evangelium als Zeugnis gegen die Geschichtlichkeit Jesu*, Jena, 1921 ; by the same author, *Die Leugnung der Geschichtlichkeit Jesu in Vergangenheit und Gegenwart*, 1926 ; R. Stahl, *Le document 70*, Paris–Strasbourg, 1923 ; G. A. van den Bergh van Eysinga, *Die holländische radikale Kritik des Neuen Testaments*, Jena, 1912 ; **CLII** ; J. M. Robertson, *The Historical Jesus. A survey of positions*, London, 1916 ; **CLIX** ; Ed. Dujardin, *Le dieu Jésus. Essai sur les origines et la formation de la légende évangelique*, Paris, 1927 ;—for the historians : **CXLVIII** ; **CXLVI**, which has an ample bibliography ;—from the Catholic point of view : M. Lepin, *Le Christ Jésus, son existence historique et sa divinité*, part i, Paris, 1930.

and originality, has more than once given an enthusiastic reception to such theories, and encouraged the amateurs by its admiring applause. For " amateurs " they nearly all are who uphold the negative and mythological point of view ; some naïve and superficial, quite unconscious of the pitiful inadequacy of their knowledge, others well documented, that is to say, conversant with the subject, sometimes even learned in it, but equally ignorant or impatient of the humble and patient discipline of exegesis. They are ever ready to thrust aside or mishandle the texts instead of cautiously and respectfully attempting to extract the truth from them; to impose upon them arbitrarily whatever conclusions their own convictions demand, instead of keeping within the limits to which a scrupulous critical and historical sense would confine them. Such flimsy and unfounded speculations may perhaps yield interesting works of the imagination, and exhibit a fascinating ingenuity, but they do no service to science, which, though it lives by hypothesis, indulges in paradox at its peril.

We are not here referring to the position that Jesus had no historical existence, which is in itself a perfectly legitimate theory entitled to serious discussion. The paradoxes we have in mind are the extravagant or arbitrary interpretations imposed upon the texts and the facts by the adherents of the mythological view, the far-fetched connexions and rash and unfounded assertions into which their abuse of the comparative method leads them.

A complete survey of the investigations, hypotheses and conclusions of the adherents of the mythological point of view, even limited to those which are still prominent today, is a task of no small magnitude, and one which has already been attempted by the writer elsewhere.[1] We shall therefore confine ourselves to giving a general idea of the position of those who deny the historicity of Christ and a brief statement of our reasons for disagreeing with them.

The radical approach is by way of what is called in Germany scientific or liberal theology.[2] The history of Christianity in Germany is in the hands of theologians of all shades of opinion, who for the most part study it scientifically, but are all too prone to seek in it the justification of their own special religious views. For example, the liberal Protestants see Jesus as the founder of true godliness amongst men, the supreme

---

[1] Notably in **CLVIII** (1914), in a criticism of **CXLIX**, in **RHR,** 1926, and in a chapter on " The Jesus of History," in a collection of lectures entitled *Jésus et la conscience moderne*, Paris, 1928, 5–28.

[2] **CLVIII,** 42 *ff.*

moral teacher, who came for the purpose of effecting, by his
own example, a moral reformation which would make possible
the advent of the Kingdom of God, that is to say, the ultimate
reign of love and righteousness in a world regenerated by the
faith of those who received him. Accordingly, they attempt
to prove that Jesus of the Gospel is identical with this " liberal
Jesus " of their ideal, that his ideas and aims are the same as
their own. This is obviously a questionable proceeding, and
the objections which were raised when the liberal thesis was
first formulated over thirty years ago (1900), by Harnack in
his *What is Christianity?* (*Das Wesen des Christentums*), have
lost nothing of their force. Harnack's authoritative statement
of the position was answered by Loisy in his *L'Évangile et
l'Église*, where he rightly maintained that the " liberal Jesus,"
born of modern religious needs and ideals and conceived in a
special credal setting, is not the Jesus of history. More recently
Bultmann, one of the most destructive critics of what is called
the synoptic tradition, has attempted to reconstruct out of the
ashes to which he had reduced it, a Jesus [1] who could have
sprung only from religious feeling and an inward compulsion
totally indifferent to the historical facts. Such proceedings
arouse the most vigorous opposition from the supporters of the
mythological view.[2] They find an inexhaustible subject for
sarcasm in " the sophistical dexterity " which reads subjective
impressions into the texts and snips up the New Testament
with its theological scissors until it ends by making of it a
completely artificial thing, because it refuses to accept it for
what it is, a document showing the development of Catholic
Christianity. The name Jesus, they declare, " has become a
mere vessel into which every theologian pours the content of
his own ideas." Each extols his own Christ, and proclaims
more or less openly : " Jesus is great . . . and I am his
prophet." The vaunted scientific research of the liberals, say their
opponents, has just two objects : to discomfit Roman Catholic
theology, and to justify their own beliefs. The Jesus it finds
is the Jesus it is looking for, but it is one without any relation
to history.

In this indictment the radicals unfairly confuse the critical
method, which has been amply justified, with the tendentious
exploitation of it of which, ironically enough, too many theo-

[1] **CXLV.** There is an important review by Lohmeyer in **TLZ**,
September 17, 1927.
[2] The terms of the indictment are borrowed from Kalthoff and
Drews, but the substance of it is the same in all, or nearly all, the
negative critics.

logians are guilty.[1] The inducement to this confusion is
obvious. Liberal criticism has destroyed the traditional conception of Jesus, and shown that, granted the assumption of
his existence, we possess only a few scattered fragments of
information about his life. Consequently, if, by attributing to
the liberal party as a whole the unfounded reconstructions of
a few of its adherents, the little which it still holds to be certain,
and the remnant of the gospel tradition to which it still clings,
could be shown to be illusory, the Galilean would completely
disappear. Accordingly, exegetes who have no interest whatever in the cause of liberal theology, for instance, Alfred Loisy
and the present writer, are, under the derogatory title of " *his-
toricists*," included in the same category as the liberal theologians, for the sole reason that in their reconstruction they
refuse to substitute Jesus the god for Jesus the man.[2]

Radical criticism of the traditional evidence concerning the
existence of Jesus is based upon two main contentions, which
have been restated by Bruno Bauer : (1) Contemporary Jewish
and pagan literature makes no mention of Jesus ; (2) The New
Testament writings, with their inconsistencies and contradictions, their obvious interpolations, and their amazing improbabilities, cannot be regarded as a trustworthy historical source.
Moreover, all that they claim to relate bears the stamp of unreality. The Gospels are apocalyptic writings, that is to say,
they reveal truth which is reputed to be divine, and are characterized by a complete indifference to history and geography.
Even apart from the miracles, which must be rejected at the
start, not one of the incidents recounted in them is attested.
A comparison of the three texts reveals that in not one narrative are they in complete agreement, and that in many they
are quite irreconcilable. These contradictions prove that the
ancient Christians did not look upon them as historical books,
recounting the life and work of a man, but as treatises relating
to a god and intended for the confirmation of the faith. Otherwise they would at least have endeavoured to remove their
inconsistencies. Liberal criticism, according to the radical
school, is entirely wrong in maintaining that the three Synoptics
are of a different type from the Gospel of John ; there is not
" a hair's breadth " of difference between them. The son of
the Virgin, conceived by the Holy Ghost, the hero of the Trans-

---

[1] They are not all Germans ; there are plenty of them in England
and America, and they are not unknown in France. Some of the
Catholic party are commencing to imitate them, with more or less
success.

[2] **CXLIX**, 186 *ff.* : " The true historian is not a ' historicist '."

figuration, the Resurrection, and the Ascension, has no more historical probability than the Johannine Christ. All that can legitimately be sought for in the Gospels, is the material of the earliest history of Christian dogma, not that of the life of Jesus. Of the latter they can tell us absolutely nothing, for all that they relate concerning it is obviously incredible.

The Epistles of Paul are not so easily disposed of, and the liberals are perhaps justified in regarding them as the fundamental evidence for the existence of Jesus. They contain several passages which appear to be based upon, and to necessitate, the belief that the Lord lived in the flesh and died upon the cross. Various arguments are advanced by the radicals to meet this evidence. The most sweeping consists in maintaining that all the Pauline Epistles are apocryphal, the product of some theological school of the second century. Another takes the contrary form of granting them the highest authenticity, as the most ancient expression of primitive Christian beliefs concerning Jesus,[1] but logically and ruthlessly disposing of all the troublesome passages as interpolations or misinterpretations.

The Jesus of Paul, say they, was revealed to him in visions, and has no resemblance to Christ of the Synoptics, the preacher and worker of miracles. Nor is he more real. He is either a god already worshipped in some Jewish sect as a self-appointed Saviour and Redeemer, or simply another manifestation of the Jahweh of old.[2] The most ancient Christian literature, that of the first and second centuries, tells us nothing of the historical Jesus. The Lord with which it is concerned is not an individual, but a kind of personification of the transcendent principle of the Church, which suggests that the ancient Christians were not themselves deceived by their myths, and did not regard the Christ as an actual man. The wall-paintings of the Catacombs confirm this impression, portraying Jesus, as they do, not in the likeness of a carpenter of Nazareth, but in that of the Good Shepherd, youthful and beardless, the symbol of the young community and its work of sustaining the weak and bringing back the strayed. Finally, it is asked, how could the obscure *nabi* of whom we get a glimpse in the Synoptics possibly have been so quickly transformed into the exalted divine Being, the Lord, of the Pauline conception ?

Since there is no proof that Jesus had any historical existence, and, on the other hand, there are many difficulties which

---

[1] " It is to Paul that we must go for the most certain information regarding the beginnings of the faith," writes M. Couchoud, **CXLIX**, 89, and it is the best thing in his book.

[2] **CXLIX**, 77–90.

suggest the contrary, the balance of probability, in the opinion of the radicals, is in favour of the latter conclusion. M. Couchoud, whose dilettantism does not save him from the inevitable tendency to dogmatism, scorns the cautious, and offers his conclusions as certainties. In return he promises " an endless and intoxicating study " [1] to anyone who will follow his revelation.

II

The Mythological Explanation of the Christian Movement

It remains only to explain the origin of the Christian movement and the gospel legend itself, and to this each of the radicals applies himself in his own way, according to his own system. Jensen, for instance, [2] sees in the gospel figure of Jesus an adaptation of the saviour hero Gilgamesh of the Babylonian epic, and since the legend of Gilgamesh represents a solar myth, the Jesus of the gospel becomes the sun surrounded by the twelve signs of the Zodiac, personified by the Apostles. Our Assyriologist takes enormous—and incidentally, quite futile—pains to fit into his general contentions all the details of the gospel story.

Kalthoff, [3] again, maintains that Christ was not a man, but the personification of a social movement. This movement was Roman in origin, due to the fact that the social organization of the Empire had created a wretched and turbulent proletariat, but Jewish in form, because the Messianic conception of the Jews, once " denationalized " and universalized, lent itself readily to exploitation by the outcasts of society, and also because the police and military organization of the imperial government made any direct uprising of the lower classes impossible. The reason that the four Gospels differ is because they represent different trends in the great social upheaval out of which they arose. Their unity consists in the fact that their combined accounts give us the total process by which the Church was established ; their variety comes from the fact that the four authors did not all witness the same phase of the movement which brought it into being. Their Palestinian appearance is only a mask ; they are in reality Roman products. The Christians of the first century mirrored their own life of trials, and embodied their own ideal, in this picture of Christ. It was made in their own image, and, once it had

---

[1] CXLIX, 186.   [2] CLVIII, 85 ff.
[3] Ibid., 78 ff.

passed from the status of fiction to that of accepted fact, it became their guide and pattern.

Robertson [1] believes that Jesus was the hero of a sacred drama which was performed in the secret circle of a company of initiates of Jewish origin, and represented the story of a god sacrificed by his father for the salvation of men. In primitive times the drama may have culminated in the real sacrifice of a man playing the part of the god. At the time when the Gospels were written it ended in a ritual feast at which the faithful were supposed to eat the god, symbolized by the consecrated bread and wine, for the purpose of assimilating his substance and becoming one with him. It was, in short, a syncretistic cult for which the Mysteries of Osiris, Tammuz, Adonis, Attis, Dionysus-Zagreus and Heracles furnished the models and the main features. The movement from which this cult sprang originated in Israel, at least a century before the beginning of the Christian era, in the lower classes of society, amongst people who were hostile to Pharisaic Judaism and who were called " the poor " (*ebionim*). One of the sects of *ebionim*, that of the Nazarenes, transported its god to Greek soil, and there he flourished. This god was, in fact, no other than Joshua, an ancient divinity of the tribe of Ephraim, who had brought his people into the Promised Land, and who, under his new name of Jesus, was to open the Kingdom of God to his followers. He symbolizes the triumphant progress of the sun. The Gospels are, accordingly, propaganda intended to systematize and to give a basis of probability to the legend operative in the sacred drama of the sect, to bring it into conformity with the mythological conventions of the age.

Another critic, B. Smith,[2] sums up the matter as follows. Jesus the Nazarene is the special god of the syncretistic and " occult " Jewish sect of the Nazarenes, or Nazoreans, who, more than a century before the time of the supposed birth of Jesus Christ, worshipped a divine Liberator, Guardian, and Saviour, or, preferably, worshipped Jahweh under that special aspect, since Jeshuah is Jahweh the Saviour. The whole gospel narrative is the concrete development of symbols and myths according to well-known processes. This pre-Christian cult of Jesus was spread by preachers, of whom Paul is the perfect type, and whose activities the Book of Acts depicts. The basis of the gospel story was probably drawn (Drews) [3] from the Oriental Mysteries, and crystallized around the myth of the young god who dies and rises again as Saviour and exemplar of

[1] *Ibid.,* 88 *ff.*   [2] *Ibid.,* 95 *ff.*

[3] *Ibid.,* 107 *ff.*

his worshippers.   Primitive Christianity is thus to be explained as a vast syncretism, in which were combined the solar myths of India and Persia, the Messianic hopes of Iran and Israel, the Greek mystery cults of a divine mediator, and numerous practices from various sources.   The origin of the story of an earthly existence of the god is to be found in the pretensions of the Judaeo-Christians of Jerusalem.   In their desire to humble Paul, they pretended that the Saviour had lived amongst them, that they had known him *in the flesh*, and were possessed, on that account, of an indisputable superiority.

Various other systems [1] have been advanced, all based on the same ideas and composed of practically the same elements. The most general conclusion, in which almost all concur, may be stated as follows : *The Jesus of the Gospels is only a mythological figure, created, in one or more of the syncretistic Jewish sects, prior to the Christian era.*   M. Couchoud distinguishes himself by seeking his explanation, not in a mere myth, but in a spiritual movement and a religious conception actually operative in Israel.[2]   On his view, Jesus is only one aspect of Jahweh—for his name means Jahweh the Helper or the Saviour —an aspect which had previously been neglected or unrealized in his worship, and of which Jewish religious feeling, or one section of it, finally became conscious.   The type of Saviour depicted was modelled on recollections of the Scriptures, and is, properly understood, only an interpretation of the famous fifty-third chapter of Isaiah, wherein are described the trials of the Servant of Jahweh.   This chapter is, in fact, the epitome of Christianity and the original source of the life of Jesus.[3]   The source of the Passion is to be found in the account of the trial of Stephen in the seventh chapter of Acts.

III

CRITICISM OF THE MYTHOLOGICAL THEORIES

Learned and ingenious though many of them are, the mythological theories have not succeeded in gaining the adherence of any of those independent and disinterested scholars who are always open to conviction by established facts, and whose support would have been of real significance.   This is a failure for which the enthusiastic reception of those unqualified to judge hardly compensates.

Jensen's theory reveals itself on first examination [4] as the

---

[1] CLVIII, 118 *ff.*   [2] CXLIX, 87 *ff.*
[3] CXLIX, 39, 43 *ff.*   [4] CLVIII, 123 *ff.*

colossal aberration of a specialist obsessed by the desire to explain everything in terms of his own particular preoccupation. Actually, the most characteristic features of the traditional life of Jesus—the passion, the crucifixion, and the resurrection—are not found in the epic of Gilgamesh, and conversely, the most prominent incidents of that poem do not appear in the gospel narrative.

The theories of Kalthoff [1] have a sociological cast which renders them at first more attractive. But all the details of the popular movements, the social unrest, of the Empire of the first century, on which the author depends, are, in reality, purely hypothetical. He has no proof that the Roman proletariat was affected by Jewish apocalyptic beliefs. It is merely assumed by him on the strength of the idea that both tend to communism—a belief which itself needs proving, especially in the case of Jewish Messianism, of which we have no reason whatever to suppose that one of its fundamental features was the hope of an economic revolution. The theory of the substantial creation in Italy of the gospel narrative seems an untenable paradox, and Kalthoff himself makes a poor show of defending it. Finally, there is the question how a social movement of revolutionary trend could have given rise to a religion of resignation, and by what precise process the Christian community came to make this projection, personification, and deification of itself.

Robertson, Benjamin Smith and Drews [2] accept the existence of pre-Christian, syncretistic, Jewish sects, an essential feature of whose cult was the worship of a sacrificed god called Jesus, who was the Saviour, Mediator, and Protector of his people. That such sects did exist is probably true, but unfortunately we know nothing of their cult, and if we may regard it as probable that it centred around the Messiah (Greek, *Christos*) expected by the Jews, we have no grounds whatever for believing that it gave him the name of Jesus. Similarly there is no documentary evidence for the belief that Joshua, whatever may have been his original character, was still regarded as a god at the beginning of the Christian era, and, consequently, no foundation for the statement that Jesus is simply a continuation of Joshua.

M. Couchoud, in deriving the Christian movement from a vision of Simon Peter, only substitutes the riddle of Cephas for that of Jesus, for if we know hardly anything about the carpenter, we know nothing at all about the fisherman up to the moment of his appearance in the synoptic narrative. His

[1] *Ibid.,* 124 *ff.*   [2] *Ibid.,* 130 *ff.*

claim that the most ancient form of the religion of Jesus is that of Paul, sounds, to a critic who has spent his life in the study of the Epistles, like a somewhat laboured attempt at humour. For the supreme influence of the fifty-third chapter of Isaiah on the story of the Passion, there is simply no evidence. It is surely significant that Mark, who makes considerable use of the Scriptures, does not appear to attach any particular importance to the ancient prophet, and makes no citation whatever of the crucial passage, the famous fifty-third chapter. Even Matthew, who is so anxious to point out every instance of the fulfilment of a scriptural text,[1] makes no reference to the chapter. The truth is, that at the beginning of the Christian era Isaiah liii. was not regarded as of Messianic significance. It was the Christians, later on, who found in it the means of amplifying their meagre tradition regarding the Passion of the Lord.

When we consider the mythological theories as a whole, problems start up on all sides. If Jesus was a god, how was it that the Christians, even Paul himself, did not regard him as one, and why this parody of humanity with which they unanimously clothe their myth ? The answer of Drews to this question is not satisfactory, for even if the people at Jerusalem had invented the earthly life of the Lord to give themselves an advantage over Paul, why should he have apparently agreed with them ? Moreover, the Christianity of the gospel is not an independent religion ; it worships the god of Israel. Why, then, should it have created for itself another divinity, and then proceeded to conceal him, for he never appears as such ? If the god Jesus is an aspect of Jahweh, why is this great truth never even hinted at ? It is suggested that we are in the presence of a Mystery, in which secrecy is the rule. But the god of the Christian cult dies openly, at the hands of the Roman authorities, after a public trial ; this has nothing in common with a Mystery, or anything like it. If the legend of the god is purely imaginary, divorced from all foundation in fact, it is strange that it should have been left so full of gaps and inconsistencies, that it should have been encumbered with the details of a common human existence, which serve no useful purpose, and are even rather shocking. Why take the trouble to speak of the brothers and sisters of the god, and even to give their

---

[1] At the very beginning of Matthew (i. 22) the characteristic formula makes its appearance : τοῦτο δὲ ὅλον γέγονεν ἵνα πληρωθῇ τὸ ῥηθὲν ὑπὸ κυρίου διὰ τοῦ προφήτου λέγοντος—*Now all this was done that the word of the Lord* (Jahweh) *that was spoken by the prophet might be fulfilled. Cf.* Matt. ii. 5, 15 and 17 ; iii. 3 ; iv. 14 ; viii. 17 ; xiii. 35 ; xxiv. 4 ; etc.

names (Mark vi. 3)? Why represent his family as believing
him " beside himself " (Mark iii. 21)? Why show him exhibiting anger and grief, and weeping over himself and others?
Why cause him to reject the designation of himself as good
(Mark x. 18), and to proclaim that God alone is good? Why
should he, who has come down to proclaim and to bring about
salvation, declare that he does not know when the great day,
his own day, from the Pauline point of view, will come (Mark
xiii. 3, 2)? And why is his last cry, at the very moment of
his consummation of the divine mystery (Mark xv. 34), one of
despair ("My God, why hast thou forsaken me?")? To
explain all this as an attempt at verisimilitude, is surely to
attribute an incredible amount of method and consistency to
men who are, in other respects, so conspicuously lacking in
either. How are we to reconcile this with so much vagueness
and ambiguity in the teaching, so that even today the exact
meaning is sometimes doubtful? Above all, why did those
who created the myth, place the hero of it in their own
time, instead of, in accordance with the universal practice of
religions, seeking to avail themselves of the enormous prestige
of antiquity?

It would be only too easy to prolong the list of such questions, to none of which can those who deny the existence of
Jesus give any satisfactory answer. If the figure of Jesus had
really been a deliberate and intentional creation of the Gospel
writers, they would naturally have been supremely interested
in him. But we have only to read the Gospels to see at once
that, as a matter of fact, they are not interested in him at all.
That is precisely why their quasi-biography of him is so inadequate. The truth is that this man, this Jesus, is already, in
their eyes, Christ, the god. His humanity is something thrust
upon them, which they have to make the best of. Their narrative is composed of mythical variations on the facts of an actual
existence, which hampers them, and which they would never
have imposed upon themselves. The Jews were in a position
to know the truth, and were restrained by no scruples in their
polemic against the Christians regarding the person of Christ.
Had there been any possibility of denying his existence, we
may be sure they would have seized upon so conclusive a retort.
But while the Talmud attempts to disparage Jesus, it never
denies his reality.

The best witness of the historical existence of Jesus is,
paradoxically, Paul, the alleged mainstay of the mythological
view. Undoubtedly his Christ is a divine being. We may
even grant, though it is straining the term, that he is a god.

But *he is a god who has been a man*, or Paulinism is unintelligible. For the mystery preached by the Apostle to have any meaning, the Lord must have been a mortal man, for the sham crucifixion of a god, the unreal death of a supernatural being, is quite incompatible with the realism of the Pauline teaching. Moreover Paul states definitely that in the flesh—and he is confident that he might have known him *in the flesh*—the Lord sprang from the race of David, that he was born of a woman, became subject to the Law, and voluntarily, in obedience to God, assumed human form, and submitted himself to a human life of suffering, culminating in the death of the cross. It is unquestionable that Paul regards him as a man, a human being capable of death and pain, for without that he cannot become the vicarious sacrifice necessary for the salvation of the world. The fact that Paul declares that the Lord was " in the flesh a man born of woman," seems of itself proof enough, but the comparison of two passages in the Epistle to the Corinthians appears to put the matter beyond all possible doubt. In the first (2 Cor. v. 16) the Apostle emphasizes the necessity of living ἐν Χριστῷ, *in the risen Christ*, and declares that he is now determined to know no other Christ, even though he had known Christ formerly *in the flesh*, that is to say, as Jesus, in his life upon earth. In other words, the divine Lord, glorified after having accomplished his work of salvation, is all that matters in the Pauline mystery, in spite of the men who set themselves up as authorities on the strength of having known Jesus in life, and who have tried to claim precedence over Paul on that account. That is why he asserts (1 Cor. ix. 1) that *he, too, has seen the Lord*, not in the flesh like the people at Jerusalem, but in the realm of the spirit, by the divine grace which would exalt his lowly status as an apostle. The desire to establish by means of this glorious compensation, the dignity of his mission against the prestige of the Twelve, proves conclusively, in the opinion of the writer, that Paul of Tarsus implicitly believed that Jesus had really lived.

It is no answer to this to say that Paul's attribution of humanity to Christ is merely ideal, a symbol demanded by his soteriological scheme. A hypothetical interpretation of that kind has no weight against a precise passage which is perfectly clear in itself—still less against a whole collection of such passages. Moreover, it is difficult to see what object men who lived in a perpetual confusion between the mythical and the real could have, in making a god into a man. As an attempt to give probability to a legend, it might be a comprehensible proceeding on the part of some mythologist of our own time, but in the case of a mystic, or even of an initiate of the first century, that explanation is absurd. To make a man into a god is, on the other hand, a characteristic step in ancient religions. It is asserted by Couchoud that such a thing is inconceivable among the Jews. This is, perhaps, not strictly true, since at the very same period Simon the Samaritan was calling himself " the Great Power of God," and had obtained a following. But in any case, the Pauline metamorphosis that transformed Jesus Christ into the Lord before whom every creature bows the knee (Phil. ii. 10) did not take place on Jewish, but on Greek soil, in the atmosphere of the salvation Mysteries and of syncretism. In the world of Palestine, in the bosom of Jewish orthodoxy, only a madman could have conceived the incarnation of the Spirit of God, and such an idea would have been received with the utmost horror and indignation.

The inevitable transmutation of the original tradition into a myth took place by several stages. First *the Messianic idea* was developed in the Jewish communities by grouping all the supposedly Messianic passages of the Scriptures around the figure of the man who had come to be regarded as the Messiah, and embodying them in events of his life. Then when it reached Greek soil, the tradition took over the conception of the *Soter*, in order to assimilate the picture of Jesus to the generally recognized characteristics of the rôle of the *Soter*. Our Synoptics are still in the first stage. Paul belongs wholly to the second. John and the author of the Epistle to the Hebrews represent a more advanced development of the same phase. The transformation of Jesus into the Saviour no more excludes his human existence than his transformation into the Messiah. In fact, it is true to say that neither of them is historically conceivable without that existence.

Christian propaganda created, developed, and elaborated a Christ myth at the expense of Jesus. But it did not invent Jesus himself, and it was Jesus himself who was in some way the inspiration of its faith in him.[1]

Those who surrender to the heady delights of theory-building may possibly see things in a different light, but this is the view that emerges when we regard the facts soberly in their historical setting, respecting the unconscious evidence of the documents, and making no attempt to extort from them findings conformable to our own desires.

[1] *Cf.* Loisy, **RHLR**, 1922, 22.

CHAPTER II

THE NAME: JESUS THE NAZARENE

I

THE PROBLEM

GRANTING the historical existence of Jesus, we are at once confronted by the problem of his name, Jesus the Nazarene. According to our Gospels, his name, properly speaking, was simply Jesus, and "the Nazarene" was a kind of surname indicating his birthplace, or perhaps merely his origin —Jesus came from Nazareth. It is a very simple explanation. In fact, it seems suspiciously so when we remember that the ancients in general, and the Jews in particular, attached to names, both of men and of things, a peculiar value, at once metaphysical, mystical, and magical. They were supposed to express the special power or virtue (*virtus, dynamis*) of that which they designated. The true name of a god, for example, whose revelation to the initiate or the believer endowed him with knowledge (*gnosis*), was supposed to contain, so to speak, the essence of his divine being.[1] A worshipper of the syncretistic Greco-Egyptian god, Poimandres, for instance, addresses Hermes in the following words: " I know thy name, Heavenly One. I know thy various manifestations. . . . I know thee, Hermes, and thou knowest me. I am thou, and thou art I." [2] Moreover, it is sometimes stated in the Bible, for instance, with regard to Ishmael (Gen. xvi. 11) and Isaac (Gen. xvii. 19), that God himself has selected in advance the name of someone for whom he has prepared a great destiny.[3] Josephus (*Ant.*, 2, 9, 5) makes the same assertion concerning Moses, and Rabbi

---

[1] See: W. Schmidt, *Die Bedeutung des Namens*; 1912; **CCL,** 235 *ff.*, the chapter entitled " Magic Use of the Names "; **CCX,** 68 *ff.* ; **XLI,** 182 *ff.* ; **VIII,** 140 and 143 ; **CCLXV,** i, 124 *ff.* ; Maspero, *Etudes de mythol. et d'archéol. égypt.*, ii, 298 ; Fossey, *Magie assyrienne*, 56, 58, 95 ; Henry, *Magie dans l'Inde*, 31. It was a belief that was prevalent throughout the whole of the ancient world.

[2] **CCXCIV,** 20 ; **CCXXVIII,** 123.

[3] On the power of divine names amongst the Jews, see **X, 184.**

Eliezer declares [1] that " six persons received their names before they were born, namely, Isaac, Ishmael, our great law-giver Moses, Solomon, Josiah, and the Messiah." It is well known, further, that the name of Jahweh was generally regarded, even outside Israel, as possessing such power that the pagans used it in their magical incantations. In Israel, it was in itself the centre of a cult.[2] Finally, the power of the name of the Lord Jesus [3] is frequently borne witness to in the New Testament. We need mention here only one passage, the most famous of all, from the Epistle to the Philippians (ii. 9–10). Paul has just been reminding his readers that the Lord showed himself obedient to God even unto death, and he adds : " Wherefore God also hath exalted him above all, and given him a name which is above every name ; that at the name of Jesus every knee should bow, of those that are in heaven, and on earth, and in hell." In other words, the name of Jesus has a peculiar power over the whole of creation, so that the spiritual beings of the world, who rule the elements and the stars, prostrate themselves at the sound of it.[4]

These brief considerations, which, as we shall meet them again, need not be elaborated here, are sufficient to warn us against any purely human, obvious, and popular interpretation of the name of Jesus the Nazarene. The most reasonable and probable explanation, if we reflect for a moment, is that the original followers of Christ, those, that is, who first recognized him as Christ, the Messiah, gave him a name which set him above humanity and expressed his divine nature.[5] Paul, at any rate, definitely understands the name Jesus in this light, and if the writers of the Gospels, or rather, the redactors whose work has come down to us, no longer appear to do so, it is perhaps because they belonged to an environment in which the meaning of the Aramaic had been lost.

[1] *Pirke R. Eliezer*, 32.
[2] On the " life of words " and the importance of the name in ancient Israel, *cf.* **XIX**, 149 *ff.* For the magical power of certain Jewish formulæ, see Origen, *Contra Celsum*, 4, 33.
[3] *Cf.* **CCX**, *passim*, and **CXCIII**, p. 107, where it is stated that in the Pauline community the cult of the name of the Lord is substituted for that of the name of Jahweh amongst the Jews.
[4] With regard to the power of Jesus' name in the realm of spirits, *cf.* Origen, *Contra Celsum*, 8, 58, and **CXCIII**, 104 *ff.*
[5] It must be remembered that the followers of the Lord Jesus are " those who call upon his name " (1 Cor. i. 2), and that " those who have received him," and to whom " he has given power to become the children of God," are " those who believe in his name " (John i. 12).

II

Jesus the Nazarene

The Greek ’Iησοῦς,[1] which we find in our Gospels and in Paul, is only the transcription of the post-exilic Hebrew word, Jeshuah, which is derived from the more ancient form Jehoshua, or Joshua, the Joshua of our Bibles.[2] In the Greek Bible, Joshua (Exod. xvii. 10), Jehoshua (Zech. iii. 1) and Jeshuah (Neh. vii. 7 ; viii. 7, 17), are all rendered by ’Iησοῦς. The old name, after a long period of obsolescence, reappeared in its new form about 340 B.C., and became very common towards the beginning of our era.[3] Its original, etymological meaning is " Jahweh is help," or, " the help of Jahweh " ; obviously, for a prophet, a vessel of the Holy Spirit, a name preordained. So thought, certainly, the editors of Matthew and Luke, both of whom attribute the choice of this name to the will of God, and associate it with the divine work which he who bore it was destined to accomplish.[4] It is to be observed that Matthew (i. 23), citing in reference to Jesus the passage of Isaiah (vii. 14) which prophesies the birth of a miraculous child who shall be called Emmanuel [5] (" God is with us "), betrays no surprise at the divine command which assigned to the son of Mary a different name, from which it is to be inferred that he regarded Jesus and Emmanuel as equivalent.

It may be contended on the basis of the text of Matthew just cited, that the parents of Christ must have given him the name of Jesus at his birth. Otherwise, had his followers christened him, they would have sought to make the application of the prophecy more direct by calling him Emmanuel rather than Jesus. The answer to this is that the Christians were not immediately aware of the use to which the text Isaiah could be put, and that apparently before they discovered it,

---

[1] Cf. XCVIII, 4.

[2] CCXIV, 820 ; EB, Jeshua and Joshua.

[3] EB, Names, para. 84 ; CCLI, 23 ff.

[4] In Matt. i. 21 the angel says to Joseph : " Thou shalt give him the name of Jesus, for he shall save his people from their sins." The author of this Gospel, then, translates the name Jesus by " Saviour." In Luke i. 31 the same angel says to Mary : " Thou shalt name him Jesus, and he shall be great, and shall be called Son of the Highest." For this author, on the other hand, it is the quality of Son of God which is in some way implied by the name Jesus.

[5] Καὶ καλέσεις τὸ ὄνομα αὐτοῦ Ἐμμανουήλ—Luke i. 31 does not mention this text, but it is evidently in his mind, for the words of the angel to Mary echo its phrasing : καὶ καλέσεις τὸ ὄνομα αὐτοῦ Ἰησοῦν.

the name Jesus had already become established as signifying the Messiah, the *Soter*, and, in Paul, the great Instrument of God's work.

The adherents of the mythological view have, of course, attempted to profit by the above considerations, and adduce them in support of one of their arguments for the non-historicity of Jesus Christ.[1] But their conclusion goes beyond what is justified by the texts, and the substitution of a sacred name for his human one hardly invalidates the existence of Jesus.

We cannot say positively that such a substitution did take place, but it is very probable. It would be perfectly consistent with the process of " mythification " which the whole figure of Christ underwent, and which is already manifest in the Gospels. From its very beginning, the tradition tended to efface the facts of the life of Jesus prior to the commencement of his mission.

The explanation of the surname " the Nazarene " is beset by the greatest difficulties.[2] The redactors of our Gospels certainly believed that Jesus the Nazarene (ὁ Ναζωραῖος or ὁ Ναζαρηνός) meant " Jesus of Nazareth." Matthew ii. 23 tells us that on their return from Egypt the parents of Jesus went to live in " a town called Nazareth, that it might be fulfilled which was spoken by the prophets ; that he should be called a Nazarene " (Ναζωραῖος). Luke i. 26 gives Nazareth as the home of Joseph and Mary. It is thence that they go to Bethlehem to report for taxation, and it is there that they return after the Nativity. It is " their town " (Luke ii. 39 ; πόλις ἑαυτῶν). Mark i. 9 states definitely that it was from there that Jesus came to join John the Baptist on the Jordan. Finally, John i. 45–6 makes Philip say, just after his conversion by the Galilean prophet : " He is Jesus, the son of Joseph, of Nazareth " (τὸν ἀπὸ Ναζαρέτ). It would be easy to multiply quotations to the same effect. The declaration of our Evangelists on the point is so clear, that right down to present times commentators and historians have accepted it almost unanimously. There is today in Galilee a little town called Nazareth,[3] situated " in

[1] *Cf.* particularly **CLXXVIII**, 15 *ff.* ; **CLXXIX**, 64 *ff.* ; **CLI**, 17 *ff.*, 47 *ff.*

[2] *Cf.* EB, art. *Nazarene, Nazareth, Nazarite* ; Keim, *Geschichte Jesu von Nazara*, Zurich, 1867–72, 3 vols., i, 319 *ff.* ; ii, 421 *ff.* ; **CLXXVI**, 464 *ff.* ; **CCLVII**, 124–56 ; **CCXXXI** ; **XLI**, 238 *ff.* ; **LXXIII**, *The Beginning*, app. i ; G. Moore, *Nazarene and Nazareth*, ap. XIII, i, 426 *ff.* ; P. Schwene, *Nazareth und Nazaraër*, ap. ZWT, 1912, 56–67 ; **CCVIII** 59 *ff.* ; **CLIV**, ii, 18 *ff.* Further bibliographical references will be found in W. Bauer, *Griechisch-Deutsches Wörterbuch zu den Schriften des N.T.*, Giessen, 1928, under the word Ναζωραῖος, col. 839 *f.*

[3] More precisely, it is called *En-Nasira*. The ancient form of the name was probably Ναζαρά rather than Ναζαρέθ. The former is what

a little open valley high up in the group of mountains which bound the plain of Esdraelon on the north " (Renan), and consisting of from three to four thousand inhabitants. It is natural to identify it with the town spoken of in our Gospels, and the majority of modern critics still, in fact, do so.[1] But grave doubts, which cannot be dismissed without examination, have recently been cast upon this identification, and seem to be rapidly gaining ground amongst the commentators.

The first disturbing observation which forces itself upon the scholar is that no ancient pagan or Jewish writing mentions Nazareth. The pagan texts may readily be disposed of, for since the straggling little Galilean village neither played an important part in the Jewish rebellions, nor attracted Greek or Roman colonists, the obscurity which surrounds it is hardly surprising. But with regard to the Jewish texts, there is no such explanation, yet the name of Nazareth is to be found neither in the Bible, nor in the Talmudic literature, nor in works of Josephus, though the latter is particularly well informed on Galilean affairs, and enumerates a number of towns and villages in that country.

The damaging effect of this unanimous silence may be mitigated, but it cannot be entirely done away with. The mythicists have naturally made the most of it,[2] and have attempted to prove that the existence of Nazareth at the time of the birth of Jesus is only a geographical fiction. Their argument, however unconvincing, has at least performed the service of stating the problem and illuminating its various aspects.

With regard to the silence of the Bible, it may justly be pointed out that when its latest books were edited Galilee was of very little importance in the Jewish world, and only some chance circumstances might have led one of the sacred writers to mention the name of Nazareth. In the case of the Talmudic literature, it has been argued that its omission of the name of Nazareth cannot be due to the fact that the town did not exist, since we have certain knowledge that it was in existence at

we find in Eusebius, *H.E.*, 1, 7, 14, on the authority of Julius Africanus. The most ancient Jewish transcription of the word known (in the hymns of Qalir, of about the year A.D. 900) gives *Natzereth. Cf.* **CCXI**, 52.

[1] " The majority " because there have been various attempts, none of them successful, to assign the native place of Jesus to some other part of Galilee than the little town of Nazareth. Cheyne held that Nazareth meant Galilee itself ; Burrage, that the name indicated a district of Peræa ; Burkitt, that it stood for Chorazin, etc.

[2] *Cf.* especially : **CLXXVIII**, 42 *ff.* ; **CLXXIX**, 285 *ff.* ; the essay entitled *Eine Stadt genannt Nazareth* ; **CLI**, i, 25 *ff.*

the time when the first treatises of the *Mishnah* were edited ; which is true. It has been contended, further, that the rabbis were likely to be interested only in towns which possessed a rabbinical school, and since Nazareth was certainly not one of these, it is not strange that they ignored it, or at least found no reason for speaking of it ; which may well be true. Josephus never intended to enumerate all the towns and villages of Galilee. Those to which he paid special attention were the ones which played a part in the beginning of the Great Revolt, during which he himself was fighting in the country (the first half of the year A.D. 67). In short, the contention is that the insignificance of Nazareth was the sole cause of its going unmentioned. Josephus and the Talmud, however, name many places which cannot have been any more important than Nazareth, nor any more interesting intrinsically, so that, on this view, the town of Jesus must have been peculiarly unfortunate. In other words, there still remains room for doubt as to its existence in the first century.

Doubt, however, is not conviction. Moreover, in default of external evidence we still have that of the New Testament, which is not to be despised. It is to be noted, however, that it is only in Acts and the Gospels that such evidence is found. Neither Nazareth nor the Nazarene are mentioned in any of the other canonical texts. This additional silence may be explained on similar grounds to that of the Jewish writings, namely, that the Galilean life of the Lord had no interest for any but Palestinian writers. The omission would be strange if the so-called " apostolic " Epistles—Peter, John, James and Jude—had really been written by Galileans, the companions or kinsmen of Jesus, but as this canonical ascription is fundamentally improbable, that point falls to the ground. The only peculiar thing is that, if, by the time of Saint Paul, the surname " the Nazarene " was constantly associated with the name of Jesus, the Apostle himself should not have employed it, though it is conceivable that he might have had his reasons for discarding it.

For the Gospel writers and the author of Acts, who is probably the same as the author of Luke, Nazareth is a town in Galilee. As a rule they are content merely to name it. Only in one passage (Luke iv. 29) do we find any kind of specification : " And they rose up and thrust him out of the city, and led him up to the brow of the hill whereon their city is built, that they might cast him down headlong." Nazareth, that is to say, is situated in high country, and so far as the general impression goes, it may be said that the text is correct enough.

But the details are too fanciful [1] to permit us safely to infer from the passage any more than that the author of it seems to have known that Galilee was a hilly region ; which is not of great importance.

We find the first specific assertion about Nazareth in Eusebius,[2] but it goes back to Julius Africanus (between A.D. 170 and 240), who had spent most of his life in Palestine and knew it well. The passage states that the family of Jesus, " hailing originally from the little Jewish towns of Nazareth and Kochabah, had become scattered about the rest of the country." At the end of the fourth century Saint Jerome and Saint Epiphanius, again, mention Nazareth quite specifically.[3] It seems certain, then, that the little town, the *viculus*, as Jerome calls it, was in existence by the last third of the second century, and as there is nothing in any text to indicate the possibility of its having been founded between the birth of Jesus and that date, the probability is that it was in existence before the beginning of our era. This being so, there would have been no need to discuss the matter, had the traditional derivation of the surname " the Nazarene " been unquestionable. But there are, amongst others, serious philological objections to that derivation.

The word which we write as Nazarene is actually given to us in three different forms : *Nazarenos* ($Na\zeta a\varrho\eta\nu\acute{o}\varsigma$), *Nazoraios* ($Na\zeta\omega\varrho a\tilde{\iota}o\varsigma$), and *Nazorenos* ($Na\zeta o\varrho\epsilon\nu\acute{o}\varsigma$) which the Gospel editors and their copyists seem to have regarded as interchangeable.[4] First of all, assuming that the name of the town was really Nazareth, none of the three forms in question seem capable of being derived from it. One would expect Nazareth to necessitate a derivative like *Nazarethenos, Nazarethanos,* or *Nazarethaios.* The dropping of the final *th* or *t* of Nazareth (which is also written *Nazaret*) [5] might, strictly, be justified as an exception which sometimes occurs, and the residue of *Nazar* might then seem to lend itself to the derivation of our three forms. But as it happens there is a further obstacle, as applic-

---

[1] The present-day inhabitants of Nazareth can, of course, point out the " precipice." On the spot, it is not very convincing.

[2] *H.E.*, 1, 7, 14.   [3] Jerome, *Onomasticon* ; Epiph., *Haer.*, 1, 136.

[4] In Mark, i. 24 and x. 47 for example, several important versions give $Na\zeta a\varrho\eta\nu\acute{o}\varsigma$, others $Na\zeta\omega\varrho a\tilde{\iota}o\varsigma$, and Codex D $Na\zeta o\varrho\epsilon\nu\acute{o}\varsigma$. *Cf.* the similar variants of Mark xiv. 67, Luke iv. 34 and xxiv. 19, etc.

[5] An example is given in **XXV**, p. 428. There is, in Galilee, a town which Josephus calls $'I\omega\tau\acute{a}\pi a\tau a$ and the Talmud, *Yotpat,* the birthplace of a rabbi who is known as R. Menahem *Yodpa'a* (*Yotpaya*) which would be written in Greek as $'I\omega\delta\pi a\tilde{\iota}o\varsigma$ or $'I\omega\theta\pi a\tilde{\iota}o\varsigma$. The feminine final *t* has been dropped in the derivation.

able to *Nazara* as to *Nazareth,* in the way of such a relation between them and *Nazoraios, Nazarenos,* or *Nazorenos.* Both words were unquestionably spelt in Aramaic with a *tsadê,* which is fairly rendered by our *z,* but which in Greek is represented by a *sigma* (σ), while *Nazoraios, Nazarenos,* and *Nazorenos,* take a *zeta* (ζ), the customary transcription of the Aramaic *zain.* The difficulty is serious enough to have convinced a scholar like Nestle that the traditional derivation of Nazarene is a misconception.[1] The substitution of *zeta* for *sigma* in the transcription of the *tsadê,* is not, however, without precedent, though it is definitely erroneous, hence we may, if necessary, give our three forms the benefit of the exception.[2] But it is hardly permissible to deal similarly with their traditional meaning.

If it is conceded, as it must be, that Nazareth or Nazara was, at the time of Jesus, an obscure little town unknown and unnoticed, the question arises why a surname derived from it should have seemed so characteristic as to become attached to the name of Jesus in the gospel tradition. To indicate the country of the prophet it would have sufficed to call him Jesus the Galilean, just as the first leader of the Zealots was called Judas the Galilean (᾿Ιούδας ὁ Γαλιλαῖος). To distinguish a certain Simon, it is quite natural to call him Simon of Cyrene (Mark xv. 21 : . . . Σίμωνα Κυρηναῖον) for everyone had heard of Cyrene. But a reference to Nazareth conveys no information. Simon or Andrew are not designated as " of Capernaum."

Moreover, there are numerous passages of our Gospels in which the epithet *Nazarene* appears, which do not lend themselves to its interpretation as " *of Nazareth.*" In Mark (i. 21 *ff.*),

[1] E. Nestle, *He shall be called a Nazarene,* in *Expos. Times,* August, 1908, xix, 523.

[2] This is, substantially, the contention of **XXV,** 427, which points out that Burkitt (*Syriac forms of New Testament proper names,* 1913) brought to light in the Old Testament ten cases of the apparent transcription of the *tsadê* by *zeta,* and that, counting the variants in the manuscripts, the list could be made even longer. There are also several examples in Josephus. It is to be noted, however, that 'Burkitt himself regards these instances as slips of the pen, and rejects the derivation of Ναζωραῖος from *noṣri* on account of the difficulty of the *tsadê.* Nevertheless, the fact that the Syriac translation of the Christian Bible (the *Peshitto*) always gives Naṣraya for Ναζωραῖος and Naṣrat for Ναζαρέθ, transcribing, that is, the *zeta* by a *tsadê,* is strong evidence for the possibility of the opposite process. If the error could occur in the passage from Greek to Aramaic, it seems reasonable to admit that it might also have done so in the passage from Aramaic to Greek. Moreover, there is the possibility that the word Ναζιραῖος, properly derived from *nazir,* may, by a kind of attraction, have been responsible for the spelling of Ναζωραῖος with a *zeta.*

for example, we have the account of the first miracle of Jesus, the healing of a demoniac at Capernaum. On seeing Jesus enter the Synagogue, the man exclaims : "What is there [in common] between thee and us, Jesus the Nazarene? Dost thou come to destroy us? I know who thou art : the Holy One of God " (ὁ ἅγιος τοῦ θεοῦ). If we compare this passage with Mark v. 7, in which another demoniac says to Jesus : "What is there in common between thee and me, Jesus, Son of the most high God? " ('Ιησοῦ υἱὲ θεοῦ τοῦ ὑψίστου), we shall notice, first, that the expression, " Son of the most high God," stands in the same place in the second passage as " the Nazarene " does in the first, and seems to be equivalent to it ; second, that " the Holy One of God " and " the Son of God " express similar conceptions, which shows that the former is simply an expansion of " the Nazarene." It looks very much as if it were a kind of Greek gloss, introduced by the editor for the benefit of readers ignorant of Aramaic. It must not be forgotten that Mark i. 21 *ff.* is recounting the first miracle of Jesus, his début, as it were, in the rôle of lord and master of evil spirits. This is his first act of hostility against the Enemy who rules over the terrestrial world. Hence it is natural, and even necessary, for the all-powerful name to be announced, or more accurately, confessed, at the very beginning, by the one who is to be defeated by its supreme power. This name is essentially bound up with the divine mission to which the new prophet, "son of God" like all prophets, is dedicated. It would be contrary to all custom to hail Jesus by a name signifying nothing but his place of origin, while, on the other hand, it seems as if he must necessarily be given, on such a momentous occasion, the title expressive of his true nature and function.

We find in John xviii. 5 *ff.* the account of the arrest of Jesus. To the soldiers who come to the Garden of Olives he says, "Whom do you seek? " and they reply, "Jesus, the Nazarene," as if the surname possessed a kind of official value and was not to be detached. And when he has uttered the words, " I am he," they all fall back, as if the avowal of the personality expressed by the name in some way at once actualized its inherent power. It is not easy to see how a mere mention of the town of Nazareth could account for this. To oppose Jesus the Nazarene is " to oppose his name," [1] and his supreme name displays its irresistible power at his will. The

---

[1] In Acts xxvi. 1 Paul is represented as confessing that he has acted " against the name of Jesus the Nazarene " (πρὸς τὸ ὄνομα 'Ιησοῦ τοῦ Ναζωραίου).

incident in John is probably only a late version of the Synoptic account of the arrest, and we refer to it only to prove that its editor, though he believed that Jesus came from Nazareth, had not yet lost the memory of the original tradition, in which the surname " the Nazarene " evoked something more than the fact of his origin in a little Galilean town.

Various other passages in Acts and the Gospels indicate the same conclusion. For instance, Mark xvi. 6, in which the angel whom the women—Galilean women—find seated in the tomb, says to them : " You seek Jesus the Nazarene, who was crucified ; he has risen again ; he is not here. . . ." Similarly, Luke xxiv. 19 ; Acts ii. 22 and Acts xxii. 8 ; where one of those who went to Emmaus, Peter in his preaching, and Christ himself, speaking to Paul on the road to Damascus, respectively use the name Nazarene as if it expressed a personal and essential characteristic of Jesus. There are, finally, two passages in Acts (iii. 6 and iv. 10) which actually exhibit the miraculous power of the sacred name in action. In the first, Peter, to heal a lame man, says to him : " In the name of Jesus Christ, the Nazarene, arise and walk." In the second, Peter again, speaking before the Sanhedrin concerning the miraculous cure of the lame man which he has performed, utters the words : " In the name of Jesus Christ, the Nazarene, whom you crucified and God raised from the dead, behold him before you, whole." It is of no importance in this connexion whether the events actually occurred as related in Acts, and Peter really uttered the words that are put into his mouth. The interest of the two passages lies in the fact that they exhibit an ancient Christian spell, full of beneficent magic power, for it is the formula itself which is supposed to have performed the miracle. It is composed of the name Jesus, the title Christ, which proclaims the Messianic rank of the Lord, and the surname, the Nazarene. The power of these three words is, so to speak, united in an inseparable combination. Clearly the market town of Galilee has no relevance here.

It is, perhaps, possible that the surname, the Nazarene, was first applied to Jesus by non-Christians, and was then adopted by the Christian movement and somehow invested with a special meaning, so that it ceased to seem strange, on the other hand, to see it used in speaking to Galileans belonging to the movement, who did not need to be told that Jesus came from Nazareth, or, on the other, to hear it uttered in circumstances in which the mention of his native place could have no significance. But it is indisputable that this appropriation would be much more intelligible in the case of a surname expressing a peculiar quality of Jesus. We may even say that such a process implies that, even if " the *Nazarene* " did mean, in the first place, " *man of Nazareth*," this significance must have practically disappeared, and given way to another, more or less similar to that suggested by Matthew's reminder (ii. 23) that the Prophets had foretold " that he would be called the Nazarene." In that case perhaps the form *Nasarenos*, or, less correctly, *Nazarenos*, would have to be regarded as the oldest, as being the nearest to the word Nasara, and because the form *Nazoraios* expresses the *personal* significance of the epithet, necessitated by the passages just cited.

Probability, however, appears to be in favour of a different explanation, namely, that the oldest form of the surname was the Aramaic·equivalent of the Greek *Nazoraios*, and expressed a peculiar quality of Jesus, and that it was only when this was no longer comprehended by the Hellenized Christians, who had ceased to understand Aramaic, that it received the interpretation " of Nazareth," and took the form *Nazarenos* or *Nazorenos*. But in that case we are faced by the problem, what did *Nazoraios* mean, and to what Aramaic word did it correspond ?

III

THEORIES AND PROBABILITIES

Several hypotheses have been advanced, into the details of which we shall not enter ; but it will be as well to give at least a general idea of their trend.[1] It has been maintained, first, that Jesus was called the *Nazarene* because he was a member of the Nazarene sect mentioned by Epiphanius, or at least had a strong resemblance to the devotees of that sect, to which John the Baptist is supposed to have belonged. This theory, which is that of Friedländer, is exposed to serious objections. The assertions of Epiphanius may be unfounded, and it is open to question whether the pre-Christian Nazarenes of whom he speaks really existed.[2] Moreover, it is highly improbable that if Jesus had only seemed to be, but was not actually, a *Nazarene*, his followers would have designated him by a name to which

[1] For the details see **CCVIII**, 67 *ff.*

[2] The best argument for the veracity of Epiphanius is the fact that there still exists a sect of Mandæans, who are not Christians, and who call themselves *Nazorenes*. On the strength of this, Lidzbarski (*Mandäische Liturgien*, 1920, xvi) has compared *Jesus der Nazoräer* with *Enosh der Nazoräer*, who was described by Brandt in *Mandäischen Schriften*, p. 93, and has come definitely to the conclusion that Jesus

he was not entitled. Other theories attempt to explain the
surname as derived : (1) from the word *netzer*, meaning branch
or off-shoot, and signifying in this connexion the off-shoot of
the stem of Jesse, the descendant of David, the Messiah ; [1]
from the word *noṣri*, meaning " one who observes," or " one
who guards, watches over " ; or (3) from the word *nazir*, which
designates a man bound to God by a vow, and may be translated
as " holy," " consecrated," " chosen," " crowned," all of which
senses are fairly close, the first, however, probably being the
oldest. [2] Each of these explanations has its probabilities and
its difficulties. Thus, the meaning of *netzer* would be appropriate to the early Christians' conception of Jesus, but the word
is spelt with a *tsadê*, for which, as we have already noted, the
zeta of Ναζωραῖος is not the proper transcription. *Ha-noṣri*
might be a fitting epithet for a man of God, that is, if we take
it in the sense of " one who guards or watches over," for Jesus
does not exactly play the part of an " observer " (Sc. of the Law)
in the gospel tradition.—It is a term that could be applied to a
strict Pharisee, but not to him.—But again we encounter the
difficulty of the *tsadê*. Nazir, on the other hand, is spelt with
a *zain*, which becomes in Greek *zeta*, and gives rise to the Greek
forms ναζίρ, ναζειραῖος, ναζιραῖος, ναζαραῖος. The Greek equivalent
of *nazir* is *hagios* (ἅγιος), [2] and certainly the characterization
" Holy One of God " would fit Jesus perfectly. It is no less
certain that he was regarded as such by his followers. We have
already quoted Mark i. 24–5 : " I know who thou art, the Holy

bore the name of that sect. Reitzenstein, *Das iranische Erlösungs-
mysterium*, Bonn, 1921, vi, regards the explanation as final. It remains
to be seen, when we have a little more light on the ancient history of
the Mandæans, whether they really afford an explanation.

[1] Siderski, in **RHR**, *Bulletin de la Soc. Ernest Renan*, May 1921
to June 1922, 51 *ff*. He bases his argument on Num. vi. 7, which he
translates as foliows : " He shall not make himself unclean when his
father dies, because he bears upon his head the crown (*nezer*) of his
God." The meaning of *nezer*, which is usually translated here by
" consecration " (Weihe, **CCXXXIII**, i, 193), he regards as conclusively
defined by 2 Sam. i. 10, which gives : " I took the crown (*nezer*) which
was upon his head."

[2] In Judges xiii. 7 and xvi. 17 the manuscripts give as equivalent
readings the two words ἅγιος and ναζειραῖος. The synonymity of the
two terms is further evidenced by the famous passage of Hegesippus,
quoted by Eusebius, *H.E.*, 2, 23, 5, which describes the virtues of
James, the brother of the Lord, as those of a *nazir*, and specifies : " From
the womb of his mother, he was holy " (ἅγιος ἦν). Judges xiii. 2
says the same thing of Samson :] ναζίρ θεοῦ ἀπὸ τῆς κοιλίας. These
passages recall the Annunciation in Luke, in which the angel says to
Mary : " Therefore the Holy One who shall be born (τὸ γεννώμενον
ἅγιον) shall be called the Son of God."

One of God," and John vi. 69 uses the same term : " And we know and believe that thou art the Holy One of God." " The Holy One of God " for the Christian is the Christ. A textual variant of the passage of John just quoted makes a kind of bridge between the two expressions : " We know and believe that thou art the Christ of the living God." Acts iv. 27 shows clearly that " the Christ " is the " Servant of God," his son, his Holy One : " Thy holy servant Jesus, whom thou hast made Christ " (τὸν ἅγιον παιδά σου ᾿Ιησοῦν ὅν ἔχρισας). Thus it is clear that the name of Holy One (ἅγιος) applied to Jesus would both express his character and, at the same time, impress upon the mind of the original community the idea of his Messiahship, and of his special relations with God.

The interpretation of *Nazarene* by Holy One of God has, accordingly, great advantages,[1] and seems to be the one suggested by the gospel texts themselves. It is, in the opinion of the writer, the most probable interpretation. Nevertheless, it is open to two objections, which must be considered. In the first place, it is questionable whether an orthodox Jew could be regarded as a *nazir* during his whole life, for, according to the rules of its institution, the *naziriteship* [2] seems never to have been anything but temporary, and no text makes any mention of a perpetual *naziriteship* in the time of Jesus. In the second place, it is difficult to see how Jesus could have been described as a *nazir*, when he apparently had taken no vow, and certainly did not lead an ascetic life. It may be conjectured that the sense of the word had become wider and less strict, and that a man who lived for God was regarded as *vowed* to him, in other words, that the meaning of *nazir* had come more clearly to approximate to that of *hagios*.[3] Unfortunately a supposition, however plausible, is not a certainty, and the derivation of *Nazarene* from *nazir*, meaning " Holy One of God," must always be open to doubt. It remains, however, the one which best satisfies the facts of the problem.

What does seem quite certain is that the epithet, " the *Nazarene*," did not mean in the beginning " the man of Nazareth," and that it was a title bestowed upon Jesus either during his lifetime or immediately after his death, at the period when his followers effected the first stage of his exaltation by asserting

[1] Salvatorelli has maintained this thesis with great ingenuity and force : **CCXXXI**.

[2] *Cf.* Num. vi. On the *naziriteship*, see **LXVI**, ii, 80–9.

[3] It is perhaps worth remarking that there were probably some distinguished nazirs in the primitive Judæo-Christian community, of whom the famous portrait of James by Hegesippus is, in all likelihood, a kind of idealized synthesis.

that God, by the Resurrection, had made him Christ. In the Greek communities which produced our Gospels and Acts, the meaning of the Aramaic word was lost, because there the conception of the Lord (Kyrios) speedily overwhelmed that of the Servant (Ebed, παῖς).[1] The Jewish epithet of the Galilean prophet was no longer worthy of the Lord Jesus. Moreover, the word had probably passed into Christian speech in its Greek form of *hagios*, as several of the texts which have been cited indicate. His followers, who continued in Aramaic communities to bear the name Nazarenes, and who still do so today in Semitic-speaking countries, were henceforth called in the Greek communities the *hagioi*, the " Saints," until they adopted a designation given to them by the pagans of Antioch, the *christianoi*, " the Christians," which finally prevailed. The word given by the original tradition, and probably transcribed as *Nazoraios*, was at first repeated without being translated, like the name Jesus itself, and, in general, any supposedly sacred name, whose power depended upon the strict preservation of its form, and it very quickly ceased to be understood. Then, in the Greek communities, it came to be interpreted, *according to Greek practice*, as referring to a town. Jesus was a Galilean ; there was in Galilee a town of Nazareth or Nazara, which offered timely assistance to puzzled and well-meaning men who cared nothing for *tsadê* or *zain*. It was perhaps then that the form *Nazarenos* sprang up alongside that of *Nazoraios*. But these questions of derivation are wrapped in obscurity, inasmuch as several words used in Palestinian religious terminology might have influenced the Greek transcription of the actual Aramaic term applied to Jesus : *nazir, noṣri, netzer*, and possibly even the name of the sect mentioned by Epiphanius, the *Nazarenes* or *Nazorenes*.[2] The more imperfectly the real, original epithet was understood, the more readily its form would be changed in the passage from Aramaic to Greek.

All, then, that we venture definitely to conclude, is that the first followers of Christ, when they called him by his name and surname, Jesus the Nazarene, did not signify by it Jesus of Nazareth, but an all-powerful divine name accompanied by a distinctive epithet, which meant approximately, " the One sent by Jahweh," " the Holy One of God."

---

[1] This might account for the fact noted above, that Paul does not use the term " the Nazarene."

[2] Some influence of this kind was probably responsible for the adoption of Ναζωραῖος, Ναζαρηνός or Ναζορηνός rather than of one of the usual transcriptions of *nazir* : ναζίρ, ναζειραῖος, ναζιραῖος, ναζαραῖος. The rendering ναςωραῖος is not found amongst these.

CHAPTER III

THE PLACE AND DATE OF THE BIRTH OF JESUS

I

NAZARETH OR BETHLEHEM

WHAT has just been said about the interpretation of the word Nazarene would of itself suffice to raise doubt concerning the birthplace of Jesus. Apart from that, however, we are already confronted, in the Gospels, with two conflicting traditions. Mark clearly gives us to understand that Jesus was born at Nazareth.[1] The first verse of chapter vi. states : " And he went out from thence and came into his native place " (ἐις τὴν πατρίδα ἀυτοῦ). The town is not named, but it is certainly in Galilee, since it was about this district that Jesus was wandering at the time when he is said to have preached in " his native place," and, since we are told in another passage (i. 9) that it was from Nazareth that he came to join John the Baptist, " his native place " must mean Nazareth.[2] Père Lagrange has attempted to invalidate this argument by maintaining that a man's " town," " country," " native place " (πατρίς), do not necessarily mean his birthplace, but merely the place of origin of his family, or, in the case of Jesus, the place where he was brought up.[3] It is in this sense, undoubtedly, that Matthew and Luke understand Nazareth to be the " native place " of Jesus, but, as we shall see, this construction was the only possible one from their point of view, while there is not the slightest indication that Mark, before

---

[1] John seems to accept this Marcan position. He says nothing to imply the belief that Jesus was born in any other place than Nazareth (see i. 45). In vii. 41 *ff.* we have the following passage : " Others said : This is the Christ. But some said : Doth Christ come out of Galilee ? Doth not the Scripture say that Christ cometh of the seed of David, and out of Bethlehem, the town where David was ? So there was a division amongst the people because of him." **CCL**, 189 *ff.*, observes rightly that if the writer of the Gospel believed that Jesus was born at Bethlehem, he would not have neglected such a good opportunity of discomfiting the sceptical Jews.

[2] **CIII**, i, 197 ; **CV**, 167 ; **XCVIII**, 8.   [3] **CI**, 141.

them, had any such idea.   On the contrary, everything suggests
that they have harmonized the Marcan tradition, which they
could not reject, with their own point of view.

Both assert that Jesus was born at Bethlehem.   " Bethle-
hem in Judæa," specifies Matthew ii. 1 ($B\eta\theta\lambda\varepsilon\dot{\varepsilon}\mu$ $\tau\tilde{\eta}\varsigma$ $Iov\delta ai\alpha\varsigma$) :
" the city of David," adds Luke ii. 4 ($\varepsilon i\varsigma$ $\pi\acute{o}\lambda\iota v$ $\varDelta av\acute{\varepsilon}\iota\delta$).[1]
According to the former, Joseph and Mary dwelt there before
the birth of the child ; according to the latter, it was there
that they came, from Nazareth, for the census, repairing to the
place of origin of their family, as commanded by the Emperor.
The little town [2] still stands today, about five and a half miles
south of Jerusalem.—There is no gainsaying the contradiction
between the two traditions.   Mark definitely believes that Jesus
was born at Nazareth, Matthew and Luke, that he was born
at Bethlehem in Judæa, the place of which the prophet Micah [2]
had said (v. 1), according to the apt quotation in Matthew
ii. 6 : " And thou Bethlehem, land of Judah, thou art not the
least amongst the chief towns of Judah, for out of thee shall
come a leader who shall shepherd my people Israel."—A prophecy which represents the longstanding Jewish hope of a
restoration of Israel by a descendant of David inspired by
Jahweh.

There was another Bethlehem, situated in the old territory
of the tribe of Zabulon, about five and a half miles north of
Nazareth, which is mentioned in the Book of Joshua (xix. 15).
Some critics [3] have inclined to the theory that these two towns
of the same name became confused, and that the best known
of the two, the one given by the prophet Micah as the native
place of the future Messiah, superseded the other, although it
was really at Bethlehem of Nazar, or Nesar, as the Galilean
town was called, that Jesus was born.   This suggestion, however, has no documentary support, and cannot possibly be
justified.   The tradition which established Bethlehem as the
birthplace of Christ did not depend upon any historical event.
It needed only the prophetic utterance of Micah to bring it
into being and confirm it beyond all question.   Since Jesus
was the Messiah foretold by the Prophets, he must necessarily
have fulfilled the prediction of Micah, and come into the world

---

[1] 1 Sam. xx. 6 and 28 gives Bethlehem as David's native town.
Grave doubts have been raised as to the authenticity of the tradition
embodied in this text (cf. EB, David, § 1, note 2), but we need not
concern ourselves with them here.

[2] EB, Bethlehem.

[3] Cheyne, for instance, in EB, Nazareth, where this opinion is set
forth in considerable detail.

at Bethlehem, the city of David. This requirement was all
that was needed to prove the event, without any other evidence.

The accounts of the childhood found in our Gospels of
Matthew and Luke, be it remembered, issue from the same
source and belong to the same family as those in the Apocryphal
Gospels ; and the *Protevangelium of James*, for example, or
the *Gospel of Pseudo-Matthew*, happening to require the setting
of Jerusalem for the beginning of their miraculous story, have
no hesitation in making that city the residence of the parents
of Jesus before his birth. In other words, hagiographers are
mainly influenced by their own requirements, and always con-
trive to adapt to them the more or less genuine recollections
of the tradition.

Setting aside, for the present, what the disciples themselves
may have known and said concerning the actual birthplace of
Jesus, the members of the movement who, some time after
them, established the main features of the oral tradition, were
evidently confronted by two conflicting prophecies : that of
Micah v. 1, " He shall come from Bethlehem in Judæa " ; and
that given in Matthew ii. 23, " He shall be called a Nazarene."
The latter prediction [1] might be related to the assertion of the
birth of Jesus at Nazareth in one of two ways—it might
either have conditioned, or been conditioned by, that assertion.
In the latter case, the assumption is that Jesus was known
to have been born at Nazareth, and that this fact was taken
as the fulfilment of the prophecy, " He shall be called a Nazarene." In the former, we must suppose that the surname of
Nazarene, which had been bestowed upon Jesus for reasons
quite irrelevant to his birthplace, came, at a time when its
original significance was no longer understood, to be interpreted

---

[1] It is not easy to find textual justification for the expression in
Matthew, " the word of the prophets " (τὸ ῥηθὲν διὰ τῶν προφητῶν)
which signalizes this second prediction. *Cf.* **XCIX**, 167 ; **CCXXXI**,
8 *ff*.—In antiquity Saint Jerome was of the opinion that Matthew
had not quoted his source literally (*non verba de scripturis sumpsisse,
sed sensum*), while John Chrysostom, on the other hand, believed that
he had made use of a prophecy which had since been lost. In modern
times it has been held (**CIII**, i, 376) that the **LXX** version of Judges,
xiii. 5, was the source of the quotation. This is the passage in which
it is said that Samson will be the *nazir* of God, and Matthew is supposed, according to his custom, to have taken from it the words which
suited his purpose without regard for their context. This is quite
possible, but in the opinion of the writer, Deut. xxxiii. 16 affords a
more probable explanation : " Let the blessing of him who dwells
in the bush come upon the head of Joseph, and upon the top of the head
of him who is *noṣri* amongst his brethren." The Vulgate, here more
accurate than the Septuagint, gives the translation : *super verticem
nazarei inter fratres suos.*

as meaning " of Nazareth." We have already shown why this explanation seems to be the probable one. Of the two prophecies in question, the second was probably the first to be connected with Jesus, because of the fact that he was already called the Nazarene. The application of the first must unquestionably have been later, since it could have been made only outside the circle of those who knew positively that the Master was *not* born at Bethlehem, and it is certain that the redactor of Mark had assigned the origin of Jesus to Nazareth before ever our Matthew and Luke associated him with the other town.

Another difficulty is that Matthew and Luke, if they agree as to the birthplace, give quite irreconcilable accounts of the birth. The respective details of the two stories cannot be fitted into a common whole, and convey very different impressions. Matthew's is full of tragic horror, Luke's, a tender and joyous idyll. The wailing of the mothers whose children are being slaughtered by the soldiers of Herod (Matt. ii. 17–18) blends ill with the hymns of the angels and the thanksgivings of the shepherds (Luke ii. 14 and 20). Apart from this, neither of these two accounts of the Nativity will bear critical examination, and it is obvious that neither is founded upon an authentic and accurate original tradition. As literature, the narrative of Luke is superior to that of Matthew in restraint and descriptive power, but as history, it is equally unreliable.[1]

The story of Matthew is entirely dictated by the prophecies, which must, at all costs, be fulfilled, and relies upon them for its whole justification. If Jesus is born at Bethlehem, it is to carry out Micah's prediction that the Messiah would come from that town (Matt. ii. 5) ; if he goes to Egypt, it is because it is written in Hosea xi. 1 : " I called my son out of Egypt " (Matt. ii. 15) ; the piteous cries of the bereaved mothers fulfil the words of Jeremiah xxxi. 15 : " A voice was raised in Ramah, lamenting and wailing long ; it is Rachel who weeps for her children, and will not be comforted, because they are no more " (Matt. ii. 18) ; the Holy Family, on its return from Egypt, goes to dwell at Nazareth in order to vindicate the prophecy : " He shall be called a Nazarene " (Matt. ii. 23). All these strained coincidences do not inspire confidence in the incidents which they are supposed to corroborate. Neither the visit of the Magi, nor the appearance of the miraculous star, nor the massacre of the Innocents, has any other basis than the imagination of the hagiographer who put the whole story together.

[1] A detailed study of the two accounts by the present writer will be found in CCVIII, 44 *ff*.

To attempt to discover the sources and analyse the elements of these incidents, may be an interesting pastime for a scholar, but it is quite irrelevant either to the actual history of Jesus or to any primitive tradition concerning it.

The study of the account in Luke (ii. 1–20) leads to exactly the same conclusion. It has nothing in common with Matthew except the anxiety to explain how it was that, though Jesus was called a Nazarene, in the sense of " a native of Nazareth," he was actually born at Bethlehem. The reason for this divergence of these two products of a common purpose, is that the editor of Luke, like the editor of Matthew, relied upon no tradition, and simply invented his own story,[1] independently of Matthew. The birth in the stable, the coming of the shepherds, the angelic visitations, all the charming pictures painted by our Evangelist, though, like the incidents in Matthew, they may be investigated with a view to discovering their components, belong, like them, to the domain of pure hagiography, and have no connexion with history. As Strauss has justly observed, the writers of the two Gospels relate the same thing in two different forms, and what they relate is a legend designed to verify the birth of Jesus at Bethlehem. Neither of these two accounts of the Nativity belongs to the original version of the Gospel in which it appears; they are both later parasitic growths.

The oldest tradition, which is found in Mark, knows nothing of the story of Bethlehem. John is perhaps acquainted with it, but does not accept it, because it is connected with the effort, already out-of-date in the Fourth Gospel, to vindicate the Messiahship of Jesus by proving that all the Prophecies were fulfilled in him. Are we, then, to assume that Mark was right, and that Jesus was born at Nazareth? It is not entirely out of the question, even insisting on the fact that the surname, the Nazarene, cannot be interpreted as meaning " the man of Nazareth," for the epithet might just have been chosen for its assonance, as having the double advantage of expressing the function of Jesus and at the same time sounding like the name of his birthplace. That, however, does not seem very probable. The original tradition, as far as we can judge from Mark, was not interested in the " private life " of Jesus, that is to say, in his birth and the period of his existence prior to his baptism by John, and the likelihood seems

---

[1] To say that he *invented* it, is perhaps slightly overstating the case. He may have found the elements of his story in the Christian tradition by which he was surrounded, as, also, may the editor of Matthew. But these elements are none the less inventions.

to be that the recollection of his exact birthplace was lost. The immediate disciples must have known it, of course, and doubtless the oral tradition also remembered it for some time. But, not being fixed in writing, and having no significance for the Christological development, it lapsed into oblivion, and that all the more rapidly and irrevocably because the generations which followed the original disciples had little interest in the human existence of the " Lord." The development of Christology characteristic of Paul and the Johannine writings, soon turned the attention of believers from any inquiry into the human childhood of the " Saviour," who came to be more and more exclusively regarded from the eschatological point of view. When, by means of the Apocrypha, such as the *Gospel of the Childhood*, the *Protevangelium of James*, the *Pseudo-Matthew*, the *Gospel of Thomas*, and the *History of Joseph the Carpenter*,[1] Christian piety was recalled to an interest in the childhood of Jesus, it was to find it all embellished with miracles and prodigies, designed to show the divine power of Christ from the time of his birth to the beginning of his mission in Israel. There was no question of establishing or supplementing historical facts ; a collection of fantastic miracles is not to be confused with biography. It was a case of a kind of hagiographic intoxication, intended to heighten the faith of the credulous, of which there were several outbreaks between the second and the fifth centuries. (For if the writings which exhibit its manifestations sometimes go back, in their original form, to the end of the second century, they have reached us in texts which continued to be revised, altered, and elaborated, down to the threshold of the Middle Ages.)

Hence, though it is quite certain that Jesus was not born at Bethlehem, as stated by Matthew and Luke, it is by no means so that he was born at Nazareth, as Mark and John believe. All that can be said is that it is not actually impossible, inasmuch as Nazareth was in Galilee and the oldest tradition preserves the information that Jesus came from that country. The critical and prudent conclusion, however, is that we have no knowledge in the matter, and in all probability never shall have. From the moment when it was perceived, on the one hand, that he " was to be born " at Bethlehem, and, on the other, that Nazarene meant " man of Nazareth," the name of his insignificant native place became indifferent,

---

[1] We purposely mention only the Apocrypha, which have been studied, edited, and translated in **CXXXVI**, i and ii. For the substance of the others, see **CXLII**, part i, sections ii, iii, and iv.

and even embarrassing, to the faith, and could not fail to fall into oblivion.

We may say, without seeking to be more specific, that Jesus was born in Galilee. The date is another obscure and much disputed question.[1] It will suffice here to give the data and general drift of the discussion, without going into details.

II

The Various Evidence of the Gospels regarding the Date of the Nativity

It is not to be expected that our Gospels will give us a definite date, for such accuracy is not one of the characteristics of this type of writing. They afford, in fact, only a few vague indications, which are either contradictory or obviously erroneous. Matthew ii. 1 places the Nativity "in the days of Herod the King" (ἐν ἡμέραις Ἡρῴδου τοῦ βασιλέως). It is unquestionably Herod the Great who is meant, for the successor of this king in Judæa was called Archelaus. But we know that Herod died in the year 750 of the Roman calendar, early in the spring, either in March or April, of the fourth year before Christ,[2] which constitutes a serious difficulty to begin with. There is nothing to be obtained from Mark, except the fact that his silence on the matter of chronology proves that the question was not one which interested the early tradition, which is a further reason for misgiving. Luke is apparently more explicit. The information he professes to give us is as follows : (1) Elizabeth, the mother of John the Baptist, became pregnant " in the time of Herod, King of Judæa," and Mary conceived six months after her cousin (Luke i. 26, 36 and 42). At the time of the latter's delivery, an imperial edict for a census made it necessary for her to go to Bethlehem, at which time Quirinius is stated to have been Governor of Syria, no further mention being made of Herod (ii. 1–2). (2) John the Baptist began his preaching in " the fifteenth year of the reign of Tiberius Cæsar," when Pontius Pilate was Governor of Judæa, Herod Antipas tetrarch of Galilee, and Annas and Caiaphas

[1] For the bibliography see : **CLXXVI**, 610 ff.; **CXLII**, 279, n. 1; and **XXIX**, i, 19 ff. Cf. also **DB**, Chronology of N.T. ; **EB**, Chronology ; **CCXXIV** ; Endemann, Die chronologischen Daten des Lebens Jesu, Leipzig, 1911. These various writings deal with the chronology of the life of Jesus in general, but the date of the Nativity is, of course, their point of departure. The problem of this date has been gone into by the writer in **CCVIII**, 23 ff.

[2] **XXIX**, i, 415, n. 167 ; **CCXXIV**, 191 ; **V**, i, 234 ff.

were High Priests (iii. 1–2). It was shortly after this that Jesus came to be baptized by John and commenced his public career, and he was then " about thirty years old " (καὶ αὐτὸς ἦν Ἰησοῦς ἀρχόμενος ὡσεὶ ἐτῶν τριάκοντα, iii. 21 and 23).—Finally, John (viii. 56–7) makes Jesus say, in the course of a dispute with the Jews : " Your father Abraham rejoiced to see my day ; he saw it and was glad " ; to which his opponents reply : " Thou art not yet fifty years old, and hast thou seen Abraham ? " This ironic question appears to imply that Jesus may have been nearly fifty at the time of his public career. On the other hand, by the Johannine reckoning itself, which is much more generous than that of the Synoptics, this public career of Jesus cannot have lasted more than three years, and the probability is, that at the most it did not cover more than one.

Several of these various chronological data are contradictory.[1] We may set down to begin with, as a practically undisputed fixed point, that Pontius Pilate was Procurator of Judæa from A.D. 26 to 36. Now what can we make of our data ? The fifteenth year of the reign of Tiberius, who was made Emperor on the tenth of August in the year 14, falls between the nineteenth of August 28 and the eighteenth of August 29. If Jesus was thirty years old between 28 and 29, he could not be nearly fifty, a year, or even two years, later, and he could barely, though just possibly, have been born under Herod the Great, which would make him at least thirty-three. However, a man of that age might be said to be " about thirty." But if the census of Quirinius mentioned in Luke is the same as that spoken of by Josephus,[2] it took place in A.D. 6 to 7, which excludes the possibility of the birth of Jesus under Herod, and, at the same time, brings him to the age, in the year 28–9, of only twenty-two or twenty-three, instead of anywhere near thirty. These are grave difficulties, and they do not include those contributed by the astronomical calculations which have professed to explain and to date the appearance of the star of the Magi.[3]

[1] CCVIII, 24 ff.—This contradiction makes quite futile the classic comparison between the Synoptic and the Johannine chronology. There is no such thing as a " Synoptic chronology," and the Johannine chronology is inconsistent. Cf. LXXXIV, 419 ff. ; CLVI, 236 ff.

[2] Ant., 17, 13, 5 ; 18, 1, 1 ; 18, 2, 1. The census here referred to is one instituted by Quirinius, legate of Syria, after the deposition of Archelaus, for the purpose of imposing the Roman tax.

[3] Kepler, De Jesus Christi salvatoris nostri vero anno natalitio, 1606, upholds the year 7 B.C. Westberg, Die biblische Chronologie nach Flav. Josephus und das Todesjahr Jesu, Leipzig, 1910, accepts the identifica-

In order to unravel this skein of contradictions, we should have to know what value to assign to each of the elements that enter into it, and that we have no means of determining. The immediate impression, however, is that at the time of the redaction of our Gospel writings, the Christian tradition itself was no longer sure of its chronological ground, for, had there been any established tradition in the matter, it would easily have compelled the acceptance of all the gospel editors. It was precisely because such a thing was lacking, that each of them attempted to supply the deficiency as best he could. Possibly one or other of them may have had some more or less authentic information at his disposal, but we cannot tell. It may be, for instance, that the original tradition vouched for the fact that Jesus was born " in the days of Herod," but the statements of Matthew are mixed up with such improbable tales that they must all come under suspicion.

We shall confine ourselves here to a few words on the chronology of Luke, because its air of accuracy has been particularly misleading, and it has been the subject of much bitter dispute.[1] The most important point in it is the statement concerning the census of Quirinius (ii. 1–5), which runs as follows :

" Now it came to pass that in those days there went out a decree of Cæsar Augustus that all in the world should be taxed ; this was the first taxing, when Quirinius was governor of Syria.[2] And all went to be registered, each into his own city. And Joseph also went up from Galilee out of the city of Nazareth, in Judæa, unto the city of David, which is called Bethlehem, because he was of

---

tion of the star with Halley's comet, and suggests the year A.D. 12, etc. Cf. H. Voigt, *Die Gesch. Jesu und die Astrologie*, Leipzig, 1911 ; **CLXXVI**, 611 *ff*.

[1] Bibliography will be found in **XXIX**, i, 508 *ff*. For the substance of the matter see : **XXIX**, 508 *ff*., which seems to the present writer conclusive ; **EB**, *Quirinius* ; **XCVI**, i, 315 ; **CIII**, i, 343 *ff*. ; **XCVII**, 32 *ff*. ; —for the conservative position : **CCXXVI** ; **LXIX**, ii, 395 *ff*., 415 *ff*. ; —for the Catholic point of view : **V**, i, 281 *ff*. ; Lagrange, *Où en est la question du recensement de Quirinius*, **RB**, January, 1911. **XXIV**, i, 46 *ff*., also defends the chronology of Luke. *Cf.* also : C. Cichorius, *Chronologisches zum Leben Jesu*, **ZNTW**, xxii, 1923, 16 *ff*.

[2] Ἀύτη ἀπογραφὴ πρώτη ἐγένετο ἡγεμονεύοντος τῆς Συρίας Κυρηνίου. The meaning here adopted is that accepted by the most modern translators (Crampon, Loisy, Goguel, Moffatt, Klostermann). It has, however, been disputed, and two other renderings proposed : " This census was the first of those which took place under Quirinius, when he was governor of Syria " ; and even : " This was the census which took place before Quirinius was governor of Syria." There seems little possibility of either of these two tendentious translations being correct, but it is true that the sense of the passage is not unambiguous.

the house and lineage of David, to be registered with Mary, his wife, who was pregnant."

We will not unduly stress the peculiarity of the mode of census-taking implied by our text, but it is to be noted that it is a very strange proceeding. The moving about of men and families which this reckless decree must have caused throughout the whole of the Empire, is almost beyond imagination, and one cannot help wondering what advantage there could be for the Roman state in this return, for a single day, of so many scattered individuals, not to the places of their birth, but to the original homes of their ancestors. For it is to be remembered that those of royal descent were not the only ones affected by this fantastic ordinance, and many a poor man must have been hard put to it to discover the cradle of his race. The suspicion, or, rather, the conviction, is borne in upon us at first sight that the editor of Luke has simply been looking for some means of bringing Joseph and Mary to Bethlehem, in order to have Jesus born there. A hagiographer of his type never bothers much about common sense in inventing the circumstances he requires. In this case, no notice is taken of the fact that " the city of David " was not the city of Mary, and that there seems to have been no necessity for her to have made such a journey on the eve of her confinement. It is all outside the plane of reality.

The actual census of Quirinius may, however, have been a fact, and one that was in some way, though how, we do not know, connected with the date of the birth of Jesus. The historical problem may be stated as follows. Josephus asserts that, Augustus having appointed Archelaus his legate in Syria in A.D. 6–7, Quirinius, the governor of Judæa, ordered a census for the purpose of imposing the Roman tax—a quite necessary and normal proceeding. It cannot be this measure to which Luke refers, since the decree there mentioned concerns " the world " (πᾶσαν τὴν ὀικουμένην), that is to say, the whole Empire, and would have to be dated at least ten to twelve years *prior to* the census recorded by Josephus, to bring it within the reign of Herod the First. The question is whether Josephus has been guilty of an omission in saying nothing of this first census (of which, incidentally, there is no mention anywhere else), or whether it is Luke who has made a mistake and assigned to the time of Herod the First an event which actually took place in the year A.D. 6–7.[1]

[1] The mainstay of the partisans of Luke is still Huschke's study : *Ueber den Census und die Steuerverfassung der früheren römischen Kaiserzeit*, 1847. Of more recent contributions to that view, the most im-

Not to go into a detailed discussion, which would be out of place here, we shall reduce the solution of the problem to a certain number of points which appear to be quite definite, or at least as definite as the present state of our evidence permits. (1) We have no authority for asserting, or even for supposing, that there was a general census of the *orbis romanus* under Augustus. (2) No text gives us any reason to believe that any proceeding of this kind, limited to Syria, was taken, except under the circumstances mentioned by Josephus, that is to say, on the establishment of direct Roman government in the country in the year A.D. 6–7. (3) The Jewish historian represents this measure of 6–7 as *something new*, which the inhabitants of Judæa received very badly,[1] because they guessed what it meant. This makes it appear very improbable that it was a mere repetition of a similar census already imposed under Herod the First. (4) There was no reason for a Roman census, which could have no purpose except revenue, in Judæa under Herod the First, for Herod, although a very obedient subject of Augustus, retained control of his own treasury and system of taxation, as is witnessed by the protests which were raised at his death against his exactions. (5) If a census had really been taken under Herod, it is difficult to see why it would need to be taken over again in A.D. 6–7. The Romans did not lightly create trouble, and they were perfectly aware that such a proceeding sometimes involved very serious trouble, wherever it was instituted. (6) Quirinius is known to have been legate of Syria between Volusius Saturninus and Cæcilius Creticus Silanus, that is to say, between A.D. 6 and 12.[2] These dates are quite consistent with the attribution to him of the census of A.D. 6–7, but they make it difficult to understand how he could have directed a similar undertaking ten or twelve years previously. An attempt has been made, on the strength of certain inscriptions, to show that he was twice legate of Syria, but the evidence is not convincing.[3] In any case, it could only have been in the year 3–2 B.C. that he first held the office in question, because that is the only year for which we do not know the name of the governor of Syria,[4] so that

portant are : Ramsay, *Quirinius, Governor of Syria*, in the *Athenæum*, August 10, 1912 ; and Barton, *Archæology and the Bible*, Philadelphia, 1917, pp. 432 *ff.* For the details of the discussion see **CCVIII**, 27 *ff.*, and notes ; and for the negative, **XXII**, 210 *ff.*

[1] Josephus, *Bell. Jud.*, 2, 8, 1.   [2] **XXIX**, i, 326 *ff.*
[3] **CCVIII**, 179, notes 18 and 19.
[4] **XXIX**, i, 322 *ff.* This is disputed by **CLIX**, 54, which argues for 12 B.C. and A.D. 6 as the two years in which Quirinius received the appointment.

it was definitely after Herod's time. This is confirmed by the fact that we know the name of the legate who suppressed the uprisings consequent upon the death of Herod ; it was Quintilius Varus. (7) It is incredible that such an unusual and disturbing proceeding as the census spoken of by Luke must necessarily have been, should have escaped all mention in Josephus.

To sum up, the probability, we may even venture to say, the certainty, seems to be that Luke made a mistake, or, more accurately, that he referred to a well-known event without being particular as to its exact date. The census of Quirinius in A.D. 6–7 was a painful memory for the people of Palestine. It was called simply " the census," [1] as in France, before 1914, the struggle of 1870–1 was spoken of as " the war." It is certainly this occurrence of A.D. 6–7 which Luke ii. 1 has in mind, and of which he makes use to bring Joseph and Mary to Bethlehem, for the purpose of establishing that town as the birthplace of Jesus. Since, however, he thinks there are reasons for placing the birth " in the days of Herod the King," he anticipates the census and governorship of Quirinius by ten years or so. Such a displacement, effected outside Palestine and a considerable time after the events in question, would hardly be likely to meet with contradiction. In any case, it is quite in the style of the pseudo-proofs and chronological data of the hagiographers, [2] which is the reason history can make nothing of them.

The other chronological details in Luke, that is to say, the connexion he apparently established between the fifteenth year of the reign of Tiberius and the thirtieth of the life of Jesus, are, unfortunately, equally unreliable. We do not even know the exact meaning of the twenty-third verse of chapter iii. in which the words " about thirty years " appear. The text usually accepted seems to require the following translation : " And Jesus himself was, at the beginning, about thirty years of age, being, as was supposed, the son of Joseph . . ." What we are to understand by " at the beginning " (ἀρχόμενος), it is very difficult to say, and numerous theories have been advanced on the subject. [3] We shall not discuss, nor even enumerate them, because there seems small probability that

[1] As Acts v. 37 testifies : " After him rose up Judas of Galilee in the days of the census " (ἐν ταῖς ἡμέραις τῆς ἀπογραφῆς).

[2] It is to be remembered that the editor of Acts v. 36 ff. calmly perpetrates an error of forty years, in placing the rebellion of Theudas before that of Judas of Galilee.

[3] **CCVIII**, 38 ff.

the estimate of the age of Jesus given in that " about thirty years," was authorized by any genuine tradition.[1] Various texts in the Bible attribute a special value to the age of thirty. Joseph was thirty when he became Prime Minister (Gen. xli. 46); David was thirty when he became King (2 Sam. v. 4). Most significantly, Numbers iv. 3, 23 and 30 fixes the eligibility of the Levites for service at the altar at from thirty to fifty years of age. To say that Jesus was thirty years old at the beginning of his career, was, therefore, to specify that he was exactly the age required by the Law for a Man of God. Similarly, when John viii. 57 says that he is not yet fifty, it asserts that he is still within the consecrated period.

When we observe, further, that Luke seems to have only an approximate and remote knowledge of Judæan affairs, and that, in particular, the chronological evidence which he professes to draw from the sequence of the High Priests (iii. 2, " under the High Priests Annas and Caiaphas ") is doubly erroneous,[2] we are led definitely to conclude that the hagiographer did not know either the exact date of the birth of Jesus or his actual age at the time of his mission. He knew, or thought that he knew, only that the Lord was born " in the time of Herod," and he attempted to support that conviction, which may have been more or less justified, by recalling facts and names well known in themselves, but whose dates were sufficiently vague in his chronology for him to be able, without scruple, to gather them all together at the point where they could be of use to him. Chronological vagueness and capriciousness are the rooted vices of hagiography, and there is nothing surprising in encountering them here.

The earliest believers, having no interest in this question of chronology, made no attempt to elucidate it, so that by the time our Gospels were edited, the Christians had no longer any verifiable data. When, in spite of this, they desired knowledge, they were obliged to create their own beliefs, which inevitably resulted in disagreements even wider, at times, than the reading of our canonical Gospels would indicate. It appears, for instance, that the Asiatic presbyters, taking literally the text of viii. 57 of their Johannine Gospel, brought down the death of Christ to the time of Claudius (A.D. 41–54). Others advanced

---

[1] Even Meyer, who, for not very convincing reasons, regards this estimate as probable, admits that it looks like a conjecture rather than a traditional belief : **XXIV**, i, 50.

[2] Annas was High Priest neither in the fifteenth year of the reign of Tiberius, nor at the same time as Caiaphas. The former was governor of the Temple from A.D. 6 to 15, the latter from 18 to 36.

it still further, to the year 59, which falls in the reign of Nero, and took the year 9 for the date of the Nativity. Others, on the contrary, placed the Crucifixion in A.D. 21, forgetting that Pilate had not received his appointment until 26, as their opponents overlooked the fact that he had lost it in 36.[1]

It is to a Scythian monk called Dionysius the Less (*Dionysius Exiguus*), living at Rome in the sixth century, that we owe the traditional dating of the beginning of the Christian era.[2] He had at his disposal no more information than we have ourselves, and his conclusion is merely the result of reasoning based entirely upon the data of Luke, and running substantially as follows. If John the Baptist began his preaching in the fifteenth year of the reign of Tiberius, and if we allow an interval of about a year between the commencement of the career of the Forerunner and that of Jesus, the latter must have been thirty years old in the sixteenth year of Tiberius. Deducting thirty years, we reach the seven hundred and fifty-fourth year of the Roman calendar, so that the date of the Nativity is December 25th of that year, which thus becomes year one of the new era. Dionysius was hindered in his calculations by none of the difficulties which we have encountered, for the simple reason that he did not admit the possibility of any contradiction between the Gospels, and, as he had no external means of fixing the exact dates of the death of Herod and of the census, he did not know that those two events were subsequent to 754.

Nowadays the Catholic chronologists, who are unwilling to give up the massacre of the Innocents or the flight into Egypt from Herod's executioners, are compelled to say that Dionysius was wrong, and that the Nativity must be placed in A.D. 6 or 7.[3] Unfortunately, the account of Matthew is also pure hagiography, and yields no basis for a positive conclusion in the matter. There is nothing to prove that the expression " in the days of Herod " was anything more than a popular approximation, a mere application of the rule by which, in that kind of writing, any facts of which the dates are unknown are associated with the name of some famous personage.

It is wisest to conclude that we do not know, within about fifteen years, or perhaps more, the time when Jesus came into

[1] Regarding these eccentricities, which merely prove the complete uncertainty of the Christian chronology on the subject of Jesus, see **CCXCII,** iii, 18 *ff.*

[2] On Dionysius the Less, *cf.* **CLXX,** i, 403 ; Von Soden, **EB,** *Chronology,* col. 807.

[3] **V,** i, 224 *ff.* For some more recent computations see **CLXXVI,** 610 *ff.*

the world. It will be hardly necessary to add that the liturgical date of Christmas (December 25) has no foundation in history.[1] It was fixed at Rome, only after long uncertainty, probably in the first quarter of the fourth century. Hippolytus, at the beginning of the third, already supported it, but at almost the same time Clement of Alexandria was championing the 19th of April. The 18th of April, the 29th of May, and the 28th of March also had their advocates, for the story in Luke, with its shepherds spending the night in the fields, suggested spring rather than winter. In the Orient, however, the 6th of January was generally accepted as the date. The fact is that nobody knew, and we know no better today.[2] It is very probable that the festival of the solar god Mithra, which occurred on the 25th of December, coincident, according to the Roman calendar, with the winter solstice, was largely influential in securing the acceptance of the same date for the Nativity of Jesus. The words of the prophet Malachi (iv. 2) find their appropriate application : " But unto you who fear my name shall the sun of righteousness arise." [3]

[1] A good collection of the most important writings on the subject is to be found in **CCLXXIV**, 96 *ff.*, of which book there is a French translation, **CCLXXIV**-*a*. See also Duchesne, *Culte*[3], 257 *ff.* ; Frazer, *Adonis*[3], i, 304 *ff.*, and *Balder the Beautiful*, i, 246 and 331 *ff.*

[2] The two rival dates of the 25th of December and the 6th of January were arrived at by computation from the date of Easter. The adherents of the former placed the Crucifixion on the 25th of March, of the latter, on the 6th of April. As it was held that the life of the Lord must have embodied chronological perfection, that is to say, have comprised an exact number of years, without a fraction, he was believed to have died on the anniversary of his Incarnation. Reckoning nine months from the 6th of April, yielded the 6th of January, and from the 25th of March, the 25th of December, as the date of the Nativity.

[3] The comparison of Christ with the sun is common in ancient Christian writings. *Cf.* **CCLXXIV**, 113, n. 3, and in particular F. J. Dölger's exhaustive study in *Die Sonne der Gerechtichkeit und der Schwarze*, Münster, 1919, and *Sol salutis*, Münster, 1920.

CHAPTER IV

THE FAMILY OF JESUS, AND THE CIRCUMSTANCES OF HIS BIRTH

I

The Relatives of Jesus: Mary and Joseph

WE shall not stop to discuss the wonders with which the editors of Matthew and Luke have thought fit to adorn their accounts of the Nativity.[1] The appearance of the miraculous star, the visit of the Magi, the flight into Egypt and the massacre of the Innocents, on the one hand; the birth in the stable, the announcement of the glad tidings to the shepherds, the presentation in the Temple, on the other, form two groups of incidents which it is futile to endeavour to blend into one, and still more futile to attempt to connect with history. They are sheer hagiography. The editors have sought to make up for their lack of knowledge by moving but fictitious narratives, founded either upon supposedly prophetic writings, or upon popularized myths or folk tales.[2] The Apocryphal gospels supplementing and elaborating these edifying tales increased their improbabilities,[3] but did not alter their essential nature, which by the deliberate intent of their authors set them outside the sphere of verifiable and probable events. Such is the fundamental character of the miraculous element in hagiography, a fact which it would be rash and ingenuous to forget.

The question of the parents of Jesus cannot be so easily dismissed.[4] The oldest tradition believed, probably rightly, that the mother of the Master was called *Mariam*. The name of his father was *Joseph*, according to the legends at the

---

[1] A brief study of the question will be found in **CCVIII**, 43 *ff.*; and a bibliography in the same work, 132. Add also **XXIV**, i, 52 *ff.*, and **LXXXVI**, 175 *ff.*, both of which are of the greatest interest.

[2] **XXIV**, i, 52 *ff.*, ably characterizes these legendary accounts.

[3] **CXLII**, 74–82; **CXXXII**, 63–76.

[4] Von Soden, *Genealogies of Jesus* in **EB**, the general lives of Jesus and the commentaries on Matthew and Luke; **CCVIII**, ch. iii. *Cf.* **CLVI-*a***, ch. lx, pp. 325 *ff.*

beginning of Matthew and Luke, and two passages in John (i. 45 and vi. 42). But this evidence is not in itself conclusive, and it is not confirmed by Mark, who makes no mention of Joseph. The tradition reflected in the Second Gospel thus appears to have had no interest in the father of Jesus, and it has been suggested, as a means of obviating this difficulty, that he was dead when his son began his preaching. Eduard Meyer justifiably questions whether we can regard the name of Joseph as authentic,[1] and his answer, which cannot be gainsaid, is that we have no means of deciding the point. Everyone today knows that Joseph was a carpenter, but it may well be that the ancient Christians were less sure of the fact than we. In Mark vi. 3 the people of Nazareth, amazed at the wisdom displayed by Jesus, exclaim : " Is not this *the carpenter, the son of Mary* ? " Matthew and Luke have both altered this passage. The former (xiii. 55) substitutes : " Is not this *the son of the carpenter* ? " ; and the latter (iv. 22) : " Is not this *the son of Joseph* ? " It is our opinion that the three editors all had before them an original text of Mark which actually read " the son of the carpenter." In Aramaic, however, the expression " the son of the carpenter " means " a carpenter," just as " a son of man " is another way of saying " a man." Accordingly, our Mark has correctly translated it as " the carpenter " ; Matthew has failed to understand, and has simply transcribed the expression as it stands ; Luke, also failing to understand, has tried to improve it by specifying the person meant by " the carpenter."

Whether the father of Jesus was called Joseph or not, and whether or not he was a carpenter or joiner, are, however, matters of small importance. The impression conveyed, and on which we may rely, is that he was a man of humble station, earning his bread by the labour of his hands. We have no means of ascertaining anything more about him, and the details of his biography and character given by the Apocrypha are completely untrustworthy.[2] As to his ancestors, we are entirely ignorant, and the two gospel editors who have professed to trace his descent from David are not even in agreement about the name of his father, one giving it as *Jacob* (Matt. i. 16), and the other as *Heli* (Luke iii. 23).

We are little better informed regarding Mary.[3] What

[1] **XXIV**, i, 72.

[2] Cheyne, *Joseph in N.T.*, in **EB**, para. 2–10 ; **CXLII**, 4–8.—For the Catholic point of view see Sonvay, *Joseph (Saint)*, in **CE**, viii, 504–6.

[3] P. Schmiedel, *Mary*, in **EB** ; **CCXX** ; **CCLXIX**.—For the Catholic point of view, A.-J. Maas, *Virgin Mary*, in **CE**, xv, 464 *ff.*

the Synoptics say about her is insignificant, and the contradictory fantasies of the Apocrypha [1] are worthless, except to convince us that the primitive tradition, having no reason to be interested in the mother of Jesus in herself, had amassed no accurate and trustworthy information concerning her. Her lineage is completely unknown. Some commentators have maintained that Luke connected her, as he did Joseph himself, with the house of David. [2] We should say, on the contrary, that, in representing her as a relative of Elizabeth, whom he makes a descendant of Aaron, he affiliates her with the family of Aaron. In any case, since the whole of the Lucan legend regarding the relationships of the Forerunner and of Jesus cannot possibly be based upon any authentic tradition, we have no choice but to give up even that shred of information concerning the ancestors of Mary. Nor do we know what became of her after the death of Jesus. In this complete absence of any genuine tradition, the imagination of the hagiographers had full scope to indulge in the most affecting or the silliest fabrications, according to their degree of literary skill. [3] The only passage in our Synoptics which might recall a real incident with regard to the mother of Jesus, is that which shows her, incapable as she is of understanding her son, attempting to get him away from his disciples to take him home (Mark iii. 20 *ff.*).

There is nothing surprising in the fact that the gospel tradition leaves us in ignorance concerning the parents of Christ, for even if, as is possible, the original disciples had possessed accurate and more or less detailed information about them, there would have been no reason for transmitting it to the second generation of Christians. Almost immediately after the Crucifixion, was begun that labour of faith which, absorbed in elevating Jesus more and more above humanity, must necessarily have contemned everything that tended in the opposite direction. Too many details about his earthly family, and its actual status, which was certainly not too distinguished, could not fail, at that time, to be very embarrassing. When Paul announces that he is interested only in "the crucified and glorified Christ," [4] he gives the exact formula for the transformation of the life of Jesus in the minds of the earliest genera-

---

[1] Schmiedel, *Mary*, § 21 ; **CXLII**, 8–21.

[2] B. Weiss, in **LIX** (1901), on Luke i. 27 ; **CIX**, 21.

[3] Epiphanius, *Haeres.*, 78, especially 11, 12, and 24, gives evidence that this creation of legends had not yet ceased in the fourth century. *Cf.* **CCLXXXIII**-*a*, 570 *ff.* and 689 *ff.*

[4] 1 Cor. i. 18, 23–4 ; ii. 2.

tions of Christians. At the same time, he reveals the secret of the rapidity with which authentic recollections concerning the family of the Nazarene and his life prior to his baptism were obliterated.

The glorious legend which was thus substituted for a humble reality is very old, because the reason for the substitution is also very old. From the moment his followers believed that Jesus was the Messiah foretold by the Prophets, the transformation of his life into myth began, and proceeded apace.

The legend in its growth has left in the text of our Synoptics traces of at least three of its stages, or, if the evidence of Acts be included, we may say, four :

(1) It was the belief in the resurrection which probably established, or·at least defined, as we shall see later, the faith in the Messiahship of Jesus. The Apostles, having *witnessed* the Resurrection, realized that he had been glorified by God, and no longer doubted that he was " the one who was to come." These beliefs, together with their scriptural justification, that is to say, accompanied by the prophecies which were supposed to confirm them, appear in the two discourses attributed to Peter in Acts ii. 22 *ff.*, and iv. 8 *ff.*[1] Such an idea was not by any means inconsistent with the phenomena of a completely human existence, and it presented itself as one which could be accepted by men who had actually lived on familiar terms with the Master. But it was not designed to satisfy for long the growing faith of men who believed in Jesus without having seen him.

(2) In the account in Luke of the event of the Baptism, we read (iii. 22) : " The Holy Ghost descended in bodily form, in the shape of a dove, upon him, and a voice came from heaven (saying) : Thou art my beloved son ; in thee I am well pleased." The most authoritative manuscript of the *Western* text, codex D, gives here the variant, borrowed from Psalm ii. 7 : " This day have I begotten thee " ($\dot{\varepsilon}\gamma\grave{\omega}$ $\sigma\acute{\eta}\mu\varepsilon\varrho\upsilon\nu$ $\gamma\varepsilon\gamma\acute{\varepsilon}\nu\nu\eta\varkappa\acute{\alpha}$ $\sigma\varepsilon$). This is certainly earlier than the accepted reading, for it exhibits the belief that God adopted Jesus as his son on the day of the Baptism. Thus, the whole life of the Lord, or at least his public career, is included in the Messianic period of his existence, but his birth, according to the rabbinical conception, remains that of a man amongst men, and a man of

---

[1] These two discourses are undoubtedly spurious, but there is every probability that the idea which we wish to bring out here is very old, and really represents the first form of the divine exaltation of Jesus.— *Cf.* Acts xiii. 33, in which it is stated that God has raised Jesus " according as it is written in the second psalm : Thou art my son, this day have I begotten thee."

humble status.[1] It was not long before the progress of the faith made intolerable to the " brethren " these prosaic ideas of an insensitive Judaism, and they substituted for them beliefs more worthy of their object.

(3) The first and third Gospels both contain genealogies of Jesus connecting him with King David. The belief that the Blessed of Jahweh, the Messiah, would belong to the race of the old national king was widespread in Israel towards the beginning of our era.[2] It is possible that the current identification of " Messiah " and " Son of David " was not taken literally in the Pharisaic schools, but amongst the people it probably was, and in our Gospels it unquestionably is. From the moment when Jesus came to be regarded by his disciples as the Messiah, it thus became necessary for him to be descended from David. The parentage of the humble Galilean workman had to go back in a direct line to the king chosen of old by Jahweh.[3] There was no question of finding out if such a relationship could be proved, or even made to appear plausible. Hagiography does not trouble itself with such details and scruples. The point was to show that the announcement of (διά) the Prophets had not been false. A hagiographer had no need of any other evidence than that of the Prophets themselves to be convinced that Jesus was a member of the house of David, and to realize his own duty, which was to embody this truth in concrete form that it might convince the sceptical.

The genealogies of Matthew and Luke represent two of these fulfilments of prophecy, and there may possibly have been others in circulation, contradictory no doubt, like the two which remain to us. But it would show lack of intelligence to apply critical methods to these reconstructions arising from credal or apologetic necessities, and directed solely towards edification.

A moment's scrutiny of the genealogy of Matthew i. 1–17 will reveal its artificiality ; in fact, it is naïvely admitted in the last verse :

> " So all the generations from Abraham unto David are fourteen generations, and from David unto the exile into Babylon, fourteen generations, and from the exile into Babylon unto Christ, fourteen generations."

In other words, for reasons unknown to us, but probably connected with the symbolism of numbers,[4] or with the desire for

---

[1] CCXVII, 223.   [2] II, 446, and CCXVII, 216 ff.
[3] XXIV, i, 61, justly observes that the Davidic descent is, under the circumstances, simply a " religious postulate."
[4] XCIX, 151, gives the principal explanations that have been suggested. Cf. CII, 2.

that equality of parts which the Orientals of those days regarded
as a form of perfection, the genealogist, taking the pattern of
his work, and the names on which he has mainly relied, from
the Bible,[1] has constructed a framework which has no historical
basis and then filled it in as he thought fit. The proof is, that
his second series, the one commencing with " David begat
Solomon," and comprising the kings of Judah, has skipped
four names. In verse 8, instead of " Joram begat Uzziah,"
we should have " Joram begat Ahaziah ; Ahaziah begat Joash ;
Joash begat Amaziah ; Amaziah begat Uzziah." That is to
say, Joram was not the father of Uzziah, as the genealogist
would have us believe, but his great-great-grandfather. Further, in verse 11 we find : " Josiah begat Jechoniah and his
brethren in the exile to Babylon," that is, " at the time of the
exile." In reality, Josiah had been dead for over twenty years
" at the time of the exile," and he did not beget Jechoniah,
who was his grandson. It is not a case of accidental forgetfulness or casual inaccuracy ; the redactor has simply cut out
anything that interfered with the regular pattern of the symbolic structure by which he professed to prove that Jesus had
fulfilled the divine promises made to his ancestor Abraham,
and had accomplished the sacred destiny of the race of David.
The prosaic facts of history mattered nothing to him.

The editor of Luke was equally indifferent to them. His
genealogy, which is found in iii. 23–38, is in reverse order. It
starts with Jesus and goes right back, through David and Abraham, to Adam " (son) of God," comprising seventy-seven names,
with God at one end and Jesus at the other. This figure also
seems to reflect an interest in numerical symbolism.[2] The
names, from Adam to Abraham, have been taken from the
Greek Bible, as is proved by the mention of Cainan (iii. 36),
who does not appear in the Hebrew text. From Abraham to
David, Luke's list, still taken from the Bible, coincides exactly
with Matthew's, but after David, instead of continuing the
descent through Solomon, it takes it through Nathan, another
son of David, whose name is given in 2 Samuel v. 14, and is,
incidentally, the only thing we know about him. Beginning
with Nathan, Luke diverges from Matthew, only temporarily

---

[1] *Cf.* Gen. v. 1 : " This is the book of the generation of men." The
names come from 1 Chron. i. 34 ; ii. 1–5 ; iii. 17 ; iii. 19 ; Esdras iii. 2.
With the exception of Zerubbabel and Salathiel those of the third series
are completely unknown to us and we do not know whence they were
taken.

[2] The Messianic number, which is 7, must be the basis of this figure,
which is probably to be interpreted as seven times eleven, or seven
times ten plus seven.

rejoining him with the two names, Salathiel and Zerubbabel, and then pursuing his own course again down to Joseph. From Jesus to Abraham, Luke enumerates fifty-six generations, while Matthew gives only forty.[1] In going back to Adam, the genealogist of Luke appears to have intended to signify the universality of salvation, and by this, no less than by his use of the Greek Bible, he reveals his Hellenic origin. It is hardly necessary to add that we do not know where he, any more than Matthew, got the names which form his list after Nathan. But it is quite comprehensible why neither of them could leave out Salathiel and Zerubbabel, names which were indissolubly associated with the Return.

By slightly different means, or, rather, with slightly different materials, the two editors have succeeded in realizing the same purpose, namely, to vindicate the Messianic status of Jesus by proving that he was a member of the house of David.

The belief in this illustrious descent is unquestionably very old,[2] since Paul already knew and accepted it (Rom. i. 3, " of the seed of David according to the flesh "), but that is no reason for believing, without further investigation, that it was correct. There are still critics, even open-minded ones, who accept the possibility of its being so,[3] but we cannot share their opinion. The Davidic descent of Jesus is impugned, to begin with, by the mere fact that it was *necessary*, an inevitable corollary of the announcement of the Messianic status of the Nazarene. But there is a more serious argument against it. The *Ebionim*, the descendants of the ancient Judæo-Christians, apparently rejected the genealogies,[4] and their opinion appears to be justified by the oldest tradition. In the Synoptic narrative Jesus never boasts of his ancestor David, nor do his disciples appear to have regarded him as a descendant of the great king. Neither the appeal of the blind man of Jericho : " Son of David, Jesus, have mercy upon me " (Mark x. 47), nor the Messianic acclamation on the entry into Jerusalem : " Blessed be he that cometh in the name of the Lord. Blessed be the kingdom that cometh, of our father David " (Mark xi. 9–10), can have the least weight against this double silence of Jesus and his companions. The blind man is supposed to divine that

---

[1] The list of Matthew, which ought to amount to forty-two names (14 × 3), actually comprises only forty. The fifty-six generations of Luke are not found in all the manuscripts. Nothing would be easier than for a copyist to make a mistake, either of repetition or omission, in reproducing this long string of proper names. See **CCVIII**, 194, n. 14, for the principal variants.

[2] *Cf.* **CLVI**, 107 *ff.*   [3] **CCXXXII**, 17.

[4] Epiphanius, *Haer.*, 30, 14.

the prophet passing by is the Messiah, and it is *his* name he bestows upon Jesus in calling him " Son of David." To bless the " kingdom of David," on the other hand, is simply to hail the dawn of the Messianic day.[1]

Another, and even more important objection, is that the author of the fourth Gospel, who could not have been ignorant of the belief in the Davidic descent, does not accept it.[2] In the seventh chapter of John, after one of the Master's sermons, the listeners exchange admiring exclamations : " This is a prophet," say some ; " This is the Christ," say others, going further, to which the objection is made :

> " But can the Christ come out of Galilee ? Hath not the Scripture said that Christ cometh of the race of David, and out of the village of Bethlehem whence David came ? " (vii. 40–2).

The fact that the writer of the Gospel does not refute the objection by declaring that Jesus *was* born at Bethlehem and descended from David, proves that he did not think either of these things to be true ; they were not believed in his circle. In his opinion Christ was much more than the son of David, he was his Lord.[3] The same impression is conveyed by John viii. 12–14 :

> " Then spake Jesus again unto them, saying : ' I am the light of the world. . . .' The Pharisees therefore said unto him : ' Thou bearest witness unto thyself; thy witness is not true.' Jesus answered and said unto them : ' Though I bear witness to myself, my witness is true, for I know whence I come and whither I go. But ye do not know whence I come nor whither I go.' "

This shows that Jesus, or rather, the writer of the Gospel, scorned the answer, which the Pharisees would not have accepted, certainly, without proof, but which would have impressed them at once : " I am the son of David."

Enough has been said to prove that the belief in the Davidic descent of Jesus found acceptance only amongst the earliest Christians, and the point need not be emphasized further. Let us now turn to the genealogies and try to evaluate their evidence.

---

[1] **CXCIII**, 4, points out that in Mark xi. 9, Jesus is not explicitly called the Son of David, but only ὁ ἐρχόμενος—" he that is to come," that is to say, the Messiah.

[2] **XXIV**, i, 63.

[3] **CXXVII**[2], 274 *ff.*—The belief that Christ is the Lord of David is easily derived from Ps. cx. 1 : " The Lord said unto my Lord : Sit thou at my right hand." The first Lord is Jahweh, the second is Christ, and it is David who is supposed to speak. *Cf.* Mark xii. 35–7, which gives the same impression as our Johannine texts, although due reservation must be made as to the genuineness of this strange outburst of Jesus. *Cf.* **CLXII**, 439.

If, as has been suggested, the two editors had gone to the public archives for their lists, they would have been the same, or at least, making due allowance for carelessness and error, approximately the same. But they are not only at variance, they are irreconcilable. From David to Jesus, Luke gives forty-two names and Matthew only twenty-six, a difference of sixteen generations, which, in terms of time, allowing an average duration for each, amounts to fully four centuries. Either Luke, that is, is four centuries too long, or Matthew four centuries too short, a divergence which the most generous allowances cannot succeed in reducing to any perceptible extent. To this first difficulty is added another, if possible even more formidable, in the fact that the two genealogies, although following different lines of descent from David, both end with Joseph.

The traditional answer [1] to these objections is that one of the two lists gives the actual members of the line of descent, the other the putative members, arrived at by the operation of the *levirate*, as was called the custom which decreed that if a man died without issue, his nearest relative should marry his widow and endow him with the posterity which he himself had not been able to provide.[2] The difficulty is, that in this case we should have to suppose that, between David and Joseph, the levirate affected all the generations except the two, represented by Salathiel and Zerubbabel, which are common to the two lists. This implies that the generations sprung from Solomon became as a result of the levirate and second marriages,[3] somehow intermingled with those sprung from Nathan, which is improbable, not to say absurd. The complications may, indeed, be reduced a little, but only at the cost of further completely hypothetical assumptions. Julius Africanus, who, if he did not originate the explanation in question, at least disseminated it, admits that it is without proof ($\dot{\alpha}\mu\dot{\alpha}\varrho\tau\upsilon\varrho\sigma\varsigma$) but says that it is the most satisfactory one he knows of, and is supposed to go back to the " dominicals," or relatives of Jesus, who apparently claimed that it was founded on family recollections. They accounted for their inability to produce records, by the assertion that Herod had malevolently destroyed them. It is difficult to have any confidence in such evidence, which could, at best, come only from the descendants of cousins of Jesus, who no longer had any definite information about their lineage, and who were, moreover, bound to believe that

[1] CCVIII, 92 *ff.*
[2] See the law of the levirate, in Deut. xxv. 5–10.
[3] Julius Africanus, ap. Eusebius, *H.E.*, 1, 7, 4.

it was Davidic for the very reason that it was that of the Messiah, " the son of David."

At a much later epoch,[1] a very different explanation was devised to reconcile the two genealogies. It was maintained that that of Matthew applied to Joseph, and that of Luke to Mary. This theory is exposed to numerous objections, of which we shall note only two, which seem to us conclusive : (1) The Jews did not admit the transmission of birthright by the mother. " It was not the custom of the Scriptures," as Saint Jerome justly remarks, " to count women in their genealogies." Hence the genealogy of Mary could be of no use for the purpose of proving that her son was descended from David. (2) It is Joseph, and not Mary, whose descent the genealogist of Luke professes to trace, inasmuch as even our present text reads : " And Jesus himself, at this beginning, was about thirty years old, being the son, as was supposed, of Joseph, (son) of Heli, etc." (iii. 23). Moreover, in i. 27, and ii. 4, it is Joseph, and not Mary, whom Luke makes a descendant of David.[2] Mary, as has already been pointed out, is, as far as Luke is concerned, a member of the house of Aaron.

Neither of these two professed explanations is valid. The two genealogies remain contradictory, resembling each other only in their common object of proving that Jesus is in fact the " son of David " expected by Israel, and in their equal indifference to historical truth and to probability. It is significant that we find in the texts no indication that the Messiahship of Jesus was ever deduced from his Davidic descent. The process was just the reverse ; the Christians first believed that he was the Messiah, and then inferred that he was descended from David.[3]

(4) The belief in the virgin birth represents a new and culminating stage of the Messianic faith, only to be superseded by the Pauline and Johannine doctrine of the Incarnation.

The selection of Jesus for his sacred mission is now taken back to his conception, or, more accurately, for the idea of *selection* is substituted that of rigid *predestination*. The child is conceived at the express command of God in order to be " the

---

[1] At the end of the fifteenth century, if it really was, as is supposed, Annius of Viterbo who was the author of this explanation.

[2] Luke i. 27 and 28 : " Now . . . the angel Gabriel was sent from . . . to a virgin espoused to a man called Joseph, of the house of David." ii. 4 : " And Joseph also went up from Galilee . . . unto the city of David . . . because he was of the house and lineage of David."

[3] CIII, i, 316 ; CXCIII, 4 ; CLXXXII, i, 164 ; CLXXX, i, 4 ; XCIX, 153.

one who is to come," and for this purpose the Virgin Mary is impregnated by the Holy Ghost.

II

How Matthew and Luke reconcile the Davidic Descent with the Virgin Birth

It is somewhat surprising to discover that the two Gospels which relate this miracle are the very ones which contain the Davidic genealogies. Why should they have taken so much trouble to connect Joseph with David, if Jesus was not the son of Joseph ? It seems probable that the comparatively late redactors whose work has come down to us, felt that they could not discard a statement which controversy with the Jews had no doubt caused to become very deeply rooted in Christian apologetics. Possibly, too, they thought that the Davidic descent of the " foster father " of the Lord was a strong factor in preserving the faith of the people.[1] In the course of time, however, copyists, less easily satisfied, began to be somewhat disturbed by the very obvious contradiction between the conclusion of the genealogies, " Joseph begat Jesus," and the story of the Virgin Birth, which was definitely intended to annul the paternity of Joseph. Accordingly, they made some very illuminating alterations in the text.[2] The original reading of the genealogy of Matthew undoubtedly concluded with the attribution to Joseph of the *procreation* of Jesus. Our certainty of this is confirmed by a text of Epiphanius,[3] which informs us that the heretics of the second century, such as Cerinthus and Carpocrates, made the genealogy of Matthew the basis of their claim that Jesus was in reality the son of Joseph and Mary ($\dot{\varepsilon}\varkappa$ $\sigma\pi\acute{\varepsilon}\varrho\mu\alpha\tau\sigma\varsigma$ $\dot{}I\omega\sigma\grave{\eta}\varphi$ $\varkappa\grave{\alpha}\iota$ $M\alpha\varrho\acute{\iota}\alpha\varsigma$). Eusebius attributes the same opinion, and the same defence of it, to the Ebionite Symmachus.[4] Our accepted text of Matthew i. 16, however, employs the following form of expression : " And Jacob begat Joseph, the husband of Mary, and of *her* was born Jesus called the Christ." In other words, the editor means to imply that Joseph was only the *apparent* father of the child of his wife Mary, and he has, in fact, wiped out with one word all the work of the genealogist. In all probability this obvious emen-

---

[1] This is the explanation already given by Origen, *In Rom.*, 1, 3, and generally accepted. *Cf.* **CIII**, i, 317 ; **XCIX**, 156 ; **XLIV**, 139, etc.

[2] For the details see Schmiedel, *Mary*, § 14 ; **CCVIII**, 97 *ff.*

[3] *Haer.*, 30, 14.   [4] Eusebius, *H.E.*, 6, 17.

dation was not the first. Two manuscripts [1] read : " And Jacob begat Joseph ; and Joseph, to whom was married the Virgin Mary, begat Jesus," which is probably an earlier form than our own, in which the editor has simply interpolated, as a kind of supplement, the assertion of the Virgin Birth. This peculiar combination is even more naïvely and awkwardly exhibited in the following reading : [2] " Jacob begat Joseph, the husband of Mary, of whom was born Jesus called the Christ, and Joseph begat Jesus called the Christ."

In the case of the text of Luke, we have been less fortunate, and the manuscripts do not permit us to trace the manner in which it has been altered. But that it has been, is self-evident, and sufficiently proved by the reading of iii. 23 : " Jesus . . . being the son, *as was supposed* (ὡς ἐνομίζετο) of Joseph." The words " as was supposed " betray an alteration designed, as Loisy justly observes,[3] " to abrogate the idea of natural son- ship which the text of this passage originally suggested." The belief in the Virgin Birth is thus unquestionably later than the desire to establish the Davidic descent of Jesus, as Messiah.

The assertion of the Virgin Birth came, in time, to occupy the central position in Christian apologetic, as forming the great proof of the divine origin of Jesus. It afforded, at the same time, the point of departure for the multifarious ideas and speculations out of which, in the course of the centuries, has grown the majestic structure of the cult of Mary. This result certainly far outran the purpose of those hagiographers who thus transposed, for the benefit of their creed, a myth that was generally current in their environment. Their inten- tion was only to provide a conclusive argument in their con- troversy with the sceptical Jews, though perhaps also, in materializing their own conception of the relation between Christ and God the Father, they were instinctively seeking to invest their Lord with the same supreme privilege possessed, according to the belief of their own adherents, by all the other Lords and Saviours renowned throughout the Hellenistic Orient. Their accounts, which are obviously outside the realm of history, would not be worth pausing over, if we were only concerned with their intentions. But the serious consequences of these accounts make it necessary for us to explain their character and define their origin.[4]

[1] The *Sinaitic Syriac* and a manuscript discovered by Conybeare in the Vatican.

[2] From the *Dialogue of Timothy and Aquila*, published by Cony- beare in 1898, p. 16.

[3] CIII, i, 327 ; LXVII, 234 ; XLI, 224.

[4] For the details and bibliography see CCVIII, iv and 196.

The first point to be established is that the Virgin Birth of Mary, which is definitely asserted in Matthew i. 18–25, and Luke i. 5–80, finds no echo in any other part of the New Testament. It has been maintained that this is not so, and no ingenuity has been spared to prove it, but it is a vain task. There are limits to the forced interpretation of texts. Mark has been cited, for instance, as a witness to the virginity of Mary, on the strength of i. 1 : " The beginning of the Gospel of Jesus Christ, the son of God " ; and vi. 3 : " Is not this the carpenter, the son of Mary ? " If Jesus is the son of God, it is argued, he is not the son of Joseph, and the insistence upon his mother to the exclusion of his father, further proves that, on the human side, his mother alone was concerned in his birth. Unfortunately for this reasoning, the following points must be taken into account. (1) The words, " the son of God," in the first verse of Mark, cannot possibly have belonged to the original version of the text. Almost all the great existing versions give them, it is true, but as is well known, these are far from being original. Moreover, the *Sinaitic Syriac*, which is of great authority, and the early patristic tradition represented by Irenæus and Origen, followed by Basil and Jerome, omit the words : " υἱοῦ (τοῦ) θεοῦ." The addition must have been made as a counterpart to the avowal of the centurion in xv. 39 : " Truly this man was a son of God " (υἱὸς θεοῦ ἦν). (2) In any case, the expression " son of God " is in all probability to be interpreted in a metaphysical and not a physical sense. (3) The phrase " son of Mary " is very naturally explained by the fact that Joseph may have been dead at the time when these people of Nazareth are supposed to have significantly designated Jesus by the name of his mother. Nothing in all the rest of Mark gives the slightest support to the interpretation which it is sought to impose upon the two passages in question. Therefore, since it is difficult to believe that the editor of our Mark did not know the story of the Virgin Birth, we must suppose that he did not accept it, otherwise there would be no reason for his not having simply added it to his Gospel. There are still traces which show that in *Urmarcus*, it was not at the moment of the conception of Jesus, but at that of his baptism, that the Holy Spirit entered his humanity.

John sets forth a similar but far more exalted conception. His point of view was entirely different from that of Matthew and Luke, hence, save for the object of conforming to historical reality, if that were in question, there was no reason why he should adhere to their account of the birth of Jesus. The two

Synoptists attempt to prove that a child was specially created
by God to be his Messiah, and that this was accomplished by
a process, the miraculousness of which is of itself an infallible
" sign." John, on the other hand, believed that Jesus was the
incarnation of the *logos*, co-eternal with God, which is a very
different thing. From this point of view, Christ is not human
at all. He is dependent upon neither an earthly father nor an
earthly *mother*, which is the exact meaning of i. 13, if the reading of Tertullian be accepted as original : " It was not of blood,
nor of the will of the flesh, nor of the will of man, but of God
that he was born." [1] To cite this passage in favour of the
Virgin Birth, is grossly to misconstrue it. The incarnation of
the *logos* in Jesus does not imply that the *man* Jesus was exempt
from the laws of human generation, for it was at the *Baptism*,
according to John, that the *logos* descended into him. John
thus elevates the idea of Mark, but he preserves its framework,
and, if we may so put it, all its external garb. Accordingly,
he never misses an opportunity of stating that Jesus is " the
son of Joseph." [2] Far from supporting the legend of Matthew
and Luke, he definitely opposes it.

We have spoken of John in this place in order to keep the
four Gospels together, but in reality, between the Palestinian
tradition which Matthew, Mark and Luke are supposed substantially to reflect, and the Fourth Gospel, come the Epistles
of Paul, which were written during the lifetime of the apostolic
generation, in contact with men who, having known Jesus and
his family, could at least testify to what was said in the Master's
own circle concerning the conditions of his birth. There is not
the smallest reference, in the letters of the Apostle, to the
Virgin Birth. What we find there is a doctrine of the incarnation of the Holy Spirit, less definite, certainly, than that of the
incarnation of the *logos* in John, but as it were, anticipatory,
and preparatory of it. " The Lord is the Spirit " (ὁ δὲ κύριος
τὸ πνεῦμα ἐστιν), declares 2 Corinthians iii. 17. Paul's actual
belief is that Christ, the divine instrument in the work of
creation, and in that of the reconciliation of men with the
Father, pre-existed with God before time was,[3] but his incarnation in the human person of Jesus did not in any way exclude
the natural and usual conditions of his birth " according to

[1] *De carne Christi*, 19 : *Non ex sanguine, non ex voluntate carnis,
nec ex voluntate viri, sed ex Deo natus est.* The *textus receptus* alters
this to a reference to the Christians, those who became *sons of God*
by following the Christ, but there is every reason for believing the
reading of Tertullian to be the oldest.

[2] *Cf.* John i. 45 ; vi. 42 ; vii. 3–5.

[3] 1 Cor. viii. 6 ; 2 Cor. viii. 9 ; Gal. iv. 4 ; Col. i. 15 *ff.*

the flesh." Paul would assuredly not have encumbered himself with his doctrine of the divine Adam, coming to redeem humanity, if he had believed that the Lord was conceived by Mary " of the Spirit." In Galatians iv. 4 he writes :

> " When the fulness of the time was come, God sent his son, born of a woman (γενόμενον ἐκ γυναικός) born under the Law, to redeem all those that were under the Law."

If this verse is read without forcing its meaning, it will appear to indicate the normal birth of a Jewish child. It is perfectly clear that if the Apostle had believed in the Virgin Birth of the child, he would have written, " God sent his son, born of a virgin " (γενόμενον ἐκ παρθένου), instead of "born of a woman " (ἐκ γυναικός).[1] On the other hand, he appears to have believed in the Davidic descent of Jesus,[2] and hence in his human generation. Finally, the prologue of Romans states that Jesus Christ, our Lord, " born of the seed of David *according to the flesh* . . . has been proved to be the Son of God, in power, *according to the spirit of holiness*, by his resurrection from the dead." This simple sentence takes us back, apparently, at least, to the Christological point of view already found in Acts, in which the Messianic exaltation of Jesus still dates from the Resurrection.

Moreover, the gospel narrative in the Synoptics themselves knows nothing of the Virgin Birth. That is to say that, omitting the two supplementary sources of Matthew and Luke, and confining ourselves to the account whose limits and general development are dictated by Mark, we shall find that not one of the incidents contained in it, in any of our three texts, alludes, even indirectly, to this outstanding miracle. If Jesus can say, in speaking of Mary, " Who is my mother ? " ; if his mother and his own brothers attempt to dissuade him from his mission ; it is because neither he, nor she, nor they, know anything of his conception by the Holy Ghost.[3] Otherwise the narrative would involve us in the greatest improbabilities and embarrassments. It is, moreover, worthy of note that the text of our Luke, on careful examination, reveals two editorial strata. In one (verses 26–33 and 36) there is no question of the Virgin Birth. The angel announces to Mary the birth of a son who will be the Messiah, the son of David, and he gives her as a

---

[1] It is perhaps worth remarking that this expression " born of a woman," is not peculiar to Paul. It is the usual way of describing normal human birth. *Cf.* Matt. xi. 11 ; Job xiv. 1 ; " Man that is born of a woman is of a short life." 4 Esdras vi. 6 ; vii. 46 ; viii. 35, etc.

[2] Rom. i. 3 ; " Of the seed of David according to the flesh."

[3] Mark iii. 31–5 ; Matt. xii. 46–50 ; Luke viii. 19–21.

" sign " the fact that Elizabeth, although old and barren, is yet in the sixth month of pregnancy. Verses 34–5 form a clear interpolation, which introduces the announcement of the Virgin Birth (" The Holy Ghost shall come upon thee "), and, following upon it, that of the divine paternity of Jesus (" And he shall be called the Son of God "), which is an entirely different thing from the Messianic " election " previously spoken of.[1]

The other writings of the New Testament which happen to allude to the birth of Jesus, show that they believe him to be a descendant of David, that is to say, born according to the laws of nature.[2]

Finally, the men who adhered to at least a portion of the original tradition long enough to be regarded as heretics in the second century, namely, the Ebionites, rejected the doctrine of the Virgin Birth. The evidence of both Justin and Epiphanius is explicit on this point.[3]

The documents and the facts thus confirm the conclusion already dictated by the logic of the development of primitive Christology, namely, that the doctrine of the Virgin Birth represents a secondary development of the faith in Christ Jesus. The Pauline doctrine of pre-existence springs from the same purpose and desire, but it takes a different form. Logically, the two conceptions are mutually exclusive and cannot be held simultaneously.

It has been asked how the idea of this particular development could have arisen.[4] To the men of the period which produced it, certainly no violation of the laws of nature would be incredible à priori, for miracles were the familiar stock-in-trade of all magic. The production of a child by a virgin was no more improbable than the rising of a corpse from its tomb. Nevertheless, it is reasonable to suppose that, for the Virgin Birth to have had any hope of being accepted as *proof* in any community, the way must have been to some extent prepared for it by the influence of more or less similar beliefs.

In our opinion, Palestine could not have offered this necessary favourable environment. It is, indeed, easy to show that the old Semitic religions were familiar with the myth of the Mother-Goddess, including the representation of her as the Virgin-Goddess, and even with that of the virgin birth of the king, the son of God and the Saviour of his people.[5] But, apart

---

[1] CCVIII, 103 *ff*.
[2] *Cf.* 2 Tim. ii. 8 ; Heb. vii. 14 ; Rev. v. 5 ; xxii. 16.
[3] Justin, *Dial.*, 48, 4 ; Epiphanius, *Haer.*, 30, 14.
[4] CCVIII, iii *ff*.
[5] CCLXXXVIII, i, 342 *ff*., deals at length with these points.

from the fact that the virginity of Ishtar is not to be taken
literally, and that, likewise, the ostensible virginity of the
human mother of the king probably merely means that her
son was mysteriously begotten by a god, without her human
husband having any part in the affair,[1] no trace of any of these
ideas seems to be left in Israel at the beginning of our era.
The Jews certainly believed that the birth of a child destined
for the work of God, might be marked by wonderful signs, for
instance that this child might be conceived, against all expectation, by a barren woman ; [2] but they do not appear to have
thought that the woman could still remain a virgin in the act
of conception. In particular, there is no indication of their
ever having held the belief that the Messiah would be born of
a virgin. It has sometimes been maintained that, if they had
not all attained to this conception, some of them, at least, came
very close to it, if only in metaphor, for instance, in speaking
of the Virgin, daughter of Sion and mother of the Messiah ; it
has also been asserted that such an idea " would tend to be
realized as soon as the Messianic faith was concentrated upon
a particular individual." This, however, is only theory based
upon a dubious possibility.[3]   In reality, there is not one scrap
of documentary evidence for any expectation in Israel that the
birth of the Messiah would be signalized by such a miracle,[4]
and one text, at least, declares that there was no such expectation. Justin puts into the mouth of the Jew, Tryphon, the
familiar statement : " For we all await the Christ, who will be
a man amongst men," [5] and makes him say, further, that,
inasmuch as the Messiah will be descended from David, he will
not be born of a virgin. It was God's promise to the ancient
king that " he who is to come " would issue " from his seed."
Are we to think that God was mocking him ? [6] It hardly seems
likely that, for the purpose of confuting the Jews of Palestine
who denied the Messiahship of Jesus, the Christian apologists
would have selected so un-Jewish a " sign." Only those believe
it to be Jewish who are virtually bound to do so, because of
their conviction that Christianity itself was essentially a purely
Jewish phenomenon.

It is not in the Jewish world, nor even in the oriental world
proper, but in the Greco-Roman, that we find the most striking

---

[1] *Ibid.*, 288 *ff.*
[2] As in the case, for example, of Isaac (Gen. xvii. 17), Samson (Judges
xiii. 2 *ff.*), and John the Baptist (Luke i. 7 *ff.*).
[3] CCXVII, 218 and 233 ; XLI, 226 *ff.* ; CIII, i, 196 ; XLVIII, 68.
[4] CVI, 12.
[5] Justin, *Dial.*, 49.   [6] *Ibid.*, 68.

parallels to the story of the miraculous conception of Jesus.[1]
It is here that we find the legend of Perseus, born of Danäe,
a virgin who was impregnated by a shower of gold. (A parallel
which was made the most of by the Jews, and proved so embarrassing to the Christians of the second century that they were
compelled to maintain that it was an invention of the Devil
to confuse men and lure them from the truth.[2]) Here, too,
we find the story of Attis, whose mother, Nana, became pregnant as a result of eating a pomegranate. It was here especially
that the birth of notable men—Pythagoras, Plato, Augustus
himself [3]—tended to be explained by some kind of partheno-
genesis, or by the mysterious intervention of a god. It is quite
conceivable that, in a community in which so many stories of
this kind were current, the Christians, desirous of adducing
conclusive vindication of their faith in the divinity of Jesus,
naturally turned to the sign by which men bearing the divine
stamp were commonly identified. There was no question, of
course, of a conscious imitation of any particular story, but
simply of the influence of a certain atmosphere of belief. We
shall often meet with this phenomenon.

It has been held by some that the whole story of the Virgin
Birth of Jesus arose from the interpretation of a supposedly
prophetic passage of the Scriptures, namely, Isaiah vii. 14,[4]
according to the Greek text of the Septuagint. This would, in
any case, make the conception a Greek development. This is
the occasion of the passage : Ahaz, king of Judah, fears a new
attack by the allied kings of Syria and Israel, who have just
failed to take Jerusalem. The prophet reassures him, and says :

> "Therefore the Lord himself shall give a sign. Behold the
> Virgin (ἡ παρθένος) shall conceive and give birth to a son, and thou
> shalt call him Emmanuel. Butter and honey shall he eat, that he
> may know how to refuse the evil and choose the good. But before
> this child shall know how to recognize good and evil, to refuse the
> evil and choose the good, the land whose two kings thou abhorrest
> shall be forsaken."

The prophet adds that the king of Assyria will be the instrument employed by Jahweh to crush the power of Damascus
and Samaria.

[1] **XXXV**, 127 ; Usener, *Religionsgesch. Untersuchungen*, 1889, 70 *ff.* ;
XLVIII, 67 *ff.* ; **DCG**, art. *Virgin Birth*, para. 3 ; **XXIV**, i, 52 *ff.*

[2] Justin, 1 *Apol.*, 54 ; *Dial.*, 70.

[3] Plutarch, *Sympos.*, viii, *quæst.* 1, 3 ; Jamblichus, *Vita Pythag.*,
2, 2 ; Ælian, 2, 26 ; Diogenes Lærtius, *Vita Platon.*, 3, 1, 1 ; Suetonius,
Octav., **94** ; **CCCII.**—It would be difficult to construct a closer parallel
to the legend of the birth of Jesus found in Matthew, than is furnished
by that of the birth of Plato. *Cf.* **XXIV**, i, 56.

[4] **CCVIII** 116 *ff.*

Considered in its context and specific purpose, the passage has no resemblance to a Messianic prophecy. The prediction has a much more immediate bearing, and it is precisely for the purpose of indicating its speedy fulfilment that the author makes his comparison. It will require only the time necessary for a child to be conceived, born, and brought to the beginning of understanding, before Jahweh will crush the enemies of Judah. It is not the birth of the child which is emphasized by the prophet, but the happy issue for which the king is waiting, and of which he may now, relying upon the comparison given him, confidently - estimate the approaching date. The child in question is probably the same one referred to again by Isaiah in viii. 3 : " Then I went in unto the prophetess, and she conceived and bare a son."

However this may be, the general sense of the passage is unambiguous. Only by isolating from its context the announcement of the birth of the child who is to be called *Emmanuel* (*God with us*), can it be given a Messianic meaning. This, to be sure, is exactly what Matthew i. 23 does, but the point is whether the Jews themselves did so at that time. There is no evidence for it in any Rabbinical writing,[1] and every probability points to the conclusion that it was the Christians who, in their search for all the prophetic utterances regarding the Messiah, discovered and gave that interpretation of this passage.

Further, the discovery could have been made only in the Greek Bible, because the Hebrew text does not contain the word *virgin* (*bethulah*), but the word *young woman* (*haalmah*), which ought to have been rendered into Greek by *neanis* (νεᾶνις) instead of *parthenos* (παρθένος). Orthodox theologians have made every effort to prove that *haalmah* might mean virgin,[2] but without success. The prophet had no thought of predicting a miracle, and the Jews, as soon as they began to attack

---

[1] It has nevertheless been argued that many a Jew, studying the text of the prophet, might have concluded that the Messiah would be born of a virgin. *Cf.* **CCLXIII**, i, 113, n. 1 ; and **XCIV**, 103. This, however, is mere unfounded hypothesis.

[2] Two passages of the Hebrew Bible determine the meaning of *haalmah*. There is, first, the Song of Solomon vi. 8 : " There are sixty queens and eighty concubines, and young women without number," which the Greek text correctly translates : καὶ νεάνιδας ὧν οὐκ ἔστιν ἀριθμός. The occupants of harems are not, as a rule, virgins. The second passage is found in Prov. xxx. 18–19, and runs : " There are three things which are too wonderful for me, yea, four which I know not ; the way of an eagle in the air, the way of a serpent upon a rock, the way of a ship in the midst of the sea, and the way of a man in a maid." It certainly cannot be a virgin that is referred to, and the Greek translation again correctly gives ἐν νεότητι.

the Christians, did not miss the opportunity of pointing out that the term to which their opponents appealed was nothing but a blunder. Possibly the first translator into Greek was responsible for it, but it is not very probable. We simply do not know when, and by whom, it was introduced into the text of the Septuagint.

Even if the Christians found it already there—which is questionable—it has still to be proved that, as has been contended, it was that which suggested to them the Virgin Birth of Christ. The main argument of Harnack,[1] who has recently come forward in support of this view, is that the Christians, convinced that Christ was born of the Spirit of God, as the accounts of the Baptism testify, must eagerly have seized upon the word *parthenos* as a means of *effectuating* this divine relationship. We cannot agree, for the reason that a mere reading of Isaiah vii. 14, even in the Greek, would not give rise to the belief that the " virgin " would remain such throughout conception and birth. The passage says nothing of that. The translator or copyist who rendered *haalmah* by the Greek *parthenos* simply meant : " a young woman will marry, conceive, and bear a child," not " a virgin will conceive and bear a child." To suggest this interpretation, the word would have to be read with such an idea in mind, in fact, with the definite belief that Mary had conceived Jesus and yet remained a virgin. Isaiah may have been regarded as conclusive prophetic witness to the miraculous sign, but it was certainly not he who suggested it.

It is, however, perhaps possible to see where it comes from. It will be observed that in Paul, John, and Mark, none of whom believes in his Virgin Birth, Jesus is characterized as the Son of God. This description of him is, accordingly, prior to the establishment of the belief in the miracle related by Matthew and Luke, and does not arise out of it. As soon as they were convinced that, not only had Jesus been raised up by God, as a man full of the Holy Spirit, to accomplish his plans, but that his birth into this life for God had been divinely predestined, and glorified by the Holy Ghost, they must have attempted to signalize and to express this special relationship between Jesus and God. They said that he was his " son," because that was the only term in human language by which they could intelligibly, if not completely and adequately, express this relation. Since the idea of the direct generation of a man by God could only appear to the Jewish mind as a monstrous absurdity, the expression was, in reality, to the Palestinians, only a manner of speaking, only a metaphor.

[1] **XCIV**, 101 *ff.* ; *cf.* **CCLXIII**, i, 113, n. 2.

A critical examination of the passages in the Synoptics in which it appears, shows that Jesus never applied it to himself [1] and that, moreover, it had not hitherto, in Israel, any Messianic significance. That is to say, the Jews did not beforehand bestow this title of Son of God upon the expected Messiah. The Messiah must have been for them not the *Son*, but the *Servant*, of God (*Ebed Jahweh*), for such was the designation of the " men of Jahweh."[2] But on Greek soil the Christological belief found an environment very different from that of Palestine. There, the idea of the procreation of a human being by a god was current, and the relation of real sonship between Christ and God the Father could shock no one (save Jews of rigid orthodoxy, and they could not have been very numerous). On the contrary, the term Son of God was more likely to arouse sympathy in that quarter than the too peculiarly Jewish, too nationalistic, name of Messiah. Hence it was, in all probability, in the first Christian communities amongst the Gentiles, that the expression arose. Possibly it did so, at first, as a simple translation of the Palestinian *Ebed-Jahweh*, for the Greek word *pais* (παῖς) means both *servant* and *child*, and it would be an easy transition from *child* to *son*. But it soon took on the colouring of an original Christological idea, the idea which met the needs of the environment which called it forth, the idea expressed in the Epistles of Paul. It found its Pauline and Johannine justification in the doctrine of divine pre-existence and of the incarnation of the Lord. The legend of the Virgin Birth is another of its justifications, sprung from a quite different intellectual environment, but analogous to the one just cited, and finding its Scriptural confirmation, when the need arose to defend it in controversy, in Isaiah vii. 14.[3] Matthew and Luke represent two concrete embodiments, different in form, but similar in spirit and meaning, of the belief : " He is the Son of God. He is born of the Holy Spirit."

Their solution, which probably dates originally from about A.D. 80,[4] prevailed and endured because there was nothing metaphysical about it, and it was in the direct line of the stages

---

[1] For this examination, see CCVIII, 121 *ff.*

[2] In the third century, Origen again bears witness (*Contra Celsum*, 1, 49) that the Jews, who were still expecting the Messiah, declared that they knew of no prophecy which referred to the coming of a *Son of God*.

[3] It may have originated in cults where virginity and continence were especially honoured. The other comes from environments more permeated with the spirit of the Mysteries. *Cf.* Schmiedel, *Mary*, § 16 ; XLI, 216 ; CCLXIX, 5 *ff.* ; XLVIII, 66 ; CCL, 214 *ff.* Contra : xciv, 101 *ff.*

[4] CCLXIX, 4.

of development which had already taken place in the progress of Christology. Above all, it appealed to the popular faith. In a sense, its success is demonstrated even more by its elaboration in the Apocryphal Gospels,[1] which found in it what they sought, than by its final incorporation in the orthodox tradition.

III

THE DEVELOPMENT OF THE LEGEND OF THE VIRGIN BIRTH

Our two Synoptic accounts do not, of course, exhaust the subject of the Virgin Birth. Faith and theology alike subsequently demanded more explicit statements, which were arrived at, occasionally, only at the cost of extremely embarrassing discussions.

It was asked, for instance, whether the miraculous conception had been precisely simultaneous with the Annunciation, and since the text of Luke gave not the smallest hint in either direction, the way was open for endless discussion. The very uniqueness of the Virgin Birth led to the question in what form the Holy Spirit had entered the body of Mary, in what precise manner the generation of Jesus had been accomplished.[2] On this point, again, the silence of the writings left a clear field for hypothesis, and placed no limit upon even the most fantastic speculations. Tertullian (*Apol.*, 21) speaks of a ray of light descending into Mary, and there becoming flesh. This suggests an adaptation of the Egyptian belief according to which the cow-mother of Apis was impregnated by a ray of light falling from Heaven (Herodotus), or a moonbeam (Plutarch).[3] In any case, it is an interesting parallel. In the fifteenth century it was even maintained that Jesus entered the womb of his mother fully formed, but this met with the opposition of the theologians.[4]

Popular belief made its own contribution to the subject according to its lights, and its customary tendencies. Amongst other fantastic ideas, it evolved that of conception by the ear.[5] This " explanation " is not met with until the fourth century, when it is found in Saint Ephraem, Saint Augustine, and Gaudentius, but its ingenuous simplicity places its date of

---

[1] CXLII, 53 *ff.*; CCVIII, 201, n. 40. For the Jewish calumnies and the legend of Pandera, the Roman soldier who is supposed to have played the part of the Holy Spirit to the wife of the gullible Joseph, *cf.* CCXVIII, 9–39; CCCII, 260; CXXXII, 38 *ff.*; CXLII, 458 *ff.*
[2] CXLII, 53.   [3] CCL, 230.   [4] CCXLV, 1, 131.
[5] CCLXXXIII–*a*, 578, n. 12; CCCII, 191, n. 3.

origin much earlier.[1] It must have been in circulation amongst
the people for a long time before being taken into consideration by the learned. It has been suggested that this device,
designed to make the conception of Jesus completely superhuman, and to place beyond dispute the virginity of his mother,
may also have been of Egyptian origin, since Plutarch (*De
Iside*) tells us that the idea was prevalent amongst the people
of Egypt that cats conceived by the ear and were born from
the mouth.[2]

The doctrine of the Virgin Birth did not fail to expose the
Christian to annoying jests and calumnies. In an Apocryphal
writing entitled *History of the Nativity of Mary and the Childhood of our Lord*, Joseph, returning from a journey, replies to
the virgins who are attempting to cheer him with the news of
the Annunciation :

> " Why do you seek to deceive me and make me believe that
> it was the angel of the Lord who got her with child ? Perhaps
> someone pretended to be the angel of the Lord in order to seduce
> her."

The foster-father, in this case, soon abandons his scepticism
and recognizes the truth, but many unbelievers received the
announcement of the decisive miracle in the same way.

Almost in modern times, the daring German rationalist
Paulus (d. 1828) again attributed the birth of Jesus to a ruse
of the ambitious *Priesterfrau*, Elizabeth, who was supposed
to have sent an unknown man to play the part of the angel
Gabriel and deceive the simple Mary. In antiquity, Jews and
pagans vied with each other in stories attacking the honour
of Mary,[3] who was represented by them as an adulteress, or
even a professional prostitute (*quæstuaria*—προακτική πορνή).[4]
The Samaritans themselves took part in this offensive chorus.
In one of their books, the *Samaritan Chronicle*,[5] there occurs
the following passage :

> " In the time of Jehonathan there was put to death Jesus, the
> son of Myriam, son of Joseph the carpenter, *ben Hanapheth*, at
> Jerusalem, in the reign of Tiberius, by Pilate the governor."

---

[1] **CXLII**, 53.—**CCL**, 233, thinks there is a trace of this belief in the
very ancient rule that Christian virgins should be veiled, to hide their
ears from evil spirits. It is an interesting suggestion, but there is no
sound documentary justification for it. 1 Cor. xi. and the beginning
of the *De Virginibus velandis* of Tertullian hardly support it.

[2] **CCL**, 230.   [3] **CCXVIII**, 9 *ff.* ; **LXX**, 6, 1900, 266.

[4] Tertullian, *De Spectaculis*, 30 : " *Hic est ille fabri aut quæstuariæ
filius.*"

[5] Published by Neubauer in the *Journal asiatique*, 1869, 11, 439.

The expression "*ben Hanapheth*," is interpreted by Clermont-Ganneau,[1] on the strength of an Arabic translation, as meaning "the son of the courtesan."

When the accusation became specific, and professed to name the real father of Jesus, a Roman soldier called *Panther*, or *Pandera*,[2] it was not easy for the Christians to adduce material proof of its falsity. The main argument of Origen is that one who came to render such services to the world could not have been born in shame. So shameless an adulteress could have produced only a madman, a monster of vice and intemperance, whereas Jesus was a pattern of all the virtues. It is hardly a convincing proof. The story of Pandera, moreover, was not the only one, nor the worst, of the anti-Christian calumnies which claimed to give the details of the charge that, if Jesus was not the son of Joseph, his mother was an adulteress. An Alexandrian story-teller makes him the issue of an incestuous relationship between Mary and her own brother.[3]

These were clumsy fabrications, no doubt, inspired by malevolence and the desire to wound, but they were the inevitable price of the controversial weapon which the Christian faith derived from the legend of the Virgin Birth, the bastard product of Jewish mentality and pagan mythology.

The elaborations and proofs, of varying ingenuity, which the necessities of polemic induced the Christians to add to the assertions of our Synoptics,[4] did not succeed in strengthening them. In spite of praiseworthy and persevering efforts, perpetually renewed, apologetic today can no longer succeed even in disguising their inconsistency.

In the last analysis, history must discard everything contained in the orthodox tradition concerning the circumstances of the birth of Jesus, and we have no choice but to conclude that we have no information on the subject. Doubtless those circumstances were quite ordinary, so much so that they attracted no attention, which would explain why, according to the oldest of our gospel narratives (Mark iii. 31–5, quoted above), the mother of Christ herself, at the very time when the memory of the decisive miracle, if such a miracle had really occurred to, and by means of, her, might have been expected to dominate her own human affection and desire, gave no sign of being in any way conscious of her son's divine destiny.

---

[1] *Recueil d'archéologie orientale*, vii, 387.

[2] *Jerus. Talmud, 'Abodah Zarah*, 9, 40. *Cf.* Origen, *Contra Celsum*, 1, 28 ; 32 ; 69.

[3] CCCII, 260.　　　　　　　　　　[4] CXXXII, 38 *ff.*

IV

THE FIRST-BORN OF MARY

The stories of the birth of Jesus in Matthew and Luke imply that he was the first-born (πρώτοτοκος) of his mother, since otherwise there could be no question of a virgin birth. But it is hardly necessary to observe that the fact that this assertion is necessitated by these two accounts, and vouched for only by them, means that we have no guarantee of it whatever. Neither Mark nor Paul is interested in this point, and it must, consequently, have been a matter of indifference to the original tradition. Possibly Jesus may have been the first of the children of Joseph and Mary, but we do not know.

We say " the children of Joseph and Mary," because our Synoptics have no hesitation in giving Jesus brothers and sisters. They refer to them in the most natural way in the world. We read in Mark iii. 31, etc. :

> " And there came his mother and his brethren, and standing without, they sent unto him, to call him, and the multitude was sitting about him, and they said unto him : Behold thy mother and thy brethren without, ask for thee." [1]

Again, in Mark vi. 2–3, the people of Nazareth are represented as saying :

> " Whence hath he these things, and what wisdom is this which is given unto him ? And these miracles which his hands perform ? Is not this the carpenter, the son of Mary, the brother of James, and Joses, and Juda, and Simon ? And are not his sisters also with us ? "

We need not stop to prove that the Evangelist certainly means " brothers " and " sisters," in the usual sense of the words.[2] There is absolutely nothing to suggest that they are to be understood in any other, and such a thing would never have been thought of, if the development of the cult of Mary had not subsequently made a different interpretation necessary. Moreover, references to these " brothers " of Jesus are fairly frequent in the New Testament, and nowhere is there any ambiguity about them. It is unquestionably blood brothers

[1] Various manuscripts also mention his sisters, who seem to be implied by 3, 35.

[2] Matt. xiii. 53–8, and Luke iv. 16–30, both recount, following Mark, but adapting him, the visit of Jesus to Nazareth, but only Matthew mentions brothers and sisters. Luke limits himself to making the townspeople of Jesus say : " Is not this a son of Joseph ? "

which they appear to signify.[1] Clearly, if there had been any risk of the words " brothers " and " sisters " misleading the reader so seriously, the editors of all the writings referred to would have taken some precaution against this dangerous misinterpretation.

The fact is, that the first Christians, even after the belief in the Virgin Birth was firmly established, were content with the assertion that Jesus was the first-born. Since, at that period, they were not interested in Mary on her own account, it was a matter of indifference to them that, her divine work accomplished, she should have become the wife of Joseph in a perfectly natural sense. It is to be observed, further, that the very insistence upon the term " first-born," for instance, in Luke ii. 7 (" And she brought forth her first-born son "), immediately suggests the birth of younger children. Finally, we have plenty of evidence of the existence of such a belief in the Christianity of the first four centuries.[2]

We may be inclined to wonder why neither the texts themselves nor this common-sense tradition managed to prevail. The answer is simply that there very shortly appeared Christians who could not reconcile themselves to the idea that the mother of the Lord, once her mission was accomplished, had reverted to the level of an ordinary woman. For the doctrine of the virginity of the *Christotokos*, that is to say, *the mother of the Christ*, was gradually substituted the doctrine of the perpetual virginity of Mary, until, finally, they arrived at that of Joseph himself, which appeared as early as Saint Jerome.[3] It was the asceticism of the fourth and fifth centuries which finally established the beliefs, henceforth to become *articles of faith*, concerning the perfect and perpetual virginity of Mary. But long before this, the Christian feeling already referred to was seeking to get rid of the brothers and sisters of Jesus. As early as the second century, the *Protevangelium of James*, and according to Origen,[4] the *Gospel of Peter*, maintained that they were the children of Joseph alone, born of his first marriage, and the husband of Mary came to be pictured as a very old man, at the time of the Nativity. Clement of Alexandria and Origen

---

[1] *Cf.* in addition to the passages just cited, John ii. 12 : " After that he went down to Capernaum, he and his mother, his brethren, and his disciples " ; John vii. 3 ; 1 Cor. ix. 5 ; Gal. i. 19 ; Acts i. 14. Finally, in a fragment of the *Gospel of the Hebrews*, preserved by Saint Jerome (C. Pelag., 3, 2), we find : " *Ecce mater domini et fratres eius dicebant ei : Johannes Baptista baptizat . . .*"

[2] Passages will be found in CCVIII, 201 *ff.*

[3] *Adv. Helvid.*, 19 : " *ut ex virginali conjugio virgo Filius nasceretur.*"

[4] *In Mt.*, 12, 55.

were completely confident that Christ and his mother, the former for men, and the latter for women, had set the example of perfect continence.

It remained only for the writings of the New Testament to support this conviction, and their texts were tortured in various ways until they were finally made to profess the contrary of what they believed. We shall not here embark upon an exposition of the discussions, in which the most arbitrary theories were supported by the most unverifiable assertions.[1] They resulted very early in three theories which it will be sufficient to recall : (1) The *Helvidian*, maintained by Helvidius in the time of Saint Jerome, which held that the " brothers " and " sisters " were children of Joseph and Mary born *after* Jesus ; (2) The *Epiphanian*, sponsored by Saint Epiphanius, which declared that the brothers and sisters were the issue of a previous marriage of Joseph ; (3) The *Hieronymian*, the theory of Saint Jerome, in which the brothers and sisters became cousins of Jesus, the sons and daughters of a brother of Joseph named *Clopas*, and a sister of the Virgin who also was called *Mary*. It was, of course, this last theory which the extension to Joseph of the perfect virginity of Mary finally made the choice of the faithful. It is neither better founded nor even more probable, and impartial criticism can see in it only a thin subterfuge, by means of which a pious elaboration, totally without historical foundation, sought to evade the limitations of the texts.

The radical critics, who profess to reduce to a myth the very existence of Jesus, have lately given the orthodox doctrine indirect and unexpected, and, on the whole, undesirable, support. They have maintained [2] that the " brothers " and " sisters " of Jesus were no other than groups of his followers, united to each other by the bonds of the mystical fraternity. It is well known, certainly, that the earliest Christians spoke of themselves as " brethren." [3] And when we read in Matthew xxviii. 10, " Go and tell my brethren to go into Galilee," or in John xx. 17, " Go to my brethren and tell them that I have ascended unto my Father," we are not tempted to give the word a family sense. The redactors have, in these cases, put into the mouth of Jesus the expression which they were in the habit of using amongst themselves. It does not follow, however, that the meaning it assumes in these two passages is necessarily to be extended to all the others, especially those

---

[1] For the details of these discussions see **CCVIII**, 133 *ff*.

[2] *Cf.* especially **CLXXXI**, 20, and **CLXXVIII**, 18 *ff*.

[3] Gal. i. 2 ; 1 Cor. i. 10 ; ii. 1 ; xvi. 20 ; 2 Cor. i. 1 ; etc.

in which the brothers of Jesus are called by their proper names (Mark vi. 3).[1]   Naturally, since the adherents of the mythological view do not concede that Jesus actually existed, they cannot admit that he had brothers and sisters.   We do not think there is much help for the orthodox position in such feats of imagination, and certainly, there is none for history.

The probable conclusions which are justified by the documentary evidence, concerning the questions we have been considering, may be summed up as follows : Jesus was born somewhere in Galilee in the time of the Emperor Augustus, of a humble family, which included half a dozen or more children besides himself.

---

[1] B. Smith attempts to get over the difficulty by suggesting that the proper names are an addition to the text.   Nothing could be more improbable.

CHAPTER V

CHILDHOOD AND EDUCATION [1]

I

THE QUESTIONS

IF we wish to picture the childhood of Jesus, we are thrown back upon our imagination. The Apocryphal writings which undertook to satisfy the faith of the second century, eager for information which the authentic tradition did not furnish, knew no more on the subject than we ourselves, and the amazing stories recounted by them [2] need not detain us. Mark makes no reference to the childhood. Matthew omits it completely, passing straight from the settlement of the Holy Family at Nazareth after the return from Egypt (ii. 23) to the account of the preaching of the Baptist (iii. 1 : " In those days came John the Baptist . . ."). Similarly, Luke, having brought the parents of Jesus to Nazareth, at the end of a series of ceremonies and prophecies of which the scene is laid in Jerusalem (ii. 39), sums up the whole of the childhood in a single, vague sentence (ii. 40) : " And the child grew and waxed strong, filled with wisdom, and the grace of God was upon him." The fact that he repeats this again (ii. 52) does not make it either more explicit or less banal. [3] After this, the gospel writer relates an incident to which we shall briefly revert (Jesus in the Temple at the age of twelve, ii. 41–52), and goes on to the mission of the Baptist (iii. 1).

The Apocryphal gospels are mainly interested in proving that their hero never was a child like other children, but that even as an infant he radiated a supernatural power, which made itself felt around him without his being conscious of it. It was thus that the faith of simple folk liked to picture him, and it was for and by them that the marvellous tales collected by our hagiographers were invented. The truth was probably

[1] For bibliography see **L–a**, i, 159 *ff*.
[2] **CXXXII**, cc. ix–xiv ; **CXLII**, pp. 87–100.
[3] **XCVII**, pp. 45 and 48.

much more sober. No doubt Jesus grew up amongst his brothers and sisters in his Galilean village without his childhood being marked by anything unusual to give his family a premonition of his future. If it had been otherwise, the Synoptic tradition would surely not have preserved the recollection, or perpetuated the belief, that the Master encountered nothing but misunderstanding and opposition on the part of his relatives when, later, he disclosed his mission.[1]

The tradition is our only authority for the statement that the father of Jesus followed the trade of a " wood-worker " (τέχτων),[2] and that he taught it to the child. It is, however, probable, that the future prophet began by working with his hands for his living. There is no question here of the Jewish custom that a rabbi should learn a trade, in order to be above the suspicion of leading a parasitic existence. The only necessity was that common to all humble folk who have to earn their bread. When Mark (vi. 3) makes the inhabitants of Nazareth, astonished at the bearing of Jesus when he returns to them for a day, say to one another : " Is not this the carpenter, the son of Mary ? " he implies that he himself took the expression literally, and believed that the Nazarene was really a τέχτων.[3] It is probable that he was right, and this is of importance in assisting us to form some idea of the original form and content of the thought of Jesus, of the direction of his central interests and the limitations of his outlook. A village craftsman, he was also a peasant, because in the East, in his time as today, a man's whole energies were not absorbed by his trade. It left him time to busy himself with a garden or a field.

It would indeed be illuminating to pierce the veil that hides this apparently humble, obscure and insignificant life, to discover the influence upon the child's mind of the ordinary events of his existence, or of some chance happenings of which we know nothing. But unfortunately, we have no means of doing so. Information is completely lacking, and we can only fall back upon more or less probable conjecture.

There is reason to believe, for instance, that Jesus did not remain entirely ignorant and uneducated, inasmuch as the *Torah* insisted upon the necessity of instilling its precepts into children (Deut. iv. 9; vi. 7 f.; vi. 20 f.; xi. 19 f. Prov. xxii. 6 also counsels : " Train up the child in the way he should go,

[1] **CCXVI**, p. 48.
[2] In Xenophon, *Hellen.*, 3, 4, 17, the τέχτων is contrasted with the χαλκεύς, who is the " metal-worker." *Cf.* **CCLXXXVIII**, p. 436.
[3] **CV**, p. 169.

and when he grows old he will not depart from it "). Originally this particular instruction was the business of the father. From Josephus,[1] however, we get the impression that there was in his time in Palestine a regular curriculum, essentially religious, certainly, but which to be of value, even from this restricted point of view, must have included some general knowledge. The child, after receiving his first instruction in the family, passed on to the elementary school, then to the synagogue, which was regarded as already providing a more advanced religious education, and finally, if he had the means, to the school of a rabbi (*Beth-hammidrash*), where he extended and deepened his Biblical studies. Whether, however, this " curriculum " actually existed, whether it was operative at the period when Jesus was a child in Galilee, whether Jesus himself followed it, and how far, are all questions which it is easier to ask than to answer.

The well-known tendency of Josephus to glorify Jewish habits and customs, arouses some suspicion on the first point. In any case, the second is decidedly doubtful. Nevertheless, it may be regarded as probable that elementary schools existed throughout the Palestinian world from before the beginning of our era. The *Jerusalem Talmud*[2] attributes to a famous doctor, Simonben-Shetach, the brother of Queen Alexandra (78–69 B.C.), an order compelling children to attend what we might call primary schools. This, however, does not necessarily prove that such schools existed, inasmuch as this Simon seems to have been an eccentric individual, and his dictum might possibly be only the expression of a personal idiosyncrasy.[3] It is difficult to tell. On the other hand, the *Babylonian Talmud*[4] attributes the organization of these schools to Joshuaben-Gamba, High Priest from A.D. 63 to 65, or more than half a century after the birth of Jesus. If our two texts leave us in doubt, however, it is still to be taken into account that the Pharisees had every interest in giving the Jews, even the common people, some idea of their studies, as a practical means of extending their influence over them. When we add to this consideration the examination of various passages of Josephus and Philo,[5] it becomes very probable, all things considered, that the Jewish children were, from the beginning of the first century, more systematically initiated into the study

[1] Especially C. *Apion*, 2, 16 *ff*.   [2] *Kethuboth*, 8, 11, 22*b*.
[3] *Cf.* **XXIX**, ii, 423.   [4] *Baba-Bathra*, 21, *a*.
[5] Josephus, *Ant.*, 4, 8, 12 ; C. *Apion*, 2, 25 ; 1, 12 ; 2, 18 ; Philo, *Leg.*, 31 and 16. *Cf.* **XXIX**, ii, 422, which cites 2 Tim. iii. 15 : ἀπὸ βρέφους ἱερὰ γράμματα οἶδας.

of the *Torah*, regarded as "the highest knowledge and the condition of prosperity," [1] than they could have been in their own homes.

The elementary school (*Beth-hassepher*) was an appendage of the synagogue, and since Galilee had synagogues, it could not have been without their Judæan accompaniment. This school was in charge of the *ḥazzân* (ὑπηρέτης—*minister*), a kind of beadle or official of the synagogue. It was to this person, in the incident of Luke iv. 20, that Jesus handed back the scroll of the prophet Isaiah, after reading from it in the synagogue at Nazareth. From the age of six, usually until that of ten, the children learnt the holy book under his direction. That, at least, is what we are able to establish for a slightly later period. Assuming that this was the case in the time of Jesus, what would he have learned from the lessons of the *ḥazzân* of his village?

He would have learned to read, and have become familiar with the most important practical parts of the *Torah*. The methods of instruction and study employed in the school of the synagogue were not of a sort designed to stimulate young minds. They subjected the children to a ceaseless repetition, a relentless reiteration, of what it was desired to impress upon their memories, without making any real appeal to their intelligence, so that the word *šanah*, meaning "repeat," finally came, in common speech, to signify "to teach" or "to learn." All that we can say is that the glimpse which the Gospels give us of the knowledge of Jesus, is quite consistent with his having attended such an elementary school, but it does not necessarily imply it. [2]

Even if there was a Rabbinical school within reach of the village of Jesus, he cannot himself have been a student (*talmid*). Otherwise it would be hard to understand why the tradition attributes to his Jewish auditors the amazement they are supposed to have displayed on hearing him preach. "Whence hath he these things, and what wisdom is this which has been given to him?" exclaim the people of Nazareth in Mark vi. 2. [3] He never became, therefore, a "master in Israel," and his religious life was entirely based, as far as education is concerned, upon an elementary instruction confined to a practical and superficial study of the *Torah*. To this may be added, however, the teaching later heard in the synagogue. The value of this supplementary instruction would naturally vary greatly

---

[1] Josephus, *Ant.*, 4, 8, 12 : μάθημα κάλλιστον καὶ τῆς εὐδαιμονίας αἴτιον.
[2] **CCXVI**, 48.
[3] *Cf.* John vii. 15 : πῶς οὗτος γράμματα οἶδεν μὴ μεμαθηκώς.

according to the competence and the inspiration of the teacher. It is an attractive conjecture that one of these preceptors especially stirred the adolescent Jesus, and thus helped to prepare and decide his vocation.

According to the Evangelists, Jesus is supposed to have been steeped in the Scriptures.[1] He may have been, but on this point we cannot place too much confidence in redactors who themselves found in the Old Testament the main justification for their faith. They give the impression that the Galilean *nabi* was especially familiar with the Psalms and the Prophets, which is not unlikely, since we know that the first of these collections was the main sustenance of the living faith of Israel, and the second the chief source of the Messianic proof-texts. We have no means of proving the point,[2] but Jesus would not have been a son of his people if the sacred book had not been the very foundation of his religious and moral thinking, although the gospel writers can hardly have failed to exaggerate somewhat the number and accuracy of his references to the text.[3] We cannot doubt, either, that he was well versed in the additions to Jahwism made by popular belief and endorsed by many of the learned : angelology, demonology, the hope of resurrection, and, above all, the Messianic expectations. But it is a waste of time to inquire which of the writings, which were more or less influenced by the innovations accepted in Israel about the time of his birth, he may have read, or heard read. It has been maintained that there are signs of his acquaintance with Daniel and Enoch, which may be true, but it is by no means incontrovertible.[4]

We may perhaps safely conclude that, apart from the knowledge that was, so to speak, indispensable to the ordinary Jew, Jesus had no education. We have no reason to think that he travelled at all, nor that his view of the world extended beyond the horizon of his own little country.[5] " The delightful impossibilities which throng his parables when he represents kings and great folk, show that his idea of aristocratic society was always that of a young villager who sees the world reflected in the mirror of his own simplicity " (Renan).

It is doubtful whether he actually knew Hebrew. He spoke Aramaic, and it was in this language that the Bible was read in his synagogue.

[1] **CXLI**, 77 *ff*.

[2] **CCXVI**, 47 ; Klostermann, *Jesu Stellung zum A.T.*, 1904 ; **L–a**, 164 *ff*.

[3] **CLXXXVI**, 1 *ff*., gives a table of the Bible references attributed to Jesus by the Synoptics. *Cf*. **XLIV**, 36.

[4] **CCXVI**, 48.   [5] **CCXXXIV**, 112 ; **CLXVIII**, 30 *ff*., 38 *ff*.

Most critics believe that he remained free from any profound Hellenistic influence,[1] and the text of the Gospels undoubtedly confirms this view. It has been suggested, however,
that he had a knowledge of Greek, which could hardly have
failed to enlarge his ideas. It is hard to see what basis the
commentators have for such a view.[2] Galilee was, certainly,
a means of transit between the Greek cities of the coast and
those of Peræa, and there were Greek merchants on the shores
of the Lake of Tiberias, but these are slender arguments, which
hardly seem capable of outweighing the impression of pure
Semitism which is given, for example, by the parables and, in
general, by the whole Synoptic tradition, in spite of the fact
that it has reached us only in Greek dress. We do not dispute
that in Galilee, as in Judæa, at the beginning of the Christian
era, Greek had its place by the side of Aramaic, but the question is, how large a place. We do not know, and the assertion
that, in Galilean custom, Aramaic was used in familiar intercourse, and Greek for purposes of public life and religious
instruction,[3] is entirely arbitrary. It would follow from this
that Jesus used Greek in his teaching, which is as great a paradox as that which would have us believe that the Nazarene
read the Scriptures in the Greek text of the Septuagint,[4] on
the grounds that the disciples, who make use of it in our Gospels,
would not, at the very beginning, have dared such a revolution
as the abandonment of the actual Book used by their Master.
Apart from the fact that we are completely ignorant of what
book the real, original disciples did make use, since nothing
of theirs has come down to us—unless, against all possibility,
we accept the traditional assignment of Matthew, John, Jude,
and 1 Peter, to four of the Twelve—there would have been no
revolution in substituting the Septuagint for the Hebrew text,
because the Greek version was commonly regarded as inspired,
which is to say, as equivalent in every way to the original. It
is worthy of note that, when the gospel writer wishes to give
us the impression of a direct utterance of Jesus, he puts Aramaic
words into his mouth. We refer to the cry on Golgotha, in
Mark xv. 34 : " *Eloï lama sabacthani,*" and the phrase in Mark
v. 41, " *Talitha kum.*"

[1] CCXVI, 48.

[2] CLXXVII, 263 *ff.* G. Dalman, *Jesus-Jeshua. Die drei Sprachen
Jesu,* Leipzig, 1922, goes still further and believes that the prophet
conversed in Hebrew with the scribes, in Aramaic with the disciples,
and understood Greek. It would indeed be marvellous if we knew
that.

[3] Roberts, *Greek, the Language of Christ and his Apostles,* 1888.

[4] LXIV, x.

The spread of the Greek language in Galilee and Judæa should not be exaggerated. We must not forget that, in order to be understood by his compatriots, Josephus chose to write his *Jewish War* first in Aramaic. It was in Aramaic that, during the siege of Jerusalem, Titus summoned the defenders of the city to surrender.[1] According to Acts (xxi. 40 ; xxii. 2) it was also in Aramaic that Paul expressed himself when he wished to speak to the people of Jerusalem, which proves at least that the author of Acts believed that to be the actual language of the Palestinians. Probably those of them whom their business or some other necessity brought into regular contact with the Greeks, usually did acquire a smattering of everyday Greek, and certainly all the Jewish upper classes had a thorough knowledge of the literary language. But since Jesus was definitely neither a trader nor an aristocrat, it is hard to see what would have induced him to acquire a knowledge that could be of no use to him. There is, of course, always the possibility of some chance reason, but it is highly improbable. It was neither in the village nor amongst the working classes that Greek was affected in Palestine. The fact that the Gospels make no mention of an interpreter in connexion with the interrogation of Jesus by Pilate, means nothing, inasmuch as, as we shall see, the whole account of the trial of Jesus is so artificial and so unreliable that it would be folly to attach the slightest significance to so minor a detail.

We may conclude that the probability is that Jesus was ignorant of Greek, and consequently uninfluenced by the ideas which that language introduced and disseminated throughout the world. When we come to study Paul, we shall be able to estimate the extreme importance of this conclusion.

II

THE RELIGIOUS ENVIRONMENT OF THE CHILD JESUS

It would be of the greatest advantage to us to know the exact religious environment in which the religious consciousness of Jesus was formed, but it is as completely unknown to us as the intellectual environment with which we have just been dealing. We are told that Jesus lived in a healthy religious atmosphere, in which the grand spirit of the Old Testament circulated freely, and so to speak, at its full strength, amongst devout men who were neither hidebound by the narrow legalism of the Pharisees, nor isolated by the separatism of the Essenes,

[1] Josephus, *B.J.*, 5, 9, 2 ; 6, 2, 1. *Cf.* **XXIX**, ii³, 63 *ff.*

nor misled by the syncretism of the Judæo-Alexandrians.[1] We may safely grant the last point. On the others we can only withhold judgment, because documentary evidence is lacking, and speculations and inferences, however ingenious, are no substitute for it.

As against this, it has been maintained, though without proof, that Jesus belonged to the Essenes,[2] but that is quite incredible. Short of admitting that the synoptic tradition has grossly deceived us, to the point of declaring the exact opposite of the truth, concerning the type of life led by the Master and the spirit of his preaching, it is impossible to confuse his doctrine with that of the Essenes. He seeks to reform life, and does not preach withdrawal from it ; it is to all the men of Israel that he addresses himself, and not to a company of elect ; his life appears to conform to the normal habits of mankind, and not to an ascetic ideal. It may be assumed that he knew members of the Essene sect,[3] since they were to be met with outside their communities in the neighbourhood of the Dead Sea, but the question is, how far, and in what way, did they influence him, how did he himself react to the contact ; and of this we have not the smallest idea. However this may be, there is not, in the opinion of the writer, the faintest trace of Essene influence in the teaching which our Gospels attribute to him.

As far as the Pharisees are concerned, we shall, in the first place, be on our guard against what the Gospels tell us of the relations of Jesus with them. It is reasonable to believe that our redactors freely endowed the Lord with the emotions and hatreds which were of necessity their own, at a time when the Jewish doctors seemed to them the arch opponents of the Truth.[4] In the second place, we must not forget that, starting from similar ideas, and even beliefs, men of different minds and temperaments can arrive at very dissimilar schemes of practical life.

We have endeavoured to show that Jesus did not attend the Pharisaic school, but Pharisaism was not confined to the schools. It did not present itself as a doctrine—although, of course, it had its doctrines—so much as a practical religious

[1] CCXVI, 48 ; CLXVIII, 34 ff.

[2] A. Bugge, in ZNTW, 1906, 99 ff. ; N. Schmidt, The Prophet of Nazareth, 1905, 255 ff., 303 ff. It is surprising to see Conybeare also admitting the possibility of this affiliation, CXLVIII, 41, n. 1.

[3] L–a, i, 167.

[4] Bultmann maintains, with reason, that the idea of this fundamental and perpetual antagonism could have arisen only on Hellenistic soil. Cf. LXXXVI, 26 ff.

discipline. Its adherents were probably less numerous in Galilee than in Judæa, and its " masters " seem rather to have looked down upon the peasants and mountaineers of the " Circle of the Gentiles." We may safely conclude from this that Jesus was not as surrounded by Pharisaism as he would have been had he lived in Judæa.[1] He was not subjected to the deep imprint of its sometimes strong but always subtle dialectic, which had a withering effect upon most minds. Renan believes that the principles of Hillel were nevertheless familiar to him, and that the famous rabbi was his true master.[2] Without going to the length of such a rash and unverifiable assertion, it seems certain that Jesus was influenced by the Pharisaic movement. His standpoint and teaching fall within the pattern of the Pharisaic faith ; it is on the Messianic hope, which was adopted and propagated by Pharisaism, that he bases his whole preaching, more, his whole mission.[3] The problems by which he is obsessed are Pharisaic problems, and he formulates them in the Pharisaic manner. It is to the forms of exposition familiar to the Pharisaic doctors that he resorts, to explain himself and make himself understood.[4] The resemblance between him and his supposed opponents is, indeed, so strong that it seriously detracts from the originality which, even to-day, is said to have marked him out from his contemporaries.

We do not mean that he accepted everything that Pharisaism offered him, and is to be regarded merely as one of its disciples. There is probably a great deal of truth in the revolt which the gospel writers attribute to him against pedantry, the pride, the exaggerated legalism, and the scholastic hair-splitting,[5] from which the sect was not always free. But it is equally exaggerated and untrue to maintain [6] that there is no bond between Pharisaism and the Gospel, and no possibility of passing from one to the other. Jesus certainly was not a Pharisee, but his career and his activities would be incomprehensible if the Pharisaic movement had not paved the way for them.

More important even than the determination of his exact relation to Essenism and Pharisaism, is that of his connexion with those Jewish sects of which we have already endeavoured to give some account.[7] It has been asked whether he owed nothing to them, whether, even, he did not spring from one, which his name is supposed to indicate, namely, the pre-Chris-

[1] CCLXXXIV, 15. [2] CLXVIII, 34 *ff.*
[3] CCLXIII, i, 78, n. 2. [4] L–a, 169 ; CXLIII, 52, 54, 78.
[5] III, 194. [6] CCLVI, 15.
[7] *Cf.* vol. xxviii of this series, *From the Prophets to Jesus*, last part.

tian Nazareans spoken of by Epiphanius.[1] We do not, ourselves, place much reliance on the statements of the bishop of Salamis, who is often careless and ill-informed. However, even admitting the truth of what he says, the resemblances between the Nazareans and Jesus which may be deduced from it, seem to be counterbalanced by equally important differences, so that we are left in complete uncertainty. It is quite possible that Jesus may have belonged to some sect in which the current ideas of the Kingdom or of the Messiah, or both, had perhaps suffered strange transformations and adaptations, but our present information does not permit us to say anything one way or the other.[2] On the whole, there was no need for Jesus to come from a Messianic sect in order to begin preaching the imminent advent of the Messiah. It is enough that he was deeply imbued with the great hope of his compatriots. In making this hope the central idea of his own thinking, he simply showed himself to be the child of his people and his time. Perhaps this Messianic belief, being opposed in Galilee by neither the restrictions of the Sadducees nor the influence of the Temple, found especially favourable conditions in an environment where deficiency of education was fortunately made good by spontaneity of feeling and a glowing hope. The frequency and stubbornness of the uprisings which the Romans had to suppress in that country, would incline us to believe so. In that case it would be all the more understandable that the Messianic belief may at an early age have become ingrained in the religious consciousness of Jesus.

Undoubtedly as soon as the child was of a suitable age, and capable of enduring the three days' journey from Galilee to Jerusalem,[3] he would go with his parents to the Holy City. Theoretically, the males of Israel were supposed to go there for the three great festivals of the Jewish year, Passover, Pentecost, and Tabernacles, and at least for the first. The women did not come under this rule,[4] but they often accompanied their husbands or fathers. It was long supposed—following Lightfoot and Wetstein, who based their conclusion upon our Luke ii. 42—that twelve was the age when the young Jew became responsible to observe the regulations of the *Torah*. But it has since been shown that some partial obligation began

---

[1] **CCLVII**, 136 *ff.*, 148, 150.
[2] **CXLVIII**, 41, n. 1 : " But it is a long way from a may to a must."
[3] Josephus, *Vita*, 52.
[4] The *Babylonian Talmud* (*Chagiga*, 1, 1) states that deaf people, idiots, children, eunuchs, bastards, and women are exempt from this journey. *Cf.* **XCVII**, 46, and **LXVI**, ii, 141 *ff.*

much earlier. The end of childhood was defined, at the time we are dealing with, by the appearance of the first signs of puberty. Later, it was fixed at thirteen years of age, not twelve.[1]

It is to one of these journeys of Jesus to the City and the Temple—perhaps the first—that the incident previously referred to, in Luke ii. 41 f., relates. Jesus is twelve years old, and goes with his parents to Jerusalem for the Passover. " The days being fulfilled," that is to say, at the end of the week dedicated to the festival, Joseph and Mary depart. They believe that their child is amongst the company of friends and neighbours who have made the pilgrimage with them (ἐν τῇ συνοδίᾳ), and miss him only after a day's journey. They then retrace their steps, and seek him for three days in the City, where he has remained. At last they find him in the Temple, surrounded by the doctors, listening to them and asking them questions, and delighting them with his intelligence and his replies. His parents are amazed. But when Mary tells him that she and his father have been looking for him in great anxiety, he replies : " Why have ye sought me ? Know ye not that I must be with my Father ? " They do not under-stand, and take him away. He follows them obediently to Nazareth, " but his mother keeps all the words (πάντα τὰ ῥήματα) in her heart."

It will hardly be necessary to point out the intrinsic im-probabilities of this anecdote as it stands. With regard to the authenticity of its substance, the numbers, *three* and *twelve*, which appear in it, would be sufficient to arouse our suspicions. *Three* is the Messianic figure, and it was at the age of *twelve* that Solomon became king and burst into prophecy.[2] At the same age, likewise, Daniel is supposed to have come into prominence,[3] and Moses, according to the legend, to have separated himself from his family.[4] It is, accordingly, to be feared that the twelve years of Jesus, in our text, represent rather a kind of formal convention than an authentic record. On the other hand, it is obvious that the redaction of Luke does not give the original form of the story, which must have been in existence before the development of the belief in the Virgin Birth. In proof of this we have the amazement of the parents, awkwardly extenuated by Luke's assertion that " His mother kept all the words in her heart." The opposition of " my Father " to " thy father," which is unintelligible to Mary and Joseph, is due to the pen of a redactor who " knew " who

[1] **XXIX**, ii, 426.   [2] Josephus, *Ant.*, 5, 10, 4.
[3] Ignatius, *Magnes.*, 3, 2, 4.   [4] *Midrash* on Exodus iv. 27.

the true father of the child was, and cannot possibly be part of the original account. Finally, the whole section is entirely in harmony with the spirit and aims of the Apocryphal Gospels. Its purpose is to show that the innate superiority of Jesus to the doctors, and his divine vocation, were manifest even before the great public revelation of them. The redactor has just said (ii. 40) that the child grew up, full of wisdom and the grace of God ; the story comes in aptly to prove and illustrate this statement, and accordingly, he concludes it (ii. 52) with the simple repetition of the idea which suggested it. It is actually a preface to the gospel narrative proper, which begins immediately afterwards.

If, as is only too apparent, the incident in Luke, of which there is no mention in the other Gospels, has no historical foundation, where did it come from ? We simply do not know. It has been suggested that it is an adaptation of some myth regarding the precocious manifestation of a hero, of which there are further echoes in the legends of Moses,[1] Samuel,[2] Alexander,[3] Buddha,[4] and various others,[5] but nothing very convincing has been said on the subject. It is possible that this isolated and improbable anecdote enshrines some reminiscence, but we are not in a position today to discern it. On the other hand, the purpose of the redactor who introduced it is plain. He wished to show that, from an early age, Jesus was impelled by his divine mission.

It will be seen that the statement made at the beginning of this chapter is, unfortunately, well founded. Concerning the childhood of Jesus, his education, his physical, intellectual, moral, and religious development, we have no direct, specific, trustworthy, documentary evidence. Our only hope, and that a very modest one, is that what the Gospels relate of his public career will assist us in imagining to some extent what he may have been at the time when it began.

[1] Josephus, *Ant.*, 2, 9, 6 ; Philo, *Vita Mos.*, 1, 5.
[2] 1 Sam. ii. 26 ; **XCVI**, i, 324.   [3] **CLI**, i, 182.
[4] **XLI**, 243 *ff.* ; **CCLXXXV**, 124, 146.   [5] **LXXXVI**, 180 *ff.*

CHAPTER VI

THE ADVENT OF JESUS

I

THE INITIAL IMPULSE

THE advent of Jesus, his appearance as the messenger of God, is doubtless to be explained by the combination of his religious temperament and one or more external influences, but since neither of these factors is known to us, we are not in a position to explain, that is, to analyse, the phenomenon. The question, as it appears to us, did not, of course, interest the gospel writers. For them the advent of Jesus was a supernatural event, the fulfilment of God's eternal purpose, which at once rendered any psychological explanation superfluous.

We cannot but be struck, however, by one feature of the Synoptic tradition, namely, the anxious and slightly shocked amazement of the family of Jesus at the activities of the *nabi*. Mark iii. 21 relates that his immediate relatives (οἱ παρ' αὐτὸν), that is to say, his mother and his brothers (iii. 31), on hearing of his preaching and the effect which it was having, went to Capernaum to seize him (κρατῆσαι αὐτόν) and bring him home by force, under the impression that he had gone out of his mind. This looks very much as if we were in the presence of one of those authentic recollections which the original disciples contributed to the tradition, and which became sufficiently deeply rooted therein to withstand both apologetic expurgations and Christological elaborations. This attitude of his family proves conclusively that his vocation was neither foreseen nor visibly foreshadowed in the circle in which his childhood and youth were spent, an impression which is to some extent confirmed by the surprise which, according to Mark vi. 2, the people of his native village displayed on hearing him preach. "Whence has he all that?" they ask, "And what is this wisdom which has been given to him?" Hence the tradition must have believed that it was not in his "home country" that Jesus first revealed himself.

It is not very helpful to attribute his advent, the shaping

of his activity and his destiny, to " a complex of feelings and ideas which first arose under the influence of the miseries of Roman rule amongst the discontented inhabitants of Galilee," [1] since it is precisely this complex which evades us, and which alone would reveal the exact origin and the true forms of the effect on Jesus of the discontent of his fellow-countrymen.

The Synoptic writers closely connect the advent of the Nazarene with the preaching of John the Baptist.[2] They inform us that Jesus was attracted by the fame of the Baptist, and came, like so many others, to be baptized by the prophet on the banks of the Jordan, and that it was at this moment that his own vocation was revealed to him and became settled in his mind. Whether this view is correct, and we are to regard the mission of Jesus as in a way a result of that of the Baptist, is a large problem, and an extremely obscure one, and the innumerable disputes to which it has given rise have not contributed much to its illumination. It is one of those questions of gospel history which discourage and baffle investigation, and the number and variety of whose solutions—all dangerously hypothetical—exhibit most clearly the futility of the efforts which, in the absence or disagreement of documentary evidence, so many critics have persisted in venturing, in the vain hope of surmising what we have no means of finding out.

It has been maintained [3] that Jesus began his work of preaching before meeting with John the Baptist, inasmuch as its whole character, as described by the Gospels, was from the very beginning entirely different from that of John, so that what they represent as the beginning of his career is merely its continuation. Furthermore, the " great reception " he receives from John is inexplicable except on the assumption that he is himself " already a teacher of considerable repute." Unfortunately, the " great reception " referred to is entirely comprised in two verses of Matthew (iii. 14 and 15), in which John, before complying with Jesus' request and baptizing him, protests that it is rather he who should receive baptism at the hands of the one who asks for it ; and these two verses are definitely inspired by the purpose of the redactor, and are out of harmony with historical probability. It is also rash to base conclusions on divergences which, if real, may be due more to differences of disposition than to the development of different methods. Moreover, it is purely arbitrary to draw conclusions

[1] CCLXVIII, i, Pref., xiv.—For the whole question, see CLVI-a, ch. x.
[2] John, that is, Johanan, meaning " Jahweh is gracious," was a very common name in Israel.
[3] CLXVIII, ch. v.

concerning anything before the beginning of the gospel narrative, since we have no information, not even an allusion, with regard to that period. Psychologically, Jesus seems to have been of the type, common enough in history, produced by an environment in which religious interests could take tyrannical and exclusive possession of the mind, and, in this particular case, in which obsession with the Messianic hope created a predisposition to an ecstatic state. Under these conditions, the slightest impulse from without was sufficient to produce a sense of vocation.

In the case of the mission of Jesus, it is possible that this impulse may have come from John the Baptist. No hypothesis has a better documentary foundation, since both the gospel traditions, the Synoptic and the Johannine, make the Baptism of Jesus the threshold of his public career. This does not, however, place the point beyond doubt, because we have only to read our Gospels to see that their accounts of the Baptism are deliberately designed to settle the question of the relations between the two prophets in a manner favourable to the Messianic status of Jesus. We know that the Gospel of Marcion omitted the incident on the banks of the Jordan, and began with the going down of Jesus to Capernaum, and it has even been suggested that neither the original version of John nor *Urmarcus* contained any reference to the Baptist at the beginning of their accounts.[1] The baptism of Jesus by John may be a fact, but since it is very difficult today not to admit that the *accounts* of it are purely mythical, the creation of credal requirements rather than authentic biography,[2] it is hardly unreasonable to believe that the event itself might easily be legendary, and represent only an artificial preface to the Gospel.[3] Our Synoptics are known to have been edited under the influence of catechetical and cultual interests. It seems natural that they, or rather the tradition on which they depended, should deliberately have placed at the beginning of the tendentious composition which they designedly represented as the life of Jesus according to the Spirit, a story intended to explain and confirm what was, in the practice of their time, the initiatory

[1] **CLXII**, 404 *ff*.

[2] **XXIV**, i. 94; **LXXXVI**, 151 *ff*. *Cf.* H. Gressmann, *Die Sage von der Taufe Jesu*, ap. Z. f. *Missionskunde und Religionswissenschaft*, 34 (1919), 86 *ff*.

[3] For the opposite view, see **CCLIX**, 139 *ff.*, whose confidence is not shared by the writer. *Cf.* **CCXXXII**, 38 ; **CCXXII**, 76 ; **CV**, 180 ; **XXIV**, i, 83. The latter concludes by saying that if Jesus did receive this baptism, it was only as one of the crowd, without John's singling him out.

rite of the Christian life. It is no small cause for suspicion to see Goguel himself, although a strong supporter of the authenticity of the incident, accepting this obvious relation between the inauguration of the mission of Jesus and that of the Christian life of his followers,[1] and subsequently admitting that the gospel writers are open to the suspicion of having made the baptism of Jesus take on the appearance of the prototype of Christian baptism.[2]

Our information about John the Baptist [3] is all contained in one passage of Josephus (*Ant.*, 18, 5, 2) and about fifteen references in our Gospels.[4] The Jewish chronicler, after having stated that the subjects of Herod Antipas saw in the defeat of their tetrarch by Aretas, the king of the Nabateans, the punishment of the crime which he had committed in putting John to death, tells us incidentally that this John was a good man (ἀγαθὸν ἄνδρα), who gave the Jews valuable advice concerning the practice of virtue, piety and fair dealing. When they should have attained to the state to which he exhorted them, he offered them a baptism, to purify the body whose virtue had already cleansed the soul, and make them acceptable to God. He was eloquent, and the crowd flocked to hear him. Herod was disturbed by the interest which this preaching aroused amongst the people, and fearing the worst, that is to say, some movement against himself, tried to prevent it by having the preacher seized, imprisoned, and executed. Taken literally, the expression of Josephus, " to unite themselves by a baptism " (βαπτισμῷ συνιέναι), implies that the Baptist wished only to gather together, in a kind of a sect or order of a purely religious type, pious men, mainly recruited from amongst the *anavim*, the " poor of Israel," who were desirous of uniting in their expectation of the " day of Jahweh." It is to be inferred that no political, or purely nationalistic, aims infected the teaching of the prophet, nor had he countenanced the desperate Messianic zealots who were so numerous in the Judaism of his time.[5] We must however hesitate in accepting the exclusively spiritual nature of the movement, inasmuch as the veracity of Josephus is always doubtful when he is dealing

---

[1] CCLIX, 227. [2] CCLIX, 290.
[3] Three especially valuable works are : CCLIV, CCXLV, and CCLIX.
[4] First, Mark i. 2–11 and 14 ; ii. 18 ; vi. 14–29 ; xi. 30–33. Second, Matt. iii. 7–17 ; Luke iii. 7–17 ; Matt. xi. 2–19 ; Luke vii. 18–27, 31–35 ; xvi. 16 ; all supposed to be derived from Q. Third, Luke i. ; John i. 19–42 ; iii. 22–36 ; iv. 1–3 ; which are of uncertain origin. There has been much futile discussion regarding the different impressions of John and his preaching conveyed by Josephus and the Synoptics. Cf. XIII, i, 103 *ff.* [5] CCLIX, 287 *ff.*

with a Messianist. But on the other hand, there is no reliance to be placed in the corrections and additions which the fragments of the Slavonic version of the *Jewish War* are supposed to furnish.[1] The gross historical errors of which they are full, together with their inconsistency, deprive them of any claim to serious consideration, and the various emendations to which their most recent, and staunchest, champion, Robert Eisler, has arbitrarily subjected them for the purpose of making them acceptable, have, in the opinion of the writer, rendered them worthless.

Josephus, then, tells us nothing of what would be most helpful in explaining the appearance of Jesus, but at least he vouches for the existence of the Baptist and the fact of his activity. His testimony, however, has not been universally accepted, and the adherents of the mythological view have denied the existence of John as stoutly as that of Jesus. Jensen, for instance,[2] sees in the Baptist a reappearance of that Eabani who played a large part in the Babylonian epic of Gilgamesh. Eabani, he points out, was clothed with hair, and lived among the cattle, feeding on herbs and various kinds of plants. Luke has merely taken the old poem and removed its marks of identification, in order to deceive us with his legend of the Baptist. Drews, after deciding [3] that the texts offer only contradictions and obscurities on the subject of John—the passage of Josephus just cited being, according to him, a Christian interpolation—comes to the conclusion that this *Johannes* is no other than the Babylonian god *Oannes* (*Ea*), the water-god, " *Wassermann und Taufgott*," and originally a solar deity, like Isaac and Samson. According to Luke i. 26 he precedes by six months Jesus, the other solar deity, each of them, that is, representing half the year. Now, at the beginning of its annual course, the sun undergoes a baptism, since it enters first the sign of Aquarius, then that of Pisces.—But we will go no further. Our intention was only to give an idea of the fantastic arguments of those who deny John's existence. There is no reason whatever to suspect Josephus of having invented John the Baptist, and in our opinion there is no trace of a Christian hand in the redaction of the text in question.[4]

[1] CLIX, ii, 1–144, for the positive case ; CCLIX, 23 *ff*., and 297–302, for the negative. *Cf.* XIII, i, Appendix C, which gives an English translation of the passage relating to John.

[2] CCXIV, 812 *ff*.   [3] CLI, 83 *ff*.

[4] On this much-discussed question, see LXXIV, i, 30–5, which observes justly that a Christian interpolator would have taken care to bring the passage into harmony with the Gospels, for instance, by introducing Jesus into it.

If, ruling out of the Synoptic narrative everything which has an obviously Christian purpose, we confine ourselves to its account of the essence of John's preaching, we shall find a very probable connexion between the inspiration of the new prophet and the Messianic hope. John announced the speedy advent of the Kingdom, or of the Reign of God, and the great purification by fire which would precede the fulfilment of the Promise,[1] and he urged men to alter their way of life and bring it into conformity with the will of God. This change of heart (*metanoia*) would influence the Judge in their favour and be of advantage to them in the coming Day. The baptism of repentance (βάπτισμα μετανοίας) thus takes on the aspect of a symbolic purification in preparation for the advent of the Messiah.[2] It is not improbable, however, that the Baptist, like the Pharisees,[3] said : " Repent *that the Kingdom may come*," instead of : " Repent *for the Kingdom is coming*." In any case, his emphasis was upon the threat of punishment rather than the announcement of " good news." [4]

Just as Josephus mentions the Baptist only in connexion with an event in the reign of Herod Antipas, and his relations with that monarch, the Gospels are only interested in the prophet as officiating at the Baptism of Jesus, and, subsequently, in the question of the contacts between the two teachers, or between their disciples. The result of this twofold bias is that the man himself remains unknown. We know neither whence he came nor what was the cause of his appearance. Luke (i. 5 *f.*) indeed relates a fine story about his miraculous birth (he was the offspring of two aged parents, the woman being barren), but the purpose of the gospel writer is so obviously to make John subordinate to Jesus, by representing him as the latter's precursor,[5] that we can have no faith in what he recounts. The attempt has been made to salvage some scraps of his narrative, to maintain, for instance, the probability of the belated birth of the Baptist in some priestly family, but the result is simply an arbitrary selection from a mass of tendentious legends.

In attempting to account for John's two main characteristics, the use of baptism and the personal practice of asceticism, affiliations have been sought for him in Israel and elsewhere. Some have maintained that he belonged to the Essenes. His very name, the Baptist, is supposed to mean " the *Essene*," the man who bathes every day in running water.[6] It is true

---

[1] For the origin of this idea and its place in Judaism, see **CCLIX**, 40.
[2] **XCVIII**, 7.   [3] **LXXIV**, i, 34.   [4] **CCXVI**, 48.
[5] Luke i. 16 *ff.*, 41 *ff.*, 76 *ff.*   [6] **XI**, ii, 261.

that Josephus seems clearly to imply that he was connected with the Essenes,[1] but his baptism appears to have been a rite undergone once and for all by the " converted," the " repentant," rather than a daily practice according to Essene custom. Moreover, if he founded a sect it must, unless our texts conceal the most important facts, have strangely declined from the communism and ritual of the " houses " of Engedi. Others [2] have associated him with the Baptist sects whose names, Hemerobaptists and Masbotheans, are supposed to have been preserved to us by Christian heresiologists, but about which we should have great difficulty in making any assertion, even that they really existed. Schürer was even moved to suspect, and not without reason,[3] that the worthy Epiphanius had invented a sect with the Jewish custom of ritual ablutions. Tertullian (de Baptismo, 15) certainly said, " Israel, the Jew, washes every day, for every day he defiles himself." [4] Still others have believed it certain that John belonged to that Nazorean sect mentioned by Epiphanius, because the Mandæans, who call themselves Nazoreans, are supposed to be descended from him, and to have succeeded the sect from which he himself came. Unfortunately, the Mandæan literature, of which certain critics [5] make a great deal, appears to be so confused, so obscure, so composite, so mixed, so impossible to date in its various parts, at least for the present, and either so vague in its terms or so general, so trite, exactly where it needs to be clear and precise, that it seems to the present writer quite unfit to be used as a basis of explanation. It is true that mention is made in it of John the Baptist, but nothing is said which implies any other source of information than our Gospels themselves.[6] Possibly a careful and unbiased critical study of the Ginzâ (the Treasure), the principal Mandæan book, may yield valuable information. Until that is done any conclusion based upon it can only be conjectural.

All these unfounded attempts to place the Baptist explain nothing and may be ignored. He belongs clearly to the great Jewish prophetic tradition ; he appeared and uttered his

[1] LXXIV, i, 34. On the Essenes, cf. vol. xxviii of this series, From the Prophets to Jesus, last part.

[2] II, 321 ; CCXLVI, 382, who is especially concerned with Samaritan baptists. Cf. CCLIX, 108 ff.

[3] XXIX, ii, 577.

[4] " Καθ᾽ ἡμέραν βαπτιζόμενοι," says Epiphanius, Haer., 17. Cf. CXCIV, 70–85.

[5] The contributors to LVII, in general, and especially Reitzenstein.

[6] An abundant bibliography and an exhaustive study of the question will be found in CCLIX, 113 ff.

message because he felt that the Spirit of Jahweh had breathed upon him—an impression which it is always easier to record than to analyse. His experience was not an isolated one in those times. The hermit Bannos, with whom Josephus spent, as he tells us, three years (*Vita*, 2), clothed and fed himself on what the trees supplied, " for the sake of purity " (πρὸς ἁγνείαν), and he also practised frequent ablutions. To be sure, he did not attain the same notoriety as the Baptist appears to have done, but other enthusiasts of more or less the same type had better success, as we are reminded by the question of the Roman centurion who arrested Paul at Jerusalem in the midst of the tumult of the populace : " Art thou not that Egyptian who didst lately incite a disturbance, and didst lead out into the wilderness four thousand Sicarii ? " (Acts xxi. 38).

All these fanatics went out into the wilderness. Accordingly, it is " in the wilderness " (ἐν τῇ ἐρήμῳ) that Mark (i. 4) puts John the Baptist in the beginning. Matthew (iii. 1), in an attempt at exactitude, specifies that it is the " wilderness of Judæa " (ἔρημος τῆς Ἰουδαίας), but this is an error, for he adds (iii. 6) that John baptized " in the Jordan " those who flocked to hear him from Jerusalem and all Judæa, and the whole of the country about the river. The desert of Judah is a forbidding region on the north-western edge of the basin in which the Dead Sea lies, a land of complete desolation, which may be seen from the top of Mount Olivet, and through which passes the unpleasant traverse from Jerusalem to Jericho. The wilderness which Mark means is unquestionably the lower valley of the Jordan, near the Dead Sea. Sand and stones are not completely victorious here. There is grass, dense brush, tamarisks, tall reeds, even real trees, especially the Euphrates poplar,[1] and on the banks of the river the vegetation becomes so luxuriant that, at the very place to which local tradition assigns, rightly or wrongly, the scene of the Baptism,[2] the famous water-course might be mistaken for some great European river. It is " the wilderness " because it has no settled inhabitants, except those of a Greek monastery, and of the inevitable shacks for the entertainment of pilgrims, which do not date from the time of John. Josephus (*B.J.*, 3, 10, 7) could truly say that before emptying itself into the sea, the Jordan crossed " an extensive wilderness " (πολλὴν ἐρημίαν). The prophet probably wandered about the whole belt of country which stretches between Jericho and the river, and no doubt

---

[1] **CXCVIII**, 118 *ff*.
[2] On the uncertainties of the tradition on the point, see **CXCVIII**, 126 *ff*.

crossed occasionally to the left bank, since, if Herod Antipas
had him arrested, it could only have been in Peræa, the territory
over which he ruled.   It is futile to attempt to be more precise.
John iii. 23 informs us that it was "at Ænon near Salim"
that John baptized, because he found plenty of water there,[1]
but according to Eusebius this locality was situated far to the
north in the valley of the Jordan, almost as high up as Scytho-
polis (Beisan), that is, on the borders of Galilee.   Certainly,
there is nothing to prevent the Baptist from having gone as
far up as that, but when it is observed that Αἰνών means
"springs," and Σαλείμ, "peace," it rather suggests that the
writer of the Gospel took the Forerunner to "the springs of
peace" for purely symbolical reasons.   It is, incidentally,
surprising that the Apocryphal Gospels made no effort to give
the exact location of the place to which the baptism of John
attracted Jesus.   They content themselves with saying "on
the Jordan."[2]

There is nothing peculiar about the mode of life which the
Synoptics attribute to the Baptist.   He was "clad in camel's
hair, with a leather girdle about his loins, and his food was
locusts and wild honey" (Mark i. 6).   This was the traditional
prophetic garb.[3]   Elijah, according to 2 Kings i. 8, was "a
hairy man, wearing a skin robe, and a girdle of leather about
his loins."   His food is that of a man who has withdrawn from
ordinary life and lives on what chance provides.   To eat locusts
was not an eccentricity.   Leviticus xi. 22 sanctioned four
varieties, of which the people of the country still make use.[4]
The honey may have been really the product of wild bees,
which is several times mentioned in the Old Testament (for
example, in Deut. xxxii. 13), and which, according to Josephus
(B.J., 4, 8, 3), was plentiful in the country of the Jordan, or
it may have been the sugary sap of certain trees.[5]   All the
items belong to the resources of a solitary existence.   Although
John may, according to Saint Jerome, have set the example
of a hermit life, he does not seem to have desired to make
anchorites, but only penitents.

His baptismal rite is a matter of great uncertainty.[6]   We

---

[1] CXX, 59 ; CCXLV, 82.   [2] CXLII, 103.

[3] Zech. xiii. 4 : καὶ ἐνδύσονται δέρριν τριχίνην—" and they will be clad
in a skin covered with hair."

[4] It is amusing to note that the Apocryphal Gospels, improving
on the asceticism of John, removed the locusts from his diet on the
grounds that he was supposed never to have eaten meat.

[5] Diodorus Sic., Bibl. hist., 19, 94 ; Gospel of the Ebionites, in XXIII,
no. 8, p. 10.   Cf. XCVIII, 8, and LXVI, i, 100.

[6] L–a, i, 171, gives a review of the opinions held in Germany.

do not even know how he administered it, nor what part he, personally, took in the ceremony. Whether the penitent himself plunged into the water, after having announced his *metanoia*,[1] whether John pronounced any invocation or prayer over the baptized, are questions to which we can give no reply. It is known that the practice of the lustral bath was common in Israel. Leviticus (xi.-xv.) and Numbers (ix.) give numerous cases of defilement in which the Jew must wash his clothing and his body. Certain sects, notably that of the Essenes, attached a special importance to this rite (which was at once a symbol and an act of literal purification) for they repeated it every day.[2] Moreover, probably as early as the time with which we are dealing, a baptism formed part of the ceremony by which proselytes were joined to the seed of Abraham.[3] But the baptism of John differs from all these in that it is apparently administered only once, and to Jews, and is connected with a general moral reformation and not with a special purification. Josephus and the Gospels are at one on this point. Unfortunately, they differ as to the true value of the rite, the first regarding it as merely a symbol of a moral event, the others representing it as endowed with an actual efficacy against sin, undoubtedly with Christian baptism in mind. It seems likely that John saw in the immersion which he practised nothing more than the outward and visible sign of the purification of the soul by *metanoia*. But we cannot be certain, for he must have known the passage of Ezekiel xxxvi. 25, in which it is written : " And I will sprinkle clean water upon you ; from all your filthiness and from all your idols ye shall be clean," and he might easily have derived from this the idea of a sacramental virtue for his rite. It has been held, indeed, that he did so,[4] but we have no means of knowing.

Josephus does not say much about the success of the prophet, but in Mark i. 5 it is stated that " All the country of Judæa went out unto him, and all they of Jerusalem." Matthew iii. 5 adds " all the region which is about the Jordan," and Luke iii. 7 and 10 speaks of " crowds " ($\overset{?}{o}\chi\lambda o\iota$), and iii. 15 and 21 of " the people " ($\lambda a\acute{o}\varsigma$) as flocking to baptism. All these impressive phrases really indicate vagueness and uncertainty.

---

[1] CXIV, 4. On the meaning of the word μετάνοια, its origin, etc., see XCVIII, 7.

[2] Josephus, *B.J.*, 2, 8, 3 ; on Bannos : *Vita*, 2.—Regarding the Jewish practice of baptism, *cf.* XCVIII, 7 ; XXIX, iii, 129.

[3] On this Pharisaic baptism, see LXXIV, i, 36 *ff.* ; CVI, 33 ; CXCIV, CLIX, 137, n. 4.

[4] XXXVII, 25 ; CCXLV, 83. For the discussion of the subject, see : III, 231 and CCXLVI, 282 ; XLI, 166 ; XXIV, i, 90.

It is hard to imagine the Pharisaic lawyers, the cautious Sadducees, and the Temple personnel, who were naturally not very well disposed towards enthusiasts, going out to seek a baptism of doubtful purity at the hands of a dangerous fanatic. Luke (vii. 30) shows an appreciation of this fact, when he states that the Pharisees and doctors of the Law refused to be baptized.[1] In our ignorance of the facts, we may nevertheless regard it as probable that the proclamation of the expected Kingdom would create a certain amount of excitement amongst the " *amhaareṣ*," the poor people, many of whom were pious folk, and that hope, and also curiosity, which is always to be reckoned with in the East, would lead a considerable number of them to flock to the new prophet.

The great question for us is whether Jesus was really of their number. The account of the Baptism given, with more or less interesting variations, in our three Synoptics (Mark i. 9–11 ; Matt. iii. 13–17 ; Luke iii. 21–2) offers plenty of problems for the commentators, but it will not detain us, because its central purpose, which is to prove that Jesus was filled with the Spirit of God, and chosen by heaven for the office of Messiah, and its miraculous details—(the heavens opening, the dove descending, the divine voice uttering a verse of the Scriptures) [2] —are all unhistorical. What we should like to know is whether Jesus actually came to the baptism of John, and felt there the stirring of his vocation, and whether he became, and under what circumstances, and for how long, the disciple of the Baptist. On all these points, interpretations, hypotheses, and assertions naturally abound ; but on none of them have we any positive knowledge.

It has been claimed that Jesus had known John before his Baptism, and even that they had worked together in Peræa. The protest of the Baptist in the account of Matthew iii. 14 (" It is I who should be baptized of thee, and comest thou to me ? ") is supposed to prove that he was well acquainted with Jesus before that event.[3] What it does prove, primarily, is

[1] This is confirmed by Matt. xxi. 32, which states that only publicans and harlots believed John (οἱ δὲ τελῶναι καὶ αἱ πόρναι ἐπίστευσαν αὐτῷ), that is to say, " unclean " people.

[2] Isa. xlii. 1, according to the words usually attributed to the voice : " Thou art my beloved son, in thee I am well pleased " ; but Ps. ii. 7, in the very interesting variant of Codex D : " Thou art my son, this day have I begotten thee," which exhibits a stage of the Christological development in which it was believed that Jesus had been *adopted* by God at the Baptism. *Cf.* **XCVII**, 55 ; **CXLII**, 121, n. 2 ; **LXXXV**, 132 *ff.* ; **XCVI**, i, 328 (for references to the Christian Fathers and bibliography) ; and **CIII**, i, 411 and note 5.

[3] **CCLVII**, 151 *ff.*

the anxiety of the gospel writer to attribute to the Forerunner an attitude of deference. Of course, it is not impossible for the two prophets to have come from the same sect, whether that of the Nazoreans or some other,[1] and, in that case, the Baptism of Jesus, if it is to be regarded as at all historical, would be only an incident in his career. But documentary evidence is lacking. There is not a passage to support the theory of any connexion between John and Jesus prior to the meeting of which the Baptism was the occasion. No account can be taken of the Lucan legend of the relationship between Mary and the alleged mother of the Baptist, Elizabeth (Luke i. 36), because it contradicts all the rest of the Synoptic tradition. To illustrate this, we need only compare Luke i. 39, 45 and 56, in which Mary and Elizabeth share the Messianic tidings, with Mark iii. 20 f., in which his family come to attempt to lay hold of Jesus, because they think he is out of his mind. On the other hand, there is absolutely nothing in the attitude attributed to the two men at the time of the Baptism and afterwards, to indicate that they were cousins and had known each other from infancy. It may very well be that Luke borrowed the first portions of his story [2] from a legend about the Baptist, but he adapted it in his own fashion so as to make it prove the subordination, we may say, the *explicit* subordination, of John to Jesus. This adaptation gives us the full development of the legend of the Forerunner. Mark says nothing about it directly but he foreshadows it in making John exclaim (i. 7): " There cometh one mightier than I after me, the latchet of whose shoes I am not worthy to stoop down and unloose." Matthew iii. 13 introduces the Baptist's scruples about receiving the baptism at the hands of Jesus, of which mention has already been made. John i. 26 f. puts into his mouth a speech in which he announces the coming of one after him, whom he later (i. 33) recognizes as soon as he appears. In Luke i. 41 the Forerunner, while yet unborn, responds to the proximity of " the one who is to come ": " And when Elizabeth heard the salutation of Mary, the child leaped in her womb, and Elizabeth was filled with the Holy Ghost." The few references found in the Synoptics to the relations between John and Jesus are irreconcilable with the story of their intimacy, as also with that of the proclamation by the one of the Messiahship of the other.[3] They do not corroborate the account of the Baptism of Jesus, and if this omission is not altogether

---

[1] Which is the idea favoured by **CLXII**, 404 *ff*.
[2] F. Jackson, *Josephus and the Jews*, London, 1930, 265 *ff*.
[3] **CIII**, i, 398.

inexplicable, it is none the less very surprising, for it is natural to expect that John the Baptist, sending to ask one whom he regarded either as his rival or his successor (Matt. xi. 2 *f.*), for some explanations regarding himself and his work, would recall the occasion of their first meeting. Whether this inquiry is historical or imaginary,[1] such a reminder would be equally in place.

The only argument which can, in reality, be put forward in favour of the Baptism of Jesus by John, is that it would be hard to understand why the tradition should gratuitously have saddled itself with an incident so troublesome to Christology, and have substituted it for the actual facts of the entrance of Jesus upon his public career (which must have been known to the original disciples) if it had not been based upon a definite and incontestable recollection, which they could not discard. If Jesus went to the baptism of John, it could not have been like his compatriots, in a state of repentance, for the purpose of preparing himself for the Great Day whose advent the prophet was proclaiming. To admit that he came to it, appears to imply that he felt, like the others, the necessity of *metanoia*, and also to place him, in a way, in a subordinate position to the Baptist, both of which beliefs were equally repugnant to the Christians of the time of our Gospels,[2] and which their account of the event of the Baptism seems expressly designed to confute.[3] The solution which ultimately prevailed, and which is incorporated in the Roman catechism, was that Jesus had himself baptized in order to consecrate the water and endow it with sacramental power, that is to say, in order to institute the rite of Baptism. Surely, if the incident had not really taken place, the simplest way would have been not to invent it. However, since the simplest way is not always the one chosen by the gospel editors, and their deeper motives are not always visible to us, it would be rash to deduce from this any positive conclusion, and we can only say that it appears *probable* that Jesus came to the baptism of John.

We must, moreover, observe, on the other hand, that Q, though including the Baptist and his preaching of repentance,

---

[1] CCLIX, 63.

[2] " *Ergo peccavit Christus, quia baptizatus est,*" writes Manes, in *Acta Archelai*, 60. *Cf.* CXLII, 110 *ff.* By way of contrast we may quote this curious fragment of the *Gospel of the Hebrews*, preserved by Saint Jerome, *C. Pelag.*, iii, 2 : " *Ecce mater domini et fratres ejus dicebant ei : Joannes baptista baptizat in remissionem peccatorum, eamus et baptizemur ab eo. Dixit autem eis : Quid peccavi, ut vadam et baptizer ab eo? Nisi forte hoc ipsum quod dixi ignorantia est.*"

[3] CIII, i, 497 ; CLXXXII, i, 399 *ff.*

does not appear to have mentioned the baptism of Jesus, and that, consequently, it is not unreasonable to hold that the whole legend, in substance as well as in form, came from the Hellenistic community, which might have composed it under the influence of its own liturgy, to represent the ceremonial investiture of Jesus with the Messiahship.[1]

Assuming, however, that the Nazarene did come to the baptism of John, we are confronted by the question of its significance for him. Did he then receive the inner revelation of his prophetic mission?[2] Did he have a vision, in which was suddenly resolved a long and obscure working of his mind, possibly as mysterious to him as to us? A psychologist would say that it was very probable; the historian must confess that he cannot tell.

II

AFTER THE BAPTISM

According to the Synoptic tradition, the Spirit which took possession of Jesus at the moment of his baptism drove him into the wilderness, where in solitude, amidst terrible temptations, his vocation matured. (Mark i. 12–13, and Syn.) He began to preach only after the arrest of the Baptist, at least, on the testimony of Mark (i. 14) and Matthew (iv. 12), for Luke (iv. 14) does not mention John in this connexion. Henceforth he did no more than repeat what was probably the theme of his predecessor : " The time is fulfilled and the Kingdom of God is at hand ; repent ye, and believe in the gospel " (Mark i. 15).

The incident of the temptation is completely legendary, and each of our three Synoptists has embroidered the main theme as he saw fit. The accounts of Matthew (iv. 1–11) and Luke (iv. 1–13) are sheer hagiographical imagination. But it is reasonable to ask whether, under the all too obvious fiction,

---

[1] **LXXXVI**, 153. Goguel writes (**CLVI**-*a*, 251) " that it is impossible to cast any doubt upon " the baptism of Jesus at the hands of John. We are far from being so easily convinced.

[2] It is to be noted that the descent of the Spirit upon a man meant no more, according to the Jewish belief, than " a special call to a given work." It is in this way that the Spirit affects Gideon (Judges vi. 34), Jephthah (Judges xi. 29), Samson (Judges xiii. 25), Saul (1 Sam. x. 6, 10), etc., and it is certainly in this way that Acts x. 37 *ff*. indicates the Baptism of Jesus when it asserts that he has been anointed with the Holy Ghost and divine power (ὡς ἔχρισεν αὐτὸν ὁ θεὸς πνεύματι ἁγίῳ καὶ δυνάμει).

there might not be some truth ; whether this supposed withdrawal to the wilderness might not reflect the actual knowledge that Jesus did not begin to preach immediately after his
baptism ; whether, in short, this space of forty days (a conventional number, used " at random " by the Jews " in their
writings and traditions ") [1] does not represent an indefinite
period of private preparation of which nothing was known. [2]

Here, again, the absence of documentary evidence reduces
our curiosity to impotence. If the tradition had really preserved the memory of a kind of period of doubt before the
beginning of the public life of Jesus, the gospel writers have
placed this recollection in a very different light. As soon as
faith arrived at the idea that the Messianic consecration coincided with the Baptism, the myth of the Temptation arose to
satisfy the accepted belief—which is embodied in the Apocalypse—that the Messiah had to strive with Satan and vanquish
him. [3] For the Jews (Isa. xiii. 21 ; xxxiv. 14 f. ; Lev. xvi.)
as for the Egyptians, [4] the favourite habitation of the powers
of evil was the wilderness. It is to be noted that the incident
does not occur in John, an omission which throws a clear light
on the purpose of the Synoptics. For the Fourth Gospel, Jesus,
being the incarnation of the eternal *logos*, was *ipso facto* master
of all the powers of the underworld. The ecstasy of the man
of God in solitude [5] is a well-known theme, and it is possible
that at least two oriental myths, that of Zarathustra and that
of Buddha, influenced the gospel account. Zarathustra, [6] too,
was thirty years old when *Vohu mano*, god as mind and spirit,
descended into him. At the same time he was tempted by
Angra Mainyu, the principle of evil, who offered him dominion
over the world if he would but renounce the law and service
of *Ahura-Mazda*. The Bodhisatva, the future Buddha, also
underwent a temptation by *Mara*, the Evil One, and his band.
It is recounted at length in *Lalita Vistara*, xxi, [7] and its similarity
to that of Jesus is undeniable. [8] This resemblance, however,
does not mean that the Synoptic legends were copies, or even
conscious imitations, but merely that they were influenced by
themes well known and widely disseminated in the East.

[1] **XVI**, ii, 134. Moses remains upon Sinai forty days and forty
nights (Exod. xxxiv. 28) ; Elijah takes forty days and forty nights to
reach Horeb (1 Kings xix. 8).

[2] See **CLXXVI**, 611, for the quite unfounded theory of Westberg,
who proposes to substitute ten years for the forty days.

[3] **CIII**, i, 185.   [4] **XXIV**, i, 94.   [5] **X**, 33.

[6] **XLVIII**, 70 ; **CCL**, 177. Texts to be found in **CCLXXXV**, 221 *ff*.

[7] **CCLXXXV**, 162 *ff*.

[8] **CCLVIII**, 50. For the opposed view, **XLI**, 247.

According to Mark, it was during this period of Jesus' meditation that the Baptist disappeared at the command of Herod Antipas.[1] Then, seeing that the great voice " crying in the wilderness " had been silenced, and feeling it impossible to leave the imminent Kingdom with no one to proclaim it, the Nazarene is supposed, in his turn, to have lifted up his voice and announced his mission. Thus John was, if we may so put it, the threefold cause of the appearance of Jesus : (1) the fame of the prophet drew him from his village, and led him, already deeply stirred, to the banks of the Jordan ; (2) the baptism revealed to him his vocation ; (3) the arrest of John put an end to his doubts, and thrust him into the path perforce abandoned by the stormy preacher. This course of development, which seems consistent enough in all its parts, has a very human quality which recommends it to the historian as well as to the psychologist. But unfortunately there is nothing to support it except the interpretation of a few verses, which in reality may have quite a different meaning, and an inference implicit in the gospel narrative.

To accept it disposes at once of the much discussed question of the personal relations between Jesus and the Baptist after the Baptism. Inasmuch as Mark i. 12 states that the Spirit *at once* ($\varepsilon\dot{\upsilon}\theta\dot{\upsilon}\varsigma$) drove the newly-baptized Jesus into the wilderness ($\varkappa\alpha\grave{\iota}$ $\varepsilon\dot{\upsilon}\theta\dot{\upsilon}\varsigma$ $\tau\grave{o}$ $\pi\nu\varepsilon\tilde{\upsilon}\mu\alpha$ $\alpha\dot{\upsilon}\tau\grave{o}\nu$ $\dot{\varepsilon}\varkappa\beta\dot{\alpha}\lambda\lambda\varepsilon\iota$ $\varepsilon\dot{\iota}\varsigma$ $\tau\grave{\eta}\nu$ $\ddot{\varepsilon}\varrho\eta\mu\sigma\nu$) there can be no question of his having tarried with John at all. There is reason, however, to be somewhat mistrustful of the impression conveyed by Mark on this point. " Sayings " attributed to Jesus concerning the Baptist and his disciples are scattered throughout the gospel narrative, and it is impossible to consider them as a whole [2] without becoming convinced that the original Christian community took a great and constant interest in these people,[3] and must have owed them a great deal—possibly, for instance, the practices of fasting and common prayer, and certainly the institution of baptism itself, adapted to their own requirements. The legend of the Forerunner is essentially an adoption of John by the Christian sect.[4] Does it not look as if Jesus simply came from John's following, as if he had been an actual disciple of the Baptist, and his own movement were a kind of offshoot and successor of the other ? These questions may, of course, be asked whether or not we accept the historical truth of the incident of the Baptism. They have, however, no answers except those based upon personal impressions, for there is no documentary

[1] **XXIX**, i, 437 *ff.*   [2] *Cf.* **CCLIX**, ch. ii, and ch. iii, 1.
[3] **CXCIII**, 46.   [4] **XXIV**, i, 90.

evidence which definitely solves them.[1] The reasoning which claims to include John, his disciples, and Jesus, under the title of Nazarenes, as indicative of their original and fundamental fellowship,[2] is very dubious. The name is not in itself clear enough to serve as the sole basis for a conclusion of such importance, and it would be difficult to find, apart from that, the smallest proof of this contention.

It may, indeed, be judged that the similarity asserted by our Gospel between the essential features of the preaching of John and of Jesus, proves that there was a spiritual relationship between the two prophets.[3] But to declare as decidedly as certain modern critics have done, that " Jesus was, for a period of which it is, unfortunately, impossible to estimate the duration, even approximately [sic], the disciple of John the Baptist," [4] we should have to add to the paltry fragments of information which may still linger in the passages just referred to, and a few others,[5] a personal conviction which the present writer cannot feel. How are we to be sure that John really said the things attributed to him by the Gospels ? Even if he did, however, say them, and Jesus repeated them after him, that hardly justifies us in concluding that they both united in saying them for a certain period in Galilee or elsewhere—who knows ?—and that during that time Jesus was the disciple of the Baptist.

Granting this relation of disciple and master between the two prophets, their separation has to be explained. The execution, or at least the imprisonment, of the Baptist might, perhaps, suffice. Jesus would continue alone the work begun by his master, and at first followed along with him. The objection to this is that he seems to have continued it quite differently, to have adopted different ways, to have spoken with a different emphasis, and to have employed different methods.[6] He leaves the desert and travels round the towns of Galilee ; he mingles with the life of the people, abandons ascetic practices, and refuses to baptize. Renan, who doubted this last point,[7] was unquestionably mistaken. In the first

[1] CLXXVI, 391 ; CCXXXII, 18 ; CCXLV, 114 ; CCLIX, 235, 252 *ff*.
[2] CLXVI, 14 ; CXLV, 26.
[3] Mark i. 15 ; Matt. iv. 17 ; Mark vi. 12 ; Matt. x. 7 ; Luke ix. 2 ; x. 9 ; passages in which Jesus is supposed to repeat the phrases previously uttered by the Baptist (Mark i. 4 ; Matt. iii. 2).
[4] CCLIX, 235.
[5] Goguel reviews them all, and treats them with an indulgence which in the opinion of the present writer they hardly deserve.—*Cf.* CLVI-*a*, 246-61.
[6] L-*a*, i, 173.　　　　　[7] CLXVIII, 107.

place, there is not a passage of the Synoptics which shows us Jesus either performing or preaching baptism, with the exception, of course, of the famous : " Go ye therefore and teach all the nations, baptizing them in the name of the Father, and of the Son, and of the Holy Ghost," which is put by Matthew (xxviii. 19) into the mouth of the risen Christ, and which no judicious critic for a moment regards as authentic. In the second place, we have in John iv. 2 a perfectly conclusive statement : " Jesus himself baptized not, but his disciples." The gospel writer would never have said that, at a time when baptism had become an indispensable rite of initiation into Christianity,[1] and its institution had necessarily to be ascribed to the Lord himself, if the evidence of the tradition had not compelled him to do so. His assertion has all the more weight in that it appears in the form of a correction, for the editor has already said (iii. 22) that Jesus baptized (καὶ ἐβάπτιζεν), and (iv. 1) that he made and baptized more disciples than John had done. These statements have been made with his mind on the results of the preaching of Jesus, and the custom which, in his own time, would have consecrated them, and not on the personal practice of the Lord, and when he thinks of the latter he at once corrects himself.[2] If Jesus was for some time the disciple and companion of John, he may, like him, have baptized, but of that we are completely ignorant. All that we know is, that when he began to act on his own account, he did not make use of baptism.

The reasons which might have severed the association of the two preachers, and have caused the kind of difference which distinguishes them, have been sought in our Gospels, and it has even been believed that they had been found. The writer, however, is completely sceptical of this discovery, and will therefore say nothing on the subject, beyond referring the reader to a book in which it is set forth with great confidence and ingenuity.[3] There seems to us no means of finding out whether John and Jesus preached together, or whether they separated,

---

[1] Cf. the pronouncement attributed to Jesus by John iii. 5 : " Except a man be born of water and of the Spirit, he cannot enter into the kingdom of God."

[2] Renan held that our John iv. 2 was only a secondary gloss, but as such, there would be no point in it.

[3] **CCLIX,** 257 ff. We are compelled to say that Goguel's thesis is more like a new edifice than a restoration. The use which he makes of the texts seems to strain them unduly, and to insert into their fragmentary accounts considerations which belong to religious psychology, rather than to verifiable history, and are always disputable because they are largely subjective.

or why, and we can only envy those to whom the situation appears less obscure.

Our first conclusion concerning this crucial problem of the advent of Jesus is that it is a clear and particularly telling illustration of the gulf that is set between our curiosity and the facts, by uncertain, vague, and inconsistent documents, which are capable of the most diverse interpretations, and may be used to support or to contradict, at will, the most dissimilar theories. Our second is that it is better to resign ourselves to ignorance than to imagine what we wish to know. There is a possibility that the vocation of Jesus was determined in some Messianic sect; there is a possibility that he awoke to his mission at the baptism of John; there is a possibility that he may have been, if one cares to put it that way, a disciple of the Baptist, that is to say, that his impulse was derived, in a manner of which we know nothing, from the obscure precedent established by the Baptist sect. This last possibility may perhaps even be ranked as a probability. But on the whole, we are so completely ignorant on the essential points, between us and the recollections which possibly still existed in the time of our Gospels there is such a tangle of thorny undergrowth, that we can, in truth, no longer find our way. Of that which appears to us as possible or probable, perhaps no portion is true, and it is the part of wisdom to admit that the final verdict of criticism is that the true explanation of what happened is for ever denied us.

CHAPTER VII

JESUS AT THE TIME OF HIS PUBLIC CAREER

IT would be of the greatest interest to us to have some definite
information regarding the personality of Jesus, his physical
and mental characteristics, but unfortunately, the first Christians took no interest in these essential biographical details,
or, at any rate, they paid no attention to them.

I

THE PERSONAL APPEARANCE OF JESUS

No description of the person of Jesus has come down to us,
except in wholly unauthenticated legends of a much later
period.[1] These legends were based upon two traditions, which
arose, one after the other, out of considerations quite unrelated
to the facts of his history. The more ancient of the two grew
out of the belief that Jesus had chosen to assume upon earth
a lowly guise, an idea which was founded upon the famous passage of Isaiah (liii. 2–3), in which the Servant of Jahweh is
described as the meanest of men, a figure totally devoid of
beauty or impressiveness. Hence it was that Justin could
write [2] that Christ " was manifested without beauty or dignity,
as said Isaiah, David, and all the Scriptures," Irenæus [3] characterizes him as *infirmus* and *ingloriosus*, and even *indecorus*.
Clement of Alexandria, arguing that true beauty is not physical,
does not fail to remind us that the Lord was not beautiful in
the flesh,[4] a belief to which he several times refers.[5] Origen
improves upon it by adding that Jesus was small, ill-favoured
and insignificant.[6] Commodian, writing for the general public,

---

[1] They have been collected and studied by von Dobschütz, *Christusbilder*, and, more recently, by G. Müller, *Die leibliche Gestalt Jesu Christi
nach der schriftlichen und monumentalen Urtradition*, 1909. See also the
same author's *Christusbilder*, in RE, iv, 63 *ff*., and CXLII, 311 *ff*.

[2] *Dial.*, 85, 1.

[3] *Hær.*, 4, 33, 12 ; *cf*. 3, 19, 2.   [4] *Pædag.*, 3, 1, 3.

[5] *Strom.*, 5, 2, 22 ; 3, 17, 103 ; 6, 17, 151.

[6] *Contra Celsum*, 6, 75 : μικρὸν καὶ δυσειδὲς καὶ ἀγεννές.

164

declares that, on the evidence of Isaiah, he was of humble and
mean appearance, and looked like a slave :

> " Hunc ipsum Esaias humilem denuntiat esse
> Et nimis dejectum, fuerit quasi servi figura." [1]

Tertullian, Saint Cyprian, Hippolytus, etc., were all of the same
opinion.[2] A very early tradition goes still further, and claims
that the Lord was a leper.[3]

The Olympian ideal of the coincidence of beauty and divinity
was, however, too widely disseminated for simple-minded
believers to picture Christ otherwise,[4] and the sarcophagi often
display a flattering representation of him. In order the better
to convey his greatness, he is naïvely represented as much taller
than those who are speaking to him or who surround him.[5]
There was, moreover, another passage, Psalm xlv. 2, which
could be cited against that of Isaiah : " Thou art fairer than
the children of men, grace is poured into thy lips." From the
time of Clement of Alexandria, the controversy was in full
swing, and contradictory assertions abounded, with no [6]
promise of a satisfactory solution. The dispute actually lasted
until the fourth and fifth centuries, with great animation on
both sides, but the partisans of ugliness eventually lost ground.
They numbered amongst them, indeed, Basil and Cyril of
Alexandria, who did not hesitate to maintain, with his customary extravagance, that Christ was " the ugliest of the children of men " ; but they had against them Gregory of Nyssa,
John Chrysostom, Ambrose, Augustine, Jerome, Theodoret,
and all the practice of iconographic art. They were, accordingly, practically vanquished, but their defeat merely represents
the triumph of Psalm xlv. over Isaiah liii., and adds nothing
to our knowledge of the appearance of Jesus.

There is not much to be expected of the supposed portraits
and descriptions, which had varying fortunes during antiquity
and the Middle Ages, and some of which have come down to
us. Their production began very early. The Carpocratian
Gnostics, according to Irenæus,[7] possessed some, and Eusebius

---

[1] *Carmen apolog.*, 335 *ff*.

[2] Tertullian, *De carne Chr.*, 9 ; Cyprian, *Testimon.*, 2, 13 ; Hippolytus, *De Antichr.*, 44 ; *cf. Acta Petri*, 24 ; *Oracula Sib.*, viii, 256 *ff*.

[3] **CXXXII**, 205.

[4] Le Blant, *Les sarcophages chrét. de la Gaule*, Introd., vii *ff*.

[5] Le Blant, *op. cit.*, 20, nos. 19, 20, and 21.

[6] *Strom.*, 2, 5, 21. Other references in **CXXXII**, 312 *ff*.

[7] *Hær.*, 1, 25, 6 : " . . . *imagines quasdam quidem depictas quasdam
autem et de reliqua materia fabricatas . . . dicentes formam Christi
factam a Pilato, illo in tempore quo fuit Jesus cum hominibus.*"

knew others,[1] as also did Saint Augustine,[2] who testifies both
to the absence of any authentic picture of Christ (*qua fuerit ille
facie nos penitus ignoramus*) and to the variety of the imaginary
likenesses (*dominicæ facies carnis innumerabilium cogitationum
diversitate variatur et fingitur*). Of these pseudo-portraits,
almost all those which pretended to authenticity ended up by
claiming a miraculous origin. The others, which early legend
freely attributed to Saint Luke, have disappeared, except
possibly one or two, for instance, that in the cathedral of
Moscow. One of these " acheiropoietic " images, that is to
say, not made by the hand of man, the Veronica, of which the
original is at Rome, exists today in thousands of reproductions
throughout the Christian world, and another, the one imprinted
upon the Sacred Shroud of Turin, has lately even been arousing
the interest of the daily press. There is no need to go into the
subject of devout frauds or pious illusions,[3] but a word must
be said concerning one description which even today deceives
the ignorant, and which the image makers of Saint Sulpice are
constantly distributing, accompanied by a portrait which is
supposed to embody it. It is necessary to mention it, because
Robert Eisler, whose love of paradox is deterred by no
anomaly, has quite recently attempted to secure for it the
credence of scholars. We refer to the Letter of Lentulus.[4]

The supposed author, a certain Publius Lentulus, who calls
himself " Governor of Jerusalem," addresses to the Senate and
People of Rome the following communication :

> " There has appeared here in our time, and still lives here, a
> man of great power (*magnæ virtutis*) named Jesus Christ. The people
> call him a prophet of truth (*propheta veritatis*), and his disciples,
> the Son of God. He raises the dead and cures the sick. He is,
> in stature, a man of middle height and well proportioned (*statura
> procerus mediocris et spectabilis*). He has a venerable face (*vultum
> habens venerabilem*), of a sort to arouse both fear and love in those
> who see him. His hair is the colour of ripe chestnuts,[5] smooth
> almost to the ears (*planos fere usque ad aures*) but above them wav-
> ing and curling, with a slight bluish radiance (*aliquantulum ceruliores
> et fulgentiores*), and it flows over his shoulders. It is parted in the
> middle on the top of his head, after the fashion of the people of
> Nazareth. His brow is smooth and very calm, with a face without

---

[1] Eusebius, *H.E.*, 7, 18, 4.

[2] Augustine, *De Trinitate*, 8, 4-5.

[3] A detailed study of all the " acheiropoietic " representations will
be found in CC. On the Holy Shroud see also CE, *Shroud* (*The holy*).

[4] For the history of the question see : CE, *Lentulus*, on the text
and its variants ; CC, 319 *ff.* ; CLIV, ii, 337, 344 *ff.*, and the references
in the index under the word *Lentulus*.

[5] We adopt the reading *permature*. *Premature*, which is that accepted
by von Dobschütz, seems unintelligible.

wrinkle or blemish, [lightly] tinged with red (*quam rubor* [*moderatus*] *venustat*). His nose and mouth are faultless. His beard is luxuriant [and unclipped] (*copiosam* [*et impuberem*]) of the same colour as his hair, not long, but parted (*bifurcatam*) at the chin. His countenance is full of simplicity and maturity. His eyes are expressive and brilliant. He is terrible in reproof, sweet and gentle in admonition, cheerful without ceasing to be grave. He has never been seen to laugh, but often to weep. His figure is slender and erect (*in statura corporis propagatus et rectus*) ; his hands and arms are beautiful to see. His conversation is serious, sparing, and modest. He is the fairest of the children of men."

The text varies from manuscript to manuscript,[1] the main points being rich in eulogistic variants. One concluding sentence is worth quoting, because it exceeds all the limits of probability with admirable ingenuity, while adhering to the main tenor of the text.

> *Ipse enim est rex gloriæ in quem desiderant angeli prospicere, cuius pulchritudinem sol et luna miratur, salvator mundi, auctor vitæ, ipsi honor et gloria in æternum. Amen.*"

It is hardly necessary to point out the details which betray the evident falsity of the document. There was no " Governor of Jerusalem " in Jesus' day ; no Lentulus plays any part whatever in the Jewish history of those times ; and in the reign of Tiberius a subordinate official would never have ventured to write directly " to the Senate and People of Rome," a form of address, furthermore, which had no longer any meaning. Moreover, what could have been the purpose of such a letter ? There is only one to be discerned, that of giving partisan evidence concerning Jesus ; but the terms in which it is couched make it impossible that it could have come from a Roman official. One of the Twelve would not have displayed such conformity to the orthodox beliefs of the future ; he would not have called his master Jesus Christ, nor have described him as the Son of God, any more than he would have identified him with the fairest of the children of men, as does this Roman who is so expert at quoting the Psalms.[2] It is probable, however, that the introduction of the name of Lentulus into the forgery does not go back very far. In the oldest manuscripts (Series " *a* " of Von Dobschütz) it begins with the words : " *legitur in annalibus libris Romanorum*," and is thus presented as an anonymous historical record. The form of a letter can-

---

[1] Von Dobschütz has examined more than seventy-five manuscripts, and a large number of printed editions and translations.

[2] One variant makes the quotation definite by introducing it with the words : " So that one might justly say of him, according to the prophet, . . ."

not have been given to it prior to the fifteenth century, and probably represents an "improvement" introduced by some Humanist. The description itself does not appear to have been known in the West before the fourteenth century.[1]

The question would be closed, but for the fact that it is possible to differentiate the portrait from its frame, and to ask if its component details may not have come from an ancient source, and possibly a reliable one. It is on the strength of this possibility that M. Eisler has reached the conclusion that, in the main, the letter of Lentulus gives us the "description" of Jesus contained in the warrant for his arrest issued by Pilate. That sounds too good to be true, and it would be difficult to explain why not one of the Christian writers of antiquity who have been preserved to us, appears to know anything about so interesting a document, which would have so effectively settled all the disputes concerning the *facies* of the Lord Jesus. Two eastern writers, Nicephorus Callistus [2] (who wrote in the first half of the fourteenth century, but reproduced a chronicle belonging to the tenth) and John Damascene [3] (middle of the eighth century), do, indeed, give portraits of Christ which they claim to have taken from the "old authors" (δι αρχαῖοι—δι αρχαῖοι ἱστορικοί), and which it has been sought to relate to that of the letter of Lentulus. John Damascene need not be considered, for he merely describes a conventional figure, such as was frequently reproduced in the religious art of his time. His Christ has, moreover, a black beard (γενειάδα μέλανα ἔχοντα) which is sufficient to destroy all resemblance to the "type" of the pseudo-Lentulus. The portrait depicted by Callistus, on the contrary, approximates to this type in several rather striking ways. The beard and hair are tawny (σιτόχρους—the colour of ripe wheat); the head has never been shorn by a human hand; the face is slightly ruddy (ὀλίγον ἐπιφοινισσομένην). A special detail which the author emphasizes is the resemblance of Jesus to his mother. None of this is, however, sufficient to guarantee the antiquity of the substance of the pseudo-Lentulus. The probability is, that the chronicler of Nicephorus Callistus, like the author of the "portrait" on which the "letter" of Lentulus was based, was inspired by some iconographic likeness well known in the East at the beginning of the Middle Ages, one of the "acheiro-poietics," or of the pictures attributed to Luke. It has been suggested,[4] and not without some show of reason, that a pagan

[1] CC, 330 ff.   [2] *Histoire ecclés.*, 1, 40, in *P.G.*, CXLV, col. 747 ff.
[3] *Epist. ad Theophilum imperatorem*, 3, in *P.G.*, XCV, col. 350.
[4] CXXXII, 205.

type well known in the decline of the ancient world, that of Serapis, which the artists endowed with a grave and serene beauty, a very noble air of majesty, a direct and piercing glance, parted hair, and a cleft beard, had served the Christians as a model when they desired to portray the features of the " fairest of the children of men." The incompatible representations of which we have spoken, and the definite statement of Saint Augustine : " *nos penitus ignoramus*," together with the silence of the Fathers concerning the contents of the letter of Lentulus, suffice to relegate this clumsy document to the company of the forgeries with which the simple-minded consoled their ignorance, and which were, in fact, expressly manufactured to please them.

We shall say nothing about the vast amount that has been written regarding the charm which is supposed to have emanated from the person of Jesus, except, flatly, that it belongs to literature, and that not of the best. The complex charm of the Gospel must not be confused with the personal impression produced by the Nazarene. The attraction of his mind, which we can, perhaps, still feel in reading the parables, for instance, is one thing ; the magnetism which may have radiated from his countenance is another, and one for which there is no evidence. A " wonderfully beautiful "[1] soul may not shine forth at all from the face of its possessor, and we do not know the " soul " of Jesus in sufficient detail to deduce from it anything about his personal appearance.

II

THE MENTAL CHARACTERISTICS OF JESUS

It has been supposed possible to obtain from our gospel writings some light on the mental characteristics of Jesus. Works of various kinds, some scientific,[2] others inexact or imaginative in method,[3] have been devoted to the examina-

[1] V, i, 316.

[2] CCXXXII, in which is to be found a brief but conclusive critical examination of earlier works : Loosten, W. Hirsch, Binet-Sanglé, Rasmussen.

[3] Binet-Sanglé, *La folie de Jesus*, Paris, 1908, which professes to examine Jesus from the point of view of clinical psychiatry. The replies to the psychiatrists by Knieb (*Moderne-Leben-Jesu-Forschung unter dem Einflusse der Psychiatrie*, Mayence, 1908), Werner (*Die psychische Gesundheit Jesu*, Gross-Lichterfelde, 1909), Sanday (*Christologies ancient and modern*, Oxford, 1910), and H. Schæfer (*Jesus in psychiatrischer Beleuchtung*, Berlin, 1910), are as much enslaved by

tion of the problem in all its aspects. " Erudite amusements,"
wrote Loisy on one occasion with regard to one of them, and
he expressed exactly the feeling of the critic who is confronted
by these inductions and deductions, which, however clever they
may be, are all equally flimsy. It must be admitted, however,
that our professional or amateur psychiatrists do not write to
amuse themselves, or even to amuse us, and they are not always
erudite. What makes their utterances unconvincing is their
lack of clinical observation, for which the texts furnish no data,
together with their failure to realize that, for the most part,
they are incapable of understanding properly what they read
in the texts. They are usually astonished to hear that, but it
is the obvious truth. A brief outline of their principal arguments will be sufficient to prove it.

The starting point of their researches is to be found in a
remark of Strauss, in his first *Life of Jesus*, to the effect that
a man who was obsessed with a Danielic vision of the world,
who called himself the Son of Man, who believed himself to be
the Messiah, and who prophesied his speedy return by way of
the skies, in divine glory, must have been mentally abnormal.
Jesus, in other words, showed signs of a well-marked patho-
logical fanaticism. Strauss, however, refrained from drawing
this conclusion, because he observed, in addition to these
extravagances, a number of other points which indicated that
Jesus was a sensible man (*ein besonnener Mann*), and also because
he realized the strong influence of Jewish Messianism upon
him.[1] When he took up the question again, in the second
Life, in 1864, he seemed to be much more impressed by the
predominance of the visionary element (*das Abenteuerliche*) in
his hero, and at that time he wrote to Lang, that he regarded
the Galilean as " on the verge of insanity " (*als dem Wahrsinn
ganz nahe*).[2] The critical researches prosecuted by liberal
theology since the time of Strauss have laid especial stress on
the eschatological character of the preaching of Jesus, and have,
in so doing, given colour to the suggestions of the veteran
scholar—excessive megalomania, visionary fanaticism, symptoms and proofs of mental disease. The following is a summary of the diagnosis made by the psychiatrists : (1) *Megalomania* : It is quite incompatible with mental health that he
should believe himself the Son of God, the future Judge of the

terms and illusions as the theories they claim to overthrow. A less
extravagant, but still unconvincing work, is that of G. Berguer, *Quelques
traits de la vie de Jésus au point de vue psychologique et psychanalytique*,
Geneva and Paris, 1920.

[1] *Leben Jesu*, 1835, ii, 1480 *ff*.   [2] **CCXXXII**, 3.

Universe, and announce his triumphal return on the clouds of heaven ; (2) *Hallucinations* : the incidents at the time of the Baptism, in the wilderness, on the Mountain of the Transfiguration, in Gethsemane, etc., are all bad symptoms ; (3) *Dromomania* : for a man to wander, for three years, about a little country, always moving from place to place, always unsettled, is not normal ; (4) *Obvious indications of insanity* : for example, the cursing of the fig tree, consigned to destruction because it did not bear fruit out of season ; (5) *Unhealthy self-absorption* : borne witness to by the fact that all the discourses and teachings of Jesus centre about the word " I " ; (6) Various physiological symptoms of an abnormal condition : (*a*) of the vasomotor system : the sweat of blood (Luke xxii. 44), which is in reality a facial " *hematidrosis* " ; (*b*) of the digestive apparatus : the attack of " *sitiophobia* " which impels him to fast for forty days ; (*c*) of the respiratory organs : the weakness which rendered him incapable of carrying his cross ; the pleurotubercular effusion revealed by the lance-thrust on the cross ; (*d*) of the genital organs : his saying concerning those who voluntarily undergo castration for the sake of the Kingdom of Heaven (Matt. xix. 12) ; his glorification of sterility in Luke xxiii. 29 : " Blessed are the barren, and the wombs which never bare, and the paps which never gave suck " ; his attitude of timidity towards women, which was not that of a true male (Binet-Sanglé), etc. ; (*e*) *Oedipism*, or the tendency to mutilation : " If thy right eye offend thee, pluck it out. . . . If thy right hand offend thee, cut it off. . . ." (Matt. v. 29–30) ; (7) *The definite testimony of his family* (" He is out of his mind," Mark iii. 21) and his enemies (" He hath Beelzebub," Mark iii. 22), which leaves no doubt that he was mentally affected. The only question is, in precisely what way, and here our psychiatrists diverge, some voting for *paranoia*, which is a very elastic term, others for *epilepsy*, which is hardly less so.[1]

Glancing through the writings from which these dogmatic conclusions have been extracted, it is at once evident that their authors, with the exception of Rasmussen, who is more judicious and better informed than the others, have not the slightest knowledge of source criticism. They quote the four Gospels indiscriminately, and on the same footing (so much so that three-quarters of the material used by Loosten, Hirsch, and Binet-Sanglé comes from John), without apparently suspecting that there are any precautions to be taken or any distinctions to be made. They do not even hesitate to use Apocryphal Gospels, and Binet-Sanglé, for instance, calmly applies for

[1] **CCXXXII**, 26.

information—how valuable, we can judge—to the *Protevangelium of James* or the *History of Joseph the Carpenter*. The Talmud, Celsus, anyone and anything, are interrogated and believed without a shadow of critical misgiving. This really amazing lack of caution is aggravated by a complete ignorance of the most elementary methods and principles of exegesis. Our psychiatrists take at its face value everything they find in the Gospels ; there is no statement too fantastic or indefensible to be accepted by them. For instance, an account as suspect as the one in Luke showing Jesus in the Temple in the midst of the doctors, at the age of twelve, is made a basis of diagnosis, especially by Hirsch. The sojourn in the wilderness, and the Temptation, which are quite unhistorical, represent for Binet-Sanglé the " hallucinatory phase " of the development of paranoia in Jesus. The most disputable incidents, even those which, to the veriest tyro in criticism, are obviously unreliable, are taken seriously and interpreted in terms of psychiatry. Binet-Sanglé has even gone so far as to say [1] that if the authors of the Gospels were not strictly accurate historians, they must have been *physicians*, to have assembled so many symptomatic details. Neurologists and alienists, in other words ! Reviewed one after the other by a competent critic, restored to their context and their actual meaning, the " symptomatic details " that are esteemed by our psychiatrists to be most conclusive, lose their point, fall to pieces, disappear, and leave behind them nothing but the obvious and complete impossibility of establishing any such diagnosis.

Nevertheless, even though the theory of a mental condition which today would call for certification be rejected as incapable of demonstration, the impression remains that a man of the people who believed himself empowered to proclaim that the Kingdom of God was at hand, who produced effects on his fellows by magical means, concerning which neurology, for once, has something to say, who came, perhaps, to believe himself chosen to play a predominant, and finally, the principal part, in the apocalyptic catastrophe of his age, who, in short, was swollen with such overweening and naïve arrogance, was not a normal person. But, by definition, a prophet is not an ordinary human being. His calling necessarily implies an exceptional nervous organization, and the presence of stimuli, so to speak, which do not occur in the psychological make-up of everyone. It has been suggested that the main one, in the case of Jesus, was habitual " ecstasy " or vision. Let us pause for a moment over this important question.[2]

[1] *Folie de Jésus,* i[3], 67.   [2] *Cf.* **CLVII,** ii, 126.

It may be observed to begin with that the phenomena of ecstasy were not unfamiliar to the Jews of that time. What Paul relates of his visions and revelations (2 Cor. xii. 1 *ff.*) agrees with what we know of other rabbis. The development of apocalyptic necessarily implies the existence of visionaries and mystics.[1] It was even sometimes supposed that the archangel Michael, prince of the angels, was entrusted with the special mission of transporting the living, in a state of ecstasy, before the throne of God.[2] Hence it is natural to ask this question with regard to Jesus, and it is clear that if it could be answered in the affirmative an effective light would be thrown upon the origin and mechanism of the religious activity of the Nazarene. A German scholar, Oscar Holtzmann, who has distinguished himself by important works on Jesus and his time, has devoted a very interesting book to the problem,[3] a brief synopsis of whose theories will be a convenient approach to the discussion.

According to Holtzmann, Jesus, whose behaviour is often quiet and normal, on other occasions shows definite signs of an ecstatic condition ; the two elements are combined in him (78 *ff.* ; 114 *ff.*). The main argument on which our critic bases this opinion is that Jesus represented himself as " the prince of the world to come," and a state of mind which can entertain such an idea is definitely " ecstatic." The vision of the Baptism from which he derives the assurance of his Messiahship ; his " eschatologico-ecstatic " conception of the Kingdom (p. 30) ; the apocalyptic discourse related by Mark (pp. 57–9) ; the indications of ecstasy, which increase towards the end of his career, such as the designation of his betrayer ; the identification of the broken bread with his own body, and the sacrament of the new Covenant expressed in the cup representing his blood (p. 63) ; the miracles indicative of an ecstatic tendency (p. 90) ; the curses, like that of the tempest and the barren fig tree (p. 99), which are similarly ecstatic ; these are all additional details which confirm what the Messianic " call " of the Nazarene has already demonstrated in general. On the whole, on numerous occasions, those, namely, on which he actually received his principal inspirations, he was probably exalted to that " supreme degree of spiritual excitement " (*im hochsten Grad geistiger Erregung*) which, according to Holtzmann, is characteristic of the state of ecstasy (p. 3). A volcano whose activity may have short interruptions, but which is

[1] II, 356 *ff.* ; IV, 211 *ff.*
[2] *Vita Adam et Evœ*, 25. *Cf.* CCLXXXII, ii, 516, and ii, 382.
[3] CCXII.

generally pouring forth lava and flames, such is the metaphor which most accurately represents Jesus.

If this really was his character, it would be hard to understand why the police of Herod permitted so dangerous a fanatic to remain at large, even for a few weeks. It is true that we do not know the exact circumstances of Jesus' public career, but the account of Mark, read without prejudice, does not give the impression of so excitable a person, or even of a man who was habitually abnormal, or whose motives and impulses were, even occasionally, the result of irrational transports. Moreover, Holtzmann uses the word " ecstatic " to designate states or characterize facts which do not belong to what is usually called ecstasy.[1] The correct meaning of the term seems to be simply *an abnormal and transitory state* of excessive excitement, in which the subject undergoes a kind of suspension of the normal faculty of thinking and feeling, and all consciousness of external things is blotted out, absorbed in an intense spiritual experience. " The subject feels at once freed from himself and possessed by the divine " (Delacroix). If this is the case, Jesus' vision of the Kingdom is not ecstatic, since it and its elements had their origin in the beliefs and expectations already present in the Palestinian community, and did not leap, fully armed, from the agitated brain of the Galilean prophet. It took possession of his mind as an obsession, but it cannot be identified with a repeated ecstasy, and did not even originally proceed from one. Moreover, there is no logical, or even empirical, connexion between ecstasy and eschatology. The one can very well exist without the other, and we may recall, for example, that Philo of Alexandria, who was so much concerned with ecstasy, had very little interest in eschatology. To particularize, it is arbitrary to regard as ecstatic manifestations the designation of Judas as the traitor, the eucharistic acts and symbols, the curses, the miracles, etc. The only incident to which the term can properly be applied appears to be that of the Baptism, with the possible addition of the Temptation in the wilderness and perhaps the Transfiguration, although " on the high mountain " (Mark ix. 2) it was the disciples rather than their Master who had the mystic vision. Perhaps we might also include Luke x. 18 *f.*, where Jesus recounts that he has seen Satan " fall as lightning from heaven," but the statement occurs in a passage (the sermon to the seventy disciples) which has no historical foundation, and even if we assume that

---

[1] **CLXXVI**, 831, n. 1. *Cf.* Delacroix, *La religion et la foi*, Paris, 1922, 250 *ff.*

the words were really uttered, they might easily be merely metaphorical.[1]

The conclusive objection to the theory of Holtzmann is that the majority of the incidents which he regards as evidence, and on which he relies, seem, to an unbiased critic, to be of extremely dubious historicity, or even entirely incredible, and amongst these we may unhesitatingly include the vision of the Baptism, the Temptation, the Transfiguration, and, in the opinion of the writer, the scene on Gethsemane.

Hence his reasoning actually proves nothing. Even admitting, however, for the sake of argument, that Jesus may have had his period of trance (*Verzückung*), like the ancient prophets before him, and Paul after, we are still not at liberty to conclude that he was " an ecstatic," in the sense of being subject to a recognized mental condition which is classed as abnormal. The texts do not give the slightest justification for believing that it was in periods of derangement, when his reason had temporarily left him, that his intimate relationship with God was established. His " experience " of the Father is not at all like a Saint Teresa's experience of Jesus. There is no mystic rapture about it ; it is spoken of quietly and without excitement. According to all the evidence, Jesus lived with God in a continuous tranquil intimacy, not in the memory of rare and in some way supernatural contacts. The life of the apostle Paul " in Christ," that is to say, the union with his Lord of a man perpetually guided by visions and revelations, has little in common with this uneventful communion. Renan has excellently expressed this generally acknowledged truth : [2] " Jesus has no visions ; God does not speak to him from without ; God is in him ; he feels himself to be with God, and what he says of his Father comes from his own heart. He lives in the bosom of God by virtue of a continuous communion ; he does not see him, he feels him." [3]

This is certainly the impression one receives from the Gospels, and there is every probability of its being correct, for the tradition would not have underrated the " gifts " of the Lord. Nevertheless, we should hardly venture to assert as decidedly as Von Soden, that " Jesus had no ecstasy ; apocalyptic imagery did not possess his soul," because impressions are not to be taken for certainty, nor the aims of the interpreters of the tradition for a faithful reflection of reality.

Summing up our conclusions : (1) We must reject the view

[1] LXVII, 141.
[2] LXVII, 142 ; CCXXXIV, 87 ; CLXXV, 75 ; CVIII, 220.
[3] CLXVIII, 75.

that Jesus was " definitely unbalanced." If he was, we do not, and cannot, know it ; (2) The intensity of his religious life, and even the exaggerated opinion he possibly may have had regarding his importance in the eyes of God, and the gifts he had received from heaven, interesting though they may be from a psychological point of view, are not sufficient, taking into account the period and the country in which Jesus lived, to indicate any deep-seated psycho-physical aberration ; (3) The whole of the gospel tradition implies an intense religious temperament, not at all abnormal in his environment, and an endowment of psychic powers which we have no means of analysing, but of which the miracles leave no doubt. All these conclusions, it must be admitted, tell us very little, and are not of much assistance in understanding the mind of the Nazarene.

That he was an enthusiast is certain, else he would have stayed quietly at home. That he was a subject to misleading illusions is equally so, for otherwise he would not have believed the Kingdom to be so near, nor have imagined that he was to usher it in. But of what there was behind these phenomena we have no knowledge whatever.

III

The Psychological Characteristics of Jesus

The most superficial inquiry into what might be called the " psychological aspect " of Jesus, his character, his mind, his religious feeling, reveals insuperable difficulties. There have, to be sure, been no lack of attempts to surmount them, sometimes attended with some show of success, but the methods employed give us small confidence in the results obtained by means of them. It has been stated, for instance,[1] that it would be better to employ the *logia* and the parables in an endeavour to reconstruct the personality of Jesus, at least on its religious side, than to subject them to rash attempts at " unification " in a coherent didactic system, in the hope of reproducing his teaching as a whole. It is his personality which is really reflected in all these sayings and incidents. Their very preservation shows that those who heard them regarded them as characteristic. Such an endeavour could be made, certainly, and would promise a great deal, providing : (1) that we had any certain means of sifting all this gospel material so as to avoid being led astray by the additions or expansions which

[1] CLX, 107 *ff.*

came from the environment of the Gospels and not from Jesus, and hence are concerned with the Christ, and not the Nazarene ; (2) that we were certain of being able to interpret correctly these *logia* and *parables*, which have come down to us detached from their setting, that is to say, the circumstances in which they were uttered, which determined their true meaning ; (3) that we could be confident that these disjointed fragments of a whole of which we are ignorant, really represented the essential features of the personality in question, and that it was possible for us to restore their original connexion.   But inasmuch as none of these conditions is fulfilled, the method recommended is obviously useless.

The same thing may be said of the attempt to arrive at an understanding of Christ through the feelings with which the primitive Christian community regarded him.   It is perfectly true that the personality of the Master made a very strong impression upon his disciples.   Otherwise the revival of their faith, after the access of despair which dispersed them at the time of his arrest, would be incomprehensible.   But that is not to say that their religious life, when they reorganized it in common, was a reflection of his own inner life.   If all that is meant is that it was the essence of the teaching received from him which remained the mainspring of their faith, we readily assent.   But that fact does not take us very far in our knowledge of the personality of the prophet.   Moreover, it was the *glorified* Jesus who was the centre of the faith of these disciples, its divine support and impregnable justification.   In other words, the real work of that faith was the laying of the foundation of the Christological structure, which could only be achieved by the gradual effacement of the Galilean *nabi*, known and loved by his disciples, in the interests of Christ, the god.   He was effaced, not perhaps from their hearts, which are inscrutable to us, but from their faith, which we know very imperfectly through the most mixed and uncertain of the New Testament writings.   It is certainly not on the basis of the information contained in Acts that we may venture any inferences as to his psychology.

There is hardly any subject whose discussion has been more, and more disastrously, beset with sentimental illusions and extravagant expressions, even in professedly scientific works. It has even been seriously claimed that " intuition " could in this case supply the deficiency of documentary evidence, that is, that the blindest and most unreliable of feelings could be substituted for the positive and objective data of historical information.   But this is not the place to expatiate on these pious aberrations, and we have mentioned them only because they still delude so many.[1]

Psychological reconstructions are hardly less difficult than those of archæology, where beautiful fragments are worth more than a new structure, which rarely goes beyond a mere resemblance, and which destroys what was still worthy of admiration. We shall not, therefore, imitate the ingenious architects who have reconstructed the mind and character of Jesus,[2] but merely content ourselves with noting some ideas which seem to emerge from the texts. To begin with the most obvious, those relating to his intellectual equipment, it is important to remember that we are dealing, according to the Synoptics, with a man of the people, born and brought up amongst humble folk in a little town in Galilee ; that he was surrounded by companions of the same class as himself ; that he, as a rule, spoke only to audiences of peasants and common people ; and that the extent of his culture was bounded by his religious education. The religious idea of the " Man-God," and even of the peerless Master, still so often accepted as dogma, has seriously obscured this fundamental fact. We have to do, then, with an ignorant man, not so much because he did not pursue liberal studies, which, as a matter of fact, would have been of little use to him in his Palestinian country, but because he had only a limited horizon. He does not appear to have known anything outside of Judaism, and he was familiar only with the social environment of Galilee. Renan makes the acute observation that " a king's court was, in his eyes, a place where people wore fine clothes." [3] Under the circumstances, the only disadvantage of this limitation of outlook was that it concealed from him the difficulties of his undertaking, which amounts to saying that it was practically the prime and essential condition of it. It has been observed that he was fundamentally optimistic. Had he not been so, he would never have attempted anything. A man of the people who initiates an important enterprise, necessarily with slender resources, is bound to believe that " it will come off," otherwise he would make no

---

[1] It will be sufficient to refer the reader to the *Introduction* of **CLXV**, xxix *ff*. A careful and thoughtful reading of these pages will afford a valuable lesson in criticism, not intended by the author.

[2] As an illustration of what their efforts can lead to, see the long article by Kilpatrick, *Character of Christ*, in **DGG**, 281 *ff*., or the essay of Paul Vigué, *La psychologie du Christ*, in *Le Christ. Encyclopédie populaire des connaissances christologiques*, published under the direction of Abbés G. Bardy and A. Tricot, Paris, 1932, 460–517.

[3] **CLXVIII**, 39. The statement is based on Matt. xi. 8, which specifically says that those who wear fine clothes are in kings' houses.

move. Further, we must take into account, to begin with, the facilities of material existence in fertile Galilee, which would be likely to give a man a tendency to optimism ; and also the "poetry of the south," which is always ready to paint in rosy hues the least promising situations.[1]

From this limited outlook proceeds also, it is true, a complete lack of capacity for abstract criticism. This is shown, as also in other ways, by his habit of being satisfied with the most rough and ready application of a text to the case it is supposed to justify. For instance, when, in Mark ii. 23, Jesus undertakes to exonerate his disciples, who have plucked a few ears of corn crossing a field on the Sabbath, and are accused by the Pharisees of profaning the sacred day, he cites the example of David, who once, when he was pressed by hunger, ate, at the invitation of the High Priest himself, the "shew-bread" stored in the house of Jahweh. There is obviously not much connexion between the hunger of a band of soldiers and the pastime of strollers. This defect, however, was no drawback in his surroundings. On the contrary, for a critical sense leads to doubt, begets hesitation, and paralyses action.

In compensation, it is perhaps to the intimate presence of a smiling and bountiful nature, from which he was separated by no intellectual preoccupation, that the Jesus of the Gospel owes the spontaneity and freshness of his images, the picturesque quality of his comparisons. Finally, in the social system of the Palestinian world where the scene of his activity was laid, the ignorant were not inevitably condemned, as in our own, to remain inferior in station. What counted in Syria in those days, as still today in undeveloped Mohammedan communities, was boldness of personal initiative, and the power of personal influence. Abstract reasoning was not congenial to the simple Oriental people, and Jesus does not employ it. Instead he uses images to express his ideas, which are few and simple. His most important ideas are embodied in trenchant aphorisms, bordering sometimes on paradox, as, for instance : Matthew v. 39 : "If anyone smite thee on the right cheek, turn to him the other " ; and Matthew v. 29, " If thy right eye offend thee, pluck it out." The speech of a man of the people is naturally pithy. The Old Testament itself had much of this quality of popular literature, and the Rabbis, modelling themselves upon it, were in the habit of speaking in an oracular style.[2] Jesus did not need to have come into close contact with them to know that.

His essential simplicity, and even his lack of education, do

[1] CCCXIII, 350.   [2] Cf., for example, the *Pirke Aboth*.

not detract from his natural intelligence, which is shown in the acuteness of his observations, the irony of his questions, even a certain shrewdness in his manner of evading the trap of an embarrassing question and turning it against his opponent.[1] All these traits are to be found in the Jesus of the Gospels, and give to his methods of discussion and teaching a somewhat Socratic character.[2] What we call the "freshness of the Gospel," which is really perceptible only in the Synoptics, can come from nothing but the freshness of the mind of Jesus, which makes itself felt in those straightforward passages whose simplicity has not been destroyed by the entirely artificial setting in which most of them have been imbedded.

A few other important, if negative, characteristics of the Synoptic Jesus may perhaps be indicated. As a prophet, the Nazarene was not of the denunciatory, gloomy, austere type which his calling might lead one to expect, and of which John the Baptist seems to have been an excellent example. There is nothing to show that he prophesied in the apocalyptic style, in spite of the thirteenth chapter of Mark, which may be a little apocalypse, but cannot possibly be attributed to him. Even if he had, during the anxiety and uncertainty of his last days, yielded to the temptation to burst into gloomy prognostications, that would be merely incidental, and quite contrary to his usual behaviour.

The Gospels attribute to him several outbursts of anger. For example, in Matthew ii. 21–3 he curses the unbelief of Chorazin, Bethsaida, and Capernaum ; in Matthew xii. 39 f. he replies very harshly to the Pharisees who have asked him for a " sign," that is to say, a decisive miracle ; in Matthew xxiii. 13 f. he is supposed to inveigh against those to whom he is especially opposed ; " Woe unto you, scribes and Pharisees, hypocrites ! " Such outbursts, with due reservations, of course, as to the authenticity of the words with which the redactor accompanies them, are not improbable ; they correspond to the " righteous indignation " which all men of God feel on certain occasions, and which even the angelic Saint Francis experienced. They reveal a very acute sensitiveness, rather than a trait of character, properly speaking. On the contrary, the synoptic tradition has preserved deep traces of the benevolence, the habitual kindliness, of Jesus, and these sober, but appealing virtues, although they were finally overshadowed in the Christological legend by more glorious qualities, were still

[1] We will cite only the famous example of Mark xii. 13–7, which contains the saying " Render unto Cæsar the things that are Cæsar's."
[2] **CLXVIII, 90 ; CLX, 107.**

foremost in Paul's conception of the Lord. "I beseech you by the meekness and gentleness of Christ" (διά τῆς πραΰτητος καὶ ἐπιεικείας τοῦ Χριστοῦ), writes the Apostle to the Corinthians (2 Cor. x. 1).

It is evident that Jesus was not interested in asceticism, that he saw no objection to marriage (in Mark x. 7 f., on the contrary, he asserts the necessity of its permanence), nor to the use—probably within the limits prescribed by the Torah —of all forms of food accessible to man.[1] He was, then, neither a despiser of life nor favourable to those disciplines, supposed to be pious and pleasing to God, which sought to restrict it.[2] It is perhaps this point which best confirms the impression of moderation and good sense conveyed by the general character of the Synoptic Jesus. It is a striking thing that Christianity should so soon and so completely have forsaken the way of the Master as regards this conception of practical life. The fact is, that his immediate expectation of the end of this perishable world rendered Jesus indifferent to evidences of piety which the postponement of his hope again endowed with value.

It has been claimed that he had supernatural will-power.[3] This is, however, not the impression given by the Marcan narratives, for they show him wandering hither and thither, breaking off his preaching, and attempting to disguise himself.[4] He must, then, have been conscious and apprehensive of danger up to the time of his embarking on the great adventure which ended in his death. The tradition attributes to him an access of weakness in the garden of Gethsemane on the night of his arrest (Mark xiv. 34, "My soul is sorrowful unto death").[5] That the incident was dramatized after the event, and was even, in the main, entirely imaginary, there can be no doubt, for who could have seen, heard, and reported it, when the only ones who might have witnessed the scene were asleep (xiv. 37, 40–41)? But the rapid development of Christology in an entirely different direction proves that the idea of the legend would never have been thought of had the disciples not pre-

---

[1] The passage of Mark vii. 15 : "*There is nothing from without a man that, entering into him, can defile him,*" is not, in our opinion, to be taken as a defence of laxity in practical life. We shall revert to this point.

[2] Matt. xi. 19 : "The Son of man came eating and drinking."

[3] **CLX,** 107 : "*er war ganz Willen und Handeln*"—he was all will and action.

[4] Mark v. 1 ; vii. 24 ff. ; vii. 31 ; viii. 27 ; etc.

[5] The meaning is not quite clear. It may be "sorrowful enough to cause death" (*cf.* Jonah iv. 9) or "sorrowful to the point of desiring death" (**CXIV,** 120).

served the memory of the state of grief and anxiety of which
it was the graphic expression. Luke xxii. 43 f. offers another
dramatization of the same feelings, when he describes the sweat
of blood upon the face of Jesus in his agony ($\varkappa\alpha\grave{\iota}\ \gamma\iota\nu\acute{o}\mu\varepsilon\nu\sigma\varsigma$
$\grave{\varepsilon}\nu\ \grave{\alpha}\gamma\omega\nu\acute{\iota}\alpha$). Such doubts and upheavals are intelligible enough,
and detract nothing from either the courage of Jesus or his
faith in his mission. But at least they do not justify us in
making an inflexible determination one of his outstanding
virtues.

Regarding his " heart " a great deal has been said, as is
not surprising. But it must not be inferred from this that the
Gospels themselves are especially interested in it. Quite the
reverse; they by no means foresaw the adoration of the Sacred
Heart. It is dangerous to deduce definite conclusions from a
few vague hints, and to interpret the very omissions of our
texts as evidence. But it has sometimes been done, nevertheless, and Renan, amongst others, was guilty of it.

For instance, he writes : [1] " His family does not seem to
have loved him," on the grounds that Matthew xiii. 57 makes
Jesus say that " a prophet is not without honour save in his
own country and in his own house." Mark vi. 4 specifies,
" among his own kin, and in his own house," and his " house "
means his family. If these passages prove anything, if they
really give his actual words, they imply only that Jesus was
not *understood* by his family, not that he was not *loved*. The
incident related in Mark iii. 33 when his mother and brothers
attempt to tear him from the circle of his disciples and bring
him back to the peace of his home, certainly does not argue
a feeling of indifference towards him. On the other hand, the
hard words put into his mouth in the same passage : " Who
is my mother and my brethren ? And he looked round about
on them which sat about him and said : Behold my mother
and my brethren. For whosoever shall do the will of God,
the same is my brother and my sister and my mother," are
neither a denial nor a kind of excommunication of his kin, any
more than those given in Matthew viii. 22, in reply to the
disciple who asked permission to go and bury his father :
" Follow me and let the dead bury the dead." They mean
nothing more than the fundamental principle that the service
of God comes before earthly affections, and no natural feeling
should avail to divert from it him who has heard its sovereign
call. " Jesus, like all men exclusively absorbed in an idea,"
continued Renan, " came to have little regard for the ties of
blood. The bond of the idea is the only one which this type

[1] CLXVIII, 42.

of nature recognizes." This psychological phenomenon is undeniable. But if Jesus was compelled to proceed in opposition to his family, he may nevertheless have suffered from their misunderstanding and the necessity, in spite of his continued attachment to them, of severing his life from theirs. It would be going rather far to conclude, from the fact that he obeyed the call of his vocation, and followed his own path in spite of the misunderstanding of his relatives, that he had no family feeling, and that he scorned it. We have no knowledge of that whatever. Renan maintains further [1] that he loved nothing except " what he regarded as his divine vocation," and that in him, " as often happens with very lofty natures, tenderness of heart is transformed . . . into infinite gentleness, into vague poetry, into universal charm." But of that, too, we have no knowledge, and the passages which Renan cites do not in the least justify his contention.[2] It rests upon the unstable verge of one of the gaps in our information. We are justified, at most, only in thinking that Jesus did not attach a fundamental importance to human loves, on the assumption that he really did describe the elect inheritors of the Kingdom as sexless beings, according to Matthew xix. 12 : " There be some which have made themselves eunuchs for the Kingdom of Heaven's sake "; and Mark xii. 25 : " For in the resurrection they neither marry nor are given in marriage, but are as the angels in heaven."

It goes without saying that it is religious emotion which dominates the whole personality of Jesus, surpassing and controlling all his other emotions. It may be said to fill his entire consciousness, and to radiate from him.[3] This will be sufficiently brought out in our subsequent study of his religion, and we shall therefore do no more here than give it its place in the list of psychological characteristics which we are endeavouring to draw up from the Synoptics. The mind and heart of Jesus were full of God, not, as might be those of a theologian, by pre-occupation with doctrine, but somehow spontaneously, by nature.[4] This is, of course, the form which piety takes in simple people. This intensity of religious feeling, this kind of identification of the religious life with life itself, does not involve in him any denial of the world, any condemnation of normal

---

[1] CLXVIII, 72.

[2] Luke vii. 37 ff. : his attitude towards the sinful woman (γυνὴ . . . ἁμαρτωλός) who has anointed him with a precious ointment : John iv. 7 ff. : behaviour towards the Samaritan woman at Jacob's well ; John viii. 3 ff. : treatment of the adulteress. These are all very dubious incidents, and, in any case, beside the question.

[3] CIII, i, 209.   [4] CLXVIII, 76 ; CLX, 109, 112.

existence, any monkish renunciation. On the contrary, the religious feeling of Jesus seems to intensify life, to illuminate it, to enhance its dignity and worth as a work of God, an earnest of and preparation for His Consummation.[1] It is not for a moment to be supposed that, although Jesus may very possibly have held up his own religious life as a model to those who listened to him, he made any such claim with regard to his practical life. The life he led seemed to him the one necessitated by his mission, and proper to him alone. At most its pattern was extended to his immediate disciples, those whom he had sought or received as companions and fellow-workers.

We must take care, however, not to fall into an exaggeration which very few of those who have spoken of Jesus have succeeded in avoiding, because it is so hard for men to rid themselves of the influence of their ancestral prejudices. It is fully exemplified in a sentence of Renan : [2] " The highest knowledge of God that ever existed in a human breast was that of Jesus." It may be so. But who can see deeply enough, or make an accurate enough comparison of all the great religious characters, to be justified in the assertion ?

We are sensible of the poverty, the incoherence, nay, more, the uncertainty, of this brief psychological sketch of Jesus which we have attempted to compose from the impressions of our gospel writers regarding him. These impressions, it must be remembered, consist already of interpretations, which may be tendentious, of recollections which may not be accurate, and of hearsay which may have no foundation in fact. Nevertheless, since there seems to be in all this nothing which reflects especial glory upon the Christ, nothing superhuman, we feel justified in believing that *Urmarcus* and the *Logia* have preserved at least a glimpse of the figure of Jesus the man.

[1] CLX, 110.   [2] CLX, 75.

CHAPTER VIII

THE PUBLIC CAREER OF JESUS

I

THE SIGNIFICANCE OF THE ENVIRONMENT

THE general features of the public career of Jesus, like everything else not directly concerned with edification or belief, are left vague by our gospel writers, and our curiosity has to be satisfied with a few meagre hints here and there, nor may our imagination supplement them with rash and unverifiable additions.

Nevertheless, with no desire to achieve a superficial vividness, we may say that the amazing changelessness of the common folk of the East in dress, food and customs, makes it easy, as far as these details are concerned, to reconstruct a very probable picture of the habits of the Galilean *nabi*. It has often been remarked how frequently the streets of the little towns and villages of Palestine evoke gospel scenes. We must hasten to make the most of them, and to fix their outline, for the hour has struck, and everything is changing rapidly. We cannot doubt it, when we see women of Nazareth coming to draw water at the Virgin's Well, no longer carrying on their shoulders the graceful pitcher, which has not yet entirely disappeared, but an empty petrol tin, thrown away by some overloaded chauffeur. The same evidence of " progress " may be seen even at Palmyra and Jerash. Before the ubiquitous motor-car the ancient customs are receding, for the car brings with it commodities previously unknown, and establishes between men hitherto strangers to one another contacts which no prejudice can long resist. A brief indication of certain points will perhaps guard us against errors of perspective, and permit us to restore the Nazarene to his true setting.[1]

A man of humble station, Jesus lived simply amongst common folk, whose daily life was wholly devoid of glamour.

[1] It will be worth while to glance through CCCIV, which, in spite of its title, contains much solid fact very clearly set forth. In this connexion, the watercolour drawings of Tissot are also worth mentioning.

We must beware of the illusions into which the sumptuous representations of certain Biblical incidents by modern painting might easily lead us. It is not to be imagined, for instance, that Veronese has given us a faithful picture of the wedding feast of Cana. The kindly hosts who received the Master and his disciples were far from being aristocrats, and Simon the Leper, who entertained them in Bethany (Mark xiv. 3), was hardly a millionaire.

We may, then, imagine Jesus clothed as the men of his people still are. His head, with its long hair, as Jews and Bedouins wear it in that country, and unclipped beard, was covered by a *kuffieh*, a piece of thin cloth drawn tight on the forehead and falling over the shoulders, for protection against the sun. His body was clad in a long tunic with sleeves, usually made of linen, and over which was worn a woollen cloak decorated with fringe or tufts, as prescribed by Deuteronomy xxii. 12. Various passages mention at least these last two garments : " If anyone taketh away thy cloak (τὸ ἱμάτιον), forbid him not to take thy tunic also," says Jesus in Luke vi. 29 (*cf.* Matt. v. 40, in which the same two articles are named). It is the fringe or tufted edge of his cloak (τὸ κράσπεδον τοῦ ἱματίου αὐτοῦ) which is timidly touched by the woman with an issue of blood in Matthew ix. 20 in the hope of being healed. A girdle permitted the tunic to be tucked up to free the legs for walking or working (Luke xii. 35 : " Let your loins be girded "), and also served instead of pockets (Mark vi. 8 : " Neither scrip, nor bread, nor money in their girdle "). On his feet were sandals, to which the ordinary footgear of the Syrian peasant probably corresponds exactly : a strong sole attached by means of thongs—those very thongs which John the Baptist, according to Mark i. 7, deemed himself unworthy to undo. Another passage (Mark vi. 9) shows us Jesus sending the Apostles out on their mission " shod with sandals " (ὑποδεδεμένους σανδάλια). To this equipment, the people of the country usually add a staff, and in Mark vi. 8–9 Jesus is supposed to enjoin the Apostles to take one.[1] He may, perhaps, not have carried one himself.

When travelling in this Syro-Palestinian country, it is a common thing to sleep outdoors ; and in the hot season it is not unpleasant to camp out. Jesus, however, apparently cannot have done so often, not only because the Gospels say nothing about it, which would not be much proof, but because, if we believe that he died in March or April, and that his career was very short, it must have been spent during the months

_____
[1] Matt. x. 10, however, says the opposite : μηδὲ ῥάβδον.

when it is not wise to sleep in the open air in Galilee. During the time of his stay in Capernaum, or near it, he used a house, that of Simon Bar-Jona (Matt. viii. 14). When Mark ii. 1 writes : " And being entered again into Capernaum, at the end of some days it was noised that he was in the house " (ἐν οἴκῳ), it is probably this same house to which he is referring. Otherwise, someone who welcomed his teaching had offered him hospitality.

This hospitality, which is customary in the East, partly, probably to a great extent, assured the material existence of himself and his followers, which involved little outlay. Incidental references help us to understand how the band of disciples eked out their subsistence. In the first place, those who composed it cannot have been entirely destitute ; there is no suggestion that they were paupers. They probably pooled their possessions, and one of them was entrusted with the common purse. If John xiii. 29 is not a fabrication, which is not certain, it was probably Judas. We must, finally, take into account the women whom Jesus won to him, and who served him with disinterested devotion. Amongst others, a passage of Luke viii. 1–3 deserves to be noted :

> " And the twelve were with him and also certain women who had been healed of evil spirits and infirmities ; Mary, called Magdalene, out of whom had gone seven devils, and Joanna, the wife of Chuza, Herod's steward, and Suzanna, and many others which helped him with their substance."

There seems no reason to reject this statement *in toto*. Though details may be disputed, there is at least every probability of its being substantially true. These women provided what was needed and looked after the domestic work. Jesus and his itinerant disciples were thus probably the first to put into practice the principle established by the primitive community : he who preaches the Gospel must live by it.

The maintenance of Jesus would, however, hardly be very expensive. His clothing was of the kind that lasts, and his staple food must have been precisely similar to that of the Galilean peasants, wheat or barley bread, and fish, plentiful by the lake, supplemented by milk and its products, vegetables, and fruit. There would be little meat, and his drink would be water ; on special occasions, wine, and *sikera* (Luke i. 15), a kind of beer, made, apparently, from fruit and corn. Possibly the Nazarene was not very strict about the food laws of the *Torah* (Mark vii. 15).

His habits were those of a *nabi*, a man who goes about spreading a message, a type still to be met with in the Moslem world. Those who did not take him seriously, either did not listen to him, or tried to embarrass him with artful questions, to entice him, if necessary, into a compromising situation. It was with this in view, that some ill-disposed persons came to him with the dangerous query : " Is it lawful to pay tribute unto Cæsar ? " If he said " yes," he would be discredited in the eyes of the strict Jews ; if he said " no," he would be fatally compromised with the Romans (Mark xii. 13–17). There is no indication that he was insulted or maltreated. The outbreak of fury against him, attributed by Luke iv. 49 to the people of Nazareth, is quite unreliable. It is only a development of Mark vi. 1 ff., and is intended to symbolize the fact that the countrymen of Jesus refused to listen to him, and that he turned away from their unbelief : " But he, passing through the midst of them, went his way." In Luke's time it was no longer to the Jews that salvation was offered, but to those more worthy of it. Probably the worst that usually.happened to Jesus was that he was not listened to. It may be that sometimes people were afraid of him. It would be quite comprehensible, for in his environment, those who did not see in him a man of God would doubtless be more inclined to regard him as a terrible sorcerer than as an inoffensive and insignificant fanatic. This feeling is shown in the sequel to an incident which in itself is highly strange and completely improbable, but which may be separated from the feeling which it illustrates. In the land of the Gerasenes, somewhere on the eastern bank of the lake, the Nazarene has just performed a miracle ; he has compelled a band of devils which were in possession of an unfortunate man to pass into a herd of swine, and the animals, suddenly seized with madness, have thrown themselves into the water and perished. The people of the neighbourhood, alarmed by the swineherds, far from being delighted by the marvellous " sign," are terrified, and beg the magician to go away as quickly as possible (Mark v. 1–20).

For a very different reason, the public authorities must have been disturbed by a preaching whose theme, the near advent of the Kingdom of God, could not have been pleasing to them. It is possible that Jesus was very soon made aware of this hostility, but we do not know how it was revealed to him. What the Gospels tell us of the evil intentions of the " Herodians," whom they couple with the scribes and Pharisees, is very vague, and cannot be analysed into definite facts. We see the prophet face to face with the authorities only at the time of the Passion, but it does not seem likely that he had never been troubled by them before.   If he had assumed the behaviour of a Messianic agitator, of the pattern followed by so many others,[1] the police would not have been long in obstructing his progress.   But since he seems to have preserved, on the whole, a calm and peaceful demeanour, since he did not talk of any warlike uprisings, and filled his teaching with injunctions to morality and piety instead of denunciations of the oppressors of Israel, since, finally, he did not create any excitement, it is conceivable that the public authorities at first left him unmolested.[2]   That this indifference did not last long, we may be certain without the explicit assurance of the gospel writers.   The rapid changes of place, and the precautions of the little gospel band implied by them, especially by the abandonment of Galilee and the journey into heathen territory, are quite sufficient to convince us.   Jesus does not appear to have been a blind fanatic, inaccessible to the suggestions of natural prudence.

II

THE MIRACLES

In that age and country, a prophet could induce people to believe in him only by means of " signs," that is to say, miracles which proved that he was possessed of more than human power.   The synoptic tradition avers that the Nazarene offered a great many of these miraculous proofs.   " The sight of the sick cured by Jesus was, accordingly, the experience which convinced the masses that he was possessed by a supernatural power." [3]   This evidence has been somewhat troublesome to the critics, and for the conservative it still constitutes a conclusive argument. [4]

Carefully considered, the argument is, however, hardly impregnable : first, because the distinction between a *good*

---

[1] It has been maintained by C. K. Kautsky, *Der Ursprung des Christentums*, Stuttgart, 1908, that he did so.   For the refutation of this view, see Hans Windisch, *Der messianische Krieg und das Urchristentum*, Tübingen, 1909.

[2] **CIII**, i, 208.

[3] **CXC**, 205, based especially on Matt. xii. 15–21.

[4] There are numerous works dealing with the question.   **CCV**, 114 *ff.*, gives a bibliography, and an interesting general idea of the ancient history of the problem.   For a general study of the phenomenon of the " miracle," *cf.* **CCCI**, and for its relation to the current Jewish and pagan magic, see **CCIV** and **CCII**.   *Cf.*, also, **CCXCIII** and **CCCXII**.

miracle, which attests the truth, and a *bad* miracle, which proves nothing but the cunning of the Prince of Error, or the adroitness of a charlatan, is a very delicate matter; next, because a miracle being, by definition, a *fact* (*factum mirandum*), it is not easy to distinguish it from another sort of fact which is merely extraordinary or surprising (*res mira oculis*). The theologians inform us that a true miracle " contravenes the laws of nature." Unfortunately, we cannot boast of knowing the laws of nature well enough to be certain whether a particular occurrence contravenes them or not. Further, such a definition does not endow a miracle with sufficiently definite characteristics to prevent the ignorant man—who, we must remember, is likely to be a witness, and often the sole witness, of the event—from mistaking for one a phenomenon which is merely unfamiliar and inexplicable to him, but which a more enlightened man would unhesitatingly assign to its proper place in the natural order. Moreover, these famous " laws of nature " have not the slightest objective reality. They are nothing more than convenient formulæ, the systematization of factual experience, and symbolize the observation of a certain regular order in the occurrence and connexion of phenomena. In reality, the only things that exist for us, that we perceive and have knowledge of, are *facts*, of which some are intelligible to us, and have been explained, while others are not, but all of which, by the very fact of their occurrence, are a part of nature. They are *natural*, or they would not *be*. Hence, to set down as a datum the " laws of nature," and regard the contravention of these laws as the criterion of the miraculous, is a mere delusion founded on a fallacy. To say that a *fact* is contrary to nature is a meaningless proposition.[1]

The order of nature is of a *physical* character. Scientific observation has never discovered any facts which violate it so far as it is really known. Hence, to the mind of an educated man, it has no metaphysical, but only a practical and inevitable necessity. This important conception is foreign to the simple, the ignorant, those unimbued with the scientific spirit. They readily believe that phenomena, the causality of which they do not understand, can be arbitrarily modified, as they are arbitrarily produced, by a superior power, divine or magical. Therefore, as soon as a phenomenon seems to them to deviate

---

[1] Augustine, *Civ. Dei*, 21, 8 : " *Portentum . . . fit non contra naturam, sed contra quam est nota natura.*" This penetrating observation does not, however, prevent Saint Augustine from believing in miracles, which shows how difficult it is to follow the logic of an argument to its ultimate conclusion.

from the normal—whose limits, it must be emphasized, vary
greatly with the capacity of the observer—they proclaim a
miracle. Renan was mistaken when he wrote : [1] " No miracle
ever took place before a sceptical audience. The condition of
a miracle is the credulity of the witness." The truth is, that
it is the *interpretation* of the fact *as* a miracle which depends
upon the credulity of the witness, and not the occurrence of
the fact itself. If Renan had gone to Lourdes, his presence
would not have prevented the cures which the pilgrims regard
as miraculous. He would himself have seen there extraordinary,
and sometimes amazing, phenomena, but which, in the majority
of cases, were easy enough to explain, and he would have
tried to account for each of them as exactly as possible. It is
hardly necessary to point out that this critical desire for information involves a doubt which faith does not ordinarily
experience, and which, at bottom, it does not want to experience. It must be remembered that the miracles of the
past, as, for that matter, those of the present, were observed,
or rather, discovered, and reported, only by believers. Moreover, very often, in fact for the most part, those who reported
the events were not those who actually witnessed them. Hence,
in a great number of cases, the historian is confronted by the
material impossibility of getting back to the exact fact which
is described as miraculous, and which the inevitable interpretation begins to distort even in the minds of the eye-
witnesses.

"In the last analysis," writes the Catholic philosopher
Blondel,[2] there is nothing more in a miracle than in the most trivial
of ordinary facts. . . . Miracles are miraculous only to those
who are already prepared to recognize the operation of God in the
commonest events and actions."

That is perfectly true, and if faith dictates the interpretation
of the fact, it likewise controls, and to the same end, the account
which is given of it.

Nevertheless, the miracle constitutes, in many religions, the
supreme argument of apologetic, because it appears to possess
an objectivity capable of convincing even the unbeliever. This
is a pure illusion, and in itself the use of the miracle as a religious
argument is worth no more than the use of the martyr. The
martyr dies for his truth, and proves thereby that he holds it
dearer than life. He does not in the least prove that it is
" the Truth," inasmuch as many different, and even conflicting truths have had their martyrs. Similarly, all the religions
which have so desired have had their miracles, the *same*

---

[1] **CLXIX**, xliii.   [2] M. Blondel, *L'Action* (1893), p. 396.

miracles, and, on the other hand, all have shown themselves equally incapable of producing certain other miracles. The unprejudiced scholar is not surprised at this, because he knows that the same causes everywhere produce the same effects. But what is strange is that the believer is not surprised at it either. He merely insists that *his* martyrs are the only ones who prove anything, and that the martyrdoms of other religions are mere acts of fanaticism.[1] Similarly, *his* miracles are the only genuine ones ; others are mere empty appearances, fabrications, frauds, uncomprehended facts, or witchcraft.

In this rapid review of the general features of the miracle from a critical point of view, our intention was, before approaching the study of the miracles attributed to Jesus, to emphasize two fundamental points : first, that the supposedly miraculous fact has no specific characteristics which enable it to be unhesitatingly identified ; second, that the interpretation of this fact as a miracle depends essentially on the attitude of the witnesses. This attitude is not merely the result of the faith, or the stupidity, or the inattention, or the credulity, or the ignorance, of individuals, but is conditioned by the state of knowledge and belief, the state of mind, so to speak, of the community from which they come. At the time when Jesus lived, at the time when the tradition concerning him was formed and fixed, the conviction that miracles, the direct and arbitrary manifestation of the Powers above or below, were not only possible, but even frequent, prevailed unquestioned in all communities.

The Olympic cults gave a large place to wonders and miracles of all kinds. Livy, for instance, relates so many that at the end of the fourth century, a certain Julius Obsequens was able, by merely collecting them, to produce at the same time a ponderous volume and a very important contribution to teratology. Certain gods were veritable specialists in everyday magic, for example Æsculapius, and the inscriptions discovered in the ruins of the *Asclepeion* at Athens, or of the temple of Epidaurus in Argolis, inform us of the marvellous cures which the god achieved in his temples.[2] Care was taken to record the principal ones, and to have an account of them engraved on the walls, for the honour—and profit—of the sanctuary, and the gratitude of those miraculously cured was expressed by votive images, often in precious metal. These images sometimes represented the part of the body restored

---

[1] It is not the suffering, but the cause, that makes the martyr (*martyrium non facit pœna sed causa*), asserts Saint Augustine.

[2] CCXLIII, 242 *ff*.

to health by the divine intervention.[1] These miracles were
the exact counterparts of those still performed daily in all
the great centres of faith-healing.

But it was not only the gods who worked miracles. Certain
noted persons, who had special relations with heaven, such as
the famous physician Asclepiades [2] (end of the second century
B.C.), the Emperor Vespasian, and his contemporary, the
philosopher Apollonius of Tyre, also performed very interesting
ones.[3] The resemblance between the miracles of Apollonius
and those of Christ is at first sight so striking that Philostratus,
the author of the *Life of Apollonius*, was long credited with
the intention of creating a kind of counterpart of Jesus for
the pietistic circle which surrounded Alexander Severus. This
opinion has been generally abandoned,[4] and it is now regarded
as probable that the resemblance was due solely to an essential
similarity of means and results. The Oriental religions, including Judaism, were even more permeated with the miraculous than classical paganism. In those times, when people
troubled themselves little with the " laws of nature," and had,
in general, lost the experimental bent which makes for science,
the performance of miracles appeared in itself to be easy
enough.[5] All that was necessary was to know the operative
words and the efficacious actions. Accordingly, the specialists
wrote books of formulas, manuals for the complete sorcerer.
(We still possess a few fragments of them.) It was known
what it was necessary to do and say, even to revive a corpse.[6]

Origen (*Contra Celsum*, 2, 57) is of the opinion that the
reason Jesus was born and lived amongst the Jews was because
they were more accustomed to miracles than any other race,
and he wanted his supremacy to be impressed upon them by
a comparison of the marvellous things they had already seen
with those which he was capable of showing them. If the
Nazarene had really reasoned in the fashion attributed to him
by the Alexandrian writer, he would have been greatly disappointed. His compatriots, the Jews, were neither over-

[1] P. Girard, *L'Asclepeion d'Athènes*, Paris, 1882, p. 116 *ff*.

[2] Apuleius, *Florida*, 19 : " *Asclepiades ille, inter præcipuos medi-
corum, si unum Hippocratem excipias, ceteris princeps. . . .*"

[3] The texts will be found in **CCII**, 15, 18, 23 *ff*.

[4] **XXXV**, 217.

[5] **CCLXIV**, 37, n. 1, rightly observes that, though we, nowadays,
are accustomed to confine the question of miracles solely to the religious
sphere, this was not the case in those times. In the absence of definite
scientific knowledge, the miraculous was found in all departments of
life.

[6] Dieterich, *Abraxas*, Leipzig, 1891, 167 *ff*. *Cf.* **XXIII**, no. 79,
p. 27 ; **CCXCIII**, 41, 3.

whelmed nor convinced by the miracles which he is supposed to have performed before their eyes. They remained true to type by demanding " signs," which it was necessary for him to produce because every man who claimed to speak in the name of God had to prove that the Holy Spirit was in him. Moreover, the *nabi* could never be sure that his most impressive miracles would not be attributed to Beelzebub. The miracles which Jesus performed, according to the Gospel writers, were in no way original : the healing of lunatics, the expulsion of devils, extraordinary cures, wonderful powers over nature, and even the resurrection of the dead, all were a part of what the faith, both of Jews and of pagans, expected of a genuine worker of miracles.[1]

It has, however, been observed [2] that in the time of Jesus exorcism could not have been common in Palestine, since there is very little mention of it in the *Mishna* and the Tannaite literature. This observation, which is well grounded, and in harmony with the Talmudic ascription to Jesus of magic powers (*Shabbat*, 104, *b*), suggests that many of the important miracles reported by our Gospels are redactional additions, for instance, the raising of the widow's son at Nain, in Luke vii. 11 *ff*.[3] Apostolic propaganda, which made a great deal of them, probably magnified their number, especially by the device, so dear to Matthew (ix. 35 ; xi. 5 ; xiv. 35 ; xv. 30 ; xix. 2 ; xxi. 14), of generalization. It is only what we might expect.

On the other hand, it is easy to see that there were, so to speak, miraculous " themes," which influenced all the miracle workers, and even more, their biographers.[4] Lucian of Samosata, who was, perhaps, much less sceptical than he imagined with regard to the popular story-tellers, was once inspired to make fun of the wonderful tales of miracles which were current in his time, and wrote the *Philopseudes*, the *Lover of Lies*. It was not only " cobblers and fullers," but very serious-minded men, who believed these incredible fables, for instance, Eucrates, " with his long beard, his sixty years, and his pronounced taste for philosophy " (*Philops.*, 5), the great enemy of all falsehood and error. In the book, other philosophers of the same type are gathered together in his house one day when he is ill, and exchange, along with the most fantastic prescriptions of empirical medicine, the most amazing accounts

---

[1] **XXXV**, 219 *ff*. ;   **CCL**, 142 *ff*. ;   **CXCIII**, 71 *ff*. ;   and especially **CCIV**, particularly p. 72 *ff*.   *Cf.* **LXXXVI**, 143.
[2] **LXXIV**, i, 110.   [3] **CIV**, 22 *ff*.
[4] **LXXXVI**, 136 *ff*. (a very suggestive study).

of miracles. We see paraded before us, one after the other, the theme of the sick man who carries his bed on his back (11), of the man who walks on the water (13) and revives " putrefying corpses," of the sorcerer who interviews the evil spirit who is capriciously dominating an unfortunate demoniac, threatens him, and finally forces him to come out (16), of the " young man of rare beauty, clad in white," the messenger of the gods (25). Anyone who has read the Gospels will at once recognize all these incidents and personages. Lucian's book cites other wonder-working themes, which are to be found in later Christian legend. Must we then conclude that it is a case of lies pure and simple, as Lucian says ? Let us say rather, of facts badly observed, distorted, and enormously exaggerated, by the unbridled imagination of those who originally bore witness to them, and also of illusions, originating we know not how, or where.

Finally, it is upon the validity of the gospel evidence that our judgment depends, on the *historicity* of the facts which they offer as miraculous, not upon their true nature. Unfortunately, there is little hope of this validity being much greater in the case of the miraculous events than in that of the others, and the most superficial examination of the texts proves, in fact, that it is not. We discover, for instance, that each of the Synoptists relates impressive miracles which are not mentioned by the others,[1] so that each has taken just what suited him from tradition or legend. The answer of apologetic, that each has chosen from amongst the numerous miracles of the Lord the ones that seemed to him most characteristic, taking especial care not to duplicate any of the other Gospels, will not hold, because several of the miracles which are related by one alone are more striking than others which are given by all three, and because the fact that they sometimes select the same ones, proves that the Synoptists were not influenced by the precaution which is attributed to them.

On closer scrutiny, we find that the Synoptics treat the

---

[1] For example : Mark viii. 22–6, the healing of a blind man ; vii. 32–7, that of a deaf-mute ; Matt. xxi. 14, the healing of blind and lame in the Temple ; xxvii. 52, the resurrections which signalize the *Ninth Hour* ; Luke vii. 11–17, raising of the widow's son ; vii. 21, various cures in the presence of the messengers of the Baptist ; xvii. 11–19, the healing of ten lepers ; xxii. 50 *ff.*, the healing of the servant of the High Priest, wounded in the commotion of Christ's betrayal ; etc., etc. As it is perhaps hardly necessary to add, the Synoptics make no mention of the two great Johannine miracles, the miracle of the wine at the wedding feast of Cana (John ii. 1–11) and the raising of Lazarus (xi. 38–44).

chronological order of the miracles in the career of Jesus in the most cavalier manner, and that they further disagree both as to their number and the circumstances which characterize them. To cite only one example : if we read the story of the resurrection of the daughter of Jairus, a very remarkable miracle, which demands the most accurate attestation, we shall find in Mark v. 23 that the young girl is " at the point of death " (ἐσχάτως ἔχει) ; it is not until somewhat later (v. 35) that someone comes to tell the father that she is dead (ἀπέθενεν). Matthew ix. 18, on the other hand, makes Jairus say at the beginning that his daughter is dead (ἡ θυγάτηρ μου ἄρτι ἐτελεύτησεν). Luke follows Mark, first stating (viii. 42) that the maiden is dying (ἀπέθνησκεν), and causing it to be announced later (viii. 49) that she is dead.

It is claimed that these are mere details, and that the facts remain. Not so, because in this case *there are no mere details*. Everything is essential to the evaluation of the story, and it is even very often what is called a detail that holds the clue to the validity and significance of the event in question. It is probable that the accounts of the miracles were already in confusion when our redactors found them in their sources, without details or reliable evidence, more like assertions of apologetic which no one thinks of verifying, or confused memories, arbitrarily forced into some sort of meaning and order by a redactor, than authentic and circumstantial reports. Of the cures, for example, it is impossible to say anything definite. We know neither exactly what diseases they operated upon, nor whether they were efficacious or only seemingly so, permanent or temporary, real or imaginary.[1]

The rationalists have, on various occasions, made great efforts to eliminate the thaumaturgical element from the life of Jesus. The veteran Paulus is noted for his frank *reductio ad absurdum* of all the miraculous incidents.[2] With infinitely more astuteness and historical sense, Bousset has revived the theory, already upheld by Havet amongst others,[3] that, with the exception of the cures, the gospel miracles proper are not historical. During the lifetime of Jesus, there was no thought of such things, but when it was realized that he was the Messiah, the prophecy of Isaiah xxviii. 18 : " Then shall the eyes of the blind be opened, and the ears of the deaf unsealed," was

---

[1] CCCI, 94 ; XXIV, i, 102.
[2] CCCXI, 17. Paulus, who died in 1851, was a professor at Jena in 1798. His great work, *Leben Jesus als Grundlage einer reinen Geschichte des Christenthums*, appeared in 1828.
[3] CCLXVIII, iv, 10 *ff.* ; CXCIII, 70 *ff.*

piously read back into the period of his activity. On this view, the gospel miracles must be regarded as a halo with which Jesus was surrounded by the faith of the primitive community. This is not the place for a detailed exposition and criticism of this conclusion, which is based upon somewhat specious exegetical arguments, and is, in the opinion of the present writer, unsound. It would be valid only if it were possible to eliminate all the miracles of the gospel narrative, and that seems a hopeless task, although, as anyone may see, the number of them preserved by the tradition was not excessive, since altogether those related in any detail by the four Gospels amount only to about forty.[1] Doubtless the men who edited our texts thought this was all too few, as is naïvely revealed in the last verse of John (xxi. 25) : " But there are also many other things which Jesus did, the which, if they should be written, every one, I suppose that even the world itself could not contain the books that should be written."

We should like to have some information as to what Jesus thought of the miraculous, of his own supernatural gifts, and of the use which he made of them, but the Gospels offer us little satisfaction. They give the impression, which is probably true, that the Master's ideas on the subject of miracles did not differ from the current beliefs of his contemporaries. There is no doubt that he believed in the " double," in demoniacal possession, and in the maladies resulting from it, and that he regarded the working of the miracles as an essential part of the life of a man of God. The Scriptures alone would have convinced him of it. Moreover, it is very improbable that if he had departed from common opinion on a matter of such importance, the tradition would not have preserved some trace of so striking an idiosyncrasy.

As a matter of fact, various Protestant theologians have believed that such a trace was to be found in two parallel passages given by Matthew xii. 38–42, and Luke xi. 29–30, of which the source was in all probability the *Logia*. The following is the translation of Matthew :

" Then certain of the scribes and Pharisees answered, saying, Master, we would see a sign from thee. But he answered and said unto them : An evil and adulterous generation seeketh after a sign, and there shall be no sign given to it but the sign of the prophet Jonah. For as Jonah was three days and three nights in the whale's belly, so shall the Son of Man be three days and three nights in the heart of the earth."

The reading of Luke, although differing somewhat in form,

[1] **LXXIX,** 226 ; **V,** i, 395.

is evidently a development of the same *logion* attributed to Jesus. Mark also was acquainted with it. He gives it in a condensed form and without the reference to Jonah (viii. 12) : " Why doth this generation seek after a sign ? Verily I say unto you, there shall be no sign given to this generation."

Matthew, finding it both in the *Logia* and in *Mark*, has copied it a second time (xvi. 4), putting in again the epithets relating to " this generation," and the " sign of Jonah," and giving to the proffered " sign " the sense of a prediction of the great event the imminence of which Jesus is proclaiming (xvi. 3).

Jesus' meaning appears to have been : " I produce no miracle as a conclusive sign : I do as Jonah did, when he was sent by God to the Ninevites : I speak and proclaim the truth : do as the Ninevites did when they heard Jonah, and believe me ! " But this decidedly does not mean that Jesus had no belief in miracles, or that he would not, and did not, perform them.[1] He only rejects them as " signs," as the *proof* of his mission. In this he is in accord with the logic of the facts, by which we mean that the most amazing miracles attributed to the Nazarene were never, on the admission of the redactors themselves, accepted by their witnesses as conclusive signs. The audience may be amazed, admiring, or fearful, occasionally angry, but their faith does not necessarily follow upon their wonder.[2] Hence Jesus would have been grievously disappointed had he hoped for any greater success. Were not Chorazin, Bethsaida, and Capernaum deservedly cursed by him, according to Matthew xi. 20, because, having seen the greater part of his miracles, they had, nevertheless, not repented ? Further, how could miracles have borne irresistible witness to the truth, when the workers of iniquity themselves (οἱ ἐργαζόμενοι τὴν ἀνομίαν) performed them, when they, too, prophesied, effected cures, expelled devils (Mark xiii. 22 ; Matt. xxiv. 24) ? In such an environment, the miraculous was too commonplace to constitute an absolute proof in any instance. We must note especially that it was not at all the idea amongst the Jews that the working of miracles, even astounding ones, would in itself identify the Messiah.[3] According to the prevalent Jewish conception, the Messiah would have no need to perform prodigies ; he himself would be the miracle.[4] On the other hand, a mere rabbi could prove his words by appropriate marvels.

[1] *Cf.* EB, *Gospels*, § 141 ; LXVII[1], 146 ; CLXV, 44.
[2] Mark i. 27 ; ii. 12 ; v. 17 and 20 ; Matt. viii. 27 ; ix. 8 and 33 ; xi. 20 ; xii. 23 ; Luke v. 26 ; vi. 11 ; vii. 16 ; viii. 25 and 56 ; etc.
[3] CLXXVI, 295.
[4] O. Holtzmann, *Leben Jesu*, Tübingen, 1901, p. 223.

There are some passages which seem at first sight to contradict these statements, but they are in all probability expressions of the religious beliefs of the gospel writers, and not of the mind of Jesus. In Matthew xii. 28, for instance, we read : "If I by the Spirit of God cast out devils, then the Kingdom of God is come unto you." This *logion*, which is not found in Mark, but which Luke xi. 20 gives in almost the same words, comes, apparently, from Q. According to it, Jesus adduces his power to cast out devils as a proof, a sign, of the divine nature and the truth of his message.[1] A general examination of the whole passage relating to Beelzebub in the three Synoptics, however, reveals Mark iii. 23–7 to be an older and more connected version, which justifies us in believing that the passage in Matthew and Luke belongs to a secondary redaction. Obviously it is inserted like a wedge into the original reading, breaking it into two parts.[2] It represents a tendentious gloss by a redactor, and is quite unreliable.

The reply which Jesus is supposed to have made to those sent by the Baptist to ask who he is, seems at first much more conclusive. In Matthew xi. 4–6 it runs as follows :

> "And Jesus answered and said unto them : Go and tell John the things that you have seen and heard. The blind see, the lame walk, the lepers are cleansed, and the deaf hear, the dead are raised up, and the poor receive the Glad Tidings."

This passage, like the preceding one, is given by Luke (vii. 22–3) almost word for word, but omitted by Mark. It must come from the *logia*, but like the previous one, from a more elaborate redaction of them than that known by Mark. Taking the passage literally, Jesus adduces his miracles, which the messengers of John are supposed to have witnessed, as the expression and proof of his Messiahship, and the fulfilment of the prophecies. Part of the alleged reply is, in fact, inspired by Isaiah xxxv. 5–6 : "Then shall the eyes of the blind be opened and the ears of the deaf unstopped ; then shall the lame man leap as a hart, and the tongue of the dumb sing." It contains also a reminiscence of Isaiah lxi. 1 : "He hath anointed me to preach Glad Tidings to the poor." The ancient prophet mentions neither the healing of the lepers nor the restoration of the dead, but those were the most wonderful miracles of all, that were ascribed by the tradition to the public career of the Lord.

If Jesus actually said those words, his reply to John the Baptist was completely contrary to that which he is supposed

[1] **LXVII,** 144.   [2] **CIII,** i, 766 ; **XCVI,** 48.

to have given the Pharisees when they asked him for a sign. The attempt has been made [1] to interpret the passage metaphorically, in a spiritual sense, on the grounds that its meaning is completely determined by the final sentence, in which no miracle is involved : " The poor receive the Glad Tidings." We have no right to juggle with perfectly definite statements in this manner, but we are justified in questioning whether Jesus really uttered the assertions reported by *Q*. It is to be noted that, if the passage is genuine as we have it, it flatly contradicts, not only the statement with regard to the sign of Jonah, but the whole of what may be called the " Messianic secret " of Jesus, all his injunctions to those who benefited by his miracles, and to the evil spirits, to say nothing of the matter to anyone (Mark i. 44 ; iii. 12 ; v. 43 ; vii. 36 ; viii. 30 ; ix. 9 ; etc.). It is particularly hard to see what could be the point of Peter's confession at Cæsarea Philippi (Matt. xvi. 13 *ff.*) that the Master was the Christ, the son of the living God, a confession of which the disciples are enjoined to say nothing to anyone, if Jesus himself had deliberately announced the same thing in public for the information of John the Baptist. It is still stranger that he offers his forerunner, as convincing proof, all that wonder-working which the Jewish tradition did not in the least expect of the Messiah [2] and which he himself does not interpret in that way in the presence of his most intimate disciples.

If he really received messengers from the Baptist—as is probable, because the proceeding is inconsistent with the legend of the Forerunner, which implies that it was forced upon the redactors of the first gospel documents by the original tradition—he could not have offered a crop of miracles as the expression and proof of his own mission, since there was nothing in that to convince John. There is no apparent connexion of fact or reason between the miracles enumerated and the assertion that the Glad Tidings are given to the poor. The combination represents nothing but the coupling of two prophecies, and it is certain that this was not the work of Jesus. It belongs to a time when the Glad Tidings meant the *Gospel*, the *Christian faith*, and when the miracles of the Lord were already regarded as proofs of his Messiahship, that is to say, they were adduced by apologetic as being essentially *signs*. To judge by the Synoptics themselves, Jesus did not share this view. He offers

[1] *Cf.* **LXVII**, 144 ; **EB**, *Gospels*, § 140 ; **L–a**, i, 307 ; **CLXV**, 44.
[2] The passage of Isa. xxxv. 5–6, just cited, does not refer to the Messiah's *personal activity*, but to the prosperity of Israel under the reign of God.

his miracles as the rewards, almost the results, of faith in him,[1] and not as manifestations of his special power. It seems particularly improbable that Jesus said " the dead are raised," when, at the utmost, our Synoptics record only *two* cases of resurrection, of which only one (that of the daughter of Jairus) is given by all three redactors. But it was quite natural that the secondary tradition should extend to death the power over the whole of life which it attributed to Christ.

These considerations lead us to believe that the passage of the *logia* copied more or less exactly by Matthew xi. and Luke vii. was already only a tendentious interpretation of the actual reply of Jesus, or, more accurately, it substituted for that reply a couple of lines of artificial apologetic. We may wonder why such a proceeding was deemed necessary. Probably it was because what Jesus had really said did not correspond in the least with what it was at that time believed that he must have said.

We shall add a word on the subject of another passage which puts into the mouth of the Nazarene an assertion of the evidential value of his miracles. It is the one which contains the cursing of Chorazin, Bethsaida, and Capernaum (Matt. xi. 20–4 ; Luke x. 13–15). The passage of Matthew is a little longer than that of Luke, and a comparison of the two affords an opportunity for interesting observations regarding the redactional methods of the two authors, but since the substance is the same, and undoubtedly comes from the *logia*, we translate the shorter of the two :

> " Woe unto thee Chorazin, woe unto thee Bethsaida ! for if the miracles [literally, the ' powers,' the ' forces '—*dynameis*] had been done in Tyre and Sidon which have been done in you, they would have long ago repented, sitting in sackcloth and ashes. And verily, it shall be more tolerable for Tyre and Sidon at the judgment than for you. And thou, Capernaum, shalt thou be exalted to heaven ? Thou shalt be hurled down to hell."

This, too, contradicts the statement about the sign of Jonah. It has been claimed [2] that the anger indicated by the passage sprang from an incident of Apostolic times, an ill-fated attempt at propaganda in a region where Jesus, according to the Evangelist, had had nothing but success. But this theory is too

---

[1] In Mark v. 35 he says to the woman with an issue of blood who has humbly touched his cloak from behind : " Daughter, thy faith hath made thee whole ; go in peace and be cured of thy plague." See also Mark vii. 29 ; ix. 22 *ff.* ; x. 52 ; etc.

[2] **CXV**, 50.

obviously inspired by the desire to get rid of a troublesome passage.

The passage reflects a feeling which Jesus cannot fail to have experienced, that of the practical futility of his preaching. Hence it is reasonable to suppose that the substance of what he said was somewhat as follows : " I have spoken ; I have proclaimed the truth to you ; you have not listened to me, for you have not repented. More, you have ignored the manifestations of the divine power that is in me ; you have achieved your own damnation." If this was Jesus' train of thought, there is no implication that the *dynameis* in question had been intended by him as " signs." But they were *facts* from which it was natural to infer the divine origin and the authority of the prophet. In other words, the passage obviously implied that Jesus believed himself to have wrought miracles—cures and exorcisms—but it does not contradict the assertion regarding the sign of Jonah. It merely intimates that the towns which he cursed, though unmoved by the spoken truth, might at least have been moved by the *dynameis*, but remained untouched even by his works of power.

From the various considerations just presented, it seems possible to draw the following conclusions :

(1) Jesus believed in miracles just as the people around him did. He regarded cures and exorcisms as miracles, manifestations of the power (*dynamis*) granted by God to his chosen ones.

(2) Believing himself to be one of these, he felt in him the power to manifest the divine *dynamis* in the ways with which his world was familiar.

(3) Nevertheless, it was not these miracles which he regarded as the most important part of his activity. It was necessary for him to perform them in order to be taken seriously, but, though he did not despise them, he never counted on them to establish his Gospel, that is to say to procure the acceptance of the Glad Tidings. They were only incidental. He must have been conscious of his failure, and perhaps on one occasion went so far as to say, in acknowledgement of the eager confidence the Jews so often accorded to " signs " : " Not even those moved them ! "

There can be no doubt that the most ancient tradition attributed to Jesus feats and actions regarded as miraculous, and that it was right. But it is equally evident that, not having the slightest suspicion that its assertions might reasonably be disputed, it took no trouble to justify them. Not only did it collect indiscriminately whatever was said about these miracles amongst the disciples, but, once more, it surrendered completely to the inevitable tendency to elaboration, which must have exaggerated their quality as well as their quantity. The gospel redactors are inspired by the " *aretalogical* " spirit.[1] What matters to them, much more than the truth and accuracy of the facts they allege, is their effect upon the reader. They take none of the precautions which would imply the slightest disposition to incredulity on his part. This is not the place to devote ourselves to a critical examination of the miracles attributed to Jesus, since we are only concerned with them here as a feature of his career. But if they are examined as thoroughly and impartially as possible, certain conclusions clearly emerge, of which we may give the following brief summary.

Jesus effected cures which were deemed by himself and his contemporaries to be miraculous. He attributed them to the divine *dynamis* which he felt within him. This *dynamis*, whose efficacy implied, or, more correctly, was the result of, the faith of the sick, did not pertain peculiarly to him ; it manifested itself wherever there was a strong faith in its existence. It still manifests itself today under the same conditions, exercising its power on diseases of nervous origin. There is no trust-worthy evidence to lead us to believe that Jesus cured any other kind of malady, and it appears certain that the authentic tradition limited his miracles to those of healing, which offers a very natural explanation why they were not regarded, in his environment, as conclusive " signs." A considerable heighten-ing of the wonder-working element was very quickly forced upon the tradition ; in the first place, because the miraculous was, if we may so put it, the accepted currency of the religious faith of the time, and because no miracle appeared *à priori* impossible ; secondly, because the Christian faith had, of urgent necessity, to discover in the life of the Lord the illustration of all the wonder-working " themes " contained in the Old Testament or in contemporary pagan legends. It was unthink-able that the *dynamis* of Christ should not reveal itself as equal, or superior, to that of all the prophets and all the pagan divinities. Finally, symbolic or allegorical modes of expres-sion [2] were customary, which frequently transformed religious ideas and concepts into myths, that is to say, which would

---

[1] ἀρεταλογία means in substance an account of the wonders wrought by a god or a hero. The " *aretalogical* spirit " is, then, in general, the *hagiographical* spirit of ancient times. " Est mendax aretalogus," wrote Juvenal, *Sat.*, xv, 16, and he expressed the common opinion.

[2] **CLXXV**, 114 *ff.* ; **CCLXIV**, 42 ; **CIII**, i, 183.

symbolize a teaching, a parable, a doctrinal point, by a more or less marvellous anecdote. Above all, we must emphasize the fact that our Gospels are not books of history. They belong to a type of literature in which the factual unreality of the narrative was justified by the deep sincerity of the writers' feelings, and vagueness, or definite inaccuracy of detail were effaced by the truth of the general impression. The attribution of a miracle sanctified by tradition and regarded as evidential, or of a striking moral characteristic, to an entirely different place, date, or personage from its original connexion, is a recognized form of procedure in writings intended for edification. Such methods were to attain their height later, in the Lives of the Saints, but our Gospels may be rightly regarded as the first essays in Christian hagiography.

CHAPTER IX

THE LENGTH OF JESUS' PUBLIC CAREER [1]

THE subject of this chapter is another of those questions of the greatest importance to us, with which our gospel writers did not concern themselves. The few meagre and careless hints they have incidentally let fall are very vague, and, in addition, difficult to reconcile. According to the Synoptics, the public life of Jesus may be inferred to have covered, at the utmost, about a year, [2] but according to the Fourth Gospel its duration must be extended to nearly three and a half years. We are justified in asking, not merely who is right, but whether anyone is right. There is grave danger, not only in John, but hardly less in the Synoptics, [3] that our calculations may be invalidated by the numerical symbolism which was so common among Eastern people.

The smallest acquaintance with the Gospel of Mark reveals its complete indifference to chronology. Its incidents succeed each other in an entirely artificial sequence, and it is usually impossible to determine their exact temporal relation to each other, and consequently to form the slightest general estimate of the period covered by the series. Here are a few examples :

We read in Mark i. 39 : " And he preached in their synagogues throughout all Galilee, and cast out devils " ; in Mark vii. 24 : " And departing thence he went into the country of Tyre " ; in Mark vii. 31 : " And again departing from the country of Tyre, he came through [that of] Sidon on the sea of Galilee to the midst of the territory of Decapolis."

It is obviously impossible for us to estimate the period of time covered by these various journeys and removals. Certainly no one seems to think that it was very long, but we cannot base a definite conclusion on such an impression, couched in such vague terms. Let us take a case in which the redactor

[1] EB, *Chronology* (von Soden), § 44 ; CXLII, 279 *ff.* ; bibliography 279, n. 1. On the principal works, see Schweitzer, CLXXVI, 613 *ff.* The most recent with which we are acquainted is that of H. Windisch, *Die Dauer der öffentlichen Wirksamkeit Jesu*, in ZNTW, xii, 1911, 141–75.

[2] CCXVI, 50 ; CCXXXII, 17 ; LXXXIX, 62.

[3] CXXVII[2], 178, 197, 202, 259 ; CV, 344.

has aimed at an appearance of precision. He has just (viii. 27–9, 1) related how Jesus received, near Cæsarea Philippi, the confession of Peter : " Thou art the Christ," and has attached to it a discourse which, moreover, has hardly any connexion with the incident. He passes next to the account of the Transfiguration (ix. 2 *ff*.) which he introduces with the following words : " And after six days, Jesus took with him Peter and James and John." The definiteness is strange and means nothing to us, unless it is simply an echo, on the redactor's part, of a verse of Exodus, xxiv. 16 : " And the glory of Jahweh abode upon mount Sinai, and the cloud covered it six days, and the seventh day he called unto Moses out of the midst of the cloud." In any case, it is merely the link between a discourse torn from its proper setting and a purely mythical incident.

There is a passage in Luke iv. 19 which has often been supposed to contain definite information. Jesus has come to Nazareth, and in the synagogue on the Sabbath he reads a passage from the *Nebiim*, in this case Isaiah (lxi. 1–2 ; lviii. 6), which, quoted freely from the Septuagint, may be translated as follows :

> " The Spirit of the Lord is upon me because he hath anointed me to speak glad tidings to the poor. He hath sent me to proclaim liberty to the captive and sight to the blind, to set the oppressed free, and announce the propitious year of the Lord."

The whole verse is very applicable to Jesus ; too applicable, in fact, for it is easy to forget that it is only a quotation and to see in it an indication of the length of the public career of the prophet, namely, one year. But the question is, exactly what this " propitious year of the Lord " means. Does it correspond to the recollection of a fact, or to the requirements of a conventional chronology, mainly, or wholly, dictated by cultual considerations, and with little relation to facts ? [1] It is difficult to decide, and in either case the suggestion rests on too slender a foundation to justify any conclusion.[2]

If we approach the matter from another angle, and ask ourselves what length of time would be sufficient to include, without crowding them, all the events related by Mark, we can readily see that it would not need to be very long. The Fathers and most of the heretics were, on the whole, of the opinion

---

[1] CXVIII, 391 *ff*.

[2] XCVIII, 63, is of the opinion that the passage has no chronological implication whatever. We have our doubts as to that, but certainly, it proves nothing. *Cf.* CIII, i, 842.

that the period indicated was one year,[1] and the majority of modern critics have agreed with them.[2] It is difficult to understand why Albert Reville, for instance, holds that twelve months would not be long enough, and, after having specifically declared that John cannot be relied upon in the matter, finally accepts [3] the period of three years indicated by that Gospel, on the grounds that it is borne out by a sentence of Luke xiii. 6–9 (parable of the fig-tree), in which Jesus is supposed to say : " Behold these three years I have come seeking fruit on this fig-tree and found none." But in the parable, it is not Jesus who says these words, but the owner of the fig-tree, and the three years merely symbolize a long period of patient waiting. It is rash to read more into them.[4]

Although attempts have sometimes been made to reinstate the Johannine chronology, it is not in very good repute. Its inconsistency with that of the Synoptics creates a difficulty which critics have attempted to remove by showing that it is the result of a faulty transmission of the Johannine text. According to the letter of the text that has come down to us, John intimates that three Passovers were observed by Jesus at Jerusalem (ii. 13 ; vi. 4 ; xi. 55). The Fathers, however, who accepted a year as the period of Jesus' career, were not disturbed by the contradiction in John, which suggests that possibly it may not have existed for them as it does for us. It is noteworthy that Irenæus, who does reckon three Easters in John, finds, as we do, the first in ii. 13, and the third in xi. 55, but the second, not in vi. 4, but in v. 1 ($\mu\varepsilon\tau\grave{\alpha}\ \tau\alpha\tilde{\upsilon}\tau\alpha\ \tilde{\eta}\nu$ $\dot{\varepsilon}o\varrho\tau\grave{\eta}\ \tau\tilde{\omega}\nu\ '\textit{I}ov\delta\alpha\acute{\iota}\omega\nu$), where the word $\dot{\varepsilon}o\varrho\tau\grave{\eta}$, that is, festival, is usually understood to mean Pentecost. We may perhaps infer that Irenæus and Origen, who agrees with him (*In Johan.*, 13, 39), had a text of vi. 4 that was different from ours. Again, we know from Epiphanius (*Hær.*, 5, 22) that the Alogi [5] thought that the Johannine narrative included only two Passovers, one at the beginning and the other at the end of the ministry of Jesus. It might, accordingly, be that John really intended to represent a period of about a year, and that the successive festivals to which he alludes—assuming, of course, our vi. 4 to be an interpolation—were distributed as follows : ii. 13 : Passover ; v. 1 : Pentecost ; vii. 2 : Tabernacles ; x. 22 :

[1] Detailed information on this point will be found in **CXLII**, 281 *ff.*

[2] There were, however, some Fathers who were, under the influence of John, in favour of two or three years, e.g. Melito, Heracleon, Tatian, Hippolytus.

[3] **CLXX**, ii, 227 *ff.*   [4] **XCVIII**, 143.

[5] Designation of the heretics who rejected the Johannine *Logos*.

Dedication; xi. 55: Passover. Certainly all the events of
John easily fall within these limits.[1]   On the other hand, however, there is always the danger that these considerations may
indicate, not the original state of the text, but a patristic
adaptation designed to reconcile the Synoptics with the Johannine tradition.[2]

It must be remembered, moreover, that the chronological
details of John may not have any direct connexion with history,
but merely represent the intentions of the author, who is very
little concerned with historical facts.   One of the best commentators on the Fourth Gospel, the American critic Bacon,
has suggested [3] that the visits of Jesus to Jerusalem mentioned
by the Evangelist are to be interpreted on the basis of the
teaching which they involve :

> " We cannot deduce from them an itinerary of the travels of
> Jesus during his ministry, but we may perhaps obtain a glimpse
> of the ideas of Christ, as they were understood and interpreted
> nearly a century after him, regarding the Jewish festivals which
> were adopted and transformed by Christian ritual."

In other words, the redaction had a cultual aim in view.   In
Bacon's opinion an unbiased reader cannot fail to receive the
impression that when, on the occasion of the last Passover,
which is the only one mentioned by the Synoptics, Jesus visits
the Temple with his disciples, it is for the first time.[4]

Modern conservative critics have gone to enormous trouble
in their endeavour to retain both the gospel chronologies
and to regard them as complementary.   Some, such as Sanday
and Stanton, have made this reconciliation as it were an *à
priori* necessity, by laying it down as a principle that no pious
Jew, such as Jesus, could possibly have missed going to Jerusalem for the great festivals.[5]   It is a well-meaning, but, as it
happens, entirely gratuitous assumption.   The truth is, that,
without straining the texts, the inference to be drawn from
John is that the period of Jesus' public life comprised three
years and a few months.[6]   It is only arbitrarily, and by means
of very questionable deletions, that this can be reduced even
to two years.   Bacon, for instance,[7] believes himself justified
in saying that there is little difference between the two appar-

---

[1] Von Soden, **EB**, *Chronology*, § 45.   On this particular chronological problem, *cf.* **CXXIX**, 278 *ff.*, 282.

[2] **CXXVII**[2], 61, is convinced that three Passovers at least, and
possibly even four, are indicated in John.   *Cf.* **CXLII**, 280.

[3] **CXVIII**, 410 *ff.*

[4] *Cf.* especially Mark xi. 11 and Luke xix. 41.

[5] **LXXXIII**, iii, 228 *ff.*   *Cf.* **CXVIII**, 358.

[6] **CXXVII**[1], 65.   [7] **CXVIII**, 409, 491.

ently conflicting chronologies, but he has paved the way for this conclusion by transferring two of the Jerusalem Passovers to Galilee, on the strength of a very forced interpretation of Mark ii. 23 and vi. 39, besides ruling out John ii. 13–25 (the first Passover), and x. 22–39 (the Dedication). These emendations made to order are inadmissible, and the solution of the problem must be sought in some other way. If John had intended to correct the Synoptics, he would probably have emphasized his assertions, tried to throw them into relief. This precaution would have seemed all the more necessary inasmuch as he was contradicting a tradition which was unquestionably established in writing and familiar to the Christian communities long before his own redaction, and which he himself was well acquainted with, and made free use of, interpreting it in his own way. Hence his motive must have been different, and the inference is that it corresponded with some symbolical intention, which would be quite in accord with his characteristic tendency, and would, besides, harmonize very well with the perspective in which he places the public life of Jesus. Three years and a half is *half a week of years*, the Messianic week consisting of seven years. It is true that he does not stress this idea either, but here we are no longer in the presence of a mere chronological computation, we are approaching the heart of the *Mystery*, which will be properly understood by the initiated for whom the book is intended, and by them alone. It is completely improbable that the preaching of Jesus, thoroughly Messianic as it appears to be in John, could have lasted so long, especially *in Judæa*, without arousing the authorities. Much less than that would have sufficed to make the Roman officials take measures for safeguarding the government. The Evangelist realizes this so well that he implies a kind of permanent miracle, by means of which the arrest of Jesus is deferred [1] until the moment when the Lord himself permits it, because " the hour is come when the Son of man should be glorified " (xii. 23. *Cf*. xiii. 1 ; xvii. 1).

The statements of Luke, if we were compelled to infer from his quotation of Isaiah in iv. 19 that he assigned to the career of Jesus a duration of one year, would inspire no more confidence than those of John. But it seems reasonable to suppose that, in default of exact dates, which they were doubtless not in a position to give, the Synoptic editors followed the contemporary Christian belief, and that this did not hold the public life of the Lord to have extended over several years. Indeed, it would be hard to conceive that the Nazarene could have

[1] **CXXVII**[1], 62–6.

gone up and down the country for three years, proclaiming an event which never came, without losing all his followers and himself ceasing to have faith in his mission. Such hopes do not endure postponements and delays for long. Judging by the probabilities, even " about a year " seems too much. The gospel narrative does not require this minimum by a long way, and it is improbable that the forbearance of Herod's police and of Roman suspicion would have lasted so long. Our own opinion is that the public life of Jesus did not cover more than a few months, or even, exclusive of the times when he was in flight or hiding, a few weeks.[1]

If we take it as probable, on the evidence of the first editor of Acts and the Third Gospel,[2] that the Baptist began preaching in the fifteenth year of the reign of Tiberius (Luke iii. 1), or between August, 28, and August, 29, and if we assume that he was arrested, as seems likely, at the end of a few weeks, or, at the most, of a few months, we can place the career of Jesus in 28, 29 or 30, and the end of it about the April of one of the two latter years, supposing that it really was coincident with the Feast of the Passover. Any more exact dating is quite arbitrary, and a matter of opinion, not of knowledge.[3] Even if the details of the Synoptic tradition regarding the chronology of Passion week were accurate, which is by no means certain, we are too ill-informed regarding the Jewish lunar calendar of those times and its exact relation to the Julian calendar to make any reliable [4] reckoning.

To give an idea of the ingenious or fantastic theories which have claimed to supply a certainty underived from the texts, we shall say a few words about two or three of them. Keim, the author of a well-known work on the history of Jesus, believes that John the Baptist perished at the end of 34 and Jesus at the time of the Passover in 35.[5] He bases his conclusion on the evidence of Josephus (*Ant.*, 18, 5, 2) from which he argues as follows : Herod Antipas having experienced great reverses in the war he was waging against the Arab king Aretas,

---

[1] This is, on the whole, the opinion of Loisy, lxxix, 62. The conclusions of Eusebius, *H.E.*, 1, 10, 6, who believes that the preaching of Jesus lasted not quite four years (οὐδ᾿ ὅλος τετραέτης), are of no importance, being based upon an erroneous calculation regarding the succession of the Jewish High Priests.

[2] **CCXXII**, 64.

[3] *Cf.* Von Soden, EB, *Chronology*, § 50.

[4] The reader is referred, for example, to the book of J. Bach, *Monatstag und Jahr des Todes Christi*, Frib. in Brisgau, 1912. The author decides in favour of the 3rd of April, 33. We can only envy his confidence.

[5] Th. Keim, *Die Gesch. Jesu von Nazara*, iii, Zurich, 1873, 489 *ff*.

in 36, the people saw in this fact a punishment for the killing
of the Baptist. Hence the execution of the prophet could not
have been very much earlier than 36. But at the Passover of
36, Pilate was no longer in Jerusalem, so that, at the latest,
the crucifixion of Jesus must have taken place at the Passover
of 35, and the death of John, which necessarily preceded it,
falls naturally at the end of 34. It seems somewhat rash to
place so much reliance on a statement of Josephus, which in
any case would be entirely consistent with a longer interval,
and to do so is to plunge gratuitously into difficulties. For
what becomes of "the fifteenth year of Tiberius"? Even
sacrificing this to Josephus, who is not usually deserving of
such confidence, we have still to attribute to the Lucan tradition an error of five years in the date of Jesus' death. Keim
seems to explain the obscure by what is still more obscure.[1]

A still more arbitrary and surprising theory is that of De
Jonge.[2] He affirms that Jesus was a disciple of Hillel, and
must have made his first appearance when he was between forty
and fifty years old, as John states (viii. 56-7).[3] If Luke makes
him thirty, it is because Luke was an artist, and wished to
picture Jesus in the full flower of his manhood. De Jonge is
equally convinced of other, and even more surprising things ;
for instance, that Jesus was a widower when he began preaching, and had a young son. It is the latter who is referred to
in John vi. 9 : " There is a lad here which hath five barley
loaves and two fishes." All these ingenuities, and others which
we leave unmentioned, leave us unconvinced, as also the
confident conviction of Voigt [4] that Jesus was baptized on the
10th or 11th of January, 27.

They are mere illusions, fairy-tales, curiosities, to which
common sense can give no credence, and which bring us back
to the only assertion justified by prudence and probability,
namely, that we cannot determine exactly the limits of the
public career of Jesus, but we may be sure that they were
narrow. We shall probably not be far from the truth if we
assign to it, at the maximum, a duration of a few, possibly
three or four, months.

---

[1] A criticism of his theory will be found in **XXIX**, i, 443 *ff*.

[2] De Jonge, *Jeschuah. Der klassiche jüdische Mann. Zerstörung des
kirchlichen Enthüllung des jüdischen Jesus-Bildes*, Berlin, 1904. For
criticism see **CLXXVI**, 352 *ff*.

[3] *Cf.* p. 102 *ff.*, 110.

[4] H. Voigt, *Die Geschichte Jesu und die Astrologie*, Leipzig, 1911.
Cf. **CLXXVI**, 613.

CHAPTER X

THE SUCCESS OF JESUS

I

DOCUMENTARY INCONSISTENCIES

IT is not easy to estimate the success of Jesus' preaching. In the period and the environment which produced our Gospels, it was hardly possible to admit that the Lord had not been listened to, and had not aroused enthusiasm wherever he went.

We get the impression from Mark that the appearance of Jesus had a tremendous effect all over the country of the Jews. From the miracle which initiated his career at Capernaum, his fame (ἡ ἀκοὴ αὐτοῦ) spread " abroad throughout all the region round about Galilee " (i. 28), and that very evening " all the city was gathered together at the door " of the house which sheltered him (i. 33). Henceforth, wherever he goes, as soon as his presence is known the multitude assembles and crowds around him. As by degrees the news of " the things he does " becomes more widely known, the throng is recruited from further afield. They come " from Galilee and from Judæa, and from Jerusalem and from Idumæa, and from beyond Jordan, and from the neighbourhood of Tyre and Sidon " (iii. 7 ff.). If he departs, they follow him (ii. 13 ; x. 46). In vain he seeks to escape by going into the desert places ; they are soon on his track (i. 45). He takes ship and hastens to the other side of the lake, only to find there a great throng awaiting him (v. 21). A " great multitude " surrounds his disciples, and watches for his return at the foot of the mount of the Transfiguration (ix. 14). Frequently it is the desire and hope of a miracle which attracts the people, but they are brought also by the wish to hear the prophet (vi. 15 ; viii. 28) and to listen to his teaching (ii. 13 ; cf. iv. 1–2). In their zeal, his followers even forget food and drink, and Jesus is compelled to perform dazzling miracles to make up for their lack of fore- sight and feed them in the heart of the wilderness (vi. 34 ;

212

viii. 1–9). This eagerness is manifested not only in Galilee, it is met with even in the country of Tyre and Sidon, where, as soon as she hears of his beneficent presence, a Syrophenician woman hastens, in her simplicity, to implore him to heal her daughter (vii. 24 *ff.*). It is the same even in the territories of Judæa and Peræa (x. 1), even at Jerusalem, where the enemies of the Galilean *nabi* dare not arrest him for fear of the multitude (xii. 12 ; xiv. 2), which " listens to him gladly " (xii. 37). In his account of the two miracles of the loaves and fishes, the Evangelist mentions the number present, which at least indicates what he means by " a great multitude " (πλῆθος πολύ) (iii. 8) : it is *five thousand souls* (πεντακισχίλιοι ἄνδρες) (vi. 44) in the one case, and *about four thousand* (ὡς τετρακισχίλιοι) in the other (viii. 9). That is no mean gathering, and one which could not have passed unnoticed by the authorities in a small country.

At times there were so many people constantly arriving to surround Jesus and his disciples, that they had no time to " so much as eat bread " (iii. 20 ; vi. 31). In order to speak to them effectively the prophet was compelled to go on board a boat a few yards from the shore (iv. 1). In town, on one occasion, the press was so great in and around the house where he was, that in order to bring a paralytic to him it was necessary to hoist the man on to the roof and let him down through a hastily contrived hole (ii. 1 *ff.*). When Mary and " his kin " come to try to tear him away from the mode of life which disturbs them, they cannot get through the crowd, and it is by word passed from mouth to mouth that his mother lets him know that she is in the street and wants him (iii. 31). Through all the country around Gennesaret the sick and disabled are brought out to be placed in his way, that they may touch the fringe of his cloak (vi. 53–6).

It is hardly necessary to repeat after Matthew and Luke what we have just heard from Mark, and they had heard before us, but it is to be noted that the Johannine tradition is quite in accord with it. The eager flocking of the people about Jesus, and their anxiety to profit by the cures he performed, are as much emphasized by the Fourth Gospel as by the second (iv. 39 *ff.* ; iv. 45 ; vi. 1–2 ; vi. 22 *ff.* ; etc.). At one time, the enthusiasm even goes so far that its object is forced to escape by a kind of flight, knowing that the excited multitude wants *to make him king* (vi. 15). According to Luke, when he leaves Jericho to go up to Jerusalem, those with him believe that the Kingdom is on the verge of appearing. Such faith and such demonstrations would not be hard to conceive of, on the part

of the *am haareṣ*, villagers and peasants, simple people, quickly
moved to extremes, who probably made up the usual audience
of Jesus [1] and whom he understood well enough to know how
to talk to them ; and some modern critics, who are not in the
habit of blindly accepting every Gospel assertion, have believed
in this enthusiasm and this success. [2] Nevertheless, it is
extremely improbable, and the gospel writers themselves give
conclusive evidence against it.

In the preamble of John we read (i. 10–11) :

> " He was in the world, the world which was made by him, and
> the world knew him not. He came unto his own, and his own
> received him not."

Plainly though the Baptist had spoken, hailing in Jesus
" the Lamb of God which taketh away the sins of the world "
(i. 29), his authority did not avail to remove this deplorable
blindness. Though the " signs," that is to say, the miracles
which Jesus consented to perform, induced a certain number
of the people of Jerusalem to believe " in his name," they
created no more than a superficial and unstable faith (John
ii. 23–4). The obstinate, malevolent, and murderous unbelief
of the majority of the Jews with regard to the divine Master
is, indeed, one of the main themes of the Fourth Gospel (vii.
1, 11, and 30 ; viii. 59 ; etc.). In the Synoptics, too, there is
no lack of evidence to contradict their apparent optimism.
We have only to recall the curse uttered against Chorazin,
Bethsaida and Capernaum, the very centres of the Galilean
activity of Jesus, whose incredulity nothing could break down,
and whose hardness of heart is declared to have been greater
than that of Tyre, Sidon, or Sodom (Matt. xi. 20–4 ; Luke x.
13–15). Be it remembered, too, that that same mob of Jerusalem which was represented as giving pause to the enemies of
Jesus, chose Barabbas instead of him (Mark xv. 11), clamoured
for his execution (xv. 14), and insulted him on the cross (xv.
29).

We are, of course, taking all the passages so far cited at
the face value given to them by the Gospel editors, and are
not subjecting them to individual criticism, which would be
the task of a commentary. It is not essential to know, for
instance, whether the bitterness of the Fourth Gospel towards
the Jews is really due solely to its knowledge of their attitude
towards Jesus. It seems certain that, if the redactor had
believed that the Lord in his own time was enthusiastically

[1] It is " sinners " whom Mark ii. 15 describes as following him.
[2] **XXVII**, 63.

received by his fellow countrymen, he would not have indicted them as he does, nor have regarded their descendants as the arch-enemies of the Truth, the very " sons of the Devil " (viii. 44). We wish merely to show that, side by side with the assertion of success, in our Gospels, is to be found the admission of failure—a true admission, and most painful to have to make, for the scepticism of those who had seen and heard Jesus long remained the most formidable argument of the opponents of Christianity.

There is not the slightest doubt that it is this admission which represents the truth. The Jews did not believe in Jesus, and did not follow him. It was apart from them, and indeed, in spite of them, that his effort achieved permanent results. It is indisputable that he might have, nay, must have, attracted the attention of the *anavim* in the little towns of Galilee, and gained the lasting adherence of some of them. We shall not venture to estimate their number, but it is doubtful that it was large enough to justify references to " crowds," or to any enthusiasm whatever. In any case, even if there were signs of such a movement in the beginning, which might possibly be granted, it certainly did not last, and it is not difficult to guess why.

As far as we can judge, Jesus did not speak to the people in the language which was expected of a Messianic prophet. He seemed not to be concerned with the temporal state of Israel; he issued no call to arms; he preached resignation rather than rebellion, and crowds are not carried away by that, least of all the crowds of Galilee. The very substance of his teaching condemned him to complete failure, or, which amounts to the same thing, to success of a kind which could attract no attention because it was necessarily *invisible*. What he said was : " Behold the Kingdom is at hand, repent," and his teaching consisted in pointing out how this *metanoia* was to be accomplished. At first people could not have believed him, or given either credence or ear to his proclamation. But at best, assuming that they did believe, what had they then to do ? Repent, in other words, achieve *metanoia*—an entirely subjective process—and then wait for the Kingdom to appear. That was all. We may wonder why anyone should have followed the *nabi*, and what reasons there were for being carried away by enthusiasm. At most a few pious men may have attached themselves to him because his words had moved them and they found comfort in his presence. But certainly the doctors, the scribes, whose profession was the study and scrupulous observance of the *Torah*, could not have had the slightest

sympathy with him ; not, as has been too often said, because
his religion and theirs were fundamentally and irreducibly opposed, but because it would have been too humiliating for them
to acknowledge as a man of God and their religious teacher,
an ignorant person who had never pursued their studies, one
of the *am haareṣ*. " He teacheth as one that hath authority "
(ὡς ἐξουσίαν ἔχων), that is to say, as a prophet speaking as
the mouthpiece of the Spirit, " and not as the Scribes," Mark
i. 22 makes the first hearers of Jesus in Galilee say. Everyone in Israel was aware that the Spirit of God " bloweth where
it listeth," but in order to accept the authority of Jesus, it was
necessary to believe that the divine *ruach* had really entered
into him.

If he had *acted*, no matter how, his influence would have
found means of asserting itself, but he merely spoke and coun-
selled. The Gospels show him perpetually coming into collision
with the Pharisees, arguing with them, evading their artful
questions, frustrating their hostility, while at the same time
bidding his own disciples beware of " their leaven " (Mark viii.
15). Sometimes the Scribes, the Sadducees, and the Herodians,
that is to say, the Schoolmen, the Temple officials and the civil
authorities, unite collectively, or singly, with the Pharisees in
opposing him, or Jesus himself includes them all together in
his antipathy (Mark iii. 6 ; vii. 1 ; viii. 15 ; viii. 31 ; ix. 11 ;
x. 33 ; etc.). When we remember that at the time when our
Evangelists wrote, it was an established tradition that the Lord
had perished as the victim of a plot of influential Jews, doctors,
priests, and members of the Sanhedrin, and that it was, in
fact, with the hateful guile of the *rabbis* or the disdainful scepticism of the Jewish aristocracy that Christian apologetic came
into sharpest collision, we shall be led to believe that, as has
already been stated, the gospel picture (heightened by John)
of the continual controversy of Jesus with Jewish officialdom
is very largely artificial. It is difficult, however, to believe that
it is entirely imaginary, because the most elementary reasoning
would arouse the suspicions of the School, the Temple, and
the Government (whatever it was), against the activities of a
man who claimed to be answerable only to the Spirit, and who
in any way whatever concentrated the attention of the people
upon the Messianic hope. What seems definitely artificial in
the gospel statement is the idea that all these people united
from the very beginning to get rid of the intruder (Mark iii. 6),
and that they laid traps for him. But that they did actually
regard him as an annoyance, and exhibit a " class " hostility
towards him from the moment they encountered him, is hardly

to be doubted. They cared little, at bottom, about his piety, his deep and sincere faith in which the Pharisees could find nothing to disapprove of. He was deemed dangerous, just as the Baptist had been, because one could never tell what would be the end of these "missions," so innocent in appearance, but nevertheless verging on the irregular, and, in reality, on the unorthodox. Experienced and prudent men are always afraid of what may happen. Since, as has just been explained, Jesus had not the enthusiasm of the people to counterbalance this ill-will on the part of the important Jews who formed the social backbone of Israel, his cause was lost from the beginning. Perhaps he was not long in finding it out. It would seem so, from his wanderings hither and thither, before, staking all on a last desperate venture, he throws himself into the lion's mouth at Jerusalem.[1]

II

THE DISCIPLES

The Gospels depict Jesus going about the country surrounded by his *disciples* (οἱ μαθηταὶ αὐτοῦ). They are his habitual companions and his chosen audience. We should like to know whence they came, who they were, and what their number was, but on these points, as on all that seem to us of primary and special importance in the life of Jesus, we have no information, and have to fall back upon hypotheses.

The tradition believed that it knew (Mark i. 16–20) how the first of these disciples had been recruited. It was by an irresistible summons on the shores of the lake of Galilee :

"Now as he walked by the sea of Galilee he saw Simon and Andrew the brother of Simon, casting [their] net into the sea, for they were fishers. And Jesus said unto them : Come ye after me, and I will make you to become fishers of men. And straightway they forsook their nets and followed him. And when he had gone a little further, he saw James [the son] of Zebedee and John, his brother, who were in their boat mending their nets, and straightway he called them, and they left their father Zebedee in the boat with the hired servants and went after him."

This Marcan account is obviously artificial. It is hard to believe that people who are supposed never to have seen or heard Jesus would have obeyed him at the first sign, to the point of leaving everything to follow him, without knowing

[1] This failure of the Nazarene is reconstructed with striking vividness and convincing probability by CLXIV, 230–52.

why or whither.[1] The narrator's purpose was to impress upon
us that these first disciples, Peter, Andrew, James, and John,
unhesitatingly renounced everything for Jesus, and that they
could not do otherwise. Their summons, presented as a kind
of miracle, belongs to a theological convention not greatly concerned with actualities.[2] While a recollection of the irresistible
" call " of Elisha by Elijah (1 Kings xix. 19–20) may have
suggested the story, it is rather the idea of the supreme authority of Jesus that has inspired the Evangelist. Nevertheless,
omitting the details, which are shaped, not by historical probability, but by the Evangelist's point of view, it may be that
there remains a kernel of fact. If we admit that Mark was
the spokesman of Peter, we are compelled, indeed, to believe
that this is so,[3] and that the incident is to be interpreted as
signifying that the two pairs of brothers were drawn to Jesus
by an irresistible force, just as, again, in the case of Levi the
son of Alpheus, whom a single word from the Master sufficed
to draw from his place at the receipt of custom (Mark ii. 14).

The tale is told differently in the Fourth Gospel, and the
first disciples called are not exactly the same as in Mark. They
are Andrew and a nameless one, who is supposed to be John,[4]
both of whom have previously been disciples of the Baptist
(John i. 35–7, 40), then Peter (i. 42), and then Philip (i. 44),
which proves that at the time of the redaction of John, the
tradition was not yet finally fixed as regards the choice of the
first disciples, and was therefore sufficiently indefinite to permit
special purposes, like those of the Fourth Gospel, to find a
place in it.

We may at least hold that the tradition conceived the
" call " of the disciples as an imperious impulse of faith, as
blind as it was irresistible, a kind of " illumination." The
question is whether this conception was in accordance with the
facts. Broadly speaking, it is possible that it was, but we
have no knowledge on the point, and it is not improbable that
our gospel writers were equally ignorant. They wrote at a
time when the Christian vocation was a stereotyped and inevitable conception. Doubtless only those followed Jesus over
whom his personal influence was strong enough to make them
believe that they would derive happiness and benefit from living

---

[1] Lagrange, CI, 19, is not unaware of the difficulty. Other critics
are somewhat disturbed by this desertion of the family, and Holtzmann,
XCVI, i, 115, thinks it necessary to point out that if James and John
leave their father *with the hired servants*, he is not left completely helpless.

[2] CIII, i, 437 ; CV, 70, 111.

[3] LXXXV, 138 ; CCXXXIV, 24 *ff*.   [4] CXX, 37.

with him. The psychological reasons which influenced them probably varied from one to another, and are all equally obscure to us. There is no *nabi* too insignificant to attract some followers, and besides, if Jesus had gone about alone, it is improbable that the tradition would have failed to exploit a circumstance which would have so emphasized the *unique* character of his mission. It is noteworthy that our redactors do not say why Jesus wanted disciples. The subsequent course of the narrative seems to imply that it was for the object of making them his collaborators and extending his influence through them, but it may easily be that this was the idea of the Evangelist rather than the purpose of the Nazarene.

It is impossible to say exactly how many disciples composed the gospel band, but neither the tradition nor probability suggests a large number. We must be able to imagine them all being invited to a meal, as they sometimes were, or crossing the lake in a single boat. We get the impression from the Gospels that the following of Jesus never greatly exceeded the number of those referred to as the Twelve, and supposed to have been selected by Jesus himself from amongst the other disciples (καὶ ἐποίησεν δώδεκα ἵνα ὦσιν μετ᾽ αὐτοῦ).[1] These Twelve and possibly two or three women,[2] about fifteen persons in all, probably composed the usual entourage of Jesus. The author of Acts seems to have been of the same opinion, since it is about fifteen persons whom he gathers together in the upper chamber at Jerusalem on the Eve of the Ascension (i. 12–14) : the Eleven, Judas having disappeared, and the women. The fact that he adds also the mother and brothers of Jesus is beside the point, since in any case, the Synoptic tradition makes no mention of the family of Jesus having accompanied him in his wanderings.

These Twelve are the ones known to us as the Apostles, who are represented in Acts as forming a kind of college, endowed with an authority over the faithful which they begin to exercise immediately after the Crucifixion, and entrusted with the responsibility for the spreading of Christianity. The Synoptic tradition believed that they had been chosen by Jesus. We read in Mark iii. 13 *ff.* :

" And he went up into the mountain and called to him those he would and they came unto him. And he ordained twelve to

----

[1] It is to be observed, however, that Matt. x. 1 seems definitely to state that Jesus has only these twelve disciples when he invests them with the power to cast out devils and cure all manner of disease.

[2] Mark xv. 41 names three " who, when he was in Galilee, followed him and ministered unto him."

be with him, and that he might send them forth to preach, and to have power to cast out devils."

The purpose of this Marcan passage is to establish the authority of the Apostles on the firmest possible basis. At the time when our Mark was written, the more or less authentic *Apostolic tradition* still furnished the whole substance and constituted the principal guarantee of Christian doctrine, but obviously, on the subject of the Apostles themselves, it offered the writer nothing more than a vague impression and a list of names. Indeed his account, taken by itself, is so completely inconsistent that neither Matthew nor Luke follows it. The former states (x. 1), in quite a different chronological connexion, after various miracles and events unmentioned by Mark : " And when he had called unto him his twelve disciples, he gave them power to cast out unclean spirits and to heal all manner of sickness and disease." Luke vi. 12 freely alters the Marcan setting, and gives his own picture of the choice. It is as if he wished to endow the incident with greater solemnity. Jesus is supposed to spend a night in prayer before proceeding to make his selection and giving to the chosen the name of " Apostles." It is hardly probable that the author of Luke was better informed on the subject than Mark, for there is good reason to believe that he was identical with the redactor who " arranged " Acts, and like him, he seems to be entirely actuated by the idea of the sanctity of the Apostolate and of the Apostolic testimony.[1] Hence we may infer that at the time of the editing of the Synoptic tradition the circumstances of the choosing of the Twelve were no longer known.

There was some doubt also as to the order in which the selection was made, and even as to the names of one or two of the chosen. We have four lists of Apostles, one in each of the three Synoptics and one in Acts i. 13. They agree in placing Peter at the beginning and Judas at the end, which may perhaps reflect rather the ideas of the post-Apostolic community than the truth. The four lists, further, seem to be composed of three sets of four names, and in all of them each set commences with the same name : Peter (No. 1) ; Philip (No. 5) ; James the son of Alpheus (No. 9). The order of the other names varies from one source to the other, as if the whole list had been formed by putting together three special lists. Most of the names are found in all four enumerations. *Thaddeus*, however, who is the tenth in Mark and Matthew, and whom certain versions of the text of the latter call Labbeus,

[1] CCLXXXII, 139.

does not appear in either Luke or Acts, which give instead
Jude, who is not mentioned by Mark or Matthew. The orthodox commentators have attempted to reconcile all these variations, and to prove that the four lists are at bottom identical,
but that is a matter of belief rather than certainty.

With the exception of Peter and the two sons of Zebedee,
James and John, we have no admissible information regarding
the men whose names appear in the lists, and it is doubtful
whether the Gospel writers knew any more about them than
we do. It is not the tradition from which we hear about these
nine companions of Jesus, it is legend, whose often fantastic
tales are sufficient proof of the lack of any tradition.[1]

It is a question whether the choice of the Twelve is really
to be attributed to Jesus. Some have imagined a kind of
special confidence on the part of the Master in some twelve
disciples, and have attributed the establishment of the Apostolic college, and even the idea of the Apostolate, to the first
Church at Jerusalem after the death of Jesus.[2] Others, such
as Wellhausen[3] and J. Weiss,[4] have gone further, and maintained that Jesus himself had nothing whatever to do with the
choice, which was a kind of symbolic representation of the
Twelve Tribes,[5] and again the work of the first community.
Lagrange is indignant at these doubts, which he describes as
an " audacious denial " which is opposed by the evidence of
the whole tradition.[6] Since, in this case, " the whole tradition " amounts to very little, the charge is hardly a grave one.
There are, however, several points that may be advanced
against the negative party : (1) the early existence of the
Twelve is witnessed by Paul (1 Cor. xv. 5) ; (2) James, the
brother of the Lord, who according to Acts was very prominent
in the primitive community, is not amongst them (John vii. 5 :
" for even his brethren did not believe in him ") ; (3) Judas
the traitor is included in the list, which he would not have been
if the first Church had made the selection ; (4) after the betrayal
Luke (xxiv. 9 and 33), Acts (i. 26), and Matthew (xxviii. 16),
no longer speak of the *Twelve*, but of the *Eleven* ; [7] (5) finally,

---

[1] DACL, *Apôtres* ; **CXXXV**–*a*, see Index.

[2] For example, Ed. Meyer, **XXIV**, i, 264 *ff*., 291 *ff*. On the problem
as a whole see **CLVI**–*a*, 318–26.

[3] **CXII**, 138.   [4] **XXXIV**, 33.

[5] This connexion is implied in Rev. xxi. 14, and definitely indicated
in Barn. viii. 3 : οὖσιν δεκάδυο εἰς μαρτύριον τῶν φυλῶν ; and in the
Gospel of the Ebionites, quoted by Epiphanius, *Haer.*, 30, 13, in which
Jesus is supposed to say : " It is my will therefore that ye shall be
the twelve Apostles, as a witness of Israel."

[6] **CI**, 144.   [7] **CI**, 61 ; **XCVIII**, 39 ; **XXIV**, i, 296.

the Apostolic fellowship appears as an established body, devoted to Jesus and dedicated to his work, immediately after his death, which would be easier to understand if it were already in existence and merely continuing what had been begun.[1]

These arguments, which Eduard Meyer regards as very convincing, do not, however, appear to us to dispose of all doubt. Certainly it would not be improbable for Jesus to have selected some men whom he especially trusted, not to *preach* (as the κηρύσσειν of Mark iii. 14 is usually translated), but to carry on and extend his own activity, to proclaim the Kingdom as he had done (Mark x. 1).[2] But to be not improbable is not necessarily to be true, and it is impossible to ignore the fact that the account of the mission of the Twelve given in Mark vi. 7-13, and, with important variations, in Matthew x. and Luke ix., is very vague and unconvincing. After suggesting that Jesus is organizing a systematic evangelization, perhaps of Galilee, Mark says nothing further about the mission of the Twelve, and leaves us in complete ignorance, which was probably his own plight, regarding the setting, the duration, the events, and the results of their expedition. What he says in vi. 12-13, has no historical value : " And they went out and preached repentance, and they cast out many devils and anointed with oil many that were sick, and healed them." This is nothing but the most commonplace and empty hagiography, and the explanation of their return to Jesus as due to the hostility of Herod (vi. 30) is not much better. It is to be feared, consequently, that the pseudo-tradition attributed to Jesus a missionary enterprise of a type that must have become common in what is conventionally called " the Apostolic period," and that it was this tradition which conceived of the group of Twelve as a kind of institute of Christian propaganda, which is the way in which the redactor of Acts [3] obviously regards it. The historical existence of the Twelve around Jesus thus finds no real support in the account of their supposed mission. The alleged evidence of Paul in its favour is also, unfortunately, not very strong, for apart from the one passage just cited (1 Cor. xv. 5), the authenticity of which is not above suspicion, the Tarsiote seems to know nothing about the Twelve. It is not they whom he calls the Apostles, and not with them that he has to do when he comes to Jerusalem (Gal. i. 19 ; ii. 9).[4] We shall see shortly that the existence of an established group immediately after the death of Jesus may be regarded as certain.

---

[1] CLIX, 65, which admits, however, that the call of the Twelve is far from being satisfactorily authenticated.
[2] XIII, i, 299.　　[3] CCLXXXII, 139.　　[4] CIV, 193 ; CCLXXXII, 167.

We do not believe in the mission of the Twelve, and have little more faith in the choice of the Twelve by Jesus. We believe that the tradition preserved, at all costs, the names of some dozen intimate and faithful companions of the Master, and are inclined to think that they represented the whole of the gospel band, the regular companions of Jesus. We must not, of course, take absolutely literally a number which may be symbolic, or at least conventional, but it gives an idea of what the " crowds " which accompanied the Galilean *nabi* must in reality have amounted to.

III

THE ITINERARY OF JESUS [1]

We may imagine Jesus, then, wandering through the country accompanied by a handful of disciples. To the question exactly where he went, what itinerary he followed before going up to meet death at Jerusalem, there is no satisfactory reply, because the gospel tradition apparently took only a very superficial interest in it. As we shall see, it is bound up with that other question which is the main subject of this chapter, that of the success of Jesus.

Evidently, if we adhere to the brief outline which is to be obtained from the Synoptics, we shall not have the same view of the matter as if we accept, together with the Johannine chronology, the journeys to Jerusalem attributed to Jesus by the Fourth Gospel. One of the latest historians, to our knowledge, to deal with the problem, the avowedly conservative English critic, Headlam, although very anxious to reject as little as possible of the Gospel accounts, admits [2] that their chronology is too vague for us to be able to extract from them any definite plan of the travels of Jesus. In addition to a few short expeditions around the lake, he believes, however, that it is possible to make out : (1) two long tours in Galilee, including visits to Nazareth, Nain, and Cana ; (2) two journeys across the lake to Gerasa and Bethsaida ; (3) a journey into the territories of Tyre and Sidon ending at Decapolis ; (4)

---

[1] The author of **CXCVII** knows the country very well, but he has no use for, nor appreciation of, scientific criticism. *Cf.* **XXIV**, i, 131 *ff.*, which shows clearly the existence of variations and doublets in the tradition.

[2] **CLIX**, 325. This author has a capacity for confidence in the gospel texts which is only equalled by his critical incompetence. See especially **CLIX**, 290.

several visits, how many he cannot say, to Jerusalem. All this is very vague and unreliable, especially in view of the decidedly arbitrary combination of the data of the Synoptics, which are themselves confused enough, with those of John. Mark alone, however, if examined with proper caution, will perhaps yield us, not certainty, which is unattainable here as elsewhere, but at least a semblance of probability.[1]

To begin with, it seems likely that there was a period of activity on the shore of the lake of Tiberias, with Capernaum as its headquarters. It was there that the boat (τὸ πλοῖον) was stationed which Jesus used for going from one shore of the lake to the other (iii. 9 ; vi. 32, etc.). It is possible, however, that the Evangelist has somewhat exaggerated the number of these crossings, using them to make the necessary transitions between the various portions of his story.[2] From Capernaum the prophet penetrated the surrounding country : " he went about the neighbouring villages, teaching " (Mark vi. 6). He probably extended his " rounds " to the whole of Galilee (i. 39), and even visited " his own country " (εἰς τὴν πατρίδα αὐτοῦ) where he had no success (vi. 1–6). It is doubtful, however, whether he went very far from the lake, because he had not time enough. Mark gives the impression that things went wrong very soon, possibly at the end of a few weeks.

Herod Antipas, tetrarch, but popularly called king, of Galilee and Peræa, heard of the new prophet, and is supposed to have wondered (vi. 14 ff.) if it might not be John the Baptist risen from the dead, and to have been troubled. The Gospel writer here clothes a very strong probability in the garb of fable for the purpose of bringing in the story of the death of the Baptist, which, as he relates it, appears to belong rather to legend than to history.[3] Herod, whose usual place of residence was Tiberias, had no difficulty in keeping himself informed as to what went on at Capernaum a few miles to the north. He had his police, who could not fail to keep watch on the actions and movements of a man of God. Mark shows us the Twelve reassembling about their Master and then going to seek " a desert place apart " (vi. 30). They went to Bethsaida (vi. 45), and from there towards Gennesaret (vi. 53), that is to say, first to the north of the lake, and then to the narrow plain which borders it on the west, and in which Capernaum is situated. It seems as if the little band were trying, by moving quickly from place to place, to baffle an alarming pursuit.[4] We can place no reliance on the details of the Marcan

---

[1] See **XXIV**, i, 131, for criticism of the data of Mark.
[2] **CV**, 230. [3] **XCVIII**, 66. [4] **CV**, 203.

narrative, which gives no definite particulars and no explanations, but the feeling of hostility towards Jesus which it attributes to the Herodians, along with the Pharisees and Sadducees,
and Jesus' sudden and frequent changes of place are too logically
convincing not to be true. In this connexion, Luke (xiii. 31)
makes a statement which is peculiar to him alone, and of which
we cannot gauge the authenticity, which is unfortunate, for it
would be worth a good deal if it were accurate. He claims that
it was some Pharisees who, at the instigation of the Tetrarch,
undertook to intimate to Jesus that it would be as well for
him to leave Galilee. Antipas can hardly have been anxious
to repeat the affair of John the Baptist, especially with a fanatic
who did not seem very formidable, and he may well have preferred to have him go and get himself hanged elsewhere.[1] At
all events, we get the impression—though it can be no more
than that—that Jesus realized simultaneously that he had
failed to succeed in Galilee and that the authorities had become
hostile to him.

He next went towards the " borders of Tyre " (vii. 24),[2]
that is, to that part of the Phenician territory which bounds
Galilee on the north, with the intention of hiding ($o\vec{v}\delta\acute{\epsilon}\nu\alpha$ $\mathring{\eta}\theta\epsilon\lambda\epsilon\nu$
$\gamma\nu\widetilde{\omega}\nu\alpha\iota$). To all appearances he ceased to preach, and seems
to have abandoned his mission. The gospel writer's story of
a Gentile woman, a Syrophenician, who came to give him an
opportunity, by demanding of him a great miracle, to authorize
the reception of Gentiles into the faith, is quite artificial. It
is probably only an allegory [3] designed to show that pagans who
believed were admitted to salvation, and has nothing whatever to do with the life of Jesus. Since this journey to the
goyim appears to have been entirely barren, nothing but this
tendentious miracle being attributed to it by Mark, it has been
suggested that it was a pure invention on the part of the Evangelist, for the purpose of introducing the miracle. The possibility
of this is undeniable, for the gospel writer has no interest in
it except so far as the prodigy required by his doctrine is concerned. Nevertheless, we feel that there is a strong probability
of some kind of withdrawal out of the reach of Antipas, and
Phenicia would not have been unappropriate for the purpose.

From this point the geographical setting of the Marcan
narrative becomes very confused. " And again departing from
the country of Tyre, he came by way of Sidon to the sea of

---

[1] LXXIX, 70.

[2] Sidon, which various manuscripts, followed by the Vulgate, add
here, probably erroneously, is mentioned further on (vii. 31).

[3] CCXV, ii, 258 ; LXXXV, 235.

Galilee in the midst of the territory of Decapolis " (vii. 31).
That is to say, he is supposed to have gone from Tyre to Sidon,
or from south to north, and thence to have returned south-
eastwards to the lake and pushed on still further in the same
direction towards Decapolis. After this we find him again on
the shore of the lake, resuming his journeyings from one side
to the other (viii. 10, 14, and 22). Immediately afterwards
(viii. 27 *ff.*) he is in the neighbourhood of Cæsarea [1] in the territory of the tetrarch Philip, far to the north of the lake, having
presumably come from Bethsaida up the left bank of the Jordan.
All this seems very confused, or would seem so, at least, if it
related to an ordinary journey. It looks, for instance, as if the
Evangelist had put *after* the excursion into Phenicia certain
Galilean incidents which must have occurred *before*; or again
as if he had arbitrarily brought Jesus *back* to Cæsarea Philippi,
inasmuch as that town was directly on his route from Sidon to
the lake ; in short, as if *Mark* had ruthlessly mixed up his times
and places. But if it were really the erratic flight of a man
who felt himself hunted, the strangeness and the incoherence—
barring the incidents with which the narrator cloaks his ignorance—would no longer be so suspicious.

He returns from there (ix. 30)—we are assuming that the
reference is still to the neighbourhood of Cæsarea—through
Galilee, and regains Capernaum (ix. 33) seeking concealment.
He doubtless does no more than pause there, because he is too
well known in the town, for he immediately (x. 1) sets out
again for Judæa, passing through Peræa.[2] Then he begins
to preach again. His courage has come back because he
has come to a heartening decision ; he is going up to Jerusalem. It is undeniable that all this Marcan itinerary remains
extremely vague, and the Synoptics shed no light upon it, as
may be seen merely by comparing its final part with the corresponding passage of Luke (ix. 51 *ff.*), which apparently sends
Jesus to Jerusalem through Samaria and Judæa, the usual
route from Galilee. All this portion of Luke also is most bewilderingly confused, and looks like a hodge-podge of everything the editor has been unable to find room for elsewhere.[3]

---

[1] This town was probably founded in 3 B.C. by the tetrarch Philip
(Josephus, *Ant.*, 18, 2, 1 ; *B.J.*, 2, 9, 1). It was called Cæsarea Philippi
to distinguish it from the other Cæsarea (the ancient Tower of Strato)
which was on the coast.

[2] This is, at least, how I interpret, in agreement with Wellhausen,
the confused text of x. 1 : ἔρχεται εἰς τὰ ὅρια τῆς Ἰουδαίας καὶ πέραν τοῦ
Ἰορδάνου. Wellhausen, following Codex D and various MSS., omits
καί. As against this reading, see CI, 241.

[3] CLXII, 420 *ff.*

Jesus is supposed to arrive at Jerusalem via Jericho (Mark x. 46), which fits in with the detour through Peræa. This country was, it is true, also governed by Antipas, but the Galilean was not known there, and it would undoubtedly be easier for him to keep under cover than in Samaria and Judæa, where the Roman police were in direct control.

It must be confessed that an examination of the movements of Jesus recorded by Mark is rarely in favour of their veracity, and that in all too many cases Mark is legitimately suspected of having taken Jesus to this place or that merely because he needed to have him go there, and not because he knew that he had actually gone,[1] and for this reason we offer the above restoration of the itinerary of Jesus in all diffidence, without pretending to vouch for its correctness. Nevertheless, it seems to us that the Evangelist, having no apparent motive for giving his readers the impression that the Master was unable to remain long in Galilee and very quickly felt himself to be unsafe there, did not invent the fundamental fact of this incessant moving about, away from the original scene of the preaching of the Glad Tidings. At most he may have arbitrarily located the various stages of it, but we do not actually know that he did so, and as he appears to have no good reason for it, except in a few special cases, it is not entirely improbable that, *on the whole*, what he says is true. Reading the first ten chapters of Mark, it is obvious that the events contained in them imply only a very brief period of time. Five or six weeks in Galilee, and the same, at most, on the outskirts, would apparently be quite sufficient, and short of the gospel editor's having been either totally ignorant or consistently mendacious, there seems no likelihood of its having been much more.

Hunted from Galilee, then, Jesus goes up towards Jerusalem. At first this is surprising, for what hope of success could he have in the city dominated by the Temple, where the doctors of the School and the priests reigned supreme, where the suspicious Roman was on the watch, and where he himself was only a provincial without influence ? The Evangelist's answer to this question is that the Nazarene went to Jerusalem to suffer and to die, as he had predicted to the Twelve (x. 33 *ff.* ; *cf.* viii. 31 and ix. 31). But that is a *post factum* explanation. The redactor is actuated by the desire to show that Jesus was not struck down unexpectedly, that he had foreseen the blow as an essential and inevitable part of his mission. A study of the Passion will easily convince us that this apologetic conception is quite untrue. It was not to die, it was to act, that the prophet

[1] CVIII, 232.

turned his steps towards the Holy City.[1] It had been borne in upon him that all he had done and said, since the day when he felt in his heart the *ruach* of Jahweh, had accomplished nothing. But God does not lie ; it was his servant who had failed to understand that a part like his was not to be enacted in the little towns of Galilee. Jerusalem was his last hope, because, according to common expectation, it was in the City of David that the Kingdom whose herald he was,[2] was to appear and be realized. Loisy well observes,[3] in this connexion, an interesting comparison between two passages of the Synoptics, one in Matthew (xix. 28), and the other in Luke (xix. 11). In connexion with the parable of the ten talents, Luke introduces the following remark : " . . . because he was nigh to Jerusalem, and they thought that the Kingdom of God should immediately appear " ; and the parable which follows is intended to prove that each will be recompensed in proportion to the zeal he has displayed before the Great Day. Matthew, amongst the other sayings which he attributes to Jesus when he is on the point of entering Judæa (xix. 1), includes the promise to the Twelve that they shall each sit upon a throne and judge the twelve tribes, which is an indirect proclamation of the imminence of the reign of God. Perhaps it would not be going too far to conclude from the comparison of these two passages that the tradition had preserved the idea that the gospel band on drawing near to Jerusalem was filled with a great exaltation and a glowing anticipation of the desired event.

According to the Marcan tradition (xi. 1–11), this enthusiastic premonition manifested itself in a very dangerous demonstration. At Jesus' bidding two of the disciples had gone to Bethany, at the southern end of the Mount of Olives, to fetch a colt.

> " And they brought the colt to Jesus and put their cloaks upon it and he sat upon it. And many spread their mantles on the way, and others, green branches which they cut in the fields. And they that went before, and they that followed cried : ' Hosanna ! Blessed be the coming kingdom of our father David ! Hosanna in the highest [of heaven] ! '[4] And he entered into Jerusalem into the Temple. . . ."

Taking this account as it stands, it is clear that Jesus wished to make a Messianic entry into the City, in fulfilment of the prophecy of Zechariah ix. 9 : " Rejoice greatly, O daughter of Zion ! Utter cries of joy, O daughter of Jerusalem ! Behold

---

[1] CLX, 101 ; CLVI, 256 *ff.*   [2] LXXIX, 101.
[3] CLXII, 422 and 424.
[4] In Job xvi. 19, the expression ἐν ὑψίστοις which we find in Mark xvi. 10, is paralleled by ἐν ὀυρανοῖς, which explains its meaning.

thy king cometh unto thee, just and bearing salvation ! He is
lowly and riding upon an ass. . . ." Matthew xxi. 4, who
cites the prophecy, does not fail, according to his custom in
such cases, to say explicitly that the incident was for the purpose of accomplishing it. The whole question is whether this
accomplishment was the doing of Jesus or of the gospel narrator.
On this point, opinions differ, for it is naturally doubtful.[1]

If Jesus and his disciples really arrived at the gates of
Jerusalem in the state of mind which we have imputed to them,
it is obviously not impossible that he himself may have wished
to " impress the masses,"[2] and to excite them to the point of
forming a procession. Nevertheless, we do not believe in the
reality of the incident ; in the first place, because it is not clear
how a *nabi*, probably unknown to the people of Jerusalem,
could have found outside the walls the people to compose such
a demonstration[3] ; in the second place, because, even if he
had, in some mysterious way, succeeded in doing so, it would
be hard to understand why the Roman and Jewish authorities
did not interfere, for the precise purpose of preventing him
from arousing the people, which was what they dreaded above
all ; and, finally, because the account appears to be, not merely
dramatized, but completely artificial. Its object is to show
that the prophecies were fulfilled, and to rob the Jews, who
subsequently refused to acknowledge Jesus, of all excuse,
inasmuch as they had had warning of his status. The very
content of the account is furnished by the passage of Zechariah
just quoted, and by Psalm cxviii. (cxvii. in the Septuagint)
which gives the substance of the alleged acclamations. It is
so definitely an invention,[4] and an end in itself, that this
triumphal entry is left without any sequel. It is as if all the
enthusiasm stopped at the door of the Temple, from which
Jesus is supposed to return quite quietly to Bethany with the
Twelve, who could hardly have created all that disturbance by
themselves (Mark xi. 11). The following day, nobody in the
City seems to have any recollection of the affair. It hardly

[1] **XCVIII**, 126 ; **XXIV**, i, 162 ; **CLVI**, 255 *ff*.

[2] **XXIV**, i, 162.

[3] Luke xix. 28–38, who follows Mark and for the most part merely
copies him, is, however, sensible of this difficulty, for he attributes the
demonstration to the " multitude of the disciples," xix. 37 : (ἅπαν τὸ
πλῆθος τῶν μαθητῶν). We might be perplexed by this, were not the
purpose of mitigating the improbability by means of this formal correction completely obvious. Luke also adds that the Pharisees intervened and asked Jesus to reprove his disciples, which is another interpolation for the same purpose, and is equally inconsistent.

[4] It is modified in John xii. 12 *ff*., but does not thereby gain any
more credibility. *Cf.* **CXLII**, 155.

seems likely that matters would have blown over in this fashion, even if only a fraction of the people of Jerusalem had believed that the Messiah had come.

Either tendentious legend or subsequent invention, this is the verdict that perpetually recurs when we are reviewing the incidents which the Synoptic tradition has bequeathed to us. It is impossible to ignore the extreme poverty and confusion of its content [1] : a few goings and comings and some miracles, accompanied by teachings bearing, for the most part, on the imminent eschatological future. Of facts which can be utilized by the historian, which really bring us near to the true Jesus, there are none, or very few, even for those who are not hampered by critical scruples. Possibly the short public career of the Nazarene may have contained nothing more, but we prefer to think that this disappointing emptiness is in the main due to the indifference, if not of the tradition, at least of the Gospel editors, to everything that did not directly serve their own ends, to everything that was not of importance for doctrine, apologetic, or ritual. For that reason they laid much more emphasis upon the drama of the Passion and the miracle of the Resurrection, which had become, by force of circumstances, the foundation of their belief in Christ, than upon all the rest of the life of Jesus.

Before examining this final act of the drama, which is said to contain the secret of the origins of Christianity, we must ask ourselves what Jesus believed himself to be when he arrived at Jerusalem, what conception he had of himself and his mission, and exactly what his teaching was.

[1] An interesting general survey will be found in **XXIV**, ii, 420 *ff.*, and a study of the main incidents in **LXXXVI**, 151 *ff.*

PART II

THE TEACHING OF JESUS[1]

CHAPTER I

OUR INFORMATION

I

THE DOCUMENTS

FOR the purpose of explaining the birth of Christianity,
adequate and reliable information concerning the teaching
of Jesus would obviously be of even greater value than an
authentic knowledge of his life. That we possess such information, however, can hardly be maintained. Practically our
only hope of enlightenment lies in the Synoptics; all that is
contributed by other sources could, as Harnack justly observes,[2]
be comprised in less than a page. The orthodox claim the
same footing for the Fourth Gospel as for the other three,
but no impartial critic can share this opinion. With regard
to the teaching of Jesus, as with regard to his life, the Johannine Gospel represents a tendentious interpretation of the
tradition; it is a treatise of a mystical rather than a strictly
theological character, on lines which may have been derived
from this tradition, but also on others which were developed
by Paul, and have no connexion with it. To regard it as
complementary to the Synoptics, and to rank its assertions
with their evidence, is a completely uncritical proceeding, and
one which can, moreover, lead only to a representation of
Christ's teaching as a whole, which is as inconsistent as it is

[1] Systematic expositions will be found in **L–a**, i, 159–420; **LXVII**,
42–187; **XLIV**, 22–189; (all three of these contain full bibliographies);
CXC; **CCXXXV**; **CCXXXIII**; E. Burton, *Source Book for the Study
of the Teaching of Jesus*, 1923. For the relations with Judaism see
LXXIV; Walker, *The Teaching of Jesus and the Jewish Teaching of
his age*, 1923; **LXXX**; and all the great commentaries on the Synoptics, especially those of Strack and Billerbeck, of Montefiore, and of
Klostermann.

[2] **CCLXIV**, 31.

artificial. Paul does not contribute a great deal, which is at
first surprising, considering how much authority he attaches,
and must necessarily attach, to the words of the Lord Jesus.
We read in 1 Corinthians ix. 14 : " Even so hath the Lord
himself ordained (καὶ ὁ κύριος διέταξεν) that those who
preach the Gospel should live of the Gospel " : and again,
in 1 Corinthians vii. 10 : " And unto those who are united in
marriage, I command (παραγγέλλω), yet not I, but the Lord
(οὐκ ἐγὼ ἀλλά ὁ κύριος), that the wife shall not depart from
her husband." On other points concerning matrimonial discipline the Apostle is careful to point out that, having no
" commandment of the Lord " on the subject, he can give only
his own opinion (1 Cor. vii. 12 and 25). We do not know
what use he made of the teachings of Jesus in his preaching,
hence we cannot tell how much of them he knew, but it is
evident from a mere comparison of Matthew and the Epistle
to the Romans that the Pauline *doctrine* was already so different
from that which our First Gospel attributes to the Nazarene,
that it could not have paid much attention to the details of
ideas which it had already left behind—any more than it did
to the incidents of a life which no longer interested it (2 Cor.
v. 16). Between the Gospel of Jesus and that of Paul intervened influences of which the Synoptics knew nothing—personal
revelations and speculative ideas from various sources—which
led Paul's mind into an entirely different world of thought.
Such considerations render the meagreness of his contribution
to our subject no longer surprising.[1]

The other writings of the New Testament yield nothing
at all, a noteworthy fact, since it gives us reason to fear that
the Christian generations to which we owe these works (Acts,
the Catholic Epistles, Revelation) did not go back to Jesus
himself for an understanding of his ideas, any more than they
drew their pictures of him from the original. They were much
more interested in what they expected the Lord to do in the
immediate future than in what he had done or said in the past,
during his earthly existence.

The earliest Christian literature, the collection of the writing
of the so-called *Apostolic Fathers*, reveals the same tendencies,
and affords us no more assistance in our inquiry.

Even the *Agrapha* fail us. They add nothing of any importance to what is contained in the Synoptics, as a glance
through the collection of Resch or White will readily convince
us.[2]

We must accordingly content ourselves with what we can

[1] **XLIV**, 27.   [2] **CXXXVII**; **CXL.**

glean from the Synoptics. Of the two primary sources on which they are based, one alone, the *logia*, is of importance in this connexion. It must not be overlooked that the attempts which have been made to restore it, by extracting its contributions from Matthew and Luke, have achieved no more than probable results, and that its very existence is still disputed in some quarters as merely hypothetical. We do not know whether the collection did not circulate in quite different forms, or, so to speak, in different editions, and in any case it must be borne in mind that our reputed informaton regarding the teaching of Jesus consists only of that portion of the contents of the *logia* which the Synoptists thought fit to appropriate.

The amount is not very large. It has been computed that it would have taken no more than an hour for Jesus to utter all the *sayings* of his that we possess,[1] and not more than six hours, the time required for two parliamentary speeches of average length,[2] for him to deliver all the discourses attributed to him in the Gospels. Hence it is indisputable that we do not possess the preaching of Jesus in its entirety. Who, for that matter, could have preserved it? During his discourses people were certainly not engaged in noting down his words. They did not see in them, strictly speaking, a doctrine for future guidance ; they were impressed only by the promise which was the basis of all his teaching, and which in fact rendered all doctrine superfluous, that of the imminent advent of the expected Kingdom. The disciples themselves do not seem to have felt that the items of the teaching had any *internal* connexion. They accepted them as independent utterances, and preserved, together with the general tenor and purport of the teaching, the most striking of these sayings.

It is not surprising that the tradition which had, in the last analysis, only their recollections to sustain it, is not more complete and systematic. The sole question is whether it is sufficiently so to enable us adequately to comprehend what Jesus said and meant. This question has received the most contradictory answers. Harnack, for instance, avers [3] that the Synoptics " give us a perfectly clear idea of the preaching of Jesus, as regards both its fundamental principles and its particular applications." Batiffol, on the contrary, maintains that it is certain [4] that, though the Synoptics may have retained the " essential principles " of the teaching of Jesus, they do not give us the whole content of this preaching. " On certain

---

[1] Platzhoff-Lejeune, *Religion gegen Theologie und Kirche*, 1905, 24 *ff.* ; L–a, i, 179, n. 6.

[2] Burkitt, **LXXVI**, 29.   [3] **CCLXIV**, 45.   [4] **CXC**, vii.

points these principles are no more than suggestions, and regarding the fundamental articles of our Christian faith, even these are lacking." We must accordingly acknowledge " the imperfection of the Gospels "; to refuse to do so is " a Protestant error " of the first magnitude. The Lord entrusted to his immediate disciples something quite different from what the Evangelists have recorded, and this something—need it be said ?—is the substance of the Catholic tradition. This diametrical opposition between the Protestant and the Roman Catholic theologian simply corresponds to that between the postulates of their respective creeds.

At first reading, the *logia* are seen to consist, at least, in so far as they are represented in Matthew and Luke,[1] of a collection of sayings and a number of discourses. Amongst the sayings, there is a distinction to be made between those which, so to speak, embody a teaching, and might belong to a doctrinal scheme,[2] and those which are nothing but *comments*, extempore utterances of restricted application, having no connexion with any preconceived and coherent system.[3] To confuse these two categories, or rather, to regard them as one, is a common error, and one from which the Gospel writers are by no means exempt. It results in taking what is merely a sally or a paradox, wholly bound up with the occasion which called it forth,[4] for a universal and absolute rule.

In a large number of cases, however, the *sayings* were preserved in detachment from the circumstances which gave rise to them, or at all events determined their exact meaning and limited their application. Under these conditions, the Gospel redactors made use of them as they pleased, sometimes combining them, in a context which was not their own, with other similar sayings, sometimes adapting them, by means of more or less drastic pruning, to a quite arbitrary use.[5] In this process, they have, to all appearances, lost their true meaning. It is further obvious that the Gospel editors handled the other *logia*, those which probably were originally intended as

[1] **XCV**; **CCL**, 107–26 ; **CLXX**, i, 430 *ff.*, gives a systematic list, which, though concise, is sufficient, if necessary, to enable anyone to ascertain the contents of the *logia* with the help of the text.

[2] Matt. v. 42 ; vii. 12 ; xii. 32 ; and a number of verses inserted in the Sermon on the Mount, Matt. v.–vii.

[3] Matt. xv. 14 ; x. 24 ; vii. 16–18 ; x. 34–8 ; x. 16*a* ; etc. *Cf.* Weidel, *Jesu Persönlichkeit*, 1909, 33 and 39 ; **L–a**, i, 176 ; **CXLIII**, 50 *ff.* ; **CXC**, xviii.

[4] What Bousset, **CXLIII**, 50, calls " *ein Augenblickwort.*"

[5] *Cf.* the commentaries in our list on Mark iv. 25 ; Matt. v. 17 ; Luke xiv. 36 ; to confine ourselves to three striking instances.

general precepts and doctrine, with no more scruples and no greater respect.

It is common in religious circles, and even outside them, to praise the beauty of the Gospel discourses :

> " They are such," it is asserted,[1] " as those of a god become man must necessarily be." We cannot fail to recognize "in both their substance and their form the mind and heart of the incarnate Word." They are especially admirable for the precision with which they express " in the fewest possible words, the most sublime, true, and practical ideas, on God the divine matters, on man and his destiny, on the present and the future life, on duty, and on perfection . . . an inimitable naturalness, clearness, and simplicity . . . a wholly divine eloquence . . . a simple and popular style . . . a marvellous aptness," so that the saying attributed to the Jews by John vii. 46, " ' never man spake like this man,' is true in every sense." The author concludes that these discourses, which are, however, "rather talks than speeches, . . . permit us to see [in conjunction with the whole public career of Jesus] and to hear, the greatest, the most sacred, the most moving thing conceivable : the Man-God living on earth, or wisdom and love incarnate revealing themselves to men and conversing familiarly with them."

All this, which is full of admirable feeling admirably expressed, is unfortunately based upon an illusion. There is not the slightest doubt that Jesus never uttered the discourses attributed to him by the Gospels. They are artificial compositions, of which the most that we can hope is that they employ authentic *logia*. Even the Sermon on the Mount, which has been so much discussed, is no exception to this rule. On the contrary, it would be sufficient to establish it, and at all events it conspicuously confirms it.

On closer examination these discourses break up into a number of disjointed sayings, or, at best, into small groups of sayings.[2] These groups appear to be for the most part the work of the primitive community, and for the rest, that of the Gospel redactors. They have been composed by putting together sayings and parables which seem to resemble each other, either in substance or merely in external form.[3] The primitive community made use in several different ways of the collection of sayings provided by the *paradosis*, which could only serve this purpose by adapting itself to aims and tendencies which were fundamentally alien to it. For instance,

---

[1] V, i, 509–13.
[2] CXLIII, 49 : " *in einzelne kleine Konglomerate, oft in einzelne Wörte* "; CLXXXV, 75.
[3] CXC, 8.

the necessity for a kind of moral instruction which could be offered in the name of the Lord to the newly converted, quickly made itself felt, and the Sermon on the Mount came into being to fill this need. Again, it was necessary to define and authorize the duties of missionaries, and this was provided for by the sermon which Jesus is supposed to have delivered to the disciples before sending them out on their mission (Matt. x. 5 *ff.*). The discourse on John given in Matthew xi. was the result of the difficulties which arose between the infant Church and the disciples of the Baptist ; and that on the Pharisees in Matthew xxiii.,[1] was called forth by the opposition of the Jewish rabbis to Christian propaganda in Jewish communities.[1]

A certain Catholic historian has maintained, not without some show of reason,[2] that these sermons composed of sayings strung together, though characterized by the " oracular " manner so dear to the Jewish taste, are not all what we should expect of Jesus, in that they are too artificial in style and too lacking in feeling and spontaneity. The actual words of the Master must have " gushed forth " in a different way. This is certainly what we should be inclined to believe, but between belief and knowledge there is a considerable gap. What we are sure of, however, is that the comparison of Matthew and Luke makes it impossible to hold that these Gospel discourses were ever uttered.

If we consider, for example, Luke xii. 1–7, or even the whole of the chapter, which contains a long instructional discourse of Jesus to his disciples, we can easily see that it is a compilation, constructed by stringing together : first, some isolated sayings detached from their setting ; second, a parable on the subject of avarice, followed by a discourse on freedom from earthly cares which has no necessary connexion with it, and is used by Matthew vi. 25 in a different context ; and third, several groups of sayings regarding the necessity of holding oneself in readiness for the sudden coming of the Kingdom, and the inevitable punishment of those who, having been given the opportunity of knowing what they should do, have refused either to listen or to obey. We have only to read these sayings, from *v.* 35 to 59, to realize their complete lack of connexion. This impression is further confirmed by Matthew, who, finding these *logia* either singly or in small groups in his source, has used them in quite a different way from Luke, dividing them amongst several chapters.

The artificiality of the Sermon on the Mount is equally obvious from a brief comparison of it with the Sermon in the

[1] **CXLIII,** 49 ; **CXC,** xvii.　　　　　[2] *Ibid.,* 14.

Plain recorded by Luke vi. 20 *ff*. The sayings and groups of sayings found in Matthew are in part repeated in Luke,[1] but sometimes in different phrasing, and in quite a different *order*. On the other hand, there are important portions of Matthew which do not appear in Luke at all,[2] and others which appear elsewhere, in a different context.[3] All this shows plainly that each redactor used the material of his source as he pleased, for the purpose of composing one or more discourses. Finally, it is obvious that nobody took notes, and that it would have been impossible to remember from merely hearing them the one hundred and seven verses of the discourse of Matthew, or even the thirty verses of that of Luke.

To sum up, the only approximately definite information which it is possible to derive from the Gospel sermons, is some idea of the main themes, not so much of the preaching of Jesus, as of the doctrine of the community by and for which the sayings were organized. This involves, of course, no assumption as to the origin of the sayings themselves. Any literary admiration is in great danger of being really directed towards some anonymous compiler, and similarly, it would be most hazardous to base any doctrinal inference upon the letter and arrangement of any of the discourses, the relative position and value of the ideas which it expresses, for they are due to the redactor and not to Jesus.

II

THE SAYINGS

We are accordingly brought back to the fundamental problem of the validity of the sayings. We might, at first, be tempted to believe that the collection of the Master's teachings must always, from the very beginning, have been the first care of the disciples, and the preservation of this precious legacy the great endeavour of the original community, but it has already been pointed out that we must be under no such illusion. For the disciples, the most important thing in the preaching of Jesus was its assurance that the time was fulfilled, and the Kingdom at hand, and the first generation of Christians lived in a constant expectation of the *parousia*. Neither it nor the

[1] For example : Luke vi. 29–30 is almost identical with Matt. v. 38–42 ; Luke vi. 27–8, 32–6, with Matt. v. 43–8 ; Luke vi. 37, 38, 41, 42, with Matt. vii. 1–5 ; Luke vi. 31 with Matt. vii. 12 ; etc.

[2] Matt. v. 17, 19, 20, 21–4, 33–7 ; vi. 1–4, 5–8, 16–18 ; vii. 6.

[3] Matt. vi. 9–15 is found in Luke xi. 1–4 ; Matt. vi. 19–21 in Luke xii. 33–4 ; etc.

disciples felt any necessity of especially remembering and preserving for the future the details of a teaching which interested
them precisely because it limited the future to a few months,
or possibly even days. Any striking phrases which Jesus may
have used, might, to be sure, remain in the memory of their
hearers, but disconnectedly, and as it were at random, and
in any case, much more by virtue of their form than of their
content. The ideas that were really important *to Jesus*, must,
we admit, have been expressed by him often enough to be
remembered. But on the other hand, many others which
would be illuminating *to us*, have vanished because they happened not to be so happily expressed as those which have
survived.

To imagine [1] that from the beginning his followers composed
little collections of the Lord's sayings, each preceded by the
formula, " Jesus said," such as we find in the papyri of the
second and third centuries, implies that the generation of the
disciples, and its successor, believed that the Master built on
earth and for the future, in other words, that the Kingdom
was to be identified with the Catholic Church. But though
that is the inevitable conviction of the whole ecclesiastical
tradition, it cannot be shared, as we shall soon see, by any
unbiassed reader of the texts. The probability is that the
members of the faith thought of making collections only when
they had begun to have doubts of the *parousia*, and when the
disappearance of those who had known and heard the Lord
aroused their anxiety. It is to be noted that Paul, who welcomed " words of the Lord," seems to have obtained them
only from the *paradosis*. The attempt to formulate and stabilize
this oral tradition itself, was probably only made when it
became necessary to particularize and extend the teaching of
the Lord, for the exhortation and training of proselytes.[2] In
other words, it was gradually effected as the Christian faith
freed itself from its Jewish swaddling-clothes and developed
in the direction of an independent religion. We may estimate
that twenty-five or thirty years would be required for this
need of a collection of the sayings of Jesus to make itself felt,
and that is a considerable time from the point of view of their
complete preservation.

We cannot be too often reminded that the men who committed to writing the deliverances of the Synoptic tradition
were not interested in recording, but in proving. What they
tried to bring out was the evidence in favour of their religious
ideas. From Mark to John, their spirit and purpose are the

[1] CXC, 14.   [2] CCXXXV, 20.

same, and their differences are only of degree. If we are no
longer able to see Jesus except through the eyes of these men,
we are likewise unable to hear him except with their ears.[1]
The whole question appears to resolve itself into that of the
accuracy of their hearing and the fidelity of their memories.
It was a saying amongst the rabbis that "the good disciple is
like a cemented reservoir, which never loses a drop of its water."
But unfortunately, we cannot in this case count upon scholastic custom, because the recipients and preservers of the
gospel tradition were the common people, the uneducated, and
our Gospels are merely religious books for popular use.[2] Further, we have to do here, not with a small group of pupils,
quietly hearing, preserving, and transmitting the words of a
master, but with an active community of believers in the
midst of the constructive period of its faith, and in the very
process of transforming its teacher into the glorified Lord.[3]
There is no question of any already formulated doctrine, but
only of a tradition gradually adapting itself to religious ideals
which are still to some extent uncertain. Under these circumstances, it seems natural that the young community, "in
making the teaching of Jesus the sustenance of its life, should
have revised that teaching and brought it into line with its
own experience, its needs, its trials, and its knowledge."[4]
When, for instance, we read in Mark ix. 41 : "For whosoever
shall give you a cup of water to drink because ye belong to
Christ ($\H{o}\tau\iota$ $X\rho\iota\sigma\tau o\tilde{v}$ $\H{\varepsilon}\sigma\tau\varepsilon$), verily I say unto you, he shall not
lose his reward," we are struck by the expression, "because
ye belong to Christ," which seems very strange in the mouth
of Jesus. Lagrange himself admits [5] that it is a Pauline mode
of expression, which is never found in either the Synoptics
or in Acts. He puts the responsibility for it on some copyist,
while Batiffol thinks it is the adaptation of a saying of Jesus
for the purpose of supporting Christian preaching. It is not
easy to see what the authentic *logion* which is supposed to
have been adapted could have been, and we are inclined to
believe that the whole thing was the tendentious creation of
the redactor.

It is at first surprising to find the lips of Jesus uttering
so many contradictory sayings, but it becomes intelligible when
we discover that all the complexities of Christian doctrine of
the time of the gospel compilers are reflected in the utterances
which they attribute to the Lord, rather than the probably

---

[1] XLIV, 22 ; *cf.* CXCIII, 47.
[2] L–a, i, 179: *Volks- und Andachtsbücher.*
[3] CXLIII, 54. [4] CXC, xvi. [5] CI, 234.

very simple, authentic words of the Nazarene.[1] It was inevitable that this should have been the case.

There is accordingly not much hope that what has come down to us of the *logia* presents a faithful and accurate record of the preaching of Jesus, a summary of the substance of his teaching. It is, on the contrary, probable that ideas, conceptions, and interests quite alien to the mind of the Master were, in all good faith, ascribed to him by the community which adhered to them, and also that many, if not all, of his authentic utterances were revised by the growing faith and adapted to purposes for which they were not originally designed.

III

REASONS FOR HOPE

The case is not, however, quite so desperate as it may seem from the foregoing discouraging remarks, because, on reflection, there are to be discerned some mitigating factors.

The first arises, if we may so put it, from the very nature of the preaching of Jesus. If he had built up a system of doctrine, for which the disciples and the primitive community had by degrees substituted another, the loss would be irreparable, but this does not appear to have been the case. Strictly speaking, we do not find any original body of doctrine in the Gospel. Jesus belongs to the religious setting of Israel, and is rooted in beliefs already long established. It is on the basis of these beliefs, and without stepping out of this setting, that he speaks of his mission and of the imminence of the great event which he proclaims. He attempts to induce his hearers, by means of appropriate but apparently very simple religious and moral exhortations, to prepare for the coming day in a manner conducive to their own advantage. The original community, of which we are given a glimpse in the first chapters of Acts, the community which lived on Jewish soil and developed the fundamental tradition out of which the Synoptic tradition arose, had no need to change the religious setting of the Gospel of Jesus, or to attribute to it any other aims and methods than those expressed by the Nazarene himself. The first " brethren " were Jews, or Jewish converts, and they awaited the appearance of the Kingdom in an effort to lead the kind of life which the Master prescribed, and which was to assure them of a place amongst the elect. Their faith was subject to no irresistible impulse towards elaboration, except with regard to the

[1] CXLVII, 405 *ff.*

figure and status of Jesus himself. They began the Christological development, and summoned all the Messianic passages
of the Old Testament to their aid in commenting upon, interpreting, and amplifying the details of the life of Jesus. This
preoccupation is reflected, for instance, in the composition of
the genealogies, the accounts of the Resurrection, and the
treatment of various details. It was only when Greek and
syncretistic influences came into play, that is to say, when
the faith entered the Hellenistic communities, that the great
work was begun which resulted in the Christian doctrine and
the Christian Church, and which can be seen in progress in
Paul and the Fourth Gospel. Accordingly, we may conclude
that in the beginning, the *teaching* of Jesus was exposed to
little change, and it seems a reasonable presumption that the
most striking sayings concerning the Kingdom and its advent,
and the efforts necessary to secure a place in it, were impressed
on the memory of the disciples, at least at random, as perhaps
they were uttered, and that, through all the adaptations to
which the *logia* were subjected, and in spite of the resulting
perversions, it may still be possible to discern the essential
substance and method of the teaching of Jesus.

It is to be noted that several important changes which
were made in the conceptions of the primitive community to
meet the needs of the Hellenistic converts, are not to be found
in the *logia*. For example, the *Kingdom* is not yet identified
with *salvation*. At the time when our redactors made use of
the *logia*, the original faith had undergone great developments,
as various details of their writings testify, but these details
give the impression of being, as it were, superimposed on a
groundwork which is quite different. Moreover, the development of the faith did not find all the teachings ascribed by the
tradition to Jesus equally hampering. The value of his precepts
concerning morality and practical life, for instance, remained
the same, or even increased, in proportion as emphasis on the
deification of the Saviour increased. The Sermon on the Mount
is nothing but a set of ethical precepts, and exhibits Jesus
only as a teacher of morals, and not at all as the god of salvation, although at the time when it was put together the
Christians were for the most part convinced that he was the
Saviour.[1] As far as we can form an idea of the document *Q*,
it did not contain anything that implied this conception. In
opposition to this, there has been cited a verse of Mark (x. 45):
"For the Son of man came not to be ministered unto, but to
minister, and to give his life as a ransom for many." But if

[1] CLXXX, 26.

this be compared with Mark xiv. 24 : "And he said unto them : This is my blood [that] of the covenant which is shed for many," which has a similar ring, it will be seen that it is in all probability a case of Pauline influence. The idea is as foreign to *Urmarcus* as it is to *Q*. It may be observed, further, that various conceptions and beliefs imputed to Jesus may well have found protection, once they were committed to writing, in the very indifference which the faith soon developed with regard to them. Thus the conception of the Kingdom was not long in giving place to that of the Church of God (ἡ ἐκκλησία τοῦ θεοῦ of 1 Cor. i. 2), but the idea of the Son of Man, which was quite unintelligible outside the Jewish communities, persisted as an obscure but venerable formula, because it was supposed to have come from the Lord.[1]

Finally, certain things which our gospel redactors must have been very reluctant to record, have nevertheless been preserved in their accounts—the inner struggle of Jesus, the misunderstanding of his family, the denial of Peter, the flight of the disciples after the arrest, etc.—which looks as if the Christological development had, on these various points, been powerless to suppress the tradition.[2]

These various considerations seem to restore a little hope. It would indeed be foolish to exaggerate it, but if, remembering that our Gospels were written by *compilers*, who were not always either very exacting or very careful, we examine closely each separate instance, it may seem not altogether impossible to discern in some of them, beneath the redactional layers and behind the tendentious adaptations, some traces of an authentic and accurate record. This is perhaps not a great deal, but it is better than nothing.

IV

THE FORM OF THE SAYINGS

We shall pause only briefly on the much disputed question of the authenticity of the form in which the *logia* are presented. It has frequently been the object of admiration, and has even been cited as a proof of the authenticity of the content. From the fact that there is recognizable throughout the same stamp, the same style, it has been concluded that they all came from the same mind, which could have been no other than that of Jesus.[3] We have already noted the objections to this argu-

---

[1] XLIV, 26. [2] LXVII, 234.
[3] CCL, 137 ; CLXXX, 24 ; CXC, xiii. *ff*.

ment,[1] to which we may add that it seems rash to overpraise
translations whose accuracy we have no means of verifying.
Nevertheless, it must not be forgotten that oral preservation
of the teachings of the rabbis was still the rule amongst the
Jews in the time of Jesus, so that it is not without significance
that the disciples of the Nazarene attributed to him a whole
collection of sayings.

They are unquestionably similar to those which the Talmud
is supposed to have taken from the teachings of the early
rabbinic teachers of Israel, and which have, indeed, every
appearance of genuineness.[2] But we have already pointed out
why it is not entirely legitimate to compare the case of the
rabbinical Fathers with that of Jesus Christ. A pure and
simple forgery, however, coming, let us say, from the second
generation after Christ, would exhibit a tendentious character,
as do the Gospels themselves ; that is to say, it would have
a purpose in view which would probably be quite visible and
would devote itself to achieving that instead of wandering off
into little stories, anecdotes, or discourses, which seem to have
no connexion with its aims. Such details have no bearing on
the justification of the Christological movement, or on the
development of the faith, and represent the fulfilment of no
prophecies. But it is easy to understand how this sort of thing
remained in our Gospels if we regard it as at least a fragmentary
survival of an earlier established tradition, sanctioned undoubtedly by its reputation of authenticity, and hence to be
respected. It is incredible that it should have been gratuitously
invented, at such risk of creating difficulties, of giving rise to
contradictions.

Two observations appear to strengthen our impression that
the *logia* are essentially orientated towards the past of Jesus'
activity, rather than towards the future of Christ's glory.
(1) Whenever a sentence or a parable appears to have preserved
its original setting, it is localized in Galilee. Does it not seem
probable that if it had been invented, even in the time of the
Apostles, it would have been attached to Jerusalem ?[3] Observe
how important the setting of the Holy City becomes in the
Gospel of John. (2) The precepts contained in the *logia* are
addressed by Jesus to his immediate disciples, without any
reference to any ecclesiastical organization or system. It is

[1] *Cf.* p. 48 *ff.*
[2] On the basis of these sayings, very plausible psychological portraits
of Hillel and Jochanan ben Zacchai, the contemporary of Paul, amongst
others, have been constructed.
[3] CCLXIV, 35.

hardly credible that this would have been the case if they had been forged by the Church at Jerusalem.[1]

When we admit that the *logia* may contain authentic sayings of Jesus, we have in mind, of course, only a general authenticity, which excludes neither rearrangements of detail nor tendentious additions, still less the more or less serious perversions and contradictions of which there is always a danger in the passage from one language to another, and whose existence, moreover, is sufficiently demonstrated by the differences between the letter of Mark and that of Luke.

As Loisy truly observes, "sayings and parables were repeated and written down according to what they were understood to mean, and in a way to make this meaning intelligible for the greatest good of the community. There was no thought of refraining from either convenient omissions, or desirable emendations, or the addition of anything which the situation, or the purpose of interpretation, seemed to demand." [2]

This is perfectly evident. Nevertheless, it does not seem too much to believe that the original tradition gathered up the teachings which had seemed most striking to the disciples, and which their Master had repeated to them most frequently and with the greatest emphasis, and those were undoubtedly the ones which he himself had most at heart. Comparative criticism is not helpless before the redactional alterations in the original meaning, as it would be if the Evangelists had been more scrupulous in the literal transcription of their sources,[3] and it is this fact which justifies our belief that the case is not entirely hopeless. Whoever will examine the texts with patience, not expecting too much of them, and not relying upon them unduly, will derive therefrom the impression of a simple unsystematic teaching, controlled by a small number of ideas, embodied in a few precepts, and based upon religious principles which were well known before Jesus ; and he will feel that he is not far from the truth.

[1] CCL, 135.   [2] CIII, i, 188.   [3] CXLIII, 46 ; CCL, 137.

CHAPTER II

THE FORM OF JESUS' TEACHING

I

The Essential Nature of His Preaching

IN the ancient Jewish world the main function of the prophet
was not to predict the future, to *prophesy*, but rather to
teach. Jesus seems to have been no exception to this rule, even
though the prophetic announcement of the imminence of the
Kingdom be regarded as the fundamental feature of his mission.
It is true that this announcement appears at first to be bound
up with the wonder-working necessitated by his environment,
but it is nevertheless ultimately expressed in a *teaching*, of which
the first thing to be determined is, not its content, but the
form, the mode of expression of that content—in other words,
how it was presented.

Our caution is aroused at the outset by the fact that our
Evangelists also taught, in fact that was the whole purpose of
their writing, and, from what we have already discovered concerning them, their teaching was not the same as that of Jesus.
In studying their evidence, we must not lose sight of the possibility of their having at times, perhaps frequently, possibly
even regularly, substituted in their accounts their own spirit
and manner for those of their Master. Further, if we are to
derive any real information from this study, care must be taken
not to allow any artificial preconception to come between us
and the documents, as, for instance, the idea that the spiritual
gifts of Jesus were so unusual, the depth of his religious
feeling and the delicacy of his moral perceptions so far
above the ordinary, that he cannot really be judged by human
standards. This way of regarding him, which is still very
common even amongst those who do not believe in him, is a
kind of tenacious survival of the inherited belief in his divinity,
which is a great obstacle to critical freedom. It is as if people
unconsciously attempted, as it were, to compensate for depriv-
ing him of his divine nature by attributing to him superhuman

245

qualities. We are not thinking merely of the sentimental effusions of Renan, which are all the more dangerous to the unwary reader in that they assume the form and the tone of objective conclusions, still less of the pronouncements of a dilettante like Houston Chamberlain,[1] or an amateur like Couchoud.[2] We have in mind particularly the statements of such an eminent critic as Holtzmann and his follower Jülicher. The former, himself, cannot resist the temptation to grow lyrical, in a way which is not characteristic of him, over the " peculiar genius " (*eigener Genius*) of Jesus.[3] His effusions are such that, beyond a certain " scientific prejudice," one can see no reason why he should stop short of believing in the miraculous birth of so superhuman a being. The Gospel, however, is not to be interpreted in the light of the whole history of the Christian Church.

It is obvious that, if Jesus preached, it was for the purpose of convincing his hearers, of bringing them to the realization of what was, in his opinion, an all-important truth. But to an unprejudiced reader of the texts, it is plain that, even for the Evangelists, this truth was a *personal belief* and not a *doctrine* ; it was a conviction regarded as an indisputable fact, and embodied in one or two definite ideas. To these ideas are attached, rather by their purpose and content than formally, some more or less detailed remarks, occasioned by various circumstances, and easily classifiable into a few types. (This involves no assumption, of course, regarding the profundity of the said ideas and the specific value of the remarks in question.) The teaching of Jesus is not to be imagined as a kind of course in theology, delivered to an audience of attentive students ; [4] we have no reason to believe even that Jesus " instructed " the Apostles, in the strict sense of the word. Why should he have done so, and what would he have taught them, since the great transformation whose imminence he proclaimed was going to make all doctrine, and all human rules, unnecessary ? The Church was brought into being by the persistence of the temporal order, which compelled it to ask and to answer questions which Jesus had never foreseen. It was led to believe, at the same time, that it was only putting into practice the special precepts given by Jesus himself to his intimate companions, and hence arose the inevitable supremacy

---

[1] *Dilettantismus*, 23 : " *Jesus stehe ausserhalb der Geschichte.*"
[2] **CXLIX**, 13 *ff*.   [3] **L–a**, i, 173 *ff*.
[4] **CIII**, i, 211 ; **CCXXXV**, 19.—On the misuse of the term " Master," as applied to Jesus, see Travers Herford, *Judaism in the New Testament Period*, London, 1928, p. 202.

of the postulate of the " Apostolic tradition." In reality Jesus,
wholly dominated by what Renan aptly calls [1] " a fixed personal
resolve," had no idea of teaching those whom we call his
Apostles ; " he swept them along with him towards the great
hope by which he himself was irresistibly attracted " (Loisy).
Whether they were aware of it or not, they were undoubtedly
much more influenced by his personality than by what he said.[2]

Properly considered, he does not look like a reformer, whose
activity is necessarily the result of observation, criticism, and
constructive purpose.[3] He frequently attacks things and
people, but in every case what he says leads back to his original
obsession with the near advent of the Kingdom, which bespeaks
the state of mind of a prophet, and not of a theologian. A
moment's consideration is sufficient to prove the truth of the
above remarks. At the very beginning of the Marcan narrative we see Jesus speaking in the synagogue at Capernaum,
and " teaching them as one that had authority " (Mark i. 22 :
διδάσκων αὐτοὺς ὡς ἐξουσίαν ἔχων), at which " they " are very
much astonished. The meaning seems to be that he broke
away—for good reason—from the form of teaching established
in the schools ; that he did not necessarily base his preaching
upon a text of the Scriptures, to be interpreted and commented
upon ; and that he did not cite the evidence of famous rabbis,
but that his own inspiration was all he had need of, even when
he appealed to the Book, and the freedom, the homeliness, and
the spontaneity of his words were hampered by nothing, not
even the attempt to organize them, because they were inspired
and justified by an irresistible inner force. It is plain that,
from the standpoint of an observer, such a method is characteristic of one who is disturbed by no doubt. The Gospel
writer shows us Jesus at the end of his career (Mark xi. 27 *ff*.)
in the Temple at Jerusalem, in the presence of enemies who
are equally astonished by this air of authority in his speech
and of power in his actions. They ask him bluntly what right
he has to speak and act in this manner, a question which he
evades by a counterthrust : " Tell me first whence came the
authority of the Baptist." But his resort to this stratagem
does not alter his own conviction that he is " authorized." In
this persuasion he commands, and the Evangelist cannot conceive of the men whom he calls as having the least hesitation
in following him (Mark i. 17 ; ii. 14). His enemies ascribe this
authority to Beelzebub, prince of the devils (Mark iii. 22). He
himself believes that he is possessed by the Spirit of God, which

---

[1] **CLXVIII**, 46.   [2] Weidel, *Jesu Persönlichkeit*, 1909, p. 83.
                    [3] **CCCXI**, 95.

amounts to the same thing. It is obviously not a doctrine by which he is inspired, but a faith, and to him all things lead back to that faith, and are comprised in it. It does more than fill his mind ; it extends its power over the realm of concrete realities (Mark ix. 23 : πάντα δυνατὰ τῷ πιστεύοντι, everything is possible to him who believes). This faith is not a *belief*, of the kind which may be applied to a dogma, but a *confidence*. When he feels himself opposed by a doubt, he makes no attempt to refute it, for there is nothing for him to say. He neither argues nor discusses, proves nor confutes ; he knows the truth and he utters it, and when he realizes that it is not believed he grows angry and depressed (Mark iii. 5 : " And when he had looked round about on them with anger, being grieved for the hardness of their hearts . . ."). Because it was hard for him to understand that his hearers did not hear the voice of God in the depths of their souls as he did, he identified this lack of religious experience with a deliberate hardening of the heart. His religion is his whole life, and God is the very breath of his being.[1]

II

GENERAL CHARACTERISTICS OF THE PREACHING

For this reason his teaching can only be a kind of spontaneous outpouring. We find in it no abstractions, no theories concerning man, life, the world, or God, in short, not the slightest interest in rational and objective knowledge. He observes the world, and quite simply records his impressions in what he says.[2] It has often been remarked how interested he seems to be in his material surroundings, in all the living aspects of them, and how much one can learn of Galilee from his utterances.[3] The attitude of Christianity, which has so often condemned the world, which has regarded it as the empire of Satan and the home of perdition, and turned from it with horror and disgust, was never modelled upon that of Jesus.

The external characteristics of his teaching are easily seen. There are no real sermons. Those ascribed to him are redactional, and represent nothing more than strings of sayings. The " saying " was in common use amongst the rabbis : a short, clear pronouncement, containing some instructive observation or piece of advice, which had the advantage of being easy to remember. The *logia*, as we remember, consisted of a

[1] CCLXIV, 49.   [2] CCXXXIV, 91 ; CCLXIV, 51.
[3] L-a, i, 161 *ff.* ; CXC, 32 *ff.*

collection of sayings of this kind. Possibly they were often accompanied, in reality, by explanatory comment, and we may wonder whether, taking them as they have come down to us, they do not lead us to attribute to the teaching of the Nazarene a quality which was perhaps in reality not quite so strongly marked. There may be something in this, especially considering that the desire to draw up a kind of compendium of the " Wisdom " of Jesus may have influenced the editor, or editors, of Q, to present their material in a special form. But this reservation does not invalidate the general conclusion that Jesus, in conformity with the taste and customs of his environment, habitually employed the " saying," which was, in addition, very well adapted to the kind of thing he had to say.

In the gospel the saying sometimes has the air of an aphorism,[1] or even of an epigram, but we have only to turn over the pages of Proverbs to see that the Galilean prophet had not far to seek for examples. A certain number of logia, which sound at first very strange, become more intelligible when we remember that, in accordance with the type of the aphorism and the epigram, they aim at vividness and energy of expression, rather than at perfectly suitable wording and illustrations of practical value. Such, for instance, are the famous aphorisms on obstacles to virtue in Matthew xviii. We are inclined to believe that Jesus also had a fondness for the dialogue,[2] which is not only associated with the Socratic technique, but is a popular custom that still flourishes in the East.

To sum up : teaching delivered " with authority," that is to say, statements supposed to come directly from God and to be indisputable ; short striking " sayings," occurring in the course of ordinary talks occasioned by the circumstances of daily life ; pithy pronouncements, sometimes deliberately exaggerated ; brief dialogues in which the interlocutor is led to analyse his difficulty, which is then resolved by an aphorism ; these appear to have been the methods by which Jesus taught. They are completely in harmony, first, with what we have ascertained of his lack of systematic doctrinal teaching and his contempt for dialectical methods, next with the customs of an environment, which, in more than one respect, survives in the East today, and finally, with the instinctive tendency to

[1] Mark ii. 17 : " I am come not to call the righteous, but the sinners.' Mark x. 25 : " It is easier for a camel to go through the eye of a needle than for a rich man to enter into the Kingdom of Heaven."
[2] Mark x. 17 ff. Of course we cannot vouch for the literal authenticity of this conversation between Jesus and the young enthusiast.

present his own unique and outstanding personality as the example and proof of his teaching.

There is, however, one device of Jesus which we have mentioned only incidentally and which deserves some emphasis, because it is the one which the Gospel writers seem to regard as most completely characteristic of the Master. It is as if it surprises them, and they do not understand it very well. We refer to his use of the *parable* or *similitude*.[1]

The word parable (παραβολή) is the one regularly employed by the Synoptics. John uses παροιμία, which in classical Greek means " proverbs " (John x. 6 ; xvi. 25 ; etc.). " *Parabolé* " is used by the Septuagint to translate the Hebrew *mashal*, which is ordinarily rendered by the elastic term " *similitude*." It is used in the Old Testament to designate obscure sayings (Ps. xlix. 4), or figurative discourses (Num. xxiii. 7 ; Job xxvii. 1), or stories which we should rather call fables,[2] or sometimes more or less allegorical comparisons.[3]

In a very general way, we may say that the " parable " of the Gospels is the story of a real or imaginary event, borrowed from nature or daily life, and so set forth as to suggest some moral or religious truth. It is, then, a comparison which uses pictorial description to convey an idea. As it is not always necessary for its purpose to state this comparison fully, the fact that it is one, is often left unspecified. For example, in Mark ii. 16 *ff.*, when the scribes and Pharisees express surprise that he should eat with publicans and sinners (ἁμαρτωλοί), Jesus' reply is : " They that are whole have no need of the physician, but they that are sick. I am come not to call the righteous but the sinners." The parallel is obvious, and needs no explanation. The same thing is true of the whole series of analogies which, in the same chapter of Mark, follow the verse just quoted : the attendants of the bridegroom who do not fast while he is with them ; the patch of new cloth which is not to be sewn upon an old garment ; the new wine which cannot be poured into old bottles ; and, iii. 24, the kingdom

---

[1] The main work is still that of Jülicher, **CCXV**, which is summarized by himself in the article *Parables* in **EB**. *Cf.* Loisy, *Études évangéliques*, 1902. A bibliography of the Catholic works will be found in **CLVII**, i, 332, n. 1. See also H. Weinel, *Die Gleichnisse Jesu* ⁴, Leipzig, 1918. For an analysis of the parables, see **LXXXVI**, 101. It will be helpful to read **CLVI**–*a*, 270 *ff*.

[2] For example, in 2 Sam. xii. 1–4, the story of the poor man and his ewe lamb, which is told by Nathan to David to make him ashamed of his conduct.

[3] 2 Sam. xiv. 6 and 8 ; 1 Kings xx. 39 *ff*. ; Isa. v. 1–6 ; xxviii. 24–8.

which cannot stand if it be divided against itself. These might be called parables in embryo, but as they stand they are no more than briefly suggested parallels. Half the gospel parables are of this type.

We must be careful not to confuse the parable with the allegory, or, which amounts to the same thing, to give the parable an allegorical interpretation. Tempting though it sometimes is,[1] such a proceeding is dangerous. " An allegory is a succession of metaphors which means something different from what it says." [2]   In order to interpret an allegory, one must possess the key to it, must be " initiated."   A parable, on the contrary, is intended to illuminate the thought of the one who uses it, and not to conceal it. To understand the difference, we have only to compare the Synoptic parables with the Johannine allegories. When John vi. 35 says : " I am the bread of life ; he that cometh to me shall never hunger, and he that believeth on me shall never thirst," he is speaking allegorically, in that he identifies the symbol with the thing signified, and what the latter is, is not discernible by common sense. No one who has never heard of the Eucharist and its Christian interpretation is in a position to understand it.

A single example will show the danger of " allegorizing " a parable, that is to say, of regarding each individual term of it as a symbol for which is to be substituted the word really meant. We take the parable of the widow and the unjust judge in Luke xviii. 2 *ff.* :

> " He said : there was in a city a judge which feared not God, neither regarded man. And there was a widow in that city and she came unto him saying : Avenge me of mine adversary. And he would not for a long time, but afterwards he said within himself : Though I fear not God, nor regard man, yet because this widow troubleth me I will avenge her, lest by her continual coming she weary me. And the Lord said : Hear what the unjust judge saith. And shall not God avenge his own elect which cry day and night unto him, and shall he delay ?   I tell you that he will avenge them speedily."

If we take the unjust judge to symbolize God, as the end of the passage might seem to suggest, we are going to get a very shocking, not to say blasphemous, interpretation. Regarding the widow as either the Church, or the soul in prayer, we are confronted by the unthinkable situation of God's yielding to

---

[1] We do not say that a parable may not have an allegorical meaning (see, for instance, that of the wicked husbandmen in Matt. xxi. 33), but merely that it is not essentially an allegory.

[2] **CIII,** i, 245 ; **LXXIX,** 171.

her entreaties only to avoid being wearied by them. We might equally well take the parable of the Ten Virgins and the Bridegroom (Matt. xxv. 1–15),[1] and amuse ourselves by trying to find out who the bridegroom is, and who the oil merchant to whom the five wise virgins send the five foolish ones, and exactly what the virgins themselves represent ; but it would be a profitless diversion. In the first parable cited, there is simply an *à fortiori* argument : if an iniquitous judge finally grants justice to a poor woman for unworthy reasons, how much more speedily and completely will God satisfy those whom he loves, and who put their trust in him ! The second parable is nothing more than a story to illustrate a piece of practical advice : do not forget that the appearance of God may be sudden and unexpected ; hold yourselves always in readiness. In both cases the parallel does not apply to all the details of the story, but only to the idea which emerges from it as a whole.

The gospel redactors regarded the parable as a method of teaching that was very freely employed by Jesus.[2] It is noteworthy that there are no real parables in the New Testament except in the Synoptics, and that the tradition did not ascribe any to the Apostles. This seems to imply that the first generations of Christians believed that Jesus alone used this form of expression, which gives us reason to hope that we have in our possession, we will not say, *the* parables of Jesus, for it is hardly conceivable that they were all preserved, but some of them. We must, moreover, unfortunately discount the redactional changes, which no more respected the original form of the parables than of the sayings. It is easy to get an idea of what these changes may have been by comparing the different renderings of the same parable given by Matthew and Luke. That of the lost sheep (Matt. xviii. 12 *ff*. and Luke xv. 4 *ff*.) will suffice as an example.[3] Hence, though we may regard it as probable that there remain to us parables which were really uttered by Jesus, we are debarred from knowing the actual form in which they were uttered. There are all sorts of parables in the Synoptics, and it is possible to differentiate many stages

[1] CXC, 22.

[2] Mark iv. 2 : καὶ ἐδίδασκεν αὐτοὺς ἐν παραβολαῖς πολλά. Jülicher estimates the number of parables in the Synoptics at about sixty. Other critics are less generous, because, in many cases, it is possible to deny that we have a parable. In the judgment of O. Schmidt, CLXXV, 25, there are about thirty.

[3] Another good example is the comparison of Matt. xxv. 14 *ff*. with Luke xix. 12 *ff*. In the former it is the parable of the *talents*, in the latter, that of the *pounds*.

between the brief illustrative reference and the fully developed parallel. The latter is, however, not very frequent, there being only four of them altogether, all in Luke (x. 29 *ff.* ; the good Samaritan ; xii. 16 *ff.* : the rich fool ; xvi. 19 *ff.* : Dives and Lazarus ; xviii. 9 *ff.* : the Pharisee and the publican) ; but that need not concern us for the present.

The Nazarene prophet did not invent the parable, nor even all the themes of which he made use in his own. The Jewish rabbis of his time regularly employed the parabolic method, and put it to similar specific uses.[1]

Jesus did not actually imitate the rabbis. It was simply that they both followed the same customs and worked with the same traditional material, which was probably of popular origin. Saint Jerome records [2] that in his day the people of Syria, and especially of Palestine, made frequent use of parables in familiar intercourse. The fact that neither Mark nor Matthew, nor, above all, Luke, discarded this Jewish technique of instruction, may be regarded as a proof that the tradition was at least Palestinian in origin,[3] and that the Hellenizing editors of the Gospels did not alter it to the point of robbing it of all its native characteristics.

Naturally much stress has been laid on the differences between the gospel parables and their Rabbinical parallels,[4] which are said to have " much less freshness and simplicity." This is not surprising, for it is quite conceivable that a rabbi sitting in his school discoursing on the *Torah*, would not have such lively impressions as a young prophet, sprung from the people, who spent his time wandering about the country. But the main difference between the two sets of parables seems to be in their content, which is much more varied in those of the rabbis than in those of Jesus, where it is almost exclusively concerned with the coming Kingdom.

When we read the gospel parables impartially, we cannot have the slightest doubt as to their purpose. Jesus, like the contemporaries of Saint Jerome, uses a comparison in order to explain a precept : the concrete example is to assist the abstract idea to penetrate into the minds of listeners who are likely to be simple people. As Mark iv. 33 ingenuously remarks, in a passage which unquestionably goes back to the earliest version, and whose naïve admission was inadvertently overlooked by the final redactors : " And with many such parables spake

---

[1] CCIII ; Loisy, **RHLR**, 1912, p. 506 ; **LXXIV**, 90 *ff.*
[2] *In Mt.*, 18, 23. [3] **LXXXVIII**, 152.
[4] Fiebig, *Altjüdische Gleichnisse und die Gleichnisse Jesu*, Tübingen, 1904.

he the word unto them as they were able to hear it." The
meaning can only be that he spoke to the simple-minded in
parables, because it was the only possible way of making himself understood by them.   Later, however, when by the inevitable development of Christology Jesus had become a divine
being, his followers, who had gradually lost all knowledge of
Palestinian customs, were unwilling to believe in such a simple
explanation, and claimed to have discovered in the parables
the deliberately obscure expression of profound mysteries, and
the oracular replies to various questions which the parables
certainly never anticipated.   Catholic criticism is very reluctant
to abandon this extraordinary and obviously erroneous theory.
Quite recently a by no means reactionary theologian [1] has
asserted that, if the parables are couched in a simple and
familiar style, they have nevertheless, for the most part, " a
hidden and very profound meaning, which few minds can
fathom " ; to them are to be applied the words of Saint Augustine
(*Ep.*, 137, 18) :   "*Omnibus accessibilis, paucissimis vero pene-
trabilis.*"

Père Fonk goes further still [2] and maintains that in the
parables Christ intentionally passed sentence of rejection upon
the people and their leaders who were guilty of unbelief ; hence,
Jesus actually inflicted on them the punishment of a teaching
which was intelligible without explanation.   It is difficult to
take such " criticism " seriously.

The parable is not an instrument of precision ; [3] it may
just as easily lead the mind astray as direct it aright.   Probably the tradition ascribed to Jesus more than one parable
that seemed far from clear, but on the other hand, the disappearance of the context of some of these sayings had contributed to their obscurity.[4]   Under these circumstances, since
it was unthinkable that the Lord had made an imperfect use
of an imperfect form, and had acquiesced in its obscurity,
people came to think that he had deliberately veiled the truth,
so that the Jews, understanding it only partially, or not at all,

---

[1] **V**, i, 469.   Catholic criticism is, however, far from unanimous on
the meaning and purpose of the parables.   *Cf.* **CLVII**, i, 332.   The
subsequent pages, in which the Jesuit Father attempts to reconcile
the two theories, that of the use of the parables for teaching purposes,
and that of their hidden meaning, are very interesting.   It is obvious
that this ingenious and subtle exposition cannot possibly represent the
true facts.

[2] Fonk, *Die Parabolen des Herrn im Evangelium*, 1904, 17 *ff.*   On
the other hand Lagrange, *Mark* 96 *ff.*, attempts to acquit Jesus of the
flagrant absurdity attributed to him by the Reverend Father.

[3] **LXXIV**, i, 106 *ff.*   [4] **CXI**, 186.

should be prevented from repenting and obtaining forgiveness. The passage on which this fantastic theory is based is found in Mark iv. 10–12 and is usually translated as follows :

> " And when he was alone, they that were about him with the Twelve questioned him about the parables, and he said unto them : Unto you is given the Mystery of the Kingdom of God, but unto them that are without (τοῖς ἔξω) all things come in parables, that (ἵνα) seeing they may see and not perceive, and hearing they may hear and not understand, lest (μὴ ποτε) they should be converted and their sins should be forgiven them."

On the face of it these statements are so shocking or so preposterous that the attempt has been made to dispose of them by maintaining that the version just quoted is a misconstruction.   Recently a neo-Hellenic philologist, Hubert Pernot, resuming and supplementing an emendation that had already been unsuccessfully proposed several times, has endeavoured to prove [1] that the word ἵνα is to be understood to mean ὅτι and translated by " because."   If we had only to explain the verses in question, the proposed interpretation, which is in itself very plausible, might be satisfactory.   But if it were accepted, it would then have to be acknowledged that the passage of Isaiah vi. 9–10, which is obviously the basis of our Mark, has been taken in quite the opposite of its original meaning, for the Hebrew runs as follows :

> " Go and tell this people : Ye shall hear, but understand not ; ye shall see, but perceive not.   Make the hearts of this people insensitive, harden their ears and blind their eyes, so that they see not with their eyes nor hear with their ears, so that their hearts may not understand nor be healed anew."

The Septuagint couches the message in somewhat milder terms, but does not alter the general sense.   On the other hand, the whole of the Marcan passage, which begins with the parable of the Sower (Mark iv. 3–9), clearly implies that the listeners, including the disciples, have not understood the meaning of Jesus.   Hence it is to be inferred that the first words of the Master, when the disciples ask him for an explanation, are intended to demonstrate and to justify the difference between *them*, who should have understood, because the Mystery of the Kingdom has been imparted to them, and *those without*, who are incapable of understanding the Truth. " They " will be saved, and " those without " will not.   But why do these unfortunate people not understand ?   The passage of Isaiah replies explicitly : because it is the will of God.   By this fact, the alteration in the meaning of ἵνα suggested by Pernot is rendered improbable, and is in danger of making

[1] **LXXXI**, 90 *ff.*

the passage even more unintelligible than it already is. It is not, moreover, only modern criticism which has accepted and upheld the alleged misconstruction ; the redactor of John showed himself equally obtuse when he wrote (John xii. 39), after speaking of the scepticism of the Jews :

> " They could not believe because Isaiah said again : He hath blinded their eyes and hardened their heart, lest they should see with their eyes and understand with their heart, and be converted and I should heal them."

For these reasons, we adhere to the generally accepted meaning.[1] In any case, the translation of ἵνα by " because " would make no essential difference in the meaning of the Johannine passage.

The explanation of the strange passage is to be sought, not in a verbal detail, but in the interests of the redactor. The Evangelist was actuated by the desire to mitigate the great affront—the unbelief of the Jews. What he knew of their behaviour towards Jesus, and later, towards his followers, made him naturally disposed to think—that is, it was the common opinion amongst the brethren of his circle—that the Jews were not worthy to believe. They came with evil in their hearts to listen to the teaching of the Lord, and he, reading their minds, chose not to be silent but to speak so that they did not understand. Further, Mark had another object, indicated by the peculiar expression " the mystery of the Kingdom of God " (τὸ μυστήριον τῆς βασιλείας τοῦ θεοῦ) which occurs in the Gospels only in this one place. It was to attribute to the idea of the coming Kingdom, a very simple conception to the Jews, the character of a specific gnosis, a revelation only accessible to the initiated,[2] in short, of an obviously Pauline doctrine. A parable like that of the Sower seemed actually much more adapted to cloak the Pauline mystery than to reveal anything. In all probability the verses under discussion (Mark iv. 10–12) are no more to be assigned to Jesus than the absurd theory of the intentional obscurity of the parables. They are both nothing more than explanations concocted by the generation of Christians from which the Apostolic tradition arose.

To conclude, the teaching of Jesus belongs in general to a type common in his environment, and displays methods well known to his contemporaries. It is simple, homely, spontaneous, sporadic and unorganized, consisting entirely of the emphatic repetition of a few ideas.

---

[1] XCVIII, 47 ; CVII, i, 103 ; C. H. Turner, *Mark*, in XLVI, 64.
[2] In the later portions of the Septuagint, the word μυστήριον has apparently come to designate an esoteric Mystery doctrine. *Cf.* Dan. ii. 27 ; ii. 47 ; Wisd. ii. 22.

CHAPTER III

JESUS' CLAIM TO AUTHORITY

I

THE PROBLEM

THERE is still a difficult problem to which we must devote a little time before attempting to analyse the teaching of Jesus. By virtue of what authority did he claim to teach? What was his idea of his mission and his status? Between him and us, as we know, the first generations of Christians intervene, and the answer to this question can only come from them. But it is to be feared that they can tell us no more than what they themselves believed, and that much care and patience will be required to discern, behind the account produced by their faith, even a few suggestions as to the true facts.

A first impartial glance through the Synoptics gives the impression that Jesus was a belated scion of the Prophets of Israel, a man filled with the Spirit of Jahweh, who came to proclaim the imminent fulfilment of the ancient Promises, and to teach the means by which each might enjoy the blessings of this event. It is as a prophet that those who see and hear Jesus seem to regard him: " Who is this ? " ask those who witness the triumphal entry into Jerusalem, in Matthew xxi. 10. " And the multitude said : This is Jesus the prophet, of Nazareth in Galilee." Doubtless because it is a long time since any prophet has appeared, the people wonder if he may not be one of the ancient stalwarts, Elias or Jeremiah for instance, sent down again to earth by Jahweh (Mark vi. 15 ; viii. 28 ; Matt. xvi. 14). According to Mark vi. 4, he himself, at Nazareth, refers to himself as a " prophet," and Luke xiii. 33–4 conveys the same impression, which is borne out by various other passages (vii. 16 ; vii. 39 ; xxiv. 19), when he makes him say that a prophet cannot perish outside Jerusalem.

Jesus might, however, have assumed the aspect of a prophet in certain connexions, and in others have manifested himself in a different and much more glorious light. Several passages,

indeed, appear to imply that he regarded himself as *more* than
the Prophets.[1] His manner of speaking, and his demands,
sometimes sound strangely out of place on the lips of a simple
nabi.[2] We need cite only Mark viii. 34 : " Whosoever will
come after me, let him deny himself and take up his cross and
follow me." He proclaims the Kingdom as if by virtue of a
personal revelation, which he does not explain, at least not in
the Synoptics, and the suggestion is natural that this revelation
may be involved in the Nazarene's very being, as an element
of the special endowment bestowed upon him by God. This,
at any rate, is what John x. 29 asserts when he makes him say :
" What my Father has given me is greater than all." [3] The
Synoptics also hold the same view ; in the coming Kingdom
he will occupy the central place ; he is already potentially the
Messiah, and he will be so in fact. This is the meaning of the
mysterious title which is given to him, " Son of Man." On
the strength of our texts we may go even a step further : Jesus
believed that between himself and God the Father there was
a special relationship, which was expressed in phrases like
" my Father" and " the Son of God." We know at least
what orthodox theology has evolved from this suggestion,
which gave birth to the doctrine of the divinity of Jesus Christ.
But we must always remember that between what the Evangelists make Jesus say, and what he actually said or thought
himself, we have the irresistible influence of the desire to exalt
the Lord, and to place his authority beyond question ; and
from that time onwards the tendency of the Christian faith
to deify him dominated the tradition.

A " prophet," the " Messiah," the " Son of God," which
of these three terms corresponds to Jesus' own conception of
himself ? On the answer to this question depends the correct
idea of the scope which he intended his teaching to have, and
the authority he attached to it. The allied question of what
the Nazarene really *was*, of course, does not concern us at this
point.

We shall not revert to the first of the three appellations,
because we have already shown that it represents at least one
aspect of Jesus ; and we shall take the two others in inverse
order, because the Galilean prophet might easily have believed

---

[1] For example, Luke xi. 32 : καὶ ἰδοὺ πλεῖον Ἰωνᾶ ὧδε, *and behold
a greater than Jonah is here.*

[2] **CLXV,** 4 *ff.*

[3] One may recall John x. 30: " *I and the Father are one* " ; xii.
49–50 ; xiv. 9 : " *He that hath seen me hath seen the Father* " ; xvi. 15 :
" *All things that the Father has are mine* " ; xvi. 28 : " *I came forth
from the Father* " ; etc.

himself to be the Messiah expected by Israel without regarding himself as the Son of God of Christian theology.

II

THE SON OF GOD

In the Synoptics the expression " Son of God " (υἱὸς θεοῦ or υἱὸς τοῦ θεοῦ) [1] is applied to Jesus twenty-seven times, and the word " Son," in what may be taken as an equivalent sense, nine times. Mark alone gives the former seven times and the latter once. Hence there is, at any rate, no doubt of what the editors intended to convey. For them Jesus was definitely the Son of God, and it is to be noted that even in Mark the expression is conspicuous in all the most important events of the narrative : the Baptism (i. 11), the Temptation in the wilderness (Matt. iv. 3), the Transfiguration (Mark ix. 7), the interrogation by the High Priest (xiv. 61), the declaration of the centurion which follows the execution (xv. 39) : " Truly this man was the Son of God "—not to mention the confessions of the devils whom he cast out (iii. 11 ; v. 7), which are also very important from the point of view of the Evangelist. It was quite correctly, therefore, that some unknown scribe headed our Mark : " The Gospel of Jesus Christ the Son of God." It is evident that Mark, at least, regards the expression as a specific designation of the Messiah, whatever may be his conception of the exact meaning of the phrase, that is to say, the actual form of the relationship which it implies between God and Jesus. It is, however, also to be noted that in Q the expression occurs only once, in a famous *logion* which at first sight seems to be a Johannine fragment : " All things are delivered unto me of my Father, and no man knoweth the Father save the Son " (Matt. xi. 27 ; Luke x. 22). In the rest of the New Testament the appellation is very common. John uses it ten times, Paul, sixteen, the Epistle to the Hebrews, ten. It is, however, not found in the Pastoral Epistles, James, Jude, and 1 and 2 Peter. For the present we are merely enumerating without inquiring whether the same words actually mean the same thing in every case in which they are used.[2] The conservatives lay particular stress on the number of these

---

[1] For a discussion of this expression see J. Weiss in **XL**, i, 76 *ff.* —in a sort of excursus on Mark x. For the use of the idea and title *Son of God, Sons of the Gods*, in antiquity, *cf.* **XCVIII**, ii.

[2] For the necessary distinctions, *cf.* **XLIV** 112, and **CXCIII**, 67.

attestations, and naturally see in it " the evidence of the primitive tradition with regard to the person of Jesus," based upon Jesus' own words and the impression produced by his personality.[1] They regard it as certain " even on the testimony of the Synoptics alone, that Our Lord claimed actual divine sonship in the metaphysical sense of the term, and consequently, a nature superior to that of created beings, and that he took the expression Son of God in its strictest and most exalted significance." [2] The title in question expresses " a relation with the Godhead so intimate that no mere man could lay claim to it without blasphemy." It comprises a definite, if not perfectly lucid, explanation of the mystery of the Trinity, for it defines the second person of it.[3] The orthodox cannot well hold any other opinion, but their statements cannot be accepted without further examination.

The first question to be asked is whether the expression was intelligible to the hearers of Jesus, for the mere utterance of a hitherto unsuspected truth is not sufficient to reveal it. It must be given in words which can be understood by those who are to be enlightened. Now Israel knew and used that august title. In principle all Jews were sons of Jahweh, and it was this which distinguished them from the rest of mankind,[4] but the name was especially applied, as it was throughout the ancient East, to outstanding personages, the mouthpieces of God, and above all, to kings.[5] It has even been held that the verse of Psalm ii. which according to Codex D plays a part in the Baptism of Jesus : " Thou art my beloved son ; this day have I begotten thee," was a part of the liturgy of the coronation rite of the Hasmonean kings.[6] During the post-exilic period, the pious man was especially regarded as the son of God.[7] In all these cases, it is clear that there is no idea of expressing anything more than a closer moral and religious connexion with the Creator than is enjoyed by ordinary human beings. There could be no question, even remotely, of any real sonship, for to a Jew that would have been the most preposterous absurdity and the grossest blasphemy. To sum up, at

---

[1] CXC, 211 ff.　　　[2] V, i, 580 ff.　　　[3] CCLXXVII, i, 249 ff.

[4] CXLI, 268. Cf. especially Ps. lxxxviii. 26 : Πατήρ μου εἶ σύ, and 2 Sam. vii. 14 ; ἐγὼ ἔσομαι αὐτῷ εἰς πατέρα καὶ αὐτὸς ἔσται μοι εἰς υἱόν —" I will be his father, and he shall be my son." It is Jahweh who says this to David, promising him in the future a glorious scion of his house. " Ye are the children of the Lord your God," says Deut. xiv. 1. Cf. Isa. i. 2 ; xlv. 11 ; lxiii. 8 ; Jer. iii. 22 ; Hos. ii. 1 ; etc.

[5] EB, Son of God, §§ 1–5, which gives the passages.

[6] Duhm, Die Psalmen. Tübingen, 1899, 8.

[7] CXIV, 6 ; CLX, 123.

the time immediately preceding the Christian era, a "son of God," in the estimation of the Jews, belonged to one of the two types who by their essential nature enjoyed a unique relationship with God—the Righteous Man and the Prince.

But the question arises whether he who was pre-eminently the Righteous Man and the Prince, the one whose coming Israel so ardently desired and awaited with such high hopes, was commonly designated as the Son of God so that anyone hearing the expression would unhesitatingly understand it to mean the Messiah. By dint of straining the texts this question has sometimes been answered in the affirmative,[1] but without carrying conviction to anyone who was not already persuaded.[2] We must not forget that the Messiah expected by the Jews was to be a *man* (ἄνθρωπος ἐξ ἀνθρώπων, as the Rabbi Tryphon says to Justin).[3] It now seems definitely established that there is not a single passage in Jewish literature giving the Messiah the title of the Son of God,[4] which can with certainty be regarded as pre-Christian.

Moreover, even if, by any chance, the belief that the Messiah had a place reserved for him in heaven, close to God[5]—and we do not know that this was widespread—had influenced a few Jews to call him the Son of God, the expression would never have been to them any more than a metaphor, a manner of speaking. For all orthodox forms of Christianity, however, Jesus is the Son of God in no metaphorical or figurative sense. This title has much more religious significance than that of Messiah, in that it contains an assertion regarding not merely the *mission* of Jesus, but his *nature*.[6] This is precisely the point. Taken in the orthodox sense of our theologians, the expression, we repeat, would have seemed to any Jew the most horrible blasphemy.

We are told, however, that the texts prove that Jesus used

---

[1] Vigouroux, *Manuel Biblique*, 10. Paris, 1897; ii, 370. *Cf.* **CLVII**, ii, 41 *ff*.

[2] **EB**, *Son of God*, § 6. Of the two most difficult passages one (*Enoch* cv. 2 : " *Because I and my son will be with you always on the paths of truth* ") is certainly an interpolation, according to the most reliable authorities (Drummond, Charles, Dalman) : the other (4 *Esdras* vii. 28 : " *For my son Christ . . .*" ; an expression which is repeated in vii. 29 ; xiii. 32, 37, 52 ; xiv. 19) is from a late text which is now only to be found in Christianized recensions.

[3] *Dial.*, 49.

[4] **LXXVII**, i, 219 ; **CXCIII**, 66. Père Lebreton gives up the struggle and agrees that the title of Son of God applied to the Messiah is not Jewish (**CCLXXVII**, 121). Lagrange (**CI**, 57) thinks that it is not at any rate a current equivalent.

[5] **CCCX**, 216 *ff*.   [6] **CLXV**, 58.

it to designate himself. That is, to designate himself specifically, for obviously, if he regarded all men as sons of God, the expression loses its significance. We must remember that he spoke, not Greek, but Aramaic, and that where our Evangelists write ὁ πατήρ μου, *my Father*, or the vocative, πατέρ μου, *O Father*, or *O my Father*, he said at most *abba*, *the* father or *father*. Consequently, the distinction which is made, for instance, in Luke xxii. 29 : " And I appoint unto *you* the Kingdom, as *my* father hath appointed it unto me," and which is so triumphantly adduced by the orthodox,[1] becomes non-existent, since the " my " disappears.

The real question, however, is whether the expression " the Son of God " was applied to Jesus either by himself or by others. But since it was not commonly used to designate a man of God—as *hadji* is in Moslem countries—nobody would have given him the title if he had not himself quite definitely set the example. Disregarding the interminable controversies to which the question has given rise,[2] let us interrogate the texts.

Two passages and no more,[3] one in Mark, the other in the *logia*, put the words into the mouth of Jesus in reference to himself, and this infrequency is of itself suspicious. We read in Mark xiii. 32 (*cf.* Matt. xxiv. 26) :

> " But of that day [the day of the appearance of the Kingdom] knoweth no man [anything], not the angels in heaven, nor the Son, but only the Father."

And in Matthew xi. 27, which is duplicated by Luke x. 22 :

> " All things are delivered unto me of my Father, and no man knoweth the Son but the Father, neither knoweth any man the Father, save the Son, and he to whomsoever the Son will reveal him."

It is hardly necessary to point out that these two passages are fundamentally inconsistent with each other, and that the

---

[1] CCLXXVII, 242 *ff*.

[2] For various views see : N. Schmidt in **EB**, *Son of God*, § 22 : **CXC**, 214 *ff*.; L–*a*, ii, 335 *ff*.; **XLIV**, 119 *ff*.; **LXVIII**, 59; **CXLI**, 270; **CIII**, i, 243; **CLXV**, 30 *ff*.; **LXVII**, 167 *ff*.; **CXXXI**, ch. viii.

[3] Little reliance is to be placed on Mark xiv. 61 (" *Again the High Priest asked him and said unto him, art thou the Christ, the Son of the Blessed? And Jesus said, I am* ") for the following reasons : 1. It is found in an episode, the trial before the Sanhedrin, of which the authenticity is suspect; 2. the wording of the passage does not ring true : *Son of the Blessed* is not a current equivalent of *Messiah*, and it seems unnecessary to put a blasphemy into the mouth of the High Priest; 3. The text itself is very uncertain : it is much less clear in Matt. xxvi. 64 and Luke xxii. 70.

title of " the Son," as it is found in both, with the significance
which is apparently given to it, would be quite unintelligible
to the Jews.   It is hard to believe that Jesus proclaimed himself to be the Son in this manner, when it could mean nothing
to his hearers and implies a Christological development quite
foreign to *Urmarcus*, a development, moreover, which is of
Greek origin.   With regard to the first passage, it does not
seem likely that the saying was subsequently interpolated in
a text which did not contain it, because that would have been
the gratuitous creation of a difficulty at a time when it had
become unthinkable that the Son had not " known of that day."
We can understand that *Q* might have preserved a sentence
containing Jesus' confession of ignorance regarding the date
of the Great Day, but it is difficult to think that he would
have coupled this unique quality of sonship with such an
avowal of ignorance.   Hence we conclude that the original
passage must have given another word, for which " Son " was
later substituted.

It is not surprising that the orthodox regard Mark xi. 27
as conclusive.[1]   Even those who realize that it is more akin
to John and Paul [2] than to the Synoptic tradition, cannot
bring themselves to reject the ascription of the words to Jesus.[3]
On the other hand, it was long ago maintained that the whole
passage was of Pauline inspiration.[4]   That is a probability
which is incapable of strict proof, but it is clear that the activity
implied by the words : " all things are delivered unto me . . ."
($\pi\acute{\alpha}\nu\tau\alpha$ $\mu o\iota$ $\pi\alpha\varrho\varepsilon\delta\acute{o}\theta\eta$) and the divine communication ($\pi\alpha\varrho\acute{\alpha}\delta o\sigma\iota\varsigma$)
of the saving secret, which is referred to in the Hellenic writings
concerning the Mysteries,[5] present an undeniable appearance
of relationship.   The language, and even the order of the ideas,
are alike, and give the impression of a gnostic formula, especially
when we read the whole passage, beginning at verse 25 : [6] " I
thank thee, O Father, Lord of heaven and earth, because thou
hast hid these things from the wise and prudent and hast
revealed them unto babes," and going on to verse 30 : " Come
unto me, all ye that labour and are heavy laden, and I will

[1] CXC, 216.
[2] John v. 17–25 ; xvii. 10 ; xvii. 26 ; 1 Cor. i. 19–31.
[3] De Grandmaison, *Études*, 1907, i, 131 ; CLXV, 8, n. 1 ; CCLXXVII,
470 *ff.* ; CX, 166.   Contra : L–*a*, i, 348, n. 1.
[4] Pfleiderer, *Das Urchristentum.   Seine Schriften und Lehren.*   Berlin,
1902, 445 *ff.*, 509 *ff.*
[5] CCLXXXIX, 277–308 ; CCXLII, 62.
[6] CVI, 65, attempts, furthermore, to limit the application of the
remark.   The following passage from Luke x. 21 must also be taken
into consideration, " *In that hour Jesus rejoiced in spirit.*"

give you rest. . . ." Nowhere else in the Synoptics do we find anything at all resembling this.[1]

That Jesus believed that he had received from God a certain "*paradosis*," and that he proclaimed this belief, is quite possible, and critics who are in no way orthodox have maintained as much, by admitting the substantial authenticity of this passage.[2] But this is not what we are interested in at the moment. The whole question is whether Jesus meant to designate himself by the appellation " the Son of God."

The whole pericope of which our passage forms a part is called " the Prayer of Thanksgiving." It is open to suspicion because, in those portions of the tradition which appear to be most historical, Jesus does not preach about himself, as he does here. The expression " the Son," as it appears in this passage, gives colour to a Christological idea which can belong only to the tradition, and not to Jesus. It implies the conception of " the immortal, or even the eternal, Christ." [3] That orthodoxy should maintain that no one knew better than Jesus his essential nature, or could proclaim it with greater authority, is quite natural, but the historical point of view is different. From that standpoint, even accepting the contents of the *logion*, and admitting that Jesus said *something like that* (which the present writer is far from doing), the actual expression, " the Son," is inadmissible, just as in the case of Mark xiii. 32.[4] The very clearly marked rhythm of the whole of the " Prayer of Thanksgiving " [5] gives it the appearance of a piece of liturgy, and definitely relates it with the formulas of the Eastern religions [6] and the current practices of Greek rhetoric. Further, the fundamental ideas and the characteristic expressions have every appearance of having come from the *Wisdom* of Jesus the son of Sirach. We can pick out no less than eight verses of *Sirach* which the redactor of the six verses of Matthew seems to have had in mind.[7] He speaks of Jesus in the same way as *Sirach* speaks of *Wisdom*. He was probably influenced by neither

---

[1] P. Schmiedel correctly calls his study of the passage (*Protest. Monatshefte*, 1900, 1 *ff.*) *Die " johanneische " Stelle bei Mt. und Lc. und das Messiasbewusstsein Jesu."*

[2] E. P. Schmiedel, Harnack, L–*a*, i, 346 *ff.*

[3] CIII, i, 909.   [4] LXXVII, i, 159.   [5] L–*a*, i, 350.

[6] XIV, 99, which compares the passage with the remark of Ea to Marduk : " My son, what I know, thou also knowest."

[7] *Sir.*, 51, 1, which indicates the beginning of the prayer—also a prayer of thanksgiving—of Jesus son of *Sirach*. Cf. Matt. xi. 28*a* and *Sir.*, 51, 23 ; Matt. xi. 28*b* and *Sir.*, 24, 19 ; Matt. xi. 29*a* and *Sir.*, 6, 24 ; Matt. xi. 29*b* and *Sir.*, 6, 28 ; Matt. xi. 30 and *Sir.*, 6, 29 ; other Old Testament passages have also crossed the Evangelist's mind, *e.g.* Isa. lv. 1–3 ; Zech. ix. 9 ; Jer. vi. 16, etc.

Paul nor John, but he coincided with about the same stage in the development of Christology as they did. The Prayer of Thanksgiving is therefore spurious, and the *logion* with which we have been dealing is the work of a Christian prophet living in a Hellenic community, and certainly unfamiliar with the apostolic world. There is no question of fraud. As we have already said, in the very early Church the Christians often adopted, in entire good faith, the contributions made by the inspired to the treasure of the direct tradition. The one in question was in harmony with the Christological development, and could not fail to be welcomed by it.

Jesus, then, did not describe himself as " the Son," and it is even more improbable that those around him designated him thus. Such a strange idea would have been beyond them. Moreover, a careful study of the various passages in which the expression appears, expecially in Mark, where it is so frequent, will easily convince us that it is not primitive, and that the passages themselves do not come from the earliest stage of the tradition.[1] We may mention especially the incidents of the Baptism and the Transfiguration, and the confessions of the devils. All this kind of fantasy, in which the voice of heaven is heard alternating with that of hell, brings under suspicion everything connected with it. Sometimes the interpolation of the phrase is evident, as, for example, in the confession of Peter, where Mark viii. 29 makes the Apostle say : " Thou art the Christ " ($\Sigma\dot{v}$ $\varepsilon\tilde{\iota}$ $\dot{o}$ $X\varrho\iota\sigma\tau\acute{o}\varsigma$), and Matthew xvi. 16 adds : " the son of the living God " ($\dot{o}$ $v\dot{\iota}o\varsigma$ $\tauo\tilde{v}$ $\theta\varepsilon o\tilde{v}$ $\tauo\tilde{v}$ $\zeta\tilde{\omega}\nu\tauo\varsigma$). We may echo the remark of Batiffol,[2] that none of these testimonies to the Sonship of Jesus are derived from the teaching of Jesus.

Those who said that Jesus was the Son of God could not have arrived at that belief except in a Greek atmosphere. It was in Greek that they said it, and under the influence of religious views quite different from the Messianic conceptions of the Jews. We shall not go into the question of how the Greeks came to call Jesus the Son of God, that is to say, how, by combining their very elastic conception of the word " god " ($\theta\varepsilon\dot{o}\varsigma$)[3] with the Jewish idea of monotheism, they found a means of at once fitting their image of Jesus into the framework of their own habits of mind, and escaping the narrow nationalism of the Jewish idea of the Messiah ; nor how, extracting from the expression, " the Son of God," a new

---

[1] **CXCIII**, 66 ; **CIII**, 243, n. 1.   [2] **CXC**, 215.
[3] For the elasticity of this term *cf.* **CCLXIII**, i, 138, which gives many examples.

description of the Lord that was more adapted to their own
aspirations, they converted the word " *Christos* " into a proper
name, and said " *Jesus Christ* " as they said " *Julius Cæsar*."
We are not concerned here with the problem of the Christological development.   What we are interested in is how these
Gentile converts could have obtained the idea that Jesus *called
himself* the Son of God, and how they could have come to
believe that this conviction was justified by the Apostolic
tradition.   It is not inconceivable that a view of faith prevalent, we may suppose, at the end of the first century, should
have projected itself back to a time fifty years earlier, but the
process must have been facilitated in some way.

It was favoured, in the first place, by the very strong sense
of the paternity of God which Jesus had with regard to all
men, but especially in his own case, because he felt himself
entirely permeated by the Spirit of God, and guided by His
will.   This idea could without much difficulty be transferred
from its original realm of discourse to some other.   In the
second place, it was assisted by a phrase which Jesus used,
and which was used by those around him, to express this
intimate relation between him and God, namely, and without
any doubt, παῖς τοῦ θεοῦ, the " child " or " servant " of God.
This expression is used in the Septuagint to designate those
who are especially devoted to fulfilling the will of Jahweh.[1]
In this sense it is often applied to Israel as a whole (Isa. xli.
8 ;[2] xlii. 19 ; xliv. 1 ; etc.), to Moses (Neh. i. 7 *ff*. : τῷ
Μωυσῇ παιδί σου), to the Prophets (Baruch ii. 20) and to David
(Ps. xvii. 1).   In all these different passages, the Greek word
pais (παῖς) is used to translate the Hebrew *ebed*, meaning
servant, which is sometimes also rendered by synonyms of *pais*
in the sense of servant, such as *therapon* (θέραπων) or *doulos*
(δοῦλος).   The former of these (Num. xii. 7 ; Joshua i. 2) has
the connotation of *attendant*, the latter (Ps. civ. 6), that of *slave*.
The word παῖς, like the Latin word *puer*, is accordingly to be
understood, when it represents *ebed*, in the sense of *servant*.[3]
παῖς τοῦ θεοῦ, *ebed Jahweh*, is analogous to the Greek proper
name ῾Ερμόδουλος, slave of Hermes, and the Arabic *Abd-Allah*,
servant of Allah.

Such an expression, so consecrated by custom and by the

---

[1] Ps. lxviii. 18 (Ps. lxix. 17, A.V.), " Hide not thy face from thy
servant " (or " from thy child " : ἀπὸ τοῦ παιδός σου) ; Wisd. ii. 13 :
. . . καὶ παῖδα κυρίου ἑαυτὸν ὀνομάζει.

[2] The text quoted by Luke i. 54 in the *Magnificat* : ἀντελάβετο
᾿Ισραὴλ παιδὸς αὐτοῦ . . . .

[3] *Cf.* Gen. ix. 25 ; xii. 16 ; Exod. xii. 30 ; xiii. 3 ; 2 Sam. ii. 12 ;
etc.

Scriptures as the designation of a Man of God, could hardly, it seems, have failed to be applied to Jesus. But on investigation we discover : (1) that παῖς τοῦ θεοῦ occurs in the Gospels only once, in Matthew xii. 18 : ἰδοὺ ὁ παῖς, "behold my servant," which is a quotation from Isaiah xlii. 1, and introduced as such by the preceding verse : " That it might be fulfilled which was spoken by Isaiah the prophet " ; (2) that on the other hand, υἱός τοῦ θεοῦ, Son of God, appears only once in Acts (ix. 20), and is there given as a characteristic teaching of Paul : " and he preached in the synagogues that Jesus was the Son of God." It looks, therefore, as if the two expressions did not both occur in the same environment, as if the one was used where the other was not. It is hardly to be doubted, for instance, that Acts says παῖς where Paul would say υἱός, as in iii. 13 : [1] " The God of Abraham and the God of Isaac and the God of Jacob, the God of our fathers hath glorified his servant Jesus " (τὸν παῖδα ἀυτοῦ Ἰησοῦν) ; iv. 27 : " There were gathered together in that city against thy holy servant Jesus " (ἐπὶ τὸν ἅγιον παιδά σου Ἰησοῦν) ; iv. 30 : " By the name of thy holy servant (τοῦ ἁγίου παιδός σου) Jesus."

It is perhaps even more illuminating to discover [2] that the expression παῖς τοῦ θεοῦ is preserved in the early liturgical writings. We read, for example, in the *Didache* ix. 2 : " We give thanks unto thee, O our Father, for the holy vine of thy servant David which thou hast made known to us by thy servant Jesus " (τοῦ παιδός σου). The same title is thus applied both to David and to Jesus. In x. 2 : " We give thanks unto thee . . . for the knowledge, the faith and the immortality which thou hast revealed to us by thy servant Jesus " (διὰ Ἰησοῦ τοῦ παιδός σου).

The expression is found again in a passage of 1 Clem. lix. 2 *ff.*, which is supposed to reproduce a formal prayer of the Roman community, and Epiphanius, at the end of the fourth century, asserts (*Hær.* xxix. 7) that the Ebionites also made use of it (κατάγγελλουσι τὸν ἑαύτου παῖδα Ἰησοῦν—" they proclaim his servant Jesus "), so that it was probably an old liturgical phrase of that sect. There can be no doubt that the two expressions were equivalent, that παῖς τοῦ Θεοῦ, servant of God, was the earlier, and that it was a Judæo-Christian form, that is to say, one that was used in the communities which sprang from Judaism. It probably already had, in them, a sense that went beyond that of " servant," for instance, it may have had that of " the servant *par excellence*,"

---

[1] Built up from Isa. lii. 13 ; liii. 11, etc.   [2] **CXCIII,** 68.

the Christ. The phrase " Son of God " undoubtedly represents a more advanced stage in the development, but it is still derived from the old expression. In the beginning the transition from one to the other was facilitated by the double meaning of παῖς, " child " and " servant," which would enable υἱός, " son," to be very easily substituted for it. We can readily imagine that the original expression, which may be supposed to have been applied to Jesus during his lifetime in accordance with ordinary custom, was retained by the Judæo-Christians, and acquired a certain elasticity in their hands, which enabled it finally to be stretched to cover the earliest Christological conceptions. Amongst the Gentile converts, where it was less clearly understood, it must have soon come to seem less precise and intelligible than the other, which was, nevertheless, only a misinterpretation of it. But it was a very suggestive misinterpretation, and by this fact its success was immediately assured.

III

THE MESSIAH

We feel justified in concluding, therefore, that Jesus did not call himself the Son of God, and was not given that title during his lifetime. The problem of his " Messianic consciousness," that is to say, the question whether he believed himself to be the Messiah, and gave himself out as such, is a more difficult one. If he did, it is this belief which is also embodied in the two expressions we have just been comparing. From an objective point of view, so to speak, our present problem resolves itself into the question whether Jesus assumed or accepted the titles of Son of David and Son of Man, which are commonly regarded as having signified the Messiah.

(1) The Jews in general believed that the Messiah would be descended from David,[1] to whom God was supposed to have promised eternal kingship : " And thine house and thy kingdom shall be established for ever before thee," it was written in 2 Samuel vii. 16 ; and Isaiah xi. 1 had prophesied : " There shall come forth a rod out of the stem of Jesse " (Jesse, the father of David), and had explicitly designated this scion as the Messiah (xi. 12 ff.). Consequently the rabbis were in the habit of saying, " the son of David cometh," for " the Messiah cometh." Hence, no title could more clearly and directly express the claim of the person who assumed it.[2]

[1] **XXIX**, ii, 527.　　　　　　　[2] **L–a**, i, 104 ff., 310.

At the outset two facts stand out : not a single passage
of our Gospels puts this title in the mouth of Jesus, and it
was neither bestowed upon him by his disciples nor contested
by his adversaries. In fact, it appears only once in the *logia*
and only once in Mark x. 47, where the blind man of Jericho
exclaims : " Jesus, son of David, have mercy upon me ! "
There is no means of verifying this solitary passage, and it
might easily have been altered by a redactor on the essential
point. It is quite conceivable that Mark wanted to convey,
by putting this exclamation in the mouth of a poor blind man
who did not know Jesus, that the blind man could discern
immediately, by divine instinct, him whom the supposedly
perspicacious Jews would not recognize.

It is important to note that, in the Marcan account of the
entry of Jesus into Jerusalem (xi. 10), it is " the coming kingdom of our father David " (ἐρχομένη βασιλεία τοῦ πατρὸς ἡμῶν
Δαυείδ), and not the " Son of David," which is spoken of.
On the other hand, it is hardly less significant that the
parallel account of Matthew introduces (xxi. 9) the words :
" Hosanna to the Son of David ! " Luke xix. 38, without
actually naming David, adds to his quotation from Psalm cxviii.
26 which Mark has in mind, the idea suggested by the name of
the ancient king : " Blessed be he that cometh [as] king in
the name of the Lord." Such additions to the source are very
significant. It is obvious that Matthew is fond of this title
" Son of David," and parades it wherever he thinks there is
a good opportunity (xii. 23 ; xv. 22 ; xx. 30), but none of the
passages in which it is introduced can be taken as warrant for
it. All of them simply represent the desire of the redactor to
multiply instances of the spontaneous testimony of the ignorant
and afflicted, as against the blindness of the Jews.

We may go further still, and assert that Jesus, far from
assuming the status and title of Son of David, definitely repudiated them. We read in Mark xii. 35-7 :

> " And beginning to speak, Jesus said, teaching in the Temple :
> ' Why do the Scribes say that Christ will be the son of David ?
> David himself said by the Holy Ghost : The Lord said to my
> Lord [that is to say, God said to the Messiah] : " Sit thou on my
> right hand till I make thine enemies thy footstool." David therefore
> himself calleth him Lord, and whence is he then his son ? ' "

The first interpretation of this passage which occurs to the
reader is as follows : Jesus believes himself to be the Messiah,
but he knows that he is not of Davidic descent, and he is protesting against the assertion of the scribes, which is prejudicial

¹ Ps. cx (cix. in the Septuagint).

to his claim. The traditionalists of all shades of opinion, who are unwilling to give up the Davidic descent of Christ, get out of the difficulty as best they can by maintaining that Jesus was perfectly aware that he was of the stock of David, but he wished to minimize this qualification, which was too closely bound up with the nationalistic idea of the Messiah, and stimulated hopes which he did not want to encourage. The remark attributed to him by Mark amounts to saying : there is something here greater than David.[1]

Whether or not we accept this explanation—which, however, in the opinion of the writer is inadmissible—the interpretation of the passage is secondary to the question of its authenticity, which is no easy one to settle. To all appearances we are probably here confronted by a projection of a very much later dispute into the life of Jesus, and the declaration attributed to the Master represents only the orthodox retort to the inevitable objection of the Jews : Your Jesus cannot be the Messiah because he is not a son of David. It must, certainly, have been a very early answer, and one confined to the first group of disciples, because beyond that circle it very soon became apparent that it was much simpler to believe and maintain that, since Jesus *was* the Messiah, he was necessarily descended from David (*cf.* the genealogies of Matt. and Luke, and Rom. i. 3). To be sure, what we have just said indicates only a possibility, not a certainty, but it is sufficient to make it impossible to base any conclusion regarding the Messiahship of Jesus on this supposed title of Son of David.

(2) The appellation " Son of Man " brings us face to face with the most involved and complicated of all the problems offered by the New Testament.[2] The origin, the history, the significance of the term, are all questions of the greatest difficulty. The multitude of theories which have been put forward in the attempt to answer them, warns us at the outset that the indefiniteness of our documents offers limitless scope for ingenious guesswork and daring hypothesis. It is the part of wisdom, however, to dispense, as far as possible, with both.

In its Hellenic form (ὁ υἱὸς τοῦ ανθρώπου), which was completely unintelligible to the Greeks in general, the expression has the appearance of a kind of password of a circle of initiates. It is a translation of the Hebrew *ben-adam*, which in Hebraic literature is usually a synonym for " man," and rarely employed

[1] CXC, 201 *ff.* ; CLXV, 27, n. 6 ; L–*a*, i, 310 *ff.*
[2] L–*a*, i, 313 *ff.* ; LXVII [1], 189 *ff.* (2nd edition, 171 *ff.*). De Grandmaison, *Jesus*, i, 317, n. 1, which gives the bibliography ; LXVIII, 55 *ff.* ; N. Schmidt, *Son of Man*, EB ; CXCIII, 6 *ff.* ; CCXCI, 31 *ff.*

except poetically.[1] It is a translation also of *ben-enosh* (Ps. cxliv. 3), and the Aramaic *bar-nasha*, which also means " a man," and has common equivalents in the various Aramaic dialects.[2] By its emphasis on the humanity of the person to whom it is applied, it is directly opposed to the expressions *ben elohim, bar ilaha*, meaning " son of God " (υἱὸς τοῦ θεοῦ).[3]

This Semitic expression should actually, it seems, be rendered in Greek simply by the word ἄνθρωπος, " man." But we must inquire whether it had not acquired, in Israel, a more complex meaning. It is found ninety times in Ezekiel, where it is Jahweh himself who thus addresses the prophet, and it is the general opinion that this repeated *ben-adam* is intended by the Scriptural writer to have a deeper significance than that of " man," that it in some way expresses the peculiar status or character of the prophet. It is as if the writer wished to show Ezekiel as, in God's eyes, a kind of representative of the human race, as Man ; as if he were imbued with a mingled feeling of humility in view of the human origin of the prophet, and of exaltation, occasioned by Jahweh's choice of him as his interpreter.

The repetition of the expression seems to be simply a feature of the author's style. It is merely a case, then, of a kind of extension of the usual sense of *ben-adam*.

Daniel viii. 17 [4] certainly gives us a similar impression. There the angel Gabriel, who is about to explain a vision to the prophet, says to him : " Understand, O son of Man ! " But in Daniel vii. 13–14, in the section written in Aramaic, " Son of Man " has a different effect from that which characterizes it in the usage of Ezekiel. The following is a translation of the passage : [5]

> " I saw in the night a vision, and behold, one like a son of Man came with the clouds of heaven, and came to the Ancient of days, and they brought him before him. And there was given him power and glory and a kingdom ; and all the people, nations, and tongues serve him, and his dominion is an everlasting dominion."

This is the reading followed by the Latin Vulgate and Theo-

---

[1] Num. xxiii. 19 ; Isa. li. 12 ; lvi. 2 ; Jer. xlix. 18 and 33 ; l. 40 ; Ps. viii. 5 ; lxxx. 18 ; etc.

[2] There is an extensive study of the linguistic question in N. Schmidt, *Son of Man*, §§ 1–5 and 36.

[3] CCLXXXVIII, 383.

[4] A late work—probably of the time of Antiochus Epiphanes— part of which is edited (from ii. 4*b* to vii. 28) in Aramaic and not in Hebrew. *Cf.* Marti's Introduction in CCLXXIII, ii, 416.

[5] XVIII, 1175.

dotion,[1] but that of the Septuagint is quite different, and gives the essential point as follows :

> " And behold : on the clouds of heaven came one like a son of Man, and he was there like an Ancient of days, and those who were with him surrounded him (καὶ οἱ παρεστηκότες παρῆσαν αὐτῷ). And there was given him power, etc."

This alteration in the real meaning, due perhaps to a copyist's error,[2] is similar to that perpetrated by Lemaître de Sacy in his translation—unfortunately, only too well known—of the passage from the Vulgate : " . . . and I saw one like the Son of Man who came with the clouds of heaven." The Septuagint suggests, and the French version makes it explicit, that the son of man in Daniel's vision is the Messiah, and consequently, that the expression designates " the One who is to come."

This interpretation was perpetuated by Enoch (xxxvii.-lxxi.) and 4 Esdras, for it is very probable that both took their idea of the *Son of Man* from Daniel. It was adopted by the Synoptics (Mark xiv. 62 and Matt. xxvi. 64), and finally became established in the Synagogue, mainly through the influence of Rabbi Akiba, the great theologian of the second century A.D., and Rabbi Joshua ben Levi. Many modern critics regard it as correct,[3] but unfortunately for this view, it is not borne out by any document that has real evidential value, that is to say, by any which is either prior to Daniel or exempt from all possibility of contamination by the Messianic interpretation of the Danielic passage, and in the last analysis the opinion that at the time of Jesus *Son of Man* was a current designation of the Messiah, has only the support of Daniel itself, which is very slender. This opinion was, to be sure, held at the time of the redaction of the Synoptics, but that does not tell us how long it had been current, and in what circles. There is no help to be obtained from Enoch xxxvii.-lxxi., because it is impossible to establish the date of that writing.[4]

If we consider the verses of Daniel and their context by themselves, the supposition that their author intended to refer to the Messiah seems very improbable. In all the rest of the book there is no further mention of the Messiah supposed to

[1] The translation of the Old Testament by Theodotion belongs to the second century A.D.

[2] **CXCIII**, 15, 1.

[3] See particularly **CLXXXIX**, 169 *ff.* ; and N. Schmidt, *Son of Man*, 19 *ff.*

[4] Baldensperger, for instance, considers this passage very old, while Bousset thinks it was influenced by Christianity. *Cf.* Beer, *Das Buch Henoch, Einleitung,* in **CCLXXXII**, ii, 252.

be indicated by them, and it is difficult to explain the introduction of such a personage if he was to play no further part
in the author's scheme.   On the other hand, it is hard to see
why Daniel's " son of man " should not mean simply " a man,"
as the expression does elsewhere ; why the passage should not
merely signify an apparition in the form of a human being,
and be properly translated : " And I saw one in the likeness
of a man who came, etc."   Whoever the man referred to may
be, there is nothing in the context to indicate that he is the
Messiah.   It has been suggested that he is a personification
of the Chosen People, as opposed to the Gentiles, or an angel,
or various other things,[1] but that is immaterial here.   We are
concerned only to prove that the interpretation of the "son of
man " of *Daniel* as the Messiah is erroneous, and that the Christian equation of " Son of Man " and " Messiah " has no other
foundation than that error.   This is today fairly generally
acknowledged.[2]

It remains to be explained how the interpretation which
is attested by the Synoptics became established.   Various
theories have been advanced, for instance, that in certain
Messianic circles of Palestine [3] the expression " Son of Man "
might have been accepted as a synonym for the Messiah from
the time of Daniel, and that the Christians adopted it because
it was the one by which they least committed themselves to
the ordinary Messianic ideas.[4]   It may also be that the very
mysteriousness of the expression caught the attention of the
Gentile converts, the readers of the Septuagint.   We shall not
undertake to decide the question, contenting ourselves with
having demonstrated that " Son of Man " was not a regular
appellation of the Messiah amongst the Jews at the beginning
of the Christian era.

The expression occurs sixty-nine times in the Synoptics,
and after this impressive total has been carefully sifted, and
the duplications weeded out, there remain about forty passages
in which the orthodox interpretation is indisputable, and Son
of Man definitely means Messiah.   John supplies about a dozen
instances, but these need not detain us, because they add nothing to the evidence of the Synoptics.   Outside the Gospels, Son
of Man is found only once, in Acts vii. 56, where Stephen just
before his martyrdom is supposed to say : " Behold I see the
heavens opened and the Son of Man standing on the right hand
of God."   Neither Paul nor the General Epistles use the term,
and it is a mistake to suppose that this is due merely to chance.

[1] *Cf.* N. Schmidt, *Son of Man*, § 6 ;   Bousset, **CXCIII**, 15.
[2] **L–a**, i, 314.   [3] **CXCIII**, 15.   [4] **CLXV**, 84.

Moreover, the expression was not popular in early Christian literature, where it is met with only two or three times.[1]

Since the Evangelists always put it into the mouth of Jesus, and never into that of anyone speaking to him, it is obvious that they wished to give the impression that it was a peculiar characteristic of the speech of the Nazarene, and his favourite designation of himself.[2] Their insistence on the point is not, however, of itself sufficient to prove it. If for the sake of argument we grant that Jesus habitually used the expression " Son of Man," we are still ignorant of the significance he gave to it. This is a bitterly disputed point,[3] but we shall not enter into the controversy, in which each participant produces passages and arguments in support of theories that are always controvertible and conclusions that are never certain. They all err in assuming that the question of the use of the expression in Israel in a Messianic sense before the time of Jesus, has been decided in the affirmative, which, as we have been attempting to prove, is the direct opposite of the truth. But it is inconceivable that Jesus should have employed, for the purpose of clearly characterizing and describing himself, a phrase which would not be perfectly comprehensible to everybody, which would not be accurately understood and defined, and which he himself would have any need to explain.

When we read through all the Gospel passages in which the words " Son of Man " appear, the impression is inescapable that they do not everywhere mean the same thing, even though in all cases, in the judgment of the redactors, they enshrine the sublime Mystery of the Messiahship. Sometimes, however, they stand for nothing more than the word " I," leaving aside, of course, the idea of himself that Jesus may have attached to the pronoun. A good example of this is afforded by a comparison of Luke xii. 8 and Matthew x. 32.[4] The first passage runs : " Whosoever shall confess me before men, him shall the Son of Man also confess before the angels of God " ; the second: " Whosoever shall confess me before men, him will I confess before my Father." The substance of the verse is found in Mark viii. 38, including the expression " the Son of Man," which Luke has retained and Matthew interpreted as " I." Another example of the same kind is given in Matthew xvi.

---

[1] Justin, 1 *Apol.*, 51 ; Eusebius, *H.E.*, 2, 23, 13.

[2] L–a, i, 314.

[3] In addition to the article of N. Schmidt quoted above, § 30, see also **CLXXV**, 66 ; **CCXXI** ; **LXXVII**, 191–7 ; **CIII**, i, 243 ; L–a, i, 314 ; **III**, 308, and **CXCIII**, 13, n. 3.

[4] *Cf.* Mark viii. 31 ; ix. 12 ; x. 33.

13, where we read : " Whom do men say the Son of Man is ? "
Mark viii. 27, however, which is evidently the source, reads :
" Whom do men say that I am ? " (τίνα με λέγουσιν οἱ ἄνθρωποι
εἶναι), and Luke ix. 18 vouches for the Marcan version, writing :
" Whom say the people (οἱ ὄχλοι) that I am ? "

On the other hand, when we read in Mark viii. 38 the following statement : " Whosoever therefore shall be ashamed of
me and of my words in this adulterous and sinful generation,
of him also shall the Son of Man be ashamed when he cometh
in the glory of his Father with the holy angels," there can be
no doubt that it is the pseudo-Danielic Son of Man who is
referred to, the Messiah in his capacity of Judge on the Great
Day.[1] In other places, however, it seems plain that " son of
man " means simply " man," in conformity with Semitic usage.
Take, for instance, Matthew xii. 31 *ff.* :

> " All manner of sin and blasphemy shall be forgiven unto men,
> but the blasphemy against the Spirit shall not be forgiven. And
> whosoever speaketh a word against the Son of Man it shall be for-
> given him ; but whosoever speaketh against the Holy Ghost it shall
> not be forgiven him, neither in this world nor in the world to come."

If we interpret Son of Man as the Messiah, or even if we assume
that the expression refers specifically to Jesus, the passage
becomes incredible, and almost inconceivable. How could the
Gospel writer have written such a thing about the Lord ? It
is certainly " man " that is to be understood here. We cannot
agree with Wellhausen,[2] in his contention that at bottom " son
of man " has everywhere this meaning, but it certainly must
be taken in this sense in several passages of the Synoptics
where the context leaves no doubt.

A careful study of the texts will enable us to reach some
suggestive conclusions, which we shall briefly summarize :
(1) In a number of cases—seventeen in all—the expression is
vouched for by only one Gospel. A comparison of the three,
or even of two, where there are only two parallel passages,
proves that the expression " Son of Man " did not come from
the source. One example will suffice : in Matthew xvi. 28 we
read: " Verily I say unto you there be some here which shall
not taste of death till they see the Son of Man coming in his
kingdom " (ἐν τῇ βασιλείᾳ αὐτοῦ). The source of this, which
is unquestionably Mark ix. 1, reads : " before they see the
Kingdom of God come," and this reading is confirmed by Luke

[1] *Cf.* Mark xiii. 26 ; xiv. 21 ; Matt. xiii. 37 and 41 ; xvi. 28 ; xix.
28.

[2] CCCXIV, vi, 1899 ; CCCXIII, 387 ; CXIV, 68.

ix. 27. Hence the editor of Matthew has supplied "Son of Man" out of his own imagination.[1]

(2) This expression is repeated with particular emphasis in contexts which must either be treated with suspicion or definitely rejected. Examples of these are to be found in Mark ix. 9 and Matthew xvii. 9 at the end of the story of the Transfiguration, where we hear Jesus forbidding the witnesses of his glorification to speak about it : " Till the *Son of Man* be risen again from the dead." Again in Mark ix. 11–13 and Matthew xvii. 10–13, two obscure passages referring to the coming of Elias and foretelling the Passion ; and in Mark x. 45 and Matthew xx. 28, which express an idea familiar to Paul (Gal. i. 4 ; ii. 20 and Rom. xv. 3 ; Phil. ii. 7–8) but decidedly foreign to Jesus, according to whom it was not his death but his life that counted, from which we were to take example : " The *Son of Man* came not to be ministered unto but to minister and to give his life as a ransom for many."

It seems likely that this reading was unknown to *Urmarcus* and in the opinion of the author this likelihood will be put beyond all doubt by a comparison of Luke xxii. 25–30 with Mark x. 41–5. In the Third Gospel there is no question of salvation through the death of the *Son of Man*. The notion of service comes up again but in a different sense : " I am among you as he that serveth," which is particularly appropriate in the context since Jesus is attempting to put an end to a dispute among his disciples on the question of who is the first among them. The probability is that Luke had in front of him a text of Mark which did not include the text with which we are concerned, and which bears all the marks of Pauline influence. In Mark xiv. 21 and xxvi. 24 we read : " Woe to that man by whom the *Son of Man* is betrayed." But this passage has the twofold drawback of being a prophecy and of supporting the historically unreliable episode of the betrayal of Judas.[2] For precisely the same reasons the prediction in Mark xiv. 41 and Matthew xxvi. 45 : " The *Son of Man* is betrayed into the hands of sinners," is also unreliable.

(3) A close examination of the passages in which the words *Son of Man* are most likely to belong to the ancient tradition, clearly shows that they only appear to have this unusual mean-

[1] *Cf.* Matt. xvi. 13, Mark viii. 27 and Luke ix. 18 ; Matt. xix. 28, Mark x. 29 and Luke xviii. 30 ; Matt. xxvi. 2, Mark xiv. 1 and Luke xxii. 1, where the expression is an editorial rendering in Matthew ; Luke vi. 22 and Matt. v. 11 ; Luke xii. 8 and Matt. x. 32, where it is redactional in Luke. The same thing applies to Luke xvii. 22 ; xviii. 8 ; xix. 10 ; xxi. 34–6 ; xxii. 48 ; xxiv. 7.

[2] *Cf.* pt. iii, ch. viii, § 1.

ing because this particular interpretation is in the minds of the editors, and is suggested by the passages where Jesus is thought to be announcing, side by side with the necessary and redemptive sufferings of the *Son of Man,* his glorious return on the clouds of heaven. In point of fact all they give us is an awkward rendering of the Aramaic *bar-nasha* ; that is to say " a man," or " man."

We have already mentioned the text (Matt. xii. 32 and Luke xii. 10) referring to evil spoken of the *Son of Man,* as a sin which will be forgiven, in contrast to that against the Spirit, which will not be forgiven. Jesus is refuting the charge that he healed by the power of *Beelzebub.* He feels that this insult passes beyond him to the source of his actions, namely the Spirit, and so he says : " Beware ! An insult to a fellow-creature can be forgiven, but not an insult to the Spirit."

It is unthinkable that he could say : " Insult the Messiah if you like but not the Spirit." The Marcan parallel (iii. 28 *ff.*) to Matthew, which says that sins and blasphemies shall be forgiven *the sons of man* (τοῖς υἱοῖς τῶν ἀνθρώπων) but never blasphemy against the Holy Spirit, gives us both the source and the complete explanation of the " Son of Man " of Matthew and Luke.

Here are a few more examples. Matthew viii. 20 and Luke ix. 58 tell us that : " The foxes have holes and the birds of the air have nests " while " the *Son of Man* hath not where to lay his head." Surely this is little more than a kind of saying or proverb which has lost its true setting, and which expresses the truism that at first sight nature seems kinder to animals than to man ? How could Jesus say at one and the same time that he is the Messiah and that he has nowhere to lay his head ? This detail has escaped the editor.

In Matthew xi. 19 and Luke vii. 3 and 4 we find : " The Son of Man came eating and drinking and they say : Behold a man gluttonous and a wine-bibber." The only possible inter-pretation of this is : The *Baptist,* when he preached, lived the life of an ascetic, and you said : " He has a devil." Here, now, comes a man who, while he preaches to you, lives like everybody else and you say : " He is a gluttonous man and a wine-bibber.

His hearers would not have grasped his meaning if he had introduced here the idea of the Messiah, and, even if they had understood, the use of it would have seemed either ludicrous or sacrilegious.

We must dwell for a moment on two passages which at first sight seem to present a certain amount of difficulty. First

of all Mark ii. 10, Matthew ix. 6 and Luke v. 24, where we
find that : " The *Son of Man* hath power on earth to forgive
sins." Second, Matthew xii. 8, Mark ii. 28 and Luke vi. 5,
which state that : " the *Son of Man* is lord also of the
Sabbath."

It seems difficult at first sight to believe that Jesus would
ascribe to man the remarkable power implied here. But let
us examine the context. A paralytic has been brought to
Jesus to be healed and he says to him : " Son, thy sins be
forgiven thee " (Mark ii. 5), that is, " I give thee a pledge that
God has forgiven thee thy sins." He does not say—and the
difference is vital—" I forgive thee thy sins."

This is not a proclamation of his power as Messiah ; it is
couched in terms which would have conveyed this idea to nobody. It is an assertion that a *man* [1] in a spirit of filial confidence in God, can guarantee the forgiveness of sins by Him.
It is quite obvious that this is not what the Evangelists understood by the passage, but their desires are hardly reliable guides
to the true interpretation, always supposing that Jesus ever
pronounced this *logion*.

It seems equally incredible that the divine precept concerning the Sabbath should be declared subject to the will of *man*.
However, when we read in Mark ii. 27 : " The Sabbath was
made for man and not man for the Sabbath," it seems natural
to conclude " so that man is master, also, of the Sabbath,"
and it is comprehensible that the *logion* wishes to convey this
idea, namely, that even according to the Law itself there are
considerations of greater importance than Sabbath observance.
An example of this is the preservation of life which comes
before the obligation to remain in one place on the Sabbath
Day. Whatever the editor may have had in mind here, it is
no more to be relied upon than in the previous example, and
we are not concerned with it.

Therefore, even though Jesus may have employed the expression "Son of Man," there is not one passage to indicate that
he used it as a special and characteristic designation of himself,
nor in which it has any definite connexion with a consciousness of his Messiahship. In short there is no use of it which
cannot be interpreted in a way entirely different from the
pseudo-Danielic " Son of Man."

The Evangelists' use of this expression is dictated, not by
historical facts but by an interpretation which grew up among
the early generations of Christians. It is not to be found in
Paul and only appears once in Acts, where it is obviously an

[1] CXIV, 17.

editorial insertion.[1]   It is therefore to be ascribed to the period
between Paul and the *Greek* editing of the Synoptics.   Hence
we may conclude that it is almost certainly nothing more than
a pious error of the Gentile Christians, and does not belong to
the apostolic times.   It gave rise to a myth, distinct from that
of the Messiah and superimposed upon it, a myth of a pagan
type, which takes Christ out of his nationalist setting and raises
him to the rôle of an immortal King of a degenerate world,
which he has come to reclaim.   There is nothing in common
between the Nazarene or his immediate disciples and such a
theory.[2]   If Jesus used the term *bar-nasha* it was only, and
could only be in the current sense of " man," " son of man."

(3) It still, however, remains to be decided whether or not
Jesus believed himself to be the Messiah.   A great deal of ink
has been spilt over this question and to go into it again requires
a certain courage in view of the confident assertions which
appear to have decided it in the affirmative.   We are told that
to question the Messianic consciousness of Jesus is to carry
scepticism beyond all limits.[3]   It would be as reasonable to
doubt the crucifixion or even the very existence of Christ.[4]
Such an attitude reduces the history of the origins of Christianity to nothing more than " a heap of absurdities, a tissue
of contradictions," [5] and destroys any means of understanding
both the activities of Jesus as a whole, and their focal point.[6]
In short, it renders the psychology of Jesus and the faith of
the disciples in his resurrection unintelligible.[7]   Such considered
opinions, selected at random, could easily be multiplied,[8] but
they all come back to the same point, namely, that it is impossible to understand the Gospel history as handed down by
the synoptic tradition without admitting the real existence of
the Messianic consciousness of Jesus.

Such a position goes beyond documentary evidence, because even if it is not possible to deny the relation between
the Messianic consciousness of Jesus and the Gospel tradition
as we know it, the relation between this tradition itself and
the truth is still an open question.   Jesus might well have had
different ideas about himself from those attributed to him by

---

[1] Acts vii. 56 ; the Invocation which follows " *Lord Jesus, receive
my spirit* " (vii. 59) is sufficient to date the editing of all the latter part
of the episode of Stephen.

[2] Loisy, **RHLR**, 1922, 81 *ff.* ; **CCLXXXVIII**, 426.

[3] **CCLIII**, 147.   [4] **LXXIX**, 76 and 109.   [5] **CCLXI**, 5.

[6] **CXLIII**, 59 *ff.*   It is noticeable that the author is much less positive
in **CXCIII**, 21 : " *Unsicher bleibt die Stellung Jesu dazu.*"   *Cf.* also p. 81
of the same book.

[7] **CLXXV**, 57 *ff.*   [8] *Cf.* **CLVIII**, i, 311 *ff.*

the editors of the Gospels. Moreover, it is quite conceivable, *à priori*, that the faith of the disciples in the resurrection of their Master sprang from another source than belief in his Messiahship. It is possible that belief in the Messiahship arose from the belief in the resurrection. Supposing that Jesus had merely proclaimed the near approach of the Kingdom, and that he was condemned to death simply as a Messianic revolutionary, might not the love of Peter combined with a natural emotional tension have been sufficient to produce the apparitions on which are based, as we hope to show, the whole of the belief in the resurrection and the explanations to which the great miracle gave rise ? It was difficult for Jews to believe that the Messiah had been crucified, but it was more difficult still for them to acknowledge that the martyred prophet had received the glorious reward of his sufferings, and that the fruit of them, his Messiahship, had been revealed to his faithful followers by his resurrection.

This is clearly the impression given by the words put into the mouth of Peter in Acts ii. 32 *ff.* :

" This Jesus hath God raised up whereof we are all witnesses . . . Therefore let all the house of Israel know assuredly that God hath made the same Jesus, whom ye have crucified, both Lord and Christ."

Later on we shall return to this question of the origins and foundations of the disciples' belief in the Resurrection.[1] On the other hand there is nothing impossible or incomprehensible in the idea that the structure of the Gospel history has been built up by working backwards from the Resurrection and the faith it brought into being. Hence it would appear that this formidable problem has not been solved, but has merely been evaded. The truly scientific standpoint seems to be to admit that it has become very difficult, if not impossible, for us to determine what Jesus said of himself and of his relation to the Kingdom he proclaimed, because the evidence produced by the Evangelists is distorted by an already developed Christology wholly foreign to his own mind.[2]

There would be no difficulty if we could be sure that Jesus had plainly said " I am the Messiah," as he would naturally have felt impelled to do if he really believed it. As a matter of fact, several passages in the Synoptics claim or suggest that he did say it, but it is safer not to take their statements without careful examination.

It must be remembered that, even if current Jewish Messianic belief was still an element in widely differing forms

[1] *Cf.* pt. iii, ch. vi.   [2] **XXVII**, 92.

of eschatology, there was no place in it either for a suffering or for a pacific Messiah. Two hypotheses have been brought forward to weaken the force of this consideration.

(1) It has been claimed that there were certain Jewish sects whose conception of the Messiah had become distorted under the influence of the dying and rising God of the mystery cults. Unfortunately we know nothing of such sects and their existence is purely imaginary.

(2) It has also been claimed that the real Jesus could never have been the preacher of pacifism portrayed in the Gospels. This theory, by no means new, has been recently revived by Robert Eisler with the help of his Slavonic Josephus.[1]

Conjectures, such as these, created to meet a difficulty, are suspect. First of all it may be remarked [2] that in the *logia* Jesus never uses the word Christ of himself, and in Mark he only uses it once. We certainly read in Mark ix. 41 : " For whosoever shall give you a cup of water to drink because ye belong to Christ " (ὅτι Χριστοῦ ἐστε) ; but the authenticity of the essential word here has been rejected even by conservative critics [3] on the two following grounds : (1) The expression ὅτι Χριστοῦ without the article is not found anywhere else in the Synoptics or in Acts, but is a common Pauline phrase (Rom. viii. 9 ; 1 Cor. i. 12 ; iii. 23, etc.). (2) Matthew x. 42, the synoptic parallel to one Marcan passage, reads :

" Whoever shall give drink unto one of these little ones a cup of water only in the name of a disciple " (εἰς ὄνομα μαθητοῦ).

This passage probably represents the original form of the saying, because it is somewhat obscure and out of place. The reading of Mark can only be a correction, a Pauline emendation.

The other passages in which Jesus is held to have used the title *Christos* of himself carry even less weight than Mark ix. 41. We shall not labour this point, but it is to be remembered that not a single case is to be found in Luke. Of the others, that is, Mark xiii. 6, Matthew xvi. 17, xxiii. 10, xxiv. 5, the first is to be found in what is called the Synoptic apocalypse, where Jesus is reported as saying : " Many shall come in my name saying : It is I." The implication here is that they will claim to be the Christ, and that Jesus therefore believed he was the Christ. This is explicitly brought out by Matthew xxiv. 5 : " For many shall come in my name saying : I am the Christ." But if, as there is every reason to suppose, the Christian writer was using a Jewish apocalypse in which the words are attributed to

---

[1] *Cf.* **CLIV** and p. 288 below.   [2] **CXCIII**, 3.
[3] **CI**, 234 ; **CLXV**, 25, n. 1.

Jahweh, the supposed proof of the use of *Christos* by Jesus automatically fails. In the second passage Jesus accepts the address of Peter " Thou art the Christ," but there is nothing equivalent to it in the parallel and basic text of Mark viii. 27–33. The addition in Matthew has been made by the editor. In Matthew xxiii. 10 Jesus plainly says : " For one is your master (*καθηγητής*) even Christ ! " But this verse is only a duplicate variation of xxiii. 8, where we find : " For one is your master (*διδάσκαλος*) and all ye are brethren." The word *Christos* is again nothing more than an editorial gloss.

But there still remain two episodes in the Gospel narrative which usually seem more convincing than all the cases we have dismissed. We read in Mark xiv. 61 *ff*. : " Again the High Priest asked him and said unto him : Art thou the Christ, the Son of the Blessed ? And Jesus said : I am."

We will not stress the peculiarity of the language attributed to the High Priest, but it is to be pointed out that the parallel passages simply say : " Thou hast said " (*σὺ εἶπας*) (Matthew xxvi. 64), and " Ye say that I am " (*ὑμεῖς λέγετε ὅτι ἐγώ εἰμι*) (Luke xxii. 71). From this we may suppose that the text of the source put into the mouth of Jesus a reply much less direct than that found in Mark. It may also be added that the whole episode is the product of the writer's imagination, devoid of any foundation.[1]

Let us now take the scene before Pilate. The text of Mark xv. 2 *ff*. reads : " Art thou the King of the Jews ? And he, answering, said unto him : Thou sayest it." The supposition is that Pilate referred to the King expected by the Jews, namely, the Messiah.

The expression appears again on the inscription or *titulus* placed on the Cross (Mark xv. 26) : " and the superscription of his accusation was written over ' The King of the Jews ' "—from which it is inferred that Jesus had been denounced to Pilate as the would-be Messiah, that he had himself confessed his claim and that it had cost him his life. But even if the Evangelist might well have known the charge which brought about the condemnation of Jesus, it is very unlikely that he could have been familiar with the details of the trial before the Procurator. Even if we accept his account we do not know the real meaning of the words " Thou sayest it." It may very easily differ from the one commonly accepted. It may, however, be urged that this does not matter. If Jesus was condemned as the pre-

---

[1] *Cf*. pt. iii, ch. viii, § iii. **XXIV**, 1, 193 *ff*., accepts the historicity of the scene and the reply ; likewise **CLVI**-*a*, 486 *ff*. ; contra : **CCLXXIX**-*a*, 315 *ff*.

tended Messiah it could only have been on his own admission or on the authority of reliable witnesses. He therefore claimed to be the Messiah. This, however, is far from being proved, and Pilate had no need of a confession in order to condemn a prophet who announced the coming of the Kingdom.

The argument drawn from the " *titulus* " on the Cross carries weight, but it does not remove all our doubts for the simple reason that since it agrees with the text containing the supposed admission, the formula of the inscription may very easily be derived from the latter, and have no foundation in fact. We must remember the statement attributed to Peter (Acts ii. 36) in which he affirms that God made Jesus the Messiah by virtue of the resurrection, which is an idea that seems closer to the original Christian conception of the Messiahship of the Nazarene.[1]

Of course it is possible to find in the Synoptics several passages in which the actors in the gospel drama apply the word Christ to Jesus, although with very different meanings. None of them, however, will bear critical examination, and they can all be traced to editorial sources.[2] Only one of them, already referred to several times, deserves special notice. It is the confession of Peter at Cæsarea Philippi, and reads as follows in Mark viii. 27–33 :

" And Jesus went out and his disciples into the towns of Cæsarea Philippi : and by the way he asked his disciples saying unto them, Whom do men say that I am ? And they answered, John the Baptist ; but some (say) Elias : and others, one of the prophets. And he saith unto them, But whom say ye that I am ? And Peter answereth and saith unto him, Thou art the Christ. And he charged them that they should tell no man of him. And he began to teach them that the Son of Man must suffer many things. And be rejected of the Elders and of the chief Priests, and scribes, and be killed, and after three days rise again. And he spake that saying openly. And Peter took him and began to rebuke him. But when he had turned about on his disciples he rebuked Peter, saying, ' Get thee behind me Satan : for thou savourest not the things that be of God, but the things that be of men.' "

The Synoptic parallels (Matt. xvi. 13–23 and Luke ix. 18–22) only add certain editorial explanations and details to Mark's

[1] **XXXIV,** 85.

[2] *Cf.* Mark xiv. 61 (the question of the High Priest) with Mark xv. 32 (the mocking of the Crucified by the Priests and Scribes, which is an artificial scene). See also Matt. xxvi. 68 and its Synoptic parallels ; Matt. xxvii. 17, which throws light on Mark xv. 9 ; and similarly Matt. xxvii. 22 in relation to Mark xv. 12. Luke xxiii. 2 is merely an editorial arrangement to make the beginning of the trial less abrupt ; Luke xxiii. 39 a mere editorial development of Mark xv. 32 ; Luke xxiv. 26 and xxiv. 46 are part of quite improbable episodes.

account, so that we may reasonably confine our attention to his version for the present. In the Second Gospel the passage quoted above is, as it were, the keystone of the arch. It is the central point of the life of Jesus according to Mark. Everything that precedes it leads up to this confession of Peter. Up to that point Jesus was only a hidden Christ. From now onwards the second half of the Gospel is to bring out the fact that he is to be a suffering Christ, going forward to inevitable victory, attaining by the way of the Cross the glory that awaits him.[1] But, as we already know, there is all the difference in the world between the purpose of a Gospel and historical reality, and the two have never been more distinct than in this passage.

On first looking at it one is struck by what appears to be a satisfactory interpretation. Jesus asks a question and Peter's answer is " Thou art the Christ." Jesus then forbids him to use such an expression and proceeds to instruct his disciples about his real destiny—not that of the Messiah. Whereupon Peter, still holding to his own opinion, takes him aside to upbraid him for not talking to them as he should, in fact for leading them astray, and Jesus reprimands him sharply for it. The historical interpretation of the passage may therefore be stated as follows : Jesus never believed that he was the Messiah. At one time his disciples believed that he was, but he tried to disillusion them. Mark has added to the record which tradition —in this case Peter himself—has preserved of this scene, an interpretation of the Passion in the spirit of Paul, which he presents under the guise of a prediction.

Unfortunately the homogeneity of this passage must be beyond question if this reasonable interpretation is to have a foundation. Even a cursory examination shows us the exact opposite. There is no coherence in the construction of it. Taken independently Peter's confession and the injunction to silence which follows are convincing, but the rest of it is suspicious. The Evangelist obviously wishes to convince us of two things : (1) That Jesus had foreseen and foretold his end, which was bound up with the great mystery of salvation ; (2) that in the beginning the apostles failed to grasp the meaning of this teaching. But the panic among the disciples at the time of his death clearly shows that Jesus had not foretold his violent end. The fact that those who were in close contact with the master had failed to grasp this, doubtless persuaded the editor· of the need to explain away the scandal of their panic. But there is every reason to believe that in the original

---

[1] **CVIII,** 269. We must naturally take into consideration the desire of the author of Mark to emphasize the faith of Peter.

confession of Peter it was a question of paying a tribute to the Apostles and not of blaming their slowness of understanding. The proper sequence to Mark viii. 31, namely the teaching of the necessity of the Passion, is Mark ix. 1 : " And he saith unto them : verily I say unto you that there be some of them that stand here which shall not taste of death until they have seen the Kingdom of God coming with Power." Everything that comes between these two passages is either put in by the editor, or at least out of place. One detail proves it. When we find another reference to the Passion in ix. 10–33, not only are we not told that it is the second one of its kind, but a remark in ix. 32 implies that it is the first. " But they did not know (that is, understood not) his saying and were afraid to ask him." These verses placed after the command to be silent, contain nothing that corresponds to historical truth, and everything in them fits in with the idea that the apostles did not understand the mystery : that the stumbling-block of the Passion was not one at all, since nothing happened that Jesus had not expected and foretold quite definitely. Subsequent events forced this view upon the Apostolic community, and its formulation bears the unmistakable impress of the influence of Paul.

On the other hand, though we may admit that the confession of Peter appears to ring true, it does not therefore follow that it is genuinely authentic. There are even more obvious inventions in the Gospels, and it would not be rash to see in the injunction to silence that followed, a proof that the primitive tradition was unaware that Peter had given an example of his insight.

In short, the disciples might love their master and place all their trust in him and yet not be convinced that he was the Messiah, since he answered so little to the current notion of " The One who is to come," of whose task he had hitherto accomplished nothing. We have actually no reason to believe that the disciples did anything but share the generally accepted notions of their time, or that their experience had led them to reconcile the current Messianic conception with the figure of Jesus.

Even if the confession of Peter were substantially authentic, all it would prove is that on the eve of the journey up to Jerusalem the disciples believed Jesus would occupy the first place in the Kingdom he had announced. And if it does not prove that even at that moment he himself had accepted that position, it provides a ground for believing that he at any rate had not previously assumed it, otherwise his question to Peter would be meaningless and the latter's reply would not be a confession.

It is perhaps not necessary to repeat that, according to Mark, Jesus does not explicitly approve the proclamation of Cephas and hence Matthew xvi. 16–19 feels the need of supplementing this reserve by means of a celebrated verse which we will discuss later.[1]

There is another passage of which much has been made (Mark x. 35–45) in which the two sons of Zebedee, James and John, come and ask Jesus for the privilege of sitting, one on his right hand and the other on his left, " in his glory," and in which he informs them, having foretold their coming martyrdom, that it is not for him to grant their request. Obviously the editor knew the facts concerning both the Passion and the death of the sons of Zebedee, so that his report cannot be taken literally. Even if the substantial truth of the episode were accepted, we could, at the most, conclude from it that James and John believed that their master was to have supreme authority in the Kingdom, and that he denied that this was the case.

Hence there is not a single synoptic passage which proves that Jesus called himself the Messiah or allowed people to call him by that title.

Commentators who are anxious at all costs to justify an idea which they consider indispensable to the Gospel tradition, bring forward other passages and facts which, according to their interpretation, *imply* that Jesus was conscious of his Messiahship,[2] but we need not waste much time on this desperate expedient.

Anybody who carefully reads the passages in question (Matt. ix. 15 ; xi. 3, 13 ; xii. 6, 41 ; xiii. 17 ; xxii. 41 and Mark ii. 35) will recognize without any difficulty that they furnish no support of the theory on behalf of which they have been used. As for the facts, namely the tone of authority of Jesus, implying that he was much greater than a prophet ; the episode of his baptism, in which it is supposed that Jesus acquired the consciousness of his status ; the retirement into the desert ; the Transfiguration ; the spectacular entry into Jerusalem ; all that can be said about them is that only a resolute tenacity of purpose can extract the desired conclusion from them. In every single instance we have to do with legendary episodes. These episodes could not have been foreseen or imagined by the immediate companions of Jesus, but their growth was inevitable. They are necessary to justify something which had been evolved from the person and work of Jesus irrespective of reality.

[1] *Cf.* pt. ii, ch. v, § ii.   [2] N. Schmidt, **EB**, *Son of Man*, § 46.

It is evident from the slightest familiarity with the Synoptics, that Jesus did not preach about himself, and that he never laid claim to the Messiahship, the proclamation of which might, *à priori*, be regarded as the central motive and the essential guarantee of his teaching.   On the contrary, on those occasions when he has been forced by circumstances to manifest in the most spectacular manner the divine power, the *dynamis*, which is supposed to radiate from his person, the Evangelists depict him as insisting, even with threats, that those who have bene-fited by it and those who have witnessed the marvel should say nothing of it to anyone.[1]   That is to say, this supposed Messiah does everything he can to hide his identity and to disguise his mission.   Any exceptions to this rule that may be invoked (Mark v. 19, for example) do not hold good in the face of an impression which is confirmed by the lack of understanding attributed to the disciples with regard to every crucial speech or action of their Master (iv. 41 ; vi. 51–2 ; viii. 18 ; x. 24).

As a rule only the evil spirits recognize and proclaim the truth.   It would seem, therefore, that such a representation of the attitude of the Messiah is so improbable as to border on the absurd.   There is only one explanation of all this.[2]   The Gospel editors, for reasons which we shall shortly explain, believe in the Messiahship of Jesus, but the tradition on which they went provided them with no certain proof that he believed himself to be " the One who is to come."   On the other hand they refused to admit that he did not know the fact or that he kept it a secret.   So they came to believe that he had really demonstrated it by *signs*, but that as a rule he refused to pro-claim it or let it be noised abroad.   The reason for this extra-ordinary reserve, we are told, is that, not answering to the current conception of the Messiah, he thought it wise not to expose himself to contempt or even to indignant opposition [3] by asking too much from the intelligence of his hearers.

There is no doubt that the Evangelists frequently insist [4] on the reluctance of Jesus to be mistaken for the warlike Messiah, victorious over the nations, whom the Jews expected.   His

---

[1] Mark i. 34 ; iii. 12 ; v. 43 ; vii. 36 ; viii. 26 ; viii. 30 ; ix. 9.

[2] CCXLI.   As early as 1883, Havet put very clearly the theory developed by the German critic.   *Cf.* CCLXVIII, iv, 15 *ff*.

[3] We may recall the indignation which, according to Mark viii. 33, he showed against Peter, when the Apostle reproached him with speak-ing of suffering and death.   " *Get thee behind me Satan : for thou savourest not the things that be of God, but the things that be of man.*"

[4] Mark viii. 31 ; ix. 31 ; x. 33 ; *ff.*, and the whole of Mark xiii., which places *after* the death of Jesus the stumbling blocks and alarms which current belief placed *before* the appearance of the Messiah.

Messiahship was of a new and personal type, formulated by himself. Most of the critics are quite prepared to accept this reversal of the common notion and are content to see in it the main originality of Jesus. They do not appear to question the reasonableness of this view, when in point of fact his lack of conformity with the generally accepted idea would require convincing proofs and detailed explanation. We are presented with the picture of a man whose personality, we are told,[1] is profoundly Jewish, whose religious genius is in perfect harmony with that of his people, who suddenly, and deliberately, so far detaches himself from the ideas of the Messiah current in Israel that even his own disciples do not understand him. None of the arguments of modern historians offer convincing proofs of the possibility of this amazing phenomenon.[2]

Of course if the evidence of the Slavonic Josephus could be taken seriously so that we might imagine Jesus to be a Messianic revolutionary who was expected by his followers to take Jerusalem by storm, and who they hoped would free them from the Roman yoke ; if it were possible to accept the fantastic deductions that the imagination and enthusiasm of Eisler have drawn from this fragmentary text, we should be able then to restore to the Nazarene the claim that the Evangelists attribute to him. We should first of all, however, have to be prepared to believe that the Gospel editors have lied shamelessly from first to last in their whole representation of the Messiahship of Jesus, and that the Slavonic Josephus must be regarded as the only authentic criterion of truth.

The combined efforts of Eisler and of Salomon Reinach have failed to convert us to such revolutionary views. They depend entirely upon a technique which we cannot accept, and we believe that every careful commentator would be of the same opinion. Therefore we must confine ourselves to the data of our canonical texts.

Let us narrow down the problem. According to the Evangelists Jesus wishes to couple his Messianic consciousness with a type of suffering and slain Messiah whose painful and willing death appears to him the chief factor in his allotted task as being "the means ordained by Providence whereby he was to make entrance to the Kingdom possible."[3] The question is not to discover whether at a given moment, when he saw that

[1] H. Holtzmann, *Das Messianische Bewusstein Jesu*, Tübingen, 1909, 99 *ff.*
[2] *Cf.* **CCVI**, 48 *ff.* ; **CLXV**, 20 *ff.* ; **CXC**, xxi *ff.* ; **CCLIII**, 109 *ff.* ; **CCXCVIII**, 33 *ff.* ; etc.
[3] **XXXIII**, 195.

things were going badly, he accustomed himself to the idea of
his coming death, and fitted the catastrophe which he saw to be
inevitable into God's plan with regard to himself. The problem
is to find out if, having from the outset discarded the popular
idea of the Messiah, he conceived and accepted, as his own, the
rôle of a suffering Messiah who was to be put to death and
thereby to accomplish a saving and truly Messianic function,
an indispensable task—in short his own appointed work. Was
he aware, as has been maintained,[1] that he was called to fulfil
the prophecy of Isaiah 53, and to be the despised and rejected
Servant ? It is hard to see how the Galilean could adapt this
particular passage of Isaiah to a Messianic hope which seemed
to belong to an entirely different plane of thought.

There would be no difficulty, had the Jews already conceived
of a suffering and dying Messiah, but in spite of the somewhat
biassed statements of certain of the modern mythological
school, they had not arrived at such a conception.[2] Later,
though not before the time of Hadrian,[3] certain Jews, probably meditating upon Deuteronomy xxxiii. 16 *ff.* (Moses' blessing of Joseph), conceived the idea of a Messiah who would be
the son of Joseph : a kind of preparatory Messiah, who, after
a glorious career, should die in his victorious encounter with
Gog and Magog (the powers of evil). Nothing, however,
indicates that he was to suffer or that his death had a redemptive
quality.[4]

Furthermore it is not at all certain that these later texts
containing this conception of the Messiah had not been influenced
by Christianity. On the other hand, Isaiah liii. was not taken
to refer to the Messiah, and was not thought to announce
his coming. The Jews believed that he was depicting the
Ideal Servant of God, the Just One suffering for righteousness' sake. It was ultimately the Christian polemic which
forced the rabbis unwillingly to interpret their passage as
a Messianic prophecy and even then not before the third
century.[5]

The Gospels, therefore, are right in one sense when they
show us the Apostles bewildered or offended by the statement that
the Son of Man must suffer and die in order to accomplish his
task (*cf.* Mark viii. 32 ; Matt. xvi. 22 ; Mark ix. 10, ix. 30 *ff.*,
and *Syn.*). But Jesus would surely have experienced the same
emotions. In point of fact the doctrine of the suffering Messiah

---

[1] CLXV, 287.   [2] *Cf.* CCXVII, 239.
[3] Dalman, *Der leidende und der sterbende Messias der Synagoge in
ersten nachchristlichen Jahrtausend.* Berlin, 1888.
[4] LXXX, 305 *ff.*   [5] CCXVII, 236 *ff.*

does not come from him. It is only a reflection of his fate and a product of Christianity.[1]

We are told [2] that Israel was not unaware of the idea of the atoning sacrifice or of that of ransom accomplished before Jahweh by the death of the Just One.[3] Nor, furthermore, were the Jews without knowledge of the idea of *substitution* common to antiquity.[4] Of this there can be no doubt, otherwise the apostolic adaptation of the Passion and the Crucifixion to the Messianic conception would not have been possible. But the question is whether Jesus himself, deliberately and from the outset, made that adaptation. All the evidence we have in favour of an affirmative reply is derived from men who, living after the event, when the fact was undeniable, could not but attribute it to Jesus.

In reality, there is not a single reliable passage or one sound argument in favour of the improbable reversal of the Messianic expectation which Jesus was to fulfil, that proves that he was conscious of that destiny.

It would be fortunate if we could see how this strange Messianic consciousness was developed in him. But this knowledge we can never hope to gain because we are without the slightest information regarding the personal factors that determined his mission. That is why Loisy is right in saying, "History has no record of the conditions under which the Messianic consciousness of Jesus was formed." [5]

It is possible to theorize on the point. For example one might say that at first the Nazarene seemed merely to be continuing the work of the Baptist, repeating his message " The time is fulfilled : the Kingdom of God is at hand ; repent." [6] Then he gradually grew more self-confident and finally was persuaded that he was the Messiah, when his disciples (confession of Peter) imposed the rôle on him. That is, in fact, precisely how things seem to happen in the Gospels as we know them. But it is clear that the New Testament documents have preserved traces of very different descriptions of the revelation of Jesus as Messiah—descriptions which had successively acquired currency among the early Christians.

If our impression derived from the speech of Peter in Acts is correct (ii. 23, 32, 34 ; and especially 36 : " God hath made that same Jesus whom ye have crucified both Lord and Christ "), the primitive tradition did not attribute the proclamation of his Messiahship either to Jesus or to his disciples during his lifetime.

---

[1] XXIV, i, 118.
[2] CLXV, 289 *ff.*
[3] *E.g.* 2 Macc. vii. 37–8 ; 4 Macc. vi. 28–9.
[4] CLXV, 290 *ff.*
[5] CCXXII–*a*, 227, n. 1.
[6] CCL, 29 *ff.*

It was only the Resurrection which revealed to them the great mystery concealed in the person of their Master.[1]

The Confession of Peter; the Transfiguration; those apocalyptic utterances in which Jesus claims to be the Son of Man according to Daniel, and the manifestation from Heaven at the time of his Baptism, most probably represent not stages— in inverse order—in the Messianic consciousness of Jesus, but stages, taken in the order of their development, in the progress of primitive Christology. This simple statement suffices to shatter all the theories. We take our stand on the evidence that we are unable to observe, during the life of Jesus, any trace of development in his consciousness, his conception, of his mission and the part he is playing. Not merely because our texts are too brief, too vague, too few, too uncertain, or too impossible to date, but chiefly because the time was too short for any great development in the mind of the Nazarene.[2] Moreover, if he really began by regarding himself as the successor of the Baptist, we must inquire by what path he arrived at the belief that he was the Messiah. For it must always be remembered that he not only had to effect a change in himself but he had also to bring about a complete revolution in the current conception of the Messiah.

But if we may suppose that Jesus never said or believed that he was the Messiah, that nobody during his lifetime recognized him as such, and that from the moment of his death, for some reason or another—in this case belief in his resurrection—his followers had come to attribute Messiahship to him, there would in that case inevitably have been an adaptation of the tradition to the new belief; and further, if at a given moment controversy had not determined and fixed the text of the Gospels, the latter would have been exposed to many other risks.

For this reason we are convinced that all the Gospel material which is arranged, usually very awkwardly and incoherently,[3]

[1] A passage from Paul (Rom. i. 4) provides further evidence in support of this primitive belief: " (he who was) declared to be the Son of God with power, according to the Spirit of holiness, by the resurrection from the dead." Cf. Luke xxiv. 25 ff.—**XXXIV**, 8; **LXXXVI**, 153.

[2] This is one of the points on which we disagree with Goguel (**CLVI**-a, 388 ff.) who attempts to retrace the evolution of the thought of Jesus after " the Galilean crisis " up to the moment when he believes himself to be the Messiah because he realizes that he is threatened with suffering and death. Not only do we fail to understand the reasoning which Goguel here attributes to the Nazarene, but we see no objective justification for it.

[3] A good example of this incoherence occurs in Mark. In viii. 29 it says : "And Peter answered and said unto him, thou art the Christ. And

to give us the impression that Jesus believed he was the Messiah, and that his disciples recognized in him that quality which the demons and God Himself had proclaimed, is the work of the editors. Its only roots are in the faith of the first Christian community, which was responsible for the revision of the Jewish ideas about the Messiah, and for their reconciliation with the fate of Jesus.

One objection comes to mind. If it is unlikely that Jesus could have upset the accepted Jewish notion of the Messiah, because he was a Jew, how could the Apostles have done it, also Jews, and apparently much less strikingly individual than he was ?

First of all one point must be made clear. His disciples were not responsible for all the work of which we see the result in the Gospels, namely, the identification of Jesus with the Messiah of current belief ; the dethronement and, as it were, the obliteration of the activity of the Nazarene during his life to make room for the prodigious mystery of his death ; the conception of the Messiah suffering and dying " for many," in other words, invested with the rôle of Redeemer, which Israel had not foreseen as that of "The Coming One " ; and the complete abandonment of all the characteristics of the traditional Messiah except the fantastic belief in his appearance on the clouds of heaven clothed with divine power. But the original affirmation that *Jesus is the Messiah*, that is, that God has granted him this status as is proved by his Resurrection, and that he will soon come again to play the part that will henceforth be his, does not go beyond the limits of what might appear possible to a Jew. When the disciples, having taken refuge in Galilee after the Passion, saw their Master again[1] they were absolutely convinced that he had risen from the dead. Why then, if God had not destined him for an unusually glorious rôle, would he have granted him such a favour ? No Jew could help thinking of the rôle of the Messiah, and since it was only in the future that Jesus was to play that part, they were not obliged to modify their traditional ideas. Nothing, in fact, would lead us to suppose that the Lord, whose manifestation was known to the early Church as the *Parousia*, was to differ in any way from the pseudo-Danielic Messiah.

he charged them that they should tell no man of him." Then immediately afterwards (viii. 34 *ff.*) Jesus announces to a *crowd* that if anyone is ashamed of him, " *Of him also shall the Son of Man be ashamed when he cometh in the glory of his Father, with the Holy Angels.*" In other words he proclaims to the world the secret he has just forbidden his disciples to tell to anybody.

[1] *Cf.* pt. iii, ch. vi, §§ ii and iii.

The remainder of the work, the various stages of which I have mentioned above, was not done by the Apostles. It took place on Greek soil and under the influence of those religions which taught a doctrine of salvation.

After finding that the expected Kingdom did not manifest itself at Jerusalem, where he had gone in search of it, it is perhaps possible that Jesus, foreseeing his death—if he really did—may have sought to reconcile it with his hope, that is, that he may have looked upon it as the divinely appointed condition of the coming of the Kingdom.[1]   But we have no absolute knowledge that this is so, and the impression which we get from the Gospel narrative of the Crucifixion—in any case suspect—does not support this hypothesis, seeing that the victim dies in despair (Mark xv. 34).   Whatever the truth of this may be, supposition that Jesus foresaw his death as an integral part of his Messianic function, as an act of redemption serving as a foundation for the future regeneration of humanity, is, from the historical point of view, not only inconsistent but inconceivable.

Taken in conjunction with the strange theory of the Messianic secret, these considerations, which render very improbable the revolution in the Messianic conception attributed to Jesus by the Synoptics, seem to lead to the conclusion that he never believed himself the Messiah and never offered himself as such.   Even when they hurled insults at him, the Jews never reproached him with such fatuous presumption.   We are not unaware that since the publication of Wrede's book (1901) which emphasized most strongly the negative argument drawn from the Messianic secret, praiseworthy efforts have been made and pressing arguments brought forward with the object of ridding the Gospels of a conclusion which so seriously undermined their authority;[2] that is to say attempts have been made to save, together with the genuineness of the Messianic confession of Peter, the truth of the Messianic avowal made by Jesus to his disciples.[3]   Attempts have been made to minimize the impression given at first sight by the command to be silent imposed by Jesus in Mark, by proving that these were only exceptional cases, and that they left the field free for the general revelation of the truth.[4]   Elsewhere the reticence of the Nazarene is accepted, but is explained on the grounds that he

[1] CIII, i, 143.
[2] Cf. with Wrede's work, that of J. Weiss, LXXXV.
[3] Ideas developed by Bousset, CXCIII, 79–82.   Cf. CLXXV, 58; CCL, 36.
[4] CLXV, 49 ff.

was obliged to be cautious because of the originality of his
conception of the Messiahship.[1] Finally, his caution is justified
by the observation that he is not the present Messiah, but is
conscious only of being "*The Coming One*," the *Messias
designatus* (Harnack) who will only reveal himself when the
Kingdom is a reality [2] and who till then conceals his status in
conformity with the esoteric plan.[3]

This is all very interesting, but it still comes up against the
very simple remark of Schweitzer.[4] It is difficult to understand why Jesus did not want people to know that he was the
Messiah if he was soon expecting to be revealed as such. On
the other hand the assumption that Mark deliberately distorted
the data of *Urmarcus* or of the tradition in order to work in his
theory of the Messianic secret seems to be quite unfounded.
What he did was to develop this idea of the hidden Messiah
to fit in with the belief that Jesus, who was accepted as the
Messiah at the time of the Evangelists, had really shown himself
to be such during his lifetime, and to meet the objection that
the Jews had not believed it and still refused to do so. He
thought that he could find a satisfactory solution by insisting
that the secret had only really been revealed to the Apostles and
that the Jews, blinded by the hardness of their hearts, had not
seen it in spite of amazing signs performed by Jesus.

Only one of the replies to Wrede, which have been briefly
outlined above, offers any probability. Might not Jesus have
regarded himself as the *future Messiah*, just as his disciples
themselves believed, after his death, that he was then actually
the Messiah ? Inasmuch as this belief would not distort the
current Messianic idea it is not contradicted by the texts. But
unfortunately neither do they afford it any direct support. In
any case, there is only one certain conclusion to be drawn,
namely that Jesus never gave himself out to be the *present*
Messiah, nor did he ever assume this character in his teaching.

Perhaps it is still possible to discern something of the
Christian idea of Jesus before the growth of faith raised him to
the dignity of the Messiah. It is to be found in the two passages
from *Acts* to which we have already referred (ii. 22–36 and
x. 37–8). It places before us the figure of a "man authorized
by God" (ἄνδρα ἀποδεδειγμένον ἀπὸ τοῦ θεοῦ) prolific in miracles,
prodigies and signs, anointed with the Holy Spirit and with
Power (πνεύματι ἁγίῳ καὶ δυνάμει) going about Galilee "doing
good and healing all that were oppressed of the devil, for God

---

[1] CCXCVII, 6 ; CCXCVIII, 34.
[2] Which is very skilfully elaborated in LXXIX, 81 *ff.* ; CV, 242.
[3] L–*a*, i, 334.   [4] CLXXVI, 396.

was with him." It is the exact definition of a prophet [1] and is confirmed by Mark i. 14–15 where it is said that he went about " preaching the gospel of the Kingdom of God " and saying that the time was fulfilled and that the Kingdom of God was at hand. He was following on the same line [2] when he went on to say " Repent ye and believe the Gospel."

Now this, the earliest tradition we can recover, was handed on by men—possibly by Peter—who were convinced that Jesus was the Messiah at the very moment of giving testimony. But in their opinion, if before his death he may have been the Messiah *virtually*—though they do not say so—he was *effectively* such only after that time. That is why, in Acts ii. 36, Peter is reported as saying that now the house of Israel should know *certainly* (ἀσφαλῶς) the true state of affairs. The first stage in the process of making Jesus the Messiah (the *Messianisierung* of Wrede) has been completed. But Jesus was not responsible for it.

We may conclude this long discussion by recalling two easily verifiable facts. The first is that Jesus is never reported to have said, " I am the Messiah ; I bring you the Kingdom," and, if he believed it, there seems no reason why he should not have done so. The second is that at the end of the Last Supper (Mark xiv. 25) when he announces the Messianic feast to the Apostles, he does not say that there is a place of honour there for him. Wellhausen [3] has every foundation for saying " At that moment he definitely does not give himself out to be the Messiah either in the present or in the future." There can be no question, therefore, that in Jesus we are dealing with a prophet, a herald of the expected Kingdom. Our first impression was right.

[1] VI, 49 *ff*.
[2] The identity of the tradition followed is easily seen by a mere comparison of Mark i. 39 and Acts x. 37–8.
[3] CXIV, 115.

CHAPTER IV

JESUS AND JUDAISM

I

THE MEANING AND PURPOSE OF THE TEACHING OF JESUS

COMMENTATORS are not agreed on that most essential point, the meaning and purpose of the teaching of Jesus. This uncertainty arises from the fact that some of them regard the Nazarene from the historical point of view, and others approach him from the credal standpoint. Between these two extremes there are numerous shades of opinion. The result is that he is sometimes regarded as the divine architect of an immortal structure, namely the Catholic church, sometimes as a dreamer, subject to the limitations of his age and his environment, the herald of an apocalyptic Kingdom which has never come. And again between these two interpretations there are various transitional stages. It is obvious that all these divergent points of view have not arisen from the documents considered by and for themselves, but from additions made to them, and from preconceived notions forced on to them, which in point of fact have very little to do with history. When, for example, Mgr. Batiffol rejects as an unacceptable paradox the " eschatological conception of the Kingdom," that is to say the theory according to which Jesus proclaims and awaits the near approach of the material transformation of the world, he is bowing to the insistent demands of the Catholic faith. He is obliged to accept the spiritual interpretation of the Kingdom without question. There would be no difficulty in producing other more or less similar examples. We will not waste time on them, however, but will rely on the facts and the documents themselves for the answers to our questions. We must avoid pseudo-logical constructions and ill-advised conclusions into which we might often be led by impatience at our inability to arrive at certainty.

It is legitimate to suppose, *à priori*, that the preaching of Jesus was characterized by a main purpose, that it was controlled

296

by a central motive, to be found in the Synoptics. The first thing to notice is that the critics do not agree on a definition of this motive.[1] The majority think that it is the Kingdom; others incline to the view that it is the need of faith in the Fatherhood of God; others again look for it in an original conception of the nature of religion, bound up with the originality of the religious character of Jesus; in which case the motive will be the production and manifestation of that character itself.

However, there seems to be no doubt that an unprejudiced reading of the Synoptics leads to the conclusion that the central motive of the preaching of the Nazarene was the announcement of the coming of the Kingdom. This motive, moreover, was in no way foreign to the religious life of Israel, since the pious Jew concentrates his thoughts at least three times a day on the promise of the Kingdom when he recites the *Shemoneh Esreh*.[2]

It is important to notice, also, that an announcement of this kind does not entail a definite system of doctrine. It could well be rounded off by a few practical counsels or precepts which might easily fall into line with a previous religious tradition. In other words, it was possible even for a strict Jew, opposed to the introduction of any innovations into the religion of his fathers, to accept the message of Jesus. In fact, as soon as we get below the surface of the Gospel history we see how right Loisy was when he said : " The object of Jesus' preaching was not to leave a written record of his doctrine for posterity, but to attract souls to the hope with which he was himself consumed." [3]

In endeavouring to estimate his position in relation to Judaism we shall be able to measure the extent of his religious originality. We shall consider him in his relation to the *Torah*, to the Temple, to the religion of the Rabbis and to that of the common people.

II

JESUS AND THE TORAH

It is quite possible, and in our opinion probable, that the editors of the Gospels have exaggerated the devotion of Jesus to the Scriptures by attributing to him their own habit of intro-

---

[1] **L–a**, i, 182, n. 1.
[2] It is the eleventh petition of this prayer which deals with the coming of the Kingdom. *Cf.* **XXIX**, ii, 460.
[3] **LXXIX**, 192.

ducing them on every occasion. Still, there is no doubt that he sought for, and found, his principle of life and the justification of his course of action in the sacred books, for such is the attitude of the pious Jew. For the same reason, argument from Scripture holds an important place in his defence of his teaching, and it is interesting to notice that he had recourse to this form of argument to justify those of his actions which seemed at first sight in direct opposition to the requirements of the *Torah*. When, for example, in Mark ii. 23, he wishes to exonerate his disciples who had gathered ears of corn on the Sabbath, he quotes the example of David and his soldiers who, driven by hunger, ate the shew-bread. In Mark x. 6 we might say that it is in the name of the spirit of the divine law that he shows his disapproval of the concession of divorce granted in the Mosaic Law. In Mark xii. 35 he bases his refutation of the doctrine of the Scribes that the Messiah must be of the house of David, on the testimony of David himself.

At this point care is necessary, and we may borrow from Mgr. Batiffol a guiding principle of caution : " Many passages from the Old Testament introduced into the thread of various discourses of Jesus . . . are not so much quotations made by Jesus himself as a kind of harmony created by the earliest tradition," that is to say, parallels between the sayings of the Master and those passages of Scripture which rounded them off and illustrated them, receiving from them in return increased meaning and value. Although these resemblances may, in many cases, seem forced, they nevertheless establish the relationship between the spirit of Jesus and that of the Bible. They are the fruit of the same tree. Nevertheless, the Synoptics show that the *legalism* of Jesus is capable, in practice, of remarkable elasticity. There is an inherent probability in such accommodations, since inspired people rarely conform unreservedly to the pattern of ordinary law. They are heretics by nature, and those of them who accept the authority of a book never submit without a secret struggle, even when they imagine that they have taken up the most correct attitude towards it. The early Prophets never quite accepted the *nomistic* point of view, and ranked religion of the heart above observance, ritual, purifications, and even sacrifices. Jesus carries on the prophetic tradition with which he was no doubt acquainted.[1]

Nor must we suppose that all traces of it had disappeared from the Israel of his day. Legalism was not everything, even to the Rabbis ; and we must not forget that the Synoptics

[1] **LXXX**, 319 *ff*.

themselves give us a picture of the good scribe as contrasted
with the bad, that is to say, the man who lives his religion as
opposed to him who lives off it, the man who finds in it the
realization of his ideal, and not merely the gratification of his
love of ostentation and of private gain. The Talmud gives us
an even clearer insight into the character of the good scribe ;
he stands for living religious feeling and moral judgment, as
opposed to the letter of the law. Hence, in this respect Jesus
is not so unique as he seems to be at first sight.[1]

He had not been through the discipline of the School, which
would have taught him to concentrate on the purely juridical
and theological interpretations of the *Torah*, and so he could
only go to the Book for the bread of his spiritual life, while
reserving to himself that freedom of choice which individuals
of deep and living piety in every religion have never surrendered.
It has been supposed that he had formulated a doctrine of his
own about the Law,[2] and that he judges it as a designedly
imperfect expedient adapted by God to the conditions of a
disobedient and corrupt people. His emendations of the old
precepts have been cited as a proof of this, for example the
reference to divorce : " For the hardness of your heart Moses
wrote you this precept " (Mark x. 1 *ff.*) ; the heightening of the
commands " Thou shalt not kill " (Matt. v. 21 *ff.*), " Thou
shalt not commit adultery," " Thou shalt not forswear thyself "
(Matt. v. 33), of the law of retribution (Matt. v. 38), and of the
law of love (Matt. v. 43). Still, all this offers no traces of a
doctrine as such. The inspired person interprets particular
instances in relation to his general principle, which is to seek
God and his spirit behind those religious formulas which satisfy
the ordinary pious person ; to let the heart speak, to fall back
instinctively upon the *ideal* which, in practice, is always weakened
by embodiment in a *precept*. The Lawgiver allowed divorce in
certain cases, but the ideal is an indissoluble union : he forbade
murder, but the ideal is the avoidance of every form of violence :
he condemned adultery, but the ideal is the suppression of
unlawful desire. The Great Commandment which calls for the
love of God and of one's neighbour seems to imply, in view of
all the individual instances to which it applies, that Jesus had
a uniform outlook which bears the appearance of a doctrine.
But we must beware of this false impression and refrain from

---

[1] L–*a*, i, 198 ; **CCXXXV**, 48, and especially the work of Abrahams,
LXXIV, in its entirety. Exception might be made with regard to
certain details, but as a whole, there is definite evidence of an obvious
relationship between Jesus and the Rabbis, especially the Pharisees.

[2] **CXC**, 70 ; **CCXXXV**, 49.

confusing the thought of Jesus with the deductions of Christian theology.

All the elaborations already quoted remain, so to speak, within the spirit of the Law, so much so that Jesus might have thought, if he was really responsible for them, that, far from contradicting the spirit of the Law, they developed and completed it. When St. Francis of Assisi drew up his Rule he had no other intention than that of expressing the Gospel in terms of contemporary life. Similarly his Master thought he was speaking the truth when he declared that he had not come to abolish the Law, but, on the contrary, to fulfil it down to the last *yod*, the smallest letter of the alphabet (Matt. v. 17–18).

An objection to this has been based on his attitude towards the Sabbath, the observance of which was clearly one of the essential requirements of the Law,[1] since the *Torah* pronounced sentence of death against transgressors (Exod. xxxi. 14 *ff.*). For the Rabbis Sabbath observance was a special privilege of Israel [2] and a signal proof of its close relation to God. Furthermore in their commentary on the divine ordinances in the *Halacha* the Rabbis had surrounded them with a network of minute regulations which increased their severity. Thus, we find that on a Sabbath day as the disciples of Jesus passed through a field they gathered ears of corn and ate them. Certain Pharisees who happened to be present upbraided the Master for allowing his followers to do *that which is not lawful*, namely to perform manual labour. His reply (Mark ii. 25) was that David, one day when he was hungry, had not hesitated to eat the shew-bread consecrated to God in the sanctuary (1 Sam. xxi. 1 *ff.*), and furthermore that " the Sabbath is made for man, not man for the Sabbath : therefore the Son of man is lord also of the Sabbath."

This passage raises considerable problems of exegesis, with which we are not concerned here ; [3] but it also raises a very serious question for a Jew. The Rabbis were agreed that the Sabbath was made for man, that is to say for the good of man, and that he should adapt it to his needs. For instance, he must not run any risks through his pious observation of it.[4] Rabbi Simon ben Menacia, commenting on the text of Exodus xxxi. 13, " My sabbaths ye shall keep, for it is a sign between me and

---

[1] Gen. ii. 3 ; Exod. xvi. 22 *ff.* ; xx. 8–11 ; xxiii. 12 ; xxxiv. 21 ; xxxv. 1 *ff.*, etc.

[2] **XXV**, i, 231 ; **II**, 21 *ff.*

[3] *Cf.* the commentaries of Lagrange, Klostermann, Strack and Billerbeck on Mark ii. 23–8 and Matt. xii. 1–8.

[4] **XXV**, ii, 30–1 ; **LXXIV**, 129 *ff.*

you," said " The Sabbath is given to you, not you to the Sabbath." Again Rabbi Jonathan, in the Babylonian Talmud, gives a picturesque rendering of the same idea, " Profane a Sabbath so as to be able to observe it better." [1] Still, this apparent laxity demanded by common sense by no means implies that man was " master of the Sabbath," that is to say, that he could regulate its observance to suit himself, since Jehovah himself, it was sometimes said, submitted to the law which he had made. Indeed, no Jew would dare to say that the Sabbath was not made for God, for his honour and service.

Nevertheless, it does not seem that the attitude to the Sabbath adopted by Jesus is particularly revolutionary. The Nazarene never spoke of doing away with it, nor did he disparage it. If we believe that he made such a statement as is attributed to him by Mark, and that the editor is not merely putting into the mouth of the Master a justification of his own lax practice, that is, taking for granted the substantial accuracy of this passage concerning the Sabbath, there is only one possible conclusion, namely that Jesus followed the broader interpretation of the Law. Of course the Pharisees might oppose him with the letter of the Law, and their own jurisprudence, which refused to adapt the observance of the Sabbath to the everyday needs of man (cf. Luke xiii. 14) ; but he was not inclined either by origin or by upbringing to find such an argument congenial, and his more humane interpretation of the divine precept would seem to him much more in keeping with the spirit of the *Torah* than the formalistic rigour of the Rabbis. In his eyes the spirit of the Law overshadowed everything, and was all contained in the Great Commandment of the love of God. [2]

This less rigid view of the Sabbath recalls the tolerant attitude of so many Roman Catholic priests towards manual labour on Sunday, or lapses from abstinence on Friday, nor need we exaggerate its importance.

The question has been raised, however, whether Jesus, anticipating Paul, had not foreseen and predicted the abolition of the Law. The point is worth considering. It has been observed [3] that the Prophets had allowed a certain freedom in interpreting the idea of the Covenant between God and his people, which would not prevent a prophet like Jesus from

---

[1] **CI,** 49 *ff.* ; **XCVI,** i, 123.

[2] The impression arises that the chief difference between the Pharisees and Jesus is to be found in his attitude towards the *Halacha*, which they respect as a kind of second *Torah*, while he, so it would seem, is inclined to treat it less seriously. *Cf.* T. Herford, *Pharisaism, Its Aim and Method*, 205, London, 1912.

[3] **CCVI,** 41.

actually believing himself in a position to conclude a new covenant with Jahweh.   We read, for example, in Jeremiah xxxi. 31 *ff.* :

> " Behold, the days come, saith the Lord, that I will make a new covenant with the house of Israel and with the house of Judah : not according to the covenant that I made with their fathers in the day that I took them by the hand to bring them out of the land of Egypt ; which covenant they brake, although I was an husband unto them, saith the Lord.   But this shall be the covenant that I will make with the house of Israel : after those days I will put my law in their inward parts, and write it in their hearts ; and will be their God, and they shall be my people."

Again, Malachi iii. 1 proclaims that the sending of the " Messenger of the covenant, whom ye look for " is imminent. Furthermore, in the past, had not the people of Jahweh, or at least their ancestors, known many covenants, each one accompanied by a sign which vouched for its genuineness ?   In Gen. ix. 17 the rainbow is a witness to the covenant between Jahweh and " all flesh upon the earth," that is, Noah and his people.   In Gen. xvii. 11 circumcision is a proof of the covenant between God and the descendants of Abraham.   In Ex. xxiv. 8 *ff.* the sprinkling of blood marks a covenant between Jahweh and the people under the leadership of Moses after the giving of the law.   Moreover, these covenants did not cancel one another out.   Each one, completing the other, served to renew, and by defining it, to consolidate, the fundamental covenant between the God of Israel and his chosen people.

Any claim on the part of the Nazarene to institute a new covenant would not therefore have implied an incomprehensible or offensive novelty.   But did he make any such claim ?   The Last Supper, and the words there attributed to Jesus (Mark xiv. 24), " This is my blood of the New Testament " (τὸ αἷμά μου τῆς διαθήκης), have been given in support of it.[1]   But even supposing that he ever uttered them, which is very questionable, and that he intended to signify the renewal of the old covenant by the shedding of blood, namely by a rite similar to that already made holy, these words could never be taken to imply the abolition of the old covenant and the introduction of a new one. There is no better proof of this than the attitude attributed in Acts (ii. 46 *ff.*) to the immediate disciples of Jesus, when they were gathered together in Jerusalem.   Their very strict observance of the Law clearly shows their ignorance of any supposed abolition of the *Torah* by their master.

There are certainly some passages in the Gospels which are

[1] **EB**, art. *Sacrifice*, § 54.

at first sight somewhat disturbing, but even a cursory examination of them shows that they are all capable of an interpretation which brings them into accord with what we have accepted as probability.   Thus we read in Matthew xi. 12–13 : " And from the days of John the Baptist until now the Kingdom of Heaven suffereth violence, and the violent take it by force.   For all the prophets and the law prophesied until John."—A passage which is echoed by Luke xvi. 16 : " The law and the prophets were until John : since that time the Kingdom of God is preached, and every man presseth into it."

The question arises whether the common source, which is Q, contained the assertion that the law and the prophets ended with John ?   If that were the case we should have to conclude that the mission of John made the law obsolete, and John is not Jesus.   But this is not the case.   For it is clear from the text that it is only a question here of the law and the prophets in relation to the coming of the kingdom, as announced by them. This probably explains the peculiarity of Matthew when, contrary to custom, he put the prophets before the law.   We must, therefore, simply take it to mean that up to the time of John it was the prophets and the law which announced the Kingdom.   Then came John, and after John, Jesus himself.[1] There is no question of the abolition of the law.

Another passage used to bring the teaching of Jesus [2] into conflict with the ancient Law is Mark ii. 21 *ff.* :

> " No man also seweth a piece of new cloth on an old garment : else the new piece that filled it up taketh away from the old, and the rent is made worse.   And no man putteth new wine into old bottles : else the new wine doth burst the bottles, and the wine is spilled, and the bottles will be marred : but new wine must be put into new bottles."

As used by Mark this passage serves to vindicate the action of the disciples in not fasting after the manner of the Pharisees, but there is certainly no question of dispensing them from the legal fasts, still less of condemning the practice of fasting itself. Strictly speaking, the only obligatory fast laid down by the *Torah* was on the day of Atonement, on the tenth day of the seventh month after the scapegoat had been sent into the wilderness (Lev. xvi. 29 ; xxiii. 27).   On the other hand, fasting as a pious custom is referred to in a number of passages in the

---

[1] The formula " *since the days of John* " connotes a lapse of time the mention of which comes more suitably from the pen of the editor of Matthew than from the mouth of Jesus.

[2] **CXC**, 75, and especially **CLXV**, 104 *ff.*

Nebiim and the *Kethubim*,[1] and it had become a common practice
in the time of Jesus.[2]   The very zealous Jews even bound themselves to fast as a rule every Monday and Thursday, without
counting the number of occasions gradually fixed by tradition.
But tradition was not law, any more than customs were binding,
and Jesus could perfectly well have condemned the practice
of pious fasting without attacking the *Torah*.   In order to know
the real scope of his parable, we must be perfectly sure of the
occasion that suggested it and of the setting in which he placed
it.   But Mark gives us neither one nor the other for certain,[3]
so that a direct interpretation of the passage is our only resource.

Those who attribute to it the great importance to which I
have just referred, take " the old " to mean Judaism, and " the
new " to mean Christianity, and consider the two to be mutually
exclusive.   " One cannot pour the generous wine of the Gospel
into the worn-out wine-skins of Judaism " (Monnier).   But if
that was really the idea of Jesus it is sadly out of keeping with
his behaviour.   Nowhere else does he appear in the rôle of a
separatist, nowhere does he withdraw himself from Israel.[4]
The odds, then, are in favour of a less general interpretation of
the comparison, that is of its application to a particular instance,
which, like so many others, has escaped us.   Possibly it refers
to certain Pharisaical practices, but there is absolutely nothing,
even in its form, which entitles us to see in it a condemnation
either of Judaism or of the Law.   There would naturally have
been a great temptation to interpret this text as a kind of
justification of the anti-legalism of Paul, but this could only
have been done by an illegitimate transposition.   We have
only to recall the episode at Jacob's well, recorded by John,
where Jesus says to the woman of Samaria (John iv. 21 *ff.*) :

> " Woman, believe me, the hour cometh, when ye shall neither
> in this mountain, nor yet at Jerusalem, worship the Father. . . .
> But the hour cometh, and now is, when the true worshippers shall
> worship the Father in spirit and in truth : for the Father seeketh
> such to worship him."

There can be no doubt that we have here an announcement
that the old Jewish law will be abandoned, and that the new
law will take its place : but it is not Jesus who says it but the
Evangelist, and his assertion is, we venture to say, a product of
Paulinism.

---

[1] Examples taken at random : 2 Sam. xii. 16 ; Isa. lviii. ; Jer. xiv.
12 ; Ps. lxix. 11 ; Esth. iv. 3 and 16 ; etc.
[2] EB, art. *Fasting* ; **XXIX**, ii, 489 *ff.*
[3] **CXIV**, 20 ; **XCVI**, i, 55.   [4] **CI**, 45.

The view that Jesus had thought of discarding the *Torah* and that he could have said that it would be replaced by another law is not supported by any genuine passage.[1] All that we find in the Synoptics is an occasional suggestion of prophetic liberty in interpreting the *letter* of the Law ; a hint of conflict between the spirit of the law and customary practice with regard to certain special points ; and so we may say that while we find contradiction in facts arising out of this or that circumstance, we find no contradiction in principle, no general opposition.

Those who disagree with this conclusion, for reasons based on ecclesiastical tradition rather than on the Gospels, are confronted by an extremely embarrassing passage in Matthew (v. 17–20) :

> " Think not that I am come to destroy the Law, or the prophets : I am not come to destroy, but to fulfil (πληρῶσαι). For verily I say unto you, Till heaven and earth pass, one jot or one tittle shall in no wise pass from the Law, till all be fulfilled. Whosoever therefore shall break one of these least commandments, and shall teach men so, he shall be called the least in the Kingdom of Heaven : but whosoever shall do and teach them, the same shall be called great in the Kingdom of Heaven. For I say unto you, that except your righteousness shall exceed the righteousness of the scribes and Pharisees ye shall in no case enter into the Kingdom of Heaven."

The only interpretation of which this passage, at first sight, seems capable, is that the Law and the prophets are, and remain, the foundation of righteousness in the eyes of God. Only by fulfilling their commandments is it possible to gain a place in the Kingdom, and the more exact the fulfilment of the precepts, the better the place. It is important to notice, however, that the verses in question act as an introduction to a development of the Sermon on the Mount, in which we find Jesus going beyond the Law, and intensifying its injunctions concerning murder, adultery, oaths, revenge, and the love of one's neighbour (v. 21–48). This apparent contradiction has been an occasional source of trouble to commentators.[2]

But at this point we find that Luke xvi. 17 in a context entirely different from the one under discussion, offers us the following : " It is easier for heaven and earth to pass, than for one tittle of the law to fall."[3] But Luke is full of the idea

---

[1] We do not take into consideration the use made of the parable of the fig-tree that was cursed (Mark xi. 12 *ff*.), nor of that of the barren fig-tree (Luke xiii. 6 *ff*.) (**CXC**, 75) with the same end in view. These two passages possibly refer to the rejection of an obstinately unbelieving Israel, but not to the abolition of the Law.

[2] **CXLI**, 103 ; **LXVII**, 81.

[3] **CIII**, i, 562.

of the Kingdom also when he writes this phrase, because the
preceding verse is that which we have already encountered :
" The law and the prophets were until John ; since that time
the kingdom of God is preached, and every man presseth into
it." On the other hand, verse 18 condemns divorce and the
remarriage of divorced people, and therefore brings us face to
face with one of the precepts peculiar to Jesus in his amplifica-
tions of the law. So we must undoubtedly conclude from this
that Luke, although he is using data from the same source in a
different way from Matthew, nevertheless keeps the same
perspective, and his evidence in this case points in the same
direction.

Before attempting to fix the meaning of this passage from
Matthew, we must remember that in the mind of a Jew there
could be no doubt about the eternity of the *Torah* [1] and consequently, any statement which insisted upon the unalterable
character of its legal obligations would only be a platitude. It
should also be observed that the meaning of πληρῶσαι, here
translated as " to fulfil," is not clearly defined, and could equally
well be rendered " to perfect," " to complete," " to deepen,"
each of which fits in better with what follows in the text.
Having said that, we may go on to observe that verses 18 and
19 seem to have been artificially interpolated between verses 17
and 20, which, when read in sequence, fit in better with the flow of
the argument. The word " for " (γὰρ) placed at the beginning
of verse 20 has no connexion at all with what is said in verse
19, and, on the other hand, connects up perfectly well with
verse 17 and fits in with πληρῶσαι. It is difficult not to feel
that these parasitic verses are directed against Paul [2] who was
playing havoc with the Law, and that they perfectly represent
the " legalism " which is attributed by tradition to the followers
of James, the Judæo-Christians.[3]

If this impression is correct, the remaining passage, which
can be traced to an authentic tradition, provides no further
difficulty. Jesus has no thought of abolishing the Law, rather
does he identify himself with it. He lives it, so to speak, in
such a way that instinctively he brings it to perfection in its
true meaning, and he is conscious of realizing it more fully than
the Pharisees ever do, who adhere strictly to the letter of it, and
fail to examine all its inherent potentialities. He lives in very
truth under the Law : Paul was right about this (Gal. iv. 4).
He is penetrated with it, without being destroyed by it. Urged

[1] References **XCIX**, 41, and **LXIV**, i, 245 *ff.*

[2] **CIII**, 567 ; **LXVII**, 82. *Contra*, on very weak grounds, **CII**, 95.

[3] Gal. ii. 12 ; Acts xv. 1 *ff.*

on by the prophet in him, while basing himself on it he goes
beyond it, but only in the direction which the Law itself
suggests.

III

JESUS AND THE TEMPLE

The Law implied a practice. It was not merely a code of
religious and moral precepts, it also ordained certain rites.
While he accepted and recommended the former, did he also
take pleasure in the latter, and demand its observance? Undoubtedly it was impossible to imagine one without the other in
Israel. But we must not forget that the Essenes, who revered the
Torah, rejected the Temple and its ritual.[1] In point of fact, two
tendencies had existed for a long time among the Jews regarding
religious practices. The one was strictly legalistic, formalistic
and unbending; the other, more elastic, was less rigorously
attached to the rites. This attitude may be called " prophetic
and moral," that is to say it was concerned above all with
conduct, interpreted according to the mind of the prophets.
For example we read in Sirach vii. 9 *ff.* :

> " Say not : To the multitude of my offerings he will look, and
> my sacrifices shall be acceptable to the Most High : cease not to
> pray, and neglect not to give alms."

And in Tobit xii. 7 *ff.* :

> " Do good, and evil shall not come upon you. The good is
> prayer, and fasting, almsgiving and justice."

And in Judith xvi. 16 :

> " Sweet-smelling sacrifices are but little, and a small thing fat
> offered in holocaust. But he who fears the Lord is great for ever."

It is to this second way of thinking that Jesus probably
belonged, both naturally and according to the tradition in
which his path was set. Without insisting on the fact in any
other way, the Evangelists give us the impression that he lived
like a pious son of his people.[2] He went up to the Temple for
the feasts ; he paid the Temple didrachma ; he kept the Passover. And there is every reason to believe that if he never
referred to all these practices it was because he took them for
granted. He might condemn poses, ostentation in speech or
behaviour, or exaggerated legalism ; but one does not find him
inveighing against ritual practices.[3] We have no means of

[1] **XXIX**, ii, 568.   [2] **XLIV**, 38.   [3] **EB**, art. *Sacrifice*, § 54.

knowing what importance or value he attached to them, but there is no question that the Evangelists depict him as giving precedence to the religion of the heart and spirit over mere ritual.[1] That is the conclusion to be drawn from the celebrated passage of the Great Commandment (Mark xii. 28), the essential part of which is :

> " And one of the scribes came . . . and asked him, Which is the first commandment of all ? And Jesus answered him ; The first of all the commandments is, Hear, O Israel ; the Lord our God is one lord ; and thou shalt love the Lord thy God with all thy heart, and with all thy soul, and with all thy mind, and with all thy strength (Deut. vi. 4–5). And the second is like, namely this, Thou shalt love thy neighbour as thyself (Lev. xix. 18). There is none other commandment greater than these. And the scribe said unto him, Well, Master, thou hast said the truth ; for there is one God and there is none other but he : and to love him with all the heart, and with all the understanding, and with all the soul, and with all the strength, and to love his neighbour as himself, is more than all whole burnt offerings and sacrifices. And when Jesus saw that he answered discreetly, he said unto him, Thou art not far from the Kingdom of God."

By adopting such an attitude Jesus placed himself alongside the old prophets, whose age had called for the same requirements as his own. Let us also add that he conformed to the best tradition of the Pharisees of his own day.[2] Rabbi Johanan, a disciple of Hillel, may be found, on the eve of the national disaster of A.D. 70, teaching that charitable works are of greater value than sacrifices and the Temple. They surpass them without rendering them superfluous, making them fruitful without abolishing them.

Jesus, the prophet, of necessity approached religion from what we may call its subjective side ; by this we mean that his primary interest was in the deeper feelings of the individual concerning God and the moral law. The objective side was overshadowed, and I think that, had he been forced to make a choice, the Nazarene would not have hesitated. But he never had to make the choice, and there is nothing which allows us to believe that, although relegating the religious rites to a secondary place, he would have been willing to dispense with them.

There can be no doubt that he relegated them to a secondary place. He probably did not attach any greater importance to scrupulous observance of the legal purifications than he

[1] *Cf.* Matt. ix. 13 and xii. 7, which attributes to him the saying in Hosea vi. 6 : " I desire mercy and not sacrifice."

[2] L–*a*, i, 199.

attached to keeping the Sabbath or to fasting. He never speaks of circumcision. He prescribes no new rites. He does not baptize,[1] and when he is supposed to be sending the Apostles out to preach (Matt. x.) he does not give them any instructions to baptize. It is impossible, from the critical point of view, to speak of his having instituted the Eucharist. Baptism and the breaking of bread are early Christian customs whose institution has been erroneously ascribed to the Master.

The Evangelists tell us very little of his attitude towards the Temple. John refers to several visits made by Jesus to Jerusalem for the major feasts (ii. 13 *ff.* ; v. 1 *ff.* ; vii. 2 *ff.*). Mark i. 44 tell us that after curing a leper he orders him to make the Temple offering prescribed by the *Torah* (Lev. xiv.). Matthew v. 23 attributes to him a remark insisting on the need of being reconciled with " thy brother (who) has aught against thee " before " bringing thy gift to the altar " ; which presumably implies that it is necessary, or at least lawful, to make an offering.

It is reasonable therefore to suppose that, in common with everybody except the Essenes, he accepted the Temple and its rites as an unquestioned part of the religious life of Israel. Had he rejected them we should have known it, since early tradition would have been concerned to retail the fact,[2] and would not have shown us the Apostles edifying the people by their devotion to the Temple shortly after their Master's death (Acts ii. 46). How far did he practise what he believed ? We may as well admit that we do not know. The commentators who refuse to admit this want of definite information have drawn frail conclusions from doubtful passages. It is intelligible that believers in the absolute originality of Jesus, and of his complete detachment from Judaism, should maintain that the Temple had no place in his teaching, that in his estimation it had no value for his religion of love.[3] But the fact that such a position is intelligible does not prove that it is true. If Jesus

[1] No attention need be paid to the last verse of Matthew, which is put into the mouth of the Risen Christ, and which would be meaningless in the mouth of Jesus. Although John iii. 22 ascribes the practice of Baptism to the Master, this statement is at once corrected by John iv. 1, which limits it to the Apostles, that is to say, which traces it to the primitive community and not to Jesus.

[2] A passage in the Gospel of the Ebionites preserved by Epiphanius (*Hær.*, xxx, 16) would be disturbing if its authenticity could be relied on : " I am come to abolish sacrifice, and until you cease to give sacrifice the wrath of God will be your portion." Nothing can be concluded from a saying of this kind, because it is unique, and comes down to us detached from its context.

[3] CLXV, 122 ; CCXXXV, 51 *ff.* ; XLIV, 40.

shared the current belief and followed the general practice with
regard to the Temple, then there was clearly no need for him to
refer to them more often than the Evangelists tell us he did.
Of course if we accept Matthew xii. 6, he announced one day,
in the presence of the Pharisees, that he was greater than the
Temple (" In this place is one greater than the Temple ") ; but
this statement, which is only found in the first Gospel, seems
so unlikely that it is not worth retaining. How could Jesus,
who does not preach about himself, at any rate in the Synoptics,
have dared to make such a statement without being immediately
assailed for his blasphemy ? This fictitious *logion* of Matthew
entirely falsifies the meaning of the parallel passage in Mark,
and represents a Christological attitude foreign to Jesus.

Finally, if, in certain circumstances, the Nazarene did predict the destruction of the Temple (Mark xiii. 1–2, and its echo
in xiv. 38) that does not mean that he despised it. It only
implies that he has taken up a message already proclaimed by
the prophets, Micah (iii. 12), Jeremiah (xxvi. 18), Enoch (xc.
28).

To sum up, his attitude towards religious practices, rites,
and even to the Temple itself is the same as his attitude towards
the Law ; he does not blame or condemn any of the principles
accepted by his people, but renewing the tradition of the
prophets, his tendency is to restrict formalistic practice in
favour of spontaneous piety. He is none the less a Jew deeply
rooted in the religion of his ancestors and wholly absorbed
by it.

Nevertheless, his conception of this religion is not that of
the Rabbis : his feeling towards it is not identical with
theirs. A layman, even a pious layman, had no time to study
the 613 written, and the 1,000 unwritten commandments of
the Law with which the scribes occupied themselves.[1] He has
no concern with the formalistic scruples which complicated
exegesis. The same can be said of the pedantry of the
" masters," an indiscreet flaunting of their knowledge of Scripture which humiliated and annoyed the layman, a claim to the
monopoly of true religion. Had not the great Hillel himself
said [2] : " Much *Torah* means much life ; much study, much
wisdom : much alms, great joy " ? A prophet spurred on and
led by his personal inspiration cannot adapt himself to the
claims of the School. A man of the people, addressing himself
to the people, under the inspiration of Jahweh, Jesus was
absolutely obliged to offer his hearers a way into the Kingdom
different from that of the Rabbis. For this reason Matthew v.

[1] CCXXXIX, 19.   [2] *Pirke Aboth*, 2, 7.

20, with every appearance of truth, puts into his mouth the following words :

> "For I say unto you, That except your righteousness shall exceed the righteousness of the scribes and Pharisees, ye shall in no case enter into the kingdom of Heaven."

The Greek δικαιοσύνη is very imperfectly rendered by our word "righteousness" since in the New Testament it is opposed to ἁμαρτία (sin), to ἀνομία (the fact of not knowing, or of despising the law), or to ἀκαθαρσία (uncleanness). According to the Evangelists, therefore, Jesus wishes to imply that the religious method of the doctors is neither necessary nor sufficient for entry into the Kingdom. He could not avoid dwelling on or proclaiming this conviction, because his whole mission was precisely to preach a "way" which turned aside from that of the scribes. Undoubtedly the meanderings of the *Halacha,* when he glanced at them, must have struck him as a particularly thorny and tortuous road to the Father. It would be unwise, however, to trust too much to the impression given by the Evangelists that a state of extreme hostility exists between himself and the scribes.[1] We must remember that when the Synoptics were being compiled, the arch-enemy of the Christian brethren was the Jewish Rabbi, who embodied the offence and unbelief of Israel. It is therefore to be feared that these compilers have made Jesus the mouthpiece of an animosity which is in truth their own. The Nazarene was sufficiently a Jew not to contest the lawfulness of the function of the teacher of the Law, which is to "sit in the Moses seat," that is, to explain and comment on the Law (Matt. xxiii. 1 *ff.*). But he distinguishes between the good scribe who practises what he preaches and does not exaggerate *legalism* at the expense of simple and sincere religious feeling, and the false scribe, who does exactly the opposite, violating it himself, seeking to complicate it, and claiming the right to hinder all its impulses in the name of the principles of the School, or of the *traditions of the elders* (Mark vii. 5 : ἡ παράδοσις τῶν πρεσβυτέρων), that is, of the Talmud in embryo. The Synoptics do not mislead us when they assert that Jesus hates the false scribe.

On one point, at least, he parts company with the good scribe ; I refer to his sympathy with the ἁμαρτωλοί, the *am-haareṣ,* defiled because they are necessarily sinners in that they do not strictly observe the law.[2] Even the tolerant Hillel would seem to have declared that : "None of the *am-haareṣ*

---

[1] *Cf.* Mark ii. 6–7, 18–22, 23–8 ; iii. 1–6 ; vii. 1–23, and the Synopsis.
[2] L–*a*, i, 188, n. 1. *Cf.* the preceding volume.

is godly." [1] And no doubt this statement may aptly be compared with that put into the mouth of the Pharisees by John vii. 49 : " This people who knoweth not the law are cursed." The children of Heaven, according to the scribes,[2] are the strict legalists, and are opposed to the children of earth, that is the *am-haareṣ*, as two socially distinct classes might be today. The *ḥaber* (companion) [3] and the *am-haareṣ* in the environment of those times, are at issue as capital and labour are with us. But Jesus is on the side of the *am-haareṣ* by virtue of his prophetic spirit as much as by that of his humble birth.[4] " They that be whole need not a physician but they that are sick " (Matt. ix. 11–13).[5] And the saying, if it is his, attributed to him in the *Logia* (Matt. ii. 5 ; Luke vii. 22), that he had come to preach the Good Tidings to the *poor* ($\pi\tau\omega\chi\grave{o}\iota$ $\varepsilon\grave{v}a\gamma\gamma\varepsilon\lambda\acute{\iota}\zeta o\nu\tau a\iota$) who are identified with the *sinners*, is a clear statement of his aims, and places him in the authentic tradition of the prophets.[6] He is addressing these who rarely bring exactness or zeal to the performance of their " Religious duties " [7] and who would have great need of transformation in order to find acceptance in the day of Jahweh ; but who are secretly capable of sincere and ardent religious feeling, are by no means sceptics, and are still susceptible to the word or *sign* which has power to move them. He does not despise their religion.   His own religion is essentially that of the best among them, of those in whom the love of God supplies the lack of theology, and faith replaces the study of the Law. Faith in what ? In the omnipotence of Jahweh and in the near approach of his Kingdom bringing blessing to Israel.

To sum up, Jesus appears to us as a belated scion of the Prophets. Such a description is the best explanation of the fact that while at heart as much a Jew as any man could be, he appears, even allowing for the misrepresentations of the Evangelists, to differ considerably from the various *types* into which Israel of that time seems at first sight to be divided.

[1] *Pirke Aboth*, 2, 5.
[2] Enoch ci. 1.   *Cf.* Matt. v. 9 ; $v\acute{\iota}o\grave{\iota}$ $\theta\varepsilon o\grave{v}$ and *Pirke Aboth*, 3, 14.
[3] **XXIX**, ii, 399.
[4] Matt. xi. 19.   " The friend of publicans and sinners " ($\tau\varepsilon\lambda\omega\nu\tilde{\omega}\nu$ $\varphi\acute{\iota}\lambda o\varsigma$ $\varkappa a\grave{\iota}$ $\acute{a}\mu a\varrho\tau\omega\lambda\tilde{\omega}\nu$).   The publican is grouped with the sinner because his duties are at variance with the moral law.
[5] *Cf.* Luke xix. 10 : " The Son of Man is come to seek and to save that which was lost."
[6] *Cf.* Micah vi. 8 ; Isa. lxi. 1 : $\varepsilon\grave{v}a\gamma\gamma\varepsilon\lambda\acute{\iota}\sigma a\sigma\theta a\iota$ $\pi\tau\omega\chi o\tilde{\iota}\varsigma$ $\acute{a}\pi\varepsilon\sigma\tau a\lambda\varkappa\acute{\varepsilon}$ $\mu\varepsilon$. The *saying* in the Gospel may owe its form and even its origin to the passage in Isaiah, but the *fact* itself is obviously reminiscent of the quotation.
[7] **XXIX**, ii, 387 *ff*,

He is different from the Sadducee, the Pharisee, the Essene, the scribe, the zealot, the revolutionary always ready to fly to arms, the dreamer obsessed by his apocalyptic fantasy. Clearly his object was neither to destroy, nor properly speaking to reform, the Jewish religion, but to introduce into it as a predominant influence a certain spirit, the active principle, if we may so call it, of the profound faith which is in him, and of the supreme hope which he proclaims.

CHAPTER V

THE PROBLEM OF UNIVERSALISM—THE CHURCH

I

THE STATEMENT OF THE PROBLEM

BEFORE we analyse the content of the teaching of Jesus, one more question must be raised which has often been the occasion of acrimonious discussion. To whom was the teaching of Jesus addressed ? To his fellow-countrymen or to the world ? Was it for his contemporaries, or for all time ? It is dangerous to claim that the question finds an answer in *the fact of the existence of the Church* as a development intended, or at least authorized by Jesus. Such an argument is a mere *petitio principii*, and though of frequent occurrence must be avoided.

By the time Jesus appeared, Jewish thinkers had long ceased to believe that though Jahweh was the god of Israel, other nations might have their own gods. Jahweh had come to be regarded as the only God, the ruler of a world created by his will, but at the same time it became increasingly difficult to maintain that the insignificant Jewish nation was the sole object of his favour, and that the rest of mankind, at least in theory, did not share in his goodwill.[1] The more liberal point of view naturally tended to prevail among the Jews of the *diaspora*, many of whom undertook the task of enlightening pagans, and of converting them from the worship of idols to that of the true God. This is obviously the whole purpose of a great part of Judæo-Hellenistic literature.[2]

Philo of Alexandria teaches that every man forsaking the worship of idols for the True God is a member of the true Israel, which is not to be confused with Israel according to the flesh.[3] In the opinion of Philo the best proof of the superiority of Judaism to all other religions is its universal character. Nevertheless, the underlying motive of this universalism is not

---

[1] **II**, 149 *ff. Cf.* Ps. xxxvi. 7 *ff.* ; cxlv. 9, 15 *ff.* ; Jonah iii.
[2] **XXIX**, iii, 114 *ff.*   [3] **XXIX**, iii, 550.

so much an ardent desire for the triumph of divine truth as a patriotic fervour, whose hopes projected themselves into the future the more they were frustrated in the present.

The hope of the Psalmist finds expression in the prophetic utterance (Ps. xxii. 27) :

> " All the ends of the world shall remember and turn unto the Lord ; and all the kindreds of the nations shall worship before thee."

Jeremiah (xxxi. 33 *ff.*) puts into the mouth of Jahweh himself the promise :

> " I will be their God and they shall be my people. And they shall teach no more every man his neighbour and every man his brother saying ' Know the Lord ' for they shall all know me."

In order to understand the real significance of these two passages we must compare them with Psalm xlvii. 1–7 :

> " O clap your hands, all ye people ; shout unto God with the voice of triumph . . . for he shall subdue the people under us, and the nations under our feet . . . for God is the King of all the earth ; sing ye praises. . . ."

In other words, if the inheritance of the Jew has become that of all mankind, it is because all mankind has first been converted to Judaism.   Hence the Kingdom, as was promised, is indeed reserved for the seed of Jacob, and this seed includes both the descendants according to the flesh and those acquired by conversion ; the true children and the adopted ones.   The universalism of Judaism is therefore but the triumphant extension of its particularism.

Those who believe that Jesus foresaw, desired, and prepared the historical development of Christianity are obliged to maintain that he was a universalist, but in the eyes of the historian the grounds for this conviction are open to question.   It is obviously difficult for anybody who is completely under the influence of dogma to admit that something entirely different took place from that which Christ himself intended, but this point of view does not concern the historian, who can rely only upon documentary evidence.

There is no doubt that the earliest Christian writings leave us with the clear impression that the Jews to whom the Good Tidings were first offered refused them, owing to their invincible hardness of heart, and that thereupon they were offered to the Gentiles, who received them more kindly.   By the time the Synoptics were edited, the faith had been transplanted into Greek soil.   On Jewish soil it found no new recruits and was everywhere meeting with relentless hostility. To those who were under its sway this state of things would naturally be accepted as part of the deliberate plan of God, and they inevitably looked for a justification of it in the words and *acts* of the Lord. It was unthinkable that he should not have foreseen and foretold it.

In the Synoptics, indeed, there are narratives and, above all, allegorical parables, of which the obvious intention is to point out that the Jews have rejected the Truth, but that the Gentiles have welcomed it and are therefore worthy of it. Take for example the parable of the wicked Husbandmen (Mark xii. 1 *ff.*; Matt. xxi. 33 *ff.*; Luke xx. 9 *ff.*). The husbandmen are the Jews; the servants of the master whom they illtreat and drive out, one after the other, are the prophets; the son who is heir to the vineyard and whom they seize and kill is the Lord himself. This parable, against all probability, is put into the mouth of Jesus, whereas in reality it agrees perfectly with the teaching of the Apostles, which is based on what they had learnt from experience and the facts of history.[1] Again, the parable of the barren fig-tree (Mark xi. 12) points, although less clearly, in the same direction, and still more so does the parable of the Marriage Feast (Matt. xxii. 1 *ff.*; Luke xiv. 16 and *ff.*). This feast, that is to say the message of the truth, had been prepared for the Jews, who refused to come, and therefore outsiders enjoyed the benefit of it. There is no need to labour the point. We have enough evidence already to enable us to see how the conditions under which the Gospel editors lived were projected back into the teaching of Jesus in the form of assertions and predictions veiled as allegories. This was made inevitable by the necessity for justifying the transference of the Jewish inheritance to the Gentiles on the authority of Jesus.

An example of this is to be found in the story of the centurion of Capernaum (Matt. viii. 6 *ff.*; Luke vii. 1 *ff.*) who, while recognizing that he was unworthy that the Lord should enter under his roof, nevertheless had sufficient faith to expect the miraculous cure that would follow one word from Jesus. Let us look at the verse put into the mouth of Jesus:

> "I say unto you, I have not found so great faith, no, not in Israel, And I say unto you, that many shall come from the East and West, and shall sit down with Abraham and Isaac and Jacob in the Kingdom of Heaven. But the children of the Kingdom shall be cast out into outer darkness: there shall be weeping and gnashing of teeth."

---

[1] *Cf.* Acts ii. 22–3.

The centurion represents the well-disposed Gentiles who have deserved the priceless benefit rejected by Israel.[1]

The episode of the Canaanite woman teaches the same lesson (Mark vii. 24 and *ff.*). When this woman begs Jesus to cure her daughter who is tormented by an unclean spirit, he replies : " Let the children first be filled ; for it is not meet to take the children's bread, and to cast it to the dogs." Nevertheless, touched by the woman's faith, he heals her daughter. This is an exception made in favour of one individual. But by the time the Gospels were being edited, the dogs had replaced the children at the distribution of bread, and the exception had become the rule. Still, the first reply undoubtedly reflects the attitude of Jesus, or at any rate that which the Evangelists had reason to attribute to him, for they would hardly have created a gratuitous difficulty for themselves. It is important to note the statement which Matthew x. 5 *ff.* puts into his mouth : " Go not into the way of the Gentiles and into any city of the Samaritans enter ye not. But go rather to the lost sheep of the house of Israel." [2]

Although Jesus may have looked with genuine favour on individual Gentiles because of their faith, nevertheless his attitude towards Universalism was the same as that of his more liberal-minded fellow-countrymen who deprecated the advent of the Gentiles into the Jewish fold. The idea of breaking down these barriers and of addressing the world at large could never have entered his head. But the Gentile Christians were bound to attribute this intention to him, since it was their only justification. For this reason Matthew xxviii. 19 gives, as the final instruction of the Risen Christ, the commandment, " Go ye and teach all nations." Mark xvi. 15 and Luke xxiv. 47 do the same, and the difference in the wording of the three versions does not alter the significance of this fictitious utterance.

For it is fictitious, and it is superfluous to point out that a correction made in the teaching of the living Jesus by the Risen Jesus does not carry conviction. We need only remember the conflict in the primitive community between the disciples, who wished to adhere to the Jewish type of Christianity, and the more liberal Jews represented by Paul, who boldly carried the Christian hope to the Gentiles even to the

[1] *Cf.* The story of the ten lepers (Luke xvii. 11 *ff.*) healed by Jesus, only one of whom shows any proper gratitude, and he is a Samaritan.
[2] *Cf.* Matt. xv. 24 (episode of the Canaanite woman) : " *I am not sent but unto the lost sheep of the house of Israel.*" **XXIV**, i, 128 *ff.* clearly indicates that this is the true point of view of Jesus. See also **LXXXIV**, 255.

point of abandoning for their sake the whole of the legalism of Israel.[1] We must ask ourselves whether the companions of Jesus would have dared to contravene his express command and repudiate his example by maintaining an attitude of inveterate hostility to the non-Judaizing Gentiles. On the other hand, if he had expressed any wish on the subject, surely the liberals would have triumphantly appealed to his example, and if it had been in their power would have confounded the recalcitrants by quoting his command.

The truth of the matter apparently is that Jesus was not only not a Universalist in the modern sense, but that he never asked himself if he ought to be. The idea of addressing himself directly to the Gentiles would have been meaningless to him. Had he claimed to be the founder of a new religion, or even to give a new form or new direction to the Jewish religion, it is reasonable to suppose that he would have wished to extend his mission over a wider field than that of Judaism. But no explanation of that kind is possible. He came to announce the fulfilment of the *Promises* and the realization of the *Great Hope*. What could an announcement of this kind mean to the Gentiles ? It could only be reasonably addressed to those who had been the recipients of the Promises, and who drew their courage from them ; to those fired by that hope ; in other words, to Jews alone. The isolated occasions on which Jesus healed *goyim* who believed in his personal *power* were merely deeds of mercy unrelated to the real scope of his mission. By remaining profoundly Jewish, and only allowing the Gentiles access to the true faith by way of Israel,[2] his immediate disciples were undoubtedly acting in agreement with the ideas of their Master. It was only later on, when, side by side with the hope, the outlines of a creed began to take shape, that adherence to this creed was looked upon as the necessary and sufficient condition of acceptance into the Christian community. But by that time Christianity had been born, and a Christological religion was taking the place of the teaching of Jesus. We shall go on to explain this statement.

II

THE CHURCH

In the minds of present-day Christians the Universalism of Jesus is proved by the existence of the Church which he is held to have intended and founded. There is no question here

[1] *Cf.* Acts xi. 13–15 ; Gal. i.–ii.   [2] Acts iii. 1 ; ii. 46 ; xv. 5.

of that body which we now call the Roman Catholic Church, which, as everyone agrees, has gradually matured in the course of centuries, but of the establishment of certain principles in which that development was implicit, to the extent that the passage of time and the experience of successive ages only resulted in the unfolding of the prophetic mantle with which Peter had been invested by his Master.

In Matthew xvi. 13 *ff.* there is a famous passage regarded by Catholic theologians as conclusive.[1] It refers to what is called *the Confession of Peter*. In answer to the question of Jesus, Peter replies :

> " Thou art the Christ, the Son of the Living God ! (17) And Jesus answered and said unto him, Blessed art thou, Simon Barjona : for flesh and blood (*i.e.* man) hath not revealed it unto thee, but my Father which is in Heaven. (18) And I say also unto thee, that thou art Peter and upon this rock [2] I will build my church ; and the gates of hell [3] shall not prevail against it. (19) And I will give unto thee the Keys of the Kingdom of Heaven ; and whatsoever thou shalt bind on earth, shall be bound in Heaven : and whatsoever thou shalt loose on earth shall be loosed in Heaven."

Taken as a whole the indications of this passage are perfectly plain. It implies that Jesus deliberately intended to found on earth his own church which would be under the supreme guidance, even in its heavenly counterpart, so to speak, of certain men to whom he delegates the necessary authority. He says nothing definite about the length of time this church is to last, but he obviously means it to endure throughout the ages until the consummation of the world.

Unfortunately this decisive passage is found on examination

---

[1] *Cf.* the various commentaries on Matthew *ad locum*, Ch. Guignebert. *La Primauté de Pierre et la venue de Pierre à Rome,* pt. i.   Paris, 1909. For a bibliography see **XLV**, i, 408, n. 1.

[2] This pun, which is easy in Greek (*Petros = petra*) is also possible in Aramaic, where *Cephas = rock.*

[3] The Gates of Hell are those of the Lower Kingdom, the gates of death, of the death which shall not hold back the believers who are destined for the blessed resurrection. *Cf.* Harnack, " *Der Spruch über Petrus als den Felsen der Kirche.*" *Sitz. Berichte der preus. Ak.,* 1918, 637 *ff.*; **XXIV**, i, 112 *ff.*; **CXI**, 153. The mention of the *keys* is said to be of Greek origin (L. Lévy) because Æacus, the guardian of Hades, is called κλειδοῦχος = key-bearer : but we must bear in mind Isa. xxii. 23 : " And the key of the house of David will I lay upon his shoulder : so he shall open and none shall shut : and he shall shut and none shall open." Nor must we forget that in current Jewish use " To give the Keys of the Kingdom to " is the equivalent of " To make Grand-Vizier." Again, to *bind* and to *loose* are technical terms used to declare an action permissible or not according to the obligations of the Law. *Cf.* **LXXXIV**, 36 *ff.*, 258 ; **CXI**, 153 *ff.*

to present certain grave difficulties, of which we shall now only consider the more important.

First of all let us examine the meaning of the expression "my Church." For us this is clear because we know what the Church of Christ is ; we have it before our eyes. But to the disciples, the word, not being explained by an existing fact, would certainly have needed amplification. Since this explanation is not forthcoming here, we might expect to find it elsewhere, as part of the essence of Christ's teaching, but not only is there no explanation of it anywhere in the New Testament, there is not even anything which corresponds to the expression "my Church."

Apart from the very notion of a church, it is surprising that Jesus should say "my Church " when he never says elsewhere "my Kingdom," [1] only the *Kingdom of God* (Matt. xii. 28 ; Luke xvii. 20 ; xix. 11) or *the Kingdom of Heaven* (Matt. xi. 12; xviii. 1). On the other hand, the word Church (ἐκκλησία) only appears in one other place in the Synoptics, in Matthew xviii. 17, in which Jesus is instructing the disciples how to reconcile an offending *brother*. The first effort must be directed to convincing him of his mistake, in private. If this is useless, an appeal for mediation must be made to certain persons of repute. If he is still obstinate it must be told to the church (εἰπὸν τῇ ἐκκλησίᾳ). But *to tell the church* means here, to tell the *assembly* of the faithful. The meaning of the word in this context is very different from that in Matthew xvi. 18. This is proved by the various steps in the method of reconciliation : a brother, several brethren, all the brethren, are called to settle the dispute. Further, we do not ourselves believe in the authenticity of the tradition which attributes to Jesus the use of a word legitimately translated *church*, even in the sense of *assembly*, in the connexion referred to in Matthew xviii. 17, for the reason that it is not given in the parallel passage of Luke xvii. 3 *ff.*, which is much the more credible of the two, that is to say, has every appearance of being earlier and more probably authentic.

> "If thy brother trespass against thee, rebuke him ; and if he repent, forgive him. And if he trespass against thee seven times in a day, and seven times in a day turn again to thee, saying, I repent, thou shalt forgive him."

[1] In point of fact, Luke xxii. 30 has the words ἐν τῇ βασιλείᾳ μου, but when we compare this text with the two Synoptic passages in Matthew and Mark we see that the use of the possessive is editorial. In the same way, in Matt. xiii. 41, *the Kingdom of the Son of Man* belongs to a secondary development, and in Matt. xx. 21, ἐν τῇ βασιλείᾳ σου is used by the mother of the sons of Zebedee and not by Jesus.

The Matthæan passage belongs to a time when the assembly
of believers under the guidance of the Spirit was, in fact,
supreme in matters of discipline as in matters of faith. Nothing
of this kind can be attributed to Jesus. We are forced, therefore, to believe that the use of the word *ecclesia*, as we find
it in Matthew xvi. 18, is unique in the Synoptics, and this
conclusion is disquieting.

A further equally disturbing conclusion to which we are
forced, is that the verses in Matthew which mention the *ecclesia*
are an interpolation.[1] In Mark viii. 27 *ff.* and Luke ix. 18 *ff.*
there is a narrative which is the exact equivalent of what we
find in Matthew xvi. 13, 14, 15, 16 and 20. This account shows
no traces of the contents of Matthew xvi. 17, 18, and 19. Again,
if we compare these three verses with the remainder of the
context, it is obvious that they interrupt the sequence. Here
is the whole passage of Mark, which also agrees with the passage
in Luke :

> " And Jesus went out, and his disciples, into the towns of
> Cæsarea Philippi ; and by the way he asked his disciples, saying
> unto them, Whom do men say that I am ? And they answered,
> John the Baptist : but some say Elias ; and others, One of the
> prophets. And he saith unto them, But whom say ye that I am ?
> And Peter answereth and saith unto him, Thou art the Christ.
> And he charged them that they should tell no man of him."

It is evident at once that the three verses of Matthew,
which have no equivalent either in Mark or Luke, represent a
different point of view from that implied in those which are
common to the three Synoptics. The latter indicate that Jesus
is uneasy, if not surprised, at the confession of his Messiahship
by Peter, on whom he imposes silence—a mode of thinking
and acting which, as we know, is in accord with what, in the
circumstances, is most likely to have been his attitude—while
the three verses in Matthew reward Peter for his insight and
reveal what was to be the result of it in days to come. It is
inconceivable that Mark, who was reputed to be the companion
of Peter, would have let slip the opportunity of recording an
honour so flattering to his master, if he had known it to be
part of the Apostolic tradition. If it was a part of that tradition, his ignorance and the silence of Peter are inexplicable.

Furthermore, while there is no passage in the New Testament to support the interpolation in Matthew, there are several
that contradict it, beginning with Matthew xviii. 15 *ff.*, which
we have just mentioned, and which, although undoubtedly
editorial, gives an entirely different interpretation of the *church*

[1] **XXIV**, i, 112 ; *eine sekundäre Erweiterung.*

from that of xvi. 18, for it shows us the church simply as a
gathering of the brethren. It is all the more perplexing to
find the Evangelist adding the following verse (xviii. 18):

> " Verily I say unto you, Whatsoever ye shall bind on earth shall
> be bound in heaven : and whatsoever ye shall loose on earth shall
> be loosed in heaven."

Surely this passage attributes to the assembled *brethren* the
privilege which Matthew xvi. 19 would reserve to Peter alone ?
It is our opinion that Matthew xviii. 18 is only a gloss borrowed,
without reflection, from xvi. 19, to explain and round off the
diatribe on reconciliation with one's brother. This transposition
proves none the less that whoever was responsible for it did
not take the *prerogative* of Peter seriously.

Later on, in Matthew xx. 20 *ff.*, we find the story of the
mother of the sons of Zebedee, who asks Jesus to give her two
sons the two chief places in the Kingdom : after which comes
the teaching based by the Nazarene on her tactless attempt,
and the enunciation of the following principle : " None among
you shall be placed higher than the others. He will be reckoned
truly the first among you who best serves the brethren."

It is impossible to reconcile a statement of this kind with
any intention on the part of Jesus to organize the brotherhood
under the authority of Peter. There is unquestionably no
sign anywhere in the Gospels of any desire to predict, define
or establish the *Church*. Even such famous and much quoted
passages as Luke xxii. 32, " strengthen thy brethren," and
John xxi. 15 *ff.*, " feed my lambs," assuming them to be
authentic, only show Jesus' affection for, and confidence in
Peter. Little reflection is needed to establish the improbability
of the tradition attributing to Jesus the interpolated passage
in Matthew. Even supposing that he had foreseen the Church
in the little group of Jews who gathered round him awaiting
the realization of the Promise—a modest hypothesis in comparison with the orthodox view—there still remains a difficulty.
By what process of renunciation did Jesus, who at first sight
appeared to be addressing the whole of Israel, arrive at the
point of isolating the insignificant group of disciples from the
mass of the Jews in order to constitute the *Church* ? When
and to whom did he confide this extraordinary limitation of
his original intention ? But this is not the real problem.
According to Matthew xvi. 18 the *Church* is not a sect within
the Jewish Faith relying on the future for its gradual development. It is " an earthly society which is neither the community
of Israel nor the Kingdom of Heaven, but which takes the place,

so to speak, of both." [1]   But what Jesus obviously expected, and that in the near future, was the advent of the Kingdom, and not the establishment, for countless centuries, of a Church constituted by a group of the elect in an apostate world.

The object of Peter's confession is to assert that Jesus was accepted as the Christ by his disciples, but what it demonstrates primarily is that this belief did not exist among the disciples in his lifetime.   The reply of Jesus is intended to prove that the existence and organization of the Christian community was in conformity with the will of the Master. [2]

If this is the case, the editor of Matthew can only have meant by *Church* the existing Christian community, which was distinct from the people of Israel and was forced both by the hate and contempt of the synagogue and by the unexpected delay of the *parousia* to organize itself on the lines of a new religion, while awaiting the day of God.   But all this is foreign to the thought of Jesus and to the ideas with which he was preoccupied.

It was the Apostles and the generation which succeeded them who, in place of the Kingdom which *he* expected and which did not come, founded *his* Church, and this by the force of circumstances, because the object of their own preaching was not the Kingdom but his own person, and also because, in the Greek world especially, the company of believers maintained a life of Sacramental communion with him.

The Rabbis believed [3] that when God wished to create the world, he had sought a solid foundation for the future and in his foreknowledge had passed all future generations in review. He had passed over the generations of Enoch and of the flood ; but when he saw Abraham rise up he had exclaimed, " Ah ! I have discovered a rock on which to build and establish the world," and he had called Abraham *the rock*.   Simon Barjona therefore is the ancestor of the new Israel which is embodied in the Church of Christ.

This conception of a *Church* occupies an important position in the Pauline teaching.   In the opinion of Paul, the various communities dispersed throughout the world constituted the *Church of God*, in the building up of which he exerted all his

---

[1] CIII, ii, 8.

[2] XXIV, i, 111 *ff.*   It is quite possible that the object of the editor in interpolating these verses was to authenticate as forcefully as possible the authority of Peter in opposition to the revelation of which Paul boasted.   *Cf.* CLXXXVII, 161, which refers us to Gal. i. 16 for the claim made by Paul.   LXXXIV, 258, prefers to see in Matt. xvi. 18 an echo of the controversy between Peter and James.

[3] CCXXXVI, 160.

missionary energies. 1 Corinthians iii. 9, " Ye are God's
building " (θεοῦ οἰκοδομή ἐστε), inevitably reminds us of
Matthew xvi. 18, " I will build my Church " (οἰκοδομήσω μου
τὴν ἐκκλησίαν). It is possible to maintain, in fact it has been
maintained,[1] that Paul took his inspiration from the *logion*
already utilized by the editor of Matthew, but it is more likely
to have been the other way round. If, as we have shown, it
is impossible that Jesus should have spoken of the foundation
of his Church, the supposed *logion* is neither authentic nor pre-
Pauline. On the other hand, the *Church of God* was already
a fact when Paul wrote his epistle. He derives the lively simile
of the existence of this *body* (Rom. xii. 5 ; 1 Cor. x. 17) from
the sense of communion which he felt with the Church of
Corinth, while in the body he was sojourning with the community of Ephesus. He knew that this communion was
realized *through the Lord Jesus* and *in* him.[2] If therefore the
question of influence arises, it seems more reasonable to suppose
that it was Paul who influenced Matthew, and not vice versa.
But this supposition is superfluous since the Church was already
in existence at the time when the editor of Matthew was writing.
He knew of its existence, he knew how it had come into being
and how it was constituted. There was no need for him to
go to the man of Tarsus for a definition. Historically it was
an anachronism to attribute his definition to Jesus, who knew
nothing of it, but from the point of view of religious instruction,
it was essential and inevitable that he should derive the idea
from Christ.[3]

One clear and certain conclusion emerges from the various
considerations brought forward : Jesus preached the Kingdom
which was to come. He announced the forthcoming realization
of the great hope of the Jews, in complete conformity with
Jewish beliefs and in the spirit of a prophet ; that is to say,
under an inspiration similar to that of the prophets of old,
without even considering what may be called the human conditions of its realization. We do not maintain that his religious
thinking was obsessed by the great eschatological drama, and
that the remainder of it is not worth studying, even if it were
possible. We simply say that his outstanding characteristic
is that of herald of the Kingdom.

[1] **CCXLIV**, 105, n. 5, following **CCLXXI**, 3.   [2] *Cf.* 1 Cor. i. 2.
[3] **LXXXVI**, 156 *ff.*

CHAPTER VI

THE CONCEPTION OF THE KINGDOM

I

EXISTING THEORIES

THAT the central theme of the teaching of Jesus is the announcement of the Kingdom is beyond dispute.[1] The Evangelists themselves treated it as such. "The time is fulfilled and the Kingdom of God is at hand : repent ye and believe the gospel (good tidings)." This is the proclamation which Mark (i. 15) puts into the mouth of Jesus at the very outset of his preaching, and Matthew iv. 17 expresses the same idea in different words. The *good tidings*, the Gospel, is precisely the announcement that the Kingdom of God is at hand : [2] there is no doubt on this point. The hope of the *parousia* which dominates the apostolic community is obviously only a transposition, necessitated by the turn of events, of the great revelation which the disciples had retained from the preaching of the Master.

Unfortunately Jesus left no theoretical definition of the Kingdom. At first sight this might be a reason for believing that he accepted the current idea of it. However, commentators have not generally been content with this explanation,

[1] An idea of the opposing views held by commentators and theologians may be quickly obtained by comparing **CCLXIV**, 57 *ff*. and **CCLXXXIII**, 35 *ff*. For further details see **CLXXVI, XV, XVI** and **XXI** ; and in opposition to these, **CLXXII** (see references in the Index under *Kingdom of Heaven*) and **CCLIII**, ch. xiv. A useful collection of passages will be found in **LXVIII**, 42 *ff*.

[2] It is assumed, first, that the expression ἡ βασιλεία τοῦ θεοῦ can be translated indifferently as *Kingdom* or *Reign of God* ; second, that the two expressions the *Kingdom of God*, ἡ βασιλέια τοῦ θεοῦ, and the *Kingdom of Heaven*, ἡ βασιλεία τῶν οὐρανῶν, which is preferred by Matthew, are synonymous. *Cf.* **LXXVII**, 76 *ff*. ; **CIII**, i, 226, n. 6 ; **XIX**, 113, 539, n. 3 ; **CXC**, 156 ; **XCVI**, i, 49. The idea of the *Reign of Jesus*, of the *Kingdom of Jesus*, which is found in several places in Matthew and Luke (Matt. xvi. 28 ; xx. 21 ; Luke i. 33 ; xxii. 29–30 ; xxiii. 42) does not belong to the primitive tradition. The *Kingdom*, for Jesus, could only mean that of God or of Heaven.

and for many years a bitter controversy has raged round the exact interpretation given by the Nazarene to the words " the Kingdom of God." The numerous theories on the subject can be classified into three groups, two of them extreme, and the third taking up a half-way position.

(1) The Kingdom is a *future material reality*. By an act of his will, God, by means of a miraculous and catastrophic intervention, will replace the present state of sinfulness and misery by a world of righteousness and happiness. God will set up his Kingdom in the place of Satan's. Those who have undergone *metanoia*, who are morally changed, will find a place at the festive board. Not so the others. " The Gospel is to the Kingdom what an invitation is to a feast." [1]

(2) The Kingdom is an *existing spiritual reality*. It consists entirely of the triumph of Righteousness, of the love of God and of our neighbour, and of divine peace in the heart of man.[2] It will not be achieved by any catastrophic event, but by the gradual and slow transformation of humanity under the influence of " a power which penetrates the soul, and which can only be grasped by the soul " (Harnack). Accordingly, Jesus does not merely announce this Kingdom, he institutes and establishes it around him. The future, namely life eternal in heaven, is doubtless a transcendent form of the Kingdom, its perfect development,[3] but it is not in the forefront of the Master's ideas and teaching. The Kingdom, therefore, must be taken to be " a spiritual state." Until such time as it is realized in heaven in the presence of God, it is the establishment by him in this world of a new moral and religious order, of which Jesus is the architect and the creator (Batiffol). It is obvious that a Christian, who cannot admit that the Saviour failed in any way to make good his promises, or that there was any fundamental error in his mission, is bound to accept this interpretation of the Kingdom. That is why the various Christian denominations, though they agree on little else, are in harmony on this point.

(3) The Kingdom is fundamentally *eschatological* in character. That is to say, however imminent its advent may be in the expectation of Jesus, we must define it as a *future material reality*. But, simultaneously, the Gospel is, as it were, the foretaste of it. In other words, its partial installation begins with the preaching of Jesus and the effects of *metanoia*. Although

---

[1] CIII, i, 247. *Cf.* CLXXVI ; CCXXXVIII, 121 *ff.* ; CLXXXIV, i, 404.
[2] CCCXIII, 388 : " *His Kingdom was not of this world. He substituted another ideal for the Messianic hope.*"
[3] CXC, 155 *ff.*, 164 *ff.*

essentially a thing of the future, it nevertheless belongs in a sense to the present. Although principally the work of God, it is, in so far as it is a *present* thing, the work of Christ and even of man as believing the word of Christ; for its perfect achievement will only be realized if certain conditions of a moral order are fulfilled, and a general *metanoia* takes place.[1]

Each of these interpretations can cite passages in its favour, as might be expected. To begin with, we know that the Gospels display a mingling of many different currents of ideas, belonging to various times and places. Again, many verses, particularly when studied apart from the context, are not sufficiently clear in meaning to prevent diversity of interpretation. Finally, it is not impossible that the ideas of Jesus himself varied, and that he wavered between two not easily reconcilable tendencies. It has been maintained[2] that his mind progressed from one interpretation of the Kingdom towards another. For example, it has been argued[3] that at the beginning of his career Jesus believed the Kingdom to consist only of the society of those who believed, a society which would gradually develop on earth. That is why the Kingdom is near without yet being actually present. Later, as the idea of his death grew upon him, he came to believe that the Kingdom would only come when he was revealed for the second time. Conversely it has been supposed[4] that his idea of the Kingdom was in the beginning apocalyptic, that later it became entirely spiritual, and finally transcendental.

There have been many other theories, all of them gratuitous hypotheses which could easily be inverted without losing any of their value. They are based on the arbitrary arrangement of passages, the true chronological sequence of which we do not know, to show the spiritual progress of a career which is too short to hold everything we are asked to believe about it. The most that can be conceded is that Jesus, during the last days of his life, was dominated by the feeling of the risk he was running in going up to Jerusalem, and that in consequence he came to believe that the Kingdom would only become a reality after his death.

But this hope, the last refuge of his faith as he realized his defeat, does not imply that his method of interpreting the

---

[1] **CCXLIX**, 66. "*The Kingdom simultaneously present and future, spiritual and material. Here we have widely differing points of view and apparently contradictory tendencies.*" Cf. **CCLIII**, 132, 141; **XXXIII**, 184.

[2] Cf. **CLXXV**, 77; **CLXV**, 216 ff.   [3] **CCXL**, ii, 307 ff.

[4] **CLXXXIX**, 254 ff. Cf. **CLXVIII**, 78 ff.

Kingdom thereby underwent any fundamental change, except in so far as it involved the modification of his idea of the way in which the great miracle would be effected.

II

JESUS AND THE JEWISH IDEA OF THE KINGDOM

It is useless to read our own interests and conceptions into passages which are impatient of them. Common sense must tell us that Jesus chose as his starting point the ideas of the world about him, and that on the whole his interpretation of the Kingdom was the same as that of his contemporaries. Otherwise, in order to avoid all misunderstanding he would have taken the precaution of giving his own particular definition of it.

Undoubtedly a considerable variation in detail persisted in the various Messianic ideas of the Jews.[1] This is not to be wondered at, seeing that most of the characteristic features of the picture were derived from *prophets*, that is, from individuals, from deuterocanonical writings which had no legal sanction, and from apocalyptic writings of visionaries whose value it is often difficult for us to assess.[2] However, putting aside these details, and making allowances for discrepancies, we find that there is a kind of general scheme common to the Messianic teaching of Israel. It implies the setting up on earth of a new order of things and of a new mode of life : a transformation of the world, beneficial not only to the righteous and the godly who are alive at the moment of its appearance, but also to the righteous dead who will rise again to enjoy the Kingdom (*malkūth*) of God. We are dealing, therefore, with an exclusively divine activity which will be accomplished at the time decided by Jahweh and as the result of the operation of his power. It is not a purely *internal* and *spiritual* development, but an *external* and *material* change. Underlying this hope there is unquestionably the desire for a moral and ideal Kingdom of God,[3] and also the idea of the necessity of human effort, of individual repentance, and a return to the exact observance of the *Torah*. But whatever importance the prophets attached to these ideas, and interesting as it might be to include them in our interpretation, they are never more than incidental to

---

[1] *Cf.* **XXIX**, ii, § 29 : *Die messianische Hoffnung* ; J. Boehmer, *Der alttestamentliche Unterbau des Reiches Gottes*, Leipzig, 1912 ; **CCXLIX**, pt. i.

[2] **XXIX**, ii, 515 *ff.*   [3] **CXC**, 151.

the expectation of the Kingdom.   This Kingdom is essentially
conceived of as a *Gift of God*, a material reality granted by
divine providence to those who have proved themselves worthy
of it, and which is to be first of all established *on earth* by an
act of divine power.   No doubt there were " masters " who
taught that if the whole of Israel were " righteous " for one
day, that is to say, kept the Law perfectly from one sunset
to another,[1] God would not delay the blessed advent.   But
on the whole the collective virtue of man was not considered
essential to the achieving of the Kingdom.   The common belief
was that Jahweh would operate its inauguration from Heaven
at the hour on which he had decided—probably when he considered that the long and severe trial to which he had subjected
his people had accomplished its purpose.   There were those
who made ingenious attempts to calculate the actual date.
But it is essential to remember that, so far as we can tell, in
all the teaching concerning the Kingdom there is not a single
speculation or vision of the future to suggest that it was only
a spiritual reality which might be mystically realized in the
present.

Again, the Kingdom could not be considered as an isolated
phenomenon, so to speak.   It was part of an eschatological
whole from which it could not rightly be separated, even though
the descriptions of it varied greatly at different times and places.
This eschatological whole was *the age to come (ôlam habba)* as
distinct from the *present age (ôlam hazzeh)*.   This fundamental
opposition could not be reduced, particularly by the simple
people from whom Jesus sprang, to the contradiction between
two *moral* states of humanity.   We must not confuse the
religious and moral content of the eschatological setting with
the setting itself, although in reality they cannot be separated
from each other.   A spiritual conception of the Kingdom was
not part of the outlook of the Jews in the time of Jesus.   This
is indisputable, and if we persist in regarding Jesus as the
prophet of a spiritual kingdom, we must attribute to him an
outstanding originality in his conception of the Promise which
could have seemed nothing short of revolutionary to his
contemporaries.

It is generally agreed, and indeed it would be difficult not
to concede, that Jesus preached the coming of the Kingdom,
the great eschatological transformation of the world.   But had
he not in mind, at the same time, the idea of another kind of
Kingdom ?   That is the point at issue [2] and it is one upon
which opinion is still divided.   Certain writers think that the

[1] **XXIX**, ii, 531.   [2] **CCLIII**, 128.

ideas of Jesus are hopelessly confused.   For example, Harnack [1] maintains that neither the conception of the Kingdom of God nor the manner of its coming is clear or consistent in the Gospel. At the one extreme, so to speak, we have the notion of the visible coming, at a future date, by an act of divine power ; at the other the suggestion that the Kingdom will be set up in the heart of man ; and between these two interpretations there are various intermediate degrees and shades of difference. That is to say,[2] in the Synoptics " the Kingdom is presented in two different aspects, sometimes as belonging to the present and sometimes to the future, sometimes as private and spiritual, sometimes as external and material." The two aspects are combined in Mark x. 15, where we read : " Verily I say unto you, whosoever shall not receive the Kingdom of God as a little child, he shall not enter therein." The first part of the passage might indeed imply that the Kingdom is of the present and is forthwith offered to man, the second that it will come to pass in the future.—Harnack further concludes [3] that the two ideas are practically irreconcilable, and we are not at variance with him on this point.   In that case, granting that the two con-tradictory descriptions exist, our task is to find out which of the two is the more predominant, which of them is, as it were, the kernel, and which the shell.

Two facts must be taken into consideration : (1) Jesus, so far as we know, gives no definition of the Kingdom.   How could such " negligence " be explained if he had discarded the common opinion on this capital point ? [4]   (2) The early Chris-tians were entirely absorbed in an eschatological expectation of the Kingdom.   How could this be if Jesus had led their minds away from any conception of this kind ? [5]   There are numerous passages in the Synoptics which prove that on all *essential* points the idea of the Kingdom as understood by Jesus was in harmony with the Messianic teaching of the Jews.   The Kingdom is a *feast* to which all the righteous shall be invited (Matt. xxii. 1 *ff.* ; Luke xiv. 15 *ff.*).[6]   The righteous at the resurrection will take their places at the Messianic banquet and constitute a company like that of the angels (Mark xii. 1 *ff.*), and this will be achieved by the actual physical removal of the unrighteous.   There is no question of a progressive growth, corresponding to the gradual growth of righteousness in the

---

[1] CCLXIV, 71.   [2] Charles, **EB**, *Eschatology*, § 83.
[3] CCLXIV, 72.   [4] CCLXXXIII, 46 ; LXXIX, 159.   [5] CCVI, 45.
[6] This parable is all the more instructive because the two Gospel editors, who are now beginning to confuse the Kingdom with the Church, transform the tradition derived from Q into an allegory representing their own point of view.

hearts of men. On the contrary, the Great Judge will make
his choice at a definite point of time. The good will be placed
on one side, the bad on the other ; many will be called and
few chosen (cf. Matt. xxv. 31–46). The Kingdom is undoubtedly
a gift of God, a sheepfold prepared for the flock, and not to
be confused with it. If the shepherd tries to rescue and bring
back the lost sheep, this is only because he loves it, and not
because the flock could not exist without it.[1] In other words,
the Kingdom is not the sum of individual virtues and repent-
ances. It can receive them all but does not depend on them :
the last comer among the workmen called into the vineyard
shall receive the same wages as the first (Matt. xx. 1–16). If
that is not the real nature of the Kingdom, what can be the
meaning of the insistence in the Gospels on the suddenness of
its coming ? We read in Mark xiii. 33 *ff.* : " Take ye heed,
watch and pray : for ye know not when the time is." This
idea appears several times in the Gospels,[2] and indeed it
dominates the whole of primitive Christianity. We find it
repeated over and over that the Lord will come when he is
not expected, " as a thief " (Rev. iii. 3 and xvi. 15 ; 2 Peter
iii. 10) or as " travail upon a woman with child " (1 Thess. v. 3).

Nevertheless in several places Jesus appears to depart from
the common Jewish idea. For instance, there is nothing
political in his notion of the Kingdom, which thereby gains in
simplicity since it is no longer associated with all the warlike
upheavals and catastrophic disturbances which were generally
expected to precede it. It also loses its strictly national character. For him it is a question of persons : persons whose
relations to God depend upon their individual deserts, and no
longer of a kind of glorified Israel.[3] But here more than anywhere, we must avoid being too definite, because, on this score,
what the Evangelists may have believed may not be what

---

[1] Matt. xviii. 10 *ff.* ; Luke xv. 1 *ff.* ; the parable of the lost piece
of money (Luke xv. 8–10) is to be interpreted in the same way.

[2] *Cf.* Matt. xxv. 14 *ff.* ; Luke xix. 12 *ff.* ; Mark ix. 1, according to
whom the Kingdom will come *with power* (ἐν δυνάμει) before " some
of them that stand here shall taste of death." Since neither Matt. x.
28 *ff.* nor Luke ix. 27 *ff.* give this ἐν δυνάμει, it has been attributed
to Pauline influence. This may be the case, but it is none the less
interesting to see that Paul, and Mark after him, is inclined to this
particular theory of the *manner* of the coming of the Kingdom. It
implies that the βασιλεία τοῦ θεοῦ will be set up *from without* by an
unforeseen, sudden and irresistible act of divine power.—Matt. xxiv.
45 *ff.* ; Luke xii. 41 *ff.* ; Matt. xxiv. 50 ; Luke xii. 35 ; xiii. 25.

[3] *Cf.* Matt. xi. 20–4 and Luke x. 13–15 : the cursing of Chorazin
and Bethsaida which will find that, on the Judgement Day, Tyre and
Sidon will be preferred to them.

Jesus thought and said.   They did not see things in the same
perspective as he did.   Thus, as far as we can judge, Jesus in
his understanding of the Kingdom, accepted in essentials the
hope of his people, though he may have interpreted it in accordance either with his own temperament or with the particular
ideas of the environment from which he sprang, and of which
we know nothing.   As Loisy[1] has so rightly remarked, "his
Kingdom is a Kingdom of Israel in a celestial form," to be
realized, of course, on earth.   Or at least the Kingdom is such
in one of its aspects, manifested catastrophically.   In the
prayer that Jesus is supposed to have taught his disciples, the
petition for the expected Kingdom, or Reign, has a foremost
place :   "Thy Kingdom come."   And when he feels the
approach of death, his whole being goes out towards the same
hope, and he says to his disciples, "I will drink no more of
the fruit of the vine until that day that I drink it new in the
Kingdom of God" (Mark xiv. 25).   In the teaching of the
Nazarene, therefore, the Kingdom does not appear as a new
revelation but as a realization of the old promises affirmed
by the common hopes.[2]   If we accept Luke xix. 11, the disciples
when going up to Jerusalem "thought that the Kingdom of
God should immediately appear."   If Jesus had in his mind
(which remains to be seen) any other ideas about the Kingdom,
it seems henceforth certain that they were only incidental to
it.   The eschatological interpretation far overshadows them.
On this point the more moderate-minded critics are in agreement, and it seems peculiarly presumptuous to describe this
eschatological theory as "an untenable paradox" in face of
the "indisputable evidence" in the Gospels of the spiritual
nature of the Kingdom.[3]   Actually the untenable paradox is
that which issues from the desire to justify a belief arising from
a profession of faith in spite of the evidence furnished by the
documents.

III

THE SPIRITUAL PRESENCE OF THE KINGDOM

Since, however, reference has been made to "indisputable
evidence," we must examine the Gospels in order to find it,
for the idea of a Kingdom *already present* is to be found not
only in the writings of a Catholic ecclesiastic, whose interpretation is too partial not to be suspect, but also in those of

[1] CIII, i, 229.   [2] CCLXXXIII, 37 ; LXXIX, 118.   [3] CXC, xx.

liberal Protestants, and similarly in those of Tolstoy. We may take Harnack [1] as an example of what may be called the *absolute view*. In his estimation, any attempt to evaluate the intention of Jesus exclusively in relation to the ideas of his time, neglects the greatness and sublimity of his own contribution, and subordinates the individual to his environment. The peculiar characteristic of Jesus is his insight that the Kingdom was already come. The expectation of the eschatological Kingdom accepted by his contemporaries is only the shell of his teaching, its kernel is the assertion of its actual presence. When he says that the Kingdom is at hand he means that it comes to individuals, that it enters into their souls, that they become possessed of it, for in reality the Kingdom is the reign of God in the hearts of men. In the parables which refer to the Kingdom it is understood to be the word of God. The coming of the Kingdom is revealed not only by the preaching of Jesus, but by the fact that he heals and forgives sins. Thus : " everything external or future is excluded : it is the individual who is saved : not the people or the State ; men will be born anew ; and the Kingdom of God is both the power which animates them and the goal towards which they are striving." Therefore " the Kingdom of God is, of its very nature, a spiritual reality, a force which permeates and can only be grasped by the heart."

Harnack, however, agrees that later on the disciples abandoned this idea of the Kingdom, and pinned their faith to a future fulfilment of their Master's promises. Nevertheless, the spiritual reality which Jesus understood by " the Kingdom " was an active force in the primitive Church. In other words, the eschatological element is entirely eliminated from the teaching of Jesus by this theory, for it is thereby reduced simply to an outward semblance, no more than it was necessary to retain in order not to antagonize from the outset the Jewish audience of the Nazarene.

The theory I have just outlined comes to us with all the appearance of a system, which at once makes us suspect it. It has every appearance of being based upon a theology anxious to adapt the ideas of Jesus to present-day needs, rather than upon a historical investigation solely concerned with an accurate representation of the past. Without, however, accepting this point of view in its extreme form, is it not reasonable to suppose [2] that *Jesus* conceived of two stages in the establishment of the Kingdom ? The first, set in motion by his preaching, is the reign of God in men's hearts and is a spiritual reality.

[1] CCLXIV, 72 *ff.*   [2] XXXIII, 187 ; CCLIII, 137–40.

The other, which is to come later, is a material reality which will be accomplished by a divine miracle.

Both the partisans of the absolute view and those who accept a compromise between the two extremes, draw their arguments from the Parables referring to the Kingdom, from which they elicit a general impression, and from various passages in the Synoptics which they read in accordance with their own ideas. Their principal passage is Luke xvii. 20–1, and this they regard as decisive. We may as well say at once that their interpretations conflict with the truth.

Of the so-called parables of the Kingdom, three call for special attention : that of the Feast (Matt. xxii. 2–14 ; Luke xiv. 16–24) ; that of the Talents (Matt. xxv. 14–30 ; Luke xix. 12–27) ; and that of the Wise and Foolish Virgins (Matt. xxv. 1–13).

It seems strange that a purely spiritual kingdom should be symbolized as a Feast. What was the original form of this parable ? We cannot tell, because, as it has come down to us in Matthew and Luke, and particularly in the former, it is no more than an allegory which applies to the Church *in their day* ; to the fact that it was recruited from those who were not expected (the Gentiles), instead of among those who were originally invited (the Jews) and who had shown themselves to be indifferent.

The same explanation holds good for the parable of the Talents—in Luke, that of the Pounds—which in its present form is merely an allegory. It announces the return of Christ the Judge, who will ask for an account of the goods he has entrusted to each. The object of Luke is to explain the delay of the *parousia*. Both versions end with a direct reference to the destruction of Jerusalem.

The parable of the Virgins, ending as it does with the warning, " Watch therefore for you know not the day nor the hour," is clearly intended to recommend vigilance lest the *parousia* should come unawares. Even stripped of their allegorical character, none of the three parables suppose that the Kingdom is already in existence. On the contrary they all consider it as a thing of the *future*. All that can be truly said of them is that they show the close relationship between the *preparation* for the future Kingdom, represented by the activity of Jesus, and the entrance of individuals into this Kingdom.

However, we come across other parables [1] which seem to

---

[1] There are three in Mark iv. 1–34, and seven in Matt. xiii. 1–52. *Cf.* **CIII**, i, 429 *ff*. It has been maintained, however (**CCXXXVIII**, 45 *ff*.), that at the outset they did not apply to the Kingdom but merely to the Gospel.

depict the Kingdom " as an already existing community, the little flock of the elect to whom the Father " has given it. " This little community is to grow as the seed grows of its own accord " (Mark iv. 26 *ff.*), " as the leaven which raises the meal " (Matt. xiii. 33 *ff.*), " as the grain of mustard seed which grows into a large tree " [1] (Matt. xiii. 31). In our opinion this is not a true interpretation, and we believe that, even if these parables do not refer exclusively to the Gospel itself, all of them deal solely with the preparation for the Kingdom. This is evidently the case in the parable of the Sower (Mark iv. 3 *ff.* ; Matt. xiii. 3 *ff.* ; Luke viii. 4 *ff.*) : " Like the labourer, Jesus sows the Kingdom by preaching the Gospel " (Loisy). We may say, if we like, that the Kingdom is already present on earth in the seed sown by the Lord, and now growing. But the crop has not yet come up and there is as yet no question of a harvest. The parable of the Measure (Mark iv. 24) suggests the same conclusion : " With what measure ye mete, it shall be measured unto you."

There are other isolated passages which are brought forward to prove that it is a question " of an internal kingdom, of a moral energy transforming the individual, and of forgiveness and the life of the Spirit." [2] One of these is Matthew xiii. 44–6 : " Again the Kingdom of Heaven is like unto treasure hid in a field, the which when a man hath found, he hideth and for joy thereof goeth and selleth all that he hath, and buyeth that field. Again the Kingdom of Heaven is like unto a merchant man, seeking goodly pearls. Who when he had found one pearl of great price went and sold all that he had and bought it." And Luke xii. 31 : " But seek ye first the Kingdom of God and his righteousness."

Now it seems that if we approach these passages without any preconceived ideas, they only suggest the idea, certainly essential in the mind of Jesus, that everything must be sacrificed to gain the Kingdom, and that man must put himself by *metanoia* into the right attitude to await the Great Day. But such preparations do not imply either immediately or remotely that the Kingdom is already in existence on earth. Still less, if such a thing were possible, that it is to be identified with the moral state prescribed for the individual in order that he may win a place of honour therein.

There are other passages from which we are supposed to be able to conclude with certainty that " the Kingdom consists of the communion of men of good will, working together for

[1] CCXLIX, 75.
[2] *Ibid.*, 74, based on Harnack, *Das Wesen*, §§ iii and iv.

the accomplishment of the will of God." [1] The first of these
is the parable of the Tares (Matt. xiii. 24–30). A man has
sown corn in his field : while he is asleep his enemy comes and
sows tares in the same field. His servants wish to remove the
tares, but he prefers to delay the separation until the harvest.
Matthew himself takes the trouble to explain this parable
(xiii. 36–43) : the teachings of Jesus and Satan meet and mingle
here below ; their respective fruits will be separated at the
day of Judgment. This is an interpretation more suited to
the Apostolic Church than to Jesus. In any case it, too, is
concerned only with the preparation for the Kingdom, which
itself is in the future. The parable of the Net (Matt. xiii. 47–
50 : the contents of the net will be sorted out when it has
been drawn in) has exactly the same purport. We add a few
further passages which have been cited in evidence :

> Matthew xi. 11 : "He that is least in the Kingdom of Heaven
> is greater than John."
> Matthew xxi. 31 : " The publicans go into the Kingdom of God
> before you."
> Matthew xxiii. 13 : " Ye neither go in yourselves, neither suffer
> ye them that are entering to go in."

All that these " *membra disjecta* " appear to convey is the
view, cherished no doubt by Jesus himself, and even more so
by the members of the established community, that belief in
his mission and adherence to the Christian faith are the *virtual*
conditions of admission to the Kingdom, while the opposite
attitude already involves its loss. It is a singular perversion
of these passages to regard them as supporting the theory of
the present existence of the Kingdom, and the view that it is
constituted by the fellowship of men of good will. The good
will, in this case, is necessary for the individual, and it can be
said that the Kingdom will result from it *for him*, but the good
will is not to be confounded with the Kingdom, a position
which the Gospel writers could not have understood.

But some writers go so far as to believe that it is possible
to conclude from certain Synoptic passages that Jesus himself
believed in the *present existence* of the Kingdom. They appeal
primarily to Mark iv. 11, " Unto you is given the mystery of
the Kingdom of God " (τὸ μυστήριον [2] τῆς βασιλείας τοῦ θεοῦ).
The word *mystery* has caused some perplexity because there
was no suggestion of mystery or personal privilege in the
contemporary notion of the Kingdom. The *mystery*, it is
claimed, must be the original idea of Jesus ; his revelation of

[1] CCXLIX, 75.
[2] Matt. xiii. 11 and Luke viii. 10 give the plural, τὰ μυστήρια.

the actual presence of the Kingdom under the guise of a moral good.[1] We have, however, no proof that Jesus ever spoke of a *mystery*, or that the word is not merely the Evangelist's.[2] It suggests the idea of the esoteric teaching of the Mysteries of Salvation, but since we come across it in Daniel ii. 19, 47, and in Wisdom ii. 22, where it has the meaning of *secret*, we may reasonably believe that it was already established in Jewish apocalyptic theology. It is perhaps from here that it found its way into the Johannine Apocalypse, where it appears four times. A much more significant fact is that it occurs twenty-one times in Paul, where it takes on something like its original meaning. As it is found in Mark and Luke, it has in all probability come from the Epistles of the Apostle, if not directly, at least through the medium of the Greek world, in which case it did not originate with Jesus. The most we can concede is that the prophet represented his preaching as a special revelation, only to be recognized by those who believe in it.

Now, however, we come to certain passages which present greater difficulties. We read in Matthew xi. 12, "From the days of John the Baptist until now the Kingdom of heaven suffereth violence and the violent take it by force." [3] Does not this mean that the Kingdom has been in existence since the time of the Baptist? This theory has been maintained,[4] but unfortunately, the verse in question is practically unintelligible [5] and rivers of ink have flowed round its obscurity to no purpose. It has undoubtedly lost its right setting, but if we examine its context (xi. 13, "For all the prophets and the Law prophesied until John ") we find that Jesus is represented as making a division of the history of Israel at the time of John, with whom a new period begins. *Before* that time the Prophets and the Law hold the first place, evidently because they foretell the Kingdom. *Afterwards* surely the implication is that the Kingdom itself is installed. This was not, however,

---

[1] **CLXV**, 214; **CCLIII**, 132, 137 *ff.*

[2] It is only found here and in the two parallel passages in Matthew and Luke, where it is weakened by being altered to the plural.

[3] Luke xvi. 16 gives a very different rendering: "From that time the Kingdom of God is preached and every man does violence to it."

[4] **CCLIII**, 134.

[5] The contrary view has practically only one supporter, **CII**, 221: but the explanation there offered, namely that everyone throws his energy into conquering the Kingdom and that βιάζομαι is not to be taken in a tragic sense, throws absolutely no light on the subject. **CLXV**, 199, gives the list of the principal interpretations. *Cf.* **CIII**, i, 672 *ff.*; **CVII**, ii, 162.

how Luke understood it, since he was content to write " the
Kingdom is announced," that is to say, the period of its coming
has begun. This brings us to the familiar idea of the close
connexion between the preaching of the Kingdom and its
coming, a connexion which is both chronological and logical.[1]

Again, we find in Matthew xii. 28, " But if I cast out devils
by the Spirit of God, then the Kingdom of God is come unto
you " (ἄρα ἔφθασεν ἐφ' ὑμᾶς ἡ βασιλεία τοῦ θεοῦ). Luke xi.
20 expresses this idea as follows : " But if I with the finger
of God cast out devils, no doubt the Kingdom of God is come
upon you." Does it not seem obvious that Jesus here refers
to the Kingdom as *present* ? [2] But what he is actually saying
is that in the eternal warfare between God and Satan, God is
definitely the victor, a fact which is proved by his own works.
He concludes that this is the *sign* that the Kingdom of God
has come. In other words, here, again, he is pointing out that
the brief period has begun, at the conclusion of which the
Kingdom will become a reality. In addition, it is worth
noticing that this passage of Matthew is out of place in its
context and is in all probability an apologetic commentary
based on the Gospel miracle, a commentary dating from the
Apostolic community or even later.

Other passages prove no more with regard to the thesis
in question than the ones just cited, and these, if our understanding is correct, prove nothing. Or rather, what they do
prove is that Jesus, or the early Christian Church, established
an indissoluble connexion between his prophetic mission and
the imminent approach of the Kingdom. The former is, so
to speak, the announcement, the antechamber of the latter.
Although it may be admitted that there was a certain *subjective*
confusion between these two, we must maintain their actual
or *objective* difference.[3]

There remains as a last resort Luke xvii. 20–1. Men as
widely apart as Renan, Harnack, and Tolstoy see in this passage
the expression of the deepest and truest thought of Jesus, the
logion which throws light on the whole Gospel. It runs literally
as follows : " And asked by the Pharisees concerning the time
when the Kingdom of God should come, he answered them :
The Kingdom of God cometh not with observation (οὐκ ἔρχεται

[1] CCLXXXII, 44.   [2] CCLIII, 133.

[3] Dewick, CCLIII, 140, gives himself away when he writes that
Jesus definitely seems to recognize " a non-eschatological, earthly, and
imperfect aspect of the Kingdom of God : and his words justify us in
speaking of the Church of Christ as the Kingdom of God on earth."
This is what preoccupies the theologians ; but the interests of theology
must not be confused with the conclusions of historical criticism.

. . . μετὰ παρατηρήσεως). Neither shall they say : Behold it is here, or it is there. For behold, the Kingdom of God is among you [or within you] " (ἐντὸς ὑμῶν ἐστιν).

There has been much discussion over the meaning of παρατήρησις and still more over that of ἐντὸς ὑμῶν. The former belongs to the language of astronomy, and refers to the observation of signs which foretell, for example, an eclipse, or to the ritual observations of the stars for purposes of foretelling the future. We must take it to mean, then, that the Kingdom will not come in such a way that it can be foretold from signs which will announce its immediate approach.[1] With regard to ἐντὸς ὑμῶν we have indicated above the two translations which may be said to sum up the debate.[2] Everyone can produce important authorities and weighty arguments in support of his own point of view. Although classical Greek contains examples of ἐντὸς used to mean *in the midst, among*, the conclusion of linguists seems definitely to favour the meaning of *within*. τὸ ἐντὸς τοῦ ποτηρίου (Matt. xxiii. 26) certainly means *that which is within the cup* [3] and the idea of *in your midst* would be better rendered by ἐν μέσῳ. On the other hand, the Oxyrynchus papyrus [4] which repeats and comments on the passage in question gives to ἐντὸς the meaning of *in you, within you* : καὶ ἡ βασιλεία τῶν οὐρανῶν ἐντὸς ὑμῶν ἐστι καὶ ὅστις ἂν ἑαυτὸν γνῷ, ταύτην εὑρήσει—*And the Kingdom of Heaven is within you and whosoever knows himself shall find it.* But this *logion* is in reality only a gloss on our Luke and there is no likelihood either that it goes back to a different source or represents a better text. As for the meaning of the gloss, it was called for by the indefinite delay of the *parousia*. The Greek commentator was already feeling the need of adapting the teaching of the Lord to what had or had not happened.

Linguistic arguments therefore seem to justify the translation of ἐντὸς as *within* : but probability is definitely against it. Jesus could hardly tell the Pharisees, without appearing absurd, that the Kingdom of God was within them, in their hearts. And ignoring the Pharisees, none of his disciples, who were all authentic Jews, could have understood such a strange utterance, which is unsupported by any teaching in the Gospels. If this *logion* is the focal point of the whole teaching of Jesus

[1] CIII, ii, 402 ; XCVI, i, 393 ; XCVII, 175.
[2] It is by no means new. Early Latin Christianity was already undecided between the renderings *in vobis, in animis vestris,* and *intra vos.* Cf. for example, Tertullian, *Adv. Marc.,* 4, 35.
[3] See also Ps. ciii. 1 : τὰ ἐντός μου, and Ps. cix. 22 : ἐντός μου. The meaning of these is clear.
[4] See the text in Klostermann, xxiii, *Apocrypha* iii. 18.

concerning the Kingdom, its isolation is incredible. These objections raise, and to all appearances dispose of, the problem of its authenticity.

Nor is this all. If we read the verse in its context with ἐντός as *within*, a contradiction results. Luke makes this utterance a kind of introduction to a teaching on the coming of the Kingdom (xvii. 22 *ff.*).[1] But the coming of the Son of Man is there referred to as destined to be sudden : xvii. 24, " For as the lightning that lighteneth shines from one end of heaven to the other so shall also the Son of Man be in his day." In the view of all his disciples the only object of his coming was the inauguration of the Kingdom. He could therefore hardly say in the same breath, that the Kingdom was in the hearts of his hearers, and that he would come to establish it suddenly, in a day when he was not expected.

The obvious conclusion then is that ἐντὸς ὑμῶν means *in the midst of you*, which seems equally to imply the actual presence of the Kingdom. But then there arises the question whether the verb ἐστὶν is the real present tense or a prophetic present, that is to say, the future. This would change everything, even if ἐντός be taken to mean *within*. The probable meaning of the whole passage is : " When the Kingdom comes no one will have any difficulty in recognizing it, or will need to ask where it is. It will suddenly be either in your midst, or in your hearts : that is, those who have suitably prepared themselves in accordance with the teaching of Jesus himself will enter into it." [2]

If, setting aside the literal reading of the passage, we try to grasp what Luke was really trying to say, recognizing at the same time the rashness of basing the interpretation of the entire Gospel on an isolated text, so disputed, so obscure and so suspect, we shall make the following discovery. The Evangelist (verses 20–4), mindful of the obsession of those for whom he is writing, is endeavouring to check more or less idle speculations concerning the date of the Lord's coming. This interpretation sets the passages in a perspective which is not that of Jesus but of the Christian community. His insistence on the sudden nature of the Messianic manifestation brings us to one of the most definite beliefs of the Gospel generation. If Jesus himself said : " *The Kingdom will come suddenly*," the

[1] The substance of this also occurs in Matt. xxiv. ; Luke joins it up with the apocalyptic discourse of Mark xiii. Q doubtless provides the basis for this.

[2] For a discussion of the various interpretations, *cf.* **CCLIII**, 144 *ff.* ; **CCVI**, 46 *ff.*

early believers naturally substituted *Jesus* for the *Kingdom* and said, " *The Lord will come suddenly*," which is the same thing. Verses 23 and 24 clearly prove that Luke understood this *event* as something outside man, and brought about through the will of God by means of a stupendous miracle. Verse 21 cannot possibly contradict this evidence.

Without a shadow of doubt, the whole of the beatitudes in Luke (vi. 20 *ff.*) take for granted and even teach that the Kingdom is a thing of the future, yet we read in verse 20 : " Blessed be ye poor for yours is (ἐστὶν) the Kingdom of God." They *possess* the Kingdom because they possess that which is necessary in order to be able to enter in on the Great Day. That is why Luke xvii. 21 can say that the Kingdom is already virtually in the midst of the disciples, or if we may so put it, that they carry their tickets of admission with them. If this is the correct interpretation, then Luke xvii. 20–1 proves exactly the opposite of what Renan, Harnack, Tolstoy and so many others take it to mean.

We may therefore conclude from this study of the documents that Jesus did not believe in the actual presence of the Kingdom, that he never taught it, that he never even said that the great and expected miracle had already been actualized around him in any form, and in particular by the enthronement of God in the hearts of the disciples. He taught, in conformity with current Jewish belief, that the Kingdom would come as a gift of God. But he perhaps believed, or at least his disciples after him believed, that, his own mission being to announce the imminent approach of this manifestation, his teaching, or from another angle, the belief in his vocation, was the outer chamber through which men had to pass to reach the Kingdom. A true disciple, therefore, was virtually in possession of the gift of Jahweh. Nothing could be more natural than that he should establish this close connexion between his preaching, willed by God, and the Grace of God which it announced. But, in admitting this, we are far from accepting the embarrassing contradiction into which the followers of Harnack believe that he fell. Loisy was perfectly right when he said [1] that Christ nowhere confused the Kingdom with the remission of sins, nor with God and the operation of his power in individual hearts, nor again with the word of God. All these things may imply, for those who know how to profit by them, the certainty of the future possession of the Kingdom, but *they are not the* Kingdom. The Kingdom is primarily and essentially the material transformation of this present evil world.

[1] **CCLXXXIII**, 48.

Attempts have of course been made to prove that the very expression *Kingdom of Heaven* means that Jesus was only concerned with a *celestial* realization of the Kingdom. We know, however, that *Kingdom of Heaven* means *Kingdom of God*, and that the hope of the Jews was not lost in a far horizon. In the Kingdom announced by Jesus, " the meek shall inherit the earth " (Matt. v. 5, μαχάριοι οἱ πραεῖς, ὅτι αὐτοὶ κληρονομήσουσιν τὴν γῆν), according to the will of God, that earth which to-day is governed by the violent. This idea of the possession of the earth, and that of the installation of the Kingdom among the living, are equally incompatible with the hypothesis of a purely heavenly manifestation. Matthew v. 12, which has been adduced in support of the latter idea, is a broken reed. , " Rejoice and be exceeding glad," it says, " for great is your reward in heaven " (ὁ μισθὸς ὑμῶν πολὺς ἐν τοῖς οὐρανοῖς). But this " reward in heaven " simply means that the origin of the Kingdom is transcendent, and that God, in view of the reward reserved for them, keeps a record of good actions performed and efforts made with the Kingdom in view. Neither the earthly nature of the Kingdom announced by the Nazarene nor its eschatological character can be seriously disputed.

With these essential points established, we can more quickly clear up various questions relating to the conception of the Kingdom as it presented itself to the mind of Jesus.

CHAPTER VII

THE SETTING-UP OF THE KINGDOM

I

How the Kingdom will Come

TO the question, How will the Kingdom come ? our Gospels furnish only one reply, contained in what is called *the synoptic apocalypse* (Mark xiii. and Synopsis). Unfortunately the whole verse has the obvious appearance of being an artificial composition which it is impossible to attribute to Jesus. Mark seems to have regarded it as a kind of introduction to the account of the Passion. He has used it to define the significance of the life of Jesus, and, by preparing for his death, to relieve in some measure its horror for the reader ; to neutralize it, so to speak, by setting it in the light of the *parousia*.

There are grounds for doubting whether the source used by the Evangelist could have been a Christian one, since it is obvious that the numerous signs announcing the coming of the Great Day, while completely in keeping with Jewish beliefs, are totally incompatible with the gospel statement that the Lord will come *like the lightning*, without warning and at an hour when he is not expected. The whole description (xiii. 5–27) is characteristically Jewish. For this reason, although the saying is clearly not authentic,[1] the author has not produced an effect of improbability in putting it into the mouth of Jesus. In fact, it is a reasonable assumption that the Nazarene thought of the consummation as it was conceived of by his fellow-countrymen, and hence that he expected a manifestation of divine power, followed by a sudden change in the world-order and, doubtless, by the exaltation of the Messiah.[2]

It would be useless to spend time over the details of this unauthentic discourse in an attempt to disentangle the elements which the Gospel tradition regarded as genuine utterances of the Nazarene from those which its editors have added on their

---

[1] For the opposite view : **CLXV**, 219 *ff.*, which attempts to save as much as possible, and **CXC**, 378 *ff*.

[2] **CIII**, i, 237.

own instance. We shall deal later with the rôle which Jesus is supposed to have attributed to himself in the great drama.[1]

Jesus appears to have avoided giving too definite an answer to the question of the exact time of the setting-up of the Kingdom. He did not offer precise calculations after the manner of the apocalyptic writers ; but it is clear that he believed and asserted that the time was at hand, since the belief and its utterance constituted the reason for his preaching (Mark i. 14–15). However, several passages in the Gospels seem to set a limit to the disciples' period of expectation. The first occurs in Mark ix. 1 : [2]

" And he said unto them : Verily I say unto you that there are some of those standing here who shall not taste of death until they see the Kingdom of God come with power."

It has been suspected (Loisy) that the word *some* was a correction due to the delay of the event and that the original reading ran : *all those who are here.* Further, it has been conjectured that the *logion* arose, after the death of Jesus, out of the desire to encourage the disciples and to confirm them in their expectation of the *parousia.* But it is difficult to believe that such a rash assertion should have sprung spontaneously, for there can be no question of deception, from the faith of the companions of the Crucified, if it had no foundation in their recollections or had even actually contradicted them.

Whatever its source may have been, it has sorely embarrassed those theologians who persist in attributing the saying to Jesus. The Fathers of the fourth century found the fulfilment of the prediction in the Transfiguration. Even the most resolute conservatives would hardly venture, we imagine, to maintain this view today, but what they offer is hardly preferable. For instance : " It is permissible to consider the fall of Jerusalem as the fulfilment of this prophecy, since the Kingdom thereafter ceased to be confined to a single nation and was extended to embrace the Gentiles." [3] It is legitimate to deny the authenticity of the passage, but if its genuineness be once admitted it must be acknowledged that its meaning is entirely unambiguous.

The same is true of Mark xiii. 30 [4] : " This generation (ἡ γενεὰ αὕτη) shall not pass away till all be fulfilled." It is idle to try [5] and persuade ourselves that this verse also does not refer to the *parousia* but merely to the fall of Jerusalem, and is hence a completely fulfilled prophecy. Some of the

[1] *Cf.* p. 481 *f.* [2] *Cf.* Matt. xvi. 28 ; Luke ix. 27. [3] **CI**, 205.
[4] *Cf.* Matt. xxiv. 34 ; Luke xxi. 32.
[5] So **CI**, 325 ; **V**, i, 456 ; **CXC**, 273 ; **CLVII**, ii, 457 *ff.*

commentators who refuse to consider the possibility that Jesus could have been mistaken fall back upon the supposition that the Evangelists misunderstood the saying, while others strain the words ἡ γενεὰ αὕτη to mean the Jewish race, or the generation of Christians, the Church, which was to last until the end of the age. St. Jerome suggested the more daring interpretation of the human race! Once the literal sense of the passage is abandoned any interpretation is possible, but it is only the preconceived ideas of the expositors which obscures the plain meaning of the words.[1]

A third passage confirms the force of the two already mentioned. Before sending out the Apostles on their mission, Jesus is reported to have said to them : " Verily I say unto you, ye shall not have gone over the cities of Israel before the Son of Man be come." It is quite possible to maintain that there was no apostolic mission, that there were no Apostles accompanying Jesus, and that consequently he could not have said such words to them ; but the gospel tradition did believe that he said these words, and therefore recorded them, even though the very gospel of Matthew which contains them relates that the Apostles returned to their Master without the Great Day having come to pass.[2] Hence it is clear that the tradition believed that the prediction corresponded to some prophetic utterance of Jesus.

In these three passages it is possible to see editorial influence going to the length of invention, and to regard the Evangelists as writing for a circle still dominated by the expectation of the *parousia* and by the hope of the blessed day when the Messiah would return in the glory of his Father, with his angels (Matt. xvi. 27). If scepticism with regard to the authenticity of these three passages, or at least the authenticity of their contents, be carried to its logical conclusion, leaving out of consideration the general frame-work of the gospel tradition, the only inference which follows is that we do not know whether Jesus foresaw or announced the precise time of the coming of the Kingdom. Such a position may be supported, if necessary, by the evidence of Mark xiii. 22 (Matt. xxiv. 36) : " Of that day and of that hour knoweth no man, not even the angels in heaven, nor the Son, but only the Father." Nevertheless, it must be pointed out that ignorance of the day and the hour does not imply ignorance

[1] CIII, ii, 437 ; CXIV, 107.
[2] CCLIII, 142, assumes that Jesus only intended a *conditional* prediction, and that the condition, which was repentance, was not fulfilled. An excellent example of the absurdities which theologians occasionally do not shrink from propounding.

of a time-limit,[1] and that this was the view of the Evangelists,
since they, or at least two of them, inserted this statement in
the very discourse in which they record Jesus as saying : " This
generation shall not pass away till all be fulfilled " (xiii. 30 for
Mark ; xxiv. 34 for Matthew, who consequently places the
statement two verses earlier).

At all events, it cannot be denied that Jesus believed in the
imminence of the Kingdom ; his insistent exhortation : Repent,
would alone be sufficient to prove it.   It was addressed to an
audience that at any moment might see the expected dawn.
This lends probability to the view that Jesus announced a time-
limit for the present age, a time-limit in the immediate future.
Two passages in the Gospels confirm this view.   In Luke xix. 11
we read that as they drew to Jerusalem the companions of
Jesus believed that the Kingdom would immediately appear
(παραχρῆμα), so much so that they were thrown into the depths
of despair when the death of their Master shattered their hopes
(Luke xxiv. 17 : ἐστάθησαν σκυθρωποί).   Thus it was not
death that Jesus was going up to Jerusalem to meet, but the
great supernatural event so earnestly desired.   The second
passage is in Mark xiv. 25 (Matt. xxvi. 29), where the Nazarene
says to his disciples during the last Supper : " Verily, I say unto
you, I will not any more drink of the fruit of the vine until that
day when I shall drink it new with you in the Kingdom of God."
Hence, for him, the day was near at hand, at least within a
year, if we are to take literally the saying which Luke xxii. 16
puts into his mouth on the same occasion : " For I tell you
that I will not again eat of it (the Passover) until it be fulfilled
in the Kingdom of God."   Whether these sayings are genuine
or not, they at least represent the belief of the disciples, and
are incompatible with the supposition that Jesus did not believe
in the approaching vindication of his message and never said
that its fulfilment was near at hand.

The course of events falsified this expectation which was
consequently and inevitably transformed by the persistent
faith of the disciples into the belief in the *parousia*.   Moreover,
since the world showed no signs of passing away, the Church
was forced to accept a further transformation of the belief.
But these recantations give us no help in reconstructing the
belief of Jesus.

[1] CCLIII, 175.

II

The Locality and Duration of the Kingdom

The next question concerns the chosen place for the manifestation of the expected Kingdom. We know that for the Jews only one answer was conceivable, Jerusalem was the appointed centre of the Kingdom. This belief finds expression in the *Shemoneh Esreh*, 17 ; it is extremely common in the Sibylline Oracles [1] and occurs also in the Johannine Apocalypse, xxi. 10 : " And he carried me away in the spirit to a great and high mountain and showed me the city, holy Jerusalem, coming down from heaven, having the glory of God."

There is every reason to believe that Jesus shared the belief of his fellow-countrymen. Only so does the account in Luke xix. 11 of the expectation of the disciples when they drew near to the holy City, become intelligible, and that Luke himself should have written thus is evidence that the belief was known to him and was still a living force among the disciples. The same conclusion may be drawn from the fact that our texts make no comment on the point, since their silence is only intelligible on the supposition that for them the matter admitted of no question ; it was already accepted by common consent.

According to Jewish belief the earthly Kingdom was not eternal. On this point our Gospels are silent, and it is remarkable that they make no mention of the *millennium,* the Messianic reign of a thousand years, which afterwards occupied an important place in Christian eschatology. It is possible that Jesus had a definite conception of the divine order of the new age. The present world would be *glorified,* and men would dwell in it like angels, in divine peace and righteousness. There is no evidence that the Nazarene believed in the Jewish dream of an intermediate stage, the Messianic age in the strict sense, and as far as we can judge, this is the reason why he says *the Kingdom will come* and not *the Messiah will come.* This fact has been used as an argument in favour of his Messianic consciousness, because it seems difficult to believe that he would have rejected what we have been accustomed to regard as the most essential element in Jewish eschatology. But it must not be forgotten that in Israel it was not before the first century of our era that the conception of the Kingdom became inseparably connected with the Messianic expectation. It is not suggested that the prophet eliminated the Messiah from his eschatological viewpoint, only that he placed the realization of the Kingdom

[1] *Sib. Or.,* 3, 657, 715, 724, 757, 772, 785 ; 5, 420.

in the forefront of his aims, and that he thought of it as the result of the direct interposition of God, not as brought about by the war-like exploits of the Messiah. For him the only natural and logical issue of his belief that the Kingdom consisted in the rule of God among men, and not of the domination of the Jewish nation over the conquered Gentiles, was the relegation of the figure of the divine hero to the second place. This was inevitable, since the more Jesus himself proved a stumbling-block to Jewish nationalism, the more the Jews tended to exalt the idea of a national Messiah.

Furthermore, it is remarkable that, as far as we know, Jesus never represented his activities as actually ushering in the Kingdom, but rather as preparing the Jews for its coming.[1] It may not be rash to infer from the words which the gospel tradition records him to have uttered during the Last Supper, that he accepted that feature of current eschatology which has been called the Messianic Banquet.[2] He says that he will no more drink of the fruit of the vine until he drinks of it new in the Kingdom (Mark xiv. 25 and Syn.). But it must also be remarked that in this solemn hour he only speaks of the Kingdom and not of the Messiah.[3]

III

THE CONDITIONS OF ENTRANCE INTO THE KINGDOM

The conditions of entrance into the Kingdom, as laid down by Jesus, are naturally ethical and religious. They consist of three requirements, to believe in the gospel, to do the will of God, and to repent, implying a moral change of life.

What Jesus meant by believing in the gospel (Mark i. 15 : πιστεύετε ἐν τῷ εὐαγγελίῳ), is not what we mean by it today, since for us the Gospel is a book, a collection of precepts. For Jesus it involved belief in the Good News which he announced, faith in his mission, a complete surrender to the hope of the Kingdom which he declared to be so near. There is no doubt that the Evangelists, as interpreters of the sentiments of the Christian communities of their time, emphasized the primary need of believing in the Messiah and of not doubting his word, and that they made the reception of the Kingdom,

---

[1] CCVI, 44 f.

[2] The righteous and the elect shall eat with the Son of Man, according to Enoch, 62, 14.

[3] CXIV, 115 : he does not declare himself to be the Messiah, not even the future Messiah.

that is, of salvation, depend on this faith. They could not do otherwise without ignoring the most vital necessity of membership of the Church. Moreover, if they were not to make Jesus deny himself, it was necessary to represent him as believing that he was himself the Truth and the Way. Hence absolute belief in the former and complete surrender to the latter were essential conditions of salvation. Nevertheless, it must be remarked that in this case his own person was invested with no special privilege : faith to him is requisite because he is the sent one of God ; hence, strictly speaking, it is God and the Good News which he has committed to his prophet that are the objects of faith.

To do the will of God (Mark vii. 21 : ὁ ποιῶν τὸ θέλημα τοῦ πατρός μου τοῦ ἐν τοῖς οὐρανοῖς), does not merely consist in words and well-meaning behaviour ; it consists in loving God with the will, keeping his commandments in a deeper sense than the scribes and Pharisees (Matt. v. 20), loving one's neighbour as oneself and forgiving one's enemies (Mark xii. 29–31 and Syn.), repentance and a sincere attempt to avoid sinning afresh (Matt. iv. 17), a complete moral change, out of love to God, producing a return to the simplicity and innocence of a little child (Matt. xviii. 3).

Such is the meaning of *metanoia*, the moral change essential for salvation. The coming Kingdom will be the reign of righteousness, hence righteousness is a condition of entrance. The Jews had always attached great importance to righteousness, the distinctive characteristic of Jahweh, and they had been accustomed to connect the forgiveness of sins and the moral renewal of the chosen people with the advent of the Messianic Kingdom. The only object of the sayings and repeated miracles of Jesus was " that they may repent " (Mark vi. 12 : ἵνα μετανοῶσιν) : the only reason of his coming was to produce this change in them, for " He who does not repent before Him," says Enoch (l. 2 f.), " shall perish." Hence, what is required is a fundamental *mutatio animi*, a change of attitude with regard to sin, that is, a determination to forsake all conduct which causes sin or results from it, repentance for sins already committed and a resolve to sin no more. A pious Jew who had kept the Law, the written will of Jahweh, thought that he had done all that was required of him ; but among the *anavim*, it was the deep sense of their unworthiness as sinners which created the heartfelt repentance for their shortcomings that drew them to God. We have already seen that Jesus was in the spiritual line of succession to these " poor in Israel."

It is probable that Jesus saw clearly how hard a thing he

asked of men when he exhorted them to seek the Kingdom first, and to forsake this present world in order to win a place in the age to come. He seems to have anticipated how strong would be the opposition of the human instincts, good and bad, to his claims, and to have demanded their suppression : " If any man come after me and hate not his father and his mother, his wife and his children, his brethren and his sisters, yea, and his own life also, he cannot be my disciple " (Luke xiv. 26).[1]

Similarly, it is the realization of the obstacles in the way of *metanoia* that finds expression in the famous passage in Matthew x. 34 *f.* : " Think not that I am come to send peace upon earth ; I tell you nay, but rather a sword. I am come to set enmity between the son and his father, between the daughter and her mother, between the daughter-in-law and her mother-in-law, and a man's foes shall be they of his own household " (*cf.* Luke xii. 51 *f.*). .

It is impossible that the saying should be authentic ; such an unlikely prominence given by Jesus to himself is bound to be suspect ;[2] but we may find in it, put into the mouth of Jesus, the actual experience of the primitive community, as a reminiscence of a prophetic utterance in Micah vii. 6 : " For the son dishonoureth the father, the daughter riseth up against her mother, the daughter-in-law against her mother-in-law ; a man's enemies are the men of his own house."

The fact that Mark x. 40 seems to regard places of honour as a feature of the future age, suggests that it was felt that reward would vary according to the degree of individual effort. We find, for instance, the two sons of Zebedee boldly demanding such places, and Matthew xix. 30 speaks of first who shall be last, and last first. Moreover, there is the clear affirmation that no man who has made sacrifices will be the loser thereby : " Verily, I say unto you that there is no man who has left house, or wife, or brothers, or parents, or children for the Kingdom of God, who shall not receive many times more in this present life, and in the world to come life everlasting " (Luke xviii. 29–30).

The form of the saying may be due to the redactor,[3] but

---

[1] *Cf.* Matt. x. 37. With reservations, of course, as to the letter of the saying.

[2] **LXXXVI**, 94. The passage is one of those which have been used as evidence for the violence which was to characterize the activity of Jesus. *Cf.* **CLIV**, ii, 254. As the context clearly shows, the mind of the gospel writer, behind which we cannot go, was only concerned with family dissensions.

[3] Mark x. 29, which has " *for my sake and the Gospel's,*" and Matt. xix. 29, which reads " *for my name's sake,*" instead of Luke's " *for the Kingdom of God's sake,*" are naturally more concerned to emphasize

the conception that the Kingdom is worth any sacrifice and that no sacrifice, however great, can fail to be rewarded, is characteristic of Jesus. It is not clear, however, what form Jesus thought the fulfilment of his promises would take. He could only have accepted to a limited extent the rewards offered by Jewish eschatology, for it is obvious that the central Israelite conception of national aggrandizement had no place in his own vision of the future. Still, it is not safe to suppose that he had realized all the difficulties that present themselves to us, or that his mind travelled along the lines of modern forms of thought.

Concerning the teaching of the early Christians about hell, the further question arises whether Jesus had a clear idea of the future of those who would be excluded from the Kingdom.[1] It might be said that he alternated between three views : the hardened sinner would be shut out from the Kingdom (Matt. xxv. 11-12) ;—he would be cast into " outer darkness," [2] where there shall be weeping and gnashing of teeth (Matt. viii. 12) ;—or he would go into Gehenna (Matt. x. 28-9), the place of destruction of both soul and body. It would appear reasonable that a reign of Satan over the wicked should correspond to the reign of God over the good ; but this view conflicted with the old idea that the actual reign of Good could only be realized through the annihilation of evil and the Evil One. The Gospel tradition ignored the problem.

The conclusions arising from our study of the Kingdom may now be summed up in the following propositions :

(1) The Kingdom of Jesus' expectation was an *eschatological* Kingdom, the gift of divine grace, to be established by the miraculous interposition of the divine will.

(2) Jesus did not believe that this Kingdom would be set up on earth as the result of his preaching, but that his preaching, by announcing the Kingdom, was preparing the way for it, and by immediately preceding it served as an introduction to it. Hence he believed that in this case there was a close link between his own present activity and the future interposition of God, but he never confounded the two.

(3) He conceived of the setting up of the Kingdom as the result of a miraculous act, but did not think that it would be preceded by all the fantastic portents and disturbances which Jewish eschatology associated with the appearance of the

the central interest of the Christian movement, the person of the Lord and the Gospel, rather than the Kingdom.

[1] **CIII**, i, 228.

[2] *Εἰς τὸ σκότος τὸ ἐξώτερον* implies the opposite of the *light* of the Kingdom. It is a common Jewish conception. *Cf.* **IV**, 278.

Messiah. It was his disciples who were induced to apply to him, in a modified form, the apocalyptic ideas of Daniel, in the belief that he had foreshadowed the future after this fashion, since they were convinced that his power, after suffering the eclipse of death, would burst upon the world in a glorious return. But it is clear that he believed that the Kingdom would be an actual realization on earth of divine righteousness and human happiness, a visible and sensible state of bliss for the true *sons of the Kingdom* (Matt. xiii. 38 : υἱοὶ τῆς βασιλείας), according to their deserts. There would be no further need of intermediary beings between them and their heavenly Father, and if we may describe such a state as *morally conditioned,* the theological phraseology need not obscure the simple and primitive nature of the conception. Such a mode of conceiving of the Kingdom could only survive in primitive minds, but it was not difficult, by the addition of a little metaphysics, to transform it into a sublime and majestic system, nor would such a transformation be the most radical of those which the Kingdom announced by Jesus has suffered.

CHAPTER VIII

THE FUNDAMENTAL IDEAS OF JESUS : GOD [1]

I

STATEMENT OF THE PROBLEM : THE MAIN QUESTIONS

WE have already touched, indirectly, upon the Synoptic representation of the mind of Jesus ; we shall now go on to deal directly with the fundamental aspects of the problem. The three following points will occupy our attention :

(1) We shall first inquire what Jesus, according to the editors of the Gospels, understood by the word God, and especially the originality of the ideas and the depth of the emotions contained for him in the expression God the Father, since the emphasis which our texts seem to lay upon it suggest that it was a characteristic note of his teaching. Modern thought tends to regard it as the essence of his message.

(2) We shall attempt to discover the kind of life which Jesus considered pleasing to God, the way of salvation. This involves the problem of the ethics of Jesus, a fundamental one for us because, owing to the fact that the apocalyptic vision of the prophet was not realized, *the way*, of which Christianity consisted before it became a dogmatic system, was based on the ethics of Jesus, and hence it was to the propagation of his ethics that the Church always directed its efforts. There are many who, although they have long since discarded the metaphysics and dogma of Christianity, still regard the ethics of the Nazarene as their most precious and inalienable heritage.

(3) We shall endeavour to define the manner in which Jesus regarded the eschatological drama which would close *the present age* and usher in *the age to come*. The question has lost something of its insistence with the passing of the generations which have watched in vain for the desired or dreaded *signs* of the coming change, but it was a burning question for the immediate disciples of Jesus, and the faith which created Christianity rested

---

[1] Bibliography : **L–a**, i, 210–48 ; **LXVII**, 3rd ed., J. Leitpoldt, *Das Gotteserlebnis Jesu im Lichte der vergleichenden Religionsgeschichte*, 1927.

on the living expectation of the *parousia* in the hearts of the primitive community.

It is possible that the ideas attributed to Jesus by the Gospel writers were not really held by him, but none the less they represent the foundations of the Christian religion which are supposed to have been laid by him, and as such they call for our careful consideration.

II

THE IDEA OF GOD

According to the orthodox theologians Jesus presented to the world a definite revelation of God, but it is not usually maintained that he offered it in the systematic form of a *theodicy*. He spoke and acted entirely as if his hearers did not need any doctrine about God, the reason being that they already did possess what was at least supposed to be a well-known and clearly defined doctrine of God.[1] Moreover, without such a presupposition, the fragmentary and sporadic teaching of Jesus about God, as recorded in the Gospels, would have thrown the disciples into the greatest perplexity about the existence and nature of the Most High. We are told that[2] " The Gospel is far less a theodicy than the expression of an intuitive apprehension of a personal God." While the truth of this assertion may be admitted, it must be added that such an apprehension is not self-explanatory and is, in fact, based on a revelation of God prior to the time of Jesus. When he spoke to his disciples about God, their common background was the " hereditary theodicy " of Israel; the God of whom they spoke was Jahweh, the God of their fathers.[3] Mark xii. 36 records Jesus as quoting the universally accepted Jewish designation of God : " I am the God of Abraham, and the God of Isaac, and the God of Jacob " (Exodus iii. 6) ; and in Mark xii. 29 he cites Deuteronomy vi. 4 in the **LXX** : " Hear, O Israel, the Lord our God is one Lord." [4] He is the God who spoke by Moses and through the Prophets (Matt. v. 17), the Lord of heaven and earth (Matt. xi. 25), who reveals himself in the Bible by his words and by his acts.[5]

Hence Jesus accepts, in principle, the scriptural revelation

---

[1] *Cf.* Schechter, *Some Aspects of Rabbinic Theology*, ap. McGiffert, *The God of Early Christians*, New York, 1924, p. 9 *f.*

[2] **CXC**, 83.   [3] **LXXX**, 201–7.

[4] The Hebrew has : " *Jahweh, our God, is one Jahweh.*"

[5] **XLIV**, 29.

of Jahweh. If he is himself the instrument of a fresh revelation
of God, he is unconscious of it ; when he prays, it is to the God
of Israel ; he is sent by him ; towards him are his aspirations
directed, and, like the Prophets before him, it is by the Spirit
of the God of Israel that he feels himself guided, impelled and
sustained. This is the reason why his utterances concerning
God lack the appearance of any systematic arrangement.[1] This
absence of metaphysics and theology is a frequent source of
surprise to the theologians.[2] Thus the love of God is only
explicitly mentioned in the Fourth Gospel, and the grace of God
only in Luke, gravely suspected of Paulinism. Moreover, Luke
himself only attributes one mention of this grace to Jesus, in
vi. 32 *f.* : " And if ye love them which love you, what thank
have ye ? " a passage where the word χάρις, grace, and the
sense of the saying, have both a Pauline flavour.

If the idea of God is not dealt with systematically in the
teaching of Jesus, it is none the less central in his teaching.[3]
For him it is not something to be defined like an abstract conception, it is a living reality, an almost sensible presence, in
which he seems to live and breathe.[4] He sees God in all things,
great or small, in nature and in man, in the clothing of the lilies
(Matt. vi. 28), in the feeding of the ravens (Luke xii. 24), in a
sparrow on the eaves, in the number of the hairs of man's head
(Matt. x. 29). For him there seems to be no distinction between
the activity of nature and of God : everything in the world and
in life is for him, in no mere manner of speaking, but in very
truth, of God or from God. Here we find the focal point of
his religion, whence his whole life and religious emotions radiate.[5]
The *pragmatism* of Jesus' idea of God is the most obvious
characteristic of the Synoptic Gospels. Hence Jesus' faith in
God does not present itself to our minds as *belief*, though of that
there can be no question, but as *trust*, and it is clear that this is
the kind of faith which he claims for himself. His soul rests
on God with complete certainty.

Nevertheless, as we read the Synoptics, we cannot fail to
observe that there is a blending of two different conceptions of
God, both equally fundamental.[6] God is seen as the Ruler of
the universe, in unapproachable glory, recalling the gorgeous
imagery of the description of the coming Day in the book of
Daniel ; but he also appears as the Father of mankind, upon
whom all their support and salvation depend. The theologians
admit that the first of these two conceptions is peculiar to

[1] *Ibid.*, 34. [2] **LXVII**, 1st ed., 138.
[3] **CLXVIII**, 73. [4] **CIII**, i, 233 ; **CLX**, 112.
[5] **LXVII**, 1st ed., 130. [6] **XLIV**, 30.

Israel, but they maintain that the novelty and originality of
the religion of Jesus is to be found in the second.   In order to
arrive at an estimate of this view it will be necessary to summarize the main features of the conception of God which was
current in Palestine in the time of Jesus.[1]

Although the spiritualization of the conception of Jahweh
had reached an advanced stage, his worshippers had not yet
arrived at the point of regarding him, so to speak, as a metaphysical entity.   Although it had become the custom to refrain
from the utterance of his name, his adherents were aware that
he possessed a special name, indicating a very definite divine
being, a *person*, vast, indefinable, but real, whose character was
reflected throughout the whole of their sacred literature.   Jahweh
was Israel's God and King (Ps. v. 2 ; xxiv. 10 ; cxxiii.) ; he is the
centre of Jewish history.   He is, moreover, the creator of heaven
and earth, the omnipotent ruler of the world, the source and
administrator of righteousness, who will execute judgment in
the day which he has laid up in his purposes.   This is the
essential and inalterable Jewish conception of God.   The
experiences of the Maccabean period resulted in a remarkable
revitalization of the ancient biblical conception of the direct
presence and help of Jahweh.

Doubtless, during the period between the Return from Exile
and the time of Jesus, under the influence of the vague and
cloudy syncretistic speculations of the Hellenistic East, the
conception of Jahweh tended to become sublimated into a
purely transcendental figure.[2]   The common people ceased to
have any contact with him and were afraid to utter his name.
He was regarded as a kind of Grand Monarch, incomprehensible
and mysterious, secure and unapproachable in his celestial
courts, like the Persian king immured in his magnificent palace,
only to be reached through the intermediary of his ministers
and servants, the angelic hierarchy.   But the point cannot be
too strongly emphasized that these " modernist " ideas, the
result of foreign contact, entirely failed to affect the narrow
circle of the *anavim*, among whom Jesus was born and grew
up.   In the pages of the Psalter [3] or the Psalms of Solomon [4]
we meet the imposing figure of Jahweh, the ever-present help
of the godly in Israel.   He is the omnipotent King, all-seeing
and righteous, the saviour of those who walk in his ways,
executing judgment upon the wicked who depart from them.
The dominant emotion experienced by the worshippers of such

[1] IV, 358–94.   [2] II, 358 *ff*.
[3] XLIV, 29 *ff*.   *Cf.* Ps. lxxiii. 25 *f.* ; xlii. 2 ; etc.
[4] CCLXXXII, ii, 130 *ff*.

a God is fear, tempered by trust in the unfailing justice of the Judge ; there would seem to be no place for the sentiment of a tender affection.

It would, however, be incorrect to suppose that the Jews knew nothing of the grace, the tender mercy, or the fatherhood of God.   In various passages of the Old Testament, even in the earlier literature, we hear God spoken of in terms of the most implicit trust.[1]   Such expressions, indeed, are somewhat hesitating and uncertain, but they do not represent the attitude of slaves cringing before a despot ; they depict rather the relation between the chief and father of the family and its members. " Ye are the sons of Jahweh your God," says the Deuteronomist (Deut. xiv. 1) ; [2] " Thou art my Father, the Rock of my salvation," exclaims the Psalmist (Ps. lxxxix. 27). It is precisely this sense of sonship which is characteristic of Israel's relation to God, and which distinguishes them as a people from all other nations.   Moreover, it seems clear that the idea of the fatherhood of Jahweh, alongside of his transcendence, tends to gain ground during the period immediately preceding the appearance of Jesus,[3] while the idea of the fatherhood of God carries with it the corollary that he loves and is loved by the godly.[4]

Briefly, among the Jews of the time of Jesus there were current three distinct conceptions of God, held separately or combined, according to shades of difference in the religious environment, not easy to distinguish clearly : (1) that of the God of the Old Testament, the omnipotent Creator, King and supreme Judge of the world ; (2) that of the Most High and unapproachable God, a blend of the Persian despot with Greek speculation ; (3) that of the God who is the Father of those who know and adore his name.   The last of these aspects was not as yet either deeply rooted or widely spread in Israel, but its infinite possibilities appealed to personal religion, and from this time onwards it took its place definitely alongside the other two conceptions.   The broad general tenet of the holiness of God served to embrace and unite all three views.

As we have already pointed out, it is unlikely that the conception of the remote and exalted God should have been current

---

[1] Deut. i. 31 ; viii. 5 ; Isa. i. 2 ; Hos. ii. 1.   *Cf.* **IV**, 377 *ff.*

[2] *Cf.* 2 Sam. vii. 14.

[3] *L–a*, i, 54, and ii, 370 *ff.*, which give the refs.   *Cf.* 3 Macc. v. 7 ; vi. 8 ; Jubil. i. 24 *ff.*

[4] *Shemoneh Esreh*, 5 and 6.   Towards the end of the 1st century A.D. the phrase " the heavenly Father " was in common use among the Rabbis in speaking of Jahweh.   The date is too early for the opinion to be maintained seriously that we have to do with Christian influence.

among the *anavim*; but side by side with the conception of
the almighty Ruler and Judge, that of the beneficent and loving
Father would have -found a ready acceptance among them,
offering for their worship a Deity at once omnipotent, righteous,
and benevolent.

It is exactly such a conception as this that is attributed by
the Synoptists to Jesus. It cannot be said that in his mind the
conception of God as King and Master, a terrible and inexorable
Judge, occupied the second place. We meet it everywhere in
the Gospels. Heaven is the throne of such a God, and earth is
a footstool for his feet (Matt. v. 34). He is in very sooth the
Lord of the Universe (Matt. xi. 25). His sovereignty, viewed
after the manner of the ancient East, knows no limits (Mark x.
27 ; xii. 24). , The attitude of man toward this God is often
expressed under the figure of the subservience of a servant to
his master (Matt. xviii. 23 ; xx. 1 ; xxv. 14 ; Luke xvi. 1, etc.).
His absolute power over nature and man is limited by no law,
so to speak, and is exercised *directly* and *personally*, in the
literal sense of the words, and arbitrarily. Thus, it is his sun
which shines upon the world : by his will alone it shines and
rises upon the just and unjust at his pleasure (Matt. v. 45). The
field is clothed with the green grass at his command (Matt. vi.
30). Examples might be multiplied indefinitely.

Similarly, many passages might be adduced to illustrate the
belief that God, as King, is also Judge.[1] The idea of the Judgment, being inseparably linked up with that of the Kingdom,
pervades the whole of the Gospels. At the appointed Day each
shall receive from God the reward of his deeds according to the
strictest reckoning (Matt. xxiv. 45 *ff.* ; xxv. 14 *ff.*).[2]

Finally, Jesus was equally imbued with the idea of the holiness of God, in conjunction with his two other aspects of King
and Judge upon which his holiness depends ; while it follows
from the fact of his holiness that he must be a righteous Judge
and a merciful King.[3]

So far we have not gone beyond the limits of Jewish religion.
At the most there appears a personal emphasis on the holiness
of God as the perfect expression of righteousness and mercy
(Mark x. 18). We may also discern in Jesus a certain softening
of the harsh rigidity of the Israelite conception of the righteousness of Jahweh.[4] Whereas the Old Testament might be said
to exhibit such an inevitable relation between a deed and its
recompense that even Jahweh cannot alter it, several passages
in the Gospels display God as breaking through the conventional

[1] **XLIV**, 31, gives several examples.
[2] **CXC**, 86.   [3] **CLX**, 122.   [4] **CXC**, 88.

limits of justice in order to increase the reward of a good deed, or to magnify his mercy towards an evil one (Matt. xviii. 23 *ff.* : the servant who cannot pay his debt ; xx. 1 *ff.* : the hire of the labourers in the vineyard ; Luke xv. 11 *ff.* : the Prodigal Son).

Such traits are not, at first sight, characteristically Jewish ; but we do not know the complete connotation of the term Jewish. And since Jesus and those who gave its shape to the Gospel tradition were Jews, it would be rash to dogmatize on the point. The more so in that there is no need for surprise if we find that any originality in these respects which distinguishes Jesus from his contemporaries springs from that religion of the heart which has its source in the Prophets.

III

THE FATHERHOOD OF GOD

The idea of the Fatherhood of God as found in the Gospels is so far from being at variance with the aspects already indicated that we find them harmoniously combined in the same sentence in Matthew xi. 25 : " O Father, Lord of Heaven and Earth." The two aspects of God blend into a unified conception. The second aspect, that of Fatherhood, shows no signs of displacing the first, that of authority. Nevertheless, it is still frequently asserted that the idea of the Fatherhood of God represents the original element in the teaching of the Nazarene. " The essence of the theology of Jesus is to be found in the definite conception of God as Father," so Renan wrote.[1] This conception, says another scholar, is a " characteristic feature of his idea of God." [2] He makes the idea of the Fatherhood of God the central element of his belief in God, nor does he regard it necessary to be a Jew in order to be a son of God, but for him God is as much the God of the outcast and the sinner as of the righteous. In short, the ideas of Jesus bear witness to a fresh and unspoiled nature ; they soar far above all the more or less similar conceptions to be met with in or beyond the realm of Jewish thought.[3] Mgr. Batiffol, forgetting the passages in which the Jews are represented as the sons of Jahweh, with the implication that he is their Father, and even ignoring Ps. lxxxix. 27, " Thou art my Father, my God and the Rock of

[1] **CLXVIII,** 76.

[2] **CXL,** 123 : *das eigentliche Wesen der Gottesvorstellung.* **CLXIII,** 393 (Anglican Modernist), informs us that we may think of Jesus as in essence the Lord who reveals God the Father.

[3] **XLIV,** 32 ; **CXL,** *loc. cit.* ; **CCXXXV,** 70.

my salvation," goes so far as to write : " The Psalms, representing Jewish religion at its highest, never venture to ascribe to God the name of Father." [1]

At the other extreme we find it maintained that the Fatherhood attributed to God by Jesus represented nothing beyond contemporary Jewish religious experience. The documents themselves, examined without preconceptions, constitute our only criterion. While they do not bring us into direct contact with the mind of the prophet, it is a matter of no small importance that they tell us what the disciples believed that he thought.

At the outset we meet with a difficulty that although Jesus often uses the term Father in Matthew and John, he rarely uses it in the other Gospels. In Mark God is only spoken of as Father in the absolute sense, without qualification, in two passages, both of which are believed to be either editorial interpolations or editorially modified. One is the famous text in xiii. 32 : " Of that day and of that hour knoweth no man . . . save the Father." The other is in the prayer of Jesus in Gethsemane, xiv. 36 : " Abba, Father ('Aββᾶ, ὁ πατήρ), all things are possible with thee." Moreover, the expression my Father is never found in Mark, and your Father is only found in xi. 25-6 (instructions concerning the right state of mind for prayer). It must also be remarked that several important MSS. (followed by most of the critical editions) omit verse 26, and even verse 25 is regarded by the commentators with some doubt. [2] It is no use quoting Mark viii. 38 : " The Son of Man . . . when he shall come in the glory of his Father," since the saying is generally acknowledged to be editorial ; it occurs in a discourse added by the Evangelist to the confession of Peter, and intended to prove that Jesus is the Messiah, but not that of current Jewish expectation. It is a piece of catechetical instruction, Pauline in spirit and phraseology, which could neither have been uttered by Jesus nor understood by those to whom it is supposed to be addressed. [3]

Hence even the few passages in which Mark attributes the use of the term Father to Jesus are doubtful and may be from the hand of the editor, who, moreover, makes no claim to have recorded the characteristic phraseology of the prophet.

[1] CXC, 96.
[2] The Matthæan expression ὁ πατὴρ ὑμῶν ὁ ἐν τοῖς οὐρανοῖς, is disturbing here, and it seems so isolated and meaningless at the end of the pericope that it has been thought that it must be out of place. Cf. XCVI, i, 163 ; CXIV, 91 ; XCVIII, 133.
[3] CXIV, 67 ff. ; CV, 250 ff.

Similarly, the few occurrences of the different forms :
Father, the Father, your Father, my Father, in the *logia* [1] are
easy to enumerate. Taking them altogether we have (1)
Matthew v. 48 (Luke vi. 36) : " Be ye therefore perfect as
your heavenly Father is perfect." This is one of the utterances
contained in the Sermon on the Mount and is clearly modelled
on Leviticus xix. 2 : " Ye shall be holy because I the Lord
your God am holy." It is possible that at some time or other
Jesus may have uttered a saying of this kind, but we have no
guarantee of its original form. (2) Matthew xi. 25–7 (Luke x.
21–2), the opening words of what has been called the Prayer
of Thanksgiving, because it begins with the words : " I thank
thee, O Father, Lord of heaven and earth," and in which the
words Father, the Father, or my Father, occur five times.
Unfortunately it also contains the term the Son, only found
in one other Synoptic passage (Mark xiii. 32), and more characteristic of Johannine phraseology.[2] Taken as a whole, it
bears the aspect somewhat of an errant fragment of the Fourth
Gospel, and if we admit its authenticity we should be obliged
to maintain that Jesus consciously regarded himself as " the
immortal, and possibly, the pre-existent Christ," [3] a conclusion
which the present writer cannot accept. We should also have
to ignore the fact that it is related to the formulæ in current
use in the Hellenistic Mysteries and the Oriental religions,[4] and
that it is made up of phrases from Ecclesiasticus, in the fifty-
first chapter of which we find the corresponding prayer of
thanksgiving of Jesus, the son of Sirach.[5] Lastly, we must
ignore the fact that it is in rhythmic form, which makes it
difficult to attribute to the Nazarene. Foreign to the spirit of
the Synoptic tradition, it must be assigned to the Christology
of a Christian community which knew Paul but had already
gone beyond him.

It is clear at a glance that in many of the passages where
Matthew has the term Father, it is not found in the parallel

[1] It may be repeated that this source (Q) can be restored with a
fair degree of probability by a careful comparison of the parallel passages
of Matthew and Luke.

[2] Matt. xi. 27 : " *All (i.e. the entire revelation) has been given me by
my Father, and no man knoweth the Son save the Father, neither knoweth
any man the Father save the Son, and he to whomsoever the Son will be
pleased to reveal him.*"

[3] CIII, i, 909.

[4] CCXCIV, 338. *Corpus hermet.*, tract. i, 32.

[5] Eight verses from Sirach, from ch. 51 and ch. 24, are connected
with this pericope. The influence of certain passages of Isaiah and
Zechariah has also been suggested. *Cf.* XCIX, 103 *ff.* ; LXVI, i, 608 *ff.* ;
CVII, ii, 177.

passages of Luke ; or that Matthew emphasizes the term where Luke seems to lay no stress on it.[1] It is clear that, if not in all, yet in most of the passages Matthew has emended the original. The main contention is that neither the *logia* nor Mark suggest that the attribution of Fatherhood to God occupies the place which it is commonly supposed to in the teaching of Jesus.

On the other hand, Matthew evinces a distinct predilection for the terms the Father, or my Father, or your Father ; he uses them frequently in those parts of his Gospel which are peculiar to him, and of whose source we have no knowledge ; in addition he makes liberal use of them in the rest of the Gospel. While it is not necessary to maintain that he has everywhere inserted them on his own authority, it cannot be doubted that he has very often done so. A glance at a Synopsis and a careful comparison with Mark or Luke will establish the fact.

The unqualified use of the term Father does not occur in the parts peculiar to Luke. There are two occurrences of Father (xxiii. 34) : " Father, forgive them, for they know not what they do "; (xxiii. 46) : " Father, into thy hands I commit my spirit " ; the fact that the sayings are attributed to Jesus on the Cross is disturbing. There are two occurrences of my Father (xxii. 29) : " And I appoint unto you a kingdom as my Father hath appointed unto me " ; (xxiv. 49) : " And behold, I send the promise of my Father upon you." The first passage is certainly secondary, and entirely Johannine ; the authenticity of the second, which forms part of a discourse placed in the mouth of the risen Christ, cannot be accepted. There is one occurrence of your Father (xii. 32) : " It is your Father's good pleasure to give you the Kingdom," a passage whose authenticity is less open to doubt. Hence the impression gained from the parts peculiar to Luke corresponds with that which we have gathered from Mark and the *logia*.

It is relevant here to give a brief consideration to John. First of all, it does not surprise us to find that John uses the term even more frequently than Matthew. Then it is to be noticed that while the terms the Father and my Father are of common occurrence, your Father has disappeared.[2] The

---

[1] *Cf.* Matt. x. 32 and Luke xii. 8 ; Matt. vi. 9 and Luke xi. 2 ; Matt. vii. 11 and Luke xi. 13 ; Matt. vi. 26 ; x. 29 and Luke xii. 24 ; xii. 6 ; Matt. v. 45 and Luke vi. 35 ; Matt. x. 20 and Luke xii. 12 ; Matt. xviii. 14 and Luke xv. 7.

[2] " *I ascend to my Father and your Father, to my God and your God* " only occurs in John xx. 17. Moreover, the word " your " only applies to the disciples, for the Devil is the father of the unbelieving Jews (viii. 38 *f.*, esp. 44 : ὑμεῖς ἐκ τοῦ πατρὸς τοῦ διαβόλου ἐστὲ).

Johannine Jesus has taken possession of the Father for himself
and his disciples, and, in the last resort, for himself alone;
he is conscious of being united to the Father by a bond which
is wholly unique : " For the Father himself loveth you," he
says to his disciples, " because ye have loved me and have
believed that I came out from God " (John xvi. 27). It is
this Johannine consciousness which explains the meaning of
the Matthæan usage whose tendency is already to monopolize
the Father for Jesus. This process, entirely foreign to the
thought of the prophet, belongs to the history of Christology.

Hence we are confronted by the question of what we may
believe Jesus to have thought and said. First of all we may
conclude what he did *not* say. He did not use the term the
Father which involves the corresponding term the Son, because
he did not think of himself as the Son in the Pauline and Johannine sense. Still less did he say my Father or our Father.[1]
Apparently he merely regarded God as the Father of all men.[2]
The relevant passages of the Gospels, as far as we can determine
their original form, are far from giving us any ground for believing that, in the teaching of Jesus, the idea of the Fatherhood of God held the place which modern theologians have
assigned to it on the strength of the evidence of Matthew and
John.

Nevertheless, the pertinent question arises whether into this
idea derived from his environment Jesus had not introduced
something new, hitherto unknown to the Jews. In the first
place, the fact must be recognized that he did not define the
term Father any more than he defined the term Kingdom, a
fact which might be adduced as at least one reason for supposing
that he used the term in the sense in which it was understood
by those around him. We must, furthermore, acknowledge
that we are no longer in a position to grasp the exact sense in
which he used the word Father, hidden as it is behind the
Gospel description, already so remote from his actual habit of
thought.

He may have been accustomed to use Father (Abba) in
prayer.[3] But from the fact that in his approach to God he
turns to the Father rather than to the omnipotent King and

---

[1] The Matthæan version of the Lord's Prayer (vi. 9) has πάτερ ἡμῶν,
but Luke xi. 2 only reads πάτερ.

[2] Matt. v. 45 ; Luke vi. 36.

[3] Luke xi. 2 : Πάτερ ἁγιασθήτω τὸ ὄνομά σου. The traditional belief
that he used the expression Father (*Abba*) in prayer, finds more or less
substantial support in the prayer of Thanksgiving in Matt. xi. 25 *ff.* ;
Luke x. 21 *ff.*, and in the prayer in Gethsemane, Mark xiv. 36 ; Matt.
xxvi. 39 ; Luke xxii. 42.

the austere Judge—although he did not forget that aspect of the Divine character—we should infer that Jesus tended to emphasize the idea of the Divine care, the idea[1] that man might always turn for help to the goodness that provided for his needs as they arose, and to the mercy that was ever ready to forgive (Matt. vi. 12).

The evidence of our text does not allow us to go beyond the above conclusions, which are not themselves absolutely impregnable. If they were it would be possible to draw from them an interesting inference, namely, that practically, that is to say in the working out of the relation between God and man based on prayer, the conception of the Fatherhood of God predominates over the other, theoretically equal, conception of the Sovereignty of God. If the God whom Jesus addresses in prayer is no longer the flaming God of the Apocalypses,[2] if man may realize the nearness of his personal presence, as of a father in the midst of his children, a father whose severity is ever tempered by love and tenderness, chastising at need, but preferring to pardon and bless, these are consequences of profound importance for the history of religion. It implies that Jesus desires to introduce men to that religion of the heart which we have already seen to be his own, the religion of the Prophets and of the *anavim*, a religion to which his personal experience may have added a distinctive element which eludes our search but which may perhaps be found in his emphasis on the mercy of God. Such a characteristic is only to be expected in the teaching of a prophet who came to urge men to repent and be saved.

IV

THE ACTIVITY OF GOD

All the evidence suggests that Jesus thought of the abode of God in the same way as his contemporaries. He speaks of heaven, angels, Gehenna, demons, with an entire absence of definition or description, as if these current conceptions were self-evident.[3] Heaven is above, hell is below. Even today, for simple folk, their locality remains unchanged, and there was no reason why Jesus should attempt to alter these ancient conceptions, which, no doubt, remained vague in his mind as in the minds of his contemporaries.

---

[1] Matt. vi. 11 (the Lord's Prayer) ; Matt. vi. 26 ; Luke xii. 24 *ff.* ; Matt. x. 29 ; Luke xii. 6 *ff.*

[2] **LXVII**, 135.   [3] **CCXXXV**, 127.

It does not appear that he regarded the relation between man and the heavenly Father as needing any kind of intermediary agency, either *personal*, through one of the heavenly hierarchy, for instance, or *ritual*, as by means of what we should call a sacrament.[1] He was aware, of course, that God was surrounded by angels, whom he used to communicate his will to men, or as instruments of his activities on earth. If he had not shared in this belief he would not have belonged to his people or his generation. Nevertheless, he also believed that there was a direct and personal relation between the human soul and God. While there is no doubt that he was actually baptized in the Jordan, there is nothing to suggest that he regarded his baptism as a *sacrament*, that is, a ritual act capable of imparting some supernatural gift. He certainly did not enjoin the rite upon his disciples, for there is no evidence to this effect in the Synoptists. Moreover, the Eucharist as a sacrament of communion with the Lord is wholly foreign to his thought. The passages which record his institution of the Eucharist (Mark xiv. 22 *ff.* ; Matt. xxvi. 26 *ff.* ; Luke xxii. 19 *ff.*), to which we shall refer again, do not go so far as to attribute to him the institution of the Pauline Eucharist, and even what they do relate is far removed from historical reality. Jesus may be said to have held that man possesses an inward sense of God, and that this consciousness naturally expresses itself in love, the love of man to God, and of God for man. Hence he felt no need for rites through which grace might be conferred or communion secured. It may be observed in passing that such a conception could only arise in the mind of one whose practical piety knew no liturgical rites, but was confined to the simple synagogue and family worship. Such a type of piety was a natural growth in the mind of a prophet reared among simple and godly folk, and who was ever conscious of the indwelling presence of God.

With regard to God's activity in Nature, it has already been shown that God's contact with Nature is as direct as his relations with man. While man has immediate consciousness of the will of God, and the prime law of his being is to live in accordance with it (Matt. vii. 21), even as Jesus himself does (Mark. iii. 35), the obedience of Nature is blind and passive. It is in this respect that the relation between Nature and God differs from that between God and man, whose unregenerate impulses, self-will and hardness of heart are often in conflict with the divine order of things.[2]

From this absolute and direct rule of God over the world

[1] CLX, 125.   [2] CXC, 100.

it follows logically that God is the responsible source of everything, including evil and suffering. Jesus does not seem to have
been troubled by this formidable problem which has so sorely
distressed the minds of many Christians. Neither does he seem
to have been greatly influenced by the belief, current in his
time, that bodily suffering was always a punishment. In a
passage which there is good ground for regarding as authentic,
although it only occurs in Luke (xiii. 1 *ff.*), he mentions the
miserable fate of the Galileans, whose blood Pilate had mingled
with their sacrifices, and refers to the fall of the Tower of Siloam,
which slew eighteen persons. He does not assume that the
victims in each case had received the due reward of their sins,
he merely asserts that they were no worse than others, and
regards their wretched fate as a warning to his hearers and an
incentive to repentance in order to escape eternal death. The
problem of evil in relation to the moral government of God
never really engages his attention.[1]

The same may be said about what we may call the demonology of Jesus. For him Satan is the enemy of God, hostile
to his activities and his creatures. The man of God is everywhere confronted by the Evil One or his emissaries, and one
of his appointed tasks is to repel them and to drive them out
of the bodies of the unfortunate individuals who are possessed
by them. Although Satan reigns over the present age and is the
cause of the victory of sin, he cannot be compared with Ahri-
man, the evil deity of the Mazdeans, co-equal in power with
Ormuzd, the good God; since the power of Satan bears no
comparison with that of God, nor even with that of the servant
of God. Hence it is not right to regard him as the sole author
of evil, since evil, in the last resort, always remains subject
to the will of God. But the difficult problem raised by these
two aspects of evil never presented itself to the mind of Jesus.
His concern was with *moral evil*, sin; as for physical evil, he
always endeavoured to cure it, without, as far as we know,
speculating on its nature and origin. Thus he held to the
absolute sovereignty of God without troubling about the serious
difficulties which it involves.

The question arises whether the absoluteness of this sovereignty is such as to involve man in utter determinism, to leave
him bound hand and foot by predestination. There are certain
passages which seem, at first, to answer the question in the
affirmative.[2] For instance, when the sons of Zebedee demand
from Jesus the best places in the Kingdom (Matt. xx. 23 *ff.*),
he justifies his refusal by saying that they belong to those for

[1] **CIII,** ii, 115; **CXC,** 100.   [2] **XLIV,** 34.

whom they have been prepared by God. In Matthew xxv. 32 *ff.*, a description of the separation of the elect from the reprobate, the sheep from the goats, in the Great Day, we are told that the blessed of the Father shall inherit the kingdom prepared for them from the foundation of the world (*ἀπὸ καταβολῆς κόσμου*), while the cursed (*κατηραμένοι*) go away into eternal fire prepared (for them) by the devil and his angels. Unfortunately this second passage, which is only found in Matthew and belongs to an apocalyptic discourse, may indeed represent significant beliefs of the apostolic generation, but cannot possibly reflect the mind of Jesus.[1] The genuineness of the first passage (with the exception of the words " of my Father "—*τοῦ πατρός μου*) is better attested, but it would be rash to build too much on so frail a foundation. The essential point is that determinism seems so foreign to the main trend of the preaching of Jesus, which becomes unintelligible and actually superfluous if it rests on a belief in predestination, that we must beware of stressing Mark x. 35 *f.* so far as to extract a Pauline tenet from it, for, if it does contain such a belief, it cannot have been uttered by the Nazarene. It is best to conclude that if Jesus really uttered the saying attributed to him by Mark, he can only have intended to say that God, upon whose absolute sovereignty the disposal of places in the Kingdom depended, knew beforehand to whom they would be assigned. When he says elsewhere that the tree is known by its fruit (Matt. vii. 16–20 ; Luke vi. 43 *ff.*), he did not imply that God who created the tree had determined beforehand the quality of its fruit. If the nature of the human trees was unchangeable, there could be no object in exhorting them to change it. Nor, to change the metaphor, would the prophet have said that he came for the sick and not for those that were whole (Mark ii. 17 and Synopsis). Metaphors are not principles, and we should not lay stress upon contradictions which only arise from the refinements of logic, which Jesus and his circle were not in the habit of using.

To sum up : if Jesus was acquainted with the conception of a remote and unapproachable God, he made no use of it ; it is absolutely out of harmony with the nature of his religious experience and of his mission. Direct contact with God is of the essence of the prophetic vocation. But the other two conceptions, that of King and Judge, and that of Father, did form part of his experience. Like many a godly Jew before him, he was able to combine them harmoniously, without subordinating the one to the other. The former belonged, so to speak,

[1] **CIII**, 482.

to the realm of theory, the latter to that of practical piety;
the former relates to the description of God, the latter to the
manner of approaching him. If he did prefer the idea of
Father, the earliest tradition is not aware of it, and it is to be
feared that the influence of the Matthæan redactor, to say
nothing of the Johannine, is responsible for a serious error in
perspective on this point. It is probable that Jesus in his
practice of prayer emphasized this aspect of Jahweh, but we
must hesitate before asserting that through reflection upon this
conception and its implications he brought about an advance
in its significance beyond that which it held for the Jews of
his time. As a matter of fact, we know nothing about the
question at all.

Undoubtedly, his emphasis on the need of loving and trust-
ing in God tended to direct religious experience towards faith
in the fatherly lovingkindness of God rather than to fear of
his judgment : but we must not confuse apostolic or sub-
apostolic implications with the actual mind of Jesus. Being
himself the Son, it was natural that they should ascribe to him
a preference for the term Father. The God of the Nazarene
must have been remarkably like the object of the worship and
devotion of every godly soul among the *poor in Israel.*

CHAPTER IX

THE ETHICS OF JESUS

I

THE STARTING-POINT: METANOIA

WE have seen that a change of heart, *metanoia*, is the essential condition of entrance into the Kingdom. Jesus spent his life in the attempt to convince the Jews of this necessity. His sole purpose in displaying throughout the cities of Israel the miraculous powers (δυνάμεις) which he possessed was to induce them to repent (Matt. xi. 20; Luke x. 13), and he upbraids them for their lack of understanding. Similarly, when he is supposed to have sent out the disciples on their mission in order to extend the range of his personal activities, we are told in Mark vi. 12 that they preached that men should repent (καὶ ἐξελθόντες ἐκήρυξαν ἵνα μετανοῶσιν). It was a Jewish belief that a time would come when Jahweh would make a new covenant with his people on the basis of a moral transformation.[1] By means of this change they would be brought into direct personal contact with God, which from the religious point of view would result in the establishment of his *reign*, the reign of his Law. Hence the connexion between the advent of the Messianic Kingdom and the moral renewal of the chosen people was no new thought to the Jews.[2] Moreover, even the least religious were aware that an inevitable judgment for sin awaited them.[3] Hence any announcement of the advent of the Kingdom was bound to be accompanied by the preaching of *metanoia*, and according to the Gospel tradition, the Baptist did so before the appearance of Jesus, since the advent of the Kingdom seems to be dependent upon individual and national repentance (Enoch l. 2–4). It was essential that there should

---

[1] Jer. xxxi.–xxxiv.; Mic. vii. 18–20; Isa. i. 18; xxxiii. 24; xliii. 25; xliv. 22; Zech. iii. 9; xiii. 1; Dan. ix. 24 (the well-known verse which foretells that the removal of iniquity and the cleansing of transgression will take place after seventy weeks).
[2] **XLIV**, 45.   [3] **III**, 446.

be repentance for the past, and the firm resolve to sin no more
(Wis. xi. 23 ; xii. 10–19 ; Sirach xxxiv. 16), that is, the strict
observance of the Law of Jahweh.

The ethical teaching of Jesus starts from the principle that
no man is free from sin, pure in the eyes of the Lord, that none
is good save God, and hence that all are in need of *metanoia*.[1]
It begins with a growth of conscience, a new sense of sin, a
fundamental change of view regarding religion and morals,
which now become inseparably connected. Doubtless there is
no reason why this fundamental change should not be manifested outwardly by tears and beating of the breast (Luke xviii.
13), as was customary, but the essential thing was a change
of heart, *re-birth*.[2] Actually the idea is only explicitly stated
in a *logion* quoted by Justin Martyr (1 Apol. lx. 4), and which,
though not found in our Gospels, has every appearance of
genuineness : " For the Messiah has said : unless ye be born
again, ye cannot enter into the Kingdom of Heaven " ("Aν μὴ
ἀναγεννηθῆτε).[3] It is, however, implied in Matthew xviii. 3 :
" Verily, I say unto you, unless ye be converted (ἐάν μὴ στραφῆτε) [4]
and become as little children, ye shall not enter into the Kingdom of Heaven." Hence it involves the emergence of a new
man. This is a very different thing from merely keeping the
Law, since it implies the recognition of an attitude of mind
which, while in accordance with the Law, may nevertheless go
beyond and even correct it, since it is the mind of a prophet
who is conscious of a divinely given authority.[5]

This repentance which issues in re-birth is not achieved once
and for all, God being the only judge of its sufficiency ; [6] even
the man who thinketh he stands may fall. Hence, in the
Paternoster, the model prayer attributed to Jesus by the early
Church, the mercy of God is invoked : " Forgive us our trespasses " (Matt. vi. 12 ; Luke xi. 4). This is why the Gospels
tell us that in addition to the first general command to repent,
Jesus lays down a number of special injunctions, the conditions
of salvation, which everyone who has believed in the Good
News must observe until the advent of the Great Day.

Any systematic exposition of the ethics of Jesus, in the

[1] **LXVII**, 162.
[2] **LXVII**, 160. It is a common idea in the Oriental Mysteries.
[3] Perhaps this *logion* is the original form from which the famous
passage in John iii. 3–5 has arisen.
[4] Στρέφω and μετανοέω may be regarded as practically synonymous.
[5] **CIII**, i, 232 ; **LXXIX**, 134.
[6] *Cf.* in Luke xviii. 10–14, the contrast between the Pharisee who
is sure of himself and the publican who smites upon his breast and
prays for mercy.

form of a code of morals [1] whose observance is necessary for salvation, is bound to be artificial, not only because the documents merely give us isolated commands (it is a matter of general agreement that the discourses which contain them are purely editorial), but because, in all probability, Jesus never drew up and expounded in his teaching an organized system of ethics.[2] In his mind there was probably no metaphysical conception of good and evil, and of human nature as such. His attitude was wholly determined by certain fundamental religious emotions which he instinctively used as the criterion of human thoughts and actions. Absorbed by the thought of the sinners whom he saw around him, he addressed his message to them, seizing every opportunity of contact with them to arouse in them feelings like his own towards what he regarded as their sins. It has been well said [3] that " the Gospel is neither a manual of ethics nor of religion. It is a pattern, a person, it is Jesus of Nazareth." In short, the mind of Jesus is his standard of morality ; instinctively it seizes on individual cases of conduct, estimates and indicates what is necessary for amendment.

In the time of Strauss and Renan it was the fashion to think of Jesus as a moral reformer.[4] It is no longer possible to hold such a view. Jesus no more sets out to reform morals than religion or ritual ; for, while he clearly wages unremitting war against whatever he regards as spiritual defilement and deals with many individual cases, he never sets himself in opposition to the morality of the *Torah*, nor to its religious or ritual tendencies, at least where these accord with what he believes to be the true spirit of the *Torah* ; in matters of detail his prescriptions are determined by no other general principle than the religious consideration, never absent from his mind, of pleasing God. A statement which brings us back to the conclusion already frequently indicated that Jesus thinks, speaks and acts as a Hebrew prophet.

It may be added that a real moral reformer could not have avoided dealing with several important problems concerning which the synoptic tradition has nothing to say, such as suicide, abortion, marital infidelity ($\chi\epsilon\iota\rho\sigma\nu\rho\gamma\iota\alpha\iota$), etc. Later on Christian morality found reasons for condemning all these practices, but, obviously, it did not find them in the commandments of the Lord.

---

[1] L–a, i, 241 : *Gesinnungsethik, Interimethik.*
[2] CXLVII, 440.
[3] W. Monod, *La morale de l'Évangile*, ap. *Morales et religion*, 120, Paris, 1909.
[4] CCCXI, 89 *ff.*

For Jesus morality does not exist, strictly speaking, apart from religion ; it is merely an aspect of religion, or, to put it in another way, it results from the contact of religion with daily life and human conduct. There are no earthly values save those which arise from religious considerations,[1] religion is both the determining factor of the moral life and its end. It is a serious falsification of the facts to speak, as is sometimes done today, of the morality of Jesus [2] as a *secular morality*. For, according to the ethical teaching of Jesus the moral life is the life lived in accordance with the will of Jahweh, and all his sayings about righteousness, kindness, mercy, or any other virtue, are wholly determined by his idea of God.[3] For if we remember that the fundamental principle of life is *metanoia*, we shall see that this conception is meaningless apart from its relation to God and his love towards men.

Furthermore, when Jesus sets forth the will of God as the one supreme guiding principle of life, he has no thought of a new legalism. This is well, for otherwise we might find cause for alarm if we were bound to take certain of his precepts, of which we shall speak later, literally as the injunctions of a divinely revealed code of law, a code severer than any tyrant could have enacted. Also we must again insist that there is no question of opposition to the legalism of the *Torah*, or of condemnation of legalism as such, but only of a rejection of an ostentatious and complacent legalism, a formalism which both withers and yet attracts because it renders unnecessary the co-operation of the heart. Jesus clearly believes himself to be in full accord with the *Torah*, and any independence of interpretation, any departure from the point of view of the majority of his fellow-countrymen [4] on his part, are wholly unconscious. His originality consists in basing his interpretation on a certain attitude of heart which goes beyond the arid rules of the Book. For such an attitude no definition of sin is necessary ; and it is in this respect that the righteousness of the disciples of Jesus must surpass that of the scribes and Pharisees (Matt. v. 20).

II

THE SPIRIT OF THE ETHICS OF JESUS

Although, in essence, the ethics of Jesus is merely an aspect of religion, his thinking appears to be completely determined

---

[1] **XXXIII**, 188.   [2] A. Bertrand, *Problèmes de la libre pensée*, 156.
[3] **CIII**, i, 233 ; **LXVII**, 166 ; **XLIV**, 83.
[4] **XLIV**, 47 ; **LXVII**, 76 : *Gesinnung nicht Gesetz* ; **LXXIX**, 157.

by the eschatological expectation of the Kingdom. The Kingdom is to be the reign of divine perfection : " Ye shall be perfect as your heavenly Father is perfect," is the demand of Matthew v. 48. Hence it is justifiable to say that in the teaching of Jesus ethics has become an essential part of the Kingdom.[1]

The acceptance of this principle explains at once those injunctions which, at first sight, seem so inapplicable to the ordinary needs of human society as to " set human experience and actuality at defiance." [2] For instance, the total prohibition of oaths, of the resort to force in resisting evil, the command to turn the left cheek to him who smites the right, to give one's tunic to him who steals one's cloak, to sell all one's possessions, to break all ties of human affection, to replace all forethought by simple trust in God, and other similar injunctions. The practical ordering of a normal life is impossible on such lines, but, for Jesus, normal life was about to come to an end, and he clearly envisaged the life of the Kingdom as being entirely God's affair. This eschatological *Interimethik* (J. Weiss) is, as it were, an anticipation of the ethics of the future. The Gospels certainly contain plenty of injunctions perfectly in keeping with the needs of ordinary life ; but, if we ignore the occasional platitude, they are, as a whole, comprised in the Law of the Kingdom, the law of love. Hence the most striking and typical of these injunctions seem to bear the stamp of a supernatural idealism which ignores the customs and necessities of life. So much is this the case, that even those who yield the most unqualified admiration to the ethical teaching of Jesus can only see in it a paradoxical exaggeration, a demand which is only capable of fulfilment in the spirit and not in the letter.

The true inwardness of the Gospel ethics can only be understood in the light of its essential relation to the Kingdom, whose coming will, in essence, *liquidate humanity*.[3]

Jesus, however, was not unmindful that during the time of waiting for the establishment of the Kingdom his message was addressed to men and that from men repentance was required. Hence he believed that they possessed the capacity to make the necessary effort. While it is certain that he had no metaphysical theory of human nature, he must have had some conception of its general character. He evidently thought that

---

[1] **LXXIX**, 144 ; **XLIV**, 78 ; **CCL**, 153, and especially **CCXXXVIII** ; Silver, *A History of Messianic speculation in Israel*, 8, New York, 1927.

[2] **CIII**, i, 236.   [3] **CCLIII**, 223.

the value of human personality resided in the *soul*,[1] extremely vague [2] as a term of reference, but standing for the immaterial principle of life, and a synonym for the spirit. For him the soul was of incalculable value, and by virtue of it man was superior to all other living creatures. This is why man is worth more than a sparrow (Matt. x. 31), or a sheep (Matt. xii. 12). It is the soul which possesses the power of making the necessary effort, an effort incumbent upon every man,[3] but difficult for the hard of heart. Jesus may have been led to think that human weakness was unable by itself to achieve salvation and needed divine help. Such at least seems to be the force of Matthew xix. 25 *ff.*, where the Nazarene replies to the question of the disciples " Who then can be saved ? " by the assertion " With men it is impossible ($\pi\alpha\varrho\grave{\alpha}$ $\dot{\alpha}\nu\theta\varrho\acute{\omega}\pi\sigma\iota\varsigma$), but with God ($\pi\alpha\varrho\grave{\alpha}$ $\delta\grave{\epsilon}$ $\theta\epsilon\tilde{\omega}$) all things are possible." A statement in which he is at one with the belief of his fellow-countrymen which considered *metanoia*, as well as forgiveness, as the gracious gift of Jahweh. It may not be irrelevant to point out that Jesus never attributes to himself an intercessory rôle, the part of a mediator between man's sin and God's forgiveness. The Creator knows the weakness of his creatures ; he pities them and loves them ; it is his prerogative to grant, postpone or refuse the gift of his mercy. On this point the Nazarene was in accordance with the teaching of the Jewish rabbis.[4]

Nevertheless, the view which ascribes to Jesus an essential pessimism with regard to human nature does not seem to be tenable. He sets forth the attitude of a child (Mark x. 14 ; Matt. xix. 14) as the necessary condition for that return to God involved in *metanoia*, which is the same thing as saying that the man who has become stiff-necked and hardened by sin must regain the softness, the simplicity, the plasticity of the child.[5] Hence, for him, the reason why no man could be called good would be due rather to a sinful life than to a sinful nature. Otherwise the question would naturally arise why, if Jesus believed that human nature was incurably bad, he should have

---

[1] Mark viii. 36–7 ; Matt. xvi. 26 : . . . $\tau\grave{\eta}\nu$ $\psi\upsilon\chi\grave{\eta}\nu$ $\alpha\grave{\upsilon}\tau\sigma\tilde{\upsilon}$. Luke ix. 25 only uses the word $\psi\acute{\upsilon}\chi\eta$ and merely says $\dot{\epsilon}\alpha\upsilon\tau\grave{\sigma}\nu$, " himself." But the thought is quite clear. As in Matthew it is a question of the permanent spiritual element in man.

[2] *Cf.* C. Guignebert, *Remarques sur quelques conceptions chrétiennes antiques touchant l'origine et la nature de l'âme*, ap. **RHPR**, 1929, no. 6, 428–50.

[3] **LXVII**, 165 ; **CCXXXV**, 106.

[4] **LXXIV**, i, 139 *ff.*, on Jewish ideas concerning divine forgiveness.

[5] The Rabbis also thought that God was with the child because the child is innocent ; this is why the *Shekinah* can dwell in him (*Yoma*, 22, *b*). *Cf.* **LXXIV**, i, ch. xv.

troubled to proclaim a message offering the illusion of healing. Far from this being the case, his every action showed that he regarded man as possessing power over his inner self. This inner man is the heart, whence, according to Mark vii. 21 and Matthew xv. 29, arise the most heinous sins, the most abominable defilements. For Jesus the heart is the real man.[1] He may have obtained the idea from the Psalmist where it occurs (vii. 9 ; xxiv. 4 ; li. 8–12) ; but apparently he placed it in the forefront of his ethical teaching. By the testimony of his heart man will be judged ; the conclusion being, doubtless, that the heart was capable of choice between good and evil, although Jesus was aware that man's has a natural tendency to evil.

By sin he understood disobedience to God, the transgression of his commandments. For him the true criterion of what was sin did not consist in comparing man's acts with the requirements of the Decalogue or the written Law, but with what Jesus conceived to be the will of God and well-pleasing to him. It is a vaguer and more subjective, but at the same time a far more elastic and comprehensive criterion of sin than the Jewish legalistic conception of sin as a breach of the *Torah*. Hence it is the testimony of the heart that discloses the existence of sin : the heart, or shall we say, the conscience, knows whether an action is or is not in accordance with the great law of love which we shall go on to define. Whence it follows that although it is easy for man to sin, the slightest movement of conscience suffices to indicate the sin. Moreover, the true origin of sin was to be found in the errors and illusions by which the craft of the devil had beguiled the heart of man. This was the belief of the contemporaries of Jesus, and accordingly the Gospels find little to say concerning the Master's views on the nature of sin.

On the other hand, the Jews were entirely unaccustomed to hear a prophet call himself the friend of sinners, the companion of the fallen. The Pharisees, for example, were afraid of any activities which might compromise their reputation, and we rarely find them engaged in any soul-saving work which might involve suspicion or temptation. Nevertheless, this trait must not be exaggerated, and rabbinic literature by no means ignores the need of helping the sinner, in that it idealizes Aaron as the patron of those who labour to bring back sinners to the *Torah*.[2]

Notwithstanding, it must not be supposed that Jesus started out with the preconceived purpose of fraternizing with a class of people who were despised in Israel ; it was merely that his large heart went out towards those who had special need of

[1] **CXC**, 113 *ff.*
[2] **LXXIV**, i, 56 *ff.* ; 60 *ff.*, which gives a number of examples,

help, and refused to be repelled by their misfortunes.[1] This was not the rabbinical point of view which aimed rather at preventing sin and defilement than at healing them.[2] In the thought of Jesus the world contains both good and bad, and upon all, impartially, God causes his sun to shine and his rain to fall (Matt. v. 45), as if he were indifferent to their actions, but judgment is none the less sure for tarrying, and men will reap the inevitable reward of their deeds at the Day of Judgment. It is clear that there are some who lend a ready ear to the seductions of the Enemy, and who are definitely working on the side of evil, whether they are aware of it or not. These are the people whom Jesus feels himself specially called to enlighten and help (Matt. ix. 12–13). It is these whom he considers best worth winning, a feeling which he thinks is shared by God himself, " for there is joy in heaven over one sinner that repenteth, more than over ninety and nine just persons which need no repentance " (Luke xv. 7 f.). Although this care for the erring (ἁμαρτωλόι) is intelligible in a prophet sprung from the *anavim*, it is doubtful whether it was always appreciated by his contemporaries (Matt. ix. 10–11). But it is an original trait in him, even if less remarkable than has been supposed, since the Pharisees, too, exalted the repentant sinner above the perfect saint (*Berak.* 34, b) ; the rabbis welcomed the penitent sinner with joy, and in spite of Proverbs xxi. 27, which says " the sacrifice of the wicked is an abomination," allowed sinners to bring their offerings to the Temple in order to incite them to contrition.[3]

III

The Law of Love

All that we have hitherto said, and all the evidence still to be drawn from the Gospels, emphasizes the obligation of love. For Jesus, morality and religion alike are based upon the Law of Love. To love God and to love one's neighbour constitute the highest duty and the loftiest virtue, the spring of all other duties and perfections.[4] God himself sets the example of the observance of this law of love of which he is the source, since he patiently bears with evil, and endures the grossest breaches of that which is his due, bestowing his benefits upon the worthless as upon the just, and ever ready to pardon every repentant soul.

[1] CCXXXV, 112. [2] LXXIV, *loc. cit.*
[3] LXXIV, i, 57 *ff.* Cf. also i, 149 *ff.*
[4] LXXIX, 138 ; LXVII, 82 *ff.* ; XLIV, 95.

Jesus is not wont, as we know, to deal in abstract definitions ; hence he provides us with no definition of love, never doubting that every one of his hearers knows what love is and why it is essential.[1] But when we come to analyse the *logia* it is easy to extract examples and, as it were, grades, of what becomes in John the *Great Commandment* ; *purity*, itself an extremely complex virtue,[2] for it is synonymous with *truth*, then purity of motive, *chastity*, purity of disposition, *tolerance* and *kindliness*, purity in estimating and judging conduct, involving the kindred virtues of *humility*, *gentleness* and *pity*, and lastly, *simplicity* of heart and *forgiveness* of wrongs. All these virtues spring from love, and the life which displays them is a life lived in accordance with the mind of God. Hence *holiness* and love are related to one another, and on the other hand, *love towards God* is inseparable from and inconceivable without *love towards one's neighbour.*

" To love one's neighbour as oneself " (Mark xii. 33) is more than all the Temple sacrifices. Further, this love must be displayed towards those who hate us and seek to injure us ; for what merit is there in loving those who love us (Matt. v. 44–7), and how can our Heavenly Father forgive us our trespasses if we do not forgive those who trespass against us (Matt. vi. 14–15) ?

It is hardly possible to maintain that the proclamation of this law of love was a complete religious innovation in Israel ; but solely by virtue of the relation established between the constituent precepts of this law, however universally accepted they may have been,[3] it acquires an absolute and binding

---

[1] According to Abrahams, **LXXIV**, i, 150, the law of brotherly love is a Hebrew conception, and is the glory of the Old Testament. It is to be found in the Pentateuch, the Prophets, and in the Wisdom literature. *Cf.* again in **LXXIV**, i, 18–29 ; *Test. of the XII Patr.*, *Gad*, vi, 1.

[2] **LXVII**, 82 *ff.*, would separate it from the rest as a complement of love itself.

[3] It must be observed that although Lev. xix. 18 certainly says, " *Thou shalt love thy neighbour as thyself,*" the neighbour (πλησίον) is Israel, the fraternity of race and religion (ἀδελφοί, *i.e.* οἱ υἱοὶ τοῦ λαοῦ σου). Rabbinic teaching emphasizes this injunction. There is no explicit statement in the *Torah* that it is obligatory to hate one's enemies ; but there are many passages in the Old Testament which express a lively hatred towards the enemies of God who are identified with those of Israel (*cf.*, for instance, Exod. xxxiv. 12 ; Deut. vii. 2 ; **CII**, 115). It is possible, moreover, that the obligation to hate such enemies was introduced into the sacred text as a gloss (see discussion in **CVII**, ii, 78 *f.*). In any case, the reputation of the Jews in this respect was well known. Tacitus tells us that, while extremely tolerant towards one another, they practised *adversus omnes alios hostile odium* (*Hist.*, 5, 5). In the Gospels it is not a question of the enemies of Israel, the enemies

importance whose paradoxical character must have surprised the Jews themselves. In order to understand its effect upon them we must imagine an insignificant group of puritans, of recluses withdrawn from the world, for this is how the Jews in general regarded them, claiming to impose upon us their impossible dream as the fundamental law of life.

While it is a question of practical life, it is not a life lived in an earthly City that is at issue, but the eternal life of the City of God. Nevertheless, the Gospels do not give us an impression of complete detachment from the world and its affairs. Matthew v. 45 speaks of sunshine and rain as desirable things, and Matthew vi. 28 expresses the thoughts of one who delighted in beholding the lilies of the field. It is no doubt somewhat of an exaggeration to find in this passage and in the metaphors of the parables the art of the poet,[1] but it cannot be denied that the Nazarene prophet displays a marked feeling for the realities of nature which surround him. Moreover, several passages show that Jesus knows the meaning of hunger and is aware that it must be taken into consideration. For example, Mark ii. 25 *ff.*, where he places the need of food above the law of the Sabbath. Elsewhere (Mark vii. 9 *ff.*), he maintains the right of parents to be supported by their children by condemning the Pharisaic abuse of *Corban*.[2] He protects the rights of the wife against arbitrary divorce (Mark x. 5 *ff.*). While such points must not be overstressed, they suffice to prove that though he might have done, Jesus felt no hostility towards the expression of earthly needs.

We have already seen that he had no special leaning towards asceticism. If St. Paul is to be believed (1 Cor. vii. 10–11, 25–6), he had given commandment concerning the sanctity of marriage, but had not enjoined virginity or abstinence from sexual intercourse, injunctions which would certainly have been difficult to impose upon his fellow-countrymen. It is no less noteworthy that the Synoptics contain no injunction concerning ceremonial fasting and abstinence from food, and Matthew xv. 11 expressly

of God, but of one's personal enemies, those who entertain private ill-feeling against us. No Rabbinic passage can be cited which enjoins love towards such; but there are passages which advise abstaining from rejoicing over their disasters, lest the anger of God should turn away from them, and there are many injunctions to forgive them. Evidence can be found in **LXXIV**, 150 *ff. Cf.* **CVI**, 71; **CII**, 127; **XCIX**, 50; **LXXX**, 59–104.

   [1] **XLIV**, 81.

   [2] *Corban* = δῶρον θεοῦ (Jos., *C. Apion*, i, 22). Anything consecrated to God may not be used for secular purposes. Hence, if the undutiful son says that he has consecrated to God that which might support his parents, they have no claim on him,

states, " Not that which entereth into the mouth defiles the man." While this may be the statement of a Hellenized Christian, and as a denial of the *Torah* would be inconceivable in the mouth of a Jew, it may not be rash to infer from it that the Master had not stressed asceticism with regard to food. Moreover, he is represented as occasionally seated at a rich man's table. While he lives austerely and displays indifference as to the pleasures of eating, he sets no example of asceticism.[1] Further, the glimpses which we have of the life of the disciples, who knew him intimately, and who do not seem to have departed from his principles, would not suggest that they were ascetics, and we learn from Paul (1 Cor. ix. 5) that Peter, the other Apostles, and the brethren of the Lord, had not separated from their wives.

Hence Jesus had not made individual salvation depend upon separation from the world and daily life ; his vision was rather of salvation through overcoming the world. Nevertheless, it must be repeated, there are a certain number of assertions, even injunctions, attributed to him by the Evangelists and which they would have no reason for inventing, which savour of asceticism and separation from the world.[2] For example, the ascetic antithesis seems to be implied in the command not to lay up treasure on earth but in heaven (Matt. vi. 19 *ff.*). This impression is strengthened by the assertion that no man can serve two masters, God and Mammon, the latter representing the God of worldly possessions (Matt. vi. 24).[3] The pursuit of gain and the various forms of property should be the objects of man's desire, and a wise regard for his welfare will lead him to renounce them utterly (Mark x. 17–27). However, a well-known incident, told in Matthew xix. 16, affords an interesting modification of this impression. A well-meaning young man came to Jesus and asked him what he must do to obtain eternal life (τὴν ζωὴν αἰώνιον) and the prophet answers by reminding him of the chief commandments of the Decalogue. When the young man says that he has kept them all, the Master adds : " If thou wilt be perfect (εἰ θέλεις τέλειος εἶναι) sell all that thou hast and give to the poor, and thou shalt have treasure in heaven ; and come, follow me." By this he implies that perfection can only be achieved by entire surrender to the spiritual

---

[1] XLIV, 51 ; CCXXXV, 123 ; CXC, 134 *ff.*

[2] At first sight they have *einen entschieden, asketischen, weltfeindlichen Charakter* (XLIV, 78).

[3] *Mammon* is an Aramaic word meaning *wealth*. Later on, but not before the Middle Ages, Mammon became a heathen god of wealth. In Matthew he is already conceived of as a person, at least metaphorically, *Cf.* CVI, 86,

life, complete freedom from earthly cares, and deliverance from all desire for wealth. Nevertheless, perfection is not essential for salvation. In the form in which it has come down to us the passage has certainly been edited : it displays a designed antithesis between the vision of Christian perfection based on love and complete separation from the world, and the Jewish ideal of perfection according to the Law ; but it is possible that if Jesus had intended to exclude from the Kingdom all those who had worldly possessions, the incident would have been otherwise presented. On the other hand, the harshly para-doxical saying that it is harder for a rich man to enter the Kingdom of heaven than for a camel to go through the eye of a needle (Matt. xix. 23–4), seems, at first sight, to be incapable of mitigation, and leaves the rich man with his riches in a hopeless position. Various attempts have been made to soften the paradox, such as the substitution of κάμιλος, a rope, for κάμηλος, a camel, or the suggestion that the Needle's Eye was the name of a low gate in Jerusalem. Such attempts are futile, since it was the object of the Gospel writer to suggest an insurmountable obstacle ; he was not concerned to seem coherent and logical.[1]

Similarly, it is a waste of time to attempt to attenuate the meaning of those *logia* which emphasize the need of taking no thought for clothing or for the morrow's food (Matt. vi. 25 *ff.*). Nor could those who laid store by family ties have welcomed such sayings as that contained in Matthew viii. 21 *ff.* : " And another of his disciples said to him : Lord, suffer me first to go and bury my father. But Jesus answered him : Let the dead bury their dead, and follow thou me."

Now we know that for a pious Jew the duty of burying his father was a paramount obligation.[2] Of a similar tenor is the well-known passage in Matthew x. 37, and especially its more elaborate form in Luke xiv. 26, which makes true discipleship depend upon complete severance of all family ties.[3] There is a distinctly disturbing element in the conception of a fundamental antagonism between those early relations which are essential to human life and the attainment of the other life, the life according to God.[4]

[1] **XCVIII**, 117.

[2] **XCIX**, 77. The attempt has been to soften the repellent severity of this *logion* by the claim that the Greek text is contradictory, and that the Aramaic means : Leave the dead to the sextons. It is an unwarrantable hypothesis. *Cf.* **CVII**, i, 134.

[3] *Cf.* **CCL**, 154, for a similar piece of advice given by Philo to a proselyte who was beset by the requirements of idolatry in his family.

[4] It must not be forgotten that Rabbinic literature is irreproachable in respect of the honour due to parents. *Cf.* **LXXX**, 249 *ff.*

It is impossible to avoid the conclusion that, when Jesus, in order to explain to his disciples how their relations with one another should be regulated, contrasts his injunction with the organization of the State (Matt. xx. 25 *ff.* : " Ye know that the rulers of the Gentiles lord it over them, and their great ones exercise authority over them. . . ."), he implies that this organization which he did not think fit to challenge directly was, in his estimation, opposed to the mind of God.

Finally, what practical value can be attached, for those who must live in human society, to such precepts as those in Matthew v. 39 *ff.*, where evil is not to be resisted by force, where violent assault and robbery are to be endured ?   Or those in Mark ix. 43 : pluck out the eye, cut off the hand which may be the occasion of stumbling ; better to enter into the Kingdom maimed than to be cast unmutilated into Gehenna ?

While an examination of each passage may not vindicate its genuineness in every case, it is difficult to see why tradition should have invented them all, since they can never have been regarded as practical directions for conduct, save by a few cloistered fanatics, an exception proving the rule.   The question of genuineness arises rather in connexion with those sayings which contradict or correct those which we have just quoted, as though attempting to evade their unpalatable severity.

The true state of the case is that from the point of Jesus his utterances involved no paradox.   For him there was no question of a petty insignificant movement, painfully and gradually striving towards perfection, but of the measures necessary to prepare for the setting up of the divine community of the Kingdom.   What was required of man was that he should co-operate to this end by practising the two comprehensive and essential virtues of love and abnegation of those worldly possessions whose claims hindered him from the attainment of *metanoia*.   While it may be admitted that the plucking out of the eye or the cutting off of the hand are metaphors, the rest of the sayings must be taken literally.

For it is clear that they constitute the pattern of a life whose perfection must be estimated in the light of the imminence of the Kingdom, the pattern of a life which is purely transitory. It must not be forgotten that the demands embodied in these sayings constitute the essential condition of such a life.   Undoubtedly they have a harsh appearance, but the attempt to soften them, to round off their sharp corners at any cost can only yield unsound and unsatisfactory results.   Nothing can obliterate the fact that they embody the ethics of an eschatological movement, the practical morality of salvation.   Jesus does not lay it down, at least according to the Gospels as we have them, as a standard to be rigorously and universally imposed, but as the only really certain means of attaining the goal, the means which must be employed by anyone who is afraid of missing it. These paradoxical utterances have been discussed either as the expression of " an ideal whose realization would constitute a separate society," [1] or as setting forth the monastic ideal (Renan). This is not the point. The agelong effort to represent the ethics of Jesus as the adequate expression of an absolute ethic does not harmonize with the freedom of mind, usually preserved in dealing with the Baptist, necessary to understand that the Nazarene could and did preach ideals of conduct for a specific movement,[2] ideals which, in general, took no account of possibilities arising out of situations which it was the very object of the movement to despise or destroy. But if that is so it would seem surprising that Jesus should contradict himself, that he should appear, in some passages, to admit the possession of wealth and of those family ties which, elsewhere, he had so light-heartedly swept away. In some cases the problem may be solved by calling such passages secondary modifications, but not in every case. When such inconsistencies embarrass us, we must remember that Jesus was not governed by our logic, and that many of the *logia* have come down to us detached from the setting which would have made them perfectly intelligible to us. Above all it must be observed that in his mind, and in the law of love which determined the form of his thinking, there was inherent a kind of principle of contradiction, by which, all unconsciously, he appears to confirm in detail what he rejects in its totality. He may have been induced, in particular cases which appealed to his emotions, to take into account the difficulties which his principles would ignore. He may have accepted individual compromises and approximations in the ascent towards that divine perfection which is the raison d'être and the goal of *metanoia*.

On the other hand, it is necessary to avoid introducing the ideas of our own time into the words which Jesus may have used. For instance, by " poor " he may not necessarily have meant the destitute : he might equally have been referring to the *anavim*. When we find in Matthew v. 3 : " Blessed are the poor in spirit " (μακάριοι οἱ πτωχοὶ τῷ πνεύματι), where Luke vi. 20

[1] De Faye, *Étude sur les origines des Églises de l'âge apostolique*, 113, Paris, 1909.

[2] It is not maintained that Jesus belonged to a sect, a matter of which we know nothing, but only that the spirit of his ethical teaching has a sectarian character.

only reads " Blessed are ye poor," the words " in spirit " (τῷ
πνέυματι), although a gloss, are a truer rendering of the meaning
of the *logion* than Luke's more literal translation. The poor
in question are those who possess the real spirit of poverty and
who, unperturbed by material cares, place their whole trust in
God.[1] They are probably not rich, but belong, as a rule, to the
am-haareṣ,[2] but their poverty does not constitute their title to
the Kingdom. There is nothing to prove that Jesus was
specially interested in poverty, any more than in wealth. It is
an extremely simple-minded point of view which would regard
Jesus as a precursor of Socialism who came to preach the Gospel
of the poor, on the basis of the saying attributed to him in
Matthew xi. 5 : " the poor have the Gospel [3] preached to them ";
for, apart from the fact that the idea is found in Isaiah lxi. 1,
it is always to the *anavim* that such passages refer. He may
have felt a natural sympathy for the lowly, while recognizing
the extent of their spiritual need, but it does not appear that
he regarded poverty as in any way constituting a title to the
Kingdom. It is a proof of the fundamental sanity of Jesus,
since, by itself, poverty is not more efficacious than wealth in
liberating the mind from terrestrial cares.[4] In truth, Jesus
was only interested with the spiritually poor, he who lives as
though he had nothing and desired nothing.

Conversely, it is only the rich in the bad sense who is the
object of Jesus' reprobation, he who is the slave of his possessions ; nor had he, as far as we know, any objection in principle
to the right to possess property and to enjoy it. He never
says that the essential condition of salvation lies in the surrender
of possessions. On the contrary, he is aware that riches render
possible many forms of good deeds which can be most profitable
to the doer.[5] Nothing could be further removed from Socialism.
What concerns him is the spirit in which poverty or riches
are accepted, and not the mere fact of being either rich or
poor.

[1] CXV, 13.   [2] CVII, ii, 33.   [3] XLIV, 96.

[4] The Rabbis found great cause for anxiety in the moral dangers
arising from poverty (*cf.* LXXX, 274 *ff.*) ; but they did not think that
it was an evil in itself, any more than riches were a good. A man
must rise above both. This was also the thought of Jesus. *Cf.* LXXIV,
i, ch. xiv.

[5] *Cf.* Luke xvi. 9–11, and Syn.; xix. 8.

II

THE PRACTICAL LIFE [1]

Similarly, with regard to work, the main problem does not
consist in finding out whether it is possible to live without
taking thought for the future, since it has been and continues
to be solved in the East to the satisfaction of those who have
tried it. It is to discover whether Jesus, inclined in the true
prophetic manner to carry trust in God to its limits, discouraged work. As a matter of fact, he never speaks about it. Nor
was it necessary, since work is the basis of the security and
organization of that human life whose approaching end he was
announcing. He lived in the midst of working-men, and though
he may have drawn some of them from their occupations to
follow him, there is no evidence that he recommended to them
the life of contemplation while they waited for the Great Day.
His standpoint never altered : what mattered to him was that
work should not absorb the whole of the religious man's attention, and if he could free himself entirely from it, so much the
better. It need hardly be added that there is no question of
regarding work as a social duty, nor is it relevant to inquire
what would be the effect of applying in a universal sense to a
stable society the injunction to take no thought for the morrow.

We are led to a similar conclusion when we consider the case
of the family. There is nothing surprising in the fact that the
prophet laid no great store by family ties in the light of his
expectation of the Kingdom.[2] But when the Christian family
came into being, believers were bound to maintain, as they do
still, that Jesus both foresaw it and founded it. If that were
so, the Gospel tradition would involve us in an insoluble contradiction. But it is not so. One passage, and one only (Mark x.
3 *ff.*), is cited as giving guidance concerning divorce. It seems
probable that ancient tradition absolutely prohibited divorce
(*cf.* Luke xvi. 18), and that it is the Matthæan redactor who
has softened the prohibition by adding " except for adultery "
(Matt. v. 32 ; xix. 9). It has been inferred from this passage that
" Our Lord recognized the institution of the family as sacred
and divine," [3] that he " preserves and purifies it by establishing
it as a union which cannot legitimately be broken." [4] Such an
inference does violence to the text, and confuses, in the mind

---

[1] Shailer Matthews, *Jesus on Social Institutions*, London, 1928.
[2] **LXXIX**, 142 ; **CLXII**, 421.   [3] **CCXXXV**, 121.
[4] **CXC**, 132. *Cf.* **XLIV**, 96, who finds in Jesus *eine hohe sittliche
Wertung der Ehe und Familie.*

of Jesus, an expression of *love* with a *law*, and the suggestion of a highly laudable state of mind with a social obligation. In the view of Jesus, to put away one's wife for any cause whatever was an evil deed, opposed to the law of love, and on this point the Pharisees were agreed with him.[1] He will not tolerate in those who desire to attain the Kingdom any tendency to profit by the leniency of the *Torah* in the matter of divorce. It is a practical direction with which we may compare the parallel case of illegal tolerance displayed by Jesus towards the adulterous woman (John viii. 3 *ff.*). None the less all the evidence goes to show that the ideal of Jesus was the renunciation of sexual relations, which, moreover, would find no place in the Kingdom (Mark xii. 25 and Synopsis).

This can hardly be called founding the family. The attempt has also been made,[2] on the basis of Matthew xix. 5 : " He made them male and female," to prove that Jesus affirmed the equality of the sexes. The interpretation goes far beyond the text ; but even if it could be taken as probable, there could be no question here of *feminism*. The kind of equality contemplated by Jesus could only have been religious, a very different matter. Even that implied some advance, since the religion of Jahweh was a religion for men.[3] Finally, it would be rash to claim that Jesus was interested in social economics because he considered it disgraceful that a son should not support an indigent father (Matt. xv. 5 *ff.*). He could only have been concerned with the problem if he had believed that there was a future for humanity, but this was not his belief.

It seems waste of time to demonstrate at length that Jesus was not interested in what we call political morality. His preaching had no relation to the normal conditions of a State and took no account of them. It has been said [4] that this was because the Jews had so long been governed by foreigners ; the true reason was because the State was an organization belonging to the temporal order of this age, with which Jesus had no concern. The well-known passage in Mark xii. 17 : " Render to Cæsar the things which are Cæsar's," namely, the

---

[1] **LXXIV,** i, ch. ix, 67 *ff.* They often quoted Mal. ii. 16 : " *For I hate putting away, saith the Lord.*" The Rabbis believed in the divine origin of marriage, created by God in heaven. Shammai limited the right of divorce to the case of adultery, as in Matt. v. 32. But in practice these excellent principles were rendered nugatory, and even Hillel allowed a man to divorce his wife for any cause.

[2] **XLIV,** 96.

[3] **CCLXXXVIII,** 437, even sees in the establishment of this religious equality one of the great original elements in the teaching of Jesus.

[4] **CCL,** 152 *ff.*

coin which bore his image and was used to pay taxes [1]—" and to God the things which are God's," has been mishandled to the point of contradiction in the attempt to prove that the prophet acknowledged the rights of the State side by side with those of God. Whereas, what he really did was to subordinate the demands of an earthly lord to the rights of God, while eluding the trap set for him by his enemies. They asked him whether it was right to pay tribute to Rome : if he said, No, he was at once in danger ; if he said, Yes, he would be condemned in the estimation of pious Jews. Hence he did not say : Do not pay, disclaim all service to the State. He did not raise the question since it did not interest him to bring about a revolution in a dying world. His attitude was that of a prophet who is not concerned with the contingent. The Roman tribute can be endured like hunger and thirst, as being an external necessity which has no bearing on the true life.[2]

It has been said [3] that "Civil or public law constitute a domain in which the first Christian generation could take its place without revolution, with the ultimate end in view of permeating them with its own spirit." The truth of the matter is that Jesus took no account of either civil or public law, which was a fortunate thing for the future of the Christian life ; for if he had attempted to apply his principles to them systematically in even the smallest degree, he would have become a kind of Doukhobor. Granted the continuance of the present age, his type of mind tended to a Tolstoyan solution of the problem thus presented. Christians such as Tertullian had in mind when he wrote the *De corona militis* would have understood him perfectly. If, on the other hand, throughout the course of the Christian era, Christianity has manifested itself as the mainstay of civil and public law, it is because the law adapted the Gospel to its own requirements at the cost, not only of the letter of its most vital injunctions, but of its very spirit. Nothing else was possible when life itself was at stake ; but Jesus was not concerned with continuance of this life.

His attitude was the same with regard to what we call *culture*. For him there was no question of science and its claims or of civilization and its amenities. No doubt, as far as he knew them, and his knowledge was negligible, he was not friendly

---

[1] *Cf.* Matt. xxii. 15 *ff.* ; Luke xx. 20 *ff.*

[2] It will be obvious that the above argument rests upon the assumption of the authenticity of the *logion*, and that it has no other ground. *Cf.* **CLXII**, 432 ; **LXXIV**, 62 *ff.*, concerning the similar idea developed in Rabbinic teaching.

[3] **CXC**, 131.

to them, and if he had been called upon to express an opinion about them, he would certainly have condemned them, as representing, so to speak, the order of this age, the age whose disappearance he proclaimed and expected. It is the height of absurdity to use the teaching of Jesus to vindicate modern civilization.

Hence there does not seem to be any contradiction in the teaching of the Nazarene, but, on the contrary, an extraordinary consistency and coherence in his basic ideas. We create our own difficulties by failing to read the documents in their historical perspective. The coming Kingdom stands opposed to the present Age ; Jesus longs for the former, he is completely indifferent to the latter ; but the law of love, his controlling and inspiring motive, leads him to a spontaneous and illogical relaxation in individual cases of the severity which the logical application of his principles would demand.

Let us now attempt a general summing-up of the ethical teaching of Jesus.

Strictly speaking Jesus has no ethics, if we are to understand by the term a reasoned, systematic code of morals, drawn up with a definite view to its application to the needs of daily life. The teaching of Jesus had no temporary or specific orientation to the present world order.[1] On the contrary, its fundamental purpose is to produce in man, one might almost say, à priori, a state of mind, a deep-seated and, so to speak, an instinctive tendency towards detachment from this life, a point of view directed wholly towards the realization of a life absolved from the claims and conditions of this present life.

The specific injunctions which the teaching of Jesus offers to meet the need of particular occasions display no originality whatever. They show affinities with biblical and rabbinical Wisdom-literature, and even with the universal fund of practical wisdom. It is a waste of time to attempt to disprove this statement.[2] From this point of view the marvellous superiority of Christian ethics is only a theological illusion.[3] This is not to say that, in the course of time and under the pressure of the needs of a life which showed no signs of coming to an end, Christianity did not ultimately build up a lofty and practical morality, nor that the teaching of Jesus, at least his law of love, did not constitute a very important ferment in this process ; what we maintain is that the thought of Jesus is not, in this respect, any more than in others, to be confused with

[1] CXLVII, 440.
[2] CCL, 152 ; XLIV, 78 ; XXXIII, 197. *Cf.* LXXIX, 136 ; CLI, 199.
[3] CLIII, 103.

the thinking of the Fathers. The real originality of Jesus consists (1) in his view of human life, with its contingencies and its claims, in the light of the coming Day, which for him was about to dawn ; (2) in his entire obsession with the Kingdom ; (3) in the supremacy of this law of love resulting from his eschatological preoccupation, or, at least, which can only be explained by it.

Theologians, compelled to admit that the nucleus of the teaching of Jesus preserved in Christian ethics are not peculiar to him, are willing to acknowledge that his is the originality of having brought them together and set them forth as the pattern of the life which must be lived by a real man.[1] Perhaps it would be truer to say, the life of a man who surrenders life by subordinating it to that coming transformation of the world in which it will be absorbed in God. In addition, it should be said that the alleged collection of the ethical precepts of Jesus does not present the appearance of anything more than an undesigned collection.

Taken by itself, this supposedly perfect ethics is strange and disturbing to us.[2] What we call Christian ethics, the system based on the sporadic and empirical moral teaching of the Nazarene, is the result of the failure of the vision of Jesus. This vision is meaningless save in relation to what he believed to be the ultimate goal of man and of the world.

[1] **CLXXX**, 51 *ff.*

[2] **CLXXVI**, 317 (according to von Hartmann): *Seine ethik ist uns fremd und ausstössig . . .*

CHAPTER X

THE ESCHATOLOGY OF JESUS

I

JESUS' CONCEPTION OF THE LAST THINGS

AT first sight the Synoptists appear to suggest that Jesus, in spite of his entire preoccupation with the final destiny of man, had formulated no system of eschatology, any more than he possessed a system of ethics. The one fixed object of his interest was the life which led to the Kingdom, and upon this he concentrated the attention of his disciples.

In the circle in which he moved, men's minds were occupied with lurid and fantastic descriptions of the events which would occur when the present age gave place to that which was to come. It was commonly believed that some or all of the unnumbered dead, each clothed with a bodily form which would preserve the individuality of its possessor, would rise from their graves. Standing before the Judge of all, each would receive the due record of his earthly life. The righteous would enter into a blessed life in the Kingdom of God, while the wicked—on the supposition that they came out of Sheol— would be banished into the abyss of darkness and misery to share the company of the Devil. The attitude of Jesus towards these fantastic pictures, which were probably never received as an essential part of the faith of Israel, is hard to determine. The main difficulty lies in the fact that the hope which was the motive and support of the mission of the Nazarene, namely, the immediate advent of the Kingdom, was never realized. It is clear that the disciples were brought by the force of circumstances to modify in some degree the point of view of their Master, and it is to be feared that our Gospels, without informing us of the fact, give us the point of view of the redactors rather than that of Jesus.

We find the clearest proof of this in the redactional differences which can easily be discerned in the parallel passages. It is equally clear that passages of the Old Testament have been used to supplement and fill out the details of the tradition, without the slightest probability that they were used by Jesus himself for this purpose. Be that as it may, it is obvious that Jesus' picture of the last things, in so far as the cursory indications of the Gospels enable us to reconstruct it, was neither clear, coherent, nor complete.

It is certainly improbable that he entirely discarded the popular apocalyptic. Indeed, it is to be noted [1] that in the passages in which he is recorded as describing the Last Day, he not only adopts the language of apocalyptic, but follows the general plan of the apocalyptic drama. There may have been later glosses or additions intended to supplement his silence concerning certain points, but it is hard to explain his silence save by the hypothesis that he accepted the views current in his time.[2] Hence the views which the Gospel writers attribute to him would probably show no great divergence from those which he would himself have expressed.

Mark xiii contains an account of the great final crisis (probably derived from the *logia* and utilized by Matt. xxiv. and Luke xxi.[3]; there would be disorder, uprisings, and tribulations preceding the appearance of the Messiah ; the " abomination of desolation " would be set up " where it ought not to be," that is, in the Temple (xiii. 14 : τὸ βδέλυγμα τῆς ἐρημώσεως),[4] followed by a period of unspeakable disasters in which all flesh would perish if God had not shortened the days ; there would be upheavals of the natural order, and then the Son of Man would appear with all the fantastic accompaniments of the apocalypse of Daniel. Unfortunately, the genuineness of this menacing passage cannot be maintained, as can easily be demonstrated by the liberties which the three redactors have taken with it.[5] The conservative critics, at least those whose courage has failed before the evidence, such as Dewick and Batiffol, acknowledge the fact, only maintaining that the redactor may have preserved some genuine *logia* in the framework of this invented utterance. It may be so, but these genuine fragments are difficult to disentangle, since the passage

---

[1] CCLIII, 216.

[2] Batiffol, CXC, 274, embarrassed by this situation, at once advises us not to lose sight of " *the purely moral value* " assigned by Jesus " *to the conceptions enshrined in the popular belief of his time.*" It is to be feared that the word " *moral* " is meaningless here, as is often the case.

[3] It is reproduced again by the two Gospel writers in Matt. x. 17–22 and Luke xii. 11–12, the one probably following Mark and the other Q.

[4] The redactor is thinking of a profanation of the Temple, without, perhaps, specifying its nature. *Cf.* CXIV, 103.

[5] There is an interesting treatment of the point in XXIV, i, 125 *f.*

does not reflect the belief of the actual disciples of Jesus but
that of men who were disturbed and alarmed by the delay of
the *parousia*, and who sought to confirm their hope by the
belief, following the pattern of Jewish apocalyptic, that such
events would be the sign of the advent of the promised day.[1]
The Jewish colouring of this picture is so strong as to lend some
probability to the view that its framework at least is derived
from a short pre-Christian apocalypse. Reason demands that
the conservative critics who refuse to admit this possibility
should acknowledge at least that Jesus here speaks exactly as
a Jew would have done. Such a view is entirely probable, for
if Jesus had spoken otherwise it is difficult to believe that the
tradition would not have shown traces of the difference and
have sought to supplement it from Jewish apocalyptic.

It was never in the mind of Jesus that the Kingdom would
be reserved solely for those of the righteous who would be alive
at the dawn of the Great Day. Various views were current in
his time concerning those who would be included in the future
kingdom, but the most conservative estimates allowed that the
righteous who had lived in earlier days, at least those belonging
to Israel, would share in the kingdom. The Sadducees seem
to have been the only Jews who did not believe in the Resurrection (Mark xii. 18). The early Jews, being *monists*, could not
conceive of a future life for man save under the form of a re-
constitution of his physical nature ; but the adoption by Jewish
thought of Greek *dualism* which despised the body and connected
immortality with the spiritual nature of man, had led to complications. Difficult questions were raised by the necessity of
reconciling the contradictory beliefs in the resurrection of the
body and the immortality of the soul, although in practice a
compromise might be possible. For example, it was difficult
to decide whether the resurrection was one of the body or of the
individual, and if of the latter, how the individuality was to
be preserved. Concerning these two points, taken separately
or in their relation to one another, Jesus, so far as we know,
said nothing. He believed in the resurrection, and he seems
to have held that there was an immortal principle in man which
our sources call the *soul* ($\psi\acute{v}\chi\eta$), without defining it ; it was
possible for an evil life to destroy it.[2] Since this principle was
distinct from the body, it might be thought that it was this
which would be manifested at the resurrection.

---

[1] **CXIV**, 107. Note in particular the prediction in xiii, 30–1 : " *This
generation shall not pass away till all be fulfilled. Heaven and earth
shall pass away, but my words shall not pass away.*"
[2] **CCLIII**, 220.

But there was still the question of what would become of it
after the death of the body. On this point Jesus made no
definite statement, [1] and it seems a rash proceeding to attempt
to construct a reply out of the few casual utterances recorded
in our sources. However, if he had believed that the essential
human personality resided in the immortal soul alone, the
expectation and preaching of the Kingdom would have been
superfluous. [2] The physical transformation of the natural order
would have been a dream without purpose. The world, in
the divine sense, since the death of the first man, was constituted by the sum of all the souls of the righteous of past generations. Hence it already existed above the terrestrial world,
and was of a wholly different order. There was no need, therefore, to speak of catastrophic change and resurrection. Since
Jesus preached with the sole purpose of announcing the eschatological Kingdom, it follows that the immortal principle, whose
existence in man he admits, is not the only object of the
resurrection. Such, doubtless, was the view current in his
time.

There is a passage peculiar to Luke (xvi. 19–31) which calls
for examination. It relates that Lazarus the beggar, presumably a pious person, after death was borne by the angels into
Abraham's bosom (εἰς τὸν κόλπον᾽ Ἀβραάμ). The rich man also
died and was buried. " And in hell (ἐν τῷ ᾅδη) he lifted up his
eyes, being in torments, and seeth Abraham afar off, and
Lazarus in his bosom." To his cry for pity the patriarch replies
that he has already received his portion on earth, and adds :
" And beside all this, between us and you there is a great gulf
fixed (χάσμα μέγα ἐστήρικται), that they which would pass
from hence to you may not be able, and that none may cross
over from thence to us."

We are not concerned at present with the style or the meaning of the parable, but only with the significance of the phrase
" Abraham's bosom." It appears to be a place where the
blessed rest as a child in its mother's arms [3] ; where they are
welcomed by Abraham, Isaac and Jacob, according to 4 Maccabees xiii. 16 ; a place of which a Targum says : [4] " like the
Garden of Eden, into which none may enter save the righteous,
whose souls shall be carried thither by the angels " ; finally,
the place which Luke xxiii. 43 calls Paradise [5] (" Verily, I say

---

[1] Christ's omission, according to **CCLIII**, 226.
[2] **CIII**, i, 238. [3] *Cf.* John i. 18.
[4] *Targum ou Koheleth*, 4, 12. *Cf.* **LXVI**, ii, 223 *ff.* ; **XCVII**, 168 *ff.*
[5] From the Persian word *pardès*, meaning a royal garden or park.
Cf. **XCVI**, i, 419.

unto thee, today shalt thou be with me in Paradise "; the promise of Jesus to the repentant thief). The " hell " mentioned in our passage is the ancient *sheol*, more or less hellenized, since souls are tormented there as in the Tartarus of the classical authors.

It is unlikely that Jesus could have envisaged the possibility of a dialogue between Paradise and Hell, or that he could have imagined Abraham as carrying on a conversation with the denizens of Hades. Such details are merely metaphors and symbols. But the passage implies the conception that after death the immortal part of the righteous enters Paradise while that of the wicked departs into hell. This in turn supposes a kind of *special judgment*, in the theological phrase, before the *general judgment* takes place. The Pharisees held some such view, believing that only the righteous would experience a bodily resurrection, while the rest would continue to suffer the punishment which they had deserved.[1] But we cannot tell whether this belief was shared by Jesus or was merely that of the Lucan redactor.

Nor do we know how the Nazarene conceived of the resurrection, nor whether he expected a resurrection of the flesh in the gross material form in which the Church finally accepted it, a belief which was so often the butt of pagan jest. With regard to this point certainty is impossible. We shall see that Paul gets away from this material conception of the great awakening. In his conception, that which would come forth from the earth would not be that which had been laid there, but something which, while resembling it, would be essentially different, a divine creation, *a glorified body*. Now a similar idea seems to be implied in Mark xii. 18–27 (Matt. xxii. 23–33; Luke xx. 27–38), since it is said there that those who rise will be sexless like the angels (Mark xii. 25). This clearly implies the resurrection of individuals rather than of bodies.[2] The evidence is certainly weak, but hardly so precarious as the conclusions which are drawn from the teaching which finally triumphed in Christian orthodoxy because it was based upon what was supposed to be known about the bodily resurrection of Christ. Jewish opposition and Docetic [3] denials forced the Church to emphasize the material aspect of the miracle and to heighten its realism. The same

---

[1] **XXIX**, ii, 391. μονογενὴς υἱ ὁ ὢν εἰς τὸν κόλπον τοῦ πατρός.

[2] **CCXXXV**, 177 ; **CCLIII**, 220.

[3] The Docetists believed that the body of Christ was only a phantasm (δόκησις) ; hence his sufferings and death were only an appearance. This view arose at a very early date.

causes brought about a belief in one fixed type of resurrection for all classes of persons.

We have already seen that there was no general agreement in Jewish thought with regard to the extent of the resurrection. There were those who absolutely denied any resurrection of the dead. Apart from the Sadducean view which maintained that the soul would perish with the body,[1] there was a tradition, represented by several of the deutero-canonical books, such as Sirach, Tobit, and 1 Maccabees, which knew no resurrection.[2] In others there is uncertainty concerning the extent of the resurrection, whether it would embrace all the righteous, all Jews, or all mankind. It would seem at first sight that, since Jesus believed in the existence of an immortal principle in man, and, apparently, expected a final judgment for all mankind, he must have held the doctrine of a general resurrection; but the Pharisees, who also believed in an immortal soul, confined the resurrection to the righteous. There were Jews, too, who believed in a general judgment, but did not regard it as necessarily preceded by the resurrection, or limited the latter to that of the righteous.[3] Our sources afford no certainty on this point. In Luke xx. 35 we read that " they that are accounted worthy to attain to that world, and the resurrection from the dead, neither marry nor are given in marriage . . ." Such are designated by the Evangelist " sons of the resurrection " (τῆς ἀναστάσεως υἱοὶ ὄντες). Unfortunately, these verses, remarkable for their unambiguity, are only found in Luke, and are therefore in all probability redactional, since there is no trace of them in Mark and Matthew. Moreover, the fact that the Lucan passage is only concerned with the resurrection of the blessed, apparently does not imply necessarily the denial of a general resurrection.[4] However, Luke xiv. 14 seems also to limit the resurrection to the righteous (τῇ ἀναστάσει δικαίων).

A final indication that there was no inevitable connexion between a resurrection and a judgment is afforded by the fairly general conception that demons and other disembodied spirits would experience the judgment. This clearly seems to be the suggestion of Matthew viii. 29 : " And they (the demons whom Jesus was casting out of the Gadarene demoniacs) cried out saying, What have we to do with thee, thou Son of God ? art thou come hither to torment us before the time ? " (ἦλθες ὧδε πρὸ καιροῦ βασανίσαι ἡμᾶς).

---

[1] XXIX, ii, 391.   [2] Ibid., 508, 542 ff.
[3] Charles, Eschat., in EB, col. 1375, which makes special reference to the Book of Jubilees.
[4] CIII, ii, 338 ff.

It would be rash to suppose that the words of the Matthæan redactor represent the mind of Jesus ; but at least we can see that he might have believed in a judgment of the wicked without admitting them to a share in the resurrection.

The fact that Mark xii. 24–7 (and Syn. par.) speaks of the resurrection of the seven husbands of the woman, who were hardly all righteous persons, seems to confirm the expectation of a general resurrection. But it would be dangerous to draw conclusions from a hypothetical case invented solely for the purpose of catching the prophet. The same is true of Matthew xxv. 31 *ff.*, where we have a description of the appearance of all nations (πάντα τὰ ἔθνη) before the Judge, since the whole section is plainly redactional and out of keeping with its context.[1]

The final position is that we are unable to determine what was the teaching of Jesus on this fundamental point, since John v. 28–9 is the only passage which unequivocally affirms a general resurrection. We may be sure that if he had emphasized it, the tradition would be less indeterminate with regard to the point. We do not, nor shall we ever know, which of the various conceptions current among the Jews in his time was held by the Nazarene.

II

THE JUDGMENT

The same statement must be made with regard to the judgment, concerning which several questions arise which we have no means of answering. From the evidence of his ethics, and its purpose of changing sinners into saints, it might be inferred that Jesus expected an *individual* judgment ; that it was the individual and not the nation who would appear before the Judge, and there are some grounds for saying [2] that such a conception has completely discarded nationalism. In the second place, he seems to have believed that the judgment would consist of such a detailed inquiry into the life of the individual as had not generally been envisaged by earlier teaching, and would embrace deeds, words, motives, and even thoughts. It has been suggested that this feature of his teaching is a return to the passion of the Prophets for the triumph of absolute righteousness.[3]

With regard to the manner in which the judgment would be carried out, the teaching of Jesus leaves us unenlightened. Batiffol has remarked [4] that in the various passages dealing

[1] XCIX, 204.   [2] CXC, 271.   [3] CCLIII, 222.   [4] CXC, 273.

with the subject, "the central idea is the correlation of the
doctrine of the Kingdom with that of Salvation. All the rest
is secondary, uncertain and relative." True, but if we ask
ourselves whether that which Jesus regarded as the fundamental element in the judgment is that which the Gospel writers
emphasize, we shall find no answer. The one passage which
contains information—slight enough—on the point is Matthew
xxv. 31–46, which describes the nations as summoned before
the throne of the Son of Man. Even if the passage in question
were not purely redactional, as it is, it would afford us no
information concerning the judgment, properly speaking : " and
he shall separate them one from another, as the shepherd
separateth the sheep from the goats ; and he shall set the sheep
on his right hand, but the goats on the left." Nothing more,
no information as to the manner in which the choice is to be
made. Hence it has been supposed [1] that we have to do with
an instantaneous separation, rather than with the conduct of
a trial. But nothing can be based upon a verse which is concerned more with the lesson to be drawn from the judgment
than with the judgment itself. Nevertheless several passages
seem to allude to a great Assize ; for instance, Mark viii. 38
(and Syn. par. ; Matt. x. 32–3 and Luke xii. 8–9), Matthew
xvi. 27 and Luke ix. 26, all of which point in the same direction,
being intended to warn those who might be inclined to despise
or deny the Son of Man in the present day, of the retribution
which they may expect in the Great Day. Such a tendency
stamps these passages at once as redactional, and as reflecting
an attitude on the part of the Christian community which was
certainly not that of Jesus ; hence they can give us no help
on the point with which we are dealing. We may be prepared
to admit that Jesus believed in a set Judgment, but apart from
impressions which have no direct justification, such an admission rests upon the following consideration alone, namely, that
the conception attributed to Jesus by the Evangelists was
current in his time and did not necessarily imply any detailed
account of the judgment. Such an admission has never been
called in question.

The question arises as to who would be the Judge at the
last Judgment. The general belief of the Jews was that it
would be God himself. However, the dislike felt by certain
schools of thought to the anthropomorphic conception of Jahweh
may well have led to the idea that the Messiah, acting on behalf
of God, would be the Judge. Unfortunately this change is
only found in writings of late date and suspected of Christian

[1] CIII, i, 237.

interpolation, such as Enoch and 4 Esdras.[1] At first sight the
Synoptics seem to waver between three views : (1) It is God
the Father who will judge, and Jesus will appear before him,
or beside him, as a *witness* (Matt. x. 32–3 ; Luke xii. 8–9 ;
Matt. vii. 22–3 ; Matt. xviii. 35 ; Luke xviii. 7 ; Matt. xiii.
30). (2) It is the Son of Man who will come with his angels,
with divine attributes such as the book of Daniel describes,
as the deputy of God, and will render to every man according
to his works (Matt. xvi. 27 ; xxv. 31 ; xxiv. 50). (3) The
angels of the Son of Man, sent by him, will purge defilement
out of his Kingdom (Matt. xiii. 41). Such activities might
almost be described as police measures, involving no apocalyptic
manifestation. The choice, if one must be made, presents
difficulties.

The position is almost hopeless from the point of view of
recovering the actual mind of Jesus, since the rapid transition
from prophet to Messiah, and from Messiah to Saviour-God,
imperatively demanded a fundamental change in the eschatological rôle of Jesus. The numerous Matthæan passages representing the function of Christ as Judge are suspicious at this
early date, the more so in that they rest on the passage with
its Pauline colouring : " All things have been committed to
him by the Father " (Matt. ii. 27. *Cf.* Matt. xiii. 41–3, 49 *f.* ;
xvi. 27 ; xxii. 11–14 ; xxv. 32). Thus, the conception of the
purging of the Kingdom of the Son of Man by *his* angels is
derived from the parable of the Tares, which, in its present
form, and in comparison with the rest of the Matthæan Gospel,
exhibits, in its obvious improbability, all the marks of redactional invention.[2]

The view is certainly not untenable that Jesus, without
believing himself to be the Messiah, may have reserved a central
rôle in the drama of the Judgment for the Coming One ; but
it is rash to seek a proof of it in the Matthæan assertion that
the Son of Man—a conception which, we must repeat, was
wholly foreign to the Nazarene—will confess or deny those
who have confessed or denied him on earth, " when he shall
come in the glory of his Father with his holy angels." Here
we are dealing with the *parousia*, and the conception of the
parousia did not come from Jesus. In short, we have no
knowledge whatever of what Jesus thought of the Messiah and
his functions.

Indeed, it would be a fruitless task to attempt to resolve
the contradictions of the Gospels : it is impossible, in the
present state of our knowledge, to go beyond the bald state-

[1] **XLIV,** 179.   [2] **CIII,** i, 780 ; **CVI,** 202 ; **CVII,** ii, 212.

ment that Jesus believed in the reality of the Judgment.[1] This may seem a meagre result of our inquiry, but the reason is not far to seek.

For obvious reasons it is useless to ask how the Nazarene conceived of Paradise and hell ; but it would be interesting to know what he thought would be the proportion of the elect to the lost. For him the elect would be the righteous, those who had been rendered so by *metanoia*. Possibly, at the beginning of his ministry, he may have hoped that many would be led by his message into the way of salvation which he offered to them. This illusion must soon have been shattered. This is why the Matthæan redactor may have been right in ascribing to him, at the close of his career, the much abused phrase which may well express the experience of Jesus : " Many are called but few chosen " (Matt. xxii. 14). It was, moreover, the verdict of the Jewish wisdom of his day.[2]

In conclusion, the Synoptic Gospels, distorted by the requirements of the apostolic and sub-apostolic creed, can no longer give us a satisfactory reply to the questions raised concerning the views of Jesus on the ultimate destiny of humanity. We are left with the probable conclusion that he was in accord with the opinions and beliefs of his environment. These were, unfortunately, various and confused, and we cannot form a sufficiently clear picture of the environment of Jesus, with its characteristic ideas, to make such a conclusion of much value to us. We are not even able to say with certainty whether his vision of the future had room for the warlike and triumphant Messiah, in whom so many of his contemporaries saw the last hope of Israel. Our sources certainly appear to predict the advent of the Messiah as an unexpected event which would immediately be followed by the setting-up of the Kingdom ; but that is not sufficient evidence for believing that this was the expectation of Jesus. Between him and the Gospels as we have them there is more than a difference of age and environment ; there is a fundamental difference of temper and a completely changed perspective.

[1] Batiffol himself (**CXC**, 273 *ff.*) admits this. Since he refuses to allow the existence of redactional changes in the teaching of Jesus, he prefers to believe that the Master used elements of apocalyptic imagery as metaphors or parabolic material. It is as difficult to accept this frank confession of defeat as the contradictory statements of Matthew.

[2] *Cf.* 4 *Esdras* viii. 3 : " *Many are created, but few are saved* " ; viii. 1 ; ix. 15 ; *Apoc. of Baruch* xliv. 15.

CHAPTER XI

THE ORIGINALITY OF JESUS

I

THE NOVELTY OF THE TEACHING OF JESUS

AS we come to the end of our study of the teaching of Jesus, two questions present themselves : (1) In what did the originality of the Nazarene consist, and what was new in his teaching ? (2) Since his teaching had as its object the preparation of his hearers for a crisis which never developed, what permanent elements did it contain ? With regard to the first point we have already arrived at several conclusions which must now be brought together. With regard to the second point we shall have to come to a decision about a matter of considerable importance, namely, whether, in the evolution of the religion which claims Jesus for its founder, the ideas of the prophet had, as some maintain, a determining influence, or whether, as others claim, they had no part in it at all.

The explanation which the Gospels give of the beginning of the ministry of Jesus as the continuation of the Baptist's mission has the merit of simplicity and clearness, but it is not so certain that it is historically true. It is impossible to ignore the difference between the spirit of the preaching of Jesus and that of his supposed precursor ; the contrast between the advent of a day of wrath heralded with threats by a fierce ascetic, and the Good News announced with comfortable words by a prophet full of tenderness and pity for sinners.[1] If the account given by the Gospel tradition is trustworthy, the contrast is too great to be resolved by reducing it to a mere difference of character and temperament. There is thus, at the very outset of the ministry of Jesus, a mystery which we cannot pierce ; the source of his characteristic outlook and beliefs remains shrouded in a darkness which all our labours leave unillumined. Concerning the episode at the Jordan a critic [2]

---

[1] The contrast is clearly indicated in Matt. xi. 18 *ff*. (Luke vii. 33 *ff*.) : " *John came neither eating or drinking . . .*"

[2] Bruce, in **EB**, *Jesus*, § 6.

has recently written that " it affords a backward glimpse into the silences of Nazareth; it is a window into the mind of Jesus." Unfortunately, even if the window is really open, that is, if Jesus actually went to Jordan, it is a window that opens into the dark. Moreover, if he did go to Jordan, there is no hope of ever knowing how far he was indebted to John the Baptist for any elements of his teaching, other than his two central themes of the nearness of the Kingdom and the need for *metanoia*. Furthermore, it is impossible to say what he could have received from a man concerning whom we do not know whether he possessed any specific doctrine, nor whether he belonged to a sect or was merely a solitary fanatic.

In the course of our study we have observed in the teaching of Jesus more than one feature which might be characterized as sectarian, that is to say which bears the marks of the outlook and spirit of a small exclusive group. His very name, the Nazarene, points in the same direction. Nevertheless, there is absolutely nothing in our sources that indicates with certainty the connexion of the prophet with some Jewish sect whose doctrines he was promulgating. Since the eighteenth century endless discussions have been engaged with the problem without result. Similarly, every attempt to connect Jesus with the Essenes has been fruitless, for, from our present point of view, nothing but contrast appears between the teaching of the Essenes and the Synoptic account of the teaching of Jesus; a statement which is equally true of the practices of the Essenes and the behaviour of Jesus. Even if we admit the possibility of Essene influence in matters of detail, an admission about which it is impossible to be specific, we cannot hope for light from the communities on the shores of the Dead Sea concerning the essential nature of the Nazarene's teaching.

Still less are we in a position to know anything about the connexion of the teaching of Jesus with that of other Jewish sects whose existence we can only suspect, even if they contained all the possibilities which we desire. Whether it be the case that the tradition has obliterated from the teaching of Jesus all those features judged to be embarrassing or irrelevant, or whether it has preserved a relatively trustworthy picture of him, in any case all that we gather from it is the impression that the Nazarene based his teaching on the common stock of beliefs current in Israel in his time. Such an impression is confirmed by the numerous instances in which we have had occasion to observe a connexion between the utterances ascribed to Jesus and the ideas current in his day, both in the rabbinical schools and in pious circles. To use an expression in vogue at the present time, we may say that in its *essence*, the content of the teaching of Jesus, if not its method of application, does not appear to differ widely, in essentials, from that of pharisaic Judaism. Modern Jewish writers emphasize this point, and we are bound to admit that they are right.[1]

Nevertheless, if there is one characteristic which stands out more than another in the Synoptic tradition it is the reiterated insistence on a permanent and fundamental opposition between Jesus and the Pharisees. We are at once reminded of the passage in Mark i. 22 : "For he taught them as one having authority (ὡς ἐξουσίαν ἔχων)"—the note of the prophet—"and not as the scribes"—whom the Gospels always associate with the Pharisees. Such a passage clearly implies that the teaching of the Nazarene, both in its spirit and in its methods, stands in opposition to that of the Schools. On their side, the Pharisees pursued Jesus with an unrelenting hatred ; they devoted themselves to an unceasing attempt to oppose, embarrass, compromise, and finally to exterminate him.

There can be no doubt that the tradition has read back into the mind of Jesus the hostility felt by the early Christian communities towards the Jewish Rabbis who were most formidable opponents of their mission. It has even been maintained [2] that the enmity existing between Jesus and the Pharisees was wholly an invention of the tradition, and that he was essentially in agreement with them.[3] In that case we should have to suppose that his teaching was influenced by pharisaic ideas and was a kind of popularization of Pharisaism. But there is need here of caution. When it is said that all his teaching finds a parallel in the Talmud,[4] we must remember that the editing of the older parts of the Talmud does not go back to an earlier date than the second century of our era, and that the oral tradition which embodies its discussions, and even the older tradition contained in the *Pirqe Aboth* which may be contemporary with Jesus, bear traces of Christian contamination. Moreover, if the Talmud contains parallels with the teaching of Jesus, it contains many other things as well which his teaching has discarded.[5] The process of selection in itself involves originality and points rather to the independence of the teaching of Jesus.

[1] **CCXLVIII**, 89.

[2] Elbogen, *Die Religions-Anschauungen der Pharisäer mit besonderer Berücksichtigung der Begriffe Gott und Mensch*, 1904.

[3] Fullkrug, *Jesus und die Pharisäer*, 1902 ; Chwolson, *Die letzte Passamahl Christi*, 118 ; there is also the well-known contribution of Abrahams.

[4] **CLXXV**, 75.   [5] **CCCXIII**, 1894, 37, n.

It is by no means impossible that Jesus, in his turn, hated
and opposed, not Pharisaism as such, but a special brand of
Pharisaism, that aspect of it to which the inquiries of modern
scholars have been too long confined, and the only aspect of
it which they have been willing to discover in the Talmud—
the Pharisaism which regards genuine piety as consisting in a
rigid legalism, a withering adherence to the letter, a lifeless
pedantry, content to all appearance with outward acts.

But side by side with this type of Pharisaism there was
another with which Jesus must have been in entire sympathy.
Among those who meticulously tithed their mint and their salt,
who would not eat without ritual hand-washing, who were
scrupulously careful about the cleanliness of their utensils, who
made the legal observance of the Sabbath burdensome by a
hair-splitting casuistry, and who patiently reared about the
Law—and this was their gravest offence in the eyes of Jesus
—a hedge of restrictions and limitations which repelled the
common people, among such as these there were some who had
arrived at the conception that there was an *essential content*
at the heart of the Law ; [1] they thought that this essential
content was very simple, and that to keep it was to do the
will of God ; nay more, it was the title of admission to the
blessings of the Covenant of Israel.

About the time of Jesus, they had also arrived at the belief
that external legalism was unnecessary and that regular attend-
ance at the Temple did not of itself bring a man nearer to God.[2]
Indeed, in its origin, Pharisaism was essentially an intensely
spiritual movement, and anything but an outgrowth of barren
formalism. As Harnack vigorously points out, Pharisaism
must not be judged by its later stunted growth (*Verküm-
merung*),[3] which may have satisfied those for whom piety consisted in a dull formality. History shows how often piety has
made shipwreck on the rock of rigid adherence to outward
forms. It is clear, then, that it was the narrow ritualists, the
representatives of a bad, stunted Pharisaism, who were the
objects of the opposition of Jesus. He could have had no cause
of quarrel with the good type of Pharisee with whom he would
have been in essential accord. And while the casuists and the
pedants may have hated the *nabi* who taught with an authority
that needed not the seal of scholastic sanction, the liberal-
minded Rabbis could hardly have failed to sympathize with
him. For if we consider the movement initiated by Jesus as
a whole and purely from the religious point of view, it displays

[1] *Die Hauptsumme des Gesetzes*, so Harnack, **CCLXIII**, i, 78, n. 2.
[2] **CLXXXIX**, 40.   [3] **CCLXIII**, i, 79.

the same outlook and is moving in the same direction as genuine Pharisaism.[1] Renan has said " Hillel was the true teacher of Jesus." [2] Whatever we may think about the literal accuracy of the statement, the idea which it expresses is fundamentally true. The Pharisees awaited with eager longing the great Day, the setting up of the Kingdom in a world reborn, the perfect righteousness of God, before ever Jesus had set these things in the forefront of his preaching. It has been said [3] that the term *righteousness* was the watchword and rallying cry of the Pharisees. Similarly they held fast to the idea of the resurrection. The ethical principles of the Pharisees corresponded with those of Jesus, including the characteristic feature of his moral teaching, the emphasis placed on the value of works of mercy. There is no suggestion here that the Nazarene was merely a Pharisee. He had and kept his own fashion of teaching—his *way*—which was not that of the Pharisees, as well as his originality of mind which was largely due to the fact that he had never been trained in the rabbinical schools. He was much simpler, in the various meanings of the word, than the Pharisees, more accessible to sinners, more sympathetic to the *am-haareṣ*; he laid more stress on the invincibility of love. But his roots, so to speak, were in the soil of Pharisaic piety, and even if he received his initial impulse from some sect unknown to us, his spiritual growth was nourished on Pharisaism. It is not necessary to go so far as to say that he had derived his ideas from the same sources from which Pharisaism had sprung, since the latter had long outgrown its origins. But, because Pharisaism had permeated Israel with its fundamental conceptions, it was possible for it to furnish the content of the religious consciousness of a prophet sprung from the people, who, doubtless, had known no other school than his village synagogue. The originality of Jesus lies mainly in this, that he had instinctively crystallized the essence of Pharisaism in a single act of faith ; all that Pharisaism stood for was realized in the instantaneousness and completeness of *metanoia*, the one and only door of salvation into the Kingdom. It was no small thing.

Moreover, such a synthesis of Pharisaic ideas could only have been achieved by a prophet. Hence Jesus presents himself to us as a Messianic prophet, unique among those of whom we have glimpses in this period. He was a Messianic prophet

---

[1] *Cf.* **LIV**, 420 ; **CCLXIII**, i; **L**–*a*, i, 169; there are also, of course, the Jewish writers whose works we have made considerable use of, *e.g.* Abrahams, Herford, Montefiore, etc.

[2] **CLXVIII**, 35.   [3] **L**–*a*, i, 170.

who said little, if anything, about the Messiah, and whose message struck no warlike note. But it is to be remarked that, so far as we know, John the Baptist issued no call to arms either, and that, apparently, the sects of which we have any knowledge exhibited the same characteristic, leaving to Jahweh the responsibility of securing his own triumph. Hence, so far as his aims were concerned, Jesus' prophetic teaching might be described as orthodox, judged by the standards of the Law and the Temple, but its inspiration had its source mainly outside what we may, by stretching the terms, call orthodox national Messianism, since, in the necessary preparation for the Kingdom, he laid emphasis on the need for an internal reformation of the individual, rather than on a popular appeal to force.

Whence he drew the guiding principles of that inward change which seemed to him indispensable, and which constituted both the central motive of his career and his real originality, we cannot tell, and all attempts at an explanation have so far proved fruitless. It may be that the answer can only be found in the vague and various influences at work in the environment where the ideas which he set in motion saturated the very air which he breathed. We have only to think of the forces which shaped the great religious innovators, Mohammed, Francis of Assisi, Ignatius Loyola : such men cannot be assigned to any particular sect or influence, but to an environment in which their temperaments instinctively selected those elements which characterized their religious personality and their activities.

At all events we may say that Jesus drew his inspiration from, and lived under the continual influence of the Scriptures. In this regard, the statements and modifications of the Gospel redactors are suspect, since they were accustomed to draw from the Old Testament vindications and arguments for their apologetic. However, Jesus cannot be explained apart from the Old Testament ; without it he could not have existed. His reverence for the Law was absolute ; but in his method of interpreting it according to what he believed to be the truth and the will of God, he availed himself of the freedom of a prophet who feels that his inspiration is drawn from the same source as that of the *Torah*. This characteristic, again, differentiated him from the Pharisees. His fundamental distinction from them lay precisely in the fact that he was a prophet, that he felt within him the moving of the Spirit which he was impelled to obey. The two imperative practical demands of the Spirit were, first, the eschatological direction of all his teaching, and, secondly, the law of love, carried to its logical conclusions, as the standard of life and the key which gave entrance to the Kingdom. Herein, so far as we can see, lay the novelty of his contribution to the religious life of Israel.

We need not discuss the claim that Jesus was beyond all comparison in the history of mankind (Deissmann), a claim which would certainly constitute an unrivalled originality.[1] We may agree with Loisy [2] that such a claim is " a mirage in which the dogma of the divinity of Jesus has involved the minds of liberal Protestants." We have no grounds on which to base an estimate of such a far-reaching claim. By common consent the Synoptics present us with an outstanding religious personality in Israel. More than this we cannot say without going beyond the limits of our positive knowledge. We must not confound the Nazarene with the ideal which he has come to represent since the birth of Christian dogma, an ideal for which he was not responsible. So far as history is concerned, he is not the Incarnate Logos, nor the Son who is consubstantial with the Father, but only a Jewish prophet. Drews remarks [3] that however much we may magnify the person and teaching of Jesus, his recorded utterances in the Gospels never rise beyond what is characteristic of human intellectual capacity. This will be admitted by any unbiassed person. It may be added that we have not even to do with what we may call a man of genius, but only with a man of singular spiritual loveliness and breadth of humanity.

II

TIME AND THE TEACHING OF JESUS

The teaching of Jesus did not possess a permanent character. It was based upon the expectation of a great eschatological event, of which either the fulfilment or the frustration would have been fatal to it, since it was not concerned with the future, and the continuance of human life was destined to undermine its foundations. In the same way the law of love, indispensable element of the life of the Kingdom, was unworkable in a normal society. But the hope of Jesus remained unfulfilled, crushed by a cruel death. His disciples, terrified by such a shattering blow, sought refuge in flight. This should have been the logical

[1] A quarter of a century ago Deissmann wrote : " Jesus is greater than the tradition about him " (quoted in L–a, i, 179, from *Evang. und Urchristentum*, 1905). How did he know ? For a similar statement, needing the same reservation, *cf.* CCLXIV, 63.

[2] RHLR, 1912, 569.

[3] *Did Jesus ever live? A religious debate on the Christ-Myth*, 42, trans. Lipman. Paris, 1912.

end of the Nazarene's movement, only its memory should have
survived, just as nothing but a memory remained of several
prophets of warlike messianism who appeared in Judæa about
the same time. This, however, was not what happened : a
new religion, Christianity, and an organization adapted to the
needs of an earthly life, the Church, were the continuation of
the message which, logically, ended at Calvary. The question
naturally arises whether they were its legitimate issue, and
whether the teaching which we have just examined contained,
all unknown to Jesus, the seeds of such a flowering. If not,
it is merely the memory of the Master which served as a nucleus
round which the new order of things grew up, an order in which
the prophet would have recognized neither his aims nor his
spirit.

It is a weighty problem by which we are confronted, nothing less than that of the origins of Christianity. It cannot
be solved without a study of the movement in question ; but
we may, provisionally, set forth certain considerations. The
renewed courage of the disciples was due to their belief that
their Master had immediately been delivered from the power
of death. Hence they continued to await the Kingdom which
he had announced, but their hope contained a new element of
fundamental importance : they believed that by resurrection
Jesus had become the Messiah, and for them, henceforth, the
advent of the Kingdom consisted in the *parousia*, the apocalyptic return and manifestation in glory of the Risen One.
Hence, when the disciples reassembled with restored hope, their
outlook was no longer that of Jesus : while he had preached
an indispensable *metanoia* and a mode of life necessary in view
of the immediate advent of the Kingdom, they preached the
person of Jesus and saving faith in his Messiahship, in view
of the Judgment where he would separate his own from the
rest.

They might indeed seem to adhere to the letter of the teaching which they had received from him during his lifetime, but
their interest was speedily transferred to their love for his
person and their confidence in his supreme power. This was
the figure whom the Easter faith had brought again from the
tomb, clothed with a few moral precepts relating to the intimate
daily life in which the disciples had lived in the company of
their Master. The two elements of the Nazarene's teaching,
the dream of the Kingdom which had sustained him, and the
mode of life belonging to it, were not destined to recover from
the shattering blow of his death, but were to be obliterated
by the dogmatic developments of the Christology.

We shall go on to amplify these brief remarks and examine more closely into their grounds, but the provisional conclusion to which they lead us is that the genuine teaching of Jesus did not survive him ; that the prophet neither foresaw nor desired the new order which replaced the immediate future of his dream ; and, although Christianity may be said to have its origin in him, since the new religion grew out of speculations concerning his person and his mission, he was not its founder. It had never even entered into his mind.

PART III

THE DEATH OF JESUS AND THE EASTER FAITH

CHAPTER I

JESUS AT JERUSALEM

I

THE PROBLEM

WE have now to deal with the central problem of the life of Jesus, the problem of his death and its unexpected issues. Secure in their faith in the resurrection of Jesus, his disciples, as they reflected on his Passion, arrived at the belief that beneath these shattering events there lay the ultimate mystery of salvation. Seen in the light of Calvary, the whole life of the Nazarene received its true significance, and the cross, the shameful symbol of his death, became the means by which the most stupendous of miracles was brought about. This, in essence, was the line of thought which kindled the first flame of the Christian movement.

If the belief of the disciples of the apostolic period concerning the Passion and the Resurrection was true ; if the objects which their faith attributed to their Master were really his ; if he had predicted, as they probably said he had, what was going to happen to him, and had clearly indicated what it implied, then there is no further cause for doubt : Christianity is really the work of Jesus ; he came into the world to *found* it, and by the cross he both realized it and vindicated it. In that case, all the evidence so far collected which appears to militate against this belief of orthodoxy is worthless and meaningless.

Unfortunately we are obliged to ask ourselves whether the disciples, whom we may provisionally call the Apostles, can really have seen and known the events which are supposed to rest upon their testimony. We must ask whether their evidence was the sober, weighty, and therefore reliable testimony of men who were capable of accurate observation, or whether it was that of men whose imagination was disordered, who were unbalanced by chronic ecstasy or by some violent shock, men who were liable to illusions, to autosuggestion, to the imaginative creations of the mystic's psychology. If we are forced to accept the latter of these alternatives, the superficial simplicity of the orthodox explanation of the birth of Christianity immediately disappears ; the Christian interpretation of the death of Jesus becomes meaningless, and even the reality of the Resurrection is found to be unsupported.

There are two tendencies, both alike worthless, which call for examination here. One springs from rationalism and the other from credulity.

The first starts with the assumption that the miraculous does not exist, that the existence of the supernatural cannot be proved. Hence the Gospel statements concerning the death of Jesus, in part, and concerning his resurrection, entirely, fall outside the sphere of reality without further discussion, and must be rejected *à priori* by the historian. It becomes necessary to substitute for them either an acknowledgment of complete ignorance, a kind of historical agnosticism which says : " We do not know what happened, but it was certainly not that," or else hypotheses which are necessarily insecure, but which possess a certain speciousness that commends them to the reason. This is the method followed by many unbelieving critics who have accepted, in the main, the historicity of the arrest and trial of Jesus, his execution and burial, but who have discarded the embarrassing miracle of the resurrection by supposing stories of simulated death, followed by revival and escape, or of the carrying off of the body by friends or enemies, and so forth.

Believing critics have dealt severely with this method of argument, already several times referred to, and often with good reason. Their error has been that of following, although in the opposite direction, along the very line of reasoning which they had refuted. To say that the Gospel statements are true because they are contained in the Gospel, that the activities of the Son of God must be miraculous, and that the Resurrection is its own infallible proof, implies that it is unnecessary to examine and sift the evidence, and that belief suffices. Moreover, while such a position is perfectly tenable, it is not one upon which history can be built. The historian knows nothing and believes nothing in advance, save that it is incumbent on him to believe nothing, and that he knows nothing.

His business is to search, and having examined all the documents, he bases his conclusions upon them and not upon any previous convictions of his own. An apology might seem to be needed for the reiteration of such platitudes, but experience shows how easily they may be forgotten in approaching the questions with which we are about to deal.

Now it is only too clear that our Gospel documents describe the Passion and the Resurrection under the forms which they had received from the imagination, the emotions and the religious experience of the post-apostolic period. While it is possible to maintain that these descriptions rest upon apostolic tradition, a slight examination of the sources is sufficient to cast a doubt upon such a view. There are too many passages which raise the question as to how the information which they contain could have been acquired.[1] We feel too often that the details presented to us have evidently been obtained by the methods which the novelist employs in order to give the appearance of reality to his characters : he gives an imaginary account of their thoughts, feelings and utterances, in accordance with his own standard of reality. The requirements of apologetic and of the polemic directed against Jewish opposition placed the Gospel writers in an extremely difficult position in dealing with those early reminiscences, which, if they ever existed, lie under the suspicion of having been collected in a disturbed and ecstatic atmosphere hardly favourable to a judicial attitude.

The three Synoptics present too many serious discrepancies, and it is mere nonsense to suggest that they only concern unessential details. The fundamental fact is that they all draw from a common source, and their threefold testimony is in reality only that of a single witness ; the freedom with which they treat the common source raises grave doubts concerning the stability and trustworthiness of the tradition. A careful study of the Synoptic documents reveals the growth of a legend to which each of the Gospel writers gives his own characteristic form.[2] We have, in Loisy's words, a labour of faith and devotion " which finds its satisfaction in such representations as it considers most worthy of its object." The climax of the process is reached in the Johannine story of the Passion, which, as it cannot too often be repeated, although more finished than the account of the three Synoptic Gospels, and possessing a

---

[1] To give one example : In the incident in Gethsemane (Mark xiv. 32 *ff.*) the Evangelist records words which Jesus must have uttered when he was alone and at a distance from the disciples, who were asleep. Who could have heard them ?

[2] CIII, i, 182.

somewhat different viewpoint, agrees with them in spirit, in tendency, and in the information which it affords. It has so far eliminated from the sacred drama every trace of the human element, that for the Jesus of John, the Christ, the cross becomes a kingly throne,[1] from which descends the proclamation that all is finished (xix. 30, τετέλεσται); the will of God has been fulfilled ; all that the Scriptures foretold has been accomplished (John xix. 28). Finally, confirmatory quotations from the Old Testament are numerous, and too frequently in evidence in important episodes.[2] As we shall go on to show, it is not difficult to understand the reason for this. The apostolic age founded its belief in the Christian hope on the view that the central events of the Gospel were the fulfilment of the promises contained in the Old Testament. Hence it gradually gathered round these events all those passages of the Old Testament which might seem to vindicate and illustrate the object of their faith, or which might give fuller substance to the necessarily meagre outlines of the tradition. It is well known to what an extent this tendency to confirmatory and explanatory elaboration has destroyed the simple truth of the original facts, even supposing that the companions of the Crucified did retain some traces of these facts in their memories. To such an extent have some of these Old Testament passages,[3] Psalm xxii. for instance, affected the Gospel narrative, that the question has been seriously raised whether the primitive tradition, represented by the Marcan document (*Urmarcus*), knew anything of an account of the Passion and the Resurrection ; [4] and whether the whole of this account, as we find it in the Synoptics, was not merely built up out of passages from the Old Testament, without any basis in fact. The adherents of the mythical view linger with special delight over this incoherent narrative of the Passion, regarding it as a notable piece of evidence against the historicity of the Gospels.[5] While such extreme views are only held by a small minority of critics, they may not be contemptuously dismissed.

---

[1] **LXXIX**, 224.

[2] Feigel, **CCI**, has carefully collected the passages of the Old Testament made use of in the narratives which concern us. Among these, Ps. xxii., which colours the whole account of the Passion, calls for special notice ; also the fifty-third of Isaiah, of which it has been said (**CCLVII**, 175 *ff.*) that during his Passion, Jesus had it continually before his mind, and fulfilled it deliberately, detail by detail.

[3] A critical examination will be found in **CLVI**, ch. ix. It is not altogether easy, however, to share the complete confidence of the author in every verse of the Synoptics.

[4] Reuss, *Les Évangiles syn.*, 82.   [5] Steudel, **CLXXXXI**, 48.

While the Gospels seem to be aware that Jesus had announced, at an early date, to the Apostles all that was about to happen to him at Jerusalem,[1] the Apostles had certainly forgotten this assurance, since they fled in dismay as soon as that which they ought to have expected began to take place.[2] The fact is that when the faith of the Apostles had been restored, they were obliged to find some explanation of *the offence of the cross*, as Paul called it. Clearly, the best explanation was to include the cross in the purpose of God and to assert that Jesus had foreseen, accepted and foretold it.[3] This tendency appears, for instance, in the prayer in Gethsemane (Mark xiv. 36), where the Nazarene declares his resignation to the Father's will, and the passage in Mark viii. 31 *ff.*, which is said to have disturbed Peter so deeply : " The Son of Man must suffer many things, and be rejected by the elders, and the chief priests, and the scribes, and be killed, and after three days rise again." [4]

Moreover, long before the Master had foretold it, the Law and the Prophets had predicted his fate. We read in Acts iii. 18, " But the things which God foreshowed by the mouth of all the prophets, that his Christ should suffer, he thus fulfilled." [5] It is well established that the Old Testament knows nothing of a suffering Messiah, but apologetic exegesis has always been able to accommodate passages to its needs.

Having made these necessary remarks, it only remains to seek what light we may from the Synoptics and from the meagre information supplied by the Acts and the Pauline epistles. If we may not succeed in dispelling the darkness, we shall at least have the satisfaction of an attempt to break through it.

II

THE JERUSALEM ENVIRONMENT

We left Jesus at Bethany, which is generally held to have been about a mile and a half from Jerusalem, on the way to Jericho, and were unable to accept the Gospel account, either of the triumphant entry into the city, or of his first magisterial visit to the Temple, when he cast a proprietary glance round

---

[1] *Cf.* Mark viii. 31 ; ix. 9–13 ; x. 33–4, etc.
[2] Mark xiv. 50 and Syn.   [3] **CIII**, i, 180 *ff.*
[4] *Cf.* Mark x. 33 *ff.*, and Syn., which repeats the whole saying during the journey of Jesus to Jerusalem.
[5] *Cf.* Acts xiii. 27 ; xxvi. 23 ; xxviii. 23 ; Rom. iii. 21 ; 2 Cor. i. 20.

upon everything (Mark ii. 11 : περιβλεψάμενος πάντα). According to the tradition, all these incidents took place during the week before the Jewish Passover. Christian liturgical usage assigned them to the exact date of the Sunday before the Resurrection, that is, Palm Sunday.

We may ask what the Nazarene could have expected from Jerusalem, hardly anything good. Since the Romans had assumed the government of Judæa the city had been dominated by the Temple. That is to say, by the priesthood, whose members, if not entirely, yet for the most part, belonged to the Sadducean party, of all the Jewish sects the most unfavourable to any Messianic movement. The priesthood with the natural conservatism of those whose interest it is to maintain the *status quo*, clerical in its outlook, could not fail to be hostile to the ecstatic, to the prophet who rudely overturned their pleasant customs and shattered their cherished peace. As a body they had at their disposal considerable material resources : they controlled the Temple police whose business it was to keep order in the Temple ; they possessed a majority in the Sanhedrin, which, as the custodian of the Jewish religion, could at any time declare this to be threatened, and set in motion the forces for its defence. In the city itself dwelt the personnel of the Rabbinical schools, swollen with pride, and from the outset unfavourably disposed towards a provincial *nabi*, of no repute as a scholar, an ignoramus who posed as a teacher. There were also the common people, although it is not likely that the *am-haareṣ* would be found in any great number in the shadow of the Sanctuary where there was no excuse for their presence. There may, however, have been *anavim*, and pilgrims were numerous. A wave of enthusiasm might have roused these lesser elements of the populace to action if Jesus had known how to stir them ; but, so far as we can judge, his message was not one which the majority of them were expecting, and, moreover, he was a Galilean, which would tend to prejudice Jews against him. No great reputation preceded him, his own country, Galilee, had not received his preaching with any great enthusiasm, and even the Gospels themselves do not attempt to prove the contrary, with the exception of the improbable Messianic entry, which, so far from correcting the impression given by the rest of the narrative, confirms it by the very contradiction which it presents. Furthermore, such a heterogeneous and unarmed rabble could have effected nothing of any significance. At the most it could only have listened to him, followed him, and gathered round him in an attempt to prevent his arrest. A Roman garrison was stationed in the city, and, if tradition may be relied on, the regular strength of the garrison in the tower of Antonia was reinforced at the time of the Passover, and the procurator himself came up from Cæsarea.

It would seem that the latter was Pontius Pilate. We know that he governed the province from 26 to 36, but our information concerning him is scanty.[1] He seems to have been a fairly good example of the Roman official, strict, scrupulous and well-disposed, confronted by a people whom he never understood, and who were, in consequence, distasteful to him. All his actions, however good their intentions, were always misinterpreted by those whom he governed, hence it is not surprising that he disliked them. He has been unfortunate in having been involved in the events of the Passion, for both Christians and Jews have united to denounce him. According to Philo,[2] Agrippa I told Caligula that he was " a man of unbending disposition, merciless and determined " (τὴν φύσιν ἀκαμπὴς, καὶ μετὰ τοῦ αὐθάδους ἀμείλικτος); he attributed to him all the vices of a bad ruler : corruption, violence, abuse of power, tyrannical oppression, illegal executions, cruelty, etc. Such statements are merely the amenities of controversy, and impossible to substantiate. The Jews related stories of him which sufficiently explain their feelings. They told how, under cover of night, the procurator, in violation of Jewish custom, had on a certain occasion brought the Roman ensigns, abhorred because they bore images, into the Holy City.[3] An angry demonstration of the populace in front of his house in Cæsarea had been roughly dispersed. Upon another occasion, wishing to construct an aqueduct, and being short of money, he had " borrowed " from the Temple treasury, considering that the future beneficiaries might contribute from their resources towards a work of public utility.[4] A fresh demonstration and further brutalities on the part of the police followed. On several of these occasions Pilate may well have been in the right, since we only hear the Jewish side of the case ; but he was undoubtedly a man who would stand no nonsense, believed in strong-arm methods, and feared the hysteria of those whom he governed. He was certainly keeping a watchful eye on Messianic tendencies, nor would the priests have allowed him to wink at them even if he had been so inclined. Hence there was not the slightest likelihood that such a man, especially

---

[1] **XXIX**, i, 488 *ff.* On the various contemporary references to him, *cf.* **XXIV**, i, 202.

[2] *Leg. ad. Caium*, 38.

[3] Josephus, *Ant.*, 18, 3, 1 ; *B.J.*, 2, 9, 2.

[4] Josephus, *Ant.*, 18, 3, 2 ; *B.J.*, 2, 9, 4.

on the occasion of one of the great feasts, when he knew popular feeling was capable of getting out of hand, would have dealt leniently towards a public or even a purely personal demonstration which might have given him the smallest anxiety.

Hence, at Jerusalem, Jesus encountered the worst possible conditions, not merely for the success of any movement, but even for initiating one. He must have been aware of this, but no doubt his mind had ceased to move in the sphere of human contingencies. It has been said [1] that he came with the intention of forcing the issue by appealing directly to the population of the Holy City. He must have been unusually simple-minded to have done so, since the Jews had no greater reason for believing in him than had the Galileans. The real reason must have been that he was expecting a crowning miracle, a state of mind which would take no heed of human obstacles in his path. We may repeat that it is unlikely that he came up to Jerusalem in the spirit attributed to him by Luke xiii. 33 : " Nevertheless I must walk today, and tomorrow, and the day following : for it cannot be that a prophet perish out of Jerusalem," with the purpose of vindicating his mission by his death.[2] And even if it is possible, it is still less likely that he thought that death was the precise object of his mission, and that he had deliberately determined to fulfil the prophecies.[3] Such explanations of his purpose are merely prophecies after the event, invented to suit the later view of his person. To attribute them to Jesus is to explain him by Paul.

According to the traditional account the Nazarene did not stay at Jerusalem but at Bethany, and only came in to Jerusalem during the day. This is explained as due to precaution, in order that he might thus be safe from an attempt on his person which his enemies would not risk in the daytime, in the midst of the people. But our sources give no indication that the populace were inclined to act as the bodyguard of the prophet ; and it would have been perfectly easy to take him by night in his hiding-place, in the absence of the people. It is, however, reasonable to suppose that the tradition has preserved a reminiscence of a stay at Bethany, and it is relevant to point out that the striking story of the cursing of the fig-tree (Mark ii. 12–14 and 19–25) requires that Jesus should have gone out of the city at least twice.

The tradition which Mark preserves has assigned to Jerusalem some of the most important of the teachings of Jesus. There is the teaching arising out of the cursing of the barren fig-tree (Israel), concerning the faith which removes mountains

[1] CCXVI, 50.   [2] CCLVII, 156. *Cf.* CIV, 375.   [3] LXIV, 371.

(Mark ii. 19–25) ; the teaching which Jesus derives, by one of
his familiar counter-attacks, from the question put to him by
the priests concerning the authority by which he acted (Mark
ii. 27–33) ; the parable, or rather the allegory, of the Wicked
Husbandmen, clearly signifying the exclusion of Israel from the
Kingdom, to which is appended a quotation from Psalm cxviii.
22–3 in order to indicate the destiny of the Son, rejected and
slain by the wicked husbandmen : he should become the corner-
stone of the temple which God would build, passing by the
people of his former choice who no longer understood him
(xii. 1–12) ; the teaching concerning the tribute and the obligation of rendering to Cæsar the things which are Cæsar's and
to God the things which are God's (xii. 13–17) ; the teaching
arising out of the question of the Sadducees, " who say there
is no resurrection," relating to the marital relations of the risen
(xii. 18–27) ; that concerning the great commandment of love
to God and to one's neighbour (xii. 28–34) ; concerning the
supposed Davidic descent of the Messiah, in opposition to the
scribes and Pharisees (xii. 35–40) ; the teaching concerning the
value of almsgiving, arising out of the incident of the widow's
offering at the Temple treasury (xii. 41–4) ; finally, the teaching concerning the last things occupying the whole of chapter
xiii. The evidence suggests that most of this teaching cannot
be attributed to Jesus, and reflects the point of view of the
apostolic generation.[1] The genuineness of their arrangement
cannot be defended, but whoever brought the material together
did so with a definite purpose in view : he wished to present
those conceptions which he regarded as fundamental for himself and for the Church of his time, as a kind of last testament
of the Lord, serving also, as was the intention of the Evangelist,
for a catechetical outline. While it is possible that the Nazarene
may have preached in Jerusalem, we do not know whether he
actually did so.[2] In any case the utterances attributed to him
by the so-called tradition have probably no relation to what
he might have said.

Leaving on one side those episodes which only serve as a
setting for the teaching, and which possess, undoubtedly, no
other reality, such as the cursing of the fig-tree, and the widow's
mite, there remain three important episodes which occur before
the beginning of the drama of the Passion, *viz.* the purging of
the Temple, the feast and the anointing in the house of Simon
the Leper, and the Last Supper.

[1] For instance, the Cursing of the Fig-tree, the parable of the Husbandmen (*cf.* **CCXV**, 385 *ff.*) ; the Apocalypse in ch. xiii.
[2] *Cf.* **CLVI**-*a*, 386 *ff.*

III

THE CHIEF EVENTS

(1) It may be admitted that the purging of the Temple (Mark ii. 15 *ff.*) is linked up with the Messianic entry ; two episodes which are usually accepted or rejected together. The narrative runs : " And they come to Jerusalem : and Jesus went into the temple, and began to cast out them that sold and bought in the temple, and overthrew the tables of the money-changers, and the seats of them that sold doves : and would not suffer that any man carry any vessel through the temple. And he taught, saying unto them, Is it not written,[1] My house shall be called of all nations the house of prayer ? but ye have made it a den of thieves." [2]

In certain cases, specified by the *Torah* (Lev. xii. 8 ; xiv. 22), worshippers at the Temple could bring an offering of doves. In the court called the Court of the Gentiles, they would find vendors of these birds, together with money-changers who would give the Jews of the Diaspora clean money for the payment of the Temple tax (Exod. xxx. 13 *ff.*). All these merchants tried to rob the pilgrim, who naturally protested, and the resulting scene was neither edifying nor in keeping with its surroundings. The priests winked at these proceedings, since for them it was, however annoying, a proof that the faith of Israel still lived.

Hence the setting of the incident is perfectly appropriate ; but, in addition to the two passages from Isaiah and Jeremiah actually quoted, it has been suspected, not without reason, that the incident reflects the influence of Zechariah xiv. 21 [3] and Malachi iii. 1 *ff.*[4] This of itself would give rise to doubts ; moreover, it is hard to believe that such a disturbance could fail to result in unpleasant consequences for Jesus. This consideration has clearly occurred to the redactor, since he immediately adds (xi. 18) that the chief priests and scribes who witnessed the proceedings, sought to destroy him but dared not take action because they were afraid of him (ἐφοβοῦντο γὰρ αὐτόν) and feared the people who were astonished at his

---

[1] Isa. lvi. 7, literal quotation from the LXX.

[2] Reminiscence of Jer. vii. 11.

[3] " *In that day there shall be no more merchants in the temple of the Lord of Hosts.*"

[4] " *Behold, I will send my messenger, and he shall prepare the way before me : and the Lord, whom ye seek, shall come to his temple, even the messenger of the covenant, whom ye delight in. . . . Who shall stand when he appeareth ? . . . He shall purify the sons of Levi.*"

teaching (τῇ διδαχῇ αὐτόν). Of course the Evangelist had no knowledge of such feelings, he merely invents them.

It is also extremely likely that the whole episode was invented, and is nothing more than a dramatization of the Messianic expectation, a fulfilment of prophecies adapted to the purpose of symbolic instruction.[1] It is not irrelevant to remark that the redactor has introduced the incident between the two halves of the story of the barren fig-tree, symbolizing Jewish unbelief. In fact, the two sections supplement one another : in the judgment of the Christian writer both the worship of Israel and her spirit alike merit rejection. It is difficult to attribute such a point of view to Jesus. But, in reality, it is not with Jesus and the original Gospel that we are dealing, but with the horizon of the Gospel writer. From this conclusion, to which we are brought at the outset, it will be hard to escape during our examination of the narrative of the activities of the Nazarene at Jerusalem.

(2) The anointing at Bethany is inserted into the narrative of the Last Supper, inasmuch as it is prefaced by the words (Mark xiv. 1) : " After two days was the feast of the Passover, and of unleavened bread : and the chief priests and the scribes sought how they might take him by craft, and put him to death. But they said, Not on the feast day, lest there be an uproar of the people."

The first indication of the end closes the discourses : it is almost brutally stated in Matthew xxvi. 1 : " And it came to pass, when Jesus had finished all these sayings, he said unto his disciples, Ye know that after two days is the feast of the Passover, and the Son of Man is betrayed to be crucified."

Words are now to be replaced by deeds to bring about the ultimate fulfilment. The second quotation raises again the historical problem which has already confronted us more than once, of how the Gospel writer could have known what he has set down. In Matthew xxvi. 1 ff. the statement of Mark is transformed into romance by the addition of elements which wear a false guise of accuracy but involve contradictions. Luke (xxii. 1–2) feeling the danger, doubtless, of over-precision, confines himself to a brief indication of the hostile designs of the chief priests and scribes. Hence we are not dealing with a genuine reminiscence, but merely with an inference *post eventum* drawn from the event itself.

While his enemies were laying their plans, Jesus is supposed

---

[1] Goguel (**CLVI-*a*,** 399) would see in the incident an attempt to dramatize a saying of Jesus protesting against the presence of merchants in the Temple, but this view is pure hypothesis.

to have announced his death and approaching burial, for this is the meaning of the anointing at Bethany. During the supper in the house of Simon the Leper, a woman comes in and pours precious ointment over his head. Some of those present regard her act as a needless waste, but the Master rebukes them and praises the lovely deed of the woman (καλὸν ἔργον). He adds : " She is come beforehand to anoint my body to the burying." [1] Luke vii. 36 ff. makes the incident take place in Galilee, in the house of a Pharisee, also named Simon, who refuses to believe in the mission of Jesus, because, so he thinks, the prophet has failed to recognize that the woman who has anointed his feet and wiped them with her hair is a notorious sinner. The Master utilizes the occasion to extol the saving efficacy of the love which. the humility of the unfortunate woman has so strikingly exemplified. Conservative critics naturally deny that the two incidents are the same ; but Luke himself refutes them by omitting the anointing at Bethany. We may well believe that he is nearer to the original source of the tradition which has preserved the episode, and that Mark followed by Matthew has displaced it and interpreted it in harmony with his own purpose.[2] It furnishes a good example, and a disturbing one, of the freedom with which the redactors have treated the traditional material.

According to the point of view of the Synoptic tradition, it was the members of the priestly and the scholastic orders who put an end to the career of Jesus, because they could no longer endure either his teaching or his person. After the purging of the Temple, they determined to destroy him but they were afraid of the people " because all the people was astonished at his doctrine " (Mark ii. 18). Moreover, if we may believe the Gospel writers, he did all that he could to irritate them : he told them the parable of the Wicked Husbandmen, who rebelled against their Master (Mark xii. 1–2) ; he replied to their carping questions in a manner calculated to excite their hostility (Mark xii. 13–17) ; he broke a lance with the Sadducees over the question of the resurrection, and

---

[1] The Synoptic Gospels do not know the name of this woman. Christian legend, here completely inconsistent, arrives at Mary Magdalene by combining this passage with John xii. 3, which calls her Mary, Luke vii. 36 ff., which attributes the anointing to a woman that was a sinner, and Luke viii. 2, which includes a Mary of Magdala out of whom Jesus had cast seven devils, among the women who had accompanied him in Galilee.

[2] CV, 391 ff. ; CVIII, 290. LXXXVI, 159, rightly points out that the incident is foreign to Mark's scheme of the Passion, since it breaks the sequence between Mark xiv. 2 and xiv. 10.

concluded with words : " Ye do greatly err " (Mark xii. 18–27) ; he clashed with the scribes on the question of the Davidic descent of the Messiah (Mark xii. 35–7) ; he even attacked them directly and held them up to derision with the words : " Beware of the scribes, which love to go in long clothing, and love salutations in the market-places, and the chief seats in the synagogues, and the uppermost rooms at feasts : which devour widows' houses, and for a pretence make long prayers : these shall receive greater damnation " (Mark xii. 38–40).

It is obvious that all these conflicts, born of the hostility towards the Jews in the mind of the Evangelist, on account of their social position or their culture, are wholly fictitious, at least, so far as their locality is concerned. Their only purpose is to explain the source of that alliance between the various elements of Jewish society which led to the death of Jesus. Three times, like a refrain, occurs the statement that the chief priests and the scribes sought how they might take him and put him to death (Mark ii. 18 ; xii. 12 ; xiv. 1). It is a serious matter to kill a man for the words which the Nazarene is supposed to have uttered ; but the Evangelist knew that Jesus was actually put to death. In his time the most formidable enemies of the Christian faith were the Jewish rabbis ; hence he does his best to make the hatred of the ancestors of these people against the Lord seem probable. Moreover, the sympathy of the crowd, as we shall go on to prove, is equally fictitious.

IV

THE CHRONOLOGICAL PROBLEM

For the present let us accept the statement of the Gospel writer that a conspiracy was being hatched. The episodes which lead us to Calvary seem to follow one another in an orderly sequence and with an accurate chronology. Unfortunately, a closer examination of the sources shows that, even if we neglect the contradictions between John and the Synoptics, and confine ourselves to the latter, the apparent sequence is purely artificial, and that actually, not only in Matthew and Luke, but already in Mark,[1] different traditions intermingle or overlie one another. We have already noticed the contradiction between xiv. 1 (" After two days was the feast of the passover, and of unleavened bread ") and xiv. 12 (" And the first day of unleavened bread, when they killed the passover "). Chapter

[1] **CIII**, ii, 489 ; **LXXXV**, 283.

xiv. as a whole seems to be drawn from two sources,[1] the one
relating to the preparation, and the other to the supper ; the
first, which is the later of the two, is occupied with the Paschal
character of the Supper ; to the other and earlier source this
conception is foreign. Broadly speaking, it seems probable
that Mark, in the composition of his narrative, has utilized
fragments based upon different chronological systems, that is,
upon two traditions, one of which placed the death of Jesus
before the Passover, and the other *after* it. The former of these
two traditions occupies the principal place in the Marcan
redaction ; but the traces of the other are to be seen in the
account of the preparation of the Paschal meal (xiv. 12 *f.*) and
in the introduction to the prediction of the denial of Peter
(xiv. 26 : the singing of the *Hallel*). The first source placed
the Supper on Thursday, the 13th of Nisan, and the death of
Jesus on Friday, the 14th, *before the Passover* ; the second gave
the 14th as the date of the Supper, now become the Paschal
meal, and the 15th as the day of the death of Jesus.[2]

It would also appear probable that the arrangement of Holy
Week, that is, the sequence of days from Palm Sunday to
Easter Sunday as given by Mark, is not primitive, and was
not known to the earliest tradition. The length of the stay
of Jesus remained uncertain, and tradition tended to make it
longer than a week.[3] This seems to be implied in the saying
of Matthew xxiii. 37 : " O Jerusalem . . . how often would
I have gathered thy children together ? " also, that in Mark
xiv. 49 : " I was daily with you in the Temple teaching," and
the saying in Mark xiv. 19 : " And when the evening was come
they used to leave the city." This thrice repeated statement,
retained by Luke xiii. 34 ; xix. 47 ; xxi. 37, attests either a
customary action on the part of Jesus, or the uncertainty of
the apostolic memories. Beneath these memories, or at least,
beneath the information of the Gospel writers, there lie, perhaps,
only these two simple statements : (1) Jesus came up to Jerusalem and died there ; (2) Jesus rose again. Hence, in order
to work these two facts into a single narrative, they started
with the Resurrection and, tracing the events backwards,[4] upon
the probable hypothesis of a brief visit to Jerusalem [5] they

[1] CCVII, 24. [2] CCVII, 27.

[3] CXXVIII, 93 *ff.* Goguel (CLVI–*a*, 384–9) brings Jesus up to Jerusalem in September or October. His reasons, based on the passages
here discussed, are not convincing.

[4] CV, 473 ; XCVIII, 92.

[5] There is a difference of opinion among the critics on this point.
For instance, Ed. Meyer reduces the stay to four days (XXIV, i, 168),
while Goguel (CLVI, 255 *f.* ; CLVI–*a*, 384 *ff.*) thinks that a week does

fitted the story of the Master's last days into the pattern of
Holy Week. Unfortunately, as we shall shortly see, the date
of the Resurrection involved difficulties, and it is to be feared
that the earliest tradition ignored the point. Sunday was
selected as the day of the Resurrection because, at a very early
date, and for reasons wholly unconnected with historical fact [1]
or with actual reminiscence, that day, as the day of the risen
and glorified Lord (κυριακή), came to be regarded as the only
possible day of the Resurrection. Moreover, the ground for
this development was already prepared by religious custom,
whose needs and suggestions determined the entire chronology
of Holy Week. In all probability the Gospel writer was only
concerned with the religious aspect of this sequence of events
in time.

Bearing this in mind, it is easy to explain the insuperable
divergence which appears between the Synoptic chronological
scheme of the events of the Passion and the Johannine scheme,
while admitting that the former is lacking in clearness and
coherence. This lack is due to the fact that, taking the Sunday
of the Resurrection as a starting-point, it was possible to
arrange the events in various ways. For instance, the prophetic
references, which we shall shortly examine, made it necessary
that Jesus should be in the grave for three days, or until the
third day. If the first form of expression was to be taken
literally, it was necessary to take the Crucifixion back to Thursday and reckon the three days as Thursday, Friday, Saturday.
If the second expression were taken as the basis of the calculation, then the death would be assigned to Friday and the
sequence would be counted as Friday, Saturday, Sunday morning. Clearly, no consideration of historical exactitude entered
into the controversy. For the system which finally prevailed
in the Synoptic Gospels and established the Supper as a Paschal
meal, could only do so in violation of historical fact and even
of Jewish custom, since the latter could never have admitted
of a trial and execution on the day of the Passover.[2]

If we turn for a moment to the Johannine chronology, a
divergence from the Synoptic tradition immediately presents
itself, giving us a glimpse into the processes by which the Gospel
writers reached their appearance of chronological exactitude.

---

not allow sufficient time for the drama of the Passion to develop. The
fact is that we are not on the plane of reality, and such calculations are
futile.

[1] **XXIV**, i, 170.

[2] All the commentators insist on this point. *Cf.* **CCVII**, 24 *ff.*;
CVIII, 290.

The Johannine narrative [1] begins with the arrival at Bethany and the anointing, which are placed " six days before the Passover " (xii. 1 ; πρὸ ἓξ ἡμερῶν τοῦ πάσχα). The last supper takes place on Thursday evening, before the feast (xiii. 1 : πρὸ δὲ τῆς ἑορτῆς τοῦ πάσχα), so that, when those who are at the table see Judas go out, they suppose that as treasurer of their little company he has gone to buy what is needed for the Passover (xiii. 29 : εἰς τὴν ἑορτήν). The trial is on Friday, and John xviii. 28 describes the Jews as refusing to enter Pilate's prætorium for fear of defiling themselves and thus being prevented from eating the Passover in the evening. Moreover, when Pilate presents Jesus to the people we are told that " it was the Preparation of the Passover, and about the sixth hour " (xix. 14). Apart from these indications of the course of events, the Johannine chronology remains indeterminate. The Holy Week of the Fourth Gospel, if it is a week, abounds in discourses but is lacking in facts. The Gospel editor conforms to his usual practice and only records that which interests him and accords with the plan of his narrative. In his case the plan was to give a symbolic significance to his chronology and especially to draw out the parallel between the death of the Lord and the sacrifice of the Paschal lamb. Jesus is the Lamb of God (John i. 29), and he must die at the precise moment appointed by the Law for the slaughter of the Passover lamb. This is why the Johannine Jesus dies, not at three in the afternoon as the Synoptists have it, [2] but towards evening. The symbolism implied by the whole scene is pointed by the Evangelist himself when he notes that (xix. 36) they did not break the legs of Jesus after he was dead, in order that the saying of the Scripture might be fulfilled : " A bone of him shall not be broken," [3] a text which refers to the Passover lamb. A little further on (xix. 41), the Evangelist remarks that the body of Jesus was laid in a tomb in the very scene of his execution, thus fulfilling the requirement of the *Torah* (Exod. xii. 46) which prescribed that the lamb should be killed and eaten *in the same place*. [4] Hence it is waste of time to discuss the question

[1] CCVII, 27 *ff.*

[2] Mark xv. 25, 33, 34, assigns the placing on the cross to the third hour (9 in the morning), the darkness to the sixth hour (midday) and the death to the ninth hour (3 o'c.). John places the condemnation about the sixth hour (midday) and, since the period of suffering in his account seems to have the same duration as in Mark, the death must have taken place about six in the evening. *Cf.* CXXVII (i), 869.

[3] Exod. xii. 46 ; *cf.* Num. ix. 12, and Ps. xxxiv. 21.

[4] CXXVII (i), 892.

whether the date of John is more reliable than that of Mark ; [1]
it was arrived at, not by following a more or less historical
tradition, but under the influence of a symbolism which the
author of the Fourth Gospel did not invent, since he found it
already existing in Paul (1 Cor. v. 7) : " Christ, our Passover,
is sacrificed for us." All that can be said about it is that it
is earlier than the Synoptic date, because of its agreement with
the ideas of Paul and with Jewish custom.[2]

It is equally useless to attempt to reconcile the two dates,[3]
for only definite historical evidence can either reconcile them
or prove their incompatibility, and that is not available : Mark,
equally with John, is preoccupied only with symbolic and
liturgical considerations. The sources do not tell us what their
editors *knew*, but only what they *believed*, nor did they always
believe the same thing. There is reason to fear that they did
not know anything at all, first, because they only began to be
interested in the question of the date at a time when knowledge
was no longer possible ; secondly, because it does not appear
that they sought to know, but merely to understand and to
explain. Their one object was to understand, to explain and
to vindicate the symbols and the credal implications of the
ritual system which had developed in their midst.[4]

The Marcan editor would seem to have regarded the sequence
of events in Holy Week as follows : Sunday, palms, and the
entry into Jerusalem ; Monday, the cursing of the fig-tree and
the cleansing of the Temple ; Tuesday, disputations and discourses in the Temple ; Wednesday, the anointing at Bethany
and the betrayal by Judas ; Thursday, the preparations for
the Supper and the Supper itself ; Friday, the trial and crucifixion ; Saturday, Jesus is in the tomb ; Sunday, the Resurrection.[5] But this order is only arrived at at the cost of coming
to a decision on certain doubtful points. For instance, Mark
xiv. 1 says, " After two days was the Passover and the Feast
of Unleavened Bread " (μετὰ δύο ἡμέρας) : this is his date for
the anointing at Bethany. We are then faced by the question
of the interpretation of the words " after two days." They
may mean " the day after tomorrow," or " tomorrow," and
in this connexion it should be noted that Mark, in referring
to the Resurrection, understands the phrase " after three days,"
as if it meant " on the third day," hence, in two days. By

[1] CVII, i, 308.   [2] CXXVII (ii), 465 ; CV, 396. *Cf.* CXIV, 108.
    [3] LXIX, ii, 516. *Cf.* IX, i, 288, n. 3, and CVII, i, 314 *ff.*, which
examines various recent theories.
    [4] Bertram, *Die Leidengeschichte Jesus und der Christuskult.* 1922.
    [5] XCVII, 124 *ff.* ; CI, 331.

accepting one or other of these interpretations it is possible to arrive at two conflicting chronological schemes.[1]

It would be useless to enter into a further discussion of the chronological discrepancy between Mark and John, a divergence out of which arose the long-drawn Quartodeciman controversy which troubled the early Church. The Quartodecimans, who were mainly Asiatic Christians, assigned the death of Jesus to the 14th of Nisan, following John ; while their opponents held to the 15th, the Synoptic date, which ultimately prevailed.

In reality we know nothing about the date of the execution of Jesus. If it is possible, or if we stretch the point, probable, that the prophet came to Jerusalem for the Passover and was crucified on one of the days of the Feast,[2] it is neither impossible nor even improbable that this point of time was chosen for the date of his death on purely mystical grounds, such as the fulfilment of the symbolism of the Paschal lamb, or for some other obscure reason of the same kind.[3] In this case the conflict between the divergent chronologies of Holy Week will correspond to " ritual differences in the observation and the interpretation of the Mystery." [4]

The divergence between the traditions appears still more serious when we attempt to determine from them the year of the death of Jesus. The reasonable view that the Nazarene was condemned by Pilate, on the supposition that, in all probability, the latter was governor of Judæa from 26 to 36, is satisfied to place the Crucifixion somewhere between these two dates. At the most, such a view, with the help of somewhat doubtful synchronisms, such as the conversion of Paul, the date of which is itself far from certain,[5] may attempt to arrive at a more satisfactory precision.[6] The Church of the sixth century was much better informed on this cardinal point than the Church of the first century, an increase of knowledge which is rather suspicious.[7] Now while the Synoptic narrative suggests a date shortly before or after 30, the mention of Pilate is the only

---

[1] For this interpretation—much disputed—of μετὰ δύο ἡμέρας, cf. CIII ; XCVIII ; CV ; CI, ad loc. ; CCVII, 22 ; CVII, i, 309 ff.

[2] CLVI–a, 414–21.   [3] CLXII, 441.   [4] CXXVII (ii), 481.

[5] CCLX, 2 ff. The attempt has been made to discover on what dates the 14th or 15th of Nisan fell on a Friday (cf. EB, art. Chronology, sec. 55) ; it has been found that in 30 the 14th of Nisan fell on Friday, April the 7th, and in 33 on Friday, April the 3rd ; the 15th of Nisan would fall on no Friday between 26 and 35 ; but it is a question whether we are limited to Friday, and how much reliance should be placed upon the very uncertain Jewish calendar. Cf. CI, 340.

[6] Cf. CLXXVI, 611 ff. ; CLXXV, 103.

[7] CCXCII, iii, 21 ; Von Dobschütz, in Texte und Unters., XI, i, 136 ff., gives the passages.

guarantee of this date, a guarantee which may itself be none too well-founded. For it is evidently possible that his name may have found its way into the Marcan tradition for a similar reason to that which led Luke to select Quirinus, namely, that he was a well-known figure and was in bad odour among the Jews. Be that as it may, there were Christian circles where the death of Jesus was placed as early as 21. We learn this from Eusebius (*H.E.*, i. 9, 3 *ff.*), who quotes a treatise " recently published," entitled *Memoirs of the Saviour* (τοῦ σωτῆρος ὑμῶν ὑπομνήματα). It has been supposed that he was referring to a pseudepigraphical work otherwise known as the *Acts of Pilate*. On the other hand, Irenæus, in his *Demonstratio apostolicæ prædicationis*, an Armenian translation of which was recently discovered, describes Pilate as the " procurator of Claudius Cæsar " (*Dem.*, lxxiv). The reference must be to Claudius, who was emperor from 41 to 54. While it is possible that Irenæus may have confused him with Tiberius (Tiberius Claudius Nero), it does not seem likely, because we know from another of his works (*Hær.*, xxii, 22, 5) that Irenæus placed the death of Jesus *in ætatem seniorem, i.e.* between 40 and 50, as an inference from John viii. 57, where the Jews are represented as saying, " Thou art not yet 50 years old, and hast thou seen Abraham ? " [1] Others placed the birth of the Lord in 9, and his death in 58, under Nero.[2]

In other words, the death of Jesus involves us in the same uncertainties as his birth. Here and there writers were found sufficiently venturous to attempt the task of supplementing the lack of accurate information by guesswork, but their attempts only bear witness to the ignorance of the earliest Christian generations. They do not set our feet upon historical ground ; we do not know, because the Gospel writers did not know either. An apologist was not concerned with chronological accuracy. The truth which rests on experience takes no account of time.

Altogether, the Synoptic narrative of the stay of Jesus at Jerusalem gives us a general impression of emptiness, an impression which is not diminished by the padding of the discourses, but rather increased. The tradition has retained hardly anything ; possibly it had never contained much, and, after all, perhaps there was not much to be known.

---

[1] On the same text is based the statement of John Chrysostom, *Homil.*, 54, that Jesus was about forty years old at the time of his death.

[2] *Passus est X. Kal. apr. Nerone III et Valerio Messala coss.* (Anonymous writing of the nineteenth century based upon Alexander of Jerusalem. The Byzantine chronicler Syncellus would support this date.) Text in CCC, II, ii, 161 *ff.*, and XII (ii), ii, 506 *ff.*

CHAPTER II

THE LAST SUPPER [1]

IN the Synoptic account of the Last Supper, where Christ is
described as having performed acts and uttered words which
still constitute the life of the religion that took its rise from him,
it is necessary to distinguish two periods, separated by the
announcement of the understanding arrived at between Judas
the betrayer and the Jewish conspirators : (1) the preparations
for the Supper ; (2) the Supper itself. The betrayal of Judas
will be passed over for the present.

I

The Preparation of the Supper

According to Mark xiv. 12–17, the preparation took place
on the day when the Passover lamb which was to be eaten in
the evening was slain ; the disciples ask him where he intends
to eat the Passover, and he sends two of them into the city :
he tells them that they will meet a man carrying a pitcher of
water, and, in the house which he enters, they are to tell the
master of the house to show them the room where the Master
and his disciples will eat the Passover. He will show them a
large upper room where they are to make ready the Passover.
Everything happens as Jesus had said, and when the evening
has come he arrives with the Twelve. [2] The figure envisaged
by the Marcan editor is not Jesus the Nazarene, but the omnis-
cient and omnipotent Lord ; the account, utterly improbable,

[1] The bibliography is immense. The reader must be referred to
the principal commentaries for a study of the passages in question :
CCVI, 1st part ; **CXCIX** and **CCLXXIX**, ch. xiii, for the present state
of the problem and the proposed solutions ; Hauck, **RE**, art. *Abendmahl*,
for the earlier bibliography (1926).

[2] The reader will observe the curious *verbal* resemblance between
the directions of Jesus given here for the preparation of the Passover,
and those which he is said to have given in Mark xi. for the preparation
for the Messianic entry. The outlook is the same, and the redactor
seems to have repeated himself deliberately. *Cf.* **LXXXVI**, 159.

aims at and attains no other purpose but edification. Nevertheless, though Luke follows the Marcan story, it is too much for
Matthew (xxvi. 17 *ff.*), who has cut out the whole of the carefully
staged prophetic setting and merely makes Jesus say : " Go
into the city, to such and such a one (*πρὸς τὸν δεῖνα*) and say to
him. . . ."

The Marcan account is clearly intended to emphasize the
Paschal character of the Supper. We shall attempt to elucidate
its presuppositions. But first of all we must realize the inconsistencies into which we are plunged by the passage. We read,
in xiv. 1, that there are still two days before the Passover,
while in verse 12, although nothing has happened except the
anointing, which accounts for no appreciable interval of time,
we have already arrived at the Passover ; [1] that is to say, the
morning of the day on which the lamb is eaten, the 14th of
Nisan. Furthermore, in xiv. 2, the priests have said that they
will not arrest Jesus on the feast-day, which is exactly what
they are about to do. Orthodox commentators have made
desperate efforts to preserve the Paschal character with which
Mark has invested the Supper. They tell us, for instance, that
Jesus might have kept the feast a day ahead of the proper date ; [2]
a useless expedient, for the clear and immediate purpose of the
editor is to convince us that we are dealing with the actual
morning of the day of the *legal* celebration of the Passover.
Hence, in the view of unbiassed critics, there is no question of a
Paschal meal, and it is even urged that the Supper is only an
artificial doublet of the supper at which the anointing took
place, a doublet clearly arising from the desire to represent the
Last Supper as a Paschal meal. [3]

Let us return to the Jewish setting. According to common
belief the Passover was in commemoration of the sacrifice
performed by the Israelites on the eve of their Exodus from
Egypt. The main lines upon which the ritual was conducted
were laid down in the *Torah*. [4] Many details had been added
by the Rabbis, and have been codified in the Talmudic tractate
Pesachim. The feast began on the evening of the 14th of
Nisan, [5] which was, for the Jews, the beginning of the 15th.
In the same way as the Friday of each week is the *parasceve*,
i.e. the preparation, for the Sabbath, so the 14th was the
parasceve of the Passover : on that day were completed the
preparations which were legally begun on the 10th of Nisan.

---

[1] **CXIV**, 110 ; **CI**, 348 acknowledges the difficulty.   [2] **CI** ; **CXCI**, 38.
[3] **XXIV**, i, 177, and **CIII** ; **CXIV** ; **CVII**, i, *ad loc.*
[4] Exod. xii. 1–20 ; xiii. 1–16 ; Lev. xxiii. 5–7 ; Num. ix.
[5] **EB**, art. *Passover* ; **CCVI**, 61 *ff.* ; **CCLXXIX**, 211.

The lamb was slain which was to be completely consumed during the night. Limiting ourselves to the details which concern us, the Paschal meal consisted of the lamb, together with bitter herbs and unleavened bread; four cups were drunk by each participant, in memory, it was said, of the four words used to describe the deliverance of Israel in the narrative of the Exodus from Egypt. The first cup was drunk when the guests took their places at the table : it was prefaced by a *eucharistia,* (both a thanksgiving and a blessing), on the wine, and a second on the feast as a whole. Then it was the duty of the eldest son to ask for an explanation of the meaning of the ceremony, and the head of the house would reply with a discourse on the sufferings of Israel and her deliverance by Jahweh. Then the second cup was drunk, and the first part of the *Hallel* (Ps. cxiii.– cxviii.), known as the *Egyptian Hallel,* was sung.[1] The supper itself was then partaken of, followed by the third cup, the blessing of the meal, and the fourth cup ; the proceedings were terminated by singing the rest of the *Hallel.* It is obvious that individual custom or special circumstances might introduce minor changes into this general arrangement, but the details remained the same. It is only necessary to read the account in Mark to see that, apart from the final hymn (xiv. 26 ; $\varkappa a\grave{\iota}$ $\dot{\upsilon}\mu\nu\acute{\eta}\sigma a\nu\tau\epsilon\varsigma$), which may correspond to the *Hallel,* there is not a single feature of the prescribed Passover ritual in the account. There is no mention of the lamb, which is the more surprising since it might have been expected that some parallel would have been drawn between the slaying of the victim and the act which Jesus is supposed to have accomplished ; there is no mention of the bitter herbs nor of the four cups. The only feature of the Passover is, strangely enough, associated with the bread, which is not, so far as we know, *unleavened.*[2]

Luke, evidently troubled by so many inconsistencies, has in some respects corrected his predecessor. He has been careful to point out (xxii. 17) that the Supper begins with the blessing of the cup ; he has discarded Mark's embarrassing phrase " while they were eating," and he closes his account (xxii. 20) with the mention of a further cup, the fourth ritual cup. These changes are not the result of fuller knowledge, but the attempt, however imperfect, to arrange the order of events in such a way as to preserve the Paschal character of the scene. Even the account

---

[1] EB, art. *Hallel.*

[2] Mark xiv. 22 : " *And while they were eating, he took bread* ($\lambda a\beta\grave{\omega}\nu$ $\check{a}\varrho\tau o\nu$), *and brake it.*" $\text{"}A\varrho\tau o\varsigma$ means ordinary bread ; for the ritual bread of the Passover the word $\tau\grave{a}$ $\check{a}\zeta\upsilon\mu a$ was used, and Mark himself (xiv. 1) designates the feast by this word : $\text{'}H\nu$ $\delta\grave{\epsilon}$ $\tau\grave{o}$ π $\iota\sigma\chi a$ (*i.e.* the lamb) $\varkappa a\grave{\iota}$ $\tau\grave{a}$ $\check{a}\zeta\upsilon\mu a$ $\mu\epsilon\tau\grave{a}$ $\delta\acute{\upsilon}o$ $\dot{\eta}\mu\acute{\epsilon}\varrho a\varsigma.$

of how, after the Supper, the little band of disciples went out of Jerusalem (Mark xiv. 26), represents a violation of Jewish custom. Obedient to the command given in Exodus xii. 22 : " And none of you shall go out of his house until the morning," the Jews were not in the habit of leaving the city during the night of the Passover.

There is, however, a still more serious inconsistency than any of those hitherto mentioned : if the Supper was a Paschal meal, it would mark the beginning of the great feast of the 14th of Nisan, yet it is on this day that Jesus is arrested, tried and executed ! On this day that Simon the Cyrenian, coming in from the country (Mark xv. 21), is compelled to help Jesus in carrying his cross ! On this day they bought the shroud ! (Mark xv. 46). Hence legal business was transacted, and work was done, in the face of the explicit injunction of the *Torah* (Num. xxviii. 18), and in spite of the fact that rabbinical elaboration had extended the prohibition to the afternoon of the previous day (*Pesachim*, iv. 2) ! [1]

The attempt to escape from these insurmountable difficulties by means of quibbles, guesses and equivocations, in order to vindicate at all costs the Paschal character of Mark's account, is useless and only leads to further contradictions. The gospel writer is not concerned either with probability, with historical facts, or with our difficulties ; his mind is not moving in the sphere of history, but in the realm of mystical knowledge and ritual symbolism. He is concerned with the eucharistic customs of his environment, whose existence he seeks to validate by referring their origin to the Lord.[2] He is totally uninterested in the actual character of the Last Supper, and his whole attention, or rather his effort, is concentrated upon two points : (1) Jesus' announcement of the fatal betrayal, an announcement which seems perfectly natural to the narrator, since Christians of Mark's time had no doubts concerning the Lord's omniscience ; (2) the report of the words attributed to the Lord as establishing the Christian rite of communion (κοινωνία), the rite which united them to their Saviour Lord, and bound them together in the bond of brotherhood (ἀδελφοί). Even if the earliest tradition had retained an exact memory of the last scene around the table between Jesus and his disciples, it has been overlaid and obliterated by the ritual and liturgical

---

[1] **CCXCIX**, 134 *ff.*, has taken extraordinary pains to raise every possible objection against the Paschal Supper. He has only shown how far astray it is possible to go with perfectly good intentions. *Cf.* also **LXVI**, ii, 812, and for the opposite view : **CCLXXIX**, 212 *ff.*

[2] **CCCV**, 43 ; **LXXXVI**, 160 *ff.*

considerations which occupied the minds of the generation of Christians which Mark represents.

It is possible that the tradition knew that Jesus died about the time of the Passover. This fact, together with the desire to connect the institution of the Eucharist with the Last Supper, brought about the transformation of the Supper into a Paschal meal. Apparently we must find in Paul the beginnings of this movement. Paul does not say positively that the Lord's last supper was a Paschal meal, but he writes (1 Cor. v. 7): "Christ is our Passover (*i.e.* our Paschal lamb); he has been sacrificed as such." In his mind this involved a theory of redemption, into which we cannot enter here, and a special eucharistic symbolism to which we shall have occasion to refer later, a symbolism which may imply the influence of pagan Mystery cults. It is evident that the significance of this symbolism would be enhanced by giving a Paschal character to the Last Supper. It has been said (J. Réville) that Jesus could not at the same time be the lamb and eat it; but this objection fails; first, because symbols cannot as a rule be so strictly interpreted; secondly, because the Evangelists were careful not to represent the lamb as being on the eucharistic table. For the Marcan editor, as the result of Pauline influence, as we shall see, the eucharistic "mystery" represents the redeeming death of Jesus, and is rightly in place in this christianized Paschal meal, since, according to Pauline teaching, the eucharist replaces the Jewish Passover, just Jesus takes the place of the lamb. Perhaps we can now understand why and how the earliest tradition has forsaken whatever it may have known concerning this matter, in favour of the seemingly Paschal character of the Marcan account.

II

The Prediction of the Betrayal

The prediction of the betrayal is given in ambiguous terms in Mark xiv. 18–21: "And as they sat and did eat, Jesus said, Verily I say unto you, One of you which eateth with me shall betray me. And they began to be sorrowful, and to say unto him one by one, Is it I? And he ânswered and said unto them, It is one of the twelve, that dippeth with me in the dish.[1] The Son of Man indeed goeth, as it is written of him."

[1] This does not mean: he who dips his bread *at this moment*, but he who does so *habitually*, one of my companions. On any other interpretation the incident would become absurd by reason of the inaction of the disciples.

No answer can be given to the questions which naturally arise concerning the presence of Judas, the disciples' comments, and such further developments as must have been inevitable. Matthew xxvi. 25 cannot refrain from indicating Judas as the traitor : " Then Judas, which betrayed him, answered and said, Master, is it I ? He said unto him, Thou hast said." And Luke xxii. 23 shows us the extreme agitation of the apostles, as they ask one another, " Who is it ? " But it is evident that we are dealing only with occasional editorial changes here and there, representing no additional information. Still more is this true of the positive assertions of John xiii. 26 : " He it is to whom I shall give the sop, after having dipped it." He then gives the sop to Judas, " and immediately Satan entered into him." Jesus tells him to go about his business quickly. He obeys and goes out. The rest are unaware of what is happening !

Many futile attempts [1] have been made to analyse the incident from an historical or logical point of view, but it is clear that Mark is writing a sacred story, with scant regard to such purely mundane considerations. His main concern is to validate the Lord's foreknowledge and omnipotence, in which aim he is guided by a prophecy whose fulfilment he feels compelled to indicate, namely, that contained in Psalm xli. 9 : " Yea, mine own familiar friend, in whom I trusted, which did eat of my bread, hath lifted up his heel against me." Evidence that Christians had observed this passage is provided by John xiii. 18, where it is quoted : " I speak not of you all : I know whom I have chosen : but that the scripture may be fulfilled, He that eateth bread with me hath lifted up his heel against me." [2] No more striking example could be adduced of the complete indifference of the gospel writers to the problems which perplex us. It may be remarked that Luke has placed the announcement of the betrayal (xxii. 21–3) after " the institution of the Eucharist " (xxii. 15–20), so that we are shown the unspeakable sacrilege of Judas' participation in the " sacrament " with the rest of the apostles. Even the theologians have been shocked by it. But Luke was far from imagining the perturbation which his peculiar treatment of the narrative would cause. He was quite unaware of the later dogmatic implications which would be read into his account, and was accordingly unconscious that he was creating so distressing a problem for posterity.

---

[1] **XCI**–*a*, 259 ; **LXXXV**, 293 ; **CIII**, ii, 515 ; etc. *Cf.* **LXXXVI**, 160.
[2] Moreover, John has taken pains to prevent any ambiguity, since in vi. 70 *ff.*, he makes Jesus say : " *Have not I chosen you twelve, and one of you is a devil. Now, he spake of Judas Iscariot. . . .*"

But no doubt exists in the minds of orthodox commentators :
" Once again Jesus displays his knowledge of the inmost secrets
of men's hearts." [1]   But such a treatment of the problem merely
substitutes one question for another.   It is true that the prediction of the betrayal falls into line with the rest of the predictions of the Passion, but for that very reason it possesses no
more historical value than we can attach to them.   In short,
the inaccuracy and improbability of the account is to be explained by the fact that it rests upon no historical reminiscence.

III

THE EUCHARIST

During the Supper,[2] according to Mark's account (Mark xiv.
22 : " And while they were eating "), Jesus performed certain
acts and uttered certain words from which Christian dogmatic
theology has drawn a wealth of significant conclusions.   Not
only has it found in this scene the institution of the Eucharist,
the great Christian sacrament of communion, but also its grounds
of belief in the Redemption, in Transubstantiation, and in the
Real Presence.   The Evangelist can hardly have foreseen these
consequences, but he was already confronted by the existence
of a cult whose central rite was the Lord's Supper, a fraternal
meal partaken of at the Lord's Table and in his presence.[3]   It
was both natural and inevitable that the institution of this rite
should be traced back to the Lord himself, and that the Last
Supper should furnish its fitting occasion, even if the occasion
itself were not invented for the purpose.   Possibly tradition had
preserved the remembrance of a few weighty sentences uttered
by Jesus at this juncture, when he could hardly hide from himself the fact that the course of events was turning against him.
Two remarks are in place here : (1) In actual historical reality
Jesus is not aware that he is about to partake of his last meal ;
(2) grounds for the validation of the Eucharist can be, and have
been, sought outside the setting of the Supper, since John, who,
in his account of the Last Supper (xiii. 2 $f\!f$.), ignores the institution of the Eucharist, attaches it to the story of the miracle of
the loaves (vi. 11 $f\!f$.), and to the discourse on the bread of life
(vi. 35, 49-51, 53 f.).[4]   These facts do not seem, at first sight,

[1] CI, 351.
[2] In order to understand the remarks which follow the reader should
have before him a Synopsis, or at least the text of the Synoptics.
[3] *Cf.* 1 Cor. x. 16 $f\!f$.   [4] *Cf.* CXX, 95 ; CCVI, 195 $f\!f$.

to support the Marcan account, an impression which is heightened by the serious divergences between his account and those given in Matthew and Luke.

We are faced by three questions arising out of this situation : Did Jesus actually say something of supreme importance during the Last Supper ? What did he really say ? What meaning did he attach to his words ? There are five passages which offer us material for an answer to them : one from each of the Synoptic Gospels (Mark xiv. 22–5 ; Matt. xxvi. 26–9 ; Luke xxii. 15–20) ; one from Paul (1 Cor. ii. 23–5) ; and one from Justin Martyr (*Apol.*, i. 66), much later than the rest (middle of the second century), but which is believed, rightly or wrongly, to be derived from another source than the canonical gospels.

Here are, first of all, the three Synoptic passages side by side :

Mark xiv. 22 : " And as they did eat, Jesus took bread, and blessed, and brake it, and gave to them, and said, Take [1] : this is [2] my body. 23. And he took the cup, and when he had given thanks, he gave it to them : and they all drank of it. 24. And he said unto them, This is my blood of the testament [3] which is shed for many. 25. Verily, I say unto you, I will drink no more of the fruit of the vine, until that day that I drink it new [4] in the kingdom of God." [5]

Matthew xxvi. 26 : " And as they were eating, Jesus took bread, and blessed it, and brake it, and gave it to the disciples, and said, Take, eat ; this is my body. 27. And he took the cup and gave thanks, and gave it to them, saying, Drink ye all of it ; 28. For this is my blood of the testament, which is shed for many for the remission of sins. [6] 29. But I say unto you, I will not drink henceforth [7] of this fruit of the vine, until that day when I drink it new with you in my Father's kingdom."

Luke xxii. 15 : " And he said unto them, With desire I have desired to eat this passover with you before I suffer. [8] 16. For I say unto you, I will not any more eat thereof, until it be fulfilled in the kingdom of God. 17. And he took the cup, [9] and gave thanks, and said, Take this, and divide it among yourselves : 18. For I say unto you, I will not drink of the fruit of the vine, until the kingdom of God shall come. 19a. And he took bread and gave thanks, and brake it, and gave unto them, saying, This is my body 19b which is given for you : this do in remembrance of me. [10] 20. Likewise also the cup [11] after supper, saying, This cup is the new testament in my blood, which is shed for you."

For notes see page 436.

At this point it becomes necessary to discuss certain technical details. The manuscript tradition of the Lucan section exhibits several important features. The text here given follows, with a few unimportant variations, the four great exemplars usually designated by the letters Aleph, A, B, C : the Greek Sinaitic, the Alexandrine codex, the Codex Vaticanus, and the Codex Ephræm ; but the famous representative of the so-called

---

[1] Several MSS. add φάγετε = eat, a copyist's addition, following Matthew.

[2] There has been endless discussion whether the word is should be understood in a real or a symbolic sense. Its interest is mainly theological as bearing on the controversy concerning transubstantiation. It need only be remarked that in Aramaic the phrase would not contain the word is.

[3] We may recall Exod. xxiv. 8 : " And Moses took the blood and sprinkled it on the people, and said, Behold the blood of the covenant " ('Ιδοὺ τὸ αἷμα τῆς διαθήκης). . . .

[4] καινός = new is probably to be understood in the sense of a new kind, as similarly in Isa. lxv. 17 : ἔσται γὰρ ὁ οὐρανὸς καινὸς καὶ ἡ γῆ καινή = " There shall be new heavens and a new earth " (CI, ad loc.), and not in the sense of a fresh, or second, covenant (CCVI, 119). Similarly, fresh wine would be expressed by νέος.

[5] The Kingdom is often compared to a feast in the rabbinical literature. CCXVII, 166 ff. Cf. Matt. xxii. 1 ff. ; Luke xiv. 16 ff.

[6] We have here an important addition to Mark. It is no longer merely a question of ratifying the covenant by blood, as in Exod. xxiv. 8, but the blood shed by Jesus has become the blood of an atoning sacrifice, as in Lev. xvii. 11 : " For the life of the flesh is in the blood : and I have given it to you upon the altar to make an atonement for your souls : for it is the blood that maketh an atonement by reason of the life (which is in it)."

[7] Of this = τούτου is possibly intended to emphasize the contrast between the wine which he holds in his hands and that which is reserved for him in the Kingdom.

[8] The character of the meal has now become fully apparent, as also Jesus' full knowledge of all that is about to happen, and the significance of all his actions.

[9] Here Jesus begins with the cup, as against Mark and Matthew.

[10] A vital addition, which institutes the Eucharist in the strict sense by enjoining the repetition of Christ's ritual act. And already we have an implied interpretation of the rite which has been instituted : it is to be a memorial. Note that the passage does not say, nor even suggest, that the rite is a sacrament, i.e. a rite imparting some special grace.

[11] A repetition of what has already been described in v. 17. This proves that the Lucan section is composed of two accounts awkwardly combined. The one, 15–18, is complete by itself ; the other, 19–20, is in the main, with the exception of the addition : This do . . . , taken from Mark.

Western Text, Codex D (the Cambridge Codex Bezæ),[1] together with several manuscripts of the same family, break off after the words "This is my body," that is to say, in the middle of verse 19.[2] Hence they give Luke xxii, 15–19*a*, with slight variations, but they omit 19*b* and 20, that is, substantially, the injunction to repeat the rite, the mention of the second cup, and " the testament in my blood." On the other hand, an important Syriac manuscript,[3] the Sinaitic Syriac, presents approximately the constituent elements of Aleph, A, B, and C, but arranged in a different order ; the verses of the text given above appear as follows : 15, 16, 19, 20*a*, 17, 20*b*, 18. This reproduces the order of Mark–Matthew, retaining Luke's preamble, but one of the cups, the first, has disappeared. Another Syriac version, known as the Curetonian, supported by two Latin manuscripts of the version known as the Old Latin, adopts the following order in agreement with the Textus Receptus : 15, 16, 19, 17, 18, and omits 20 ; *i.e.*, the second cup and the testament in the blood.

A third Syriac version, the Peshitto, supported by a late Latin manuscript of the Gospels (eleventh century),[4] retain verses 15, 16, 19, 20, but omits 17 and 19, that is to say, the first cup. Finally, Marcion (second century) makes use of yet another text,[5] which contained only verses 15, 18 and 19 : there is no cup, no testament and no injunction to repeat the rite. We cannot attempt to explain, for the present, all these divergences, nor to discuss all the endless controversies to which they have given rise ; [6] we shall content ourselves with the inference that at this point the Lucan tradition is not very certain, and that those early Christians who arranged it to suit themselves did not think that Luke's text was sacrosanct and merely the completion of Mark and Matthew.

We come next to the passage from Paul (1 Cor. xi. 23–5) :

" For I received from the Lord that which also I delivered unto you, that the Lord Jesus the same night in which he was betrayed took bread : 24. And when he had given thanks, he brake it, and said : [7] " This is my body which (is given) for you : this do in remembrance of me : 25. After the same manner also he took the cup, when he had supped, saying, This cup is

---

[1] These MSS. are described in **LV**, 60–88.

[2] **LV**, 88–97.

[3] Concerning the three Syriac MSS. here referred to (The *Sinaitic Syriac*, the *Curetonian*, and the *Peshitto*), *cf.* **LV**, 151 *ff.*

[4] Ad. Merx, *Die vier canon. Evangelien, nach ihren ältesten bekannten Texte*, ii, 2. Berlin, 1911, 439.

[5] **LXXI**, ii, 490.   [6] *Cf.* **CCVI**, 112 *ff.*

[7] Several MSS. add here λάβετε, φάγετε = *take, eat*, from Matthew.

the new testament in my blood : this do ye, as oft as ye drink it, in remembrance of me." [1]

The relation between this passage and the received text of Luke is obvious.

Finally, let us glance at the passage from Justin Martyr, *Apol.*, 1, 66, 3 : "The Apostles, in the memoirs which have been handed down from them (ἀπομνημονεύμασιν) and which are called Gospels, relate that they received this from him: he took bread and, having given thanks, he said to them : Do this in remembrance of me ; this is my body. And having taken the cup likewise and given thanks, he said : This is my blood. And he gave (it) to them only."

It may be asked whether Justin is giving an abridgement from memory (there is no mention of the testament), or whether he is drawing from a special source. Naturally, various answers have been given to these questions,[2] but it will suffice here to point out that the passage is in the line of the Pauline tradition.

So many statements, varying so greatly in content, both in respect of the amount and the character of their information, involve us in a very perplexing situation. We may wish in vain that we could know what was actually said and done in the apostolic group, in direct contact with Jesus. But our information is unreliable and dates from a far later period than those origins in which we are interested. However, we find in two early documents, the Acts of the Apostles, and the Teaching of the Twelve Apostles (the *Didaché*),[3] certain valuable material relating to these questions.

From the Acts we learn (ii. 42) that the Jews converted at Pentecost through the preaching of Peter " continued steadfastly in the Apostles' doctrine (τῇ διδαχῇ τῶν ἀποστόλων), and communion (τῇ κοινωνίᾳ), and in the breaking of bread (τῇ κλάσει τοῦ ἄρτου) and in prayers (ταῖς προσευχαῖς)." *The Apostles' doctrine* denotes the distinctive Christian hope and belief ; the *communion* implies the fraternal bond of union ; while by *the breaking of bread* and the *prayers* are indicated the religious observances of the community. Verse 46 gives further details concerning this last point : " And they, continuing daily with one accord in the temple (ἐν τῷ ἱερῷ ὁμοθυμαδόν = einmütig),

---

[1] This means : *Do this in memory of me, each time that you drink* (*it*). *Contra* : **CCVI**, 119.

[2] For instance, **CCVI**, 125, favours the first solution, while **CCXCIX**, 10 *ff.*, favours the second.

[3] A Palestinian (?) document, probably belonging to the end of the first or the beginning of the second century.

and breaking bread from house to house (*κατ' οἶκον*),[1] did eat their meat with gladness and singleness of heart." Whence we infer that their prayers were the usual Jewish prayers which they offered individually in the Temple ; and that the *breaking of bread*, denoting the fraternal bond which united them in distinction from the Jewish community, was also an actual meal, or, possibly, a rite introducing a meal, and concerning which the editor gives no information. The suggestion has been made that the words " with gladness " (*ἐν ἀγαλλιάσει*) indicate that the fraternal meal was a kind of anticipation of the Messianic banquet. But the suggestion is unnecessary ; the gladness of the brethren arose from their religious life, and from the sustaining hope, concerning which no doubt had as yet arisen to disturb their simple minds.

In this meal, not spiritual but material, the distinctive rite was the *breaking of bread*. There is no mention of a cup, nor the smallest indication that this rite was connected with the person of Jesus, nor even that it was in memory of him. We should probably see in it a purely Jewish custom, in which the meal partaken of together around the table symbolized and denoted the fraternal bond which united them,[2] and nothing more than this.

The *Didaché* is ostensibly a manual of Christian practice ; hence its evidence is of special value. We learn from it (ix. 2 and 3) what prayers and benedictions were to be said in connexion with the cup (*περὶ τοῦ ποτηρίου*), and subsequently with the breaking (*περὶ τοῦ κλάσματος*) of bread. Both were of a Jewish character. They occurred in the course of a meal which no doubt had a liturgical character, but which was none the less a real *private* meal. Nothing suggests that it was symbolical and, although the non-baptized were excluded from it (ix. 5), we have " no reason to believe that the rite was the fulfilment of an injunction of Christ, or that it was in commemoration of the death of the Lord, still less that it established between the participants a communion with the same Lord through the symbols of his flesh and his blood." [3] After having rendered thanks to God for material nourishment, they did no more than give thanks also for spiritual food, for the " holy vine of David, for life and knowledge " (ix. 2 and 3), without any

---

[1] Codex D has the plural *κατ' οἶκους*. It should perhaps be rendered : *now in one house and now in another*. Apparently *κατ' οἶκον* is in contrast with *ἐν τῷ ἱερῷ*. *Cf.* Acts v. 42 : a contrast between Jewish religious life and that of the Christian sect.

[2] CCVI, 130 *ff.* For the rabbinical ideas about this communion, *cf.* LXXIV, 55 *ff.*

[3] CCVI, 240 ; CCCVI, 175.

suggestion of a mystical relation thereby established between them.

However, we hear of a gathering which takes place on Sunday (κατὰ κυριακήν) : this *synaxia* affirms the fraternal communion of the believers, whose numbers had become too large to allow of all eating together daily, and, as in Acts, its distinctive rite is the *breaking of bread*. There is no mention of the cup. And, as in the case of the private eucharist of ch. ix., there is no word of the institution of the rite by Jesus, nor of any relation established between the rite and the body, the blood, the death, or the person of the Lord. The only difference is that, since the separation from Judaism has become more marked than in Acts, this eucharistic gathering takes the place, for the editor, of the sacrificial gathering of the Jews.[1] Moreover, since the *parousia* had already been considerably delayed, the author emphasizes his longing for the Kingdom (ix. 4 ; x. 5-6). In the main, however, we are still in the atmosphere of Acts. We are still on Jewish ground, where the infant community is endeavouring to build its own special dwelling-place.[2] Hence, it is not in the Gospel stories of the Supper, but rather in those of the miracle of the loaves that we should look for the link with this *breaking of bread* as it was practised among the Palestinian apostolic and subapostolic communities.[3] Nevertheless it was inevitable that Christian thought, as it diverged increasingly from Judaism, should occupy itself with this rite, and seek to give it a distinctive interpretation. It was equally inevitable that reflection on the life and death of Jesus, on his resurrection and his abiding presence in the midst of his own until the day of his speedy return,[4] should, as the prospect of that return became increasingly remote, affect the significance of the symbol of the communion of the Church. The fraternal meal assumed the guise of a continuation of those meals which the disciples had shared with their Lord, and especially of the last, which took on a unique importance. They began to think that it must have differed from the other meals, and this belief made it easy for interesting credal associations to attach themselves to it : indeed it was inevitable that the Last Supper should receive

---

[1] This is the meaning of the words : ὅπως καθαρὰ ἡ θυσία ὑμῶν ᾖ = *in order that your sacrifice may be pure* about which there has been much discussion. A comparison of ch. xiv. with ch. viii. leaves no doubt on the point.

[2] **XXXV**, 225.

[3] **CCXXII**, 80, n. 2.

[4] It should be observed that the appearances of the Risen One are related to this fraternal meal (John xxi. 9, 12, 13 ; Luke xxiv. 30-1, 41-2, and even John xx. 19-26).

such accretions.[1]   The first step in the process was the growth of the idea that the meal was a memorial.[2]   When a family has lost its head, or a group of friends its leader, they cannot help being occupied with his memory.   When they meet they speak of him, they recall his last words, they think of his last wishes, they idealize him and feel the presence of his spirit with them. So it was with the Christian brotherhood.   The first step led to others; the rite of fraternal communion became a memorial of the life, and above all of the death of Jesus; then it grew into the visible sign, first of spiritual communion, then of corporeal union, with the Lord.   Then it became the witness of a covenant made *by* him, the carrying out of the testament which he had bequeathed, the symbol of a promise whose terms must be repeated until it be fulfilled ; a mysterious and effectual operation—let us say sacrament—connected with baptism and essential for the making of a Christian ; and so we might continue.   Here, then, we have the rudiments of the evolution of the Eucharist, regarded, so to speak, from an external point of view ; it is a natural development.

When we pass on from the Jewish-Christian environment to an examination of the Pauline eucharistic teaching, we meet with instructive developments.   The passage from 1 Corinthians xi., quoted above, is not the only place where Paul speaks of the Eucharist.   We have another utterance in 1 Corinthians x. 16–17 :

" The cup of blessing which we bless, is it not the communion of the blood of Christ ?[3]   The bread which we break, is it not the communion of the body of Christ ?   For we being many are one bread, and one body : for we are all partakers of that one bread." [4]

Here a different note is struck from that in the Acts and the *Didaché*.   The feeling of brotherhood experienced by the Christians in the Acts and the *Didaché* arose from the fact that when they ate together they shared in the same hope and participated in the same prayers.   But, according to the passage just cited, it is because they drink of the same cup, whose wine represents the blood of Christ, and because they eat of the same bread, symbolizing the body of Christ, that they have become a single corporate body.   The reason for such a remarkable change of view calls for explanation.

---

[1] **CCXXII**, 79 *ff.* ;   **CCVI**, 133.   [2] **CCVI**, 173 *ff.*

[3] This should be understood as the participation in the blood of Christ, by which the communion of the brethren, *i.e.* the community, is brought into being.   *Cf.* Lietzmann, in **LVII**, 1 Cor. xlix.

[4] That is ;   *Many though we are, we are one loaf, one body.*

When we examine the two passages in 1 Corinthians x. 16–17 and xi. 23b–25, we find : (1) *The idea of fraternal communion* (x. 17 : *we are one bread, one body*). This need not be emphasized, as we have already observed it to be the natural consequence of the primitive *breaking of bread*. (2) *The idea of communion in the Lord* (x. 16 and 17 : the cup . . . communion of the blood : the participation of all in the one loaf). We use the term *communion,* communion of all believers *in,* and not merely *with* the Lord, a simpler, more natural, and at the same time, earlier conception, which is sufficiently explained by the primitive *breaking of bread.* Here the union is not only the result of *the action of the Lord,* but is *in him,* since it is effected by the eating of the bread which is his body and the drinking of the wine which is his blood. The question arises whether we are already dealing with the idea of transubstantiation, that is to say, the transformation of the consecrated kinds into the actual body and blood of Christ. There can be no doubt that this is not the case, for we should then be obliged to explain why such a miracle was not more familiar to early Christianity. Nor is it a question of mere symbolism ; the eucharistic table is *the table of the Lord,* in opposition to *the table of demons,* just as *the cup of the Lord* is contrasted with *the cup of demons* (1 Cor. x. 21). Now, for Paul, eating and drinking at the table of demons does not signify eating the flesh and drinking the blood of demons, but entering into communion with them (*κοινωνία*), since the ritual act implies surrender to their influence and entrance into their sphere of activity. Paul's comparison (1 Cor. x. 16, 17 and 21) clearly proves that in his view the Eucharist occupies the same place in the Christian religion as is held by sacrifices and sacred feasts in pagan cults. Hence, the Eucharist must be thought of as recreating for the Christian the actual circumstances of Christ at the moment when, according to the Apostle's Christology, he was about to accomplish the great sacrifice of redemption. It must be thought of as reproducing his very acts, as repeating his very words, mysterious indeed, but signifying for Paul that the redeeming death of Jesus is about to be consummated. For him the bread which Jesus distributed to the Apostles symbolizes his body, and the contents of the cup his blood ; so that the repetition of the consecration of the bread and the cup in the spirit in which he himself performed these acts, is to recall the participants to the conception of the redemption and to effectuate their mystic union with the Lord.

The act of placing on the Lord's table the bread and the contents of the cup, identifies them with him, informs them with that divine power (δύναμις) which has conquered death and by virtue of which those who believe on him will conquer it likewise.[1] Hence the viands on the table of demons, harmless in themselves if eaten without intent (1 Cor. x. 23 ff.), become a fatal food to those who partake of them in order to enter into communion with the demons. The passage in 1 Corinthians xi. 27 ff.: "Wherefore whosoever shall eat this bread, and drink this cup of the Lord, unworthily (ἀναξίως) shall be guilty of the body and blood of the Lord. . . . For this cause many are weak and sickly among you, and many sleep," seems to prove that all this is realistically conceived, and not as a spiritual process; and that an actual magical potency is attributed to the elements in the Pauline Eucharist.

Hence the eucharistic food is conceived of as possessing a kind of *tabu*; it operates beneficially to those who partake of it in the due *ritual*—in this case *spiritual*—state, but it is harmful, that is, fatal, to others.[2]

It will be agreed that if Jesus intended to imply all this in the words which 1 Corinthians xi. 23–5 attributes to him at the Last Supper, he must have had great faith in the intelligence of the Apostles, and that it is astonishing that they should have understood him.[3] But it is extremely doubtful whether he ever said: "This is my body" and "This is my blood," even with the intention of calling up the idea of his approaching death, since in themselves these words are meaningless, apart from the conception of the Redemption, or that of the communion of the body and the blood. It can only have been by considering it in the light of subsequent events, as yet unknown to Jesus and his disciples, that the Last Supper can have been transformed into a kind of mournful feast of farewell. The Apostle may well have believed that he was transmitting the actual words of the Lord (1 Cor. xi. 23: "I received of the Lord that which also I delivered unto you"); but we do not know the source from which he derived them. The question, to which we shall return later, arises whether he was referring to a tradition or to a special revelation.

(3) *The idea of atonement and redemption* (xi. 24–5: "This is my body which (is given) for you. . . . This cup is the new testament in my blood").[4] Thus Paul thinks of the death of

---

[1] CCL, 261.   [2] *Ibid.*   [3] CCI, 51.

[4] *Cf.* Rom. v. 9: "*Much more then, being now justified by his blood* (ἐν τῷ αἵματι αὐτοῦ), *we shall be saved from wrath through him.*" Eph. i. 7: "*In whom we have redemption through his blood* (τὴν ἀπολύτρωσιν διὰ τοῦ αἵματος αὐτοῦ), *the remission of sins* (τὴν ἄφεσιν τῶν παραπτωμάτων) *according to the riches of his grace.*"

Jesus as an atoning sacrifice, conferring upon men the forgiveness of sins, reconciling them to God, and assuring them of eternal life. The Eucharist recalls this sacrifice, is the symbol and expression of it, and in some sense, perhaps, re-enacts it by the consecration of the elements (1 Cor. xi. 26: "For as often as ye eat this bread and drink this cup, ye do show the Lord's death until he come "). The simple brethren in Acts and the *Didaché* can hardly have seen such wonders in their *breaking of bread*. Nevertheless, the question whether such ideas were in the mind of Jesus and were expressed by him in words, requires an answer. In the light of the Synoptic presentation of his teaching as a whole such as supposition is impossible, and there are absolutely no grounds for believing that the first generation of immediate disciples interpreted the death of their Master in this way. For them his death, at first seen only as a stumbling-block, was merely the necessary condition of the glorification of Jesus by the resurrection, and his exaltation to the position of Messiah (Acts ii. 31–3 and 36).

(4) *The idea of the New Testament* (xi. 25 : " This cup is the new testament in my blood," by which we must understand : My blood establishes a new covenant, after the manner of the one mentioned in Exodus xxiv. 8).[1] While the idea finds its natural expression in the teaching of Paul, for whom the reign of the Law is ended, and for whom Jesus the new Adam has inaugurated a new order of humanity, it is foreign to the thought of Jesus. The latter never claimed to have abolished the Law (Matt. v. 17), but conformed to it, or at least, believed that he did so, and, as we learn from Acts, imbued his disciples with his own reverence for it. It was the Kingdom that Jesus expected, not a new Covenant.

(5) *The injunction to continue the rite* (xi. 24 : " This do in remembrance of me "). Again the question arises whether Jesus could have given such a command, a command which amounts to the institution of a commemorative rite, probably of his death interpreted as a mystery of salvation in the Pauline sense, and of a symbol of the union of believers. The institution of a symbol of union could only have been possible if he had believed that the Kingdom was to be delayed. But the burden of his message was the imminence of the Kingdom. Nothing was further from his intention than the founding of a new religion. Hence it is difficult to imagine what meaning the

---

[1] Perhaps 'Paul is thinking of the covenant between God and Abraham (Gen. xvii. 11) the sign of which is circumcision. On the meaning of διαήκη = *covenant* and not *testament*, *cf.* Gal. iii. 17, and iv. 22–4.

Apostles could have attached to such a command from the lips of Jesus.[1]

Paul certainly believes in the truth of his statement that he received all this from the Lord ; but he could only have received it in the same way in which he received what he calls his gospel and his call, namely, by an immediate revelation (Gal. i. 11–12, 15–16), a personal revelation, which, apparently, happened conveniently to validate a practice which had already come into existence around him.[2]

(6) *The idea of a sacrament.* It must be admitted that the idea of a sacrament is implied in the assertion that Christians are one body because they eat of the same loaf. It is made more definite by the further conception that the bread and the cup bring the believer into a vital communion with the dying Christ, that is, according to Paul, with Christ in the act of accomplishing his most essential function. It is hardly necessary to point out again that there is nothing of this kind in Acts or in the *Didaché*. We are obliged to acknowledge that a *revolution* in the idea and practice of the Eucharist has taken place between what we find in these two primitive documents and what we find in the Pauline epistles.[3]

Moreover, the main problem lies, not in discovering whether Jesus really said the words which Paul attributes to him— (which cannot be seriously maintained), but in discovering the source from which Paul derived them. When we realize how the Apostle's mind was obsessed with the parallel between the *table of the Lord* and the *table of demons,* the question arises whether the Pauline eucharist did not spring from his Hellenic environment, and whether it may not represent *a fragment of paganism* introduced into primitive Christianity.[4] The idea of a covenant is undoubtedly Jewish ; Jewish, too, are the ideas of an atoning sacrifice and of vicarious atonement (Lev. xvi. 10, 21, 22). Possibly rabbinical tradition had already begun to interpret the sacrifice of Isaac in a way which suggested the significance which Christian tradition later gave to it as a type of the sacrifice at Calvary ; while the Essenes furnish us with an example of the practice of sacred fraternal meals.[5] But the essential point does not lie in any of these ; it is found in the idea of *the sacramental communion in the body and blood of the Lord.* This is the characteristic feature which we find in

---

[1] **CCXXII**, 77 ; **CXIV**, 113 ; **LXVII**, 67.   [2] **CCCVI**, 171.
[3] **CCVI**, 186 *ff*.   [4] O. Holtzmann, **ZNTW**, 1914, 107.
[5] Some have held that this will suffice to explain the Pauline conception (*cf.* **XLI**, 191). We cannot agree : it may have helped to complete it.

the Mystery religions, at that time abounding in the Hellenistic
world. The inevitable comparison becomes clearer if we
remember that Paul's doctrine of the Eucharist is inseparable
from his conception of Baptism : the baptized person *puts on*
Christ (Gal. iii. 27) ; he becomes a partaker of his life [1] and of
his death, or rather, he lives, suffers, dies, and above all rises
again with Christ ; and this is *the central idea in the Mysteries.*[2]
In several of them, such as those of the Great Mother and of
Attis, those of Mithra, or of the Syrian Baals, or of the Egyptian
gods, there were sacred meals which were regarded as a renewal
of the bond of union which initiation had established between
the members of the cult, and also between each individual and
the god.[3] Sometimes they were a mere external symbol of
brotherhood, like the *breaking of bread,* but " sometimes other
effects are expected from the food partaken of in common : by
eating the flesh of an animal which is regarded as divine, it is
believed that the participant identifies himself with the god and
partakes in the divine essence and qualities." [4]

Paul was familiar with such meals as these (1 Cor. x. 20) [5]
and warns the Corinthians against them.

In several of these Mysteries of salvation, particularly the
Mysteries of Attis, the symbolism of blood played a very important part. It was an extremely common belief in the ancient
world that by drinking the blood, or, later on, by immersion in
or sprinkling with the blood, it was possible to absorb the
qualities of the god whose blood was so used.[6] The blood is
the life, or at least, possesses life-giving qualities ; it is the food
of gods and demons, the essence of relationship, and, when it
is exchanged, it becomes the bond of blood-relationship between
those not otherwise related.[7] Moreover, it has a magical
potency over the soul of the person who drinks it.[8] The blood

---

[1] Gal. ii. 20 : ζῶ δὲ οὐκέτι ἐγώ, ζῇ δὲ ἐν ἐμοὶ Χριστὸς = *I live, no
longer I, but Christ liveth in me.*

[2] **XXXV**, 224; **CCXLII**, 100 *ff.*; **CCXCII**, ii, 94 *ff.*; **CXX**, 95.

[3] **VIII**, 37 and 219 (n. 43); **CCCIX**, 212 *ff.*

[4] **VIII**, 65 and 230 (n. 74).

[5] It should be observed that Justin, 1 *Apol.* lxvi. 4, immediately
after the passage in which he speaks of the Eucharist, refers to the
existence, in the Mysteries of Mithra, of a similar ceremony, in which,
in the course of the initiation, there occurs the offering of bread and
a cup, with certain ritual formulas.

[6] **VIII**, 64. *Cf.* **CXIV**, 113.

[7] **CCL**, 257 *ff.*, and the Index to the *Lehrb. der Religionsgeschichte* of
Bertholet and Lehmann (1925), on the word *Blut.*

[8] **CCXXVIII**, 51 and 204, which quotes several very interesting
papyri, to show the frequent occurrence of symbolic uses of blood
similar to that in the Pauline Eucharist.

of Christ holds such a place in Paulinism ; a fact which is the
more remarkable in that Jesus did not die a bloody death. The
Fourth Gospel, alone (John xix. 34), with a symbolic purpose
in mind, has described the soldier's spear piercing the side of
the Crucified, whence there flow forth both the Eucharistic blood
and the Baptismal water. It is the symbolic significance of
the blood which pervades the whole of the Pauline eucharistic
system, giving it its wealth of doctrinal meaning, and throwing
the significance of the bread into the shade.[1] Finally, it should
not be forgotten that all the Mystery gods are intercessors and
saviours, and that the object of the initiates was to attain,
through identification with the god, a share in his blessed
immortality. In such a way did Paul conceive of the work of
Christ and of the operation of the two rites of Baptism and the
Eucharist. We may say that it was inevitable that he should,
in all good faith, attribute to Jesus the institution and the
meaning of the eucharist ; but he was unconsciously influenced
in this, as in his whole conception of Christ, by the ideas current
in his environment concerning salvation and the means of
obtaining it.[2] Hence it is to Paulinism rather than to Jesus
that we owe Paul's teaching on the fundamental significance
of the Eucharist, a body of teaching which rests on no historical
tradition. When the attempt is made to connect the essential
elements of this doctrine with the teaching of Jesus, they
become improbable and inconceivable. On the other hand,
Paul's eucharistic teaching becomes perfectly intelligible when
considered as the logical consequence of the mystical operation
of the sacrament which secures salvation to its participants, a
sacrament which is implicit in the Pauline Christology. Like
the Christology itself, it springs, not from the synoptic tradition, but from a syncretistic gnosis.[3]

IV

Conclusion

Clearly, the origin of Justin's account of the Eucharist is
to be found in Paul, while Luke appears, upon examination,
to be an artificial conflation of Mark and Paul. The only
important difference between Mark and Matthew consists in

---

[1] CCI, 8.
[2] For a description of the environment of Tarsus, where he was
born and brought up, cf. Böhlig, *Die Geisterkultur von Tarsos in Augus-
teischen Zeitalter*. Göttingen, 1913, 24 *ff*.
[3] CCXXII, 78.

the addition in Matthew xxvi. 28, of the words "for the for-giveness of sins " (εἰς ἄφεσιν ἁμαρτιῶν) which has every appearance of being a secondary Pauline addition. If we examine the form of Mark which Matthew has followed, we shall find that it falls into two parts : (1) *vv.* 22–4 : the consecration of the bread, the cup and the covenant ; (2) *v.* 25 : the declaration that Jesus will not again drink of the fruit of the vine until the Kingdom has come. Apart from the injunction to repeat the rite, the first part contains all that is essential in 1 Corinthians xi. 23–5, and it is quite possible that its source is Paul himself.[1] Those commentators who refuse to accept this view, and who persist in believing that " This is my body " and " This is my blood " are the very words of Jesus, offer laborious explanations which all break down when confronted by the obvious fact that the disciples could not have understood these words at all. They maintain that Jesus intended to indicate the imminence of his death by comparing himself to a victim whose blood was shed in order to establish a new covenant.[2] But this is an inter-pretation of the passage based upon the subsequent events which the Apostles at the time could not have been aware of. It may be added that it is only by following the same method of reasoning that it is possible to attribute to Jesus a concern with and a knowledge of things only shared by the Greek environment of Paul's time and our conservative critics.

On the other hand, the second part of the Marcan passage strikes an entirely different note : it expresses nothing more than a hope, the same hope which had sustained the prophet throughout his career and had brought him to Jerusalem : the near approach of the Kingdom. It seems only natural that Jesus, in his hour of trial, should cling to it as the divine negation of human despair ; we can understand that he could have thought and said : the expected miracle will be accomplished, and, from the earthly meal the disciples will pass with me to the Messianic banquet.[3] The conception could not be found in Paul's teaching because it had no place there : it could have no place in the outlook of Paulinism, which was determined by the historical situation. The only way in which it could be retained in the Pauline scheme, in spite of an incompatibility too familiar to commentators to occasion surprise, was by doing what Mark has done, and reducing it to a position of secondary

---

[1] **CCL**, 270 ; **CV**, 405. We need not linger over the hypothesis of a common source formerly maintained by **CCVI**, 84 *ff.*, and recently put forward again by **CXCV**, 11 *ff.* It complicates the problem un-necessarily.

[2] **CCVI**, 191 ; **LXVII**, 173. *Cf.* **CXIV**, 114.   [3] **CV**, 402 *ff.*

importance in relation to the central features of the Pauline teaching. The variants in the text of Luke, already pointed out, and especially those of Codex Bezae, prove that before the *textus receptus* came into existence, Christians had become aware of the presence of serious difficulties. The probabilities are that the earliest tradition attributed to Jesus at the Last Supper nothing more than an assurance which may be expressed substantially as follows : " Be of good cheer : the Kingdom which I have always promised to you, and which the difficulties of the present moment may seem to have deferred, is really close at hand, for the next meal of which we shall partake together will be in the Kingdom." [1] The belief in the *parousia* made it possible for the disciples to accept with patience a temporary postponement ; but when its indefinite delay became apparent, it was necessary to discover other reasons for confidence. This much at least seems certain ; while Jesus may not actually have expressed himself in the terms suggested above, he did not use the words attributed to him, with some variation, by the three Synoptic Gospels. These words can only represent a *cult legend.*[2]

[1] *Cf.* **CCXXII**, 77.
[2] Bultmann, " *Eine Kultus-Legende* " ; **CCCV**, 43 : " *The account of the Last Supper is but an etiological cult story.* . . ."

CHAPTER III

THE PASSION
THE BETRAYAL—THE ARREST—THE TRIAL

I

THE BETRAYAL

IF we are to believe the Gospels it was a conspiracy on the part of the Temple authorities, aided by the treachery of one of the Apostles, which put an end to the career of Jesus. We have already seen that the directors of the Temple were opposed on principle to anyone who tried to introduce innovations, so it was not necessary for the Galilean prophet to have incited them wantonly, as the synoptic tradition has it, for them to have shown themselves ill-disposed towards him. But, once this point has been settled, several questions arise from a study of the synoptic narrative : (1) We are told that his enemies dare not take any decisive steps against Jesus because they fear the reaction of the people who delight in his teaching. They shrink from arresting him in the midst of the feast *lest there be an uproar of the people* (Mark xiv. 2) and seek to take him by *craft*. It is difficult to see what was to be gained by that, as, if the people feel as we are told they do, it is the arrest of the prophet and not the circumstances in which he is arrested that will affect them. (2) Have they any real reason to fear the popularity of the Nazarene ? If it is as great as Mark affirms, why are the Romans not alarmed also ? Why has Pilate not yet appeared on the scene ? Would not the first action of the plotting Jews in their own interest be to warn him at once if his own police have suspected nothing ? Would not that be a very simple way of preventing the people from suspecting their complicity in the matter ? (3) And if, as seems likely, Jesus' popularity is only the Evangelist's invention, what is the meaning of the hesitation and precautions of the priests ? And above all why should they show such hatred against a mere Galilean ? But in reality the narrator is describing his own feelings, his rancour against the Jews, who in his time were bitterly opposed to the Christian heretics and harmed them whenever they could. It is not therefore the poor Galilean that the Pharisees, Sadduces and Herodians, in league with the priests, are assailing, but the Saviour who is the object of the Evangelist's adoration and hope. This transformation changes both the relations of the actors and the scale of the drama. (4) The narrator might even have been in the confidence of the conspirators, so well informed is he of their most secret thoughts and conversations, matters which he could not possibly have known. His appearance of accurate information is merely the result of inferences based on probability and on the false grounds of his fundamental assumption, on reasons drawn from the event itself. (5) In spite of their evil designs the Jews appear much embarrassed (which does not accord with their reputation for wily astuteness), when Judas very opportunely comes to their assistance (Mark xiv. 10–11 and Synopsis). He offers to deliver his Master to them. Mark says that they promise him money, but Matthew xxvi. 14–16 goes further and says that he asked for it. Luke xxii. 3–6 adds the final explanation: "*Then Satan entered into Judas.*"

The question arises whether this base and hateful story of betrayal springs from actual reminiscence. The narrative of the prediction made during the Last Supper of Judas' betrayal has already raised doubts; it sounds too much like the fulfilment of a prophecy, and common-sense reflection confirms them. It is difficult to see why the Iscariot's crime was necessary for the accomplishment of the evil designs of the " Chief High Priests." And if they pay for this unnecessary villainy they are made to appear both foolish and richer than they ought to be. At first sight the objection appears to be well-founded that tradition would never have invented the awful fall of an Apostle, and that historical fact alone could have caused it to be accepted.[1] Let us, however, attempt to come to grips with the statements in the Gospels concerning Judas and his crime. It is a thankless task as we have no other document than the Gospels to depend on.[2]

To begin with, the tradition of the traitor's name is uncertain. It is not *Judas* but *Iscariot* which presents difficulties.[3] At first, the mention in John xiii. 26 suggests a patronymic

---

[1] **CXLIV**, 18 ; **CCVI**, 73 ; **CCLXXXII**, 179.

[2] Many critics deny the historicity of the episode. *Cf.* **CLXXIX**, 295 *ff.* ; **CCXVI**, 51 ; G. Marquardt, *Der Verrat des Judas Ischariot, eine Sage.* Munich, 1900 ; G. Schläger, *Die Ungeschichtlichkeit des Verräters Judas,* in **ZNTW**, 1914, 50 *ff.* ; **LXXXVI**, 160 *ff.*, 170 *ff.*

[3] Ἰούδας Ἰσκαριώθ, in Mark xiv. 10 ; Ἰούδας Ἰσκαριώτης, in Matt. xxvi. 14 and Luke xxii. 3. *Cf.* **EB**, art. *Judas,* cols. 2623 *ff.*

Ἰούδας Σίμωνος Ἰσκαριώτου = *Judas, the son of Simon the Iscariote*) ; but this leaves the meaning of Iscariot unexplained. Then there is the possibility that it indicates a place of origin, and in fact several manuscripts give ἀπὸ καρυώθου, ἀπὸ καριώτου, ἀπὸ καριώθου = of *Keruoth* (?) or of *Kariot* or *Karioth*.[1] *Ish-Kerioth = the man from Kerioth*, the man born in a town or village called Kerioth, must then be understood. But what town or what village ? The simplest and most honest thing to do is to confess that we do not know. But commentators, rather than abandon the attempt, have discovered in Joshua xv. 25, a *Kerioth* whose only drawback is that it is not, apparently, in Judæa ; then they have found in Josephus, Ant., 14, 3, 4, a *Koreæ* which may perhaps be found in the valley of the Jordan [2] but which could scarcely yield the form *Kerioth*. Others have tried to correct the Gospel reading. Thus Cheyne proposed to read [3] *Judas the Jerichoite* (ὁ Ἰεριχωτής = *the man from Jericho*), an arbitrary and tendencious emendation. Judas might not in point of fact be a Judæan but come from the Kerioth of *Joshua* ; and many commentators [4] hold that opinion. However, we do not even know whether the biblical writer was thinking of a town or a *group of places*.[5] There is certainly the capital of Moab, mentioned by Amos ii. 2, though only in the Hebrew text, and by Jeremiah xlviii. 24 (Καριώθ in the *Septuagint*) ; but if Judas were a Moabite it would certainly be known, and as he was one of the Twelve he was much more probably a Galilean. The important fact is that the search for Judas' birthplace leads to no certain or even probable results.

On the other hand the validity of the derivation *ish-Kerioth = the man from Kerioth* has been contested on good grounds.[6] According to Wellhausen, the word *ish* had at the time of Jesus long disappeared from the Aramaic dialect and in any case *ish-Kerioth* would not mean the *man of Kerioth* but the *people of Kerioth*. Hence the famous German scholar favoured the idea of a nickname, meaning bandit or sicarius. Research has been conducted along these lines by Benjamin Smith with as much ingenuity as persistence. Starting with the group of consonants SKR, considered as the root of Iskariot,[7] he observes [8] that the meaning *deliver up* (*überliefern*) can be extracted from it. And he refers to Isaiah xix. 4, " *And the Egyptians will*

---

[1] A variant of the synoptic forms occurs : ὁ σκαριώτης, ἰσκαριώδ, σκαριώθ. *Cf.* EB, art. *Judas*, introduction.
[2] *Cf.* EB, art. *Zarethan*.   [3] EB, *Judas*, sec. 1.
[4] CE, *Judas*, col. 539 ; DCG, *Judas*, col. 908.
[5] EB, *Kerioth* ; CLXXIX, 296.   [6] CLXXIX, 296 ; CXIV, 298 *ff.*
[7] Brewer, *The Open Court*, Aug. 1909.   [8] CLXXIX, 298 *ff.*

I give over into the hand of a cruel lord " which the Septuagint translates : καὶ παραδώσω τὴν Αἴγυπτον . . . It is the word which Judas uses, according to Matthew xxvi. 15, in his proposals to the priests : " *And I will deliver him unto you* " (κἀγὼ ὑμῖν παραδώσω αὐτόν) ; Paul also uses it in 1 Corinthians xi. 23 : " *The Lord Jesus the same night in which he was betrayed* . . ." (ἐν τῇ νυκτὶ ᾗ παρεδίδετο. . . .). The surname of Judas would then mean *the deliverer up, the betrayer*.

But for it to have been possible for the Evangelists to transcribe the word without understanding its meaning, the story of the betrayal must date from very early times and have been told in the Aramaic environment of the earliest Christian Church. It is the best argument in favour of the historicity of the betrayal. It must be noticed, however, (1) that the Marcan tradition is far from going back everywhere to the origins, and that a legend is quickly established ; (2) that Paul, who seems to speak of the betrayal in 1 Corinthians xi. 23, says nothing of the traitor. There is some force in the reply that everyone certainly knew him. However, in 1 Corinthians xv. 5 the same Paul assures us that after the resurrection Jesus appeared to the *Twelve*. Judas was then of the number ? Or must we consider that by the *Twelve* the Tarsiot only meant the *Apostles*, without any special regard to their number ? Whatever force the argument possesses is not strengthened by the silence of 1 Corinthians xi. 23, and it is difficult to believe that if Paul had possessed a vivid remembrance of Judas' betrayal, as he must have done if the crime had actually occurred, the necessity of a correction such as : *he was seen of the Eleven, for Judas* . . . would not have forced itself on him. From which we may conclude that Paul might well have spoken of the arrest of Jesus without explaining it by the treachery of one of the *Twelve*.[1] It should also be observed that the Gospel of Peter [2] says that after the feast in which Jesus perished " *we, the twelve disciples of the Lord, wept and were afflicted*." If, as Conybeare suggests, the writer of this apocryphal work had followed the lost ending of Mark, the *Twelve* (δώδεκα) is significant. There is nothing decisive to be drawn from the passage in Acts i. 26, which records the election of another Apostle to fill the place of Judas, because the

[1] The word παραδιδόναι which he uses is the one Mark i. 14 employs to describe the arrest of John the Baptist : καὶ μετὰ τὸ παραδοθῆναι τὸν Ἰωάννην, . . . without there being any question of betrayal.

[2] 14, 59, of Klostermann, *Apocrypha*, I², of **XXIII** (1908), 8, and 337 ; **CXXXIX**, which tries to prove, with the support of 1 Cor. xv. 5 —a double-edged argument—that in the case at issue *Twelve* and *Eleven* are the same thing.

passage may easily fall into line with a legend which was well established by the time that it came to be written down.

Furthermore, considered on its own merits, this story of Judas's betrayal is surrounded with such serious difficulties that it has awakened doubt in the minds of men not usually attracted by revolutionary conclusions ; Jülicher, for example, writes : " *It sounds like a later invention*," [1] and Klostermann considers that even what might be historical in the story remains doubtful.[2] The most serious objection is that the betrayal appears wholly useless and inexplicable. What need, asks B. Smith,[3] had Jesus' enemies of Judas and his kiss ? None whatever. The prophet was at their mercy and the people whom they are supposed to have feared would be the first to shout " crucify him," as Mark xv. 13 himself asserts. On the other hand, a Catholic theologian [4] very justly points out that "*All the textual difficulties and questions of detail appear insignificant beside the great moral problem of the fall and treachery of Judas.*"

Mark does not venture on any explanation. Matthew xxvi. 15 puts forward the motive of cupidity : Judas bargains for 30 pieces of silver. The amount is ridiculous and it is evident that Matthew is making a show of accuracy which has no foundation in fact : he is merely glossing Mark. It is vain to attempt to guess at the character of the traitor and then to explain his treachery by his psychology, since the latter must be imagined and deduced from the act of treachery.

The most charitable of the motives imputed to Judas would be that he wished to force Jesus to display his power, to hasten the expected miracle ; his treachery would then be in a way an act of faith. When he realizes his terrible mistake he kills himself (Matt. xxvii. 3 *ff.*). But what do we know of all this and what is the historical value of this story of suicide ? Less than nothing, because we cannot help feeling that this is a secondary legend unknown to the first tradition about Judas.[5] Or perhaps he was possessed and that is the explanation offered by Luke and John ; it is entirely satisfactory to those who believe in possession, except that it remains to be explained how and why the Christ should have consented to sacrifice one of his friends to the Devil.

Strauss pointed out [6] long ago that if it was greed which

[1] CCXVI, 51 : *Das klingt wie spätere Dichtung.*
[2] XCIX, 342. *Cf.* CCLXVIII, iv, 39.
[3] CLXXIX, 302.   [4] CE, *Judas*, col. 547.
[5] CIII, ii, 625 (*contra* : CII, 513, who gives no reasons) ; XCIV ; CVII, ii, *ad loc.*
[6] CLXXXII, ii, 415.

incited Judas he would have found it more profitable to abscond
with the common fund of the little community, than to sell
his Master for 60 or 70 sovereigns. Moreover, it is certain
that the sum of 30 pieces of silver is not based on memory but
on a text of Zechariah, xi. 12 : " *And I said unto them, If ye
think good, give me my price ; and if not, forbear. So they
weighed for my price* 30 *pieces of silver.*"

The ambition and jealousy which have also been suggested
explain nothing. Ambitious of what, jealous of whom ?
Ambitious of being the most beloved and esteemed of the
Apostles ? Jealous of those who surpassed him in both ways ?
Peter or John, for instance ? But how could the deluded
wretch have imagined that he could accomplish his ends by
giving Jesus up ? Was it fear which urged him ? [1] Did he
see more clearly than the others the growing peril and decide
on extreme measures to escape it ? Had he lost faith in the
Nazarene ? But in either case what was there to prevent him
from discreetly disappearing ? We are confronted by nothing
but questions and arbitrary suppositions unsupported by any
trustworthy passage. The very number of them is sufficient
to discredit them, and they merely vie with another in flights
of imagination. Even if we combine all the motives of greed,
ambition, jealousy, fear and failing confidence, and dress them
out in high-sounding epithets,[2] we cannot deduce from them
any well-founded and therefore acceptable conclusions. The
interminable discussions which we have touched on appear
lamentably futile. The betrayal remains purposeless, useless
and unintelligible, whichever way we turn.

These are, however, only negative arguments and we may
always suppose with Loisy that the disciples did not know the
traitor's motives, but recorded the treason. That may be so,
but there are other alternatives. As Loisy himself suggests
Judas may be the personification of incredulous and false
Judaism, the incarnation of Satan, who for the time being
appears to have conquered Christ.[3] In other words, one may
see in him the symbol of the fact asserted by tradition : *Jesus
perished at the hand of the Jews who delivered him to Pilate.*

Why this personification ? It is impossible to reply to this
question without making certain more or less probable assump-

---

[1] CI, 347 ; CV, 394. [2] DCG, *Judas*, sec. iv.

[3] CXXVII[1], 482. It is the opinion which B. Smith has vigorously
urged in an attempt to make it conform to his mythical explanation
of the life of Jesus. His modifications are not convincing, but the
arguments seem to have some weight : CLXXIX, 304 *ff.*—*Contra* :
CLVI–a, 480 *ff.*

tions : (1) In legends the responsibility for action is always definite, and centred in an individual. (2) No better current personal name than Judas (*'Ιούδας*) can be found to represent the man of *Juda* (*'Ιούδα*) or Judæa (*'Ιουδαία*), *the Jew* (*ὁ 'Ιουδαῖος*); the transition from one form to the other is quite natural. (3) The arrest of Jesus by night on the Mount of Olives, timed in such a way as to suggest that the police were informed had to be explained ; and what could be easier than to imagine that this had been done by one of the prophet's intimate associates ? Further, two prophetic passages of the Old Testament led them in this direction.[1] We read in Psalm xli. 9 :

> " Yea, mine own familiar friend, in whom I trusted, which did eat of my bread, hath lifted up his heel against me," and in Psalm lv. 12 : " For it was not an enemy that reproached me ; . . . but it was thou, my guide and mine acquaintance."

Nor must we forget that Acts i. 16 clearly states the betrayal to be necessary for the fulfilment of the Scripture :

> " Men and brethren, this scripture must needs have been fulfilled, which the Holy Ghost by the mouth of David spake before concerning Judas, which was guide to them that took Jesus."

We may conclude, therefore, that while the story of the betrayal cannot be absolutely proved to be only a legend, it is open to many serious objections. Matthew xxvii. 3–10 assures us that the traitor hung himself (like Ahithophel, the evil counsellor of Absalom, in 2 Samuel xvii. 23), after having cast down the 30 pieces of silver in the Temple, whence the priests collected them in order to buy the *potter's field* with them and so fulfil the Scriptures (Zech. xi. 12–13) ; [2] and Acts i. 18 affirms that Judas himself bought the *potter's field* with the *reward of iniquity*, that he then became swollen and *burst asunder in the midst*. These two legendary accounts, although they differ, are in keeping with the general trend of the story.

[1] **LXXXVI**, 171.

[2] Verse 13 is specially striking : " *the Lord said unto me, Cast it unto the potter : a goodly price that I was prised at of them. And I took the thirty pieces of silver, and cast them to the potter in the house of the Lord.*" This is not the authentic text of Zechariah, as the prophet wrote it ; it has been altered by a copyist's error who mistook the Hebrew word which means *treasure, treasure room*, for that which means *potter*, because the two readings are very similar. But it was the latter which the Evangelist had in his text, and which he combined with two passages of Jeremiah (xviii. 2–3 and xxxii. 6–14), where it is a question of a potter and a field that has been bought. On this curious problem of exegesis, *cf.* **CIII**, ii, 628 *ff.*, and **XCIX**, 217–19.

They are intended to satisfy a belief which could not have allowed Judas to go unpunished. If the episode is founded on fact, which is doubtful, it remains unintelligible to us.[1]

II

THE ARREST

According to Mark xiv. 26 *ff.*, when they had finished the meal and sung the *Hallel* the participants went away to the Mount of Olives, a ridge about 200 feet high which dominates Jerusalem on the east beyond the Kedron. The road to Jericho runs along the southern side and the road to Bethany crosses it. There are still some olives growing but the trees are receding before the advance of the Jewish tombs from the Kedron valley and the invasion of various buildings which claim to exalt Gospel memories and hallow these illustrious stones. At the time of Jesus the trees reigned supreme.[2] The little band of disciples settles down probably to pass the night under their branches. It could not, however, have been very warm at the time of the Passover, and we wonder why Jesus has not returned to Bethany, or even why he has not remained there to celebrate the feast, why he has left Jerusalem during this sacred night, contrary to the law ; but these details do not cause the Evangelist any hesitation in pursuing the plan of his narrative.

Jesus is supposed to have come as far as Gethsemane, or rather to an oil-press which stood there, according to the fourth century tradition,[3] at the foot of the hill close to the Jericho road. A famous episode takes place here (Mark xiv. 32–42) : Jesus withdraws a little from the disciples to pray. As the consummation of the great sacrifice draws near he hesitates, disturbed, and afraid :

> "And prayed that if it were possible, the hour[4] might pass from him. And he said, Abba, Father, all things are possible unto thee ; take away this cup from me : nevertheless not what I will, but what thou wilt."

---

[1] On the various explanations and elucidations attempted by ancient and modern commentators, *cf.* **CXLII**, 173 *ff.* ; **CXXXII**, 135 *ff.* ; **DCG**, *Judas*, col. 912 *ff.* On Judas in folklore : O. Dähnhardt, *Natursagen*, ii : *Sagen zum Neuen Testament*, 235 *ff.*, 300 *ff.* Leipzig, 1909.

[2] All the essential facts concerning the past and present history of the site are to be found in **EB**, art. *Olives (Mount of)*.

[3] The Gospel topography of Jerusalem and the surrounding district dates from the time of Constantine, and is very doubtful.

[4] The hour marked by destiny, in the astrological sense : *die Schicksalsstunde* (**CXIV**, 120).

From the critical point of view, no evidence for this prayer exists, since there is no one at Jesus' side to hear it, and Peter and James, who are not far away, are asleep (xiv. 37) ; but this very dramatic and moving episode probably held a special place in the liturgical celebration of the Passion. The gloss which Luke xxii. 43–4 adds to the Marcan text is worthy of notice,[1] since it indicates its true character :

> " And there appeared an angel unto him from heaven, strengthening him. And being in an agony he prayed more earnestly : and his sweat was as it were great drops of blood (ὡσεὶ θρόμβοι αἵματος) falling down to the ground."

The Evangelist does not suppose that the Apostles saw this double marvel any more than, according to Mark, they heard the agonized prayer ; but he has dramatized the scene in the same manner as his predecessor and has surpassed him.

It is of course easy to give an air of probability to the scene in Gethsemane by invoking Peter's memories.[2] Jesus takes his disciples near the small building which contains the oil-press ; he leaves them there and withdraws a little to pray ; when he returns he finds them asleep. Legend has subsequently embellished the story. That this view offers no difficulty does not prove its validity. It is preferable to believe that the episode, which recalls others such as the *Temptation* and the *Transfiguration,* is to be understood like them in the light of the great Mystery of the Redemption which fired the imagination of the Greek world at the time of the subapostolic generation. It has nothing to do with an actual historical reminiscence.[3] While we should gladly believe that in spite of its unreality the story expressed " in an admirable allegory what passed in the mind of Jesus," [4] we have no proof that it is true.

In Mark's narrative it serves as a transition : the prediction of the denial of Peter (xiv. 27–31) which undoubtedly Jesus must have foreseen, occupies the time on the way from the guest-chamber to Gethsemane ; the scene which we are describing allows time for the band, whom Judas has gone to warn, to assemble and reach the spot.

Jesus once more predicts to the Apostles what is going to happen to him (Mark xiv. 41).[5]   (*It is enough, the hour is come ; behold the Son of man is betrayed into the hands of sinners. Rise*

---

[1] Its authenticity is, moreover, doubtful. Some important manuscripts (*Sin. Syr.*, *Alexandrinus*, and the *Vatican Codex*) omit it. Arguments and authorities for and against are equal. *Cf.* **CIII**, ii, 572 *ff.*
[2] **XCI**–*a*, 269.   [3] **LXXXVI**, 162.   [4] **CLVI**–*a*, 479.
[5] *Cf.* the commentaries and especially **CXIV**, 120, and **XCVIII**, 168, on these verses 41 *ff.*, which are very perplexing in many respects.

up, let us go ; lo, he that betrayeth me is at hand), when the traitor arrives with "*a great multitude with swords and staves from the chief priests and the scribes and the elders*" (xiv. 43).

There is no question of a body of regular police, still less of Roman soldiers, but of a band which had probably been collected from among the servants of those who were taking the initiative in the arrest. This is Mark's (xiv. 44–52) description of the scene :

> "And he that betrayed him had given them a token,[1] saying, Whomsoever I shall kiss, that same is he ; take him, and lead him away safely. And as soon as he was come, he goeth straightway to him, and saith, Master, master ; and kissed him.[2] And they laid their hands on him, and took him. And one of them that stood by drew a sword, and smote a servant of the high priest, and cut off his ear. And Jesus answered and said unto them, Are ye come out, as against a thief, with swords and with staves to take me ? I was daily with you in the temple teaching, and ye took me not : but the scriptures must be fulfilled. And they all forsook him and fled."

They, are the Apostles, and their collapse is related with considerable reserve.

The other two Synoptics have worked on this text, adding edifying rhetoric (for example, the little homily which Matthew xxvi. 52 *ff.* makes Jesus address to the disciple who cut off the servant's ear), or details which have no historical value (for example, Luke xxii. 50 knows that it was the *right* ear, while John xviii. 10 asserts that it was Peter himself who cut it off and that the victim's name was *Malchus*). Taken literally the Marcan account is full of strange and unlikely statements ; but he is much less interested in the exactness of the facts than in the impression he wants to give and his anxiety to save appearances. He knows that the believer, unmindful of the foreordained necessity of the Passion, according to God's plan, will be shocked at the Apostles' cowardice and will cry : Then they merely looked on and did not resist ? The Evangelist replies : Yes, they resisted, but Jesus himself reminded them that the scriptures had to be fulfilled and the will of God obeyed.[3]

---

[1] τὸν σύσσημον is the equivalent of the Latin *tessera: word of command, agreed signal*.

[2] It is the kiss given by the disciple to the Master as a mark of respect and affection ; it is the normal practice (*cf.* CCCXVII, 339). Moreover, it is the hand and not the face which the disciple kisses. *Cf.* EB, *Salutations*, sec. 2.

[3] Matthew and Luke stress this point : the former by inserting the surprising speech which he imputes to Jesus and which all the people are supposed to listen to respectfully ; the latter by making Jesus the means of healing the wounded ear.

That is why the disciples could flee without guilt or remorse. The double intention of the account therefore appears to be to show the Lord asserting in his full sovereignty the necessity for accomplishing his mission—a point much stressed by John —and excusing and exculpating his disciples. The most that historical accuracy can, strictly speaking, retain of all this is that Jesus was arrested on the Mount of Olives, and that his disciples abandoned him in dismay.

But by whom was he arrested ? That is the main question ; leaving aside the problems concerning the place, time and circumstances of the arrest. The three Synoptics, which draw on a single source, are unanimous in assigning the responsibility to the Jews. Lawyers have been specially interested in it as a *case* and have taken delight in complicating it, by treating the Gospel statements with a strictness applicable to the articles of a code but quite irrelevant to the preoccupations of the redactors and out of place in view of the inconsistencies which they present.[1] They have, for example, affirmed that an arrest by the Jewish authorities was in this case illegal because a capital offence was involved. The procurator alone was competent and able to act.[2] The statement is not accurate, for in religious matters the Sanhedrin was competent in all cases and it had full authority to apprehend the prophet.[3] Besides, the Synoptic account does not give us the impression of a regular act but of a sudden disorderly affair carried out privately. It is unnecessary to emphasize a point which cannot be pressed where allegations are so vague. It goes without saying that if Jesus was tried first by the Sanhedrin he must have been arrested by Jews acting on the orders of the Temple authorities, or on the initiative of other zealous members of the priesthood, for Roman soldiers would never have taken him before a Jewish tribunal. But, as we shall see, nothing is less certain than the trial before the Sanhedrin and it is not impossible that some prominent people of the City may have taken it upon themselves to seize the Nazarene and hand him over to Pilate as a dangerous agitator.

The Fourth Gospel takes a different point of view. It tells us (xviii. 3) that Judas " *having received a band* (λαβὼν τὴν σπεῖραν) *of men and officers* (ὑπηρέτας) *from the chief priests and Pharisees*," went to the place where he knew he would find his Master. The band (σπεῖρα) is the Roman force garrisoned in the Antonia tower, for a little farther on its commander

---

[1] *Cf.* on this point the very judicious remarks of **XVI**, ii, 134, n. 2.— Very full bibliography, 137 *ff.*

[2] **CCXXVII**, 90 *ff.* ; **CCXXX**, 149 *ff.*   [3] **XVI**, 138 *ff.*

is called chiliarch ($\chi\iota\lambda\iota\alpha\rho\chi\circ\varsigma$), a term which the Vulgate rightly renders as *tribunus*.[1] There would therefore be a force of Roman police followed by a more or less disorderly band of people. In this case it appears that it is the Romans who have arrested Jesus. But what authority had Judas to summon the *cohort* and why should there be an appeal to a large armed force when a troop would have sufficed ? Underlying the Evangelist's show of accuracy is his usual desire to magnify Jesus by showing him supremely superior, both to Romans and to Jews : everyone is amazed at hearing him answer " *I am he* " when they have said that they are seeking Jesus of Nazareth (xviii. 6). The story has been questioned.[2] The objection has also been raised that, as John always tends to exculpate the Romans and charge the Jews, it is strange that in these tragic circumstances he should assign to the former an unpleasant part, if they had not actually played it,[3] simply because it suited his purpose. Various objections have been raised to the documentary evidence for the hypothesis of his arrest by the Romans.[4] But they appear to carry little more weight than the arguments alleged in defence of the hypothesis.[5] All that can be admitted is that the Synoptics *may*, in their desire to place the whole responsibility on the Jews, have systematically disregarded all memory of the Roman police ; but it remains equally possible that John introduced them to heighten the effect. The suggestion that the Fourth Gospel had access to a source unknown to the others in this instance appears unlikely.[6] Perhaps the examination of the circumstances of the trial will shed some light on the obscure point we have just been studying.

III

THE TRIAL

The *schema* of the synoptic tradition regarding the trial may be given as follows : (*a*) Jesus is taken to the High Priest's house by the band which has arrested him, and the Sanhedrin assembles there at once, in the middle of the night. (*b*) He is questioned by the High Priest, confronted with supposed

---

[1] **CXIX**, 205. [2] **CIII**, ii, 578 ; **CCLXXIX**–*a*, 321. [3] **CCVII**, 75.

[4] *Cf.* Spitta, *Das Johannes Evangelium als Quelle der Gesch. Jesu.*, 359 *ff.*, **CCXXVII**, 92 *ff.* Göttingen, 1910.

[5] **CCVII**, 74 *ff.*

[6] Goguel (**CLVI**–*a*, 448–65), who examines the question carefully and believes in collusion between the Jewish and Roman authorities. The supposition tends to contradict our texts and to favour John.

witnesses, ill-treated and finally condemned to death for blasphemy. (c) In the morning there is another meeting of the Sanhedrin which decides to take him before Pilate. (d) The trial is reopened before the Procurator on a charge which in Luke xxiii. 2 is only of inciting the people to revolt, forbidding them to pay tribute to Cæsar and claiming to be the Messianic King. Further, the really judicial part of this second trial is reduced almost to nothing. It can be divided into four episodes : the interrogation ; the comparison before the people of Jesus and Barabbas ; the sentence given under pressure from the Jews ; the scourging.

This succession of events appears at first fairly probable if the details are not subjected to a careful and critical examination, but this impression is dispelled by study of the passages. It immediately becomes obvious that the *schema* already mentioned is only obtained by neglecting the glaring disagreements between the Evangelists ; or more exactly, by exclusively following Mark and Matthew (and Matthew merely follows Mark). The order of the events is given differently by Luke, and conveys a different impression. Thus the Third Gospel only speaks of one meeting of the Sanhedrin, in the morning ; it mentions no witnesses ; the accusation is only brought on the grounds of Jesus' Messianic claims ; no judgment is pronounced ; the prisoner has confessed. They are satisfied with taking him to Pilate ; the Sanhedrin has neither judged nor condemned.

The Lucan narrative gives the impression that this is a *case* which concerns the Procurator, or has at least been tried by him, although here again there is no question of sentence having been passed, only that Jesus has been abandoned to the Jews. Does it mean that Luke had access to a private source or preferably,[1] has merely worked over the *Urmarcus* which Mark must have modified in order to throw the blame on the Jews ? It is difficult to reply, but even if it were easy we should still not know which of the two accounts comes nearer the truth.

In John another presentation is given : Jesus is conducted to " *Annas first ; for he was father in law to Caiaphas, which was the high priest that same year* " (xviii. 13). The awkwardness and vagueness of the Johannine passage (xviii. 13–24) prove that the first redactor had probably written " *to Annas the high priest that same year,*" and that the mention of Caiaphas is only a later correction after Matthew xxvi. 57. From which

[1] Especially with regard to the observation that he has transferred to the morning session what he found in Mark in the evening session. *Cf.* **CIV**, 539, and **LXXXVI,** 164. The whole Lucan verse shows traces of artificial redaction.

it follows that tradition was uncertain of the name of the High Priest who was thought to have presided at the Jewish trial of Jesus.[1] Annas questions the accused prophet " *of his disciples, and of his doctrine* " (xviii. 19), which is the vaguest of formulas ; then he sends him bound to Caiaphas, but nothing happens there (xviii. 24 *ff.*). In the early morning *they* take the prisoner to the prætorium. It is Pilate who is to try and, by implication, to condemn him (xix. 16). *It has never been a question of the Sanhedrin.*

The divergences just noted can only be reconciled artificially by placing them arbitrarily in a chronological sequence and supposing that the episodes supplement each other.

Let us return to the *schema*. It contains serious difficulties, over which the harmonizing school of commentators has expended much subtlety without great result. These are the chief difficulties : (*a*) Jews do not begin a trial on the day of the Passover.[2] Why are all the actors in the case rushing about the streets instead of celebrating the feast in a suitable religious way, since according to the Marcan chronology at least the arrest and appearance of Jesus before the Sanhedrin took place on the Passover night ?[3] (*b*) The Johannine chronology does not remove the difficulty, since a nocturnal sitting of the Sanhedrin is out of all probability. Jewish custom does not allow of a nocturnal judgment ; it also prohibits a judgment from being given on the same day as the interrogation.[4] (*c*) Further, has the Sanhedrin the right to pronounce a capital sentence ? The point has been much discussed,[5] but I believe the question has now been settled in the affirmative, that the Sanhedrin had authority to pass a sentence of capital punishment for a religious crime.[6] (*d*) However, when the Jews take Jesus before Pilate a fresh trial commences, *as if the Sanhedrin had neither tried nor decided* the case. Nor does this trial resemble in any way the handing over of a heretic to the secular arm by an ecclesiastical tribunal (Loisy). Again, if Pilate had only to confirm the decision of the Jewish tribunal, as some have maintained, the punishment would also have been Jewish : stoning, the stake, strangling

---

[1] Mark does not name him ; nor Luke xxii. 53. But Luke iii. 2 gives Annas, likewise Acts iv. 6. *Cf.* **CCXXVII**[2], 458.

[2] **XXIX**, ii, 210.   [3] **LXXXIII**, ii, 198 *ff.*

[4] Goguel, *Juifs et Romains dans l'histoire de la Passion*, **RHR**, lxii, 1910, 42.

[5] *Cf.* **XXIX**, ii, 208 *ff.* ; **CCXXVII**, 62 *ff.* ; Goguel, *Juifs*, and *ff.* ; **CCXXX**, 149 *ff.* ; **CCXIII**, 110 *ff.*

[6] Mommsen, **ZNTW**, 1902, 199 ; *Droit pénal*, i, 279 *ff.* Decisive proof rests on **XVI**, ii, 135 *ff.* **XXII**, 219, however, still contests it.

or decapitation ; but crucifixion was Roman.[1] The first two Synoptics give the impression that the real condemnation which was followed by death in a Roman manner was pronounced by the Roman procurator.   It seems extraordinary that in the detailed account of the trial before the Sanhedrin, stress should be placed on the crime of claiming to be the Messiah (Mark xiv. 61 and Synopsis) which was the only one of the accusations brought against Jesus which could interest Pilate.   The Marcan account of the same trial pays special attention to three episodes : (1) the deposition of witnesses (xiv. 55 ff.) ; (2) the interrogation of the prisoner (xiv. 60 ff.) ; (3) the ill-treatment inflicted on Jesus by the audience and the servants (xiv. 65 ff.). Now these three episodes are repeated in the trial before Pilate : Jewish testimony (xv. 1) ; questioning by the Procurator (xv. 2) ; insults of the soldiery (xv. 16–20).   This parallelism is disquieting.   There is certainly duplication and everything leads us to believe that it is the trial before the Sanhedrin which is redundant.[2]

This trial appears to be nothing but an artifice, which is clumsily introduced with the object of laying the main responsibility for the death of Jesus on the Jews, just as the episode of Barabbas, which we are about to come to, is only brought in to make Pilate a guarantor of the innocence of Jesus.   The question arises, moreover, how the Evangelist could have known what was said and done at the supposed nocturnal meeting of the Sanhedrin, since the only disciple near enough to the scene, Peter, was at that time occupied in the courtyard of the High Priest denying his Master at cockcrow (Mark xiv. 53–72).   Of course there is always the possibility of a later testimony by Joseph of Arimathæa or some other member of the Sanhedrin converted after the Resurrection, but that is a desperate resort and was certainly not assumed by the Evangelists.

Ingenuity and a certain disregard of the texts are all that is needed for finding ways of reconciling even the worst contradictions.   We need not dwell on those which the Gospel accounts of the Passion have undergone.[3]   The trial before the Jewish tribunal [4] remains quite contrary to all probability. The only concession that can possibly be made would be to

---

[1] **CXLIV**, 149.　　　　　　　　[2] **CCLXXIX**-a, 316.

[3] *Cf.* the different works concerning the trial of Jesus, quoted above. The latest one published : Max Radin, *The Trial of Jesus of Nazareth*, University of Chicago Press, 1931, is not convincing.   It is a triumph of the *subjective* method.

[4] **CXLIV**, 53, who has made a special study of the question and concludes that the whole story of this trial is a pure fiction (*Dichtung*). —*Contra* : **CLVI**-a, 486–95.

follow Luke in regarding the sitting of the Sanhedrin, on the
morning of the Passion (Luke xxii. 66), as a kind of meeting
for consultation in which the Jews would take precautions
against Jesus before bringing him before Pilate. It would still
be necessary first of all to admit that the arrest was made by
the Jews, which is more than doubtful.

In reality, if starting from Mark, all the Gospel passages
concerning the respective responsibility of the Procurator and
the Jews in the Passion are placed in chronological order, a
systematic effort to clear the former and implicate the latter
at once becomes apparent. Let us examine the passages :

Matthew.	Luke.	John.
Insistence on Pilate's desire to free Jesus (xxvii. 6–18) ; dream of the Procurator's wife (xxvii. 19) ; assertion by Pilate that the Jews are acting out of envy (xxvii. 18) ; washing of the hands ; acceptance of responsibility by the Jews (xxvii. 24–6).	Sending of Jesus to Herod (xxiii. 6–16). It is he and his soldiers who insult Christ and not those of Pilate (xxiii. 11). Positive assertion of Jesus' innocence by Pilate (xxiii. 14), who does not condemn him but abandons him to the Jews because they insist (xxiii. 21–5).	Proclamation of Jesus' innocence by Pilate three times over (xviii. 38 ; xix. 4, xix. 6) ; he abandons Jesus because the Jews make him fear a denunciation to the Emperor, but he does not formally condemn him (xix. 12–16).

It does not seem rash to suppose, in view of this instructive
glossing of the tradition between Mark and John, in the direction of incriminating the Jews, that the earliest Christian
records attributed all the responsibility for the death of Jesus
to the Roman procurator. However this may be, it is at any
rate impossible for us now to know what happened on this
important point, and in particular we cannot find the true facts
in Mark's account.

The Nazarene now stands before Pilate, the *procurator* of
Judæa.[1] The latter is an official of equestrian rank, possessing the
jus gladii. Josephus (*Ant.*, 18, 1, 1) subordinates him to the
legate of Syria, but he is probably mistaken and must be confusing special missions in the country entrusted to the governor
of Syria and, perhaps, a kind of appellate jurisdiction granted
specially to him, with the regular exercise of a superior authority.[2] He resides generally in Cæsarea, on the coast, but he
comes to Jerusalem for the great feasts because of the danger
of possible trouble from the influx of pilgrims. He then takes

[1] Cf. **XXIX**, i, 454 *ff*. on the government of the procurators in Judæa.
[2] Mommsen, *Hist. romaine*, ix, 91, n. 1 of the translation. *Contra* :
Marquardt, *L'organisation de l'Empire romain*, ii, 356 of the translation.

up his residence in the fortress of Herod's palace in the west of the city.[1] It is there, no doubt, that Jesus is taken, since the prætorium was always in the governor's residence. Mark's account (xv. 1 *ff.*) of the scene is as follows :

> " And straightway in the morning the chief priests (*that is to say the priests belonging to the great sacerdotal families as well as the high priest for that year and his predecessors*) held a consultation with the elders and scribes and the whole council, and bound Jesus, and carried him away, and delivered him to Pilate. And Pilate asked him, Art thou the King of the Jews ? And he answering said unto him, Thou sayest it. And the chief priests accused him of many things : but he answered nothing. And Pilate asked him again, saying, Answerest thou nothing ? behold how many things they witness against thee. But Jesus yet answered nothing ; so that Pilate marvelled."

There are many objections to the probability of this account : Are we to suppose that Pilate places himself at the Jews' disposal, sitting in his tribunal from dawn on a feast day when he knows there can be no trial ? that without preliminary questioning he confronts Jesus with the capital charge : Dost thou claim to be the Messiah ? Roman justice was a more orderly affair. Moreover, it may well be asked whether the governor had ever heard of the Nazarene before seeing him that day. Moreover, at the first question put by this pagan, Jesus confesses what he had always forbidden his disciples to say, that he is the Messiah. Truly an unfortunate moment for such an avowal. The words *Thou sayest it* (σὺ λέγεις) have been much discussed ; but the Evangelist certainly took them to be a confession, because he has interpreted it in advance for us in the trial before the Sanhedrin (xiv. 61 *ff.*) :

> " Again the high priest asked him, and said unto him, Art thou the Christ, the Son of the Blessed ? And Jesus said, I am : and ye shall see the Son of man sitting on the right hand of power, and coming in the clouds of heaven."

But we must remember that Mark does not trouble to observe judicial forms ; he is only concerned with the attitude which it was fitting for the Lord to maintain before a Roman judge, and with his own purpose which was to prove that the Nazarene was the Messiah. The Jews then seem to multiply their accusations, but the Evangelist does not state what any of them were ; and from the evidence we must conclude that he knew nothing about the questioning. It is, moreover, impossible that a Roman judge should not have been more precise

[1] Philo, *Leg.*, 38 and 39 ; Josephus, *B.J.*, 2, 14, 8 ; 15, 5.—*Cf.* XXIX, i, 458.

in his examination. There has been much talk of a *parody of justice*, but what reason could Pilate have had for parodying his own justice ? The probable and decisive accusation is given in Luke xxiii. 5 : "*He stirreth up the people, teaching throughout all Jewry, beginning from Galilee to this place.*" While Luke records this accusation *he does not know that it was actually brought forward* ; *he simply infers it from the circumstances.*

The rest of the Marcan account is intended to give us the impression that Pilate was favourably disposed towards Jesus and only yielded to the implacable animosity of the Jews (xv. 15) ; but this is not historically true. However unimportant the life of a Galilean *nabi* might be to him, he was not the man to be intimidated by the clamouring of the Jewish mob, and the episodes already quoted from Josephus prove it. If he had been convinced that Jesus was dangerous in the smallest degree he would have condemned him ; if he had thought the contrary he would have acquitted him. But the Evangelist *cannot* say the one and *will not* say the other. And so he attributes to Pilate a weak leniency which renders him incapable of either condemning or acquitting Jesus, so that in the end he abandons him to the murderous hands of his accusers. Matthew xxvii. 17 *ff.* and Luke xxiii. 13 *ff.* have no more knowledge of the affair than Mark, but simply improve on his statements in the direction which he has indicated and which the exigency of Christian apologetics required at the time the Evangelists were writing.

We shall not dwell on the episode of Pilate's action in sending Jesus back to Herod Antipas, the tetrarch of Galilee, who is also supposed to be at Jerusalem for the feast. This is an addition which is peculiar to the third Evangelist (Luke xxiii. 6 *ff.*), and whose futility does him scant credit. It is a piece of pure hagiography. It is impossible to imagine the procurator giving such an example of renunciation at Jerusalem. The case can only be tried by an official in whose jurisdiction the crime has been committed. Such a transference of the accused would be at the same time illegal, absurd and dangerous to Pilate's authority. We need not be surprised that a reference to this legendary appearance of Jesus before Herod should occur in Acts iv. 27, since Luke and the Acts probably proceed from the same pen ; but it also figures in the *Gospel of Peter*, where the tetrarch is represented as one of Jesus' judges ; it is he too who orders Jesus to be removed for execution : [1] "*All that I have commanded you to do to him, do it.*" There was therefore a legend which implicated Herod in the heinous crime,

---

[1] Beginning of the first fragment.

and finally made him completely responsible for it. It corresponds closely to the fiction of the trial before the Sanhedrin and represents another mode of achieving the same end. This is proved by the fact that Luke omits the trial : Herod represents for him the Jewish authorities as did the Sanhedrin for Mark. It may have been fear of flatly contradicting the Marcan tradition that restrained him from going as far as the *Gospel of Peter*.

In the eyes of the Evangelists their Lord had been condemned by an appalling and immeasurable sacrilege, although vitally necessary and ordained by God ; Pilate thought he was only suppressing a Galilean visionary who, though probably not very dangerous in himself, should not be left to play with fire too long. The sentence and its consequences must have troubled the judge far less than the narrator. In reality we never find ourselves on the plane of history because the narrator is wholly outside it himself. The probability is that *the Nazarene was arrested by the Roman police, judged and condemned by the Roman procurator, Pilate or someone else.*

IV

THE MINOR EPISODES

Before partially admitting this conclusion the Marcan redactor, in order to emphasize the responsibility of the Jews, introduces the episode of Barabbas (Mark xv. 6–11) :

> " Now at that feast (at every Passover ?) he released unto them one prisoner, whomsoever they desired. And there was one named Barabbas,[1] which lay bound with them that had made insurrection with him, who had committed murder in the insurrection.[2] And the multitude crying aloud began to desire him to do as he had ever done unto them. But Pilate answered them, saying, Will ye that I release unto you the King of the Jews ? For he knew that the chief priests had delivered him for envy."

---

[1] This name means *the Father's son*. The coincidence has sometimes appeared singular. It was still more so in the manuscripts which Origen claims to have seen and in which the person under discussion was called *Jesus Barabbas*. On the questions which these comparisons may raise, *cf.* **CCXCII**, i, 339 ; **LXXXIV**, 136. But Barabbas is not a rare name (**CXIV**, 128).

[2] This insurrection about which Mark apparently knows nothing and we, if possible, still less, is considered by Mr. Eisler as one of the chief scriptural supports of his dissertation on the revolutionary attitude of Jesus before Jerusalem, a thesis which is based principally on the Slavonic Josephus. *Cf.* **CLIV**, ii, 439 *ff.*, and the index at the word στάσις. We should note that Luke xxiii. 19, instead of *the insurrection*, says more cautiously *a certain sedition made in the city*.

When the crowd, urged on by the priests, shout for Barabbas and cry out against Jesus : *Crucify him !* Pilate asks : *Why, what evil hath he done ?* But they only cry out again : *Crucify him !* Then Pilate yields, setting Barabbas free and condemning Jesus to death.

This is another very strange episode.[1] First, we have no other evidence beside our Gospels for this astonishing custom. It is incredible that no other Jewish writer should speak of this outrageous privilege that a criminal *must* be released if the people should claim him. Various attempts have been made to find instances of clemency exercised on behalf of criminals in certain circumstances.[2] That is, however, not the question here. Mention has also been made of the *abolitio*, which in Roman law could annul the proceedings which had been begun in a case, either on the initiative of the plaintiff (*abolitio privata*), or by the intervention of the state represented by the Emperor or the Senate (*abolitio publica*). The case of Barabbas falls outside this custom. All that remains is a free pardon (*indulgentia*) ; but if perhaps the Senate had the right to grant it (Mommsen's view), it was actually the Prince who exercised that prerogative under the Empire, but it is extremely unlikely that his procurator would have the right to exercise it in his place.[3] Doubtless Pilate could have dropped proceedings against an accused but uncondemned man, even if he thought him guilty,[4] but how can it be supposed that he would wish to do so for a revolutionary taken in the act ?

The real problem lies in the absurdity of the very conception of this privilege of the Jews : in the difficulty of understanding the sudden change in the attitude of the crowd obtained by the priests, when, according to Mark, it has been favourable to Jesus up till then.[5] The scene appears more like a stage effect in a childish play than a piece of historical reality.[6]

There has been no lack of explanations of the supposed custom, and of attempts to discover its origin,[7] but none are satisfactory, because we have not the requisite knowledge. On the other hand it is clear that the redactor's intention is to acquit Pilate and throw the blame on the Jews. If we must

[1] Merkel, *Die Begnadigung am Passahfeste*, in **ZWT**, 1905, 293–316. *Cf.* **XIXX**, i, 468 *ff.* ; **CLVI**-*a*, 500 *ff.*

[2] Livy, 5, 13 ; Athenæus, 14, 15. *Cf.* **CI**, 414, and **XCVIII**, 177.

[3] *Contra* : **CCXXVII**, 129 *ff.* ; **CCXXX**, 256 *ff.*

[4] **CCLII**[4], 229, quotes an Egyptian Papyrus of the year 85 which makes the judge say to an accused man : " You deserve the whip, but I will make a present of you to the crowd."

[5] *Cf.* **CI**, 389 *ff.*, who wastes much labour. [6] **CIII**, ii, 644.

[7] *Ibid.*, 652 ; **CXLIV**, 94–105 ; **EB**, art. *Barabbas* (P. Schmiedel).

choose between the different suppositions, it would be preferable
to see in the story of Barabbas an application of the principle
of symmetry and contrast of which the Evangelists often avail
themselves : the Jews have to choose between the way of God
and that of the Devil ; they preferred the Son of their father
the Devil to the Son of God (*cf.* John viii. 44).[1]

Matthew xxvii. 19 inserts the story of the dream of Pilate's
wife into the episode of Barabbas :

> " When he was set down on the judgment seat, his wife sent
> unto him, saying, Have thou nothing to do with that just man :
> for I have suffered many things this day in a dream because of
> him."

This verse plunges us into the apocryphal legends which
know much more than Matthew about this woman and her
strange disturbing dream. They tell us that her name was
Claudia Procula and that she was a Jewish proselyte ($\theta\varepsilon o\sigma\varepsilon\beta\eta\varsigma$,
$\iota o\upsilon\delta\alpha\dot\iota\zeta o\upsilon\sigma\alpha$) ; the Greek and Ethiopian churches canonize her.[2]

We are confronted by a legendary variation of Pilate's
favourable attitude. The symbolical gesture of washing the
hands,[3] mentioned also by Matthew xxvii. 24, is in the same
category and the procurator himself explains it : " *I am innocent
of the blood of this just person : see ye to it.*" And the Jews cried
with one voice (xxv.) : " *His blood be on us, and on our children.*"
It was to fall on them, and heavily. Few of the sayings of the
Gospels have done more harm than these, and yet they are only
the invention of the redactor ! It is a mistake to suppose that
the Evangelist wished to emphasize the cowardice of Pilate ;
he was only thinking of the Roman's good intentions and the
hatred of the Jews, because those are the only sentiments which
immediately affect him at the time of writing. He not only
makes a Roman official express his sympathy with the prisoner
by a symbolical gesture that is purely Jewish, but he has been
naïve enough to put into the governor's mouth what is almost
a quotation from the scriptures (2 Sam. iii. 28), in the Septuagint
of course, because that was the version which the author himself
read. The people also, to show that they can do the same,
complete the context.[4]

---

[1] CCI, 116.   [2] CIII, ii, 648 ; XCIX, 221 ; CII, 521.
[3] The action and the symbol are both Jewish (Deut. xxi. 6 ; Ps.
xxvi. 6 ; lxxiii. 13). *Cf.* XCIX, 221 ; LXVI, i, 1032.
[4] 2 Sam. iii. 28 (it is David who speaks) : $'A\theta\tilde\omega\varsigma \varepsilon i\mu\iota, \dot\varepsilon\gamma\dot\omega \kappa\alpha\dot\iota \dot\eta$
$\beta\alpha\sigma\iota\lambda\varepsilon i\alpha \mu o\upsilon, \dot\alpha\pi\dot o \kappa\upsilon\rho i o\upsilon \kappa\alpha\dot\iota \dot\varepsilon\omega\varsigma \alpha\dot\iota\tilde\omega\nu o\varsigma \dot\alpha\pi\dot o \tau\tilde\omega\nu \alpha\dot\iota\mu\dot\alpha\tau\omega\nu 'A\beta\varepsilon\nu\nu\dot\eta\rho \upsilon\dot\iota o\tilde\upsilon N\dot\eta\rho$
= " *I and my kingdom are guiltless before the Lord for ever from the
blood of Abner the son of Ner* " (*cf.* Matt. : $'A\theta\tilde\omega\varsigma \varepsilon i\mu\iota \dot\alpha\pi\dot o \tau o\tilde\upsilon \alpha\dot\iota\mu\alpha\tau o\varsigma$
$\tau o\dot\upsilon\tau o\upsilon$). And David adds : " *Let it rest* ($\kappa\alpha\tau\alpha\nu\tau\eta\sigma\dot\alpha\tau\omega\sigma\alpha\nu$) *on the head of
Joab, and on all his father's house.*"

Finally, however, as it is necessary to tell the truth, which is that Pilate has condemned Jesus, Mark xv. 15 concludes : " *And so Pilate, willing to content the people, released Barabbas unto them, and delivered Jesus, when he had scourged him, to be crucified.*" The text mentions no sentence, but the governor must have passed one since his soldiers proceed to carry out the execution.

The Gospel account of the arrest, trial and condemnation of Jesus swarms with impossibilities, improbabilities and inconsistencies, and is quite unintelligible from the juridical point of view. Nothing is settled by saying that every form of law and justice was violated, that Jesus was not judged but assassinated, and that Pilate in a panic, condemned him to death by a monstrous miscarriage of justice.[1] We should have to explain first why this was so, but no explanation is possible. All hypotheses which support the veracity of the documents make the initial error of assuming that veracity is an article of faith, and hence treat as historical what is only hagiography directed to apologetic ends. It is quite evident that such a distortion of the truth could only have been risked at a time when Caiaphas, Pilate and the Apostles had all disappeared.

The truth, in so far as it may be discerned through these fantastic imaginations, would appear to be that Jesus was arrested by the Roman police, perhaps on the denunciation of the Temple authorities, as a Messianic preacher.[2] He was brought before the Procurator, confessed what he thought to be his mission, and was convicted on trumped-up evidence. No one defended him and the people were unmoved when they saw a prophet, a herald of the Great Miracle, suffering himself to be taken by the *goyim*, and stripped at a blow of his authority and prestige. Jesus, then, was condemned. If we ask under what law, we are referred to the *lex Julia maiestatis* (*Dig.*, 48, 4, 1), which, according to the lawyer Paul (*Dig.*, 18, 19, 38, sec. 2), entailed crucifixion or, *pro qualitate dignitatis*, exposure to wild animals or banishment to an island. It is not likely that

---

[1] CCXXVII, 110 ; CCXXX, 238.

[2] Lietzmann (CCLXX–a, 321) supposes that the initiative comes from Pilate, who is alarmed by the tumult of the Messianic entry and the sympathy which the people show towards Jesus (*er hat Anhang im Volke gefunden*). Jesus is arrested because *als messianischer Kronprätendent*, he has been a disturber of the peace. The hypothesis would be convincing if it were possible : (1) to omit arbitrarily four days of Holy Week, for how can we suppose that the police delayed taking action at the risk of seeing the disorder spread ? (2) to disregard the objections against the triumphal entry drawn from the arrangement of the narrative, as well as those which have a bearing on the *Messianic consciousness* of Jesus.

Pilate, or any other procurator, would have troubled to base
his decision on a statute. He was responsible for the maintenance of order and would take what measures he thought
necessary to that end, by virtue of his general powers. In this
case he did not need to trouble about strict legality and the
Jews would no doubt have been surprised if he had.

CHAPTER IV

THE PASSION—THE CRUCIFIXION

I

THE PRELIMINARY EPISODES

JESUS has been condemned to death. There is no reason to suppose that he was not executed. The Gospel tradition believes that he was crucified. But before his account of the last agony Mark introduces the two episodes of the scourging and the mocking.

In itself it is not unlikely that Jesus was scourged, that is to say, severely beaten with *flagella,* whips made of leather thongs. The ordeal which was sometimes so terrible that the sufferer died from its effects (Horace, *Sat.,* 1, 3, 119 : *horribile flagellum*), seems to have been inflicted usually on provincials who were not citizens, as an aggravation of capital punishment.[1] The disturbing point however is that the Evangelist merely indicates the scourging by a single word ($\varphi\varrho\alpha\gamma\epsilon\lambda\lambda\acute{\omega}\sigma\alpha\varsigma$), which is probably incorrect :[2] the *flagra,* which were iron chains ending in little metal balls or cords knotted over small bones at the ends, were only used in exceptionally serious cases or for the punishment of slaves. Jesus did not deserve this refinement of cruelty, but it was part of the Evangelist's purpose that he should suffer it. The rest of the account of the Passion piles up every incident capable of moving listeners and readers in the deepest possible way. Hence, if Jesus was condemned to be crucified, flagellation as a preliminary ordeal was not unlikely ;[3] and since it was inflicted in public the disciples may have known about it later.

The same cannot be said of the mocking. According to Mark xv. 17-20, the soldiers led Jesus inside the courtyard of Pilate's palace, where the entire cohort was assembled :

" And they clothed him with purple, and platted a crown of

---

[1] **CI**, 390 ; **XCVIII**, 179.   [2] Codex D corrects to $\varphi\lambda\alpha\gamma\epsilon\lambda\lambda\acute{\omega}\sigma\alpha\varsigma$.
[3] *Cf.* Josephus, *B.J.*, 2, 14, 9, who describes the execution of Jews : $\mu\acute{\alpha}\sigma\tau\iota\zeta\iota\nu$ $\pi\varrho o\alpha\iota\varkappa\iota\sigma\acute{\alpha}\mu\epsilon\nu o\varsigma$ $\grave{\alpha}\nu\epsilon\sigma\tau\alpha\acute{\upsilon}\varrho\iota\sigma\epsilon\nu =$ " having lacerated them with whips, he crucified them." *Cf. B.J.*, 5, 11, 1.

thorns, and put it about his head,[1] and began to salute him, Hail, King of the Jews ! And they smote him on the head with a reed, and did spit upon him, and bowing their knees worshipped him. And when they had mocked him, they took off the purple from him, and put his own clothes on him,[2] and led him out to crucify him."

These verses have caused a great deal of discussion, but history has not much to gain from it.

Those who have admitted the historicity of the episode accept the insulting mockery, supported by other details which we learn from early documents, as a comparatively accurate report.[3] For example, we have the grotesque scene prepared by the people of Alexandria to insult Agrippa, the Jewish vassal king, as he passed through their city.[4] They seize an idiot named Carabas and deck him with mock royal insignia. They hail him with the title of *Marin*, which in Syriac means *Lord*, and pretend to render him homage and demand justice from him.—Others have thought of a passage in Dion Chrysostom [5] about the King of the Sacœa (*Sacaea*). A festival was celebrated in Babylon, at the time of the Persian domination, which was perhaps derived from an ancient feast in honour of Marduk. It lasted five days, about the 25th of March. A prisoner was chosen who was given all the honours and privileges of a king during the period of the festival, after which, however, they stripped him of his finery, scourged and hanged him. The name given to him was *Zoganes*.—Others again have thought of the *king of the Saturnalia* who was drawn by lot and who presided over the festival with every fantastic extravagance possible ; and they have tried to conclude from the story of Saint Dasius [6] that in the fourth century a rite was practised in the Roman army in which a soldier chosen by lot was raised to the dignity of king of the Saturnalia. At the end of the festival he was

---

[1] Christian tradition has represented this crown as a further torture : the thorns sink into the victim's head under the lashes of the reed. There is no suggestion of that in our text : the crown appears there solely as derisive, like the lashes. The soldiers are not represented as rushing away to pick thorny plants and pricking their fingers in plaiting them. We should not forget that ἀκάνθινον στέφανον may mean *a crown of acanthus*.

[2] Note that it is not said that they left the crown of thorns on his head. The iconographic tradition which represents it on the head of the Crucified is not ancient. The earliest representations of the Crucifixion (fifth century) are without it.

[3] **LXXXVI**, 164, 2, for the bibliography.   [4] Philo, *C. Flaccum*, 2.

[5] *De Regno*, 4, 66.—*Cf.* J. Frazer, *The Golden Bough*, London, 1914 ; iv, *The Dying God*, 113 *ff.* ; ix, *The Scape Goat*, 102.

[6] Published by Cumont, in *Analecta Bollandiana*, xvi, 1897, 5 *ff.* It is thought to have taken place under Diocletian about 303 at Durostolum, on the Danube.—*Cf.* Frazer, *Golden B.*, ii, 310 ; ix, 308 *ff.*

sacrificed on the altar of Saturn, or he killed himself there. This Dasius, a Christian convert, was, according to his *Passio*, designated to play the rôle of the comic king, who seems to have represented Saturn, but he refused and was put to death.— Finally, some have referred to the feast of *Purim* (= *the Lots*), to explain which the *Book of Esther* [1] (*Ishtar* ?) was written : Mordecai (= *Marduk*) and Haman share the rôle of Zoganes of the *Sacæa*. Up to the time of Diocletian, who forbade it, the Jews had crucified and burnt in effigy a *Haman* each year at the days of *Purim*, which in reality was probably only a festival derived from the Sacæa. Mordecai's ride (Esth. vi. 11) would be comparable to the Spring procession of the beardless king, that is to say of the young king Sun, in Babylon and in Persia.[2] Other customs of the same kind might also be found in the ancient world.

It is undeniable that there are striking resemblances between some of the features which compose these different stories and the points most emphasized in the gospel story of the mocking. But *resemblance* is not the same as *connection*, and in this case it is the connection, the derivation which concerns us.

Some suppose [3] that Pilate's soldiers are performing a rite in treating Jesus as they do : they confer on the condemned prophet the dignity of a king of the Saturnalia or of the Sacæa, or of Karabas. There are serious objections to this hypothesis : (1) The story of Karabas given by Philo does not give the impression of a custom or a rite, but on the contrary suggests a grotesque parody improvised on the particular occasion of Agrippa's passing through the town. The idiot is not put to death, and it would be arbitrary to correct his name of Karabas to Barabbas to suit the case as S. Reinach would do. (2) The royalty which the tormentors are supposed to attribute to Jesus in mockery bears no visible resemblance to that of the prince of the Sacæa. (3) If we are to suppose that the soldiers identified Jesus, by the strangest of transpositions, with the king of the Saturnalia, it would surely be necessary for the episode to have taken place at the time of the Saturnalia which was about the 17th December, but there is no evidence for this. And above all we have no reason for thinking that the king of the Saturnalia would be known in Judæa among the Oriental soldiers who apparently composed the cohort.[4]

---

[1] Esth. ix. 17–32.—*Cf.* **EB**, *Purim* ; Frazer, *Golden B.*, ix, 360 *ff*.
[2] **CCXCII**, i, 335.   [3] *Ibid.*, 332 *ff*.
[4] We are not convinced by Reinach's argument that Pilate would never have dared, even ironically, to address Jesus as *King of the Jews* unless custom allowed it, because it is neither certain nor probable that Pilate did give him that title.

All that we can say is that there is evidence for the sporadic existence of the custom of a mock kingship ; we might also suppose a certain mythical element in the episode, although it would not be easy to say where, for what purpose, and to what degree.

Hence, common sense would seem to demand that before discussing the episode, we should be certain that it happened, and that the account of it is reliable. It is difficult to imagine Pilate's soldiers indulging in such foolery as to make a wretched butt of a man condemned to death, whom the scourging must have left exhausted, and that under the eye of the procurator, since it took place in the courtyard of the prætorium. We have probably to do with another of those hagiographic inventions in which *Martyria* and *Passiones* abound, and its chief aim is to show in the most moving manner, by means of the liturgical drama of the Passion, how the divine royalty of Jesus was despised and insulted by blinded men ; [1] and also to what extent the Lord could humble himself and suffer for the salvation of those who should believe on him. Confirmation of this hypothesis is to be found in a passage in the *Gospel of Peter* iii, 6 *ff.*) :

"Let us take the Son of God since we have power over him. And they clothed him in purple and placed him on the seat of judgment (*Pilate's own seat !*) saying : Judge justly, O king of Israel ! And one of them, having brought a crown of thorns, placed it on the Lord's head. And some who stood there spat on his face and others struck him on the cheek, or pricked him with a reed, and others again struck him with a whip, saying : Thus do we honour the Son of God (ταυτῇ τῇ τιμῇ τιμήσωμεν τὸν υἱὸν τοῦ θεοῦ)."

It is no longer the soldiers who speak and do this but the people of Jerusalem (*cf.* v. 5 : "*And he delivered him over to the people*"). The apocryphal account improves on the canonical, but follows its method and explains its intention. It is moreover probable that Christian imagination has not simply invented the details, and that it was enough to record the formula *King of the Jews*, a title of derision to Pilate and the Jews, to suggest a connexion with the king of the *Sacæa*.[2] This does not imply that the story of the mocking is derived from a reminiscence of the Sacæa.

On the other hand it is very probable that here, as in so

---

[1] **CXLIV**, 106 *ff.* ; **XCI–a**, 286.

[2] A comparison is at once suggested between the *Gospel of Peter*, 7 : καὶ ἐκάθισαν αὐτὸν ἐπὶ καθέδραν κρίσεως = *and they set him on the throne of judgment*, and Dion. Chrys., *De regno*, 4, 66 : καθίζουσιν εἰς τὸν θρόνον τὸν τοῦ βασιλέως = *they make* (the King of the Sacæa) *sit on the King's throne. Cf.* **CXXXIX**, 225.

many of the episodes already recounted, legend has not forgotten the necessity of *fulfilling the scriptures*. We are reminded of Isaiah liii. in connexion with the insults, ill treatment and suffering which the Servant of God endures, either in anticipation or in retrospect. We find a link with the first interpretation, suggested for the episode of the mocking in the emphasis of this famous passage on the blindness of men towards the unique figure whom they are insulting and torturing:

> " He is despised and rejected of men ; a man of sorrows, and acquainted with grief : and we hid as it were our faces from him ; he was despised and we esteemed him not " (liii. 3 ; *cf.* liii. 2 and 7).

Two other appropriate passages come to mind :

> Micah v. 1 : " They shall smite the judge of Israel with a rod upon the cheek," and Isaiah l. 6 : " I gave my back to the smiters, and my cheeks to them that plucked off the hair : I hid not my face from shame and spitting."

It is possible that this painful episode which takes place in Pilate's prætorium goes back to the time when tradition attributed the responsibility for the Passion to the Romans. Later, when it came to be felt that the Jews alone were guilty, the scene of these outrages was assigned to the high priest's house (*cf.* Mark xiv. 65), while it was also possible to attribute them to the guard of Herod Antipas (Luke xxiii. 11). Through an oversight, of which the Gospels offer more than one example, Mark has preserved both versions, while Luke more logically or more carefully does not speak of the scene at the prætorium. The *Gospel of Peter* develops the tradition still further by saying that *the whole Jewish people disown, mock, insult and maltreat the Lord of Glory*. The episode, in its various forms, belongs rather to the sphere of the Mystery-religions, of Symbolic rites, or of the sacred drama, than to history.

II

THE CRUCIFIXION

When the soldiers weary of their shameful sport, they take Jesus away to be crucified (Mark xv. 20). Is it certain that Jesus was crucified ? At first sight the question seems even more surprising than the question : *Did he ever exist ?* because in the synoptic tradition the Nazarene's death has a more historical appearance than his birth and remains the strongest guarantee of his having lived. It is impossible for us to obliterate from our minds the vision of Christ on the cross, we recognize it as one of the incontestable fundamental facts of history. Yet it has been denied more than once. Arguments of unequal weight have been urged against its reality, the first of which are drawn from the silence of ancient writers. We need not attach much weight to this argument because it is not legitimate to measure the importance of the event in contemporary eyes by that of its consequences for us.

The death of Jesus has been compared to that of the King of the Saturnalia and the King of the Sacæa in the hazardous explanation of the mocking already referred to, but at that time these rites were probably only carried out in effigy. Such comparisons are superficial, and are disposed of by the fact that the mythical colouring of an event must never be confused with the actual event to which it is supposed to refer.

An argument of greater apparent weight has been put forward : it is incontestable that many striking events in the Passion are due to the desire to exhibit the fulfilment of various prophecies, and do not correspond to any reality and therefore to no authentic memory. From this point of view the influence of Psalm xxii. is particularly interesting. Now we read the following in verse 16 of this Psalm : [1] " *For dogs have compassed me : the assembly of the wicked have inclosed me : they pierced my hands and my feet* " (ὤρυξαν χεῖρας μου, καὶ πόδας). Should we not think that the Crucifixion is only the fulfilment of this *word* and has no more in common with reality than the parting of the garments (Mark xv. 24), which proceeds from Psalm xxii. 18 ? This plausible hypothesis [2] would seem well founded if it were not that Paul on several occasions (1 Cor. i. 23 ; ii. 2 ; ii. 8 ; Gal. ii. 19 ; v. 24 ; vi. 12 and 14) positively bears witness to the historicity of the Crucifixion. It is no ground for objection that Paul does not say that Jesus was crucified at Jerusalem, since that was obvious to him and his readers. On the other hand it may be asked what possible meaning Paul's preaching, or the Gospel he claimed to announce, could possess, if it be denied that our Lord died on the cross. It is evident that if Paul lived, wherever or whenever he lived, he knew how Jesus died. We may add that if the Jews from whom the tradition comes, or the Tarsiot himself, had been

---

[1] In the Septuagint. The Hebrew is different, but the Hebrew text does not matter here as the Greek editors of the Gospels did not know Hebrew.

[2] S. Reinach (**CCXCII**, ii, 437) was led away by it before Eisler had converted him to his views. *Cf. Aux clous de la croix*, in *Congrès d'hist. du christianisme* (Alfred Loisy Jubilee), i, 114 *ff*. Paris, 1928.

inventing the death of Jesus, they would have chosen some other mode of death than the cross, which brought Jesus under the doom of the words : " *He that is hanged is accursed of God* " (Deut. xxi. 23). No one creates difficulties on purpose when they can easily be avoided. But if the reality of the Crucifixion be admitted, it is easily understood that Hellenistic Christians, seeing in it the fulfilment of Psalm xxii. 16, would expect from the rest of the Psalm as usual the information which tradition refused them, and which would appear to them to be at least as valuable as the reminiscences of tradition.

Hence it does not seem legitimate to doubt the historicity of the Crucifixion ; but exception may be taken to the details of the Gospel account.

In its origin crucifixion was an Oriental form of execution used by the Persians, Phenicians and Carthaginians. The Greeks probably took it from the Persians and the Romans from the Carthaginians, although Cicero attributes its introduction into the City to Tarquin the Proud. In Rome it is the *slaves' punishment*, which is gradually extended to other categories of criminals, for example to thieves and those condemned to death in the provinces. It was considered an outrage to inflict it on a Roman citizen.[1] In Cicero's opinion it is *crudelissimum teterrimumque supplicium*; it is also ignominious (Gal. iii. 13 ; Heb. xii. 2). Usually a cross was made in the form of a T and was not very high. The condemned man was hoisted on to it with his hands nailed or tied to the crossbar (*patibulum*) and his feet to the pillar. A strong peg passed between his legs and driven into the pillar supported the body, without which precaution the weight would have quickly torn the hands. The tradition which later fixed the form of the cross of Jesus (✝ = *crux immissa*), suppressed the peg and placed the feet on a support, has no authority for doing so.

Mark xv. 22 indicates what he knows of the place of punishment in these words : " *And they bring him unto the place* (called) *Golgotha, which is, being interpreted, The place of a skull.*" A small rounded eminence is probably intended.[2] " *The authenticity of the traditional calvary is not questionable,*" writes P. Lagrange.[3] We reply that each day it becomes more so. It rests chiefly on the worthless opinion of the officials of Con-

---

[1] Cicero, *In Ver.*, 5, 66.　　　　　　　　[2] **XCVIII**, 182.
[3] **CI**, 426.—*Cf.* **EB**, art. *Golgotha* ; **CXCVIII**, 450 *ff.* ; J. Jeremias, *Wo lag Golgotha und der heilige Grab?* in *Aggelos*, 1925, 141–73. The recent case made out by Father Vincent, *L'authenticité des Lieux Saints*, Paris, 1932, p. 54 *ff.*, who deals with sceptics impatiently, seems to be founded on shaky arguments.

stantine. Eusebius, who relates the discovery (*Vita Constantini*, iii. 25), dares not tell us that Christian tradition guaranteed the accepted identification : he merely adds an unctuous phrase about the duty which Constantine felt was his to " *make visible to all, the blessed spot of the saving resurrection and to make it available for veneration.*" Christian Faith, determined to know the whole topography of the Passion, has successively recovered all its details. It even knows that Peter, after his denial, went to weep over his cowardice in the grotto of the *Gallicantus*.[1] The Holy Sepulchre is more famous, but its site is not more certain, and Calvary, which is only about thirty yards away, is as doubtful. The expert archæological knowledge of P. Vincent or P. Abel, which has disclosed to us so much of ancient Jerusalem, is not sufficient to convince the impartial observer that the rocky eminence traditionally regarded as Golgotha was within Herod's precinct, since it is incontestable that the authentic Calvary was certainly outside it.[2] At first sight it is surprising that Christian tradition did not preserve an exact record of the place where Jesus died, but it must be remembered that the Christians abandoned Jerusalem at the time of the great Jewish revolt (in 66) [3] and that after many years only a small community returned, when the topography of the ancient town which had been overthrown by Titus after the great siege, and then by Hadrian, was irrecoverable by the newcomers. The fourth century believed that Hadrian's great religious buildings, his temples of Aphrodite and Jupiter for example, arose from the desire to profane the holy places of Christianity. Therefore they sought and of course found the latter on the same site as the former, and thus Calvary was disclosed under the temple of Aphrodite. There is naturally no reason to impute any such evil designs to the emperor of the second century and the reasoning founded on them has no value. It is only a very minor issue, upon which we need not dwell.

According to Mark xv. 21, Jesus had to carry or drag his cross to the place of execution. Such was indeed the Roman custom.[4] Possibly because Jesus is exhausted by the scourging [5] the soldiers commandeer a certain " *Simon a Cyrenian, who passed by, coming out of the country, the father of Alexander and Rufus* " to carry the burden in his stead. People have seen

---

[1] *Cf.* **RB**, 1905, 155.

[2] Heb. xiii. 12 : (Jesus) " *suffered without the gate* " (ἔξω τῆς πύλης ἔπαθεν).

[3] Eusebius, *H.E.*, iii, 5, 3.

[4] **CXLIV**, 172 ; **XCVIII**, 181 ; **LXVI**, i, 587.   [5] **CI**, 425.

in the precision of this episode a reassuring guarantee of the reality of the Crucifixion. Too much insistence should not be laid on this. First of all Matthew xxvii. 32 and Luke xxiii. 26, who also mention the episode, named neither Alexander nor Rufus, from which it follows that the text of Mark, which they had before them, did not name them either, and that this detail was added later, we do not know where or when. Neither John (xix. 17) nor the *Gospel of Peter* mention the episode. We know nothing about this Simon whom legend numbers among the seventy disciples spoken of in Luke x. 1.[1] The episode may possibly have been taken from some legend or tradition, the rest of which has not reached us. Later, the *docetic* sect of gnostics, who believed that the body of our Lord had only been a *semblance*, imagined that this Simon who was compelled to bear Jesus' cross, was changed by him into his own resemblance and crucified in his stead, while the Christ under the features of Simon himself stood beside the cross and mocked the executioners.[2] Contrary to S. Reinach's[3] former opinion, there is no trace of this extravagant interpretation being the first form of the account and we cannot explain Mark by it, which is as much as to say that we do not know what to make of Simon the Cyrenian. We have no other example of a similar requisition to that which perhaps associated him with the Passion, but we have no need of such evidence to be convinced of the historicity of the Crucifixion.

The Evangelists realized that they could not dismiss the fact with a bare affirmation of it and so they gave details of the Crucifixion. The wisest course would be to ignore them, but since their account is universally known something must be said about it.

Mark xv. 23 writes : " *And they gave him to drink wine mingled with myrrh : but he received it not.*" It was evidently a kind of anæsthetic or narcotic. Proverbs xxxi. 6 said : " *Give strong drink unto him that is ready to perish,*" and, according to rabbinical tradition,[4] women of high social rank in Jerusalem considered it a pious deed to prepare a drink of this kind and offer it with their own hands to men condemned to death. The custom is not Roman and, if we pass over certain difficulties, it remains a possibility. There is also, unfortunately, the likeli-

[1] On the efforts made to identify Alexander and Rufus, *cf.* **CIII,** ii, 659.

[2] Irenæus, *Hær.*, i, 24, 4 ; *cf.* **CXXXV**–*a*, i, 195 *ff.*, 204 ; iii, 427 ; **CXLII,** 240.

[3] **CCXCII,** iv, 181 *ff.* Reinach has apparently given up this view. Eisler's opinions, **CXLIV,** ii, 529, are, on this point at least, orthodox.

[4] **CXLIV,** 177.

hood that the incident may merely have been taken from the
verse just quoted from Proverbs. Luke has omitted this detail,
while Matthew xxvii. 34, by replacing the *myrrh* by *gall* (οἶνον
μετὰ χολῆς μεμιγμένον), has given it the opposite meaning. He
has suggested that they were deliberately adding a further
torture by giving Jesus something extremely bitter to drink.
The reason is because he is not thinking of Proverbs xxxi. 6,
but of Psalm lxix. 21, where we read : " *They gave me also gall*
(χολήν) *for my meat : and in my thirst they gave me vinegar to
drink.*" [1] We shall find the second ingredient in a moment.

When Jesus is on the cross the soldiers part his garments
among them by lot (Mark xv. 24). The custom, well established
by the time of Hadrian (*Dig.*, 48, 20, 6), of regarding the clothing
of those who had been executed as the perquisite of the executioners, may easily have already been in operation. From
which we must not conclude that the Marcan redactor knew
that this had happened at Golgotha ; he knew, what was far
more important, that it could not have happened otherwise,
since he read in Psalm xxii. 18 : " *They part my garments among
them, and cast lots upon my vesture.*" Moreover, John xix. 24
quotes the prophecy and records its fulfilment.[2]

According to Mark xv. 25, it was then the *third hour*, that
is nine o'clock in the morning. This detail, which neither
Matthew nor Luke reproduce, and may therefore have been
posterior to their redaction, is contradicted by John, who has
placed the appearance of Jesus before Pilate at the third hour
(xix. 14). We need not suppose that John is better informed
than Mark, and it is preferable to believe that this third hour
corresponds to the systematic arrangement of the day of the
Passion by the second Evangelist. He divides it into four
periods as he did with the preceding night ; the Crucifixion
marks the second period.[3]

It was the Roman custom to carry a placard before a condemned man as he walked to the place of execution, or to hang
round his neck or place in his hand a tablet stating the reason
for his condemnation.[4] Synoptic tradition claimed to know
(Mark xv. 26 ; Matt. xxvii. 37) that a *titulus* was nailed to his

---

[1] Many MSS. of Matthew continue : " *And they gave him vinegar
mixed with gall to drink* " (ὄξος instead of οἶνον). It is a mixture of
this kind which the *Gospel of Peter* says was offered to Jesus on the
cross.

[2] Some MSS. of Matt. xxvii. 35–6, which also mention this, seem
to have borrowed it from the Fourth Gospel.—*Cf.* CCI, 36.

[3] CV, 458 *ff.*—On the possibility of a copyist's error in Mark, *cf.*
XCVIII, 183.

[4] Texts in CI, 429 and XCVIII, 183.

cross with the *superscription of his accusation* (Mark) in these words : The *King of the Jews*, according to Mark ; *This is Jesus the King of the Jews*, according to Matthew xxvii. 37 ; *This is the King of the Jews*, according to Luke xxiii. 38 ; *Jesus of Nazareth the King of the Jews*, in Hebrew, Latin and Greek, according to John xix. 19 ; *This is the King of Israel*, according to the *Gospel of Peter* xi. There is therefore a certain vagueness in the records about the exact form of wording, which suggests that the text of the *titulus* was simply invented in accordance with what seemed probable to each narrator, and that the *titulus* was attached by tradition to the cross because it was expected to be there. In other words, if the details are not improbable, they are not, however, proved to be historical.

Tradition further said that Jesus was not crucified alone, that two thieves,[1] one on his right and the other on his left, were executed with him (Mark xv. 27). This in itself is not impossible, but the passage Isaiah liii. 12 inevitably suggests itself : " . . . *he hath poured out his soul* (that is to say *his life*) *unto death : and he was numbered with the transgressors.*" Other copyists had already thought of it and introduced the quotation into the text of Mark, with the formula : *and the scripture was fulfilled which saith. . . .*[2] Unfortunately the *two* thieves may be taken from another passage of the Old Testament (Gen. xl.), where Joseph, a *type* and precursor of Jesus in the Christian interpretation of the Old Testament, was imprisoned with the chief baker and chief butler of Pharaoh.[3] Hence the episode, although not improbable, very likely represents nothing more than the fulfilment of so-called prophecies. It is hardly necessary to point out that the Evangelist knows nothing about these two malefactors. Legend was not slow to prove itself better informed than he[4] : its pretensions to accuracy may make us smile, but it is to be feared that they leave us on the same legendary plane as Mark.

Death on the cross was a particularly cruel punishment, because it might last a very long time. If the unfortunate man had a strong constitution he might last two or three days. A picket of soldiers remained at the place of execution and passersby stopped, stared and made remarks. Such is the scene which Mark xv. 29 *ff.* describes : the people insult Jesus, crying : " *Ah, thou that destroyest the temple, and buildest it in three days, save thyself and come down from the cross !* " The chief priest and

---

[1] καὶ σὺν αὐτῷ σταυροῦσιν δύο λῃστάς . . . λῃστής is an armed robber, while κλέπτης is an ordinary thief.

[2] Luke quotes the passage from Isaiah earlier : xxii. 37.

[3] CCI, 62.   [4] XCVIII, 184 ; CXXXII, 95 ; CXLII, 221.

the scribes, who have also come to see their victim suffer, exchange coarse and clumsy jibes at his expense : " *Let the Christ the King of Israel descend now from the cross, that we may see and believe* " [1] (Mark xv. 31). At this point it is interesting to compare the Synoptic accounts. It is evident at the first glance that they are based on Mark, but the redactors have each enriched their source by a very instructive process.

Luke xxiii. 35–7, beginning with his own form of the story, which made a large sympathetic crowd follow Jesus to Calvary (xxiii. 27 *ff.*), shows us the people round the cross watching, while the rulers (ἄρχοντες) mock the crucified, and the soldiers also taunt him and offer him vinegar to drink. Matthew xxvii. 39–43 adds to the words which Mark assigns to the members of the Sanhedrin, the remark : " *He trusted in God : let him deliver him now, if he will have him : for he said, I am the Son of God* " : an addition which is arrived at by joining Psalm xxii. 8 (*He trusted on the Lord that he would deliver him : let him deliver him, seeing he delighted in him*), to the Messianic confession which Matthew (xxvi. 63 *ff.*) put into the mouth of Jesus before the Sanhedrin. Both redactors have therefore improved on Mark, not from fresh information, but by drawing on their own assumptions or on some scriptural passage. Hence their expansions have no more value than the Marcan account. The question arises how the Evangelist could have known, not merely the remarks of the passers-by, but those which the members of the Sanhedrin are supposed to exchange *among themselves* (πρὸς ἀλλήλους). Moreover, by an obvious artifice, the passers-by simply repeat what the witnesses said before the high priest. The presence of the members of the Sanhedrin in such a place on a feast day is improbable ; their most urgent desire must have been to escape from such an unclean sight, but the redactor wishes to incriminate them to the utmost. [2] The whole section is cast, so to speak, in the atmosphere of Psalm xxii., which not only inspires the account of Matthew xxvii. 43, as we have just seen, but also that of Mark in xv. 29, where the passers-by wag their heads (κινοῦντες τὰς κεφαλάς), as in Psalm xxii. 7 : " *All they that see me laugh me to scorn : they shoot out the lip, they shake the head* " (ἐκίνησαν τὴν κεφαλήν). [3]

For a vivid example of the way each Evangelist calmly

---

[1] **CXIV**, 131, very justly remarks that the use of πιστεύειν (ἵνα πιστεύσωμεν) in the absolute sense is rather surprising here.

[2] **CXIV**, 131. That is why some distinguished critics (**CIII**, ii, 670) consider verses 31–32a to be an *excrescence* (*eine Wucherung*).—*Contra* : **LXXXV**, 336.

[3] *Lam.*, 2, 15, has also been suggested : " *All that pass by clap their hands at thee ; they hiss and wag their head at the daughter of Jerusalem.*"

follows out his own design, regardless of history, we have only
to compare Mark xv. 32 : " *And they that were crucified with him
reviled him*," and Luke xxiii. 39–43, which tells us the edifying
story of the penitent thief, of whom there is no mention in the
other two Synoptics. The reason for this curious difference,
which greatly embarrassed early commentators,[1] is that Luke
has elicited a symbolic meaning from the contrasted behaviour
of the two thieves : the wicked thief represents hardened
judaism, the penitent one is believing and repentant paganism.
Such an atmosphere is far removed in time from Golgotha. It
is probable that a reminiscence of the above mentioned imprisonment of Joseph with the chief baker and chief butler, together
with the words : " *But think on me when it shall be well with
thee* " (Gen. xl. 14),[2] suggested to the Evangelist the line which
he has followed.

It was not possible that Jesus should die without some
convulsion of nature as a sign of the accomplishment of a mighty
mystery. Hence in Mark xv. 33 we find : " *And when the sixth
hour* (that is *noon*) *was come, there was darkness over the whole
land until the ninth hour.*" It is quite illegitimate to seek a
natural explanation [3] for this great miracle. The Evangelist
only adduces it as a *sign*, probably derived from Amos viii. 9 :
" *And it shall come to pass in that day, saith the Lord God, that I
will cause the sun to go down at noon, and I will darken the earth
in the clear day.*" Moreover, the ancients regarded this sudden
darkening of the day as the usual sign of nature's grief at the
death of great men.[4] The death of the Messiah could not yield
in significance to that of the great ones of the earth.

At the ninth hour, that is at three in the afternoon, Jesus
expires with a great cry after having uttered *with a loud voice*
(φωνῇ μεγάλῃ) in Aramaic the first verse of Psalm xxii. : " *My
God, my God, why hast thou forsaken me ?* " (Mark xv. 34 and
37). Luke xxiii. 46 prefers to make him say : " *Father, into
thy hands I commend my spirit,*" a quotation from Psalm xxxi. 5,
a perplexing variant. P. Lagrange [5] calmly says that the third

---

[1] **CIII**, ii, 672.

[2] *Cf.* Luke xxiii. 42 : " *Lord, remember me when thou comest into
thy kingdom.*"

[3] *Cf.* **CI**, 432, who, although he recognizes that this is a miraculous darkness, compares, for the benefit of sceptics, the phenomenon of the *black
sirocco* which darkens the sky of Jerusalem at the beginning of April.
We are back again in the tradition of the old German rationalists of
the type of Paulus.

[4] **XCVI**, i, 114. *Cf.* in particular Virgil, *Georg.*, i, 463 *ff.* ; *Consolatio
ad Liviam*, in Bährens, *Poetæ minores*, i, 104.

[5] **C**, 592.

Evangelist omitted the Marcan exclamation because he thought it would be difficult for his readers to understand. He does not put another in its place, " *but, according to the tradition which he followed, he says what this great cry was of which Mark had spoken.*" Happy the commentator who can be satisfied with such explanations ! But explanations are superfluous. It is useless to point out that the anguished breathing which overwhelmed the sufferer from the first moment of crucifixion renders the utterance of a loud cry after several hours quite improbable,[1] because with the Evangelists we are outside the sphere of historical reality. The Evangelist possesses the knowledge that God seemed to have abandoned Jesus and that Psalm xxii. pointed out for the prophet the *via dolorosa* which he must tread in, order to accomplish the purpose of God. The quotation of the first verse of this poem is fitting from his pen, but it has no place in the mouth of the dying Jesus, because for Luke it is not a cry of despair but the supreme proof of the truth and fulfilment of the prophecy ; whereas in the mouth of Jesus it could only mean the shattering of all his hopes.

Clearly it is useless to probe the mind of the Crucified during the horror of his execution ; but we can doubtless discern the attitude of the early Christians who had to interpret the Crucifixion so as to make it endurable to their emotions and intelligible to their reason. They saw in this terrible catastrophe the fulfilment of the scriptures and therefore a Messianic necessity. Now the scriptures are in this case Psalm xxii. which the redactor has in mind all through his account of the Passion. It may be that the quotation given as the content of his cry is a duplicate of the cry and is secondary to it. But there is every likelihood that the cry itself corresponds more closely with the purpose of the writer than with an actual memory. The first purpose that suggests itself is the fulfilment of " *a scripture,*" namely, Joel iii. 16 : " *The Lord also shall roar out of Zion, and utter his voice from Jerusalem : and the heavens and the earth shall shake.*" This is the more probable since the preceding verse tells us that " *the sun and the moon shall be darkened, and the stars shall withdraw their shining.*" If our scriptural comparison is correct we must understand the Evangelist's idea to be that the cry marks the victory which Jesus on the cross has won over death and the Devil.[2]

It has already been suggested that the vinegar offered to the dying Jesus to drink (Mark xv. 36) came from Psalm lxix. 21 :

---

[1] CCI, 64 ; **CLXXIV**, 399, 412, 414, who emphasizes the medical aspect of the Crucifixion.
[2] CCI, 75.

" *in my thirst they gave me vinegar to drink.*" Mark introduces
it awkwardly between the exclamation and the cry as if he
were repairing an oversight and wished to include everything.
We have seen that Luke introduces the vinegar at the beginning
of the episode (xxiii. 36).

The Synoptic tradition omits two notable features which are
given in John xix. 32 *ff.*: the soldiers break the legs of the two
thieves in order to kill them, but seeing that Jesus is dead they
refrain from giving him a *coup de grâce*. Nevertheless, one of
them with a spear pierced his side and " *forthwith came there
out blood and water* " (καὶ ἐξῆλθεν εὐθὺς αἷμα καὶ ὕδωρ). The
redactor partly acknowledges the truth when he writes (xix.
36 *ff.*) :

> " For these things were done, that the scripture should be ful-
> filled, A bone of him shall not be broken. And again another
> scripture saith, They shall look on him whom they pierced."

In reality the breaking of the legs (*crurifragium*) is in no
way a complement of crucifixion : it is a special torture of
which we hear in several sources.[1] There is no evidence that
this barbarous act put an end to the sufferings of the crucified ;
but perhaps it was supposed to do so ;[2] its chief purpose was
to make sure that the victim was really dead.[3] These considerations, however, do not interest the redactor. He has
placed the death of Jesus at the hour fixed by Jewish custom
for the sacrifice of the paschal lamb, *between the two evenings*
(Exod. xii. 6), that is to say, between sunset and twilight, about
six o'clock, or between the declining (three o'clock) and setting
of the sun's orb. Now Jesus signifies for John the paschal lamb
of the New Covenant, and Exodus xii. 46 enjoins that no bone
of the lamb shall be broken. But what the Evangelist does
not tell us is that the water and the blood which flow from
the side of Jesus are only symbolical and represent the water
of Baptism and the blood of the Eucharist :[4] it is therefore
the spring of eternal life which flows from the body of the
divine Lamb. With such conceptions we pass beyond history.

But the Synoptics have not kept us within its sphere, nor
do they bring us back to it when they recount the various
wonders which are supposed to take place as soon as Jesus
has expired (Mark xv. 38 ; Matt. xxvii. 51 *ff.*).[5] They are in

---

[1] **CXIX**, 219. [2] **CXXVI**, 498. [3] Quintilian, *Declam. maiores*, 6, 9.

[4] **CXXVII**[2], 492 ; **CXIX**, 220, and even **CXXVI**, 500, who however
believes in the historicity of the occurrence as based on the *ocular
witness* of the Evangelist.—*Cf.* John vii. 38.

[5] **CIII**, ii, 689 *ff.* ; **LXXXV**, 339 ; **CI**, 436 *ff.*—Matthew improves on
Mark as usual.

the same category as the conventional *signs* which in Jewish
and pagan antiquity announced and accompanied events in
which the divine will seemed to be directly revealed.[1] Their only
significance lies in the conclusion drawn from the Passion by
the Roman centurion (Mark xv. 39 ; Matt. xxvii. 54) : " *Truly
this man was the Son of God.*" [2] These words would have
represented nothing intelligible to the mind of a Roman soldier.[3]
But the Evangelist is not concerned with historical truth nor
with probability : the centurion represents the testimony of
Gentile faith.   It is also the redactor's faith and it rises towards
the glorified Christ ; the Christ whom Mark pictures according
to Paul, and whom his whole Gospel has sought to set forth.[4]
It is possible to think that at one stage of the editing of
Mark, the Gospel ended with this phrase, since it corresponds
exactly to the one with which his book now opens ! Luke's
account (xxiii. 48), which shows us the crowd dispersing over-
come with sorrow and smiting their breasts, is drawn from
Zechariah xii. 10 : " *And they shall look upon me whom they
have pierced, and they shall mourn for him, as one mourneth for
his only son. . . .*"

We have dwelt at length on the growth of legend round
the story of the death of Jesus, because the details are so
familiar, and their very familiarity seems to render criticism
superfluous.   But none of the details will bear close examination, and all in the end fall outside the realm of history.   All
are more or less open to the charge of being entirely derived
from passages of the Old Testament.

It must be admitted that the circumstances under which
the Passion took place were extremely unfavourable to the
formation of a body of authentic reminiscences.   Early tradition could only avail itself of scattered, vague and indirect
testimonies, but it has not succeeded in welding them into an
organic whole.[5]   The Evangelists clearly felt the weakness of
their evidence, since in place of the disciples who had fled, they
stationed at Calvary the women . . . "*who also, when he was
in Galilee, followed him, and ministered unto him ; and many
other women which came up with him unto Jerusalem* " (Mark
xv. 41).   They are supposed to watch what is happening from

---

[1] Examples : in **XCVIII**, 186 *ff.* ; **XCIX**, 225.

[2] Luke, generally more reasonable, merely makes the centurion say
(xxiii. 47) : " *Certainly this was a righteous man* " ; that is, *innocent,*
which is something quite different.

[3] **CCI**, 74.

[4] **LXXXV**, 88 ; **CIII**, ii, 693 *ff.* ; **CV**, 471 *ff.* ; **CCI**, 74.

[5] **LXXXVI**, 166 *ff.*, and on the details of the story of the Passion,
158 *ff.*

afar, and their real object is to guarantee by their presence
the truth of what has already been said and still more of what
is going to be added.[1] The guarantee appears singularly fragile
as soon as we begin to examine it, while the presence of the
women that constitutes the guarantee is so necessary to the
tradition that it was practically bound to be inserted. It is
less dubious, doubtless, than the Johannine scene (John xix.
25 *ff.*) where we see the mother of Jesus and his beloved disciple
with the holy women *near the cross*, receiving the last instructions which fall from it ;[2] but it represents the same anxiety
—to establish a testimony. As a matter of fact, early tradition,
with or without the guarantee of the women, was not in a
position to do more than assert the essential facts : Jesus was
arrested, tried, condemned and executed. *Of that alone are
we certain.*

The needs of Christian apologetics, changing with the growth
of Christology and its tendency to apply more and more literally
to Jesus those Old Testament passages which were supposed
to be Messianic prophecies, that is to say which concern the
Messiah, have at the same time eliminated some authentic but
inconvenient details, and introduced into the Gospel pattern
details and even whole episodes which appeared truer than the
historical facts, because the scripture required them. What
must happen did happen ; what *must* be said was said.

The whole Gospel tradition clearly collapses in the face of
the positions here established. It is, however, the account of
the Passion which is most seriously involved because the expansions and accretions of the Christian faith, in dealing with the
Passion and the Resurrection, rapidly created a fabric of
tradition wholly foreign to historical reality.

[1] Luke xxiii. 49 candidly admits this intention by saying that they
are there with all those who know Jesus, to see what is happening (ὁϱῶσαι ταῦτα). The Lucan redaction is probably influenced by
Ps. xxxvii. 11–12.

[2] The mother of Jesus here means the Judaic community ; the
disciple, the Hellenic community which must, in the redactor's judgment, be the former's legitimate guide and offspring. *Cf.* **CXXVII**[2],
488.

CHAPTER V

THE RESURRECTION

I

CRITICISM OF THE SOURCES

SYNOPTIC tradition believed that devout hands took the
body of Jesus down from the cross and laid it in the tomb
on the Friday evening; that Jesus came forth triumphantly
on the Sunday morning and that after an earthly sojourn,
during which his disciples may have seen him several times,
he ascended to heaven, and returned to God the Father who
had sent him to men. By combining the different statements
in the four Gospels, the Acts, Paul's Epistles and the first
Epistle of Peter, the Christian creed has constructed an account
of these essential events, that seems at first sight fairly consistent.[1] But this impression disappears before the most superficial examination of the texts and reveals instead a mosaic
artificially composed of contradictory fragments, which have
only been combined in disregard of their discrepancies by
exhibiting as a sequence what are really alternative narratives.

The problem is complicated: (1) because actually the
Resurrection in the strict sense, that is the accounts which
claim to establish it and relate to the discovery of the empty
tomb on the Sunday morning and to the whole series of appearances of the Risen Lord, cannot be separated from the *burial*
which preceded it and the *Ascension* which followed it; since
they are three inseparable parts of the same whole; (2) because
the sources themselves are confused and difficult to handle,
requiring a detailed examination which would be out of place
here. Hence we shall merely indicate the chief difficulties
which they raise.[2]

---

[1] v. 1, 778 *ff*.

[2] Vast bibliography. We may refer to the great commentaries
which have been utilized here: those of Loisy, Klostermann, Wellhausen, Montefiore, J. Weiss, W. Bauer, and to Goguel, *Le Christ
ressuscité et la tradition sur la résurrection dans le christianisme primitif*,
in *Actes du Congrès international d'histoire des religions*. Paris, 1923, ii,

For convenience the evidence is divided into two parts which will be considered in order : (1) the burial and the resurrection ; (2) the appearances and the ascension.

II

THE BURIAL

The study of the Synoptic accounts soon reveals that Mark —our Mark or another older one—has served as the groundwork for Matthew and Luke. They have corrected and modified him as they pleased, but their version only represents a personal adaptation and not additional, better or more complete information. A brief examination will convince us of this. Mark xv. 42–7 relates :

" And now when the even was come, because it was the preparation, that is, the day before the Sabbath,[1] Joseph of Arimathæa,[2] an honourable counsellor which also waited for the kingdom of God, came, and went in boldly unto Pilate, and craved the body of Jesus. And Pilate marvelled if he were already dead : and calling unto him the centurion, he asked him whether he had been any while dead. And when he knew it of the centurion, he gave the body to Joseph. And he bought fine linen, and took him down, and wrapped him in the linen, and laid him in a sepulchre which was hewn out of a rock,[3] and rolled a stone unto the door of the sepulchre. And Mary Magdalene and Mary the mother of Joses beheld where he was laid."

The sepulchre is therefore duly closed and its site is known. There is no need to quibble over exact archæological details

225 ff. ; by the same author, **CLVI**, ch. xi ; L. Brun, *Die Auferstehung Christi und die urchristliche Ueberlieferung*, Oslo, 1925. The remarks of Burkitt, in *Christian Beginnings*, 86 ff., London, 1924, may also be read with interest, and the study by G. Bertram, *Die Himmelfahrt Jesu vom Kreuz aus und die Glaube an seine Auferstehung*, in *Festgabe für A. Deissmann*, 187 ff., Tübingen, 1927.—*Contra :* Lagrange, *Mark* ; *Matthew* ; *Luke* ; *John, ad loc.*, **CLVII**, ii, bk. v, ch. iv.

[1] The redactor has forgotten that we have reached the day of the Passover and that the feast required the Sabbath rest for the whole day.

[2] Arimathæa is a town, from which the prophet Samuel came, according to 1 Sam. i. 1 ; this person appears and disappears suddenly in the Gospel. He must have been an important man to obtain access to Pilate thus : Mark therefore makes him a *counsellor* ($\beta ov\lambda ev\tau \acute{\eta}\varsigma$), forgetting that he ascribed the condemnation of Jesus to the whole Sanhedrin.

[3] Should we not think of Isa. xxii. 16 : " *thou . . . that graveth an habitation for himself in a rock*," in this case *a sepulchre* ? And again in Isa. liii. 9 : " *And he made his grave with the wicked, and* (he has been) *with the rich in his death.*"

which prove nothing at all : we may assume that Mark knew what a Jewish tomb was like.

An account or mention of the burial is to be found also in Matthew xxvii. 57–61 ; Luke xxiii. 50–6 ; John xix. 38–42 ; 1 Corinthians xv. 3–4 ; Acts xiii. 29.

Matthew abridges Mark or else he has an earlier redaction than ours before him, but he is probably correcting our source. As it might seem curious that a member of the Sanhedrin should be interested in Jesus, Matthew only says of Joseph that he was *a rich man*. Since the words : *which also waited for the kingdom of God* are ambiguous he states more precisely : *who also himself was Jesus' disciple*. As it might seem surprising that Pilate should not know of Jesus' death two or three hours after it had occurred, he suppresses the procurator's astonishment and the calling of the centurion. He passes quickly over the preparations for burial but adds a definite fact, saying that the tomb belongs to Joseph and is new.

Luke also omits Pilate's astonishment and his questioning of the centurion. He knows that Joseph, a member of the Sanhedrin, is *a good man and a just*, who has not consented to *their* counsel and *their* deed, that Arimathæa is *a city of the Jews*, which is a piece of information for his Gentile readers. The women prepare unguents but rest on the Sabbath day.

John embellishes the story. He tells us that Joseph was *a disciple of Jesus, but secretly* ; he gives him a collaborator, Nicodemus, of whom we have already heard in John iii. 1, as a *ruler of the Jews* ($\check{\alpha}\rho\chi\omega\nu$ $\tau\tilde{\omega}\nu$ $'I\upsilon\delta\alpha\acute{\iota}\omega\nu$). This man brings a hundred pounds of myrrh and aloes and it is he and Joseph who embalm the body, while the Synoptics attribute this to the women. The Evangelist wished that Christ should receive from the great ones of the world those honours which were reserved for the great.[1] Since it is late and the prohibited time is near, Jesus is laid provisionally in a new sepulchre which was near by in a garden.

Paul says simply (1 Cor. xv. 3) that Christ " *died for our sins according to the scriptures ; and that he was buried* ($\dot{\epsilon}\tau\acute{\alpha}\phi\eta$), *and that he rose again the third day according to the scriptures.*" For all that the Apostle tells us Jesus might have been thrown into the common grave of executed criminals. There is nothing to show that he knew the synoptic account. We must not forget that according to Acts xiii. 29 the Jews themselves who crucified Jesus took him down from the cross and laid him in the tomb, which might be an earlier form of the tradition than the Marcan one. The Jews do this in order to hide the burial

---

[1] **CXXVII**[1], 897.

place of their victim, but God frustrates their precautions by raising him from the dead (xiii. 30). One fact, however, remains evident : the whole of Christian antiquity as far as we know was ignorant of Jesus' tomb, and it was only *rediscovered* under Constantine in 326,[1] *by the inspiration of the Saviour* and as the result of a divine revelation.

If we place our texts in the probable chronological order of the traditions or beliefs which they represent, we obtain this sequence : (1) Paul's evidence : *he was buried.* No details, no evidence, nothing more than a probable assertion necessary to an understanding of the Resurrection. (2) Evidence of the Acts : *he was laid in the tomb by the Jews,* who were anxious to dispose of him. (3) Evidence of *Urmarcus* : he was laid in the tomb by *a Jew,* a good man and in authority, who wished to render him fitting honours. (4) Evidence of Mark, Matthew, Luke and John, who have no new source, each one arranging it in his own fashion in order to make it more probable and convincing. From this preliminary examination we may conclude at least provisionally : (1) That the Synoptic tradition of the burial is suspicious because it only produces unreliable evidence, and because in Paul it is reduced to a bare statement whose apparent precision does not seem to be drawn from any recollection and may not presuppose one ; (2) that it was inevitable that the tradition should crystallize into a definite pattern, even if it did not represent any historical reality, as soon as they were convinced that the tomb was found empty, and consequently that they should make this discovery the chief argument in the apologetic proof of the Resurrection.

Our mistrust increases when Matthew xxvii. 62–6 tells us that *the chief priests and the Pharisees* ask Pilate to place a guard before the tomb so that the disciples of the impostor cannot come and take away the body in order to claim afterwards that he had been raised as he had predicted. Our mistrust arises not only from the fact that Matthew is the only canonical Gospel which contains this information, nor from the fact that the apocryphal Gospels have more of the same kind of information,[2] but because the episode clearly displays a tendency to make the discovery of the empty tomb more convincing.

[1] Eusebius, *Vita Const.,* 3, 26.
Gospel of Peter, 29–34 ; *Pilate's letter to Claudius,* in **CXXXIV,** 76.

III

THE DISCOVERY OF THE EMPTY TOMB

On the Sunday morning, *at the rising of the sun*, the holy women come to the tomb to perform for the corpse those last offices which the Sabbath had prevented on the preceding day. They find the stone removed and go into the sepulchre : Jesus is no longer there, but *a young man* is *sitting on the right side, clothed in a long white garment*,[1] who announces the Resurrection to them and commands them to go and tell the disciples. He adds that the Nazarene is preceding them into Galilee where they will see him as he had told them. They flee in terror and fear keeps them silent (Mark xvi. 1–8). The Resurrection itself is not related in the Marcan source, nor is it in the other canonical writings, but a time came for this reserve to be broken through and the apocryphal Gospels supplied the missing information.[2]

The account in Matthew xxviii. 1–10 runs as follows : on the Sunday morning two of the holy women come *to see the sepulchre* ; there is a great earthquake and in the confusion an angel descends from heaven and rolls the stone away and sits upon it :

> " His countenance was like lightning, and his raiment white as snow : and for fear of him the keepers did shake, and became as dead men."

Then the angel briefly addresses the women in words which are an obvious doublet of those in Mark. They are sore afraid, but also full of joy, and are on their way to tell the disciples when Jesus himself meets them and confirms the angel's words. " *Go tell my brethren that they go into Galilee, and there shall they see me* " (xxviii. 10).

According to Luke xxiv. 1–11, the women arrive at the tomb and find it empty ; while they are perplexed *two* angels appear who reassure them and instruct them :

> " He is not here, but is risen : remember how he spake unto

---

[1] The usual Jewish description of angels.

[2] In a Latin MS. of the fifth or sixth century, the *Codex Bobiensis*, we read in complement of Mark : " Subito autem ad horam tertiam diei tenebrae factae sunt per totum orbem terrae, et descenderunt de caelis angeli et surgentes in claritate vivi dei simul ascenderunt cum eo et continuo lux facta est." This passage is placed between *vv.* 3 and 4 of ours. It cannot be discussed of course, but it shows an interesting tendency and gives us first-hand information concerning the respect with which the early Christians regarded both the text and the facts of the Gospels and the events.

you when he was yet in Galilee, saying, The Son of man must be delivered into the hands of sinful men, and be crucified, and the third day rise again."

The holy women go and tell the disciples, but the latter doubtless forgot the angels' instructions, for they did not believe in the miracle.[1]

According to John xx. 1–18, Mary Magdalene is the only one who comes when it is *yet dark* to the sepulchre and sees that the stone which closed it has been removed. She runs at once to tell Peter and the beloved disciple, believing that wicked people had stolen the body. The two disciples in great agitation hasten towards the sepulchre and discover, one after the other, that only the linen clothes remain. They did not yet know that according to the scripture Jesus must rise again : however they believe that the miracle has been accomplished and return whence they came, leaving Mary Magdalene behind weeping, because she still believes the body has been stolen. Then suddenly she sees two angels in the tomb, and as she turns Jesus reveals himself to her, and announces his approaching ascension : "*but go to my brethren, and say unto them, I ascend unto my Father . . .*" (xx. 17). An examination of this episode (11–18) clearly shows it to be a redactional arrangement of details borrowed from the Synoptics : there is someone in the tomb (Mark) ; two angels (Luke), Jesus appears from behind (Matthew) ; he speaks to Mary (John).[2]

The discovery of the empty tomb must be connected with the account in Matthew of the bribing of the soldiers who had been on duty at the sepulchre to keep silent (Matt. xxviii. 11–15). The chief priests and the elders, having heard from the soldiers themselves what had happened, pay them heavily to lie : they are to say that it is Jesus' disciples who removed his body during the night while the sentinels were sleeping. The bargain which has been concluded does not, however, remain a secret : "*And this saying is commonly reported among the Jews until this day*" (xxviii. 15). And this last phrase reveals that the object of the redactor who composed these two interdependent sections, namely the placing of the guard

[1] Some important MSS. add here that Peter goes instantly to see for himself that the tomb is empty and only contains the grave clothes ; but the verse cannot belong in this context, since it is at variance with the episode of the pilgrims of Emmaus which follows.

[2] The borrowing from Matthew is revealed by the use of the word " brothers " to indicate the disciples : Matt. xxviii. 10 : . . . ἀπαγγείλατε τοῖς ἀδελφοῖς μου . . . John xx. 17 : πορεύου πρὸς τοὺς ἀδελφούς μου . . . The expression is too rare in our Gospel sources for it to have occurred by chance.

at the tomb and the bribing of the guards, was to counteract
a Jewish allegation against the Resurrection : *his disciples
removed the body*.[1]

There are many serious contradictions in the canonical
accounts of the Resurrection. It is evident at once that the
statement which they have in common : *the tomb in which Jesus
was placed the night of his death was found empty the next morning*, has been amplified by various details intended to explain
how it took place, and which, because they vary so greatly in
the different accounts, are all suspect—at least of not corresponding to any memory and of arising from apologetic considerations. We might be tolerant of several contradictions
which would be considered negligible in secular sources, but
there are some which cannot be overlooked : Matthew says
that the tomb was guarded, but Mark and Luke know nothing
about it since they ascribe to the women the intention of going
to anoint the body of the Crucified and show them to be only
anxious (Mark) about the weight of the stone which may
prevent them from entering. John is no better informed when
he represents Mary Magdalene alone before the open tomb.
Who is right ?—How many women come to the sepulchre ?
One, according to John ; two, according to Matthew and Mark ;
three and others with them, according to Luke.—Are the
disciples commanded to go into Galilee ? Mark and Matthew
assert that they are ; Luke says nothing about it and the only
word of the command which he retains is *Galilee*, in a statement
that this is the place where Jesus predicted his resurrection,
which has now been accomplished.—According to John, Mary
Magdalene is commanded to go and tell the disciples something,
but not what is commanded in Mark and Matthew.—What are
the results of the message entrusted to the women ? None,
according to Mark, since they say nothing ; according to
Matthew xxviii. 16, the disciples obey and go away into Galilee ;
according to John, the first announcement made to Mary brings
two disciples to the tomb ; we do not know what effect the
second has since it is not translated into action ; according
to Luke, the disciples do not believe the women's story.

These are only details, reply the apologists, it is the fact
which counts. Livy and Polybius relate the crossing of the
Alps by Hannibal in different ways, but they agree that he
crossed them, and moreover as we see him at a certain moment

---

[1] In the *Gospel of Peter*, the argument receives another legendary
accretion : the Jews who have guarded the tomb with the soldiers
go to Pilate and ask him to command the centurion and the guards
to keep silent.

in Gaul and a little later in Italy he really must have crossed them. Such reasoning is fatal. The elimination of details would leave us confronted by a *fundamental* affirmation invalidated by facts. Doubtless it is no sounder if it rests merely on contradictory evidence and is surrounded by irreconcilable circumstances, but that is just the question. Neither is it legitimate to compare the discrepancies of Livy and Polybius in the passage about the crossing of the Alps with those of the Evangelists about the Resurrection, since the uncertainties and contradictions of the two secular historians are attributable to the fact that they are writing long after the event and that they are working on different *written* sources which they have no longer any means of comparing with the event.

In fact everything leads us to believe that the first Evangelist who related the discovery of the empty tomb said all he knew or thought he knew, and that the others took their point of departure from his account with no new sources at their disposal. They followed him, not faithfully, nor with the idea of elucidating his account by a commentary which respected its integrity, but with that of arranging—or disarranging—it, in order to render it more convincing, of embellishing it or merely of altering it, in order to produce an appearance of independent information, for after all none of the discrepancies have any apparent meaning. All the departures from the account of Mark—leaving aside the question of *his* reliability —proceed from the imagination or tendencious invention of the Gospel redactors. The meaning and nature of this work of adaptation become more evident after an examination of the extra-canonical accounts.

We must first note—what is now generally acknowledged —that not one of them is earlier than Mark. They all show an anxiety to improve on the evidence of the canonical sources and to anticipate sceptical objections. The *Gospel of the Hebrews*,[1] for example, states that Jesus gave his shroud to the high priest's servant on coming out of the tomb—a convenient piece of evidence—and then appears to his brother James. The *Gospel of Peter* explains (28 *ff.*) that the scribes, Pharisees and priests, after seeing Jesus die amidst marvellous prodigies, are persuaded that they have destroyed a righteous man (δίκαιος). But they fear that their terrible mistake may be disclosed. They therefore ask Pilate for a band of soldiers to watch at the tomb in order, they say, to prevent the secret removal of the body. Then, accompanying the officer, whose name is, of course, known to the narrator, they go to help the

[1] Fragment preserved by Jerome, *De viris ill.*, 2.

guards to strengthen the entrance to the sepulchre with a heavy stone, on which they place their seals, and they too keep watch beside the monument. On Saturday morning a large crowd comes up from Jerusalem to look at the stone and its seals. However the precautions have no effect and on Sunday morning the Resurrection occurs triumphantly and the apocryphal Gospel describes it.[1]

It also knows that both guards and Jews go to Pilate and confess that *in truth he was the Son of God,* to which the Roman replies that the murder of the Son of God was their affair and not his. Yet he agrees to order the soldiers to keep silent, since the Jews prefer to answer for their crime to God rather than to the people. The whole story is plainly absurd, and displays a combination of the details given by the canonical Gospels with other extravagant inventions ; [2] but its intention is clear. Christ must be shown triumphing over all the futile obstacles opposed to his power, the miracle must be irresistibly authenticated and the Jews overwhelmed, becoming thus genuine witnesses of the Resurrection and the Risen Lord. The most astonishing thing is that the disciples leave Jerusalem in sorrow and tears, still ignorant of the great consolation, probably because the women who came to the tomb and who were addressed by an angel have said nothing or have not been believed.

It is useless to linger over the additions invented by the other apocryphal Gospels,[3] from which nothing is to be gained. It is important, however, to note that they do not invent their method, they merely carry out *ad absurdum* the process set in motion by the canonical sources. We are thus brought back to the fundamental question of the historical value of Mark's narrative, or, if the Marcan additions be discounted, of *the value of the tradition relative to the discovery of the empty tomb.*

To say [4] that the Jews accused the disciples of taking away the body of Jesus, hence that it is certain that the tomb was empty when the stone was rolled away, is futile because the Jewish assertion was not made in Jerusalem nor on the day after the Resurrection. That assertion represents an argument in a later controversy, a reply to the Christian proof of the empty tomb. Those who used it were not in a position to deny with certainty that the tomb had been found empty nor could they ever verify the fact they asserted. The arguments

---

[1] Two angels descend from heaven to prepare it ; *the Ascension of Isaiah,* iii, 15 *ff.,* knows that there are *three* and gives their names.

[2] On details *cf.* **CXXXIX.**

[3] **CXLII,** 243 *ff.*   [4] **CX,** 420, n. 1.

and replies in the controversy followed like this : *He is risen?
—The proof?—He has been seen.—By whom? By his disciples?
By you? But that proves nothing.—It proves that he was no
longer in the tomb.—Then his followers had removed him to establish
their fraud.* Such an exchange of assertions would seem inconceivable if it were placed in the time and place of the events
under discussion. It is obvious that if the fact of the Resurrection was not accepted while the discovery of the empty tomb
was admitted, then the reason for its being empty had to be
explained.

As our sources are naturally opposed to any rationalist
interpretation it is necessary, if an explanation is to be found,
to create an imaginary one by distorting the real meaning of
some detail or other in the Gospel accounts. Much ingenuity
has been wasted in an attempt to establish the probability of
the removal of the body either by the Jews,[1] or by Joseph of
Arimathæa who, having provisionally deposited the body near
Calvary, would come and remove it in order to give it a final
burial place elsewhere ; [2] or by one of the women ; or by some
disciple without the knowledge of the others.[3] The ejection
of the body by the owner of the tomb has also been suggested ;
or that Jesus was only apparently dead, and that, having fallen
into a comatose state, he might have been awakened by the
chill of the tomb, escaped, and taken refuge with the Essenes,
or elsewhere, and survived forty days or more. We need not
delay over such theories. The variety of the solutions proposed [4] suffices to reveal their inconsistency. There is not the
slightest objective evidence for any of them.[5] It would be a
waste of time to discuss such hypotheses since the discovery
of the empty tomb seems improbable.

By itself this discovery proved nothing ; to bring out its
significance an explanation was needed, based on the most
stupendous of miracles. Mark has no hesitations and introduces an angel in order to provide such an explanation. This,
however, would hardly convince a sceptic, hence the legend
develops in the direction of the direct description of the Resurrection and the multiplication of eye-witnesses. Another line
of evidence is felt to be needed : Jesus, who is no longer dead,
must show himself in the neighbourhood of the empty tomb

[1] Here Renan qualifies with a " *perhaps* " (**CLXIX**, 42) ; it is also
A. Réville's view, **CLXX**, ii, 46.
[2] Accepted by Holtzmann, **XCVI**, i, 105.
[3] Renan thought of it (**CLXIX**, 40).
[4] Paulus, Venturini, Schleiermacher, Hase, etc. *Cf.* **CCCXI**, 18 ;
CLXXVI, 324.
[5] **CIII**, ii, 720 ; **CLXXXIV**, ii, 441 *ff.*

or at least in Jerusalem; and that is what he does according
to three of our canonical Gospels and even according to all
four if we take into account the end of Mark (Mark xvi. 12
and 14). Now we shall go on to show that the earliest tradition assigned the first appearances of Jesus exclusively to
Galilee. *Therefore the story of the discovery of the empty tomb
is secondary* and corresponds with a stage in the apologetic
proof of the Resurrection *posterior* to that which might be called
the Galilean stage.[1] This secondary character is also revealed
by an examination of the episode itself; the discovery of the
empty tomb, we repeat, has no value in itself, it is subordinate
to the appearances and it has no real effect on the disciples
until one or other of them has *seen* the Risen Lord. This
proves that *the belief in the Resurrection was founded first on
the appearances.* This being so, the discovery of the empty
tomb, useless as far as the disciples' faith is concerned, falls
into the category of an apologetic or polemical invention and
is eliminated from the realm of history.[2] We must also note
that neither Paul (1 Cor. xv.) nor the Acts (ii. 14–36, and xiii.
16–41) seem to know it. Paul's silence can be explained—
with difficulty; the silence of Acts, attested by two discourses
on the Resurrection, one attributed to Peter at Jerusalem, the
other to Paul at Antioch in Pisidia, is only conceivable if the
source used by the redactor contained nothing about the
episode. The stories of the burial and of the discovery of the
empty tomb are connected, the first prepares the way for the
second and arises out of it. They could only have come into
existence far from Jerusalem and outside the circle of the
original disciples, forty years *at the earliest* after the death of
Jesus,[3] that is to say shortly after the destruction of Jerusalem,
when it was practically impossible for anyone to undertake the
smallest research on the spot. The truth is that we do not
know and in all probability the disciples knew no better where
the body of Jesus had been thrown after it had been removed
from the cross, probably by the executioners. It is more likely
to have been cast into the *pit* for the executed than laid in a
new tomb.

The belief in the Resurrection upon which Christianity has
been founded did not rest in the beginning on the assertion

[1] **CXCIII,** 79 *ff.*; **XXIV,** 66. On the fact that the tradition of the
Galilean appearances was originally independent of the tradition of the
finding of the empty tomb, *cf.* **XCIV,** 112; **XXXIV,** 63 *ff.*

[2] **CXLVI,** 16, n. 1.

[3] *Cf.* **XXXIV,** 63, who thinks about ten years after the redaction
of 1 Cor., or thirty-three to thirty-five years after the death of Christ.

that *Jesus, laid in the tomb on the Friday evening, came forth living on the Sunday morning* ; but on the statement that *Jesus, after his death, was seen by several disciples.* Does not Paul assure us that " *he was seen of Cephas, then of the twelve* " ? (1 Cor. xv. 5).

IV

The Appearances of the Risen Lord

The appearances of the Risen Lord, which alone can prove the reality of the Resurrection, are attested by various discrepant sources. Here Mark forsakes us, for his canonical ending (xvi. 9–20) is clearly artificial. Although many eminent critics (Zahn, Loofs, for example) still place the first appearances in or around Jerusalem, there can be no reasonable doubt that the earliest tradition assigned them to Galilee. In Mark xiv. 27 *ff.*, Jesus says to his disciples on their way to the Mount of Olives after the Last Supper : It is written : " *I will smite the shepherd, and the sheep shall be scattered. But after that I am risen,* I WILL GO BEFORE YOU INTO GALILEE." These words in themselves would suffice to establish the only valid hypothesis. It has been supposed, with some grounds, that Mark did not end his Gospel with the silence of the women, but went on to relate the appearances in Galilee, and that this ending, having been suppressed, was replaced by the one which has come down to us, at the time when the appearances in Jerusalem [1] were accepted by tradition. It is, in fact, inconceivable if this tradition were the earliest—and Luke seems to regard it as the only one—that the other should have been substituted for it, seeing that the Galilean tradition, which is complete in itself, has no meaning *as an interpretation* of the Jerusalem tradition. If the disciples saw the Risen One in Jerusalem, as Luke claims, it is incomprehensible that an angel, and Jesus himself, should tell the disciples to go into Galilee to see him (according to Mark and Matthew). The first and second Gospels have noted the dispersal of the disciples at Gethsemane after the arrest, while Luke, conscious of the difficulty that that created, has carefully omitted it in order to keep his wit-

[1] CCL, 311, based on the *Gospel of Peter*, of which the mutilated end supposes that the first appearances took place in Galilee, since it shows us the Apostles returning from there. It should be noted that there is another shorter Marcan ending, which does not speak of the appearances in Jerusalem, to say nothing of the various combinations which the complicated redactional activity visible in the last page of Mark suggests. *Cf.* Huck, *Synopse* [8], 1931, 222.

nesses close at hand. The earliest tradition considered that the disciples were no longer in Jerusalem at the time of the Resurrection and had already returned to Galilee.

The substitution of the tradition of the appearances in Jerusalem for those in Galilee arises purely from apologetic requirements. At a certain stage it seemed advantageous to place the appearances nearer to the time and place of death and to link them up with the discovery of the empty tomb which, if it were to prove anything, could not be left isolated and in the air. It is possible [1] that the earliest tradition occupied an intermediary position : Christ *first* showed himself in Galilee, *later* in Jerusalem ; because it is natural that the belief that Christ was alive should have prompted them to return to the City and to await there the imminent *parousia*. Mark would not clash with this arrangement which at least presupposes the priority of the Galilean appearances.

The earliest source to mention the appearances is Paul (1 Cor. xv. 3 *ff*.). It appears in the form of a catalogue :

" For I delivered unto you first of all that which I also received, how that Christ died for our sins according to the scriptures ; and that he was buried, and that he rose again the third day according to the scriptures : and that he was seen of Cephas, then of the twelve ; [2] after that he was seen of about five hundred brethren at once ; of whom the greater part remained unto this present, but some are fallen asleep. After that, he was seen of James ; then of all the apostles. And last of all he was seen of me also, as of one born out of due time." [3]

Paul says of these details that he has *received* and *delivered* them *first of all* (ἐν πρώτοις) ; that is to say, as the central and fundamental teaching. The Resurrection properly speaking is proved by the scriptures ; [4] but the appearances confirm it and Paul knows them from the tradition. He is evidently naming them in chronological order ; his repetition of the words *after that* (ἔπειτα) proves it as well as the concluding words : *and last of all* (ἔσχατον). He does not describe these appearances, and it is doubtful whether he thought it possible to describe them, for the word he employs : ὤφθη = *he was seen*, does not lend itself to a complicated expansion such as

[1] CCLV, 7.

[2] It is only here that Paul uses the expression *the Twelve* ; there is therefore reason to suppose that he is repeating a tradition of the primitive community. *Cf.* Lietzmann, in LVII, 1 Cor., *ad loc.*

[3] *As of one born out of due time* means *as of an apostle born out of due time* (*cf. v.* 9).

[4] We should notice that the Gospel tradition makes no mention of this evidence, which therefore represents a later stage in the tradition.

that of a common meal, or of long discourses, like those which are connected with the *second earthly life* of Jesus, *i.e.* his dwelling amongst his disciples for forty days. It is difficult to see why Paul should not have given the details if he had known of any. It is noteworthy that he does not mention any women. Why should he have allowed a single one of the essential and necessary proofs [1] which he had *received* from the disciples to escape ? He would have been still less likely to omit the evidence of the appearances to the women, since, on account of their time and place, they would seem specially convincing. He could not therefore have known of them, nor could Peter and James, since he had talked with them in Jerusalem (Gal. i. 18 *ff.*).

We must finally note that the appearances enumerated by Paul are evidently not connected with the Resurrection nor with the Ascension ; neither the place nor the time are mentioned : that is, he only places them in a general chronological order.

We read in Matthew xxviii. 16–20 :

> " Then the eleven disciples went away into Galilee, into a mountain where Jesus had appointed them.[2] And when they saw him, they worshipped him : but some doubted. And Jesus came and spake unto them, saying, All power is given unto me in heaven and in earth.[3] Go ye therefore, and teach all nations, baptizing them in the name of the Father, and of the Son, and of the Holy Ghost [4] : teaching them to observe all things whatsoever I have commanded you : and, lo, I am with you alway, even unto the end of the world."

The last formula explains the whole section. It is a beautiful and profound expression of the fundamental belief that Christ lives and will continue to live in the Church until the

---

[1] 1 Cor. xv. 14 : " *If Christ be not risen, then is our preaching vain.*"

[2] We do not know which mountain is meant. Everything a little out of the ordinary which Jesus did has been placed by Matthew on *the mountain* : it was not the time to change a convention. *Cf.* **CVIII**, 16.

[3] It is in the apocalyptic manner : Dan. vii. 14 : " *And there was given him dominion, and glory, and a kingdom, that all people, nations, and languages . . .*" ; Rev. ii. 26 : " *To him will I give power over the nations.*"—*Cf.* Matt. xi. 27, who has already said something like that.

[4] This formula appears to bear some relation to that of the *Didaché*, 7, 1. It would be sufficient in itself to condemn the authenticity of the passage in which it occurs and which is written for it. It is evident that the Apostles were unacquainted with this last command (*cf.* Gal. ii. 8, and Acts x.–xi.) ; the author of the *Didaché* does not refer to it. In the time of Eusebius another form of the text was known : " *Go and teach all nations in my name, teaching them to observe all that I have commanded you.*" *Cf.* Conybeare, in **ZNTW**, 1901, 275 *ff.*

end of the world. The Evangelist wished to bid farewell to his reader on this essential note. He therefore gathered all the appearances of tradition into a kind of magnificent theophany, of which the disciples are only the speechless and adoring witnesses. However, he did not feel it possible to ignore another humiliating fact, which finds expression also in the famous Johannine episode of Saint Thomas (John xx. 26–9), *viz.* that the Resurrection found some of the disciples incredulous. The *Easter faith* apparently grew out of a gradual reaction, which the Evangelists tend to transform into a sudden event which grows ever nearer to the death of Jesus, as the successive stages of the tradition develop. The picture given by Matthew will not help us in solving the problem of the appearances in Galilee ; his synthesis only serves to prove the existence of the belief in their reality, and that in a form which is sufficient to make them incredible to us.

The episode related in the twenty-first chapter of John (1–14) is much more interesting. This fragment, which is inserted as a kind of appendix to the Gospel, is by another hand, and in fact upsets the plan of the book which clearly ends with verses 30 and 31 of chapter xx.[1] It is a secondary and tendencious addition, clumsy and inconsistent, and probably intended to make the Gospel acceptable to the churches which adhered to the Synoptic pattern. The author of the Fourth Gospel accepts the tradition of the Jerusalem appearances, while the author of the appendix follows the tradition of the appearances in Galilee although he places them *after* the others (xxi. 1). The juxtaposition of chapters xx. and xxi. which constitutes an inexplicable contradiction for us, certainly only appears to him as an additional body of useful information.[2] This is the scene which he depicts : The disciples have returned to Galilee and seven, including Peter and the sons of Zebedee, go out by night, as of old, to fish in the sea of Tiberias. There is, thus, a complete change of scene from that of chapter xx. (*cf. vv.* 22 and 23) ; it is the situation disclosed by the last words of the *Gospel of Peter*.[3] We are no longer dealing with the triumphant Apostles whom the breath of Christ has consecrated as his substitutes on earth, filling them

---

[1] **CXXVII**[2], 514 ; **CXIX**, 184 ; **XLV**, ii, 286. No doubt is possible, and the desperate attempt of Lagrange (**CXXVI**, 520 *ff.*) to save the Johannine authenticity of ch. xxi. is ineffectual.—It is worth while to read **XLV**, ii, ch. viii in its entirety, and **CXXI**, ii, 687 *ff.*

[2] **CXXIX**, 435 *ff*

[3] *Ev. Petr.*, 60 : " *As for me, Simon Peter and Andrew my brother, we took our nets and went to the sea. And there was with us Levi, son of Alpheus, whom the Lord . . .*" There the fragment ends.

with the Holy Spirit,[1] but of disappointed humble folk, scattered in terror at the arrest of their Master, and forced to take up again their former life of toil:

> "But when the morning was now come, Jesus stood on the shore: but the disciples knew not that it was Jesus.[2] Then Jesus saith unto them, Children, have ye any meat? They answered him, No."

They have caught nothing during the night. Then he tells them where to cast their net, and they cannot draw it in on account of the quantity of fish. The miracle opens their eyes:

> "Therefore that disciple whom Jesus loved saith unto Peter,[3] It is the Lord. Now when Simon Peter heard that it was the Lord, he girt his fisher's coat unto him (for he was naked), and did cast himself into the sea."

Meanwhile the others turn the ship and bring the net to land. Peter alone draws the net to shore and counts the 153 large fish which it contains. A fire is lighted and the fish are cooking and

> "Jesus saith unto them, Come and dine. And none of the disciples durst ask him, Who art thou? knowing that it was the Lord. Jesus then cometh, and taketh bread, and giveth them, and fish likewise. This is now the third time [4] that Jesus shewed himself to his disciples, after he was risen from the dead."

The episode is connected with a miraculous draught of fish. Luke knew about it and used it in another connexion (v. 4–11).[5] He doubtless found the scene interesting but he could only make use of it by transposing and adapting it to another setting, since his plan obliged him to omit the Galilean appearances. We need not be surprised that "*he has rationalized a supernatural appearance*" (Lagrange). The form in which the Johannine tradition has reached us is far from satisfactory. We do not know what emotions it ascribed to Peter when he

---

[1] John xx. 22: "*And when he had said this, he breathed on them and saith unto them, Receive ye the Holy Ghost. . . .*"

[2] On account of the distance or the imperfect light? The text perhaps suggests it, but does not state it.

[3] A feature has almost certainly been added to the original tradition in order to magnify the beloved disciple; the use of the word *Lord*, which could not be primitive, may perhaps prove it. It is possible that the original tradition attributed to Peter the merit of being the first to recognize Jesus.

[4] It is actually the third appearance if we count the two described in the preceding chapter; but it is not chronologically related to them; it belongs to a different tradition.

[5] *Contra:* C, 162.

met Jesus on the shore. Probably he threw himself at his feet,
as in Luke v. 8, with some expression of shame for his denial
at cockcrow (Mark xiv. 66–72), such as : " *Depart from me :
for I am a sinful man* " (Luke). Nor do we know what took
place after Jesus' eucharistic act of distributing the bread and
fish ; [1] the redactor probably cut his account short because he
was specially interested in the conversation which he assigns
to the end of the meal. But it is likely that the account is
from a very early tradition, that is to say, it refers to the earliest
appearance, the one, in fact, which Paul connects with Peter.
The actual arrangement of the episode reflects secondary
interests, but it may also show the original element in the story.
Jesus appears to Peter one morning beside the lake, and perhaps
to the other disciples immediately afterwards (*then of the twelve*,
says Paul). Of all the appearances related in the Gospels it
is the one that is most likely to correspond to a remembered
historical fact. It is not impossible that Mark related it in
the original authentic ending, now lost, and which has been
replaced by the apocryphal passage which has come down to
us (Mark xvi. 9–20) in support of the tradition which placed
the appearances in Jerusalem.

The appearances in Jerusalem are attested in two passages
in Luke which follow each other (Luke xxiv. 13–53), in the
twentieth chapter of John, and in the canonical ending of Mark.

The first Lukan passage, the most celebrated of all, relates
the episode of the pilgrims to Emmaus. Two of the disciples
are going " *to a village called Emmaus, which was from Jerusalem
about threescore furlongs*," [2] and are joined by a traveller who
walks with them and enters into conversation. They tell him
about their disappointment, how they had followed a great
prophet from whom they had expected the deliverance of Israel
(xxiv. 21), and how he had perished at the hands of wicked
men. Certainly some women had come and said they could
not find his body in the tomb on the morning of the third day,
and that angels had appeared who told them that he was alive,
but they did not know what to believe. The stranger reproves
them for their lack of understanding and explains to them the
Prophecies which foretold all that has happened. [3] Delighted
with his company they invite him to supper :

[1] The probability of this symbolism is rendered greater by relating
the appearance to the miraculous draught of fishes. **CXXIX**, 444.

[2] A great deal of trouble has been taken to identify this village,
but without entire success. *Cf.* the Commentaries, especially **C**, 617 *ff.*,
and **CXCVIII**, 290 *ff.*

[3] We must not forget that that is the chief argument of the first
Christian apologists.

" And it came to pass, as he sat at meat with them, he took bread, and blessed it, and brake, and gave to them. And their eyes were opened, and they knew him ; and he vanished out of their sight " (30–1).

They hasten back to Jerusalem where they find the disciples assembled ; they tell them what has happened and declare : " *The Lord is risen indeed, and hath appeared to Simon.*" [1]

We do not know from what source this episode of the pilgrims of Emmaus has come. Since Mark xvi. 12–13 refers to it, its source probably belongs to the tradition of the Jerusalem appearances, but the evidence is weak. As presented by Luke, it has a symbolical purpose, viz. to indicate : " *that belief in the resurrection of Christ and in his presence among his disciples, in the communion feast, were established at the same time.*" [2] We must therefore conclude that nothing at all took place at Emmaus and that the appearance in question is only a " *transposition of recollections of the Galilean appearances.*" Such a literary effort would have presented no difficulties to Luke.

The pilgrims of Emmaus have not finished their story when Jesus in person enters the room where they are assembled and says : " *Peace be unto you!* " (xxiv. 36). Those present are terrified thinking they see a spirit ($\pi\nu\epsilon\tilde{\upsilon}\mu\alpha$). He reassures them and calms them by showing them the wounds in his hands and his feet, and he tells them to touch him that they may be convinced that he is not a spirit. They are still doubtful ; they are too astonished to believe immediately ; then he expresses a wish to eat with them. After that he gives them a brief discourse, during which he opens their minds so that they may understand the scriptures, makes them his witnesses on earth and declares that they shall receive *power from on high* (44–9). Then he takes them towards Bethany, blesses them and disappears. What is probably a later addition adds : " *he was carried up into heaven.*" The interest of the fragment lies in the evident anxiety to emphasize all the material proofs of the Resurrection, by way of reply to sceptical objections. There may also be seen the desire to vindicate the Church and to establish its authority. We have before us a " *discourse of the immortal Christ to the already constituted Church : it represents the growth of the faith and the development of the Gospel mission, about fifty years after the death of the Saviour.*" [3]

---

[1] The commentators have taken much trouble to explain this *Simon*. It may be an awkwardly introduced reminiscence of the priority of Simon Peter in the list of disciples to whom the Lord appeared. *Cf.* the Commentaries, *ad loc.*

[2] CIII, ii, 767 *ff.*   [3] *Ibid.*, 776.

The contradiction has often been stressed between this *second life* of Jesus, which in Luke only lasts a few hours and ends with a quiet disappearance, and the account in Acts i. 3–9 where it consists of forty days of familiar intercourse with the disciples, ended by the Ascension. It may be that the expansion in Acts only represents a redactional activity which has developed the two purposes which we have recognized in Luke xxiv. 36–49. Neither in Luke nor in Acts are we in the first stage of the tradition.

The two connected episodes which we find in John xx. 19–23 and 26–9 exhibit the same point of view as Luke and very likely come from him. A comparison of the two sources hardly leaves a doubt on this point : Mary Magdalene has come to tell the disciples that Jesus had appeared to her (xx. 18) ; but we do not know how they received the news. As they are assembled together on the Sunday evening with the doors shut, Jesus is suddenly in the midst of them and says to them : " *Peace be unto you!* " He shows them his hands and his side,[1] and they rejoice to see him. He ordains them as his substitutes and breathing on them he imparts to them the *Holy Spirit* with the power to forgive sins ;[2] in other words, he establishes the apostolic authority which they are to wield. The Evangelist does not relate the end of the appearance which has no more interest for him. But Thomas, one of the Twelve, is not there ; he does not believe the account given by the others, and demands proofs of a more material kind ; he must place his finger in the wounds of the Crucified. Eight days later Jesus reappears in the same place to convince the disciple who has become a symbol of the sceptic (24–9), and, having done so, he concludes : " *Because thou hast seen me, thou hast believed : blessed are they that have not seen, and yet have believed.*" The Church is founded on this declaration.

It is very evident that Thomas' exclamation (xx. 28) : " *My Lord and my God!* " could never have come from the mouth of a Jew. It implies the development of a christology which carries us far from the Resurrection and Jerusalem.[3] To the conception of *Lord*, which was only developed, as we shall see, in the Hellenistic community, it adds that of *God*, which clearly marks a still later stage in Christian speculation which cannot go back farther than the second century.[4] Once the narrator

---

[1] This is the feature which reveals the source of the account : Luke xxiv. John abridges his source.

[2] John therefore combines Easter and Pentecost.   [3] **CXIX**, 183.

[4] It occurs in the so-called *Epistles of Ignatius*, which unfortunately are difficult to date. *Cf.* **CXCIII**, 301 *ff.*

has made Jesus say what he wants him to say, he abandons
him and we do not know how the Risen Jesus took leave of
the Apostles. Altogether the account gives an impression of
a tendencious creation whose setting is borrowed from Luke,
belonging to no particular tradition or genuine recollection.

The canonical ending of Mark (xvi. 9–20) gives us another
appearance of Jesus at Jerusalem. We read there that on the
Sunday morning Jesus appears to Mary Magdalene.[1] She goes
to tell the disciples who "*mourned and wept*"; they do not
believe her. Meantime he has appeared "*in another form*" to
two disciples "*as they walked*" (we recognize the disciples of
Emmaus).

> " And they went and told it unto the residue : neither believed
> they them. Afterward he appeared unto the eleven as they sat
> at meat, and upbraided them with their unbelief and hardness of
> heart,[2] because they believed not them which had seen him after
> he was risen."

A short discourse follows, similar in tendency and style to
that in Matthew xxviii. 19, and also to that in John iii. 5 and
18, and then comes the Ascension.

The account does not name the place expressly, but as it
is in the same setting as Luke, we may probably place it in
Jerusalem. Its author was not content to follow Luke, but
had the four Gospels and the Acts before him from which he
has constructed a kind of mosaic. This fact, which disposes
of the Marcan authorship of the section, also destroys its claim
to antiquity.[3] His aim is clearly the same as that which we
have found in different forms in Matthew, Luke, and John :
to validate the existence of the Church by a formal act of
Christ. Some of the most important manuscripts (the *Vatican
Codex*, the Greek *Codex Sinaiticus*, and the *Sinaitic Syriac*)
have not this canonical ending, while others have a different
one. In the fourth century, Eusebius said[4] that "*in the
accurate manuscripts*," Mark ended with the words : *for they
were afraid* (xvi. 8). A little later Saint Jerome[5] confirmed

---

[1] There is no question of that in the Marcan account which precedes
(xvi. 1–8). We have in mind John xx. 14.

[2] καὶ ὠνείδισεν τὴν ἀπιστίαν αὐτῶν καὶ σκληροκαρδίαν . . . These three
terms do not belong to the style of Mark.

[3] It is known to Justin, Tatian and Irenæus, perhaps from Hebrews ;
it is already current in the second century. For the weak orthodox
defence of its authenticity, *cf.* **V**, i, 75 *ff.* ; **XLII**, ii, 50, is more cautious.
There is a detailed study in **CI**, 456 *ff*. *Contra :* Loisy, Klostermann,
ad loc., and the latest examination of the question so far, in **LIV**[7], 309 *ff*.

[4] *Ad Marinum*, 1 (*P.G.*, xxii, col. 937).

[5] *Ep.* 120, *ad Hedibiam*, 3.

this, and the Greek fathers of the same period, Athanasius, the two Cyrils, Basil, and Gregory Nazianzen, do not mention our passage ; they therefore did not consider it authentic. Neither Tertullian nor Cyprian, writing on baptism, cited verse 16, which would have been useful to them. It is probably a well-meaning attempt, dating from the first part of the second century, to bring Mark into agreement with the tradition of the appearances in Jerusalem while completing it according to the ending of Matthew.

However that may be, this pseudo-ending affords the weakest possible evidence for the appearances, since it is clearly only a kind of mosaic made up of various earlier accounts.

It is quite useless to insist on the very much later legendary productions which improved on the evidences for the Resurrection contained in the canonical writings.[1] Among the early Apocrypha, the *Gospel of Peter*, as we already know, places the first appearance to the disciples in Galilee. On the other hand, the *Gospel according to the Hebrews* is in favour of Jerusalem,[2] but in a new setting : Jesus as soon as he comes forth from the tomb hands his shroud to the high priest's servant and goes to find his brother James, because he knows that this excellent relative has taken an oath not to eat or drink until he has seen the Lord raised from the dead.

> " Bring a table and bread, then said Jesus. He took the bread, blessed it, broke it and gave it to James the just and said to him : My brother, eat your bread, for the Son of Man is risen from the dead."

This story became a favourite one in the early Church.[3] It only interests us because of the emphasis it lays on the appearance to James, which may be indicated in 1 Corinthians xv. 7 (ἔπειτα ὤφθη ᾽Ιακώϐῳ)—although the identity of the person in question is not specified—and because of its obvious purpose of distinguishing James. Now the legend of James the brother of our Lord must not be confounded with the apostolic tradition, which did not share the knowledge of the compiler of the *Gospel according to the Hebrews*, that this James had *drunk of the cup of the Lord*. It is possible that there was an appearance to James which convinced him, and that it was the cause of the prestige which he enjoyed later—if it is the same man —in the Christian community at Jerusalem. But these are secondary phenomena.

---

[1] The subject is well treated in **CXLII**, 258–74.
[2] In Hieron., *De viris*, 2.
[3] *Cf.* Greg. Turon., *Hist. Francorum*, 1, 21 ; J. de Voragine, *Legenda aurea*, 67.

A comparison of the various sources which we have passed under review leads us to the following conclusions :

(1) There is no agreement among our redactors as to where the apparitions took place : some say in Galilee, others in Jerusalem. Paul may be interpreted in either sense, and probability definitely turns the scale in favour of Galilee, but as no source says *first* Galilee, *then* Jerusalem, any chronological arrangement of the two groups must be purely arbitrary.

(2) There is complete disagreement regarding the number of appearances, but it appears probable that the earliest tradition attributed the first to Peter and the Apostles.

(3) The differences are no less concerning what Jesus did and said during these miraculous appearances ; but in the majority of the sources a special anxiety is displayed, although expressed in different ways, to establish apostolic authority and to justify the existence of the Church, which did not correspond with what Jesus had expected and announced during his life. The diversity of the ways in which this is done condemns the genuineness of the tradition, and their unanimous tendency proves that all the redactors were swayed by the same apologetic necessity.

(4) The hesitation, fear and even scepticism attributed by many of our sources to the disciples seems to preserve in tradition the memory of more or less obstinate doubts which belief in the Resurrection encountered first in the little evangelical band.

(5) As in the case of the date, the place of the Ascension varies greatly from one source to another, but the general tendency is to connect this glorious phenomenon as closely as possible with the Resurrection. Acts i. is the only exception.

(6) The list of appearances given by Paul cannot all be found in the other sources, and much energy has been expended in trying to discover all his instances in the Gospels.[1] It is evident that if this list represents a tradition known to Paul it does not coincide with that which the most generous criticism can succeed in extracting from the canonical Gospels : in one respect it is too long, in another too short ; too long because the appearances to the 500 disciples, to James, and to all the Apostles—at least—are not in the Gospels ; too short because it does not include the disciples of Emmaus.

(7) Harnack's [2] very pertinent remark should not be forgotten : " *The discovery of the empty tomb complicated and confused the tradition of the appearances and Paul knew nothing of this discovery.*" Nor is Paul the only witness to the fact that

---

[1] Lietzmann, in **LVII**, 1 Cor. 78 *ff.*   [2] **XCIV**, 112.

the tradition of the appearances is independent of the tradition of the discovery of the empty tomb. Mark's account which breaks off (xvi. 8) with the silence of the women ; that of the *Gospel of Peter* which takes us into Galilee to show us the first appearance, and even that of Matthew, which reduces the appearances to one, in Galilee (xxviii. 16), all really bear witness to the same fact. All three doubtless mention the discovery of the empty tomb, but in relating it they give the impression of reserving an argument which may be of use rather than that of strictly following the order in which the first vindications of the faith in the Resurrection came into existence.

The study of the earliest evidences for the appearances excludes therefore the discovery of the empty tomb from the primitive historical tradition, and clearly shows that belief in the resurrection of Jesus rests on these appearances. It leaves no other foundation for what is called *the Easter faith* than the appearances themselves.[1] We must now attempt to explain and interpret them.

---

[1] *Contra :* **LXXXVI,** 166, who really offers nothing but impressions.

CHAPTER VI

THE EASTER FAITH

Θάνατωθείς μὲν σαρκὶ Ζωοποιηθεὶς δὲ πνεύματι = put to death in the flesh, but quickened in (his) Spirit (1 *Pet.* iii. 18).

I

THE STATEMENT OF THE PROBLEM

DENIALS of the Resurrection are as old as Christianity itself. An examination of the sources has led us to believe that many of the episodes related and many details in them all owe their origin and arrangement to the necessity of countering Jewish scepticism. A little later Christian apologetics had to reply to pagan scepticism. Thus Celsus [1] asks whether the story of the Resurrection could not be explained by visions produced from the agitated brain of Mary Magdalene or of one of the disciples ; the suggestion of deliberate fraud also occurs to him. Since that time the supreme miracle has encountered innumerable contradictions. Believers however maintain that only rationalist prejudice could deny it, seeing that it is the most strongly attested *fact* in history. We know what to think of this assurance and that independent criticism has the best reasons for not accepting such a dogmatic assertion. The sober critic disclaims rationalist prejudice but believes it necessary to mistrust religious prejudice, realizing also that nothing should be rejected without adequate grounds.

Here a distinction must be made between the process of explaining the alleged fact itself, that is of giving a reasonable critical interpretation of it, and the process of explaining the grounds upon which *faith in the reality of the fact* rests.

To explain the fact of the Resurrection is to admit that the faith which accepts it rests on a reality. But this is not the same as an explanation of the kind of reality upon which it rests. When once the purely miraculous hypothesis has been discarded, support for all kinds of hypotheses may be found in the sources, because they favour none of them. It becomes a

[1] Origen, *C. Celsum*, 2, 55.

question of showing that out of certain assumptions, whose elements are taken in their natural order, the faith in the Resurrection could have grown and the story of the Resurrection taken shape. This is a problem which every student solves according to his understanding of it, with varying degrees of probability ; but the point must be emphasized that these probabilities themselves depend on a process of imagination ; the sources neither give nor suggest them ; and it is no argument to say that they do not reject them, because accounts created by belief, with the sole purpose of proving the reality of the Resurrection, are by their very nature unfitted for any other purpose. At the most a few legendary details which, moreover, are peculiar to one or other of the narratives, may appear to afford grounds for certain inferences. For example, the confusion which Mary Magdalene makes between Jesus and the gardener, in John xx. 15, or the giving by Jesus to the high priest's servant of the shroud which he takes off on leaving the sepulchre, according to the *Gospel of the Hebrews*. On the whole, the process is an arbitrary one.

Up to the present time almost all rationalistic critics have been content with this process, because they have accepted the general outline, common to the different accounts : the burial, and the discovery of the empty tomb ; and above all because they admit this to have been the *chronological order* and not merely the *logical order* of the episodes. That is why it was necessary to explain the empty tomb. The utmost ingenuity remained fruitless so long as the statement of the problem remained unchanged. As soon as the rejection of the historicity of the essential facts of the burial and the discovery of the empty tomb becomes possible, the problem becomes one of explaining, not the significance of the *fact*, but the origin of the *belief*.

This new problem of the cause, origin and growth of the Christian faith in the Resurrection wears a very different appearance. This belief is evidently a *certainty* to the first Christian generation ; but certainty is a state of mind which is not always based on material facts. On the other hand certainty always tends to *materialize*, that is to say, to justify itself by facts and by reasons based on experiences. The essential thing is not to be misled by this secondary process but to recognize that it is secondary. Let us admit that the belief in the Resurrection of Jesus *may have* been established under other conditions than those given in our sources, and these sources *may* represent nothing more than the creation of material support for a certainty which came into being independently of them.

Let us define our starting-point. We have established :

(1) that the appearances preceded the supposed evidence for the empty tomb [1] ; (2) that the appearances in Galilee preceded those in Jerusalem ; (3) that it is the appearances which first gave rise to the belief in the Resurrection. Our problem resolves itself then into the two following points : (1) What were the appearances and how did they beget the belief in the Resurrection ? (2) How did the narratives of the Great Miracle acquire their present form ?

II

THE NATURE OF THE APPEARANCES

If we believe our Gospels blindly, the disciples expected the Resurrection, because the certainty that it would happen was guaranteed by the predictions [2] of the Old Testament and of Jesus himself. [3]

But we must admit that at the time of the Passion the disciples of Jesus behave as if they had never heard anything about the glorious future reserved for their Master : they mourn over his death and the first announcement of the Resurrection finds them sceptical. Moreover, when Jesus tried to instruct them in advance about the Great Miracle they did not understand him, as, for example, in Mark viii. 31 ; ix. 10 and 32. From which, unless we admit the absurd, we must conclude that Jesus predicted nothing of the kind, but that later, when faith found it impossible that the Lord should have been unaware of the fate that awaited him, it could find no better way of declaring that he had known it than by making him predict it.

On the other hand we cannot see what scriptures foretold the Resurrection of the Messiah. The Jews had no current belief that *He who was to come* must die and rise again. [4]

Everything, therefore, goes to prove that the disciples, fleeing from Jerusalem in fear and grief, had received a totally unexpected blow and that they returned to Galilee, [5] persuaded

---

[1] XXIV, 66.

[2] Matt. xii. 40 (Symbolical interpretation of the story of Jonah); Luke xxiv. 27 (Discourse to the pilgrims of Emmaus).—*Cf.* 1 Cor. xv. 4 : ". . . *he rose again the third day according to the scriptures.*"

[3] Mark viii. 31 ; ix. 9–10 and 31 ; x. 34 ; Matt. xii. 40 ; xvi. 4 and 21 ; xvii. 9 and 23 ; xx. 19 ; xxvi. 32, and Syn.

[4] We do not know if any sect believed it, and in any case eccentric views of sectaries must not be confounded with the teaching of the Old Testament.

[5] The declaration which Mark xiv. 28 puts into the mouth of Jesus : " *I will go before you into Galilee,*" is sufficient to prove that it was there that the first tradition took them back. The end of the *Gospel of Peter* bears out the same testimony. *Cf.* EB, *Gospels* (Schmiedel), 138.

that Jesus was really dead. How then did they arrive at the assurance that he was dead no longer ? It is obvious that the idea of the resurrection presented itself to these men very differently from the way in which we regard it. It was familiar to them and they accepted it without difficulty, as many early thinkers did.[1] Had we been in their place, our attitude would have been sceptical *à priori*, so to speak, but it was not so with them. In their environment the resurrection anticipated at the end of time was expected to take the form of a material restoration of the body and to be a renewal of earthly life. The resurrection of Lazarus and the idea that Jesus was John the Baptist returned to life represent this conception.[2]

On the other hand the disciples certainly believed in spirits and were convinced that the souls of men who have met a premature or violent death wander restlessly and terrify the living. Luke xxiv. 37 tells us that the disciples thought they saw a ghost ($\dot{\epsilon}\delta\acute{o}\varkappa o\nu\nu$ $\pi\nu\epsilon\tilde{\nu}\mu\alpha$ $\theta\epsilon\omega\varrho\epsilon\tilde{\iota}\nu$) when Jesus appeared in the guest-chamber, just as they thought they saw a phantom when he walked on the water and joined them in their boat (Matt. xiv. 26 : $\lambda\acute{\epsilon}\gamma o\nu\tau\epsilon\varsigma$ $\varphi\acute{\alpha}\nu\tau\alpha\sigma\mu\acute{\alpha}$ $\dot{\epsilon}\sigma\tau\iota\nu$). A spirit, a phantom, a ghost, are kindred conceptions, and at that time there was a general belief in them.[3]

We may add that people were then generally incapable of distinguishing a *subjective* experience, an hallucination or even a dream from a really *objective* experience implying a basis of tangible reality. A nightmare is still commonly considered as a revelation from the other world.[4] In particular they had not the slightest idea of the mechanism of hallucination.

If the disciples who *witnessed* the Resurrection had written down their impressions from day to day and these records had come down to us, much that remains obscure would probably be clear to modern minds in the light of experimental psychology ; but the earliest testimony available, that of 1 Corinthians xv., is twenty-five years later than the death of Jesus and remains totally vague. The first conceptions changed rapidly, involving equally swift changes in the original reminiscences. Very soon the disciples, confused by the growing christological distortion of their testimony, became incapable of restoring it in its original form. It cannot be too often repeated that what we find in the sources is the conviction of those who thought they

---

[1] CLXX, iii, 454 ; CCL, 286 ; XLVIII, 77 ; CCXCII, ii, 163.
[2] XXXIV, 61.
[3] XXXIV, 62 ; Swete, *The Gospel according to St. Mark*, 131, London, 1898 ; DCG, art. *Apparition*, col. 111.
[4] CCL, 289.

had established the truth of the facts, and not the *facts* themselves. And this unshakable conviction must not be confused with the legendary form in which it was clothed by the Gospels. We can agree with Loisy when he says [1] :

> " The accounts in the canonical and apocryphal Gospels do not represent the original appearances, but the way in which the belief in the resurrection of Christ became conscious, took shape and justified itself half a century and more after the birth of Christianity."

There is not the shadow of a doubt that the disciples believed in the reality of the appearances, nor can we deny that they possessed some kind of reality, but it remains to discover what kind of reality. We must note that in this case, *to see* and *to believe one sees* are two separate *facts* which tend to coalesce, but we cannot think we see without some cause, and every appearance possesses material or spiritual, objective or subjective reality. We need not linger over the insistence on material details displayed by Luke and John (exhibition of wounds, and meals taken with the disciples), because they are nothing more than an apologetic device intended to authenticate the Resurrection, and reflect neither fresh nor distant memories. To convince ourselves of this, it is sufficient to compare them with Paul's list (1 Cor. xv.) and with Mark xvi. 1–8, or even with Matthew xxviii. 9–20, which already shows signs of expansion : not one of these three sources gives any of the above-mentioned details, which would obviously have destroyed the illusion.

If we think of the resurrection-experience as an hallucination, we must suppose that it was repeated and under varying circumstances. It is possible that the disciples, perceiving on the distant shore of the lake in the haze of dawn a vague form, strangely resembling their Master, might think they saw him, but this will not explain the other occasions. We must imagine the circumstances of each. And even the attempt does not take us far, for if by chance it contains the possibility of an explanation we cannot grasp it clearly. Candidly, the interpretation of " sacred stories " by common-sense and material contingencies is unconvincing : there is never much to be gained by confusing modes of approach which differ so widely.

Moreover, if the disciples were deluded by false appearances they must have been predisposed by some cause, and their state of mind must have inclined them to accept a vision as a necessary phenomenon, and hence their mistake was only the almost inevitable realization of an inner expectancy ; in other words, it was caused and authenticated by this expectancy. If the minds of the disciples were in such a state of expectancy might

[1] **CLXII**, 467.

not that be sufficient, without the medium of any exterior
phenomenon, to produce visions ? *Subjective* visions, doubtless,
but perfectly real to those who experienced them. If this were
so, we should be confronted by one of the most perplexing,
definite and over-mastering phenomena to which an unbalanced
mind is liable ; most inexplicable to ignorant and credulous
people ; that of *hallucination* and probably of collective hallucination.

Would visions of this kind be an adequate foundation for the
Easter faith ? The majority of independent critics, if not all,
reply in the affirmative.[1] It is perhaps permissible to find
support for this idea in Acts x. 41, where it is said that God,
after raising Jesus, did not manifest him to all the people, but
only to those witnesses whom he had chosen beforehand. And
we are well aware that *in the history of religious enthusiasm
nothing appears more contagious than visions.* In the narrow
circle of enthusiastic believers it is enough for one to say with
the ardour of conviction that he has *seen* the object of the collective mystical desire for all to see it also. Even in our times the
Roman Catholic Church has to be cautious in the matter of
apparitions of the Virgin, the reality of which is readily attested
by enthusiastic groups of people. It is a common phenomenon
of mental contagion which has been the object of much study.

But the question might be raised why the disciples did not
go to the tomb to verify their visions ?[2] There is little force
in this objection, because the very idea of verifying presupposes
doubt, and there is no ordinary connexion between the exaltation of the vision and the uninspired business of verification.
On the other hand, was there even a tomb ? Reasons have
already been given for thinking there was none, and for rejecting
both the burial and the discovery of the empty tomb. There
is another more serious objection :[3] Why did this supposed
exaltation of the disciples subside after having engendered some
ten visions at most ? Reputed *visionary* sects such as the
Montanists, Jansenists and Camisards were much more prolific.
Doubtless, but in these sects the exaltation which produced
visions and ecstasies—the two go together—was an essential
element of their normal life. In their case visions and ecstasies
were a manifestation of the Spirit, an answer to their per-
plexities.[4] But it was logical that the visions should cease for
the disciples, once the affirmation of the Resurrection—*he
lives*—had been made. Observe, they did not merely say : *he*

---

[1] After Strauss, Renan, Réville, etc., *cf.* **CXCIII**, 20 *ff.* ; **CCL**, 43.
[2] **CLXXXIV**, ii, 474 *ff.*   [3] *Ibid.*, 477.
[4] *Cf.* the visions of Paul and those of Peter in the Acts.

lives, but : *he lives in the glory of God* ; he is *exalted* (Acts ii. 32 *ff.,* 36). He appears often enough for his followers to be convinced ; but his glory itself prevents him from multiplying those appearances which were reserved for the *parousia.* " *Blessed are they that have not seen, and yet have believed* " (John xx. 29). In the above-mentioned sects, it was a regular habit ; in the apostolic group, it was only a sad and agonizing crisis which might have ended in the abandonment of their hope, but found its completion in exaltation : there it must cease. If, therefore, visions, or more accurately apparitions of Jesus, rose before the *mind's eye* of the disciples and created the illusion of *physical vision,* the explanation must be sought in the state of mind in which these men were at the time the phenomenon was produced.

The authorities who had struck at Jesus doubtless thought it useless to pursue his disciples : logic and experience told them that *it was finished.* Everything leads us to suppose that the wretched disciples, driven by fear and despair back to Galilee, thought the same.[1] There can be no doubt about their *fall.* The alleged prediction of Jesus in Mark xiv. 27 : " *All ye shall be offended because of me this night : for it is written, I will smite the shepherd, and the sheep shall be scattered,*" would not have been invented on purpose to humiliate the Apostles. On the contrary, it was intended to justify them ; their cowardice disappeared before the necessity of fulfilling the scriptures. Moreover, this fall implies, not loss of faith, but loss of courage ; terror at the overthrow of the hope which had sustained them on their way up to Jerusalem (the hope of seeing the advent of the expected Kingdom) and not loss of confidence in their Master. They fled because they were afraid and did not understand. If it had been otherwise, and in their despair they had descended so low as to deny Jesus as an impostor or a madman, nothing of all that we are considering now would have happened. When P. Lagrange translates [2] the πάντες σκανδαλισθήσεσθε of Mark xiv. 27, as *You will all be demoralized,* he no doubt over-emphasizes the interpretation which he wishes to suggest, but he has grasped the essential meaning of the situation, as we must conceive of it. We seem to catch a glimpse of the wretched fugitives, with heavy hearts and streaming eyes (*Gospel of Peter*), in the two pilgrims to Emmaus, sadly comparing the tragedy of the death of Jesus with their shattered hopes : " *But we trusted that it had been he which should have redeemed* Israel " (Luke xxiv. 21). And yet they cannot believe that it is all over. They go on to say that

[1] **XXXIV**, 9. [2] **CI,** 383.

what happened had to happen ; that if they did not understand, it was their fault and their Master must be right. We must not forget that these men are Jews who are accustomed to thinking that the greatest good may come out of the greatest evil and who find in reflection on each fresh disillusionment, the source of some new hope, some fresh vision of cheer.[1] Since the blow which struck Jesus down did not crush them completely, it was of the nature of such a movement as theirs that a strong reaction should set in after a gathering up of all the encouraging elements of the past, and making the impossible seem possible.[2]

In this case one important factor must be taken into account : the influence that Jesus had acquired over them and the confident affection which bound them to him, their estimate of his personality and of the rôle God was reserving for him.[3] The constituent elements of this factor escape us ; but of its strength there can be no doubt, since it was sufficient to draw these men after so strange a prophet. It must have seemed to them *à priori* impossible that death could utterly destroy such a person and dissipate such an influence. Hence, as their hope and their confidence recovered from the catastrophe of the death of Jesus, it was to be expected that their first preoccupation would tend to recreate the figure of the Crucified. But it is certain that other forms might and did occur to their minds before that of the Resurrection.

If they had considered him during his lifetime as the present or future Messiah, their reaction and its direction would perhaps be more easily explained,[4] although the fact of the death of the Messiah—of which Israel had not the slightest idea—must have been singularly embarrassing to them. Indeed, it might be supposed that they would bring him to life so that he might assume his Messianic rôle. But we have given the reasons which hinder us from attributing such a conviction to them before the Resurrection, and which suggest, on the contrary, that this conviction arose from the Resurrection itself according to the pattern of the belief expressed in Acts ii. 22–4 and 32–6 : "*God hath raised that same Jesus to make him . . . both Lord and Christ.*"[5] The disciples must have reasoned as follow : We have seen him, therefore he lives ; if he lives, it is because God has raised him

---

[1] CLXIV, 271.　　　　　　　　　　　　　[2] CXCIII, 20.
[3] XLVIII, 77 ; XXXIV, 15 ; CXCIII, 20.
[4] CCXXII, 74. *Cf.* XXXIV, 22 *ff.* ; CLVI, 299 *ff.*, who attempts to prove that the Messianic faith of the disciples preceded and determined faith in the Resurrection.
[5] Rom. i. 4 still bears a trace of the same idea : (Christ Jesus who was) "*declared to be the Son of God with power, according to the spirit of holiness, by the resurrection of the dead.*"

for no less a purpose than to be the Messiah. They could assign no more exalted destiny to him and it must have been the first which occurred to them. It cannot be denied that such a transformation of current Messianic expectation seems hard to accept, but it is even more difficult to conceive of the transformation of the Messiah into a Galilean *nabi* who was unable to withstand the slightest attack of the *goyim*. Nevertheless the idea of ascension was not necessarily connected with the Messiahship : Moses, Enoch, Elijah, and Isaiah were supposed to have been translated, yet they were not Messiahs.

III

The Mechanism of the Appearances

If we are to believe Paul's assertion, it is not the assembled Apostles who see Jesus first, but Peter by himself. And if we consider the matter it certainly seems that the belief in the Resurrection springs from Peter's experience. This appears to follow, not only from the evidence of 1 Corinthians xv. 5, but from the peculiar phrase in Luke xxiv. 34 introduced into the story of the pilgrims of Emmaus : "*The Lord is risen indeed and hath appeared to Simon*"; from the account now very much rearranged of the miraculous draught of fish in John xxi. and also from the statement of John xx. 6 *ff.*, according to which Peter was *the first* to discover that the tomb was empty and to infer the resurrection of Jesus. The appearances to the women, placed first by some of our accounts, belong solely to the later expansion of the discovery of the empty tomb. Peter was probably the earliest of Jesus' actual disciples, as he was certainly the first in the matter of affection and confidence. As far as we can ascertain from the sources he seems to have been of a sensitive and emotional nature, and probably extremely suggestible. The story of his denial (Mark xiv. 66–72) does not merely suggest that he could be lacking in courage, it also shows that he was regarded as the only one who did not utterly forsake his Master, in spite of the danger. He possessed a deep instinct of devotion and faith which no catastrophe could wholly obliterate. We read in Luke xxii. 31–2 :

"Simon, Simon, behold, Satan hath desired to have you, that he may sift you as wheat : but I have prayed for thee, that thy faith fail not : and when thou art converted, strengthen thy brethren."

This text clearly proves two facts ; that Peter quickly recovered from his weakness and that he strengthened his *brethren*, the disciples, in their terrible trial.   We may interpret the " *Feed my sheep* " of John xxi. 15 *ff*. in the same sense.

We must think of him as having returned to his home at Capernaum and resumed his fisherman's calling, with the boat which had so often taken Jesus across the lake.   Everything there calls up memories of those days of hope and joy.   The vision of his Master pursues him and indeed fills his whole life. His entire being centres in the thought that it cannot all be ended, that something will happen and happen through Him, that he has not deceived us nor forsaken us, he will come back to us.   And while his grief at the loss of Jesus grows, and a hope that has no form, becomes keener, the expectation of the inevitable miracle surges in his heart.   Reason demanded that this miracle should be a personal manifestation of the Crucified. Need we be surprised that Peter *saw* Jesus ?   Where ?   Probably by the shore of the lake and under conditions favourable to hallucination : in the morning mist or the dazzling blaze of noonday.   Perhaps he was alone when it happened, but not necessarily.   He had already been able to gather round him some of the most steadfast of the disciples, the Twelve as Paul calls them (1 Cor. xv. 5), and nothing would be more natural than that they should have *seen* immediately after him.

In a process of this kind the initial impulse is all that is needed.   As soon as that is assured the rest follows, for contagion is the rule.   It would work still better in this case because Peter's companions are in a state of mind similar to his own. Contagion could only fail to be produced if all these men had completely lost their faith or if they possessed a *scientific* conviction that the appearance of a dead person was an impossibility.   We know that neither of these things was so.   And even incredulous people such as Jesus' own family seem to have been, might in their turn feel a contagion, to which their mental outlook was favourable.   None of the appearances enumerated by Paul are improbable, not even the one which speaks of the 500 brethren together, if we realize that it is a question of such an appearance as is suggested by the word ὤφθη = *he appeared, he was seen*, and not of such actualities of real life as those into which Luke and John introduce the Risen Lord.

If we ask ourselves what Peter *saw* and what he concluded from it, we certainly shall not find any satisfactory reply in the Gospel sources because—as we have already seen—the Gospels offer us only later expansions developed in relation to credal considerations unconnected with historical facts.   We must notice, however, that Paul, closing his list with the appearance by which he was himself converted, makes no difference

between that vision and those which convinced Peter, the
Twelve and a number of disciples. He uses the same word to
describe it : ὤφθη = *he was seen.* This word does not necessarily imply the actual appearance of a person, but may only
indicate an unusual phenomenon ; faith, conscious or unconscious, but expectant, accepts it as the revelation of the real
presence of the Master. Paul does not tell us that he saw the
Christ *in person* on the road to Damascus, but that he was
dazzled by a great light and that he heard a voice which spoke
with authority : how could he have doubted that this was a
manifestation of the Lord Jesus, as indisputable to him as if
he had seen the radiant countenance ? The use of the same
word ὤφθη in enumerating the other visions in the Pauline list
certainly does not prove that they took place under the same
conditions as the one on the road to Damascus, but it excludes
such details as prolonged conversation, meals, and resumption
of ordinary life, on which the Gospels dwell. If he intended a
visual phenomenon he does not define it. He does not represent it as something that needed no explanation, like the actual
apparition of a ghost. On the contrary, it is a conception that
can easily receive the interpretation given by faith, and which
can give definiteness to vague visual impressions. In 1 Corinthians ix. 1 Paul exclaims : " *Am I not an Apostle ? Have
I not seen* (οὐχὶ ἑώρακα) *Jesus Christ our Lord ?* "
He is certainly referring to the vision on the road to
Damascus, as is shown by the connexion between the two
assertions, for it was on the road to Damascus that Paul was
invested with his apostolic status. But in none of the accounts [1]
which we have of this miracle are we told that Paul literally
saw Jesus Christ.
It is therefore possible that Peter had a visual hallucination,
but it is also possible that the state of anxious expectancy in
which he lived and the indefinite but irresistible hope which
sustained him may have created their object for him, that is
to say caused him to interpret some visual phenomenon, much
more indeterminate than an hallucination, as a manifestation
of the presence of Jesus. Many modern apparitions have been
thus conditioned. We shall not attempt to define the phenomenon more closely ; since it is not possible and the hypotheses
or analogies thus produced could not be *objectively* convincing.
Let us rather try to discover what conclusions Peter, and afterwards the other disciples, may have drawn from their vision if
it was really what we have suggested it to be.
It is clear that Paul did not imagine he had seen a mani-

[1] Acts ix. 3 *ff.* ; xxii. 6 *ff.* ; xxvi. 12 *ff.*

festation of Jesus the Galilean on the road to Damascus, but a communication from the glorified Lord. We read in 2 Corinthians iv. 6 :

> " For God, who commanded the light to shine out of darkness, hath shined in our hearts, to give the light of the knowledge of the glory of God in the face of Jesus Christ."

It was, then, a divine light radiating from the face of the Lord which dazzled Paul. There is no reason to believe that he attributed to Peter's *experience* any other character than that of his own : Peter, like him, had seen his Master glorified, that is, speaking symbolically, exalted to the right hand of God, and shining with celestial light.

If Jesus is thus *exalted* and dwells in the abode of his Father, it means that' he could not be holden of death, and has really risen again. From this we may infer that Paul thought of this resurrection in terms of the general resurrection which he expected, since for him Christ's resurrection is the guarantee of ours (1 Cor. xv. 17–20 ; Rom. vi. 8) and that the distinctive feature of our resurrection will be our *glorification* (1 Cor. xv. 42 *ff.* ; 52 *ff.*) But it is not easy to understand how he imagines this general resurrection. He seems to use the word *resurrection* (ἀνάστασις) as a term in general use and not in its strict sense, just as we say the *rising* and the *setting* of the sun, although we know perfectly well that the sun neither rises nor sets.[1] Many passages in the Epistles, indeed, strangely limit the meaning of the word. For example, 1 Corinthians xv. 50 concludes a long exposition of the idea, unfortunately consisting mainly of metaphors and comparisons, with this statement : " *Now this I say, brethren, that flesh and blood cannot inherit the kingdom of God.*" What he means by " *this* " and by his metaphors is, apparently, that it will not be the body laid in the earth which will rise again :

> " Thou fool, that which thou sowest (the grain of corn) is not quickened, except it die : and that which thou sowest, thou sowest not that body that shall be, but bare grain. . . . It is sown a natural [2] body ; it is raised a spiritual body " (1 Cor. xv. 36 *ff.*).

But Paul does not go so far as to imply that a new body grows in the earth, as a new ear of corn rises from the decaying seed. He doubtless believes that God performs an act of creative will, by which he restores a body to us, but in the strict

---

[1] CXCIII, 76.

[2] A body animated by a *soul*, therefore a *living* body. *Cf.* Guignebert, *Remarques sur quelques conceptions chrétiennes antiques, touchant l'origine et la nature de l'âme*, in **RHPR**, 1929, 432 *ff.*

sense nothing of that which went into the tomb comes out of it.
He may perhaps imagine that this new body awaits God's time
in heaven. That at least is the conclusion which can easily be
drawn from 2 Corinthians v. 1 : " *For we know that if our earthly
house of this tabernacle were dissolved, we have a building of
God . . . eternal in the heavens.*" It is obvious that he is
speaking of a body (*cf.* v. 2 and 4). Therefore the spirit only
of the original man, properly speaking, survives. If our comparison between the Pauline conception of the general resurrection and the Apostle's idea of Christ's resurrection is correct,
then Paul was interested in the spiritual reality of the Risen
Lord and not with the fate of the corporeal body of Jesus.
That is what the post-Pauline redactor of 1 Peter (iii. 18) meant
when he said of Christ that he had been " *put to death in his
flesh* (θανατωθεὶς μὲν σαρκί) *but quickened in his spirit* "
(ζωοποιηθεὶς δὲ πνεύματι), an exact counterpart of the verse
from 1 Corinthians xv. 44, just quoted : " *It is sown a natural
body* (σπείρεται σῶμα ψυχικόν) ; *it is raised a spiritual body* "
(ἐγείρεται σῶμα πνευματικόν). A modern spiritualist would
say that the Risen Lord had an astral body.[1]

Paul therefore does not say that Jesus is raised *in the flesh* ;
he even positively states the contrary, and there is a striking
difference between the conception of the Great Miracle reflected
in the Pauline texts and that which may be gathered from the
Gospels and the Acts. The Tarsiot is not interested in Jesus'
return to a terrestrial life nor in the restoration of the natural
conditions of a renewed human existence. In reality, *resurrection* means for him *exaltation to the presence of God, glorification.*[2]
It is curious that in the only passage in which the Apostle
explains in detail his ideas on the being and nature of Christ,
from his pre-existence to his exaltation (Phil. ii. 5 *ff.),* no
positive mention is made of the resurrection but only of the
exaltation (ii. 9 : διὸ καὶ ὁ θεός αὐτὸν ὑπερύψωσεν = "*wherefore God also hath highly exalted him* "). One may then be
certain that the Jesus *seen* by Paul in the conditions described is the *glorified* Lord, unfettered by the bonds of the
flesh. There is no need to speak of *Ascension* here ; Jesus is
risen because he is glorified ; the two processes blend in some
way. It is only the materialization of the glorified body which

[1] CCL, 294.

[2] **XXXIV**, 61 : *Auferstehung, Auferweckung = Verherrlichung* and
Erhöhung. This equivalence is found in Paul and his followers; to
the idea of *resuscitation* (ἀνίστημι, ἀνάστασις, in Rom. vi. 5 ; 1 Cor. xv.
21 ; Phil. iii. 10 ; 1 Peter iii. 21 ; etc.), of *awakening* (ἐγείρω, in 1 Cor.
xv. 15 ; 2 Cor. i. 9 ; Rom. vi. 8, etc.), corresponds that of *exaltation*
(ὑπερυψόω in Phil. ii. 9) and of *glorification* (ἀναλαμβάνω, in 1 Tim. iii. 16).

would make Ascension necessary, and with Paul we are still far from a realistic conception of the Resurrection. It is because he has seen the exalted Christ that he believes in his Resurrection " according to the scriptures."

We must not confound Peter and the Galilean disciples with Paul and the Hellenistic Christians to whom the idea of the resurrection of the flesh was unacceptable ; and we are not as well documented about the former as we are about the latter. Acts ii. 23 *ff.*, however, calls for some comment :

> " Him, being delivered by the determinate counsel and fore-knowledge of God, ye have taken, and by wicked hands have cruci-fied and slain : whom God hath raised up, having loosed the pains of death : because it was not possible that he should be holden of it."

It is doubtless a confused passage, in an artificially arranged setting, yet its verses may well reflect something of the disciples' first impressions : It was impossible that Jesus should be held by the bonds of death ; God withdrew him from its awful grasp, and if he abandoned him at first, he did so with a purpose. The explanation, the theology of these fundamental affirmations and their spiritual justification, already adumbrated in this passage of Acts (*cf.* ii. 26–7 and 31), were to come later ; [1] but essentially they imply nothing more than Paul has said. It is sufficient to refer to the conclusion given in verses 32 and 36 :

> " This Jesus hath God raised up, whereof we all are witnesses.— Therefore let all the house of Israel know assuredly, that God hath made that same Jesus, whom ye have crucified, both Lord and Christ."

The formula bears a Pauline stamp, but it none the less expresses the truth that it was the certainty of the Resurrection which buoyed up the disciples, strengthened their assurance that the Master had not deceived them, convinced them that he was the Messiah and suggested the satisfying explanation of what had been their great stumbling-block. He died because he had to die, because that was God's plan and because his ignominious death was in reality only the first stage of his glorification. [2]

Let us sum up our facts and our conclusion therefrom. The

---

[1] The redactor of the Acts is thinking of a useful passage in Ps. xvi. (xv. of the Septuagint) 10 : " *Thou wilt not leave my soul* (τὴν ψυχήν μου = *the source of my life*) *in hell ; neither wilt thou suffer thine Holy One to see corruption.*"

[2] The idea appears clearly in the parable of the Talents, in Luke xix. 12 *ff.*, where " *a certain nobleman went into a far country to receive for himself a kingdom* " ; he returns indeed as king and punishes those who tried to oppose his enthronement.

disciples returned to Galilee perplexed, troubled, and afraid; discouraged, too, because none of their hopes had been realized and they had sustained a crushing blow; but *they did not despair.* They were too deeply attached to the person of Jesus and remained too confident in his promises to lose hope completely. After the first shock those deep feelings rose again to the surface when they were back in their homes where their hopes were revived by so many memories.

The promised future which had attracted and bound them to Jesus was bound up with his person : to admit that he had disappeared for ever was to abandon all hope. Their faith was centred in, and, we might say, hypnotized by this idea : it is not possible that he should have deceived us, that he should have forsaken us, or that he should be irrevocably dead.

Such a tension of desire and faith in the minds and hearts of uncultured men, inclined to mysticism, inflamed by moral suffering and anxious expectation, has only one logical outcome—the occurrence of visions. Peter sees Jesus first and the others see him afterwards and in the same way.

It matters little whether they have true hallucinations or whether they interpret visual phenomena and turn them into hallucination. They *perceive* their Master. There is no question of material contact nor of a resumption, however fleeting, of ordinary life and intercourse, but, if we may call it so, of an illusory externalization of this deep conviction : he cannot be dead, therefore he is alive.

The disciples do not actually conclude from this conviction and the visions which authenticate it, that Jesus has come forth from the tomb in flesh and blood, but that he has been *glorified,*[1] that all that is still living of him has been transported into the *glory* of God and remains with the *Most High* awaiting the hour of the inauguration of the Kingdom. This very vague expression : *all that is still living of him,* is used deliberately because the reality imagined by Peter and his companions lacks sharpness. They probably do not attain Paul's comparative definiteness of statement because their minds are filled with popular realistic ideas of the resurrection and also with superstitions concerning *spirits* and *ghosts.* Moreover, it is doubtful whether they attempt to systematize their impressions. They are satisfied to possess a definite *sign* which proves that the Nazarene has not failed them. They are not concerned with logic and criticism.

The *sign* restores to their faith not only all its assurance but all its vigour. That faith finds a leaping-off place, so to speak,

[1] *Cf.* **CLVI,** 284 *ff.*

from the idea of the Resurrection, which gave its initial impulse
to the apostolic preaching and remained its firmest foundation.
It is not likely that the Old Testament, or myths of a dying
and rising God in the pagan Mysteries, played any part in
the birth of the belief in the Resurrection. It arose solely
from a psychological phenomenon, whose mechanism we have
attempted to understand. But it is no longer possible to rely
on this proof as soon as the preaching of the Resurrection
extends outside the narrow circle of its immediate witnesses.
It becomes necessary to prove that the Resurrection was God's
purpose, and to justify it from the Old Testament which must
have predicted it.

It is naturally contested, especially by the Jews, and must be
demonstrated by proofs and arguments. Opposition engenders
proof which, contested in its turn, provokes a further proof;
and this apologetic development, already in an advanced stage
in the Gospels, expands when it escapes from the apostolic
circle where it is no longer hampered by any actual memory of
the historical reality. Moreover, a certain popular conception
of the Resurrection soon tends to obtrude itself and become
superimposed on the first account.

As soon as Christian propaganda is carried outside the
strictly Jewish world it encounters immortality Mysteries,
religions of salvation, the saviour gods of which die and rise
again, all of which cannot fail to react on the earliest presentation and setting of the Resurrection although they pave the
way for its acceptance.

Through the operation of these inevitable and irresistible
influences the narratives of the Resurrection came into existence,
and grew more complicated and incredible, until they finally
lost all semblance of historical reality.

IV

THE GROWTH OF LEGEND

We must now endeavour to gain some insight into the
process of legendary expansion. Early belief was not expressed
in such a statement as : *he rose again in the body ; he came out
from the tomb*, but thus : *God has exalted and glorified him until
the time appointed for his return.* He has *left this world and gone
back to the Father*, says John xiii. 1.[1] If such a conception had
continued to prevail generally, there would have been no need

---

[1] There remain traces of this first stage of belief, outside the Epistles
and the Acts, even in our canonical Gospels : In Luke xvi. 22 the dead

to describe the burial, the miraculous rolling away of the sepulchral stone, and all the material elements of the Resurrection. And it is because this account was not original but was composed of many new and imaginary incidents and modifications, originally independent of each other, and equally devoid of all historical foundation, that the stories of the Resurrection contain so many contradictions. Even considered individually on their own merits, they do not succeed in giving us a coherent picture of the Risen Lord,[1] who is represented in the same source, now as a mere spirit which passes through closed doors (Luke xxiv. 36, and particularly John xx. 19 and xx. 26) and now as a perfectly palpable being of flesh and blood who performs the functions of ordinary life (Luke xxiv. 40–2 ; John xx. 20 and 27).

It has already been said that the earliest mode of conceiving of the Resurrection could not last because it could always be challenged by outsiders who, not having seen, could always argue that there had been fraud or empty illusion, and it was this state of mind which led those who believed to *materialize* the Resurrection, because it was only when it was presented thus that material proof of it could be furnished.

The inevitable effect of the Jewish environment is seen in the tendency to render the fact of the Resurrection more acceptable by assimilating it to current conceptions of the Resurrection; that is to say, by seeking to prove the reality of the glorification of Jesus by a preliminary Resurrection conformable to popular ideas. But when we pass to the Hellenistic environment, we find that the Greeks, though willing to accept the glorification or the apotheosis of the central figure, are averse to the idea of a resurrection of the flesh.[2] Hence it becomes necessary to multiply irrefutable *proofs* for their benefit. It is therefore the opposition encountered by the fundamental affirmation, *He has risen again,* which gradually forced Christians to develop the legend of the Resurrection. This process must not be confused with the clever creation of fictive narratives, deliberately

---

Lazarus is *carried by the angels into Abraham's bosom,* without there being any question of burial or resurrection. In Luke xxiii. 43 Jesus on the cross says to the penitent thief : " *To-day shalt thou be with me in paradise,*" as if he expected to go straight up to God after his death. To go up *in the spirit,* of course, and that is why he says in Luke xxiii. 46 : " *Father, into thy hands I commend my spirit.*" *Cf.* **XXXIV,** 19 ; **CXCIII,** 76 *ff.*

[1] G. Bertram, *Die Himmelfahrt Jesu vom kreuz und Glaube an seine Auferstehung* (Festgabe für Adolf Deissmann), 188 *ff.,* Tübingen, 1926.

[2] **XXXIV,** 63, which refers to the evidence of *Acts* xvii. 31–2. Later on the question became insistent.

intended to deceive. It was nothing of the kind. Each added detail represents a conviction, however ill founded, unverified and indeed unverifiable, which in the mind of the apologist is sufficiently justified by its necessity and its logical probability. Once the first step has been taken the others follow naturally.

The first step would seem to have been taken somewhat as follows : [1] As soon as the assertion was made, *He has risen again,* even if *in the spirit* were understood, the objection arose : *But was he really dead?* And no doubt the best reply that could be given was : *He was actually buried.* But then it became necessary to state *at what time* and under what conditions he came out of the tomb. It was obviously impossible to rely upon facts in making such a statement. That is why Paul makes the burial and the resurrection on *the third day* (1 Cor. xv. 3) clearly dependent on the scriptures. As far as we know there does not exist in the Old Testament any teaching concerning the resurrection which could be applied to Jesus, and the theory, often maintained, that it was a tradition peculiar to the Nazarenes, is quite unfounded, and has apparently been invented *ad hoc.*[2] But, on the other hand, there were two useful passages [3] which gave an answer to the question : *at what time?* We read in Jonah i. 17 : " *And Jonah was in the belly of the fish three days and three nights,*" and in Hosea vi. 2 : " *After two days will he revive us : in the third day he will raise us up, and we shall live in his sight.*" The two quotations do not entirely agree and Christians had some difficulty in reconciling them, that is to say, in subordinating the first to the second,[4] but on the whole the third day seems to be indicated by both. Moreover, if Jesus came out of the tomb on the third day, must he not have been interred on the first day ? And must not the antecedent condition have been as definitely guaranteed by scripture as its consequence ?

Even though the principle of a material Resurrection had been accepted, they did not at first venture to give detailed accounts of the phenomenon, as in the case of the Passion,[5] and we have already noticed that it is only the later apocryphal Gospels which describe the coming out from the tomb.

It is evident that the affirmation of the discovery of the empty tomb, introduced in Mark xvi. 2 *ff.* with an awkwardness which reveals its novelty, could only satisfy very credulous

---

[1] **XXXIV,** 71 *ff.* ; **CXCIII,** 79 *ff.*

[2] **XXXIV,** 71. This theory, developed by Maurenbrecher in particular, has been favourably received (Zimmern, Gunkel, A. Meyer, Fiebig), but it has no documentary support. *Cf.* **XLVIII,** 82 ; *contra,* **XLI,** 148.　　　　[3] **CIII,** i, 176, and **LXXIX,** 200.

[4] L–*a,* i, 382, and 427 *ff.* ; **CXCIII,** 29, n. 1.　　　[5] **LXXIX,** 254 *ff.*

believers. Something better had to be discovered. They ended by justifying the Resurrection by pseudo-rational comparisons which make us smile but which satisfied certain requirements of the Greek mind.[1]

Once launched the legend naturally fed on elements borrowed from its environment; and thus it remembered that Adonis and Osiris rose again on the third day, and details were taken from the myths of the dying and rising gods.[2]

It seems possible to trace four stages in the evolution of this legend : (1) Visions persuade Peter and the disciples that Jesus is living, that he lives in his spirit ($\zeta\omega o\pi o\iota\eta\theta\epsilon\grave{\iota}\varsigma\ \pi\nu\epsilon\acute{\upsilon}\mu\alpha\tau\iota$), glorified by God. (2) If he is living, it means that he is no longer dead ; he has therefore risen again and popular belief as well as the necessity of finding a defence against the accusation of an illusion soon make themselves felt : he rose again with a body. Moreover, as soon as an answer is given to the question *when?* even if it refers only to the date of glorification, by means of Jonah i. 17 and Hosea vi. 2 it becomes necessary to admit a resurrection since these passages suppose one. The first witnesses, let us say the Apostles, can accept so much, *but nothing more*, because they are supported by scripture. Outside their circle the same limitation is not felt. (3) Material details multiply in reply to objections : the burial, the guarding of the tomb, the sealing of the stone, the appearances on the third day in the neighbourhood of the tomb, the apocalyptic emergence of the risen Lord, etc. (4) Various expansions occur, the result of reasoning which already bears the stamp of theological speculation. Three are particularly important : *the descent into hell*, the fixing of the date of the Resurrection, and the *Ascension*.

The descent into hell is the answer to the question whether Jesus was really dead, in the earth, during the time that elapsed from the evening of the burial till the morning of the resurrection ? A time came when faith could not be satisfied with this belief. Perhaps some prophecy, unknown to us,[3] decided

[1] **CCLV**, 99. *Cf.* a curious passage in Clement of Rome : 1 *Cor.* xxiv. 2–25, 5 : " *Day and night are symbols for us of resurrection : the night falls asleep and the day rises ; the day passes away and the night succeeds it.*" The point at issue is that of the general resurrection, but the author begins by saying that God has given us the grounds for the hope by raising the Lord Jesus Christ from the dead.—Theophilus, *Ad. Autol.*, 1, 13 ; Tertullian, *De resurrectione carnis*, 12 ; *Pseudo-3 Cor.*, 28, in **XXIII**, no. 12.

[2] **XXXIV**, 70 *ff.*

[3] Justin, *Dial.*, 72, 4, reproaches the Jews with having suppressed a passage in Jeremiah which was supposed to run : " *The holy Lord God of Israel has remembered his dead who sleep in the earth of the grave*

the question of how the interval was spent : preaching to the righteous dead. The only authentic trace of this curious addition [1] to be found in the whole of the New Testament is in the post-Pauline 1 Peter where it is said that (iii. 19) Christ "*being put to death in the flesh*" went to preach "*unto the spirits in prison*" (ἐν φυλακῇ), and a little farther on (iv. 6) that "*the gospel* (was) *preached also to them that are dead*" (καὶ νεκροῖς εὐαγγελίσθη). The origin of this legend [2] has been much discussed ; but it is sufficient here to notice that it was not an early one and results only from later speculation.[3]

The date of the Resurrection was not fixed without some difficulty, because *the third day* of Hosea vi. 2 and the *three days and three nights* of Jonah did not agree when taken separately,[4] but appeared at first to demand a difference of a day between the respective dates. But in the time of Jesus there was a popular belief that the soul of a dead person remained in or near his body for three days, at the end of which it departed and corruption set in.[5] Since Psalm xvi. (xv.) 10 asserts that God will not suffer his Holy One to see corruption, Jesus cannot remain longer than three days *in the heart of the earth*. It may be that the remembrance of the resurrection of Osiris on the third day after his death, or that of Attis on the fourth, exercised some influence on Hosea and Jonah,[6] but that did

and has descended to them to tell them the good news of their salvation" (transl. Archimbault, i, 349). Irenæus repeats this passage which cannot possibly have any foundation ; but the pseudo-prophecy may have had some currency.

[1] *Contra :* Loofs, *Christ's Descent into Hell*, in *Proceedings of Congress on Hist. of Religions* at Oxford (1910) : he quotes several texts in allusion to the descent into hell which are not convincing.—*Cf.* **CXLII**, 246 *ff.* ; J. Turmel, *La descente du Christ aux enfers*[2], Paris, 1905, and J. Kroll, *Beiträge zum descensus ad inferos*, Königsberg, 1922.

[2] On the discussion, *cf.* the Commentaries on 1 Peter, particularly Windisch, *Die Katholischen Briefe*[2] (in **LVII**), 71 *ff.*, and R. Perdelwitz, *Die Mysterienreligion und das Problem des I. Petrusbriefes*, 81 *ff.* ; Giessen, 1911, **CXCIII**, 32 *ff.* ; Loofs, *op. cit.*

[3] The *Odes of Solomon* (probably belonging to the first quarter of the second century) mention it (xlii. 15–16). It cannot have been very long in existence.

[4] The following support τῇ ἡμέρᾳ τῇ τρίτῃ : 1 Cor. xv. 4 ; Matt. xvi. 21 ; xvii. 23 ; xx. 19 ; Luke ix. 22 ; xviii. 33, and μετὰ τρεῖς ἡμέρας : Mark viii. 31 ; ix. 31 ; x. 34 ; Matt. xii. 40 decidedly supports the same formula, but does not adhere to it.

[5] **III**, 341 ; **CXCIII**, 30 ; **CIII**, i, 177 ; **XXXIV**, 70 ; **CCL**, 296.—*Cf.* John xi. 39, where Martha, the sister of Lazarus, says to Jesus : "*Lord, by this time he stinketh : for he hath been dead four days.*"

[6] **CCXLVII**, 36 ; **CXCIII**, 30. Perhaps the resurrection of Adonis was also celebrated in Phœnicia on the *third day*. *Cf.* Baudissin, *Adonis und Eshmun*, 409. Leipzig, 1911.

not directly determine the Christian belief; the idea was in the air. There is scarcely any probability that the fixing of the death of Jesus on the Friday depends on a reminiscence, and we have no indication that the Resurrection was ever placed on any other day than Sunday. In other words, as soon as it was stated that the Master rose on such and such a day, *Sunday* was selected as the day. This was apparently the first detail of Holy Week to be fixed, and indeed it determined all the others.[1] It is the orthodox view that the Resurrection of Jesus made Sunday the *Lord's day*; but the critic may be permitted to ask whether it was not the contrary which happened, and whether the Resurrection was not fixed on the Sunday because that day was already considered as the Lord's day. No scriptural passage suggested Sunday as the Resurrection day.[2] On the other hand, it appears that the first day of the week was the one on which a religious meeting [3] was held, from the very earliest Christian times, and that it was *the Lord's day*, or if you prefer *the risen Lord's day*, but the risen Lord's day is not to be confused with that of the Resurrection,[4] and nothing points to the idea that the memory of the Resurrection had any influence in fixing the religious service on that day.

It is generally said that Sunday was chosen to distinguish the Christian meeting from the Jewish sabbath. It would then point to a later arrangement which took place after the separation of the religions and in a Hellenistic environment. The desire of not being confused with the Jews appears clearly in the *Didaché* (viii. 1). But for pagans Sunday was the *day of the sun* (*dies solis*): could a connexion have been established between the glorified Lord and the sun?

Adherents of the mythological school do not hesitate. For them Jesus is the sun God.[5] Without going to this extreme it remains true that an analogy was early perceived between Christ in glory and the sun; he is pre-eminently the essence of light.[6] We remember the passage in Luke i. 78 *ff.*, in the song of Zacharias: "*the dayspring from on high hath visited us, to give light to them that sit in darkness,*" and in Revelation xix. 12: "*his eyes were as a flame of fire*"; and especially in John viii. 12: "*I am the light of the world: he that followeth me shall not walk in darkness, but shall have the light of life*" (*cf.* ix. 5). On the other hand, at the time of the rise of Christianity sun gods were honoured everywhere, gods of salvation,

---

[1] CCI, 61.   [2] CIII, i, 177.
[3] The expression ἡ κυριακὴ ἡμέρα occurs in Rev. i. 10.
[4] Loisy, **RHLR.**, 503, 1912.
[5] CLVIII, i and ii.   [6] CCXXII, 82.

for the most part, for whom it seemed natural—and necessary
—to substitute the true *sol salutis*, the radiant Christ, the
conqueror of the evil shades of darkness in which the *Black
One*, the Devil,[1] reigns. Philo had already often spoken of the
Logos as the sun (*cf.* John i. 9 : " *That was the true light* "
= φῶς τὸ ἀληθινόν, which is the equivalent of ἥλιος ὁ ἀληθινός).
The transference of the symbol to the Logos-Jesus was equally
inevitable. Once this preliminary assimilation had been accomplished, it became almost unavoidable that the day of the sun
should be the day of the glorious Lord, as a result of his glorification. This explanation forces itself upon us as soon as we
look for the origin of the religious observance of Sunday by
believers.[2] Thus the connexion of the Resurrection with the
Lord's Day, which is the starting point of the liturgical organization of Holy Week, resulted from a desire to justify established
religious custom and from the reasoning which tended to confuse the day of the Resurrection with the day of the Risen
Lord.

The Ascension explains by a necessary miracle the return
of the Glorified Lord to heaven after having assumed a material
form on earth.

At first it is confused with the Resurrection, as we have
seen. The Synoptics know nothing about it, for Luke xxiv.
51, which mentions it, placing it however on the first day of
the week, is probably a late passage.[3] John and the *Gospel
of Peter* suppose an immediate ascension, and we read again in
the *Epistle of Barnabas* (first quarter of the second century)
xv. 9 : " *That is why we celebrate with joy the third day on which
Jesus rose from the dead and on which, after showing himself,
he ascended into heaven.*" Apparently the question soon arose :
why the risen Jesus did not remain on earth to establish the
Messianic Kingdom. This explains the compromise expressed
in Acts i. 3 *ff.* where Jesus is described as spending forty days
among his disciples, " *speaking of the things pertaining to the
kingdom of God.*" And this second terrestrial life is brought
to a close by the Ascension, which inaugurates the expectation
of the *parousia*, that is, of the great manifestation of the Messiah

---

[1] The passages are collected and carefully explained in F. J. Dölger,
Die Sonne der Gerechtigkeit und der Schwarze. Münster, 1919, particularly 100 *ff.*

[2] CCXXII, 85 ; XLVIII, 74.

[3] *Cf.* XCVII, 243 ; LXXXIV, 143, still maintains that the suppression
of xxiv. 51 is a correction which harmonizes Luke and Acts. This is
possible. With regard to the divergence between Luke and Acts as
to the date of the Resurrection and the attempts at reconciliation,
cf. XLV, iii, 156, n. 1.

prophesied by Daniel. He and God alone know the time of this final return and it is useless to attempt to guess it. The death of the Lord, the first great stumbling-block, is then explained by the necessity of redeeming man and the Cosmos. That is Paul's thesis and the core of his preaching which he himself calls (1 Cor. i. 18) the *preaching of the cross* (ὁ λόγος ὁ τοῦ σταυροῦ); but this carries us beyond the boundaries of Palestine and the apostolic point of view. The same is true of the legend of the second terrestrial life, which the original disciples could not possibly have accepted.

The legend of the Resurrection continued to undergo expansion, but we may say that it had assumed its essential form by A.D. 60 or 70. It was the result of a continuous process inspired by an inward logical necessity which transformed the spiritual manifestation which illuminated and strengthened Peter, into the material manifestation described by the sources. The impulse of the process is to be sought in the attempt to meet sceptical objections and hostile criticisms.

V

CONCLUSION

We do not know what happened to the body of Jesus after his death. Synoptic tradition was no better informed and the story of the burial which it reports is only a deduction resulting from apologetic necessities. In its earliest form, the belief in the Resurrection was the result of a return of confidence in Jesus on the part of Peter and his companions, which the unexpected arrest and crucifixion of their Master had almost shattered. This process was the result of certain conditions in their environment, which also helped to determine the conclusion they reached and to ensure their success.

The evolution of the legend was a complicated process in which were combined details produced by apologetic needs, inferences arising from the Christological development of the faith, and expansions resulting from theological speculation. The completed result bears the impress of the different stages and the varying environments through which it passed. Nothing of all this will surprise the historian of religions; both the creation of the belief in the Resurrection and its transformation into legend are familiar processes. Its chief originality lies in the peculiar process of its development which started from the subjective phenomenon of the visions and worked back to their objective justification.

There would have been no Christianity if the belief in the Resurrection had not been founded and systematized. Wellhausen is therefore right in saying that Jesus would have left no mark on history had it not been for his death. *The Apostles' teaching is really that of the death and resurrection of Jesus.*[1] The whole of the soteriology and the essential teaching of Christianity rests on the belief in the Resurrection, and on the first page of any account of Christian dogma might be written as a motto Paul's declaration (1 Cor. xv. 14) : " *And if Christ be not risen, then is our preaching vain, and your faith is also vain* " (ματαία ἡ πίστις ὑμῶν ἐστίν).

From the strictly historical point of view, the importance of the belief in the Resurrection is scarcely less, in so far as it concerns the foundation, development and expansion of the Christian religion. By means of that belief, faith in Jesus and in his mission became the fundamental element of a new religion, which, after separating from, became the opponent of Judaism, and set out to conquer the world. It also rendered Christianity a favourable soil for syncretistic influences, by virtue of which the Jewish Messiah, unintelligible and uninteresting to the Greeks, became the Lord, the Saviour, the Son of God, the supreme Master of the Universe, before whom the whole creation bends the knee.[2] The ground was prepared for it throughout the oriental world by the ancient myth of the dying and rising God ;[3] it sustained and fostered the doctrine founded on the conviction of the apostolic *witnesses* and made possible the victorious career of Christianity. It is doubtful, however, whether the dogma of the Resurrection, which has so long been the mainstay of Christianity, has not, in our day, become too heavy a burden for it to bear.

[1] **CXLI**, 235. *Cf.* **CXII**, 149 *ff.*
[2] *Phil.* ii. 10.—*Cf.* **XXXV**, 220 *ff.*
[3] Frazer, *The Golden Bough* [2], iii, 197.

EPILOGUE

THE Last Things which Jesus expected did not happen. The Kingdom which he announced did not appear and the prophet died on the cross instead of contemplating the expected Miracle from the hill of Zion. He must then have been mistaken. By all the canons of probability and logic his name and his work should have fallen into oblivion, as happened to many another in Israel at that period who thought himself to be *someone*. What could remain of a movement which foundered in disaster after its brief day, without having succeeded in deeply stirring the people of Palestine ?

But this man, who could not or would not rouse the people by his message, this prophet, who at most had been able to stir a ripple of sympathetic curiosity and perchance a fleeting hope in the toilers of Galilee, had so touched the heart of a few disciples, that their attachment to his person survived his death. Their love and trust brought him to life and gave him a future, though not that which he had anticipated. Nothing of him has survived save the memory of his existence and the influence of his work on his intimate associates. We see his figure transformed into the vindication of events which he could not have foreseen, and of institutions which, to say the least, would have seemed strange to him. From the moment of his Resurrection his person began to undergo a transformation which removed him ever further from reality. The divine legend, which was rendered necessary by the evolution of the faith which followed its development, even to the point of identifying the Nazarene with God, very soon obliterated and submerged the few fragments of human reality preserved in the memory of the Galilean disciples. They were of no interest to believers who only wanted to know the crucified Saviour, the Glorified Christ, the Lord who was God's representative in this world. Nothing, or very little, of his work remained, nor could it be expected to survive the unparalleled transformation of his person. A few vestiges survived, perhaps, in the imposing edifice of Christian doctrine, but they lost their meaning when they were separated from their original connexion, and inserted into a religious setting which was not that of the Nazarene.

Although it is an unquestioned fact that Jesus' dream of the future which embodied the expectation of the Poor in Israel, ended in failure, it is, nevertheless, true that the rise of the Galilean prophet marks the beginning, however accidental, of the religious movement from which Christianity sprang. The lowly spring which pours a slender trickle over the stones neither promises nor foresees the great river to which it gives rise, nevertheless, from it the river has its origin and being.

And yet it remains true that the Christian religion is not the religion which filled the whole being of Jesus; he neither foresaw it nor desired it. Wellhausen[1] is right when he says that enthusiasm engendered Christianity, but it was the enthusiasm of the disciples, not that of Jesus.

[1] CXII, 150.

BIBLIOGRAPHY

DICTIONARIES AND REVIEWS

Archiv für neutestamentl. Zeitgeschichte und Kulturkunde
(Leipoldt, Leipzig, since 1925). . . . . ΑΓΓΕΛΟΣ

The Catholic Encyclopedia (16 vols., New York, 1917 *seq.*) CE

Christliche Welt . . . . CW

Dict. d'archéologie chrétienne et de liturgie (Dom. F. Cabrol
and Dom H. Leclercq, Paris, 1903 *seq.* The work has
reached letter M, in the CXVIIth part.) . . DACL

Dict. of the Apostolic Church (J. Hastings, 2 vols., Edinburgh, 1913–18) . . . . DAC

Dict. of Christ and the Gospels (J. Hastings, 2 vols., Edinburgh, 1906–8) . . . . DCG

Dict. of the Bible (J. Hastings, 5 vols., Edinburgh,
1897–1904) . . . . B

Encyclopedia Biblica (Cheyne and Black, 4 vols., London,
1899–1903) . . . . EB

Encyclopedia for Religion and Ethics (J. Hastings,
Edinburgh, 1908–21) . . . . . . ERE

The Expositor . . . . EX

Journal of Biblical Literature . . . . . JBL

Journal of Theological Studies . . . . . JTS

*Real-Encyklopaedie für prot. Theologie und Kirche*³ (Alb.
Hauck, 22 vols., Leipzig, 1896–1909) . . HRE

*Die Religion in Geschichte und Gegenwart. Handwörter-
buch für Theologie und Religionswissenschaft*² (H.
Gunkel and L. Zscharnack, 5 vols., 1927–32) . RGG

Revue Biblique . . . . RB

Revue Critique . . . . RC

Revue des Études juives . . . . . REJ

Revue d'Histoire et de Littérature religieuses . . RHLR

Revue d'Histoire et de Philosophie religieuses (The
Protestant Theological Faculty of Strasburg) . . RHPR

Revue de l'Histoire des Religions . . . . RHR

Revue Historique . . . . RH

Theologische Jahrbücher . . . . . . TJ

Theologische Literaturzeitung . . . . . TL

Theologische Rundschau . . . . . . TR

Zeitschrift für die neutestamentliche Wissenschaft . ZNTW

Zeitschrift für Kirchengeschichte . . . ZKG

Zeitschrift für wissenschaftliche Theologie . . ZWT

1.—GENERAL BOOKS

BARDENHEWER, *Gesch. der altkirchlichen Literatur*²,
Fribourg-in-Br., 4 vols. have appeared, 1913–28 . I

A. BERTHOLET, *Biblische Theologie des Alten Testaments.
Die jüdische Religion von der Zeit Esras bis zum Zeitalter
Christi*, Tübingen, 1911. II

W. Bousset, *Die Relig. des Judentums im neutestament-lichen Zeitalter²*, Tübingen, 1906 . . . . **III**

W. Bousset, *Die Relig. des Judentums im späthellen-istischen Zeitalter*, edited by H. Gressmann, Tübingen, 1926. A revision of the previous book . . **IV**

Brassac, *Manuel biblique*, Paris, 2 vols., 1908–9 . **V**

A. Causse, *Les prophètes d'Israël et les religions de l'Orient*, Paris, 1913 . . . . . . **VI**

R.-H. Charles, *Apocrypha and Pseudepigrapha of the O.T.*, Oxford, 2 vols., 1913 . . . . **VII**

F. Cumont, *Les religions orientales dans le paganisme romain⁶*, Paris, 1929 . . . . . . **VIII**

Duchesne, *Histoire ancienne de l'Église*, vol. i, Paris, 1906 . . . . **IX**

Dussaud, *Introduction à l'hist. des religions*, Paris, 1914 **X**

Graetz, *Hist. des Juifs*, tran. M. Wogue, vol. i, Paris, 1882, vol ii, 1884 . . . . . . **XI**

A. Harnack, *Gesch. der altchristlichen Literatur* . . **XII**
   2 parts : *Ueberlieferung und Bestand*, Leipzig, 2 vols.,
      1893 . . . . **XII¹**
       Die Chronologie, 2 vols., 1897 and 1904 . **XII²**

F. Jackson and K. Lake, *The Beginnings of Christi-anity*, London, 3 vols., 1920, 1922, 1926 . **XIII**

A. Jeremias, *Das A.T. im Lichte der Alten Orients²*, Leipzig, 1906 . . . . **XIV**

H. Jordan, *Gesch. der altchristlichen Literatur*, Leipzig, 1911 . . . . **XV**

J. Juster, *Les Juifs dans l'Empire romain. Leur con-dition juridique, économique et sociale*, Paris, 2 vols., 1914 . . . . **XVI**

C. Kirch, *Enchiridion fontium historiæ ecclesiasticæ antiquæ*, Fribourg-in-Br., 1910 . . . **XVII**

Rud. Kittel, *Biblia hebraica²*, Leipzig, 1913 . . **XVIII**

R. Kreglinger, *La religion d'Israël²*, Brussels-Paris, 1926 . . . . **XIX**

G. Krüger, *Handbuch der Kirchengeschichte. Das Alter-tum²*, Tübingen, 1923 . . . . . **XX**

P. de Labriolle, *Histoire de la littérature latine chrétienne*, Paris, 1920 . . . . **XXI**

M.-J. Lagrange, *Le Judaïsme avant Jésus-Christ.*, Paris, 1931 . . . . **XXII**

H. Lietzmann, *Kleine Texte für theologische und philo-logische Vorlesungen und Uebungen*, Bonn, 1905 seq. . **XXIII**

Ed. Meyer, *Ursprung und Anfang des Christentums*, Stuttgart, 3 vols., 1921–3 . . . . . **XXIV**

G.-F. Moore, *Judaism in the first Centuries of the Christian Era*, Cambridge (Mass.), 3 vols., 1927–30 . **XXV**

K. Müller, *Kirchengeschichte²*, Tübingen, vol. i, 1929 . **XXVI**

O. Pfleiderer, *Die Entstehung des Christentums²*, Munich, 1907 . . . . **XXVII**

A. Puech, *Histoire de la littérature grecque chrétienne*, Paris, 3 vols., 1928–30 . . . . . **XXVIII**

E. Schürer, *Gesch. des jüdischen Volkes im Zeitalter J.C.*
[Citations are from I⁴ (1901), II² (1898), III³ (1898)]   **XXIX**

H. von Soden, *Urchristliche Literatur-Geschichte*, 1905   **XXX**

G.-B. Smith, *A Guide to the Study of the Christian Religion*,
University of Chicago Press, 1917   .   .   **XXX** *bis*

O. Staehlin, *Die altchristliche griechische Literatur*,
Munich, 1924 (p. 1105–502 of vol. ii of *Gesch. der griech.
Literatur*)   .   .   .   .   **XXXI**

J. Turmel, *Histoire de la théologie positive depuis l'origine
jusqu'au Concile de Trente³*, Paris, s.d. (1904).   .   **XXXII**

L. Vénard, *Les origines chrétiennes*, after J. Bricout,
Où en est l'histoire des religions. Paris, 1911   .   **XXXIII**

J. Weiss, *Das Urchristentum*, Göttingen, 2 pts., 1914–
1917   .   .   .   .   **XXXIV**

P. Wendland, *Die hellenistisch-römische Kultur in ihren
Beziehungen zu Judentum und Christentum²*, Tübingen,
1912 (*Hdb.* of Lietzmann.)   .   .   .   .   **XXXV**

P. Wendland, *Die urchristlichen Literaturformen³*,
Tübingen, 1912 (*Hdb.* of Lietzmann)   .   .   .   **XXXVI**

P. Wernle, *Die Anfänge unserer Religion²*, Tübingen,
1904   .   .   .   .   **XXXVII**

P. Wernle, *Einführung in das theologische Studium²*,
Tübingen, 1911   .   .   .   .   .   .   **XXXVIII**

II.—THE NEW TESTAMENT

1.—General Books

B. W. Bacon, *The Making of the N.T.*, London, 1912 .   **XXXIX**

O. Baumgarten, W. Bousset, H. Gunkel, etc., *Die
Schriften des N.T. neu übersetzt und für die Gegenwart
erklärt³*, Göttingen, 4 vols., 1917–20   .   .   .   **XL**

C. Clemen, *Religionsgeschichtliche Erklärung des N.T.*,
Giessen, 1909 ; 2 edit., 1924.   .   .   .   .   **XLI**

Cornely and Merk, *Manuel d'introduction historique et
critique à toutes les Saintes Écritures*, vol ii, *Nouveau
Testament*, Paris, 1928 .   .   .   .   .   .   **XLII**

P. Feine, *Einleitung in das N.T.⁴*, Leipzig, 1929   .   **XLIII**

P. Feine, *Theologie des N.T.⁴*, Leipzig, 1912   .   .   **XLIV**

M. Goguel, *Introduction au N.T.*, 5 vols. have appeared,
Paris, 1923 *seq.*   .   .   .   .   .   .   **XLV**

Ch. Gore, H. Leighton, etc., *A New Commentary on
Holy Scripture, including the Apocrypha*, London, s.d.
(1928)   .   .   .   .   **XLVI**

A. Gregory, *The Canon and Text of the N.T.*, New York,
1907   .   .   .   .   **XLVII**

H. Gunkel, *Zum religions geschichtlichen Verständnis
des N.T.²*, Göttingen, 1910   .   .   .   .   **XLVIII**

H. Holtzmann, *Die Entstehung des Neuen Testaments*,
Halle, 1904 (*Relig. gesch. V.B.*, no. 11 of the 1st series)   **XLIX**

H. Holtzmann, *Lehrbuch der historich-kritischen Einleitung in das N.T.³*, Fribourg-in-Br., 1892   .   .   **L**

542 BIBLIOGRAPHY

H. Holtzmann, *Lehrbuch der neutestamentl. Theologie*², edited by A. Jülicher and W. Bauer, Tübingen, 2 vols., 1911 . . . .   **L bis**

E. Jacquier, *Histoire des livres du N.T.*, Paris, 4 vols., 1903. Since republished . . . .   **LI**

E. Jacquier, *Le N.T. dans l'Église chrétienne*, Paris, 2 vols., 1911–13 . . . .   **LII**

M. Jones, *The N.T. in the Twentieth Century*, London, 1924 . . . .   **LIII**

Jülicher, *Einleitung in das N.T.*⁶, Tübingen, 1913, 7 edit., in conjunction with Erich Fascher, 1931 .   **LIV**

F.-G. Kenyon, *Handbook to the Textual Criticism of the N.T.*², London, 1912 . . . . .   **LV**

R. Knopf, *Einleitung in das N.T.*², Giessen, 1923 .   **LVI**

H. Lietzmann, *Handbuch zum N.T.*², Leipzig, 1912 seq.   **LVII**

Ernst Lohmeyer, *Kritisch. exegetischer Kommentar über das N.T.*, Göttingen, 1930 (in course of publication)   **LVIII**

H.-A.-W. Meyer, *Kritisch. exegetischer Kommentar über das N.T.*, Göttingen, 16 vols., 1897–1913 . .   **LIX**

G. Milligan, *The N.T. Documents*, London, 1913 .   **LX**

J. Moffatt, *Introduction to the Literature of the N.T.*², Edinburgh, 1912. Republished in 1919 . .   **LXI**

Eb. Nestle, *Einführung in das griechische N.T.*³, Göttingen, 1909. A revised ed. by Von Dobschütz appeared in 1924 . . . .   **LXII**

E. Preuschen, *Analecta. Kürzere Texte zur Gesch. der alten Kirche und des Kanons*, Fribourg-in-Br. and Leipzig, 1893 . . . .   **LXIII**

E.-C. Selwyn, *The Oracles in the N.T.*, London, New York, Toronto, s.d. (1912) . . . .   **LXIV**

A. Souter, *The Text and Canon of the N.T.*, New York, 1913 . . . .   **LXV**

H. Strack and P. Billerbeck, *Kommentar zum N.T. aus Talmud und Midrasch*, Munich, 4 vols., 1922–8   **LXVI**

H. Weinel, *Biblische Theologie des N.T. Die Religion Jesu und des Urchristentums*, Tübingen, 1911, 2 edit., 1928 . . . .   **LXVII**

B. Weiss, *Lehrbuch der biblischen Theologie des neuen Testaments*, Stuttgart and Berlin, 1903 . . .   **LXVIII**

Th. Zahn, *Einleitung in das N.T.*, Leipzig, 2 vols., 1907   **LXIX**

Th. Zahn, *Forschungen zur Gesch. des neutestamentlichen Kanons und der altkirchlichen Literatur*, Leipzig, 9 pts., 1881–1916 . . . .   **LXX**

Th. Zahn, *Gesch. des neutestamentlichen Kanons*, Leipzig, 5 pts. in 2 vols., 1888–92 . . . .   **LXXI**

Th. Zahn, *Grundriss der Gesch. des neutestamentlichen Kanons*², Leipzig, 1904 . . . .   **LXXII**

2.—The Gospels in General

E. Abbott, *The Fourfold Gospel*, Cambridge. *Introduction*, 1913; I. *The Beginnings*, 1914; II. *The Proclamation of the New Kingdom*, 1915; III. *The Law of the New Kingdom*, 1916; IV. *The Founding of the New Kingdom*, 1917 . . . .   **LXXIII**

J. Abrahams, *Studies in Pharisaism and Gospels*, Cambridge, 1 series, 1917 ; 2 series, 1924 . . . **LXXIV**

F.-C. Burkitt, *The Earliest Sources for the Life of Jesus*, Boston and New York, 1910 . . . . **LXXV**

F.-C. Burkitt, *Gospel History and its Transmission*, Edinburgh, 1906 . . . . **LXXVI**

G. Dalman, *Worte Jesu*, i, Leipzig, 1898 . . . **LXXVII**

M.-J. Lagrange, *L'Évangile de J.-C.*, Paris, 1928 . **LXXVIII**

A. Loisy, *Jésus et la tradition évangélique*, Paris, 1910 . **LXXIX**

C.-G. Montefiore, *Rabbinic Literature and Gospel Teachings*, London, 1930 . . . . . **LXXX**

H. Pernot, *Études sur la langue des Évangiles*, Paris, 1927 . . . . **LXXXI**

K.-L. Schmidt, *Die Stellung der Evangelien in der allegmeinen Literaturgeschichte* (in *Mélanges* offerts à Gunkel), Göttingen, 1923 . . . . . **LXXXII**

W. H. Stanton, *The Gospels as Historical Documents*, Cambridge, 3 vols., 1903, 1909, 1920 . . . **LXXXIII**

B.-H. Streeter, *The Four Gospels. A Study of Origins*, London, 1926 . . . . **LXXXIV**

J. Weiss, *Das älteste Evangelium*, Göttingen, 1903 . **LXXXV**

3.—The Synoptic Gospels

R. Bultmann, *Gesch. der synoptischen Tradition*, Göttingen, 1921 . . . . **LXXXVI**

D. Wilhelm Bussmann, *Synoptiche Studien.* Halle : I. *Zur Geschichtsquelle*, 1925 ; II. *Zur Redenquelle*, 1929 ; III. *Zur den Sonderquellen*, 1931. . . **LXXXVII**

H.-J. Cadbury, *The Making of Luke-Acts*, London, 1927 **LXXXVIII**

J.-M. Creed, *The Gospel according to St. Luke*, London, 1930 . . . . **LXXXIX**

M. Dibelius, *Die Formgeschichte des Evangeliums*, Tübingen, 1919 . . . . **XC**

M. Goguel, *La nouvelle phase du problème synoptique*, RHR 1907 . . . . **XCI**

M. Goguel, *L'Évangile de Marc et ses rapports avec ceux de Mathieu et de Luc*, Paris, 1909 . . . **XCI** *bis*

A. Harnack, *Die Apostelgeschichte*, Leipzig, 1908 . **XCII**

A. Harnack, *Lukas der Arzt*, Leipzig, 1906 . . **XCIII**

A. Harnack, *Neue Untersuchungen z. Apostelgesch*, Leipzig, 1911 . . . . **XCIV**

A. Harnack, *Sprüche und Reden Jesu. Die zweite Quelle des Mt. und Lk.*, Leipzig, 1907 . . . **XCV**

H. Holtzmann, *Handkommentar zum N.T. Die Synoptiker²*, Tübingen, 1901 . . . . . **XCVI**

E. Klostermann, *Das Lukasevangelium³ (Lk.)*, Tübingen, 1929 (*Hdb.* of Lietzmann) . . . **XCVII**

E. Klostermann, *Das Markusevangelium² (Mk.)*, Tübingen, 1926 (*Hdb.* of Lietzmann) . . **XCVIII**

E. Klostermann, *Das Matthäusevangelium² (Mt.)*, Tübingen, 1927 (*Hdb.* of Lietzmann) . . **XCIX**

M.-J. Lagrange, *Évangile selon saint Luc*, Paris, 1921 **C**

M.-J. Lagrange, *Évangile selon saint Marc⁴*, Paris, 1929 **CI**

M.-J. LAGRANGE, *Évangile selon saint Matthieu³*, Paris, 1927 . . . . **CII**

A. LOISY, *Les Évangiles synoptiques*, Ceffonds, Paris, 2 vols., 1907–8 . . . . . . **CIII**

A. LOISY, *L'Évangile selon Luc*, Paris, 1914 . . **CIV**

A. LOISY, *L'Évangile selon Marc*, Paris, 1912 . . **CV**

A.-H. MC NEILE, *The Gospel according to St. Matthew*, London, 1915 . . . . . . **CVI**

C.-G. MONTEFIORE, *The Synoptic Gospels²*, London, 2 vols., 1927 . . . . . . **CVII**

F. NICOLARDOT, *Les procédés de rédaction des trois premiers évangélistes*, Paris, 1908 . . . **CVIII**

A. PLUMMER, *A Critical and Exegetical Commentary on the Gospel according to St. Luke*, Edinburgh, 1896 ; 3 edit., 1909 . . . . **CIX**

A. PLUMMER, *An Exegetical Commentary on the Gospel according to St. Matthew*, London, 1909 . . . **CX**

B.-T.-D. SMITH, *The Gospel according to St. Matthew*, Cambridge, 1927 . . . . . . **CXI**

J. WELLHAUSEN, *Einleitung in die drei ersten Evangelien²*, Berlin, 1911 . . . . . . **CXII**

J. WELLHAUSEN, *Das Evangelium Lucæ*, Berlin, 1904 . **CXIII**

J. WELLHAUSEN, *Das Evangelium Marci²*, Berlin, 1909 **CXIV**

J. WELLHAUSEN, *Das Evangelium Matthaei²*, Berlin, 1914 . . . . **CXV**

P. WERNLE, *Die Synoptische Frage*, Tübingen, 1899 . **CXVI**

ZIMMERMANN, *Die historische Werth der ältesten Ueberlieferung von der Gesch. Jesu im Markusevangelium*, Leipzig, 1905 . . . . . . **CXVII**

4.—THE FOURTH GOSPEL

B.-W. BACON, *The Fourth Gospel in Research and Debate*, New Haven, 1910 ; 2 edit., 1918 . . . **CXVIII**

W. BAUER, *Evangelium . . . des Johannes²*, Tübingen, 1908 (*Hdkomm.* of Holtzmann) . . . **CXIX**

W. BAUER, *Das Johannesevangelium*, Tübingen, 1925. (*Hdb.* of Lietzmann) . . . . . **CXX**

J.-H. BERNARD, *A Critical and Exegetical Commentary on the Gospel according to St. John*, Edinburgh, 2 vols., 1928 . . . . **CXXI**

R. BULTMANN, *Das Johannesevangelium in der neuesten Forschung*, **CW**, XL, ii (2 June 1927), 502–11 . **CXXII**

J. GRILL, *Untersuchungen über die Entstehung des vierten Evangeliums*, Tübingen, i, 1902 ; ii, 1923 . . **CXXIII**

W.-F. HOWARD, *The Fourth Gospel in recent Criticism and Interpretation*, London, 1931. (Excellent bibliography at the end of the volume.) . . . **CXXIV**

H.-L. JACKSON, *The Problem of the Fourth Gospel*, Cambridge, 1918 . . . . . . **CXXV**

M.-J. LAGRANGE, *Évangile selon saint Jean*, Paris, 1925 **CXXVI**

A. LOISY, *Le Quatrième Évangile*, Paris, 1903 . . **CXXVII¹**
12 edit., entirely revised, 1921 . . . . **CXXXVII²**

H. ODEBERG, *The Fourth Gospel interpreted in its relation to contemporaneous Religious Currents in Palestine and the Hellenistic-Oriental World*, Upsala, 1929 . **CXXVIII**

Fr. Overbeck, *Das Johannesevangelium*, ed. C.-A. Bernoulli, Tübingen, 1911 CXXIX

J. Wellhausen, *Das Evangelium Johannis*, Berlin, 1908 CXXX

Gillis P : Son Wetter, " *Der Sohn Gottes*," *Eine Untersuchung über den Charakter und die Tendenz des Johannes-Evangeliums. Zugleich ein Beitrag zur Kenntnis der Heilands Gestalten der Antike*, Göttingen, 1916 CXXXI

5.—Apocryphal Books

D. de Quincey, *The Apocryphal and Legendary Life of Christ*, New York, 1903 CXXXII

E. Hennecke, *Handbuch zu den neutestamentlichen Apokryphen*, Tübingen and Leipzig, 1904 ; 2 edit. in course of preparation CXXXIII

E. Hennecke, *Neutest. Apokryphen*, Tübingen and Leipzig, 1904 ; 2 edit., 1923–4 CXXXIV

R. Lipsius and M. Bonnet, *Acta apostolorum Apocrypha*, Leipzig, pt. i, 1890 ; ii, 1898 ; iii, 1903 . . CXXXV

R. Lipsius, *Die apokryphen Apostelgeschichten*, Leipzig, 1883 (Supplement in 1890), 4 vols. . . . CXXXV bis

Ch. Michel and P. Peeters, *Les Évangiles apocryphes*, Paris, vol. i, 1911 ; ii, 1914 CXXXVI

A. Resch, *Agrapha²*, Leipzig, 1906 CXXXVII

Tischendorf, *Evangelia Apocrypha²*, Leipzig, 1876 . CXXXVIII

L. Vaganay, *L'Évangile de Pierre (Études bibliques collection)*, Paris, 1930 CXXXIX

Ev. White, *The Sayings of Jesus from Oxyrynchus*, Cambridge, 1920 CXL

III.—THE LIFE OF JESUS

1.—General Books

D.-F. Barth, *Die Hauptprobleme des Lebens Jesu⁴*, Gütersloh, 1911 CXLI

W. Bauer, *Das Leben Jesu im Zeitalter der neutestamentlichen Apokryphen*, Tübingen, 1909 . . . CXLII

W. Bousset, *Was wissen wir von Jesus ? ²*, Halle, 1906 CXLIII

W. Brandt, *Die evangelische Gesch. und der Ursprung des Christentums*, Leipzig, 1893 . . . CXLIV

R. Bultmann, *Jesus*, Berlin, 1926 CXLV

S.-J. Case, *The Historicity of Jesus*, Chicago, 1912 . CXLVI

S.-J. Case, *Jesus*, Chicago, 1927 CXLVII

F.-C. Conybeare, *The Historical Christ*, London, 1914 . CXLVIII

P.-L. Couchoud, *Le Mystère de Jésus*, Paris, 1924 . CXLIX

G. Dalman, *Jesus-Jeschua*, Leipzig, 1922 . . CL

A. Drews, *Die Christusmythe*, Jena, 1910 . CLI

A. Drews, *Le Mythe du Christ* (trans. Stahl), Paris, 1926 CLII

K. Dunkmann, *Der historische Jesus. Der mythologische Christus und Jesus der Christ*, Leipzig, 1911 . CLIII

R. Eisler, *ΙΗΣΟΥΣ ΒΑΣΙΔΕΥΣ ΟΥ ΒΑΣΙΔΕΥΣΑΣ*, Heidelberg, 2 vols., 1930 CLIV

R. Furrer, *Leben Jesu Christi³*, Leipzig, 1905 . CLV

M. Goguel, *Jésus de Nazareth, Mythe ou histoire ?*, Paris, 1925 CLVI

M. Goguel, *La vie de Jésus*, Paris, 1932. (This important work was only available to me while I was correcting the proofs of the present book.) . .   CLVI *bis*

L. de Grandmaison, *Jésus-Christ, son message, ses preuves*, Paris, 2 vols., 1928 .   CLVII

Ch. Guignebert, *Le problème de Jésus*, Paris, 1914 .   CLVIII

A.-C. Headlam, *The Life and Teaching of Jesus the Christ*, London, 1923   CLIX

W. Heitmüller, *Jesus*, Tübingen, 1913 . . .   CLX

S. Krauss, *Das Leben Jesu nach jüdische Quellen*, Berlin, 1902   CLXI

A. Loisy, *Jésus et la tradition évangélique*, Paris, 1910   *cf.* LXXIX

A. Loisy, *La légende de Jésus*, in RHLR, 1922 .   CLXII

J. Mackinnon, *The Historical Jesus*, London, 1931 .   CLXIII

M. Maurenbrecher, *Von Nazareth nach Golgotha*, Berlin, 1909   CLXIV

H. Monnier, *La Mission historique de Jésus²*, Paris, 1914   CLXV

A. Omodeo, *Gesu il Nazoreo*, Venezia, s.d. .   CLXVI

A. Omodeo, *Gesù e le Origini del Cristianestimo²*, Messine, 1925 . . . . . .   CLXVI *bis*

R. Otto, *Leben und Wirken Jesu nach historisch-kritischer Auffassung*, Göttingen, 1905   CLXVII

E. Renan, *Vie de Jésus⁶*, Paris, 1863 . . .   CLXVIII

E. Renan, *Les Apôtres*, Paris, 1866   CLXIX

A. Réville, *Jésus de Nazareth²*, Paris, 2 vols., 1906.   CLXX

J.-M. Robertson, *A Short History of Christianity*, London, 1902   CLXXI

W. Sanday, *The Life of Christ in Recent Research*, Oxford, 1908   CLXXII

K. L. Schmidt, *Der Rahmen der Gesch. Jesu. Literarkritische Untersuchungen zur ältesten Jesusüberlieferung*, Berlin, 1919   CLXXIII

P.-W. Schmidt, *Die Geschichte Jesu*, Tübingen, 2 vols., 1901   CLXXIV

O. Schmiedel, *Die Hauptprobleme der Leben-Jesu-Forschung*, Tübingen, 1906   CLXXV

A. Schweitzer, *Gesch. der Leben-Jesu-Forschung²*, Tübingen, 1913   CLXXVI

A. Schweitzer, *Gesch. der paulinischen Forschung*, Tübingen, 1911   CLXXVII

B. Smith, *Der vorchristliche Jesus*, Giessen, 1906 .   CLXXVIII

B. Smith, *Ecce Deus*, Iena, 1911   CLXXIX

Von Soden, *Hat Jesus gelebt?*, Berlin, 1910 . .   CLXXX

Fr. Steudel, *Im Kampf um die Christusmythe*, Iena, 1910   CLXXXI

D.-F. Strauss, *Vie de Jésus*, trans. Littré, Paris, 2 vols., 1839   CLXXXII

D.-F. Strauss, *Nouvelle vie de Jésus*, trans. Nefftzer and Dolfus, Paris, 2 vols., 1864   CLXXXIII

Wabnitz, *Histoire de la vie de Jésus*, Paris, 2 vols., 1904 and 1906   CLXXXIV

P. Wernle, *Die Quellen des Lebens Jesu*[3], Tübingen,
1913 (*Relig. gesch. V.B.*, 1 series, pt. i)   .   .   **CLXXXV**

P. Wernle, *Jesus*[2], Tübingen, 1916   .   .   .   **CLXXXVI**

2.—SPECIAL SUBJECTS

B.-W. Bacon, *Jesus and Paul*, New York and London,
1921 .   .   .   .   **CLXXXVII**

W. Baldensperger, *Das Selbstbewusstsein Jesu im
Lichte des messian. Hoffnungen s. Zeit.* 1 half : *Die
messian. apokalypt. Hoffnungen des Judentums*, Strasburg, 1903 .   .   .   .   **CLXXXIX**

P. Batiffol, *L'enseignement de Jésus*, Paris, 1910   .   **CXC**

P. Batiffol, *Études d'histoire et de théologie positive.*
2 series : *l'Eucharistie, la présence réelle et la trans-
substantiation*, Paris, 1906   .   .   .   .   **CXCI**

G. Bertram, *Die Leidengeschichte Jesu und der Christus-
kult*, Giessen, 1922 .   .   .   .   .   **CXCII**

W. Bousset, *Kyrios Christos. Gesch. des Christus-
glaubens von den Anfängen des Christentums bis
Irenæus*, Göttingen, 1913 ; 2 edit., 1921   .   .   **CXCIII**

W. Brandt, *Die jüdischen Baptismen*, Giessen, 1910 .   **CXCIV**

Y. Brilioth, *Eucharistic faith and practice, Evangelical
and Catholic*, London, 1930 .   .   .   .   **CXCV**

D. Chwolson, *Die letzte Passahmahl Christi und der
Tag seines Todes*, Leipzig, 1892 ; 2 edit., 1908   .   **CXCVI**

G. Dalman, *Orte und Wege Jesu*[3], Gütersloh, 1924   .   **CXCVII**
French tr. : *Les itinéraires de Jésus, Topographie des
Évangiles*, trans. J. Marty, Paris, 1930 .   .   .   **CXCVIII**

M. Dibelius, *Das Abendmahl. Eine Untersuchung über
die Anfänge der christlichen Religion*, Leipzig, 1911.   **CXCIX**

D.-E. von Dobschütz, *Christusbilder*, ap. *Texte und
Untersuchungen*, iii, 1. Leipzig, 1899 .   .   .   **CC**

Fr.-K. Feigel, *Der Einfluss der Weissagungsbeweises und
anderer Motive auf die Leidensgeschichte*, Tübingen,
1910. (Collection of O.T. passages dealing with this
subject.) .   .   .   .   **CCI**

P. Fiebig, *Antike Wundergeschichten zum Studium der
Wunder des Neuen Testaments* (*Kleine texte*, no. 79),
Bonn, 1911 .   .   .   .   **CCII**

P. Fiebig, *Die Gleichnisreden Jesu im Lichte der rabbin.
Gleichnisse des neutestamentlichen Zeitalters. Ein
Beitrag z. Streit um d. " Christusmythe " und eine
Widerlegung der Gleichnistheorie Jülichers*, Tübingen,
1912 .   .   .   .   **CCIII**

P. Fiebig, *Jüdische Wundergeschichten der neutestamentlichen Zeitalters* (*Kleine Texte*, no. 78), Tübingen, 1911   **CCIV**

A. Friedrichsen, *Le problème du miracle dans le Christianisme primitif.*, Strasbourg-Paris, 1925 .   .   **CCV**

M. Goguel, *L'Eucharistie des origines à Justin Martyr*,
La Roche-sur-Yon, 1910 .   .   .   .   .   **CCVI**

M. Goguel, *Les sources du récit johannique de la Passion*,
Paris, 1910 .   .   .   .   **CCVII**

Ch. Guignebert, *La vie cachée de Jésus*, Paris, 1924   **CCVIII**

A.-C. Headlam, *The Miracles of the N.T.*, London, 1914   **CCIX**

548 BIBLIOGRAPHY

HEITMÜLLER, *Im Namen Jesu*, Göttingen, 1903. . **CCX**

R.-T. HERFORD, *Christianity in Talmud and Midrash*,
London, 1903 . . . . . . **CCXI**

O. HOLTZMANN, *Was Jesus Ekstatiker?*, Tübingen, 1903 **CCXII**

R.-W. HUSBAND, *The prosecution of Jesus, its Date,
History and Legality*, Princeton, 1916 . . **CCXIII**

JENSEN, *Das Gilgamesch-Epos in der Weltliteratur*,
Strasbourg, 1906 . . . . . **CCXIV**

A. JÜLICHER, *Die Gleichnisrede Jesu*², Tübingen, 1902 **CCXV**

A. JÜLICHER, *Die Religion Jesu und die Anfänge des
Christentums bis zum Nicaenum*, in *Die Kultur der
Gegenwart*, published by P. Hinneberg, part i, sec. iv, 1,
p. 42 seq. . . . . . . **CCXVI**

A. JÜLICHER, *Hat Jesus gelebt?*, Marburg, 1910 . **CCXVI-a**

M.-J. LAGRANGE, *Le Messianisme chez les Juifs* (150 B.C.
to 200 A.D.), Paris, 1909 . . . . **CCXVII**

LAIBLE, *Jesus Christus im Thalmud*², Berlin, 1902 . **CCXVIII**

K. LAKE, *The Historical Evidence for the Resurrection*,
New York, 1907 . . . . . **CCXIX**

D.-A. VON LEHNER, *Die Marienverehrung in den ersten
Jahrhunderten*², Stuttgart, 1886 . . . **CCXX**

H. LIETZMANN, *Der Menschensohn*, Tübingen, 1896 . **CCXXI**

A. LOISY, *L'Évangile de Jésus et le Christ ressuscité*,
RHLR . . . . **CCXXII**

—— Republished in *Les Mystères païens*², p. 199 *ff.* . **CCXXII-a**

SHAILER MATHEWS, *Jesus on Social Institutions*, London, 1928 . . . . . . **CCXXIII**

MOMMERT, *Zur Chronologie des Lebens Jesu*, Leipzig,
1909 . . . . **CCXXIV**

E. NORDEN, *Die Geburt des Kindes. Gesch. einer religiösen
Idee*, Leipzig, 1924 . . . . . **CCXXV**

W. RAMSAY, *Was Christ born in Bethlehem?*, London,
1905 . . . . **CCXXVI**

H. REGNAULT, *Une province procuratorienne au début de
de l'Empire romain. Le procès de Jésus-Christ*, Paris,
1909 . . . . **CCXXVII**

R. REITZENSTEIN, *Hellenistische Wundererzählungen*,
Leipzig, 1906 . . . . . **CCXXVIII**

A. RESCH, *Paulinismus und die Logia Jesu*, Leipzig, 1904 **CCXXIX**

G. ROSADI, *Le procès de Jésus*, trans. Mena d'Albola,
Paris, 1908 . . . . . . **CCXXX**

L. SALVATORELLI, *Il significato di Nazareno*, Rome, 1911 **CCXXXI**

A. SCHWEITZER, *Die psychiatrische Beurteilung Jesu*,
Tübingen, 1913 . . . . . **CCXXXII**

E.-S. SELWYN, *The Teaching of Jesus*, London, 1915 . **CCXXXIII**

VON SODEN, *Die wichtigsten Fragen im Leben Jesu*,
Berlin, 1904 . . . . . . **CCXXXIV**

G.-B. STEVENS, *The Teaching of Jesus*, New York, 1902 **CCXXXV**

Ch. TAYLOR, *Sayings of the Jewish Fathers*², New York,
2 vols., 1897 and 1900 . . . . **CCXXXVI**

A. WALKER, *The Teaching of Jesus and the Jewish Teaching of His Age*, New York, 1923 . . . **CCXXXVII**

J. WEISS, *Die Predigt Jesu vom Reiche Gottes*[2], Göttingen, 1900 . . . . **CCXXXVIII**

J. WELLHAUSEN, *Die Pharisäer und die Sadducäer*, Hanover, 1874 ; 2 edit., 1924 . . . . **CCXXXIX**

H. WENDT, *Die Lehre Jesu*[2], Göttingen, 1901–12 . **CCXL**

W. WREDE, *Das Messiasgeheimnis*, Göttingen, 1901 ; 2 edit., 1913 . . . . **CCXLI**

IV.—SUPPLEMENTARY LIST

S. ANGUS, *The Mystery-Religions and Christianity*, London, 1925 . . . . **CCXLII**

S. ANGUS, *The Religious Quests of the Græco-roman World*, London, 1930 . . . . **CCXLIII**

P. BATIFFOL, *L'Église naissante et le catholicisme*, Paris, 1909 . . . . **CCXLIV**

C.-A. BERNOUILLI, *Johannes der Taüfer und die Urgemeinde*, Bâle, 1917 . . . . . . **CCXLV**

W. BOUSSET, *Hauptprobleme der Gnosis*, Tübingen, 1907 **CCXLVI**

M. BRÜCKNER, *Der sterbende und auferstehende Gottheiland in den orientalischen Religionen und ihr Verhältnis zum Christentum*, Tübingen, 1908 . . . . **CCXLVII**

S.-J. CASE, *The Evolution of Early Christianity*, Chicago, 1914 . . . . **CCXLVIII**

A. CAUSSE, *L'Évolution de l'espérance messianique dans le Christianisme primitif*, Paris, 1908 . . . **CCXLIX**

F.-C. CONYBEARE, *Myth, Magic and Morals*, London, 1910 . . . . **CCL**

A. DEISSMANN, *Die Urgesch. des Christentums im Lichte der Sprachforschung*, Tübingen, 1910 . . **CCLI**

A. DEISSMANN, *Licht vom Osten*[2], Tübingen, 1909 ; 4 edit., 1923 . . . . **CCLII**

E.-C. DEWICK, *Primitive Christian Eschatology*, Cambridge, 1913 . . . . **CCLIII**

M. DIBELIUS, *Die Urchristliche Ueberlieferung von Johannes dem Taüfer*, Göttingen, 1911 . . **CCLIV**

D.-E. VON DOBSCHÜTZ, *L'âge apostolique* (trans.), Paris, *s.d.* . . . . **CCLV**

M. FRIEDLÄNDER, *Die religiösen Bewegungen innerhalb des Judentums im Zeitalter Jesu*, Berlin, 1905 . **CCLVI**

M. FRIEDLÄNDER, *Synagoge und Kirche in ihren Anfängen*, Berlin, 1908 . . . . . . **CCLVII**

R. GARBE, *Indien und das Christentum*, Tübingen, 1914 **CCLVIII**

M. GOGUEL, *Au seuil de l' Évangile : Jean-Baptiste*, Paris, 1928 . . . . **CCLIX**

M. GOGUEL, *Essai sur la chronologie paulinienne*, Paris, 1912, RHR . . . . **CCLX**

M. GOGUEL, *Les chrétiens et l' Empire romain*, Paris, 1908 **CCLXI**

A. HARNACK, *Erforschtes und Erlebtes*, Giessen, 1923 . **CCLXII**

A. HARNACK, *Lhb. der Dogmengeschichte*[4], Leipzig, 3 vols., 1906–9. Since republished . . . . **CCLXIII**

A. HARNACK, *L'Essence du Christianisme* (trans. of *Das Wesen des Christentums*), Paris, 1907 . . . **CCLXIV**

550   BIBLIOGRAPHY

A. Harnack, *Mission und Ausbreitung des Christentums in die drei ersten Jahrhunderten*², Leipzig, 2 vols., 1906. Since republished . . . .   **CCLXV**

E.-S. Hartland, *The Legend of Perseus*, London, 3 vols., 1894–6 . . . .   **CCLXVI**

W. Haupt, *Worte Jesu und Gemeinde Ueberlieferung*, Leipzig, 1913 . . . .   **CCLXVII**

E. Havet, *Le Christianisme et ses origines*², Paris, 4 vols., 1873–84 . . . .   **CCLXVIII**

G. Herzog, *La Sainte Vierge dans l'histoire*, Paris, 1908   **CCLXIX**

G. Hoennicke, *Das Judenchristentum im ersten und zweiten Jahrhundert*, Berlin, 1908 . . . .   **CCLXX**

H. Hort, *The Christian Ecclesia*, London, 1897 .   **CCLXXI**

E. Kautzsch, *Die Apokryphen und Pseudepigraphen des Alten Testaments*, i. *Die Apok.* ; ii. *Die Pseud.*, Tübingen, 2 vols., 1900 . . . . .   **CCLXXII**

E. Kautzsch, *Die Heilige Schrift des Alten Testaments*³, Tübingen, 2 vols., 1909 . . . .   **CCLXXIII**

H. Kellner, *Heortologie*³, Fribourg-in-Br., 1911 .   **CCLXXIV**

—— *L'année ecclésiastique et les fêtes des saints dans leur évolution historique*, trans. J. Bund, Paris-Rome, *s.d.* (1910) . . . .   **CCLXXIV bis**

G. Kittel, *Die Probleme des palästinischen Spätjudentums und das Christentum*, Stuttgart, 1926 . .   **CCLXXV**

K. Kohler, *The Origins of the Synagogue and the Church*, New York, 1929 . . . . . .   **CCLXXVI**

J. Lebreton, *Les Origines du dogme de la Trinité*⁴, Paris, 1919 . . . .   **CCLXXVII**

J. Leitpoldt, *Sterbende und auferstehende Götter*, Leipzig, 1923 . . . .   **CCLXXVIII**

H. Lietzmann, *Messe und Herrenmahl. Eine Studie zur Gesch. der Liturgie*, Bonn, 1926 . .   **CCLXXIX**

H. Lietzmann, *Der Prozess Jesu.* Sitzungsberichte der preuss. Akad. der Wiss., 1931, XIII, XIV, 313 *ff* .   **CCLXXIX–a**

Les Livres apocryphes de l' A. T., new anonymous trans. published by the Société Biblique de Paris, 1909 .   **CCLXXX**

A. Loisy, *L' Apocalypse de Jean*, Paris, 1923 . .   **CCLXXXI**

A. Loisy, *Les Actes des Apôtres*, Paris, 1920 . .   **CCLXXXII**

A. Loisy, *L'Évangile et l'Église*³, Paris, 1908 . .   **CCLXXXIII**

Lucius, *Les origines du culte des saints dans l'Église chrétienne*, trans. Jeanmaire, Paris, 1908 .   **CCLXXXIII–a**

A.-C. MacGiffert, *A History of Christianity in the Apostolic Age*, Edinburgh, 1897 . . .   **CCLXXXIV**

A. Metzger et de Milloué, *Matériaux pour servir à l'histoire des origines orientales du Christianisme*, Paris, 1906 . . . .   **CCLXXXV**

G. Milligan, *St. Paul's Epistle to the Thessalonians*, London, 1908 . . . .   **CCLXXXVI**

Moulton and Milligan, *The Vocabulary of the Greek Testament*, London, New York, Toronto, 8 parts, 1915–29 . . . .   **CCLXXXVII**

Nielsen, *Der dreieinige Gott*, vol. i, Copenhagen, 1922   **CCLXXXVIII**

Ed. Norden, *Agnostos Theos*, Leipzig, 1913 . .   **CCLXXXIX**

Ed. Norden, *Die Geburt des Kindes*, Leipzig, 1924 .   **CCXC**

A. Omodeo, *Paolo di Tarso, apostolo delle genti*. Messina, *s.d.* (1923) . . . . **CCXCI**

S. Reinach, *Cultes, Mythes et Religions*, Paris, i², 1922; ii, iii and iv, 1906–8 . . . . . . **CCXCII**

R. Reitzenstein, *Die hellenistischen Mysterienreligionen.* Leipzig and Berlin, 1910; 2 edit., 1920 . . **CCXCIII**

R. Reitzenstein, *Poimandres. Studien zur griechisch-ägyptischen und frühchristlichen Literatur*, Leipzig, 1904 . . . . **CCXCIV**

E. Renan, *L'Antéchrist*, Paris, 1873 . . . **CCXCV**

Rendel Harris, *Testimonies*, Cambridge, 2 vols., 1916–20 . . . . **CCXCVI**

A. Réville, *Histoire du dogme de la divinité de Jesus-Christ*, 3 edit., Paris, 1904 . . . . . **CCXCVII**

J. Réville, *Les Origines de l'épiscopat*, Paris, 1894 . **CCXCVIII**

J. Réville, *Les Origines de l'Eucharistie*, Paris, 1908 . **CCXCIX**

Routh, *Reliquiæ sacræ*, Oxford, 5 vols., 1846 . . **CCC**

P. Saintyves, *Le discernement du miracle*, Paris, 1909 **CCCI**

P. Saintyves, *Les Vierges mères et les naissances miracu-leuses*, Paris, 1908 . . . . . . **CCCII**

L. Salvatorelli, *From Locke to Reitzenstein. The His-torical Investigation of the Origins of Christianity.* Reprinted from *The Harvard Theol. Review*, xxii, no. 4, Oct. 1929 . . . . **CCCIII**

R. P. Schwalm, *La vie privée du peuple juif à l'époque de Jésus-Christ*, Paris, 1910 . . . . . **CCCIV**

Preserved Smith, *A Short History of Christian Theo-phagy*, Chicago, 1922 . . . . . . **CCCV**

W. Soltau, *Das Fortleben des Heidenstums in der alten christlichen Kirche*, Berlin, 1906 . . . . **CCCVI**

H.-L. Strack, *Jesus, die Haeretiker und die Christen nach den ältesten jüdischen Angaben*, Leipzig, 1910 . **CCCVII**

D.-F. Strauss, *Gesammelte Schriften*, ed. Ed. Zeller, 12 vols., 1876–8 . . . . **CCCVIII**

Volker, *Mysterium und Agape*, Gotha, 1927 . . **CCCIX**

P. Volz, *Jüdische Eschatologie von Daniel bis Akiba*, Tübingen, 1903 . . . . **CCCX**

H. Weinel, *Jesus im 19. Jahrhundert*, Tübingen, 1913 . **CCCXI**

O. Weinresch, *Antike Heilungswunder. Untersuchungen zum Wunderglauben der Griechen und Römer*, Giessen, 1909 . . . . **CCCXII**

J. Wellhausen, *Israelitische und jüdische Gesch*, Berlin, 4 edit., 1902; 6 edit., 1907 . . . . . **CCCXIII**

J. Wellhausen, *Skizzen und Vorbereiten*, vi, Berlin, 1899 . . . . **CCCXIV**

P. Wernle, *Paulus als Heidenmissionär. Ein Vortrag²*, Tübingen, 1909 . . . . **CCCXV**

H. Windisch, *Der messianische Krieg und das Urchristen-tum*, Tübingen, 1909 . . . . . . **CCCXVI**

Wunsche, *Neue Beiträge zur Erklärung der Evangelien aus Talmud und Midrasch*, Göttingen, 1878 . . **CCCXVII**

INDEX

Acts of the Apostles : authorship and date, 22 *ff.*
evidence of : concerning the life of Jesus, 23 *f.* ; concerning his teaching, 232 ; concerning the betrayal, 456 ; concerning the trial before Herod, 467 ; concerning the Resurrection and manifestation as Messiah, 534 ; concerning the post-resurrection life of Jesus, 534 ; concerning the *fellowship* (κοινωνία) of the Apostles, 438 *f.*

Adoration of the shepherds, 94

Ænon, near Salem, 153

Agrapha : definition of, 58
documentary value of, 58 *f.*
on the teaching of Jesus, 232

Am-haareṣ (the common people), 155
the relations of Jesus with them, 214, 311 *f.*

Anavim (the poor in Israel), 148
in relation to the preaching of Jesus, 215, 368
their conception of God, 356, 358, 364

Andrew, the Apostle, call of, 217

Annas (the High Priest), Jesus before, 461

Annunciation, the, 119 *f.*

Apocalypse of John : evidence concerning Jesus, 26
evidence concerning his teaching, 232

Apocalyptic teaching of Jesus, *see* Eschatology

Apocrypha, New Testament : definition and value of, 57 *ff.*
stories of the childhood of Jesus, 133 *f.*
on the Crucifixion, 481
on the site of the tomb, 493

Apocrypha, New Testament : on the discovery of the empty tomb, 498
on the Resurrection, 510

Apollonius of Tyana, miracles of, 193

Apostles, 217 *ff.*
lists of, 220 *f.*
their flight at Gethsemane, 459 *f.*

Appearances of the Risen One :
scriptural evidence of, 501 *ff.*
basis of the Easter faith, 512
mechanism of, 521 *ff.*

Aramaic, the language of Jesus, 137

Archelaus, 96

Arrest, the, of Jesus, 457–61
historical probability of, 471

Ascension, the, 509 *ff.*, 525, 581

Asclepiades, miracles of, 193

Asclepios, wonder-working of, 192

Attis, sacred meal of, 446

Augustine, St., on the appearance of Jesus and his portraits, 166

Bannos, the hermit, 152, 154

Baptism among the Jews, 150 *f.*

Baptism of Jesus, 146 *f.*
locality of, 152 *f.*
scene of, 155 *f.*
variant reading of Codex D, 108 *f.*, 260

Baptism, Christian : unknown to Jesus, 162
according to Paul, 446

Barabbas, 462, 468–71, 475

Beelzebub and Jesus, 194, 199, 277

Bethany : Jesus stays at, 229, 413, 416
anointing at, 419 *f.*, 425

Bethlehem of Judah : the town of David, 91
scene of the birth of Jesus, 90 *f.*, 95

552